500
CROSSWORD
PUZZLES

500 CROSSWORD PUZZLES

This edition published in 2022 by Arcturus Publishing Limited
26/27 Bickels Yard, 151–153 Bermondsey Street,
London SE1 3HA

AD010325US

Printed in the UK

Contents

Introduction 7

Puzzles 9

Solutions 509

Introduction

Good things come in small packages—diamond rings, cell phones, and the little puzzles in this book.

The crosswords you're about to solve are 11x13 squares in size, which is smaller than the standard 13x13 or 15x15 puzzles you normally see in your local newspaper. They're designed for you to knock out in one sitting—why, you might even see fit to take care of two or three of them before you get up from your chair! How's that for a sense of accomplishment?

But these puzzles are still every bit as full of good stuff as their larger cousins. These crosswords also have all the fun wordplay, clues and answers you've come to expect from a top-quality crossword. Answers, as ever, are found at the back of the book.

Note that the clues contain a hint when the answer has more than one word, like the clue "Casual greeting: 2 wds." for the answer HI THERE.

The game's afoot—so grab a pen or pencil and jump right in! The puzzles are small but the book is large, so you've got many hours of solving fun ahead.

1

Across

1 Scandinavian language
8 Mule of song
11 Former Brazilian president Geisel
12 Spanish pronoun
13 Gilded silver or bronze
14 PC command
15 Lover of Ares in Greek mythology
16 Humor or frivolity
18 Ogle: 2 wds.
20 Starts
23 Nabokov book set in upstate New York
26 "What did ___ deserve this?": 3 wds.
27 Lorna of Exmoor
28 Two, in Berlin
29 Ventilating passage in a mine
30 Frozen fruit-flavored dessert
32 French brandy
34 St. Louis squad from 1995 to 2015
38 Windy City rail inits.
39 The quality of sounding
41 Amex transaction, briefly
42 Russian horse-drawn vehicles
43 Mauna ___ (Hawaiian volcano)
44 Praise excessively

Down

1 Masters winner Ballesteros
2 Tiny warbler
3 Mr. 'iggins
4 Act of pulling down
5 Suffolk suffix
6 Ezra who founded Rhode Island College
7 Button-___ (sewing machine attachment)
8 1950s Edward R. Murrow news show: 3 wds.
9 Like some D.A.s
10 Delicate
17 Artificial cloud created by an aircraft: 2 wds.
19 Brian of rock
20 Profession, slangily
21 One of eight Eng. kings
22 Loses it: 2 wds.
24 ___ bit: 2 wds.
25 French marshal in the Napoleonic Wars (1769–1815)
27 Stop running
29 Fastest Finger options on "Who Wants to Be a Millionaire?": 5 wds.
31 Haile Selassie follower, for short
32 350, to Galba
33 Roman emperor after Galba
35 "Put Your Head on My Shoulder" songwriter
36 Hurdle for some univ. seniors
37 Mobutu ___ Seko
40 "___ Turn" (road sign): 2 wds.

2

Across

1 Mgrs.' helpers
6 Guam's capital, old-style
11 Area of expertise
12 Ripley's last part?: 2 wds.
13 Nasal grunt
14 The Friendly Islands
15 Direct opposite
17 Salty Greek cheeses
18 Reduces to small shreds
21 Those, in Mexico
25 Some flashlight batteries
26 Many a state name in D.C.
27 Doesn't fold
29 Stretch out
32 Texas cook-off dish
34 Gymnastic moves
39 Indiana basketballer
40 Noted jazz bandleader born Herman Blount: 2 wds.
41 Van Gogh locale
42 ____ President
43 Paris divider
44 Dateless

Down

1 Looped handle on an ancient vase
2 ____ Féin
3 Edinburgh resident
4 Frugality
5 Sofa
6 Great Barrier Island of New Zealand
7 ____ Pointe, Mich.
8 ____-Frid Lyngstad (former member of Abba)
9 December drinks
10 One day ____ time: 2 wds.
16 Elev. spots
18 Fuel
19 Singer Carly ____ Jepsen
20 Widow in "Peer Gynt"
22 Manuscript encl.
23 Gardner of "On the Beach"
24 But, to a Roman
28 Hide
29 Bro, e.g.
30 Blood component
31 Ceremony
33 Cowboy's companion
34 Alpine stream
35 251, to the Romans
36 Chinese leader?
37 Prefix in many juice names
38 Ditto
39 Pops

3

Across

1 The Grateful Dead's Phil
5 July 4th 1776, for example
9 Provoke
11 King and Norman
12 Annapolis frosh
13 Put the rowboat in motion
14 New Deal org.
15 Lennon's in-laws
16 Figures drawn simply: 2 wds.
18 St. Paul, for one
19 Fourth-year high school students: abbr.
22 Sta-___ fabric softener
23 Danger in Afghanistan, initially
24 Greek F
25 Literary collection
26 Mustard family flower
28 Like a game within reach
30 Ancient Roman garment worn at some college parties
31 State capital of North Carolina: abbr.
32 Indonesian island
33 Stagehands
36 Gray
37 "The Great Forest" painter Max
38 2 for Helium, e.g.: abbr. 2 wds.
39 Old Soviet secret police org.

Down

1 Edge
2 Film developing order: abbr.
3 1992 Al Pacino film: 4 wds.
4 Excessive self-confidence
5 Early American diplomat Silas
6 Executive producer of "Dynasty": 2 wds.
7 Uno y dos
8 Group of schools in one area, for short
10 Opponent of progress or reform
11 Became more important: 2 wds.
16 Twirled (around)
17 Fashion designer Calvin ___
18 River that forms part of the Paraguay-Brazil border
20 Taekwondo great Jhoon ___
21 Pitcher Fernandez
27 Pizza restaurant chain
29 Peter and Gordon's "___ Pieces": 3 wds.
30 List
32 Org. doing pat-downs
34 Sony handheld device, initially
35 1950s–60s TV star Erwin

4

Across

1. Big record label, once
7. Sidi ____, Morocco
11. Movement
12. Accomplishes
13. Compound thought to increase the risk of heart attacks
15. Small finch
16. Composer Camille Saint-____
17. Brightest star in the constellation Auriga
19. Like life, supposedly
22. ____ Spin (classic toy): 2 wds.
24. "____ Turn" (road sign): 2 wds.
25. Scientist's workspace, briefly
27. West who said "I generally avoid temptation unless I can't resist it"
28. Homepage address starter
30. Twofold
32. Islamic chiefs
34. Conger cousin
35. Composer Grofé
39. Easily upset: hyph.
41. Plane part
42. Axle application
43. Mo.-end document
44. Becomes fully recognized, and seems likely to continue: 2 wds.

Down

1. Gremlins, Pacers and Hornets, initially
2. Architect Mies van der ____
3. "Click ____ ticket" (NHTSA campaign): 2 wds.
4. Flint is a form of it
5. One of five on a foot
6. Years, to Yves
7. Epitomes
8. Front leg
9. All about babies
10. Small land masses: abbr.
14. China's Lao-____
18. Gucci rival
19. Wildcats's sch.
20. Only mediocre: 3 wds.
21. Art movement of the 1910s
23. Napoleonic marshal Michel
26. Outdoor blaze
29. Jupiter, e.g.
31. Online newsgroup system
33. Athletes Cobb and Warner
34. "White" peaks in N.H.
36. Genetic strands, initially
37. First name in 1950s TV comedy
38. Hebrew for "delight"
40. Metric wts.

5

Across

1 Scrutinize accounts
6 Dickens's Uriah
10 Rare and wonderful
12 Vehicle hire organization, initially
13 Cheese made from ewe's milk
14 Stat start
15 "Off ___?": 2 wds.
16 El ___ (1961 Charlton Heston role)
18 Acting award
21 Fundamentals
25 Judd and Grossman
27 Serving two functions: hyph.
29 "Yeah, right!": 2 wds.
30 California's Santa ___ Valley
31 Clinch: 2 wds.
32 Sch. group
33 2016 award for Carmen de Lavallade
37 Cube creator Rubik
40 It goes to air without delay: 2 wds.
42 Ham option
43 No-goodnik
44 Address fit for a king
45 Like Boston accents, as it were: hyph.

Down

1 Dynamic start?
2 Latin wife
3 "___ arigato" ("Thanks a lot" in Japanese)
4 "I'll consider ___ honor": 2 wds.
5 10th anniversary material
6 Printed version of computer data: 2 wds.
7 Military formation, briefly
8 Prior to
9 "The Languages of ___" (Jack Vance novel)
11 Tropical tree: 2 wds.
17 Munich's river
19 Supreme Egyptian god: var.
20 Ascent
21 Naval rank, briefly
22 Purchases
23 ___ noir
24 Dawdler
26 "Oh yeah? ___ who?!"
28 Look down
33 Curved geometric shape
34 Nota ___
35 Reply to "That so?": 2 wds.
36 December 24 and 31
37 Hesitant syllables
38 "Vive le ___!"
39 Big mfr. of A.T.M.s
41 Suffix with cash

6

Across

1. "Devil Dogs" org.
5. "Countdown" broadcaster
10. Artist Matisse
12. Tree held sacred by the Maya
13. Double-S curves
14. Criticize continually: 2 wds.
15. One way to treat disease
17. BBC nickname, with "the"
18. Berate: 2 wds.
22. Sewing case
26. Led Zeppelin singer: 2 wds.
28. Coin depository
29. Possible response to "where's the pie?": 3 wds.
30. Puncture sound
32. Garnet for January, e.g.
38. Niles's ex on "Frasier"
39. Old laborers
40. Sword lilies, for short
41. Rush
42. Sal who co-starred with James Dean
43. Coppertone nos.

Down

1. "This is bad!": hyph.
2. Utah's ___ Canyon
3. Memory: comb. form
4. Algonquian language
5. Major League Baseball manager and player Hal
6. Plane safety device: 2 wds.
7. Approaching
8. Hip-hop dancer: hyph.
9. Pink-slip
11. Weather map line
16. Childishly bad-tempered
18. Pennsylvania and B. & O. in Monopoly
19. Yahoo! competitor
20. Ethnic group of Nigeria
21. Montell Jordan album: 2 wds.
23. Menlo Park inits.
24. Prefix with cycle
25. TV cousin
27. Overtakes
31. "___ kind of you to ask": 2 wds.
32. Indonesian isle
33. Country whose capital is Tehran
34. An oz. has six
35. "Movin' ___" ("The Jeffersons" theme song): 2 wds.
36. Soft ball brand
37. Calculates roughly: abbr.
38. "The Wizard of Oz" studio

7

Across

1 Bistro
5 Pungent
10 Lena in "Havana"
11 Commercial cost, briefly: 2 wds.
12 Sportscaster ___ Albert
13 Beyond the limit: 2 wds.
14 "The ___ Love" (R.E.M. song): 2 wds.
15 ___-80 (old computer)
16 Medulla oblongata locale
21 Brave
23 Magi's origin
24 Utopias
25 Lumberjack
26 Wax-coated cheese
27 Browsing mammals of Central Africa
28 High-stakes draw in Las Vegas: 2 wds.
30 "___ did not!": 2 wds.
31 ___ la Douce
34 "___ be the day!"
37 Poverty
38 Come to pass
39 Gardner of mystery
40 Steps that lead over a fence
41 Brit. awards

Down

1 "Hot Diggity" singer
2 Actor and game show host Thicke
3 Land kept clear to stop the spread of flames
4 Relating to the natural world
5 Decorate
6 Closely questioned a hostile witness in court: hyph.
7 Brit. mil. heroes
8 Suffix for señor
9 Aachen article
11 Overhead storage spot
17 "___ for Alibi" (Sue Grafton mystery): 2 wds.
18 Interfering types
19 Actor Morales of "NYPD Blue"
20 Great heights, for short
21 "David Copperfield" character Uriah
22 Tuber of taro
25 Police blotter abbr.
27 "Darby ___ and the Little People" (1959 Disney film)
29 "Tell them Esther sent you" actress
32 Prefix with dramatic
33 Cool drinks
34 Cookbook amt.
35 ___ up (riled)
36 Movie org. with a "100 Years..." series

8

Across

1. Fed. accident investigators
5. Brad and William, e.g.
10. Sacred: prefix
12. Clinch a deal: 2 wds.
13. Montreal university
14. ___ Wafers
15. It's used to pay for online purchases: hyph.
17. Brain test initials
18. Channel that shows "Family Feud": inits.
20. Brew
22. Big-mouthed Martha
24. Feeling of pity
27. Actress Mitchell, Sister Robin on "Malcolm X"
29. Go on and on
30. Olympics cheer: 2 wds.
32. Suffix with diet or synth
33. Age
35. Que. neighbor
36. ___ tai (cocktail)
38. "If ___" (Beatles song): 2 wds.
40. Church part
42. Bring up to speed: 2 wds.
45. Actress Christina of 2012's "Bel Ami"
46. "Roots" subject Kunta ___
47. "Nuts" cartoonist Wilson
48. Phisher's acquisitions, for short

Down

1. Art Ross Trophy org.
2. Primo's mother
3. "The ___" (Marilyn Monroe/Tom Ewell movie of 1955): 3 wds.
4. Bric-a-___
5. Dope
6. Here, to Henri
7. Certain camera attachment: 2 wds.
8. Mosaic piece
9. Like some dinners
11. Endings for gran and can
16. Racecar additive
18. Gray, in Germany
19. Baseballers Bando and Maglie
21. Peut-___ (maybe: Fr.)
23. Pins and needles holder
25. "What's going ___ your mind?": 2 wds.
26. Split-off group
28. It's a relief
31. W.W. I army, initially
34. Adam's apple spot
36. "CSI" actress Helgenberger
37. Others, to Ovid
39. "Los Olvidados" director Buñuel
41. Code breakers' org.
43. Brit. news network
44. Pioneering game console, for short

9

Across

1 "Facing the Night" diarist Ned
6 In the hay
10 As a friend, to François: 2 wds.
11 Vase, in Versailles
12 Increasing by successive additions
14 F.I.C.A. funds it
15 TV's "Are We There Yet?" co-creator Ali
16 Slough
17 Shag rug made in Sweden
20 Flower lover's field
23 Classical Library founder
24 Resonant metallic sound
25 Iranian money
26 Not fer
27 TV title role for Brandy Norwood
28 North Carolina city: abbr.
29 Communally owned
30 Prefix with meter
32 Gridiron goals: abbr.
35 Woman's handbag
37 Diminish
38 Golden song
39 "That's not ___!" (parent's admonition): 2 wds.
40 "Snowden" director Oliver

Down

1 CDs and LPs
2 Load to bear
3 Avatar of Vishnu
4 Outback roamer
5 Grinding, as pepper
6 "Other" in Orléans
7 Vigor
8 Neighborhood
9 Low grade
13 Light and insubstantial
16 LPGA Hall of Famer Carol
18 Beatles refrain word
19 Start of a magician's cry
20 Mazda sub-compact vehicle: hyph.
21 One of Chekhov's "Three Sisters"
22 Man's formal evening garment
23 Baloney
25 Frito-Lay product
27 Remote button
29 Pleasing to the ear: 2 wds.
31 Plasm prefix
32 Commotion: hyph.
33 Bump off: 2 wds.
34 ___-Ball (arcade game)
35 Tenpin org., initially
36 Diner sandwich letters

10

Across

1 Spooks

6 Logos and the like: abbr.

9 Go away

11 Prefix meaning one tenth

12 Writer/director Nora

13 Tavern, old-style

14 Baseball Hall of Famer Aparicio

15 ___ State, New Jersey's nickname

17 Baseball field cover

18 ___ end point (fix a limit): 2 wds.

19 Chemical compound suffix

20 Oscar-winning movie score composer Piovani

21 In other words: 2 wds.

23 Fight, casually: hyph.

26 Hug and kiss in Kensington

30 Pick any number from ___ ten: 2 wds.

31 Au ___

32 Ascend

34 Will Varner's daughter-in-law in "The Long, Hot Summer"

35 Buckwheat pancake

36 Murders: slangily, 2 wds.

38 Place for a breath of fresh air?

39 Go over

40 Latin examples, briefly

41 Chicago airport

Down

1 Slim

2 New Guinea native

3 Speedy Suzuki

4 Extremely loud: hyph.

5 Pou ___, basis of operation

6 Care for

7 Bill ___ (Phil Hartman's "NewsRadio" character)

8 Reddish brown

10 Famous twin

11 Words quoted as actually said: 2 wds.

16 Garage sale warning: 2 wds.

20 India neighbor, briefly

22 Many comedy teams

23 Increase twofold

24 Disconnect from an electricity supply

25 Finches related to canaries

27 Sartre novel

28 More greasy

29 Rio ___ (Gulf of Mexico feeder)

33 Ethnic group of Vietnam

37 Grater maker

11

Across

1 Strategy board game
6 Bert Terhune's collie
9 Simile, metaphor
11 Paul Newman role in "Exodus"
12 Seafood go-with: 2 wds.
14 Old-fashioned music halls
15 "Doggone it!"
16 Portray
17 ___ Rivoli, Paris: 2 wds.
18 Part of UNLV
19 Elementary school textbook
21 Armada
22 To the extent that: 3 wds.
25 Deprive of by deceit: var.
28 Some citrus fruits
29 "What ___ you thinking?!"
30 Fast motion on film
31 Rial spenders
33 Motto advising caution: 2 wds.
35 Little one
36 Hasty dismissal: hyph.
37 Longest river in Scotland
38 Braying beasts

Down

1 Muslim women's quarters
2 City on the Missisippi north of St. Louis
3 It may require collateral
4 Team VIPs, shortly
5 Affirmative votes: var.
6 Oliver Hardy's partner Stan
7 Video game place
8 One who restricts food intake
9 Midway Islands, e.g.
10 Comaneci with five gold medals
13 Not for minors
17 Roger of "Cheers"
19 Some cameras, initially
20 Thimblerig prop
21 Laissez-___
22 Venn diagram part
23 Member of the Siouan people
24 As soft as down
25 Types
26 ___ Spring (brand of soap)
27 Pasta topper
29 Forgo
31 Court official's cry: var.
32 Degs. for performers
34 "J to ___ L–O" (Jennifer Lopez album)

12

Across

1 In a cool manner
6 B-52, e.g.
11 Liv Ullmann movie of 1992
12 Maori canoe
13 Poorly planned
15 Tart plum
16 Ernie who's won the U.S. Open twice
17 Car part
22 Position
25 XXX counterpart
26 Daughter of Michael Douglas
27 Bouquets
29 Mentalist Geller
30 1922–73 comic strip
31 Period of inactivity (with "the")
34 I.R.S. employee: abbr.
35 Catcall
39 Temporary
43 Politician Sarah or comedian Michael
44 Bold
45 Attention-getting sounds
46 Up ___ (trapped): 2 wds.

Down

1 Doctrines
2 Heating device
3 Assuming that's true: 2 wds.
4 ___ Bell (first rung on July 8, 1776)
5 "___-haw!"
6 ___ Peaks, ski resort in Indiana
7 "___ luck!" ("Knock 'em dead!")
8 A.B.A. member: abbr.
9 Born, in bios
10 Suffix with Salvador
14 H.S. diploma alternatives
18 Czech. neighbor
19 Binge, casually
20 Dutch astronomer who proved the galaxy rotates
21 Looking up
22 Skim along swiftly and easily
23 Poi source
24 Seed appendage
27 New age chant
28 Hand around: 2 wds.
30 Lather
32 Small crane on a ship
33 Spoils
36 Verb type: abbr.
37 Postpaid encl.
38 Real last name of Roy Rogers
39 Very softly, in music: abbr.
40 Dormitory overseers, initially
41 They protect QBs
42 Supermarket with a red oval logo, initially

13

Across

1 One of The Feds: hyph.
5 Accessories for vampires
10 Droplets
11 "___ of Two Cities" (novel by Charles Dickens): 2 wds.
12 Order
13 Encourage to attack: 2 wds.
14 Soft & ___ deodorant
15 PBS benefactor
17 Not hers
18 Get-___ (starts)
19 Truck section
20 Spanish bear
21 Historic periods
23 Back-talker
25 Latin clarifier: 2 wds.
27 Empty-___ (having gained nothing)
30 Juicy fruit
34 Fair-hiring agcy.
35 "The Little Drummer Boy" syllable
37 Palindromic conjunction
38 Change the position of words, letters, etc.: abbr.
39 Coll. in Troy, N.Y.
40 The Eagle, e.g.
41 Sir or madam
43 Malice
45 Noted Tombstone brothers
46 Kind of shooting
47 King and Shepard
48 Supervisors, briefly

Down

1 Great fear
2 ___ Tomei, Molly Fawcett in "Cyrus"
3 Boise's county
4 Group that performed at Super Bowl XXXV
5 Winter melons
6 Put away
7 Feeling of pity
8 Horror movie directed by Robert Legato
9 Security system part
10 Emblem of office
16 Relaxed: 2 wds.
22 Gillman in the Pro Football Hall of Fame
24 Racing initials
26 Lower
27 Chinese restaurant freebie: 2 wds.
28 Above the ground
29 Cosa ___
31 Harder to grasp
32 Alpine ridges
33 Convened anew
36 Divine name in showbiz: 2 wds.
42 Hosp. employee, perhaps
44 FedEx pickup: abbr.

14

Across

1 Yogurt containers
5 Having prongs
10 Zhou ___, prime minister of China 1949–76
12 What a meter tracks
13 Fraught with difficulty
15 Three vowels that mean "you'll get your money"
16 56 in Roman numerals
17 GI-entertaining gp.
18 Metric units of volume: abbr.
19 Roadside bomb letters
20 Tape deck button: abbr.
21 "How Do I Live" singer Rimes
23 Romance in verse
24 Tennessee football player
26 "Get outta here!"
29 Take washing off the line
32 Pig
33 Some batteries, initially
34 Slangy dissent
36 ___ Dubarry (cooked with cauliflower): 2 wds.
37 1959 Kingston Trio hit
38 Lit up in a car: abbr.
39 Certain grammatical tense: 2 wds.
42 Famed 1950s flop
43 Popular potato
44 Symbol of freshness
45 Opera "Moses und ___"

Down

1 Lukewarm
2 Open, in a way
3 Alternative to a shirt
4 Religious day: abbr.
5 Puffy
6 "This ___ travesty!": 2 wds.
7 Flora and fauna
8 Armor breastplates
9 Boil down
11 Fighting footballers
14 Happen finally
22 Long-distance inits.
23 Economist's stat.
25 Aziz of "Parks and Recreation"
26 Molded
27 Cocktail made with rum, pineapple and coconut, pina ___
28 2003 Australian Open champ
30 Make lovable
31 Pampas cowboy
33 More than adequately
35 Single out: 2 wds.
40 French possessive
41 Pharmaceutical watchdog grp.

15

Across

1 Attorney F. ___ Bailey
4 They have Xings
7 Weather-affecting currents: 2 wds.
9 Rate at which computer data is transferred, initially
12 Flavoring obtained from the crocus
13 Monetary unit of Romania
14 Foreign currency
15 Lens settings: hyph.
17 Related through the mother
19 Santa ___, California
20 Japan's money
21 How a homey home looks: 2 wds.
24 "The Boating Party" painter Mary
26 Crossways
28 Book after Phil.
31 Junho preceder
32 Goo
34 Lose
37 Conquistador's chest
38 Suffix with Capri
39 One who's "just looking"
41 Native land
42 Criticized strongly
43 Birthplace of Robert Burns
44 RB's stat.

Down

1 "It's My Party" singer Gore
2 "Seinfeld" pal
3 Granted voting rights
4 Time off, initially
5 It may be pitched
6 Tax IDs
8 "___ first you don't succeed...": 2 wds.
9 Marked by eagerness to resort to violence
10 Coke competitor
11 "The Volcano Lover" novelist Sontag
16 Shipping allowance
18 Lioness of literature
22 Med. land
23 Big containers at a winery
25 G.I. delinquent
26 Tracers, bullets, etc.
27 Japanese video game developer
29 Hosted
30 ZZ Top features
33 Congress passes them
35 "Dancing Queen" band from Sweden
36 Every 12 mos.
40 Dinghy mover

16

Across

1 Big name in restaurant guides
6 Pet protection grp.
11 Popular vodka, briefly
12 Kind of center: abbr.
13 Assign as a share
14 Hesitant remark
15 TV puppet surname
17 W.W. II beach assault vehicle
18 Feudal estate
20 Ancient Greek coin
22 BBC rival
23 Decorate
26 Not as many
28 Grps.
29 Not accurate
31 "Where ____ begin?": 2 wds.
32 Dict. info
33 Actress Talbot
34 Harebrained
36 Important exam
38 Accused's need
40 Have a cow
43 Rushed, as to attack: 2 wds.
44 Indian ____
45 2003 Ben Affleck/ Jennifer Lopez movie
46 Bit of a branch

Down

1 Doubled, a Gabor
2 U.S./U.K. divider
3 Fiftieth anniversary of a marriage: 2 wds.
4 Removed
5 Jackson 5 member
6 Career soldier's kid: 2 wds.
7 Hemingway book "The Old Man and the ____"
8 "Pink Motel" star: 2 wds.
9 They can be hailed
10 Assist illegally
16 1988 Meg Ryan film: inits.
18 Poodle name
19 Coast-to-coast highway: 2 wds.
21 Light settings
23 Drawings sprayed on public buildings
24 Contemptible sort, slangily
25 Chinese dynasty circa 2070–1600 B.C.: var.
27 River of Devon
30 Vegas-based crime show, initially
33 They award the Spingarn Medal, initially
34 Helgenberger of "Erin Brockovich"
35 Part of a court game name
37 Sgts. and such
39 Dance, in Dieppe
41 Rock guitarist Steve
42 Famous twin

17

Across

1 G.I.'s headgear, slangily: 2 wds.
7 Golf targets
11 Cleave
12 "I'm working ___!": 2 wds.
13 More slippery
14 Some learning
15 Rural
17 Hiker's path
20 Dance, in France
21 Rhubarb
22 7th-century B.C. Greek city
25 Naval rank, briefly
26 Mil. aide
27 Malicious
30 Vacuum cleaner maker
32 Laughing sound
33 Beat around the bush
34 Las Vegas Strip feature: 2 wds.
37 Make ___ for it (flee): 2 wds.
38 Cognition
42 Pending, as a legal decree
43 Robin Williams' role in a 1982 movie: inits., 2 wds.
44 Witnessed
45 "Gimme a break!"

Down

1 South Korea's Roh ___ woo
2 Fish of the carp family
3 Flyers' org.
4 Baseball Hall-of-Famer Manush
5 Cactus feature
6 Fork-tailed marine bird
7 Capture and confine (a group)
8 Free
9 Hummus holder
10 Submachine gun
16 Where, in old Rome
17 Govt. agent: hyph.
18 Stigma borne by Nathaniel Hawthorne's Hester Prynne: 2 wds.
19 Charitable dwelling for the poor
23 Homeland Security org.
24 "Harry Potter" lizard
28 Bark component
29 Jr. and sr.
30 "My word!": 2 wds.
31 Go back on a promise
34 Opera singer Merriman, et al.
35 Foe of the Iroquois
36 QB's misthrows
39 Freelancer's enc.
40 Tax-collecting org.
41 Geom. solid

18

Across

1 Den
5 Phoenix neighbor
9 Like some suspects
11 Tropical palm
13 Losing come-out roll in craps
14 Crew member
15 Data compression format letters
16 Sanctuary
18 Addams Family member
19 Provoke
20 Prefix meaning "ten": var.
21 "___ won't be afraid" ("Stand by Me" line): 2 wds.
22 Kitchen item: abbr.
24 Make short quick movements from side to side
26 Point (an arrow, for example) towards a target: 2 wds.
28 "The Ballad of ___" Tennyson poem
30 Kind of team
33 Paunch
34 Spawn
36 Corporate V.I.P.
37 TV series that takes place in Miami, initially
38 Animated film unit
39 Consumed
40 "___ a trip on a train..." (Benny Goodman lyric): 2 wds.
42 Formal response to "Who's there?": 3 wds.
44 Cape Cod resort town
45 "___ a gun!": 2 wds.
46 X ___ "xylophone": 2 wds.
47 Start of a counting-out rhyme

Down

1 Light brown fur
2 F equivalent: 2 wds.
3 Clandestine
4 Menlo Park initials
5 Former monetary units of Finland
6 Ending for pistol or haban
7 Tailor's tool: 2 wds.
8 Colorless ketone
10 Advantage, in sports
12 Clarinetist Shaw
17 Mend, as a rug
23 When doubled, a Teletubby
25 JPEG alternative
27 "___ Wood" (Eddie Floyd song): 2 wds.
28 In the work already quoted: abbr., 2 wds.
29 Raised platforms
31 Sanity
32 Change, make different
35 Actresses Landry, Lohan and Larter
41 "It must be him, ___ shall die" (song lyric): 2 wds.
43 Foot digit

19

Across

1. But, to Nero
4. "...then ___ monkey's uncle!": 2 wds.
7. Minor player
10. 1990 Robert Morse Tony-winner
11. Popular Indian snack food
12. ___-Locka, Fla.
13. Latin foot
14. "Yes!": 2 wds.
15. Bugs's voice
16. Unstable, changeable
18. G.I. grub
19. Practical rather than attractive
21. Dolt
22. Early capital of Macedonia
23. Subatomic particles
25. Hoosegow
27. Thatching palm
30. Capable of producing an intended result
32. Arnold Bax composition of 1907, "Symphony ___": 2 wds.
33. Purposes
34. "Pink Panther" films actor
35. The, to Germans
36. Want ad palindrome, initially
37. LAX letters
38. Suffix with rep or rev
39. Humdrum existence
40. Room of the house
41. Internet protocol, initially
42. CO and CT, e.g.

Down

1. Minnesota twin?: 2 wds.
2. "Are you" in Andalusia: 2 wds.
3. "Tootsie" star: 2 wds.
4. Last Supper query: 3 wds.
5. European sea
6. Green shade
7. Representatives of a supreme authority
8. "Fidelio" and "Rigoletto"
9. Chief ore of lead
17. High-pH chemical
20. "The Day the Earth Stood Still" star Michael
24. Came to a conclusion
25. Lined the roof of
26. Deserving attention: 2 wds.
28. Extinguished: 2 wds.
29. Stocks and such
31. "Save" shortcut on a PC: abbr., 2 wds.

20

Across

1 Vincent van ____ (painter of "Irises")
5 Silencing device
10 Thought: prefix
11 Dylan or Denver, e.g.
12 Dryer deposit
13 "Well!": 2 wds.
14 Debris
16 Décolleté: hyph.
20 City in Mercer County, Illinois
22 Truckler
23 River-blocking structure
24 Suffix for jambo or kedge
25 Grant-____: hyph.
28 Courses for horses
30 Certain farm female: 2 wds.
32 Oily, volatile hydrocarbon
35 James Cameron movie
38 Swedish furniture chain
39 Provide with new electric cabling
40 One, in Vienna
41 Stupefy
42 Make-or-break time: hyph.

Down

1 Embellish
2 Comics canine
3 Gallant sort
4 Racing car: 2 wds.
5 Ballroom dance
6 Agency the U.S. rejoined in 2003
7 France's high-speed rail service, initially
8 Wide spec.
9 Grammar-school trio, initially
11 ____ Sleep (mattress retail chain): 2 wds.
15 The Battle of ____ Jima
17 Martial arts movie of 1984 (with "The"): 2 wds.
18 Henry James biographer Leon
19 Colors
20 Result of an ace on a deuce: abbr., 2 wds.
21 Tinseltown's Turner
26 Ab ____ (from the start)
27 "L.A. Law" actor Richard
28 Dr. Wonmug's caveman, Alley
29 Diverse
31 He came after Quayle
33 1980s German pop star
34 Carefree
35 Wall St. wheeler-dealer
36 Flight formation
37 Sympathetic sounds

21

Across

1 Basket fiber
6 Financial records, briefly
11 Of the country
12 "Edges" novelist Skolkin-Smith
13 Boom source, for short: 2 wds.
14 Not intended seriously: 2 wds.
15 Hard-shell clam
17 "By the look ___...": 2 wds.
18 "___: Deadliest Roads" (reality TV series)
19 Org. that publishes American Hunter
21 Dir. opposite WSW
22 Stitched (together)
24 State
26 What the Titanic struck
28 Self-assurance
30 Beam
33 Fleur de ___ (French sea salt)
34 Hippie's hangout
36 Formula ___
37 Expectorate
39 Bring to a humbler state
41 "___ Little Prayer" (Aretha Franklin hit): 3 wds.
43 Ancient city in Egypt
44 Foolish people, casually
45 Put an ___ (cause to stop existing): 2 wds.
46 Map within a map
47 "It's a power play goal!" sportscaster Sam

Down

1 Baghdad residents
2 Seam used in surgery
3 "Everwood" star: 2 wds.
4 Punishment for a sailor, maybe
5 John of rock
6 Thrilla in Manila boxer
7 Prefix meaning "common"
8 Remains in the kitchen: 2 wds.
9 Bringing into alignment
10 River that flows through S. Carolina into the Atlantic
16 Rail fixed to a bathroom wall: 2 wds.
20 Pale ___ (kind of beer)
23 Cpl. or sgt.
25 Shirt size: abbr.
27 Title of Japan's Akihito: abbr.
28 St. Francis' birthplace
29 Digestive enzyme in the stomach
31 Move or provoke to action
32 "Next of Kin" costar Liam
35 Discourage
38 Sort
40 Soap actress Linda
42 Bermuda clock setting, initially

22

Across

1 Toni Morrison book "____ Baby"
4 Dockworker's org.
7 Show to a seat, informally
8 ____ de plume (pen name)
9 Univ. degrees
12 "Rock in ____" (2001 Iron Maiden album)
13 Silklike fabric
15 Tennis star Rafael ____
17 Peninsula in SE Asia
18 "Young Frankenstein" role
19 Soft shoes, slangily
20 Sound file available on the Internet
24 Neb. neighbor
25 Hearing distance
27 Former name of the cable network Versus, initially
29 In an offensively bold manner
32 Infirmary count
34 "I ____ Dark Stranger" (1946 movie): 2 wds.
35 Chilean pianist Claudio
37 Libreville's land
38 Small aquatic bird
40 Apt. feature, in the classifieds
41 Author Rand
42 Masi of "Hawaii Five-0"
43 Prevaricate
44 Lyndon Johnson dog
45 Even score

Down

1 Rutabaga's cousin
2 Pungent cheese
3 Shrub with large clusters of flowers
4 Worldwide: abbr.
5 Mauna ____ (Hawaiian volcano)
6 Radio switch: hyph.
9 Unfair, casually: 3 wds.
10 City in Chisago County, Minnesota
11 Final word: hyph.
14 Relatives, slangily
16 Conquistador's chest
21 Wall St. figure
22 Kazakhstan letters, once
23 "____ Carter" (Lil Wayne album)
26 Mountain in Thessaly
27 Bush successor
28 Conductor Anderson
30 Pope who crowned Charlemagne emperor of the Romans: 2 wds.
31 Mariano Rivera once, e.g.
33 Patriotic org.
36 "Looks like trouble!": hyph.
37 Watchdog's sound
39 Just manage, with "out"

23

Across

1 Alan of "M*A*S*H"
5 Cover, in a way
10 Actresses Marsh and West
11 Goof: hyph.
12 "Look no further!": 2 wds.
13 Elongated cluster of flowers
14 Reduce the intensity of (as a conflict): hyph.
16 Fight the powers that be
17 Heads in Paris
19 Actor Kevin, Captain Dylan Hunt in "Andromeda"
24 Part of a popular palindrome: 2 wds.
25 Turn
26 Small racing vehicles
28 Nocturnal South American rodents
29 Ancient Roman magistrate
31 Tabulated numerical facts
36 Second of January: 2 wds.
37 Singer Novello
38 Serving dish
39 Señora's baby girl
40 Aptly named English novelist Charles
41 Rowing machine units

Down

1 In the center of
2 In the wee hours
3 Army absconder
4 Opinion opener: 4 wds.
5 Handy-andies: hyph.
6 Brown & Haley candy, Mocha ____
7 Aid a crook
8 Apple or pear
9 Letters in a help wanted ad
11 Highlands hillside
15 Certain radios, initially
17 Steele's partner in Smif-N-Wessun
18 Ours is the Cenozoic
20 Malty drink brand
21 Listening device
22 "Luck ____ Lady Tonight": 2 wds.
23 Surg. workplaces
27 Parlor piece
28 Gumshoes, briefly
30 Naturalist Fossey
31 "Leaving Las Vegas" costar
32 When tripled, a 1970 war film
33 "Girl With ____ Hat" (Vermeer): 2 wds.
34 D.C. group
35 Mrs.'s counterparts, in Mexico
36 Symphonic score abbr.

24

Across

1 Brimless hat
6 Annoyed
11 ____ gum, resin used in making varnish
12 Brownish gray
13 Bay window
14 Oxford doctorate, briefly
15 Nestling hawk
17 Donald Duck, to his nephews
18 Slowing, in mus.
20 Chance in a game
22 P.T.A. concern: abbr.
24 One of a ship's main masts
28 Field Marshal of World War II, ____ von Bock
30 Prefix with surgery or transmitter
31 Suitable
33 Attys.' degrees
34 Those, in Mexico
36 Chase scene maneuver, slangily
37 San ____, Italy
40 Iranian coin
42 Automatic transmission setting
44 Closes in on
47 Broadcast
48 Funnel-shaped
49 Bit of laughter
50 "The ____ near!" (doomsayer's phrase): 2 wds.

Down

1 M.M.A. fight finale
2 Pole with a blade on one end
3 Peacefulness
4 Manhattan Project scientist
5 Southernmost city of Israel
6 "____ be an honor!"
7 German fairy tale girl
8 "The Structure of Scientific Revolutions" author Thomas
9 "Giant" for example
10 Boxing's Oscar ____ Hoya: 2 wds.
16 Dim ____
18 Football game "zebras": abbr.
19 Nantes notion
21 ____ Tin Tin
23 Drop in: 2 wds.
25 Natal section, once
26 Earth, to Mahler
27 Like a yenta
29 19th-century literary inits.
32 Shostakovich's "Babi ____" Symphony
35 Afterwards
37 Vitamin amts.
38 "____ Go Bragh!" (Irish)
39 Joan of art
41 "____ Flux" (Charlize Theron film)
43 Summer hrs. in D.C.
45 King, in Portugal
46 Certain 1960s protesters, initially

25

Across

1 Hanoi bowlful
4 Basic chess tactic
7 To the point
9 Automobile
12 Restaurant that makes its own ale
13 "Star Trek: Deep Space Nine" shapeshifter
14 El Paso coll.
15 Mil. head honcho
16 Alcoholic, for short
18 E-mail icon
19 Albuquerque college letters
20 Mary's upstairs neighbor, in 1970s TV
22 According to the teaching of the gospel
26 Football Hall-of-Famer Greasy ___
27 Moniker
28 Illegal firing
30 Mexican mother
32 "(Love Is) The Tender Trap" lyricist Sammy
33 "___ fan tutte" (Mozart opera)
34 The Engineers' sch.
35 Travels past (on horseback, e.g.): 2 wds.
38 Bark
39 Cloying sentimentality
40 Note after fa
41 Damascus' land: abbr.

Down

1 Banned chemical compound
2 Opposite of vert.
3 Practice of successfully outdoing a competitor
4 Church instrument, often: 2 wds.
5 "The rest ___ to you!": 2 wds.
6 Kan. neighbor
8 20ths of a ton: abbr.
9 They store digital information: 2 wds.
10 Supplementary: abbr.
11 "Marco Polo" star Calhoun
15 100 pesewas in Ghana
16 Fitting
17 Patent holder, often: abbr.
18 One worthy of imitation: 2 wds.
21 Norse goddess
23 Element seen in Las Vegas
24 Swiss river
25 Big T-shirt size: abbr.
28 "___ From Within" (2014 horror movie): 2 wds.
29 ___ Iti (island of French Polynesia)
31 On a deck, perhaps
33 Opera by Francesco Cavalli
35 A.C.L.U. concerns: abbr.
36 Nellie ___, pen name of Elizabeth Jane Cochran
37 "___ Blues" ("White Album" song)

26

Across

1 Area for users new to a website, initially
5 Magazine contents, briefly
9 "Be-Bop-___" (1956 Gene Vincent hit): hyph.
11 Drag through the mud
12 Amphitheater levels
13 "___ Frutti" (Little Richard hit)
14 Magazine: abbr.
15 Combine chemically with water
17 Zinger
18 Meditation sounds
19 Country singer McDaniel
20 "Peer Gynt" dancer
22 Coal carriers
23 Honorary U.K. title
24 "That's neither here ___ there"
25 Actress Sofer who played Rocky on "Loving"
27 Edible legume
30 Suffix with Caesar
31 PepsiCo soft drink brand
32 "Makes you wonder…"
33 Swagger
35 Facing: abbr.
36 Eastern Christian
37 Supermarket section
39 Plants with leafy fronds
40 Former
41 Liberate
42 "___ sow, so shall…": 2 wds.

Down

1 Youngest daughter of the prophet Muhammad
2 Bluegrass singer Krauss
3 Market research instrument
4 Camera inits.
5 River that flows into the Sea of Okhotsk
6 Transformation of a larva into an adult
7 Tangled
8 Architectural projections
10 On land
11 Yardsticks: abbr.
16 "The Peruvian Songbird" Sumac
21 TV schedule letters, at times
22 "___ was I supposed to know that?"
24 "Forget it!": 2 wds.
25 Blunt turndown
26 Bread maker
27 Rotter
28 Put to work
29 Current amount
31 Kit ___ (candy bars)
34 Barn topper
38 Sinn Féin's gp.

27

Across

1 "When Will ___ Loved" (The Everly Brothers hit): 2 wds.
4 ___ culpa
7 Mythical sleep-bringer
9 G.I. grub
12 Most provocative
13 "Ten thousand saw ___ a glance" (Wordsworth): 2 wds.
14 Will Varner's daughter-in-law in "The Long, Hot Summer"
15 "Valse ___" Sibelius orchestral piece
17 After a fashion: 3 wds.
19 Tries: 3 wds.
21 Meat approver, for short
23 Old English letter
24 King in a Steve Martin song
26 ___ tree (trapped): 2 wds.
27 Soda brand
29 Little feeling, as of pain or guilt
31 Unfounded criticisms
33 Disappear without ___: 2 wds.
34 Jerk: var.
37 Canadian TV channel, initially
38 Kelly's prince
40 River at Ghent
41 Donny and Marie
42 "The shakes," initially
43 Fair hiring letters, for short

Down

1 "Interesting": 2 wds.
2 "On & On" singer Erykah
3 Instruments of the oboe family
4 Fr. title
5 Abilene to Waco direction: hyph.
6 Cavern, in poetry
8 Goddess of the hunt
9 "Little" title role of 2006: 2 wds.
10 Suitable for most audiences: 2 wds.
11 Summer, in St-Tropez
16 Shiba ___ (dog breed)
18 Man in Black, e.g.: abbr.
19 Lady lobster
20 In a proficient manner
22 Tooth-doctors' org.
25 Date minimum
28 "Let's call ___ night": 2 wds.
30 "___ Good" Depeche Mode song: 2 wds.
32 Catch of the day, maybe
33 Popular ISP
35 Native of Media
36 Around: 2 wds.
39 Types online notes to, for short

28

Across

1 Strengthen, with "up"
5 Broadway backer
10 Sea east of the Caspian
11 Foolishness
12 Learning style
13 Pieces for nine
14 Former Eur. carrier
15 Assayed material
16 Trance-inducing practice
20 Pay: 2 wds.
23 Lacking points of prominence
24 ____ T (exactly): 2 wds.
25 Hit (a ball) in a high arc
27 Medical suffix
28 Turner and others
30 City in NE New Jersey
32 Brunch order
34 Lens solution brand: 2 wds.
35 Trackside barrier
39 Choice
41 Deaden
42 Bing rival
43 Prefix with logical
44 Reporter Goldman and author Godin
45 They may be audiovisual

Down

1 Fishhook's end
2 Ending for smack or smash
3 "____ Peach" (The Allman Brothers Band album): 2 wds.
4 Slender church spire
5 Deck out
6 ____ diamonds (red playing card): 2 wds.
7 Doesn't speed: 2 wds.
8 Shock treatment: inits.
9 River of France and Belgium
11 Ill-timed
17 "Futureworld" costar Brynner
18 "____ Barbarian" (Edgar Rice Burroughs novel): 3 wds.
19 Hang in there
20 Periodic table fig.: abbr., 2 wds.
21 "On Language" author Chomsky
22 French fry alternative: 2 wds.
26 Halloween flyer
29 Santa's conveyance
31 Weightlifter's pain
33 Some organic compounds
36 Car company with a four ring logo
37 Contacted online, briefly
38 Wall St. deals
39 Some guys in rap songs, initially
40 Author Edgar Allan ____

29

Across

1 Suffix with utter or annoy

5 On ____ (equipotent): 2 wds.

9 Nuts

11 Start of a song's refrain: hyph.

12 Spin doc., often: 2 wds.

13 "Brave New ____" (Huxley novel)

14 Chance

15 Soprano Sumac

17 Sportage and Sorento maker

18 Have something to complain about

19 Written account

21 U.S.-born Japanese

23 Eliminate

24 Tidbits

26 TV Chihuahua

27 Daedalus' nephew

29 Men in Madrid

31 Japanese electronics giant, for short

33 Summer D.C. setting

34 "Take your pick"

35 "Law & Order: ____" (police drama series), initially

36 Rested

38 "You've got mail" message receiver

40 Animation artist Eyvind

41 Nasty look

42 Real last name of Roy Rogers

43 Female sheep

Down

1 Greek leader?

2 Forecast words golfers like to hear: 2 wds.

3 Free

4 Disney deer

5 River of Venezuela

6 Cynical observation that work will expand so as to fill the time available for its completion

7 Joined by treaty

8 Detector

10 Late talk show host Tom

11 "Jabberwocky" opener

16 Wet

20 Push, as merchandise

22 Sound-related prefix

25 Classes you barely attend: 2 wds.

26 Give out again, as cards

28 Forbidding

29 Four-time Australian Open winner Monica

30 Bank posting

32 Ringlets

37 Mets and Marlins div.

39 Half and half

30

Across

1 Highway sign abbr.
4 Comedian Philips
7 Former federal agency for carriers: inits.
10 Portable sunshade
12 ____ Tae-woo, 6th president of S. Korea
13 Straggler's question: 3 wds.
14 "Should I take that as ____?": 2 wds.
15 Arrogantly self-assertive
16 Extraordinary, in Scotland
17 Soapmaker's materials
18 Mountain fortresses: var.
20 Campaign
21 Popular painkiller
24 Meat from a deer
25 "Are you" in Spain: 2 wds.
26 EarthLink and AOL, initially
30 Not being used
31 Small stream
33 It isn't the truth
34 Choral composition
35 Suffix with appoint or assign
36 Home perm brand
37 E.R. workers: abbr.
38 Show off, as a motorcycle's engine, shortly
39 Letters on a Cardinal's cap

Down

1 Billionaire Getty: 2 wds.
2 Like some humor
3 Drivel
4 Spanish pronoun
5 Bertolt Brecht title character: 2 wds.
6 Cheer for a toreador
7 From Teheran, e.g.
8 Yield
9 Pick
11 "Aladdin" prince and namesakes
16 Bears: Lat.
19 10 jiao
20 Outlay
21 More technologically obsessed
22 1970 hit, "____ Bell to Answer": 2 wds.
23 Wood shop gripper
24 Hidden
26 Like JFK
27 Poles, e.g.
28 ____ four
29 "Delphine" author Madame de ____
32 Part of A.A.U.W.: abbr.
34 ____ anglais (English horn)

31

Across

1 Robert ___, Jeff Haffley on "The West Wing"

5 Harmonious vocal style of music developed in the 1950s: hyph.

11 New World abbr.

12 Recently: 2 wds.

13 Clean-shaven: hyph.

15 Israeli port

16 Brazilian palm

17 "Come on, be ___!": 2 wds.

19 Fixed sock holes

22 "___ Death" (from Peer Gynt Suite No. 1)

26 Result that follows its cause

28 Architect ___ van der Rohe

29 The LO of baseball's LOB: 2 wds.

30 Sitar master Shankar

31 Compound derived from ammonia

35 TV actress Georgia

39 Wheeled support for a piece of artillery: 2 wds.

41 Funny business

42 "___ yellow ribbon…": 2 wds.

43 Places to sleep

44 Inmates' exercise area

Down

1 Carry's partner

2 Muslim community

3 Fifth-century pope who was canonized: 2 wds.

4 Treats with irreverence

5 Line from Homer

6 Internal organs of an animal

7 Endings for can and caramb

8 G.I. Janes

9 "Cup ___" (1970s Don Williams song): 2 wds.

10 Foot: prefix

14 Get to the point?

18 Daughter of William the Conqueror

19 Obstruct

20 Movie-cataloging grp.

21 State hwy.

22 Spontaneous feeling of kinship

23 Go down

24 System starter

25 El stop: abbr.

27 High temperature

30 Respond

31 Food thickener

32 Red cyclops on "Yo Gabba Gabba!"

33 Go ___ detail

34 Mark Harmon series on CBS

36 Greek goddess, daughter of Chaos

37 Elbe tributary

38 Starring role

40 System for distributing news to Web users, initially

32

Across

1 Attach, as a patch: 2 wds.

6 Garden pest

11 "Uncle Vanya" woman

12 Jungle vine: var.

13 Astronaut Neil Armstrong's middle name

14 Crete's tallest summit: abbr., 2 wds.

15 Longish skirts

16 Tijuana toast

17 "___ the Air" (novel by Walter Kirn): 2 wds.

18 A puppy has three

19 Form 1040EZ info.

20 Pound and Klein

23 Utensil used in the kitchen

26 Dry

27 Med. country

29 Saudi king until 2005

31 Spice rack selection

32 "You beat me": 2 wds.

34 Stocking material

35 Keep from desiccating

36 "To recap...": 2 wds.

37 Surgical tube

38 Headache intensifier

39 Afternoon in Andalusia

40 Shoe-factory employee

Down

1 ___ Heaney, Irish poet who wrote "The Haw Lantern"

2 Oval

3 Party before a marriage: 2 wds.

4 Words before a million: 2 wds.

5 Opera singer Merriman, et al.

6 Offering

7 Heartbeat: hyph.

8 Leader worshiped by Rastafarians: 2 wds.

9 ___ course: 2 wds.

10 Resolved issues, slangily

20 Diminish

21 Sleep unit?

22 Data compression format letters

24 Very helpful event

25 Loner

28 German auto, slangily

29 Coming before all others

30 Longtime comic strip queen

31 Lesser in importance

33 Room or sermon ender

34 Dryer discard

33

Across

1. Low-___
5. Falsify (a document, e.g.)
11. Jazz singer Laine
12. Mount Holyoke graduate, e.g.
13. Swedish automaker once owned by NEVS
14. Attaches anew
15. Trade stoppage
17. Like some textbook publishing: hyph.
18. Body underwriting private bank accounts, initially
22. Filmmaking technique that gradually introduces a picture: hyph.
24. Greek cheese
25. 1969 Peace Prize group letters
26. Benin native
27. Chimney channel
29. Fresh
32. Borgia in-law
33. Like some profs.
34. "Forget it!": 2 wds.
37. Big name in small planes
40. "You've Got a Friend ___": 2 wds.
42. Lack of acknowledgement
43. Con
44. Moon goddess
45. Records of brain activity, initially

Down

1. IV units
2. Wings, anatomically
3. Rebuked fiercely, in slang: 2 wds.
4. Decoration on a hat
5. Samantha's "Bewitched" husband
6. Cassini of fashion
7. Disconnect, isolate: 2 wds.
8. "That's more than I needed to hear!," initially
9. Latish lunchtime
10. ___ Tafari (Haile Selassie)
16. Pacific tuna
19. Respect
20. "Send ___" (Disney's Friends for Change song): 2 wds.
21. Quitter's word
22. Small flute
23. Shakespeare title starter
28. Tiny: var.
29. Flea market deal
30. Former big record label initials
31. Color of ripe cherries
35. ___ equal basis: 2 wds.
36. Drudge Report, e.g.
37. Some savings accts.
38. Big foot meas.
39. TV show with skits
41. Dash lengths

34

Across

1 Sgt. Joe Friday's force
5 1982 World Cup site
10 "Dies ___" (hymn)
11 TV's "The George & ___ Show"
12 It's used to thicken sauces
14 Popular craft
15 Sheet music abbr.
16 1960s civil rights activist Brown, familiarly: 2 wds.
20 Some formal wear: 2 wds.
24 Docker's union, initially
25 "On ___ to know basis": 2 wds.
26 Immune system lymphocyte: hyph.
28 Obese, short-legged god of Egyptian myth
29 Support (a cause, e.g.)
31 Jedi antagonist in "Star Wars"
33 "Solaris" author Stanislaw
34 Secret
39 Way to get rid of things you don't want: 2 wds.
41 Bowl
42 Clumsy boats
43 Container for water
44 Feeler

Down

1 Pass the tongue over
2 "East of Eden" brother
3 ___ passu (at an equal rate)
4 Having a toothlike edge
5 Molière's metier
6 Builder's need
7 Cry of frustration
8 Mag for execs
9 "Uh-uh!"
13 Pace
17 Modern waltz violinist André
18 Shakespeare title opener
19 Appear inferior by comparison
20 Jazz vocalist Gonzales
21 "The ___ Wrote For You" (2014 movie written by David Kauffman): 2 wds.
22 ___ Bank
23 Tampa neighbor, briefly: 2 wds.
27 Attacks: 2 wds.
30 Motto
32 "___ Johnny!"
35 One-time bathroom brand, ___-Flush
36 Exceptional
37 Exploits
38 "___ la guerre"
39 Chat
40 Southern constellation

35

Across

1 Runner Zatopek
5 Trans-Siberian Railroad city
9 Patsy's pal on "Absolutely Fabulous"
10 "Slow down, it's not ___": 2 wds.
11 Near the back of a derby field
12 H.H. ___ (Saki's real name)
13 Route letters
14 Salt
16 Go on and on
17 Radial fill
18 Cecil Campbell, a.k.a. ___ Kamoze
19 Home of the Cox Sch. of Business
20 Pan's partner
22 In danger: 2 wds.
24 Area prone to flooding
26 Cheap
28 Broken-off branch
31 "Baby ___ Star" (Prince song): 2 wds.
32 Book before Neh.
34 Rap's Dr. ___
35 Most preferred
36 Grant-giving grp.
37 Letters between M and Q
38 Kind of acid
40 Volleyballer/ model Gabrielle
42 Oscar-winning actor Colin
43 Arise
44 Oktober follower?
45 Sleep roughly, in British slang

Down

1 Blissful
2 Dasani and Ferrarelle, e.g.: 2 wds.
3 CD earnings
4 Christine, Eileen in "Hateship, Loveship"
5 Tulsa sch. with a Prayer Tower
6 Condition of having several aspects: hyph.
7 Beats it
8 County seat of Lee County, Iowa
9 Lab heaters
10 Drink of the Hindu gods
15 Consider in detail
21 Begin to drowse off
23 Hosp. workers
25 Jerk
26 Piece of information given confidentially
27 Audrey Tautou movie
29 Early spring bloomer
30 Portable home
33 Rose (up), oater-style
39 One of the Addams family
41 Musician Brian

36

Across

1 ____ Nui (Easter Island)
5 Calculates the total: 2 wds.
11 Pat baby on the back
12 Bust, in a way
13 Cannonball metal
14 Accumulate
15 ____ Kramer, Michael Richards' role in "Seinfeld"
17 Erstwhile MTV countdown program, initially
18 Motel come-on: 2 wds.
20 "Wheel of Fortune" request: 2 wds.
21 Inexpensive, poor quality item
23 How some pkgs. are sent
24 T or F: abbr.
25 Your, in Italy
28 Doff: 2 wds.
30 Fishing aid
33 Brat
34 Prefix with sphere
35 Excites (the imagination)
36 Reno's county
38 "____ Island" (2008 movie starring Abigail Breslin)
41 Celtics head coach between Chris Ford and Rick Pitino: inits., 2 wds.
42 "Amazing!"
43 Bibliographical phrase: 2 wds.
44 Lynx and Sparks org.

Down

1 Baseball stat.
2 Gold: prefix
3 Move ahead
4 Sleep problem, to Brits
5 First kicker to play in five Super Bowls (winning four of them): 2 wds.
6 Art ____
7 Hip hop group, Run-
8 A bit, colloquially
9 About-face: hyph.
10 16th century English dramatist George
16 Ireland's patron, for short: 2 wds.
18 License giver, initially
19 Pi follower
22 Glacial ridge
25 Twisting of shape or position
26 Weather balloon or military aircraft, maybe
27 Continent of Burundi, briefly
29 Before the present: 2 wds.
30 "Brand ____" (John Michael Montgomery song): 2 wds.
31 Ennoble
32 Opera about an opera singer
35 "Bless me, Father, ____ have sinned": 2 wds.
37 "2001" computer
39 Kind of rule
40 ____ Na Na

37

Across

1 Baseball great Musial
5 Con: var.
8 "___ of Honey" (Shelagh Delaney play): 2 wds.
10 L.A. to Las Vegas dir.
11 Cactus with large fruits: 2 wds.
13 Anatomical canals
14 Farm sound
15 Seating area
16 Former ABC TV president Jamie
18 Greek winged goddess of the dawn
19 "I swear!"
20 Acclaim
21 Alligator's cousin
23 "Give ___ break!": 2 wds.
26 Informal conference with an enemy
27 Compaq competitor
28 Black cat, to some
29 Buzz off
30 One making spectacles: 2 wds.
33 Decked, slangily
34 Golfer Els and comic Kovacs
35 Hill builder
36 Teetotalers

Down

1 Start of a French oath
2 Scolder's sounds
3 Pac.'s counterpart
4 Napoleonic marshal Michel
5 Banded rock
6 Caught, like fish: 3 wds.
7 Becomes more lively (with "up")
8 ___ Detoo ("Star Wars" android)
9 1970s icon Cheryl ___
11 Accumulate (with "up")
12 Skin openings
16 NBC morning show
17 At another time
19 Actor Cronyn, Joe Finley in "Cocoon"
20 Furnaces for drying bricks
21 Joined: 2 wds.
22 "The Human Condition" author Hannah
23 Gettysburg general
24 Santa's little helpers
25 One of the Sox, e.g.
26 Beer Barrel dance
27 Patron saint of France
29 Ruled
31 H.S. alternative
32 Grammar school basics, for short

38

Across

1. Isle of ___, English county
6. Obeys
11. Others, in Mexico
12. New York Knicks basketballer Stoudemire
13. "___ Mio": 2 wds.
14. Discompose
15. Home of the Seminoles, initially
16. Global positioning meas.
18. Dialect spoken in New Orleans
19. "My boy"
20. Suffix with sulf-
21. "Take Me Bak ___" (1972 Slade song)
22. TV physician: 2 wds.
24. "___ out?" (question to a pet at the door): 2 wds.
25. "Ricochet" actor: hyph.
26. ___ Go, poker tournament with no scheduled starting time: 2 wds.
27. Deity representation
28. Fit together
29. Popular online portal, initially
30. Footnote abbr.
31. School grouping in some states, initially
34. Pistol, in old gangster movies
35. "Aladdin" monkey
36. Center opening
37. Song line
39. Ply
41. Win by ___: 2 wds.
42. Take ___ (don't stand): 2 wds.
43. "Nine to Five" actress Parton
44. "___ Business" (Tom Cruise movie)

Down

1. Barks
2. "___ kind of you to ask": 2 wds.
3. "___ to Major Tom..." Bowie line: 2 wds.
4. Computer that sang "Daisy"
5. "Ash Wednesday" poet: 2 wds.
6. Like some cuisine
7. Burst of radiation generated by a nuclear explosion: inits.
8. Good-looking: 4 wds.
9. "Yeah, sure!": 2 wds.
10. Irish ___ (dog breed)
17. Tool with a curved head
23. Catholicism or Hinduism: abbr.
24. Grafton's "___ for Innocent": 2 wds.
25. "If you asked me..." follow-up: 3 wds.
26. Worldly
27. "That's good news": 2 wds.
28. Group gone wild
30. Cagney's TV partner
32. Orate
33. Below-the-belt
38. Geog. feature
40. "___ recall...": 2 wds.

39

Across

1 Collect $200, in Monopoly: 2 wds.
7 Centers for G.I.s, initially
11 Keep possession of
12 Final Four gp.
13 Suitable for growing crops
14 "War for the Planet of the Apes" star Steve
15 Hither's partner
16 Words at the start of a countdown: 2 wds.
18 Style of music popular in the 1950s: hyph.
21 Deep red color
23 Windhoek's land, once: inits.
26 "So what else ___?": 2 wds.
27 Clarified butters
29 N.F.L. linemen: abbr.
30 Polished
32 "Casablanca" crook
33 Remove chaff from grain
36 USNA rank, briefly
39 "Ripley's Believe ___ Not": 2 wds.
40 Fakes (a signature)
43 Star of Bethlehem followers
44 Disconnect from an electricity supply
45 Raindrop sound
46 Least believable

Down

1 Beseech
2 Prefix with space or dynamic
3 Subs: hyph.
4 Day of rest and worship: abbr.
5 Jazz pianist Evans
6 Pair of punches in quick succession: hyph.
7 Open, as a purse
8 Glance over
9 Pearl Harbor locale
10 Without: Fr.
17 Suffix for fish or war
19 Cockney residence
20 New York county
21 Round fig.
22 Letters before U
23 Fish-eating bird: 2 wds.
24 Skin blemish
25 Curaçao clock setting letters
28 Summit: abbr.
31 Licit
32 Tear open
33 Cowardly sort
34 Romance lang.
35 Canceled, in NASA-speak: hyph.
37 Apollo or Saturn, e.g.
38 N.C.O. rank
41 Out ___ limb: 2 wds.
42 Tachometer stat.

40

Across

1 Some transmittable files, initially

5 Plato, for one

11 Fit for the job

12 French exclamation of surprise: 3 wds.

13 Association

14 Advantages

15 Ending for opal or fluor

16 Word meaning "born" seen in wedding announcements

17 ____ the boards (acted)

19 ____ opera (daytime show)

23 Brave and persistent

26 Cold call?

27 "Lady ____ Train" (1945 film): 2 wds.

28 "So there you are!"

29 Lucky Roman number?

30 Simple sack

31 Exceptional courage when facing danger

33 Chemical suffixes

35 Prefix for bite or taph

36 Daughter of Loki, in Norse myth

38 Currency named for a continent

41 Conductor Toscanini

44 Suffixes of origin

45 Milk-derived

46 Detrained, say

47 "Jack Reacher: Never ____" (Tom Cruise movie): 2 wds.

48 Sandberg of baseball

Down

1 Clip

2 Sluggers' hits: abbr.

3 Go up and down irregularly

4 Belmondo's "Breathless" costar

5 Nonstop: 3 wds.

6 ____ Logan, "The Bold and the Beautiful" character

7 Someone ____ (not yours)

8 Skater Babilonia

9 Vintage

10 ____ Strait (Canadian waterway named for an explorer)

18 Anticipatory cry: hyph.

20 Unmistakably

21 Onassis and Emanuel

22 Governessy

23 12 in Tarragona

24 "____, U of K" (college fight song): 2 wds.

25 Auld lang syne

32 "In ____ and out the other": 2 wds.

34 "…a boy who never would ____ door": 2 wds.

37 Clapton who sang "Change the World"

39 Horse halter?

40 Bone in comb. form

41 High school subj.

42 Indian P.M., 1991–6

43 Elvis Presley's band, initially

41

Across

1 Brit. dictionaries
5 Video chat need
11 ___ Tzu (toy dog)
12 Not seeing eye to eye: 2 wds.
13 To be, in old Rome
14 Aid to loading a muzzle
15 Sports squad
17 Common clown name
18 Grasp tightly
20 Home of Iowa State University
21 Shannon Lucid's home for 179 days
22 They follow bees
24 Of considerable importance
29 Pol. divisions prior to 1991
30 The Engineers of the Liberty League, briefly
31 Vincent van ___ (major Post-Impressionist painter)
34 Prepare for sleep: 2 wds.
36 Arm bone
37 Smoked delicacies
38 Kind of crustacean
40 Island close to Mull
43 Say again, as a story
44 Actor Sharif
45 Eventually: 2 wds.
46 They come before Octs.

Down

1 Carbohydrate ending
2 Hesitant sounds
3 Agitate
4 Item of bed linen
5 In a sympathetic and kind way
6 Capt.'s guess
7 Pompous talk
8 Software mailing, perhaps: hyph.
9 Mexican brick
10 C: prompt program: hyph.
16 Financial records, briefly
18 Ruler divs.
19 Actress Lucy of "Elementary"
23 Come to pass
25 Like some curves: hyph.
26 Annoying
27 Energy trade organization, initially
28 Basketball's Jeremy ___
31 Musical instrument scraped with a stick
32 Merlin of football and TV
33 $1,000 bill, slangily: 2 wds.
35 Advertising awards
39 Commercial suffix with Motor
41 Fuzz
42 ___ Antiqua

49

42

Across

1 Seven-time All-Star pitcher Dave
6 Stomach
9 Helping
12 Paleozoic. e.g.
13 Sizable lot: 2 wds.
14 Palme ____ (Cannes award)
15 Vintner's prefix
16 Element that occurs in uranium ores
18 Breakfast dish from Paris: 2 wds.
20 Mrs. Andy Capp
21 Bonneville Salt Flats locale
22 Game boundary
24 Cain killed him
25 Reasoned
26 The "S" of R.S.V.P.
27 Small loan
32 "To reiterate…": 3 wds.
33 Genetic messenger material, briefly
34 Gun, as an engine
35 Leave in the lurch
37 Diagnostic proc.
38 Underwater breathing device
39 Socialite's clothing initials
40 Mooring sites

Down

1 "Airplane!" or "Spaceballs"
2 Coloring solution
3 Castle of the turkey trot
4 Pilot's announcement, briefly
5 Pedaled vehicle
6 Umpire
7 Awakening
8 Chill killer
10 Garden products brand
11 What remains after deductions, British style
17 Russian unit of currency
19 Saints and Cardinals, e.g.
22 Parents, e.g.
23 Lacking good manners
24 Supplies parachuted from a plane
25 Unctuous
26 Offspring
28 Blockheads
29 Circumnavigator Sir Francis
30 Contract signer, e.g.
31 Asian weight units
36 ____ Lankans

43

Across

1 Seagoing vessel, in myth

5 Frat. whose mission statement is "Building Balanced Men": abbr.

10 "National Lampoon's ___" (Ellis Weiner novel)

11 An archangel

12 Big fuss

14 Disfigured, misshapen

15 "Wheel of Fortune" request: 2 wds.

16 Hydrocarbon suffixes

20 Large seabird

23 Floor model

24 Enero to enero

25 RCA former competitor

26 Dam destroyed by the R.A.F. in 1943

28 Be deliberately ambiguous

31 "Christ of St. John of the Cross" artist

32 "Peer Gynt" character

33 Fresh way of doing things: hyph.

38 Judicial officer

40 Madison Square Garden, e.g.

41 Opera by Umberto Giordano: 2 wds.

42 Least satisfactory

43 Kitty

Down

1 What Ritalin treats, for short

2 Bounder

3 Pebble Beach pastime

4 Like some non-permanent art exhibits: 2 wds.

5 Yield to another's wish or opinion

6 "Dies ___" (hymn)

7 Covered thinly with gold leaf

8 Classified ad letters

9 Mahmoud Abbas's grp.

13 ___ Carlson (Minnesota governor before Jesse Ventura)

17 Hair removal brand, once

18 One-named "More to Love" host

19 Pierre's evening

20 "Went," in Scotland

21 One-two connector: 2 wds.

22 Holiday song

27 Person's double

28 Plays with, like a puppy: 2 wds.

29 Gofer: abbr.

30 Proceed without restraint: 2 wds.

34 One, in Germany

35 Korea Bay feeder

36 Posts: abbr.

37 Wide widths, initially

38 Gullet

39 Spanish hoop

44

Across

1 Japanese noodles
5 Hostel, in Anatolia
11 Kind of wave
12 Grinding teeth
13 Upswing: abbr.
14 Hester of "The Scarlet Letter"
15 Mawkish sentimentality
17 Steve Antin movie of 2010
21 True inner self
23 Actress Linney
24 ____ for tat
25 "Absolutely" and "positively," for example: abbr.
26 Black Sea port, new-style
29 Hard to pin down
31 Element #40
33 Denoting an important route
36 Sylphlike
39 "It's either him ____!": 2 wds.
40 ____ a button: 2 wds.
41 Make a hole bigger
42 Big name in publishing
43 Horned vipers

Down

1 ____ Tzu (toy dog)
2 Wine: prefix
3 Malicious gossiper
4 Circulatory chamber
5 Urge
6 Choice bit
7 Milano of "Who's the Boss?"
8 Fled
9 Coastal flier
10 Canadian market inits.
16 Gun owner's org.
18 Boggy places
19 Language of Pakistan
20 Gutter locale
21 From ____ (completely): 3 wds.
22 Spiders' nests
27 Periodontal scraper
28 Main lines
29 Fight (for)
30 Light show
32 Explosive experiment: abbr., 2 wds.
34 "Do I have to draw you ____?": 2 wds.
35 NASA craft, initially
36 RPI, e.g.
37 Saturn ____, sport utility vehicle
38 LAX info

45

Across

1 Stammerer's syllables
4 Lay to rest
10 Tennyson's "Idylls of the King" for one
12 Complainer
13 Club of song
14 Patriot Allen and author Canin
15 Drunken state
17 Sensational
19 "Oz" network
22 Feeling
24 Suffix with arbor or app
25 Authority responsible for educational institutions: 2 wds.
27 Miner's treasure
28 Place where clothes and linens are washed
29 Sun. speech
30 ___ on (encouraged)
31 Gilberto who sang "The Girl From Ipanema"
34 Moon stages
39 Wine: prefix
40 Some farm machines
41 One sixty-billionth of a min.: 2 wds.
42 Process sugar
43 Barbecue sound

Down

1 Lines at the register?: inits.
2 Debatable
3 Burial chamber
4 TV chef whose books include "Louisiana Real and Rustic": 2 wds.
5 "___ so fast!"
6 Island where Brando lived: abbr.
7 ___ roll: 2 wds.
8 Checkers, e.g.
9 Apt. ad info
11 Capital of Mozambique
16 American League East bird
18 Removes errors from
19 Tiara, e.g.
20 Roseanne Arnold, nee ___
21 Song popularized a considerable time ago
22 General ___ Chicken (Chinese menu dish)
23 Farm measure
26 2,000 pounds: 2 wds.
32 Ones in Quebec
33 Medicos: abbr.
34 Retro hip beer, initially
35 Have, in Edinburgh
36 TV ET
37 Tre + tre
38 Suffix with north, south, east or west

46

Across

1 Criticize severely
5 Some trucks
8 Tommy's baby brother on "Rugrats"
11 First barbarian king of Italy
12 Lennon's love Yoko
13 Cotton fiber used to make yarn
14 Tap
16 Bank
18 Mark Harmon series on CBS
19 Jonson work
20 Milan music mecca: 2 wds.
23 Barricade
25 Degree of disorder or randomness in a system
27 PC monitor type
30 Horse rider's handful
31 Allergic reaction
33 Exhausted person's utterance: 2 wds.
36 Defraud
37 Dopey picture?
38 Weird
40 Have, in Edinburgh
41 Beer, slangily
42 Cinema can content

Down

1 Fish that lays an egg case called a mermaid's purse
2 Director Jean-____ Godard
3 Big galoots
4 Fig. on a car sticker
5 Ristorante offering
6 "____ a Thousand Times" movie starring Jack Palance: 2 wds.
7 Able to be changed
8 Municipal pound employees: 2 wds.
9 One way to saute: 2 wds.
10 "____ luck!" ("Knock 'em dead!")
15 Augmentation: abbr.
17 "Sesame Street" muppet
21 PC program
22 "Don't ____ word": 2 wds.
24 "Rise, Glory, Rise" composer
25 "Love Story" author Segal
26 Greek valley where games were held
28 "The Fountainhead" character Howard
29 "My Cousin Vinny" actress Marisa
32 Move like rush-hour traffic
34 Shortened form, for short
35 Get bushed
39 Center of Arizona?

47

Across

1 King in an Elgar composition

5 Upset with: 2 wds.

10 Jay with a jaw

11 One thing after another

12 Stargazing, in college course books: abbr.

13 Battle hero: 2 wds.

14 Shore

16 Humorist Bill and comedian Louis

17 Roman-fleuve, e.g.

21 Loses prestige

23 Surf partner, on some menus

24 Lucrative

25 Animal tranquilizing drug, initially

27 "___ Freischütz" (Weber opera)

28 First name in horror

30 Gives it a shot: 3 wds.

32 Seafood selection

33 Battery type: abbr.

34 Free from contamination

37 Indicates

40 Bring ___ end (conclude): 2 wds.

42 Unabridged

43 Attraction

44 Bill of Microsoft

45 Spot

Down

1 Commercial suffix with Rock

2 Discounted

3 Before birth

4 Raids

5 Fermented honey

6 Nab

7 24 horas

8 N.R.C. forerunner

9 Follower of Mao?

11 Emmentaler, e.g.: 2 wds.

15 Penetrate slowly

18 Daring

19 US cyclist LeMond, first American to win the Tour de France

20 Big do

21 Bombers' or fighters' locations, initially

22 Pressure prefix

26 Insect's feeler

29 Hardly Mr. Nice Guy

31 Quieten

35 Orch. section

36 Complain gratingly

37 Master Mind game piece

38 ___ lark (without planning ahead): 2 wds.

39 TV cousin

41 Marshal at Waterloo

48

Across

1 Toshiba product, e.g.: abbr., 2 wds.
5 Mil. ranks
9 Billion extension
10 Actor Sal and family
12 Jordan's Queen ____
13 Mario Puzo bestseller
14 Joseph of ____ (follower of Jesus)
16 Nabisco brand
17 Old home loan org.
20 Display ostentatiously
23 Artist Mondrian
24 Showed, as a seat: 2 wds.
25 Engage in a Renaissance Fair sport
26 "Well, Did You ____!" (Cole Porter song)
27 Person skilled in handwriting
28 Doo-____ (1950s music style)
29 ____ street" (state of financial security)
30 Made disapproving sounds: hyph.
35 Curly-tailed dogs
37 Atmosphere
38 Beautiful
39 Swing voters: abbr.
40 CEO, often: abbr.
41 Mother of Levi and Judah

Down

1 Mandlikova of tennis
2 Christian of fashion
3 Deanna ____, Marina Sirtis's "Star Trek" role
4 Wine flavored with herbs
5 Old-fashioned knife
6 Plant also known as cranesbill
7 Tad
8 Govt. agency that has your number
10 Bach art form
11 Internet commenter's letters
15 River through Florence
18 "____ Rebel" (1962 hit): 2 wds.
19 Business letter abbr.
20 Traveled by air
21 On or to the left prefix
22 Capable of changing
23 Tied-back hairstyle
25 "____, Joy of Man's Desiring"
27 Easy mark
29 End-of-list abbr.: 2 wds.
31 Some Beehive Staters
32 It can be whistled
33 "Ring Cycle" goddess
34 Morse morsel
35 Monte Viso, e.g.
36 N. ____ (Kim Jong-un's country): abbr.

49

Across

1 One-time TV workers' union
6 Some 1980s Chryslers: 2 wds.
11 Certain 1960s protest: 2 wds.
12 Drawing support
13 Runs out of gear?
14 Davis of "The Matrix Reloaded"
15 Two-time U.S. Open winner Fraser
16 ___ Qs (good manners): 2 wds.
17 Some trees
18 Ten to a buck
19 The Divine, to da Vinci
20 "Hurry!," shortly
22 Flying through the air: 3 wds.
26 Golf cart noise-maker
27 Earthlink competitor, initially
29 Similar: prefix
32 Part of the eye
33 Pioneering 1940s computer
34 Fathom
35 Playoff spot
36 Laughter sounds: hyph.
37 January, to Mexicans
38 Run off together
39 Bullriding venue
40 Curve shapes

Down

1 Like some flared skirts: hyph.
2 Beethoven opera
3 Sculptural figure of a man used as a column
4 Cambodian coins
5 "As I Lay Dying" father
6 Suppress: 2 wds.
7 Fashion designer Oleg
8 Indian state near the Himalayas
9 French queen
10 Kids go down hills on them in the winter
20 Thomas the Tank Engine, to tots: hyph.
21 Boulogne-sur-___
23 Shakespearean building
24 Natives of New Mexico and Arizona: var.
25 Flips out: 2 wds.
28 Failures
29 Hymn writer Reginald
30 Brief bridge bid: 2 wds.
31 Stuck
32 Russian range
34 Clarified butter in Indian cookery

50

Across

1 Civil War general defeated by Grant at Chattanooga
6 Beau
11 Not a crime
12 "___ dead!" (worried kid's words): 3 wds.
13 Venus when seen at dusk: 2 wds.
15 Univ. degrees
16 Steelers quarterback Roethlisberger
17 Farm female
18 City SSE of Buffalo
20 Audacious
23 Relax: 2 wds.
27 Wings of an insect
28 Geraldine Chaplin's mother
29 Site of the Allied conference in February 1945
31 Pig's nose
32 Competes in a slow race
34 Kind of camera, initially
37 Alphabetical sequence
38 Careless
41 Certain wind direction pointer
44 Excessive
45 "Have another slice ___": 2 wds.
46 Called like a cow
47 Wind-deposited soil

Down

1 Air bubble in glass
2 Guns (an engine)
3 A long, long time
4 Ramat ___, city east of Tel Aviv, Israel
5 In a slick way
6 Instruct by gestures
7 Used to be
8 Recipe info: abbr.
9 Jack narrowly beat him in the 1980 U.S. Open
10 Scand. country
14 Previously
18 British track star Steve
19 Many bar signs
20 No vote, in Congress
21 Guidonian note
22 North Carolina city: abbr.
24 Also
25 Burma's first P.M.: 2 wds.
26 Political commentator Buchanan
30 Having a curved symmetrical structure
31 Unsaturated alcohol
33 Poem
34 Like the beginning of triathlons
35 Late-night host Jay
36 "Hair" co-author James
38 Easy pace
39 Galatea's love in Greek myth
40 Classic Jags
42 Day between Mon. and Wed.
43 Corp. money handler

51

Across

1 Alaska's Iditarod, for one
5 Ben & Jerry's alternative
9 Run off and get hitched
11 "These ___ Are Made for Walkin'" (Nancy Sinatra hit)
13 Shared psychological attributes of mankind: 2 wds.
15 Wallach of "The Magnificent Seven"
16 Not specific
17 Repeated phrase
19 Have a bite
20 German physicist Ohm
22 Z preceder?: 2 wds.
23 Hotel amenities
25 Equestrian
27 ___-Magnon man
28 Involuntary twitch
30 ___ Lingus (Irish carrier)
31 Harmonizing: 2 wds.
34 Humbled
37 ___ juice (milk, slangily)
38 Building with space projections
40 New York restaurateur of old
41 Bright circle?
42 Steinbeck's "East of ___"
43 Dangerous time

Down

1 Lengthen a pant leg
2 "Be-Bop-___" (1956 Gene Vincent hit): hyph.
3 Stepping up: 2 wds.
4 Air-quality monitoring org.
5 Israel's Abba
6 Give a ton of affection to, with "on"
7 "That's just what I was thinking!": 4 wds.
8 Streaked
10 Absorb the interest of
12 Pie chart part
14 ___ East
18 Kiosk purchase
21 Mother's mother, in the past
23 Hustles tickets
24 Biological rings
26 Habitable artificial satellite, briefly
29 Painter Mondrian
32 "Don't even bother": 2 wds.
33 States of torpor
35 Michael ___, German writer of fantasy and children's fiction
36 Checking line
39 Sporting goods retailer

59

52

Across

1 Australian state, initially
4 201, to Caesar
7 Actress Derek and singer Diddley
10 Melody
11 Pearl producers
13 Feature of the "Tom Thumb" locomotive: 2 wds.
15 Wholly: 2 wds.
16 Brit. awards
17 People ordained for religious duties
19 Suffix used with numbers
21 Adhere with paste: 2 wds.
25 "What's Cooking?" costar Mercedes
28 Dizzying gallery displays: 2 wds.
29 Image-recording tapes
31 Coll., e.g.
32 "What ___ to Say" (Wade Hayes song): 2 wds.
35 HuffPost, e.g.
38 Having removed clothing
41 Combined appliance: hyph.
43 Out of control: 3 wds.
44 One of the Stooges
45 Miss. neighbor
46 Somme summer
47 Old Spanish queen

Down

1 Cooked rice in Indonesian cuisine
2 ___ Go, poker tournament: 2 wds.
3 Deserving or inciting pity
4 French philosopher Auguste
5 Humanoid creature
6 Prefix with metric
7 Units of sound intensity
8 Creme cookie
9 Lat., Lith., and Ukr., once
12 Get rid of clutter: 2 wds.
14 Popular ISP
18 Mop & ___ (floor cleaner)
19 R&B record producer Gotti
20 "Dolly Girl" fashion designer Anna
22 Town near New London, Conn.: 2 wds.
23 "Lord of the Rings" monster
24 Utmost degree
26 Elevation
27 Military award, initially
30 Pointillist painter Georges
33 Orchestra founder Rieu
34 Big maker of A.T.M.s
35 Cuddly "Return of the Jedi" creature
36 "Every ___ King" (autobiography of Huey Long): 2 wds.
37 Saying: "… straight ___ arrow": 2 wds.
39 Millions of centuries
40 Actress de Matteo
42 Shoe designation

53

Across

1 Sound heard twice in "geology": 2 wds.
6 Annoyance
10 French cathedral city
12 Play to ___, draw: 2 wds.
13 Filthy, squalid
14 Common: prefix
15 File menu option
17 San Francisco to San Jose dir.
19 Masi of "Hawaii Five-0"
20 "___ for Innocent" (Sue Grafton novel): 2 wds.
23 Kind of box
25 Organ-playing singer from Kaka'ako: 2 wds.
27 North Carolina university
28 Environmental sci.
29 Magna cum ___
31 Become the legal parent of
32 W.W. II vessel, briefly
33 Lick
35 Due + quattro
36 Ford model
38 "Moonstruck" Oscar-winner
41 Read into, as motives
44 Pop singer La___ Jackson
45 Became less bright
46 Bygone depilatory
47 Thoreau work, "Faith in ___": 2 wds.

Down

1 Promgoers: abbr.
2 "Well, lookee here!"
3 Uncover: 2 wds.
4 Environmental conservation concern
5 Key of Bach's Sonata No. 1: 2 wds.
6 Rate
7 Stuffed in one's mouth
8 "Am ___ your way?": 2 wds.
9 Newcomer, briefly
11 Minn. neighbor: 2 wds.
16 Crazy
17 Odor
18 "___ Marner"
20 Dressed up for Halloween: 2 wds.
21 "In a perfect world…": 2 wds.
22 Longtime Chicago Symphony Orchestra conductor
24 It may be bitter
26 U.K. reference set
30 Little green men, initially
31 Inability to name objects
34 It might be nitric or hydrochloric
36 The "E" of Q.E.D.
37 Dashboard measures, for short
38 Big box: abbr.
39 Long-handled implement
40 Keep watch on
42 Tick (off)
43 Leno's former announcer Hall

54

Across

1 State tree of Iowa and Maryland
4 Military meal, initially
7 Fed. aviation service
10 "Today" rival, briefly
11 Company that owns MapQuest
12 Member of Cong.
13 "E.T." actor: 2 wds.
16 Expose
17 It might be heard in an empty room
18 Fruit farmers' bane
20 Compose
22 Port on the Loire
26 Ground cover in woodland
29 "The ___ of July"
30 Ore. neighbor
31 Equal-angled geometric figure
34 Superlative suffix
37 Responds
40 Demand and take for use or service
42 One of the gp.
43 VCR button: abbr.
44 Nonsense syllable of song
45 "___ Lay Me Down" (1995 hit): 2 wds.
46 Puebla pronoun
47 Big mouth

Down

1 Pre K.G.B. group
2 "I hear ya!"
3 Bob Seger song of 1975
4 Wetland
5 Kids' indoor rides: 2 wds.
6 1970s band inits.
7 Part of the Bible: abbr.
8 "The Herculoids" creator Alex
9 The goldfish in "Pinocchio"
14 Literary monogram
15 Like some questions: 2 wds.
19 ___ es Salaam (African city)
20 Sta-___ fabric softener
21 Brian of Roxy Music
23 Minneapolis, for one: 2 wds.
24 Runway guess, for short
25 Doo-wop syllable
27 Aria from "Un Ballo in Maschera": 2 wds.
28 Some N.F.L.ers
32 Car insurer, initially
33 Little piece in a feedbag
34 "My Friend ___" (1949 flick)
35 Some shoe sizes
36 Area of 640 acres: abbr., 2 wds.
38 When said three times, a W.W. II film
39 Crack
41 More than exasperation

55

Across

1 Police rank: abbr.
5 Takes place
11 Part of a day
12 Before the appointed time
13 Senorita's other
14 Thick sweet liquids
15 Park shelter
17 Brit. station wagon: 2 wds.
21 Converted into animal fodder
23 French story
24 Despot Amin
25 Catch in the act
26 Isaac Bashevis Singer story
29 Fiery gems
31 Experiencing pain or suffering
33 Ignores, as a fault: 2 wds.
36 "Charmed" costar Milano
39 Handheld CPUs
40 Land, as a fish: 2 wds.
41 ___ Laszlo skin care products
42 2004 Olympics site
43 Some breads and whiskeys

Down

1 Company that makes money in stacks
2 ___ bene (pay close attention)
3 Measuring for mapping purposes
4 Express respect toward God
5 Alternative version, in music scores
6 Wild dog
7 Trumpet cousin
8 Three-time Burmese prime minister: 2 wds.
9 Dem. rival in DC
10 AARP members, briefly
16 Inc., in England
18 Soft drink company known for ginger ale: 2 wds.
19 "Got ___ named Sue..." (Tutti Frutti lyric): 2 wds.
20 Civil War side
21 "Howdy"
22 Gulf port
27 Scrap
28 ___ wait (prepares to ambush): 2 wds.
29 Cries at a circus
30 Salt's buddy
32 O'Casey and Connery
34 Sound
35 General ___ Chicken (Chinese menu dish)
36 Celestial altar
37 Court call
38 "Sure"

56

Across

1. Bank acct. report
5. Castilian hero: 2 wds.
10. Girl scout group
12. Simple musical instrument
13. Highly
14. "The Seven Year Itch" actor Tom
15. Popular snack cakes
17. Animal that meows
18. Suffix with meteor
20. Move with a splashing sound
22. Mountain pool
24. Coypu
27. In disguise: abbr.
29. Former little kids
30. Toasts
32. Fix, in a way
33. Swahili for "freedom"
35. Handling
36. Alphabet chain
38. Founded: abbr.
40. Got off the fence
42. Volunteer's statement: 2 wds.
45. Florida's Key ___
46. R. D. ___, "The Divided Self" author
47. "___ Macduff, and damn'd be him...": 2 wds.
48. Precursors to Euros

Down

1. Disco ___ (character on "The Simpsons")
2. Erstwhile MTV countdown program, initially
3. Nation in relation to its colonies: 2 wds.
4. Foe for El Cordobés
5. Manages: 2 wds.
6. Esquire's field of study
7. Landlocked European country: 2 wds.
8. Kansas county seat
9. Buffoon
11. Oom-___ (tuba sounds)
16. TV channel relaunched as "Versus" in 2006
18. "Really?": 2 wds.
19. Aquarium
21. Holy Fr. women
23. Wordsmith Webster
25. Balin and Claire
26. "___ sow, so shall...": 2 wds.
28. Attached, in a way: 2 wds.
31. Yearbook sect.
34. Gas, e.g.: abbr.
36. Slump lazily
37. Assigner of Gs and Rs, initially
39. Wings, anatomically
41. Kind of trip
43. Bearded antelope
44. Old-school tough guys in rap songs, initially

57

Across

1 Little devil
4 Not Macs, briefly
7 King Features competitor
8 Fall winner
13 Trickery
14 Get ready
15 Approximation word
17 Relating to the pontiff
18 Deerlike water buffalo
19 Zaire's Mobutu ____ Seko
20 "Good evening", in Grenoble
24 River to the Mississippi
25 Height
27 Medical suffix
29 Fussy about one's needs
32 Brandy Norwood song: 2 wds.
34 Word before gras
35 Village matchmaker in "Fiddler on the Roof"
37 Vice ____
38 1967 Oscar winner Parsons
40 Welfare org.
41 Legislative period
42 CPR specialist
43 Actor Byrnes
44 Juan Carlos, e.g.

Down

1 Occupying a taxi: 3 wds.
2 Hardy breed of sheep
3 George to England, and Andrew to Scotland, e.g.: 2 wds.
4 Sandra Denton's stage name
5 Household cleaning product, initially
6 Percolate
9 Calculating types, for short
10 Device used in some interviews: 2 wds.
11 Expunge
12 Caught congers
16 Threw or throw
21 Dunce
22 "Lord, is ____?" (Last Supper question): 2 wds.
23 Hasten
26 Epidemic
27 "I just remembered...": 2 wds.
28 Reagan aide Ed
30 Romantic request: 2 wds.
31 In a state of turbulence
33 Holy Fr. women
36 Nobelist Wiesel
37 Peddle
39 Former Israeli airport name

58

Across

1 Capital of Yemen
6 Part of a play: 2 wds.
11 Smart guys?
12 Heard cases
13 Star in Virgo
14 Goddesses of the seasons
15 GMC pickup truck
17 "La Scala di ___" (Rossini opera)
18 Rogers, Hines and others
20 Froth
23 Front of the body between the neck and chest
27 Big name in kitchen foil
29 Stand out
30 Have no choice in the matter: 2 wds.
32 "Just ___!": 2 wds.
33 First-stringers: hyph.
35 Agency responsible for highways, initially
38 Remover of frozen water: hyph.
42 Mar
44 Issuance from Uncle Sam: hyph.
45 Some sharks
46 "Cool!"
47 Respecting
48 "Cafe Terrace at Night" setting

Down

1 Cheek
2 Gravy Train competitor
3 Not "ja"
4 Available space for occupation
5 "Ditto": 3 wds.
6 Part of N.C.A.A.: abbr.
7 One who questions in great detail: hyph.
8 Drain
9 "___ my peas with honey...": 2 wds.
10 Creative spark
16 Diplomat: abbr.
19 Hot blood?
20 Autograph seeker, perhaps
21 Bullfight huzzah
22 Hole in one
24 Room coolers, for short
25 Visualize
26 Nursery schooler's need, for short
28 Letters in a long-distance company's number
31 Library ref.
34 Prudential competitor
35 Gen. Patton's alma mater
36 Attention ___
37 "Okey-___!"
39 "___ Miner's Daughter" (Loretta Lynn biopic)
40 Ending for cigar
41 Antique autos, initially
43 D-day troop carrier, briefly

59

Across

1 Teacher's deg.
4 Duffer's goal
7 ___ Schwarz (toy store)
8 Rapper Dr. ___
9 Letters on a sunscreen bottle
12 Job that involves putting out blazes
15 Erga ___ (towards everyone, Lat.)
16 Paris pastry
17 Churn up
18 Cancel
19 Channel owned by Viacom
20 Depleted: 2 wds.
23 Aromatic root credited with medicinal properties
25 They fish with rods and lines
27 ASCAP rival
30 Prefix for tics or sci
31 Ford Explorer Sport ___
32 "I'm on ___" ("Saturday Night Live" song): 2 wds.
34 Bel ___ cheese
35 Heedful of potential consequences
37 "Grand" ice cream name
38 Abbr. between a first and last name, maybe
39 Playwright Akins
40 Masthead names, briefly
41 Airport guess, initially

Down

1 Attempt
2 Antagonist in the "Dark-Hunter" book series
3 Climbing plant with trumpet-shaped flowers: 2 wds.
4 Some printable files, initially
5 Shapiro of NPR
6 Col.'s command
9 6 on the Beaufort Scale: 2 wds.
10 ___ point
11 "The Godfather, Part II" character
13 Long fish
14 "You ___ a good time?"
20 "Wheel of Fortune" purchase: 2 wds.
21 Early role-playing game co., initially
22 Suffix with detain or deport
24 ___ artery
25 Chop-chop
26 "I pass" in bridge: 2 wds.
28 Lucky charm
29 Chilled drink: 2 wds.
31 Spigot
33 Ditty
34 They're trident-shaped
36 2500, to Caesar

60

Across

1 Seed coverings
6 Eucharistic plate
11 Lisa of "Biker Boyz"
12 Literally, "dwarf dog"
13 "Ditto": 2 wds.
14 Highland dagger, ____ dhu
15 Chinese dynasty established by Yu the Great: var.
17 "The Sweetest Taboo" singer
18 Keats piece
20 Cleveland basketballer, briefly
22 Old geographical inits.
23 Trunk growth
25 Brand of contact lens solution
27 Sporty Mazda
29 Fit again
32 Turkish hors d'oeuvre
34 Lap dog, for short
35 G.I. grub
37 Cable inits.
39 Pampered one?
40 Digital way to record shows
42 NFL star Michael who was the basis for the movie "The Blind Side"
44 "Alas…": 2 wds.
46 "Every wall is ____" (Ralph Waldo Emerson quote): 2 wds.
49 Very minor movie stars: hyph.
50 "Bring On the Empty Horses" author David
51 "Fiddler on the Roof" matchmaker
52 Parenting challenges

Down

1 Rocket interceptor, briefly
2 Eggs
3 Similar: 4 wds.
4 Thirteen popes
5 Zeno, notably
6 Mac rivals, initially
7 Astronauts' affirmatives: hyph.
8 Hidden store of valuables: 2 wds.
9 "Holy smokes!"
10 Nickname for a San Francisco football team
16 Swiss river to the Rhine
18 Canadian mil. award, initially
19 "And how!": 2 wds.
21 Chapter part: abbr.
24 Véronique, e.g.: abbr.
26 Tiny knot of fiber
28 Zidovudine, familiarly
30 When doubled, a 1965 Dixie Cups song
31 Comprehend
33 One of Roxy Music's Brians
35 Charley Weaver's hometown: abbr., 2 wds.
36 Winchester gun
38 U ____, U.N. Secretary-general 1961–71
41 Hops kiln
43 Actress McClurg
45 Way to go: abbr.
47 Vintner's prefix
48 O.R. workers

61

Across

1 Young socialites
5 Long overcoat
11 Gulf of Aqaba resort: var.
12 Complaint
13 Frank: hyph.
15 Joe of "Home Alone"
16 Rubberneck
17 "The Mocker Mocked" painter Paul
19 Mainstay
22 Agree
26 "I Love Lucy" actress: 2 wds.
28 ___ arms (agitated): 2 wds.
29 Precious metal, symbol Ag
30 Laura whose albums include "Smile" and "Nested"
31 Evacuate
35 Garden bulb
39 Cause (someone) to realize that a belief is false
41 Patrick Henry, e.g.
42 Ending for destruct or deduct
43 Portioning (out)
44 Grandson of Sarah

Down

1 Lily-Rose ___, daughter of Vanessa Paradis
2 Fashion periodical
3 Sounds from the meadow
4 It's worn to keep a tie in place
5 Hems and haws
6 Oversight
7 Place on the schedule
8 "We'll ___ kindness yet, for auld lang syne..." (Robert Burns): 2 wds.
9 Dam destroyed by the R.A.F. in 1943
10 1984 NL MVP Sandberg
14 ___ Wafers
18 Insignificant, slangily
19 Dragunov ___, Russian marksman rifle: inits.
20 Tilt slightly
21 "X-Men" producer Arad
22 Slatted window structure
23 Bill, briefly
24 Letters used (by some) for dates
25 Alway
27 Expertise in the fine arts
30 Parachute material
31 Ancient Palestinian land
32 What's wallowed in
33 10th- or 11th-graders' exam letters
34 South American monkey with a long tail
36 Ad ___
37 Kansas county seat
38 Tire in Toulouse
40 California-based clothing brand, initially

62

Across

1 Iraqi port
6 Joel Schumacher movie of 1983: 2 wds.
11 Preface to a book
12 Hotel offerings
13 Full of flesh, as a dish
14 Aegean region
15 One who gets asked a lot of questions
17 ___ the Bear (Muppets character)
19 Port city of Ukraine, new-style
22 "I get it now": 2 wds.
23 Forced out
25 ___-en-Provence
26 Cleopatra biter
27 "___ Lay Me Down": 2 wds.
28 Force
30 French silk center
31 Routine
32 Frontier and Suddenlink, e.g.
33 "___ of the King" (Tennyson poem)
35 Blackmore title name
38 Baby grand, e.g.
41 Plant tissue
42 Photo finish?
43 ___-France (sheep breed): hyph.
44 What a plant often grows from: 2 wds.

Down

1 Way to measure pulse rates, initially
2 "___ we alone?"
3 Platforms for public speakers
4 Captured back
5 ___ nitrate, fuel additive
6 Withered: hyph.
7 Aussie calls
8 Deceive
9 "What ___ doing?": 2 wds.
10 Explorer's org.
16 In a relaxed manner, not rigid
17 Brit. Airways, once
18 Buckeye State sch.: 2 wds.
20 Doesn't lose it: 2 wds.
21 Noted moralist
24 Rackets
26 Campus life
29 Completely spoiled
30 Monet subject
34 Women's tour grp.
35 511, to Nero
36 Olive ___ (Popeye's love)
37 Chihuahua cheer
39 Never, in Neuss
40 Disorder in which someone feels obliged to do things repeatedly: inits.

63

Across

1 Frightful phantom
6 Bridge positions
11 "Stuck ___" Elvis Presley hit: 2 wds.
12 Mushroom-cloud creator: abbr., 2 wds.
13 Computer storage circuits: 2 wds.
15 Financial institution
16 Peruvian pronoun
17 Botanist Gray et al.
19 Golfer Tony who won the 1964 British Open
23 States confidently
26 Chop (off)
27 Short-lived
28 "Go on, ___ you!": 2 wds.
30 Nonpro. sports org.
31 Container for footwear
33 "With God ___ witness": 2 wds.
35 "___ Time at All" (Ronnie Milsap single): 2 wds.
36 Nocturnal bird of prey
38 "Jurassic Park" terror, briefly: 2 wds.
41 Gab: hyph.
45 Commencement
46 ___ level (honest): 2 wds.
47 Watch faces
48 Confronts

Down

1 Explosive device
2 Fit to fight: hyph.
3 Place for physical exercise
4 Brief peek, slangily: hyph.
5 It's north of Afr.
6 Items included in envs.
7 ___ Fugard, playwright whose works include "The Road to Mecca"
8 Sicilian six
9 Prescribed amt., sometimes
10 AZ and AR, e.g.
14 Past time, briefly
18 Saluki sounds
20 Complex and detailed
21 Aldo ___, 38th Prime Minister of Italy
22 Pinnacle
23 Four-line rhyme scheme
24 Married ladies of Spain: abbr.
25 Priory of ___ (group in "The Da Vinci Code")
29 Gum brand with the varieties "Pure" and "Shine"
32 Sword's handle
34 Bumpkin
37 Hoses down
39 Rhinelander's "real"
40 Classic Jags
41 Smallest Hebrew letter
42 "Wheel of Fortune" buy: 2 wds.
43 Civil War side, initially
44 ___ Kippur

64

Across

1. Fancy neckwear
4. Greek vowels that look like an H
8. Small African antelope
11. "A Walk in the Woods" costar Nick
13. Relating to the Earth
15. Bill
16. Sunscreen ingredient, for short
17. Vigor
20. Suffix for tact or class
21. "Spy vs. Spy" magazine
22. Mark into squares
25. Unhappy fan
29. Horse's food
31. Aid group, often: initials
32. Door material, at times: 2 wds.
36. Huntsman Center team
37. Got bigger
38. Principal character in a work of fiction
42. Proofreader's mark, sometimes
43. Where Hawkeye served
44. Exhale like a dog
45. Suffix with ether or id

Down

1. Automated performer of computer tasks
2. Miner's quarry
3. Place for fighter jets
4. Type of MD
5. Destroyer destroyer
6. Low profile maintainer
7. Attempts
9. ____ Fox
10. "____ Your Skin" (1964 cult horror film): 2 wds.
12. Guidonian note
14. Study quickly
17. Fruit juice-flavored drink: hyph.
18. Military formation, briefly
19. Put the cuffs on
23. Reprove
24. Kit ____ Club ("Cabaret" setting)
26. "Bird ____" (1990 movie): 3 wds.
27. Latin abbrs.
28. Trinidadian musician and bandleader Edmundo
30. Peterman
32. Sink fitting: hyph.
33. Feminist author Tanenbaum
34. Comprehend, slangily
35. Jay of late-night talk
36. Help for checkers, initially
39. Part of an 800 collect call number
40. Red ____
41. Chess champion Mikhail

65

Across

1 Carbon arc lamp used in filmmaking
6 ___ monde
10 "CSI: Miami" costar Eva
11 Cloying sentimentality
12 Nonconformist
14 Door word
15 Señorita's emphatic "yes": 2 wds.
16 "Pow!" response
17 Dust Bowl denizen
21 City in Israel: 2 wds.
25 They, in Toulouse
26 Use a pen
27 French city where Van Gogh painted
29 Veiled vow?: 2 wds.
30 Encountered suddenly: 2 wds.
32 Half of an Orkan farewell
34 Home of the Bulldogs, initially
35 Tire in Tours
37 Inexperienced
40 Science room
43 Fraternal gp.
44 Flax-like fiber
45 Pig's cheek
46 Falls

Down

1 "America's Got Talent" judge Heidi
2 Runner's track
3 Vitamin tablet supplement
4 Belgium's continent: abbr.
5 Improves in health: 2 wds.
6 Open-enrollment grps.
7 Part of a TV feed
8 G.I. entertainers
9 Abbr. at the end of a note
13 Stereo system: hyph.
16 Kind of grass
18 Place to fire pots
19 "___ the Music Speak" (Abba song): 2 wds.
20 Brand name in a blue oval
21 Double
22 Mother of the Valkyries
23 Animal with a mane
24 Foremost division of an advancing army
28 Estuary
31 Teacher of Heifetz, Leopold ___
33 Cellist's stroke: hyph.
36 Christmas song
37 Former Cowboys' quarterback Tony
38 Doesn't give ___: 2 words
39 They come after exes
40 President after J.F.K.
41 Mil. address
42 Road crew's supply

73

66

Across

1 Muscle twitch
6 Class of organic nitrogen compounds
11 Ban
12 Desserts, to many dieters: hyph.
13 Big turtle of the Amazon
14 "Star Trek: First Contact" actress Woodard
15 Woman whose husband is away often: 2 wds.
17 Hebrew letter: var.
18 Hasbro action figures: 2 wds.
21 Castle for Kasparov
25 Harem chamber
26 Cultivate
27 Like a slick
29 Turn to bone
32 Virtual meeting of a sort
34 Guard
39 ____ Deering, Buck Rogers' romantic interest
40 Mushroom-cloud creator: abbr., 2 wds.
41 Pick up the check
42 Take after
43 Nixon commerce secretary Maurice
44 Receive a ____ welcome

Down

1 Just for men
2 Catherine who outlived Henry VIII
3 "East of Eden" woman
4 Such that: 3 wds.
5 Dessert made of eggs and cream
6 Grant-____: 2 wds.
7 Crumble
8 Dirt, so to speak
9 Neighbor of Swed.
10 Suffix with legal
16 Had existence
18 Bit of baby talk
19 Infamous Amin
20 Tokyo carrier, initially
22 "____ believe in yesterday": 2 wds.
23 Sock-in-the-gut reaction
24 E or G, e.g.
28 Navy enlistee
29 Common flooring wood
30 Unpleasant smell
31 Burn up
33 Mild oaths
34 Scuttlebutt
35 Olive genus
36 Orchard fruit
37 Brand name in an ellipse
38 Ways to go?: abbr.
39 Gym set: abbr.

67

Across

1. 1940s Soviet secret police org.
5. Hung down loosely
11. Mantra assigner
12. Cespitose
13. ___ about (approximately): 2 wds.
14. Actor Peter of "The Lion in Winter"
15. Loan shark
17. Because: 4 wds.
21. German port on the River Ems
22. Lariat
23. Cheerleader's syllable
24. Inc., in Britain
25. Like a maple leaf
28. Have for sale
30. 1961 Jimmy Dean chart-topper: 3 wds.
32. Interstice
33. Skeleton parts
36. Kind of race
39. Loathing
40. Old English letters
41. Animals' scent trails
42. Pitching great Nolan ___

Down

1. Aid group, often: initials
2. Former Hungarian president Béla
3. "___ Day" (movie starring Bill Murray)
4. Anatomical friction reducers
5. Blow hard
6. Filmmaker with great creative control
7. It weighs on astronauts: 2 wds.
8. Ronny & the Daytonas hit of 1964
9. Slippery fish
10. Presidential inits.
16. "Anchors Aweigh" gp.
17. ___ ware (Japanese porcelain)
18. Plant that survives all but a severe frost: hyph.
19. When some have brunch: 2 wds.
20. Baghdad's ___ City
21. Jewish eve
26. Food court pizza chain
27. Bread maker
28. Spanish "eye"
29. Container for loose papers
31. Resolved issues, slangily
33. "Quiet down!" sounds
34. Make use of
35. Purview of 10-down
37. "Gotcha!"
38. Channel owned by DirecTV and Sony Pictures Television: inits.

68

Across

1 Lawyers' degs.
5 Jettison
11 "… have to watch what ___ on this diet": 2 wds.
12 Jasper Johns genre: 2 wds.
13 Italian sportswear brand
14 Spaghetti westerns
15 Part of Manhattan, New York City: 2 wds.
17 Context or conflict ending
18 Some cassettes, briefly
22 Female entertainer
26 G.I. grub
27 "I Love a Parade" composer
28 Actionable words
30 Atmosphere: prefix
31 Breed of dog
33 Baseball great Sammy
35 Slowing, in mus.
36 In unison: 3 wds.
41 Unhealthy looking
44 Insurable item
45 Greek letters
46 Letters after Q
47 Component of RNA
48 "Vampire Blood" author Darren

Down

1 Long sentence
2 Han's love
3 Danse events
4 Rule of an institution
5 Mars, ruins
6 Laundry amount
7 Made a choice
8 Fujairah's locale, initially
9 "Why you little!"
10 Elev. areas
16 Composer Camille Saint-___
19 Prefix meaning "both"
20 Oak or elm
21 Be a vendor
22 Lukas of "Rambling Rose"
23 Cookie with florets on it
24 Certain cameras: inits.
25 Done in
29 Sobbing: 2 wds.
32 Jonah ___, character in TV's "Jericho"
34 Finnish architect Alvar ___
37 On condition that: 2 wds.
38 Sled dog command
39 Start with boy or girl
40 Proper word
41 Short orchestral section?
42 Yellowfin tuna variety
43 Independent nat. since November 1941

69

Across

1 Aqualung
6 Slap on
10 "You got it": abbr., 2 wds.
12 Russian saint
13 Fighting ___ (Big Ten team)
14 Alike, in Paris
15 "___ Hear a Waltz?" (Broadway musical): 2 wds.
16 De-chalk
18 World's first rocket-powered full-size aircraft
20 In a dull way
23 Life ___ know it: 2 wds.
25 Double-crosser
26 Not up to scratch
30 The Magic, on scoreboards
31 State, to Pierre
32 City in southern King County, Washington
34 Cut
38 New ___ (capital of India)
40 Unit of electrical conductance
41 Visiting the Lincoln Memorial, say: 2 wds.
43 "___ Forever" (Lynyrd Skynyrd album): 2 wds.
45 Banda ___ (Indonesian city)
46 Gad about
47 High spots
48 Climb

Down

1 Snippy, as a remark
2 Monetary unit of Costa Rica
3 Illuminated from below
4 Man's nickname
5 Top of the line: hyph.
6 ___ 180 (reverses course): 2 wds.
7 "x + y = z" study
8 Home of the Bulldogs, initially
9 ___ Harbour, Florida
11 Ornithologist
17 Field
19 Federal warning system, initially
21 Gibbon species
22 From Jan. 1
24 Creep
26 Letters of distress
27 Ultravox singer Midge
28 ___ wrack, common brown seaweed
29 Some initial football positions?
33 PC supporters: abbr.
35 Tiny organism
36 "___ Stop the Rain" (movie starring Nick Nolte)
37 Free of charge: 2 wds.
39 Argonaut who slew Castor
41 "Can ___ least sit down?": 2 wds.
42 Sgt. or cpl.
44 Big inits. in trucks

70

Across

1 Bangladesh's capital, old-style
6 Swedish auto
10 Toothbrush brand: hyph.
11 Annual TV awards, with "The"
13 Doctor's directive: 2 wds.
14 First Lady before Michelle
15 "Where ___?" (Frank Sinatra album): 2 wds.
17 General ___ Chicken (Chinese menu dish)
18 Ramat ___ (Israeli city)
19 "ER" extras
21 Bug-eyed ones, maybe: inits.
22 Mount near Messina
24 Prevailing weather
26 Hug, usually with fondness
28 Vice president after Hubert
29 Swing voters: abbr.
32 Cow or sow
33 157.5 degrees from N.
35 French pronoun
36 Dadaist artists Jean and Hans
38 Easy to don shoe: hyph.
40 Fools
42 Parry
43 They are a sorry lot
44 "227" sitcom star Gibbs
45 Picked from a stack of cards
46 Signed

Down

1 Amount of medicine
2 Where Noah landed
3 Culinary seasoning: 2 wds.
4 Art class material
5 Detest
6 Salt: Fr.
7 Part of a Latin trio
8 Dollywood, e.g.: 2 wds.
9 Through habitual repetition: 2 wds.
12 Guff
16 Straighten, as one's legs
20 N.Y. org. that enforces alcohol laws
23 Friend of Napoleon
25 In this localité
27 Abbr. in condo sale ads
28 Hide from view
30 Daydreamer's doing
31 "Nothing Compares 2 U" singer O'Connor
32 Baghdad suburb: ___ City
34 Bursera resin
37 Sun-cracked
39 "Terrible" tsar
41 Lincoln-to-Lubbock dir.

71

Across

1 "Jesus loves me, ___ know": 2 wds.
6 Very warm person's declaration: 2 wds.
11 Joke subjects
12 "I love you," in Spain: 2 wds.
13 Alaskan native
14 Like an anchor just clear of the bottom
15 Folding area in the rear of a car: 2 wds.
17 Warning signal
18 Like Cheerios
21 Some N.C.O.s
24 Phone six letters
25 Web browser entry letters
26 Owner's guidebook
30 Light and insubstantial (poetic)
31 "McHale's Navy" star Borgnine
33 With the top at the bottom
37 Felipe, Jesús and Matty
38 Bond girl Roberts
39 John Thomas ___, portrait painter
40 MP quarries
41 Platforms for Ancient Athenian orators
42 Prefix meaning "nine" that can precede -gon

Down

1 Way to the top?: hyph.
2 Website to watch old shows
3 Bookkeeping entry
4 Short and blunt
5 Plant fiber used for nets and cordage
6 State Park in Minnesota
7 Falling star
8 Aggressive and lengthy speech
9 Forget about
10 Toy that spins
16 "___ in elephant": 2 wds.
18 Saturday morning TV show, initially
19 "Devious Maids" costar Ortiz
20 Orchestral piece with a rhapsodic theme: 2 wds.
22 Stumble
23 On the ___
27 "The Left Hand of Darkness" author Le Guin
28 Liqueur flavorers
29 Certain digital watch face, initially
30 Early in the morning: 2 wds.
32 Bristles
33 Peter Fonda title role, 1997
34 "___, U of K" (fight song at the University of Kentucky): 2 wds.
35 Noah of "ER"
36 Discovery grp.
37 "Be on the lookout" message, initially

72

Across

1 Dye-yielding shrubs
6 Response to a playground challenge: 2 wds.
11 Credit card lure: 2 wds.
12 Calls for attention
13 Cloth spread under a sleeping bag
15 Brit. news network
16 Volleyball barrier
17 Sixth-century date
18 Khmer Republic leader
19 1996 Summer Olympics locale
21 "Green Darkness" author Seton
23 Macerich and GCP, e.g.
24 Rational belief in God
26 Hiccup, for instance
28 The like
32 Imaginary beings
34 Bud's comic buddy
35 City of Honshu, Japan
36 Chemical suffix
37 C&W cable channel
38 Baptism
41 Second-oldest Marx brother
42 Shakespeare title character
43 Keeping an ___ the clock: 2 wds.
44 Clipped (like sheep)

Down

1 Heart condition
2 Wrestler Scott or boxer Ken
3 Phrase spoken with hindsight: 2 wds.
4 Money in Moldova
5 Plant with laxative properties
6 Rooks, in chess
7 Expression of pleasure
8 "You ___ worry about it"
9 Salmon relatives
10 Old port on the Tiber
14 Disadvantage, harm
20 Intends
22 Month before Nisan
25 1988 NFL MVP Boomer
26 Walk with confidence
27 ___ Trudeau, former Canadian P.M.
29 Proximo's opposite
30 Dennis, winner of the America's Cup
31 Kept the phone line open: 2 wds.
32 Flat sheet of microfilm, familiarly
33 Prophets
39 Wall St. debut
40 Kabuki kin

73

Across

1 "Assuming yes...": 2 wds.
5 Exclamations of wonder
9 Copier company
10 Inspiration for poets and musicians
12 Individual mark on a painting
15 Solothurn's river
16 Fractional ending
17 "Gee whiz!"
18 1990 arcade-style action video puzzle game: 2 wds.
20 Astern
21 Person to who money is owed
23 Bay of Naples isle
26 Flower seed bearer
27 Confrontational: hyph.
29 Raft
30 More courageous, slangily
34 Beer variety, initially
35 Volkswagen hatchback
36 Phone six letters
37 Power tool with a rapidly rotating disk: 2 wds.
40 Flummox
41 Area around the altar of a church
42 River deposit
43 "Put ___ writing": 2 wds.

Down

1 "… when ___, I'm better" (Mae West): 2 wds.
2 Celebrating: Swed.
3 ___ und Drang
4 Alliance created in 1948, initially
5 Certain terrier, informally
6 Branch of dentistry
7 Major event of 1812
8 Leaf apertures
11 Emeka of the Charlotte Bobcats
13 Seabird with black-tipped wings: 2 wds.
14 Contest effort
19 Height, in combination
22 "As I was going to St. ___..."
23 Baby's affliction
24 Sightlessness
25 Explosive devices used to blast holes in walls
28 Means of expressing one's talents
31 "No more for me, thanks": 2 wds.
32 As a friend, to Pierre: 2 wds.
33 "Girl Meets World" actress Blanchard
38 Fifth-century date
39 Subj. of Rule 10.04 in baseball

74

Across

1 As blind as ___: 2 wds.

5 Be able to spare

11 Bitty

12 English landscape painter (1775–1851)

13 "Hud" Oscar winner

14 Excessively showy

15 French wave

16 W.W. II craft letters

17 ___ Grumman, aerospace company

22 Another name for God

24 Language of Nigeria

25 Shot of whiskey with a beer chaser

27 Boxing promoter D'Amato

28 Expected to place, as in a tournament

29 French isl. south of Newfoundland: 2 wds.

31 ___ premium (scarce): 2 wds.

32 Founder of the Church of Scientology Hubbard: 2 wds.

36 Root vegetable

39 Central American rodent

40 Bible book before Song of Solomon: abbr.

41 Samsung product, e.g.: abbr., 2 wds.

42 On dry land

43 "My word!": 2 wds.

Down

1 ___ time: 2 wds.

2 Well for the French

3 Take out ___ in the paper (publicize): 2 wds.

4 Advil alternative

5 Law enforcement and tax collection agency, initially

6 One working 40-hour weeks: hyph.

7 College newbie

8 Refusing to work, as a protest: 2 wds.

9 Hi-___ monitor

10 Like some wine

18 Small carriage: hyph.

19 Not so common

20 Agreed to, slangily

21 "___ favor" (Spanish for "please")

22 August, in Paris

23 Official report on military affairs

25 College football ranking format: inits.

26 Long Island university

30 Novelist Calvino

33 Physics units

34 Prefix with -hedron

35 Branch of the armed forces

36 Shooter ammo

37 Mil. training site

38 Suffix for sugars, in chemistry

75

Across

1 ____ avis, unique person
5 Last-minute greeting: hyph.
10 Final, e.g.
11 Cinema film
12 Overcome (a problem or difficulty)
14 Foot feature with phalanges
15 House of Lords member
16 "Let me say that again": 2 wds.
18 Neighbor of Minn.: 2 wds.
22 Ratio words: 2 wds.
24 Dutch city
25 Canon competitor
27 Play (to)
29 N.Y.C. subway line
30 Fine material used for tutus
32 Radar's favorite pop
34 "That's fine!": abbr., 2 wds.
37 Gender abbr.
39 Inlet
40 Omen of destruction: 2 wds.
43 Without a ____ stand on: 2 wds.
44 Organic compound
45 Golf's "Slammin' Sam"
46 Boxes, briefly

Down

1 Linear opening?
2 "If it ain't broke, don't fix it," e.g.
3 Kind of element: 2 wds.
4 Onetime Jeep mfr.
5 ____ Honeycutt, "Queer as Folk" character
6 Bay
7 Certifies
8 Seafood restaurant sign "Oysters ____ season": 2 wds.
9 Michigan's biggest city: abbr.
13 Immediately following, as on TV: 2 wds.
17 Nigerian native
19 Preventative measure
20 Stock follower
21 "____-plunk"
23 According to the timepiece
25 Mark, as a ballot: 2 wds.
26 Palindrome for poets
28 Austrian peak
31 Not wearing shoes
33 Candidate's concern
35 Pour ____ troubled waters: 2 wds.
36 Spherical objects
38 Encouraging preceder of "boy" or "girl"
40 Metric units of volume: abbr.
41 Poetic contraction
42 IBM competitor

76

Across

1 First Fiesta Bowl winner, initially

4 Goal

7 37th president, initially

8 Radical 1960s org.

9 Computer monitor, for short

12 Wks. and wks.

13 Men of Mexico

15 Pennsylvania's ___ Mountains

17 "I ___ Song Go Out of My Heart" (Duke Ellington song): 2 wds.

18 Raking ___ (getting rich): 2 wds.

19 Early year: 2 wds.

20 2000 Jennifer Lopez movie: 2 wds.

23 Dominant opener?

24 Overnight (as a delivery): 2 wds.

26 To the point

28 Sweet syrup served in England

31 Lions' homes

33 Met song

34 Kodak competitor, once

35 "Shining Through" writer Susan

37 Trusted male friend, slangily: 2 wds.

39 "___ me?"

40 Response card, e.g.

41 "___ to Pieces" (1965 hit): 2 wds.

42 Pasture land

43 Cry loudly

44 "That's right!"

Down

1 Deodorant place

2 Polished

3 Illogical, lacking method

4 Pt. of PGA

5 Thought: prefix

6 AOL alternative

9 Worm or spider: hyph.

10 Smooth over

11 Hebrew letter: var.

14 Canadian TV channel, initially

16 A single time

19 Quaint shop adjective

21 Some business card nos.

22 Missive: abbr.

25 Very small battery letters

26 "That's ___ excuse!": 2 wds.

27 Heathen

29 Small fruit with scented flesh: var.

30 "___ pie": 2 wds.

32 Sought office

35 Cassio's rival

36 Hoity-toity person

38 Scale notes

77

Across

1 Jewish word of disapproval
4 World financial grp.
7 TV schedule letters, at times
10 ___ Stone
12 TV chef Martin ___
13 Filled with great emotion
15 Tolkien's Quickbeam and Treebeard, e.g.
16 Raipur wrap
17 "Dynasty" costar: 2 wds.
20 Former pro wrestler Anderson
21 Fargo's state: abbr., 2 wds.
22 So far: 2 wds.
24 Storage container
28 Alliance
30 Hot temper
31 Hitchcock movie of 1928: 2 wds.
34 Like some skiing
35 Juárez ones
36 Process of changing words from one language into another
40 Parisian pronoun
41 Dial 911: 2 wds.
42 Country whose capital is Damascus: abbr.
43 Follower of Mao?
44 Time off, initially

Down

1 J. Edgar Hoover once ran it
2 Freddy Krueger's street
3 Old English coin
4 Without delay or hesitation
5 ___ up (botched the job)
6 "Just so it's known…": inits.
7 1979 Alda senatorial role
8 Boxing brothers Max and Buddy
9 "___ quote …": 2 wds.
11 "We the Living" author Ayn
14 Honshu port
17 "___ note to follow soh…": 2 wds.
18 Number crunchers of April, initially
19 Produce immunity by inoculation
23 "Barnaby Jones" star Buddy
25 More scatterbrained
26 Joanne of "All the King's Men"
27 "___-haw!"
29 Small eggs
31 N.F.L. Hall-of-Famer Hirsch
32 "___ of Blue Eyes" (Thomas Hardy novel): 2 wds.
33 "Portnoy's Complaint" author Philip
34 Lawyers: abbr.
37 Driller?: abbr.
38 Former name of the cable network Versus, initially
39 "All Songs Considered" network

78

Across

1 Happen
6 Handel opera, "____ and Galatea"
10 "Swanee" singer Al
12 Osbourne of Black Sabbath
13 Tooth: prefix
14 City of northwest Spain
15 River to the Rhône
17 Org. that monitors health
18 "Later!"
20 Fairway neighbor
22 Big ref. works, for short
24 Drinks noisily
27 Harness racer
29 Ratio words: 2 wds.
30 First
32 "____ and Away" (Fifth Dimension hit): 2 wds.
33 Stair part
35 Quick turnaround, slangily
36 "Quietly Brilliant" phone company letters
38 Nuclear weapon: hyph.
40 Waters, in France
42 Hole in your shoe
45 Giant slain by Odin, thus creating the Earth
46 Dog
47 Stiff hair
48 Words on a Renault 5: 2 wds.

Down

1 Ixtapa eye
2 Massachusetts' Cape ____
3 Like some TVs: hyph.
4 Annapolis sch.
5 Chopper part
6 Earthlink competitor, initially
7 Country, capital Prague: 2 wds.
8 Kind of shirt
9 Harmony: abbr.
11 They're taboo: hyph.
16 Girl's name
18 Hale-____ (comet seen in 1997)
19 Calendar span
21 Mentor
23 Big rig
25 Dugout sound
26 Traditional Mexican dish
28 Impulsive
31 Mountain Community of Kern County, Calif.
34 ____ flush (powerful poker hand)
36 Attention-getters
37 Domestic
39 Word on the wall, in Daniel Chapter 5
41 Overseas Mrs.
43 Disney deer
44 Dutch painter Gerard ____ Borch

79

Across

1 Spanish snacks
6 Emerald City princess
10 Tree with gourdlike fruit
12 Spring
13 Tea brand
14 Table d'___
15 Well-rehearsed
16 U.S.N. clerk
18 1936 Loretta Young title role
21 Silver-gray metal used in alloys
23 Evil
26 Scent trail of an animal
27 Levi's "Christ Stopped at ___"
29 Hit the jackpot
30 Promising good fortune
32 "Boogie Motel" band
33 A ___ (based on logic)
36 Herbert of the "Pink Panther" movies
39 Ste. Jeanne ___
40 Chicago university
43 Herr's helpmate
44 French novelist and dramatist Alain-René ___
45 Impudent stuff
46 As ___ the hills: 2 wds.

Down

1 Med. dose
2 Miniature battery, initially
3 Coward, historically
4 Attorneys' org.
5 Feeling blue
6 Golfer Lorena
7 Lens type
8 Copier brand name
9 Jimmy Van ___, founder of the International Tennis Hall of Fame
11 Louisiana wetlands
17 Tangle
19 Blood letters
20 Reflect
21 Australian state letters
22 Wall St. news
23 Large amount, so to speak
24 Cockpit reading: abbr.
25 "___ Hard" (Bruce Willis movie)
28 Cole Porter's "___ Clown": 2 wds.
31 "Darby ___ and the Little People" (Disney film)
32 Lens adjustment
33 Some transmittable files, initially
34 Avis adjective
35 Keogh alternatives, initially
37 First name in gymnastics
38 Actresses Marsh and West
41 Fair-hiring agcy.
42 Letters on a bottle of Mon Paris

80

Across

1 Big stinger
5 Web destination
9 Ghana's capital
11 "Get outta here!"
13 Teen drama series: 2 wds.
14 Galway's instrument
15 Jailbird
16 Faxes again
18 Frankfurter served in a soft roll: 2 wds.
20 Click in telegraphy
21 ___ Boingo, "Deadman's Party" band
23 "___ tu" (aria for Renato)
24 Bats
26 Del ___ County, California
28 ___ Peron (musical Madonna role)
29 Certain teaching degs.
31 Impact sound
32 Motown's Franklin
35 "Almost done": 3 wds.
38 W.W. II fliers
39 Turkish burden bearer
40 Steam bath
42 Satisfy
43 Theme park at the Walt Disney World Resort
44 Hosiery mishap
45 Merle Haggard's "___ From Muskogee"

Down

1 Item on a wrist
2 Allergy-season sound
3 1992 Al Pacino film: 4 wds.
4 Maven
5 Piz Buin nos.
6 Anglesey or Royale
7 Extremely shocked
8 Grovel, slangily: 2 wds.
10 It stands for something
12 Certain terrier, informally
17 Grade A item
19 Distinction, slangily
22 "The ___ (That's Left in My Heart)," Johnny Cash song: 2 wds.
24 Distances from top to bottom
25 Statements of belief
27 Petrarch work
30 Wilt
33 Vietnam capital
34 ___ worse than death: 2 wds.
36 Bangladesh currency unit
37 Designer for Jackie
41 PFC's address

81

Across

1 It can be scrambled
4 1959 Kingston Trio hit
7 Author Lewis et al., initially
10 Actor Billy ___ Williams
11 ___ nova (musical style)
12 "Well done!"
13 Warm ocean currents: 2 wds.
15 English writer Arthur
16 Without protection
18 Chippewa or Cherokee
20 Nomadic tents
21 Tennis's Mandlikova
22 Final countdown starter
23 Feature of 007's Aston Martin: 2 wds.
28 Word with mess or press
29 "Take ___ a sign": 2 wds.
30 E. M. Forster's "___ With a View": 2 wds.
33 Cartoon genre with wide-eyed characters
34 Pierce and make holes in
36 Partners' go-between
37 Having hooked claws
40 Outdoor sports store
41 Summit: abbr.
42 Day break?
43 Pipe joint
44 River in Somerset, England
45 Hospital sections, initially

Down

1 Ethnic group of Vietnam
2 Shaving option
3 True, real
4 Dog annoyance
5 Pranksters drop it
6 Analyst who tests metals
7 Rank below capt.
8 Wintry downpour
9 Beginnings
14 Behind: 3 wds.
17 Collides with: 2 wds.
18 Most common word in English
19 British rule in colonial India
22 Palindromic kid
24 Disciple of St. Paul
25 ___ Lantier, central character in Émile Zola's "Germinal"
26 Weapon fired from a plane, initially
27 Literary monogram
30 Into pieces
31 Zellweger of "Jerry Maguire"
32 Do ___ situation: 2 wds.
33 Finnish architect Alvar ___
35 Blow up
38 One of two on the head
39 Two-out plays, in baseball stats.

89

82

Across

1 Complain
5 Mark achieved in a test
10 Fragrance
11 Big turtle of the Amazon
12 Certain gambler: 2 wds.
14 Wolfgang ___ Mozart
15 Movie theater showing experimental films: 2 wds.
20 Last Supper query: 3 wds.
23 Prehistoric tombs
24 Salk's conquest
25 As ___ Methuselah: 2 wds.
26 Indian instrument like a cello
27 Accepted practice
28 It accepts all ships: 2 wds.
30 Roy Orbison song of 1964: 2 wds.
34 Saccharin and aspartame, e.g.
37 Barrier that encloses an area
38 Itinerary info
39 Canadian physician Sir William ___
40 Chronic drinkers

Down

1 End piece in music
2 Take ___ view of: 2 wds.
3 Brown & Haley candy, Almond ___
4 Lion's skill
5 Parisian toast
6 Short-lasting program of instruction: 2 wds.
7 Suffix with direct or deposit
8 Charlotte of "The Facts of Life"
9 Where Brit. is
13 Historical drama: 2 wds.
16 Sharpening devices
17 Meat approver, for short
18 Without women
19 To be, to Tiberius
20 Facto lead-in
21 Zest or Irish Spring, e.g.
22 "___ pastore" (opera by Mozart): 2 wds.
29 Fish-eating creature
31 Denial
32 Q.E.D. part
33 Blog feeds, initially
34 BART stop
35 All-Pro Patriots receiver Welker
36 Make bigger, as a photo: abbr.

83

Across

1 Liquid used to stimulate evacuation
6 Young bird
11 Chart holder
12 Cozy
13 Phrase used to signal a startling revelation: 3 wds.
15 F.I.C.A. benefit
16 Architect Saarinen who designed the St. Louis Gateway Arch
17 German beer
18 Musical notes
21 Basketballers' offensive drive: 2 wds.
23 Restaurateur Toots
25 "Good heavens!": 2 wds.
26 Member of a legislative body
30 The "good" cholesterol, initially
31 Dilbert coworker
32 Battle Born State school letters
33 Gull
36 Express pity
40 Firing offense?
41 Small drum
42 Parasitic flatworm
43 45th president of the USA

Down

1 Seals' meals
2 Inner cell of an ancient temple
3 Morales of "Paid in Full"
4 Rest room sign
5 Trees of the birch family
6 Innocent
7 Foil-wrapped chocolate dessert: 2 wds.
8 "That's what I think," when texting
9 Frame
10 "The Spanish Tragedy" dramatist
14 Lick
17 Owl's hangout
18 Comic Lew
19 Way to shoot down a plane, initially
20 Blue hue
21 Call from home?
22 Certain crow
23 Univ.
24 Coal carrier
27 Conical tooth
28 Small land masses: abbr.
29 Musical Lyle
32 "Er, yeah": 2 wds.
33 He played Mowgli in "Jungle Book"
34 Hanna-Barbera's heroic Ant
35 Cop's catch: abbr.
36 Half-____ (coffee mix): abbr.
37 The Magic, on scoreboards
38 2014 Rose Bowl winner, initially
39 Archival file format, initially

84

Across

1 Sun follower?
4 A.M.A. members
7 Noodlehead
10 Prefix for -logist
11 Dried river bed
12 Author LeShan
13 Atlantic game fish
15 "Thanks a ___!"
16 Reveals the true nature or identity of
17 One of two ways
18 1999 U.S. Open champ
19 Portuguese king
20 Austere
21 "Cheers" actor Roger
22 Shipments
24 Light: prefix
26 Scorch
29 Charley ___, author of "The Winning Hitter"
30 Subatomic particle
31 Hosp. areas
32 Make desolate
33 Fleischer of the West Wing
34 Sprites
35 Sequel title starter
36 Royal son of comics
37 A.E.C. successor
38 "Gross!" sounds
39 Nine-digit no. issuer
40 Inst. in Nashville

Down

1 Shared by two or more parties
2 Citrus fruit
3 Famed world peace advocate (1915–90): 2 wds.
4 Movie that earns a specified profit level
5 Scissors used to cut a zigzag edge: 2 wds.
6 Freshness
7 Temperateness: hyph.
8 Actress Renée of silent movies
9 Talk of the town?
14 Tortellini and rigatoni
21 Person who loves books
23 Wind instrument
24 Beggar's cry
25 Cultivating tool
27 Hangs in the air
28 George ___, Romanian composer of the opera "Oedipe"
32 Performing arts degrees, initially

85

Across

1 Like some tea or coffee
5 Preening fellows
9 ___ Sad (capital of Vojvodina, Serbia)
10 Fencing needs
12 Ottoman Empire founder
13 Third monastic hour
14 Wish harm upon
15 "Rhoda" actress Valerie
16 Kind of testing, for short
17 Big screen letters
18 Japanese capital, once
19 Spanish sirs
21 Sensed
22 Looked forward to with fear and dismay
24 Kind of pad
26 Hardly used
29 Prefix for dynamic
30 ___-cone (carnival purchase)
31 Tax returns pro.
32 "Happy Birthday, Sweet Sixteen" singer
34 Forehead-slappers' cries
35 Renowned football coach Rockne
36 Dutch symbol
37 Conductor Sir Georg
38 Three islands off the coast of Ireland
39 Detach from dependence
40 Collaborator with Engels

Down

1 Totally nuts
2 Control compartment of a spacecraft: 2 wds.
3 2008 AL Rookie of the Year Longoria
4 Noise
5 Kind of position
6 Phone abbr.
7 Upright
8 Leave the union
11 Asian goat-antelope
12 Probability
15 Exclamation of praise to God
17 "___ we having fun yet?"
20 Sierra Madre treasure
21 Royal Botanic Gardens site
23 ___ volente
24 Substances used for perfume
25 Heretofore: 2 wds.
27 Statue with the body of a lion and the head of a man
28 Padlock piece
30 Entanglement
33 Boy or girl lead-in
34 ___ mater (brain part)
36 One may be worn with a kilt

86

Across

1. Bank acct. report
5. Gold coins of Old Rome
11. Galway Bay's ___ Islands
12. "Dancing on the Ceiling" singer Richie
13. Including bad qualities: 3 wds.
15. Sundial number
16. Classification
17. Lucy of "Charlie's Angels," 2000
18. Port on the coast of Panay in the Philippines
20. Some AOL communications
21. Golfer who won the 1964 British Open
23. Never, in Berlin
24. Rich type of coffee
27. Russian negatives
29. Road reversal, familiarly
30. Russian pop duo
32. Author Tolkien's initials
33. Anti-aircraft fire: hyph.
37. Suffix for Darwin or defeat
38. "Now I'm onto you!"
39. ___ Angelico, Early Italian Renaissance painter
40. "Jeopardy!" phrase: 3 wds.
43. Burnt ___ (Crayola color)
44. Enthusiastic volunteer's shout: 2 wds.
45. Displace
46. Abound (with)

Down

1. 2005 horror sequel: 2 wds.
2. Bring up the rear
3. Author Puzo
4. Explosive inits.
5. Winter Olympics event
6. Farm cry
7. City southeast of Tel Aviv
8. Queueing: 3 wds.
9. Set the boundaries of
10. Mistreats: hyph.
14. Like Fatty Arbuckle's films
19. Dockworkers' gp.
22. Honeydew-producing aphid: 2 wds.
24. Japanese system of unarmed combat
25. Dirigible craft
26. Dutch painter (1632–75)
28. Loud laugh
31. Sounds some approval from a distance: 2 wds.
34. "There's no such thing as ___ lunch": 2 wds.
35. TV news staple
36. Top-40 DJ Casey
38. "Step ___ pets" (animal-friendly palindrome): 2 wds.
41. Year abroad
42. One with defib. training

87

Across

1 Serving to punish
6 Shows appreciation (for)
11 "I ___ Walrus": 2 wds.
12 Ladies' man
13 "This has me feeling blue!": 2 wds.
14 Ogler's pastime
15 Twin peaks in the Rocky Mountains: 2 wds.
17 "Little" Dickens girl
18 Crows
22 SALT subject
26 "Rebel Without a Cause" costar Sal
27 Letter-shaped opening for a bolt: hyph.
28 Guess
29 For the full length of a pregnancy: 2 wds.
30 1960s–70s pitcher nicknamed Blue Moon
32 Dockland district
38 Opening episode of a miniseries: 2 wds.
39 Kind of space
40 "Good ___!"
41 "___ Psyche" (poem by Keats): 2 wds.
42 Imitative behavior
43 Most trifling

Down

1 Couple
2 Flaubert heroine
3 Fed. accident investigators
4 Melville's obsessive whaler
5 Guided beyond the threshold of: 2 wds.
6 Angler's basket
7 Fervent supporter of a person or institution
8 Mideast ruler: var.
9 Composes
10 Soak, old-style
16 French possessive
18 Songwriters' org.
19 Suffix with human
20 "Wheel of Fortune" purchase: 2 wds.
21 Aquatic marine mammal: 2 wds.
23 Ending for corpus or cuti
24 City division, for short
25 "Lou Grant" production co.
27 Blockhead
29 Windswept spot
31 Idealize
32 Time ___
33 India.___, singer of "Cocoa Butter"
34 "How ___!"
35 "Cup ___" (1970s Don Williams song): 2 wds.
36 Fishing equipment
37 Gait between walk and canter
38 Org. for Justin Thomas

88

Across

1 Ginger, who partnered with Fred Astaire
7 Consumer protection agcy.
10 Baked goods brand that "Nobody doesn't like": 2 wds.
11 Canyon or ranch ending
12 "Back to the Future" actor: 3 wds.
14 Split 50/50: 2 wds.
15 Long stretches
16 A little lamb?
17 Thug
18 Cut out
19 Brochure
21 One way to fall in love
22 Ridicule: 2 wds.
25 Ernie of golf fame
28 High moorlands, to Brits
29 Tinker Bell capturer
30 Others, in Latin
31 Calculator feature
33 Act quickly, so to speak: 2 wds.
35 Pittsburgh to Baltimore dir.
36 Altogether
37 Onetime lottery org.
38 Pet name for a gander

Down

1 Ruin, as one's parade: 2 wds.
2 Flower used in traditional medicine
3 Cartoonist Wilson
4 Israir alternative: 2 wds.
5 Diver's domain
6 French seasoning
7 Pollute
8 "Jane Eyre" author
9 Collection of similar items packaged as a single unit: 2 wds.
10 "Say cheese!"
13 Uneven
17 Hightail it
19 Places for happy hours
20 ____ Mae Brown (Whoopi Goldberg's "Ghost" role)
21 "M*A*S*H" extra
22 Tools used for beating metal into shape
23 At a minimum: 2 wds.
24 "In" groups
25 "The ____ Strikes Back"
26 In a meager way
27 Covered with rushes
29 Wanda who played Rita in "Evan Almighty"
31 Green Hornet's aide
32 Opposite of endo-
34 Prayer ____

89

Across

1. Deity
4. Rand who wrote "The Fountainhead"
7. Afrique du ___
10. Celebrate
12. Opposite of post-
13. Cancel an online service
15. Quahog, e.g.
16. Hubert Gerold Brown, familiarly: 2 wds.
17. Good name
20. "Now ___ theater near you!": 2 wds.
21. Photographer Goldin
22. Godzilla film series character
25. Some I.R.A.s, informally
29. ___ Arann (former Irish carrier)
31. "___ can say that again!"
32. Just barely legit
36. "Lulu" composer
37. Debtor's claim
38. LXXXVIII: hyph.
42. Snow, in Scotland
43. Big name in antacids
44. U.S. job application datum
45. T or F: abbr.
46. Phillies' and Braves' grp.

Down

1. Steve Carell's "Despicable Me" character
2. Suffix with harp or lamp
3. Rotating power tool part
4. In the box: 2 wds.
5. Flunky: hyph.
6. Govt. agency whose official early history is entitled "Controlling the Atom"
7. Vice president before Gerald
8. Type of legend
9. Heavy
11. Kirk's helmsman
14. Zoo heavyweight: abbr.
17. Computer file format, initially
18. Eisenhower's command, for short
19. Roadway material
23. Cry of frustration
24. Nancy Drew's beau
26. Making a segue (to): 2 wds.
27. Doll: abbr.
28. Try to get damages
30. Trust: 2 wds.
32. Hippie happenings: hyph.
33. Heart or liver
34. Cambodian currency
35. Luke's "Star Wars" twin
36. Eleanor's successor
39. "La la" preceder
40. The "good" cholesterol, initially
41. Lao-___

90

Across

1 Broad-topped hill, in the Southwest
5 Kin of P.D.Q.
9 Tree that bears catkins
10 Salon employees
12 French school
13 Deli specification: 2 wds.
14 Mother Teresa, for one
15 Ballroom activity
17 Magician's name ending
18 "Death ___ Salesman" (Arthur Miller play): 2 wds.
19 "Wheel of Fortune" buy: 2 wds.
20 Per
22 Substance used to repair cracks
24 "Woman With ___" soap opera: 2 wds.
26 Oil from orange blossoms
29 Small river fish
33 Rough stuff
34 TV planet
36 Jazzman Adderley
37 Very small, in slang
39 Magazine no.
40 Opposite of liability
41 "___ Deadwood Stage is a-rollin' on..." ("Calamity Jane"): 2 wds.
43 Martin or McQueen
44 Former Iraqi Deputy Prime Minister Aziz
45 Reserve soldiers' org.
46 Port of Algeria

Down

1 Missing portion in a book
2 Like fresh air
3 "High Anxiety" director Brooks
4 City in Parker County, Texas
5 Shelley poem
6 Lip-___ (pretend to sing)
7 Type of gymnastics maneuver
8 "The Scarlet Letter" woman
9 "Iceland" star
11 Rock and Roll Hall of Famer Bob
16 International ___ (diplomat's area)
21 Former Vietnamese coin
23 Inc. overseas
25 Conspirator
26 "___ We" (Alanis Morissette song): 2 wds.
27 "Are you" in Aragon: 2 wds.
28 Peanut butter cup brand
30 "Peer Gynt" character
31 Make a mint, so to speak: 2 wds.
32 Footnote abbr.: 2 wds.
35 Nijo Castle's city
38 St. Petersburg's river
42 Laugh syllable

91

Across

1. Daly TV role
6. 1450, to Caesar
10. Flaming
11. Rosalind of "Star Trek: Deep Space Nine"
12. Certain discrimination
13. Ethereal
14. Fiddle stick
15. Fair-hiring letters
17. ___ Magnon
18. Steals from
20. Five-cent coin
22. Left speechless: 2 wds.
24. Ms. Helmsley
25. Rep. rival
26. "The Subject Was Roses" director Grosbard
27. Newton or Stern
29. In the ___ one's stomach: 2 wds.
32. Group of seven
34. "___ extra charge": 2 wds.
35. Drain, as strength
36. Suffix with arbor or app
38. Returns org.
39. WWW addresses
41. Chemical indicator
43. Zeno of ___
44. Hints
45. Part of R&R
46. Put away

Down

1. "The Blue ___" 1980 movie starring Brooke Shields
2. They spoil the bunch, it's said: 4 wds.
3. 102, in Roman numerals
4. Scots Gaelic
5. Aden's land
6. Longtime record label letters
7. Latest hours for vacating a hotel room: 2 wds.
8. Actor Criss (Blaine Anderson on "Glee")
9. Ignatius of ___ (Catholic saint)
12. Rock shelter at the base of a cliff
16. Do a lube job on: 2 wds.
19. Worry
21. Character in Shakespeare's "As You Like It"
23. One running the show
27. Periodical publisher
28. Dramamine manufacturer, now part of Pfizer
30. Charge
31. ___ State Park, Custer County, Oklahoma
33. Soothing sprinklings
37. Cheery song
40. Convened
42. Your, in Roma

92

Across

1 Eight, in Oaxaca
5 Tab
9 "Band of Gold" singer Payne
11 ___ Brennan, "One Life to Live" character
12 Big name in bleach
13 Galway Bay's ___ Islands
14 Rule for society
15 Short sleep phenomenon?
17 Org. monitoring auto emissions
18 Brit. news network
19 Convertible car, so to speak
21 ___ up (invigorates)
23 Playing card expert John
24 Curtain holder
26 Ransom Olds's middle name
27 Postscript
30 On or to the left prefix
33 Wild drinking spree, slangily
34 ___ Cotto, character in "Babylon 5"
35 Catchall abbr.
36 Fink
38 Whatever number of
39 Motorist's choices: abbr.
41 High seating area in a sports arena
43 "Schindler's ___"
44 French W.W. I soldier
45 Site for crafty entrepreneurs
46 Roman goddess of hope

Down

1 Recently: 2 wds.
2 Female heir to a throne: 2 wds.
3 That woman
4 Skunk's scent
5 Bus. school degree
6 Impossible to get back
7 Quickly mount: 2 wds.
8 Delaware Indian
10 Lumberjacks
12 Film fragment
16 Mugger disabler
20 Rub the wrong way
22 Auctioneer's last word
25 Procrastinator's opposite
27 Glenn Miller Orchestra vocalist Ray
28 Former cager Bob
29 Comprehend
31 Resembling wine
32 African antelope
37 W.B.A. calls
40 Pen on the farm
42 Poodle's cry

93

Across

1 Soliloquy starter: 2 wds.
5 "Any Day Now" singer Ronnie
11 Ancient Palestinian land
12 They produce mushroom clouds, briefly: 2 wds.
13 Super Bowl XLVIII outcome, scorewise
14 Almost
15 Prefix with dexterity
16 N.Y.C. rapid transport system, once
17 Short lecturer?
19 "___ Came Back Again" (Johnny Cash song): 2 wds.
23 1985 Pointer Sisters hit: 2 wds.
25 Red or Cardinal, for short
26 Wedding phrase: 2 wds.
27 Atlantic crosser letters
29 "…good witch ___ bad witch?" (question from "The Wizard of Oz"): 2 wds.
30 Banish to Hades
32 In addition: 2 wds.
34 Big name in photography, once
35 "Happy Days Are Here Again" composer
36 "Can't Help Lovin' ___ Man" (song from "Show Boat")
38 Latch (onto)
41 Sushi condiment
44 Contributed
45 With hands on hips
46 River the Chinese call Heilong
47 Filter
48 Tachometer readings, initially

Down

1 Prefix with watt
2 Lamar of "Khloé & Lamar"
3 Strong enough to resist explosives
4 Dominion
5 Appearance of a ghost
6 Coast-to-coast highway: 2 wds.
7 Opener: hyph.
8 Outdated atlas letters
9 U.S./Eur. divider
10 "Gentleman" singer
18 Sounds of Brahma, Vishnu, and Siva
20 Tall device for giving light: 2 wds.
21 Deli sandwich
22 Part of Q.E.D.
23 "Baby ___ Bad Bad Thing" (Chris Isaak song): 2 wds.
24 "Epitaph to ___" (Byron poem): 2 wds.
28 Dress (up)
31 Blavatsky or de Pompadour
33 Change is important to him
37 French clergyman
39 Egg cell
40 Seas, to the French
41 Occurred
42 "Canine Good Citizen" org.
43 Respected fellow

94

Across

1 Snake on the Nile
4 Pompous fellow
7 Controller of corp. purse strings
10 Extremely cold
12 Bible bk. after Nahum
13 Rooftop energy sources: 2 wds.
15 Phnom ____
16 Have a fling?
17 Left desolate or empty
20 Indian tree with multiple trunks
23 Chip in some chips
24 Jan Brady portrayer ____ Plumb
25 Outburst from Homer Simpson
27 Tony-winning Hagen
28 Org. that sues pirates
30 Continued: 2 wds.
32 Grotesquely carved figure
34 Prepared to drive, with "up"
35 Frigate's front
38 Derived from custom
41 Sue Grafton's debut mystery novel "____ for Alibi": 2 wds.
42 Of the appetites and passions of the body
43 Abbr. on a business card
44 Playground game
45 Banned chemical compound

Down

1 Reno and Holder, for short
2 Food for pigs
3 Whitish
4 Flighty scatterbrained simpleton (slang)
5 Softhead
6 Blackboard material of old
7 Edible item often roasted on an open fire
8 Unnaturally high voice
9 No longer used, as a word: abbr.
11 Sweet food made with sugar
14 Author-director Ephron
18 Like the top of Everest
19 Head of a college
20 Ice in the sea
21 Amy Johnson, e.g.
22 Lebanon's locale: 2 wds.
26 Giving assistance
29 Got on in years
31 ____ Circus (old Vatican area)
33 Keats, for one
36 "Step right ____!": 2 wds.
37 W.W. II server
38 ____-Bo (exercise system)
39 Tetley product
40 Degree for an att.

95

Across

1 "If I Could Turn Back Time" singer
5 Boot out
10 Gesturing performer
11 Mediterranean island, capital Valletta
12 Priests' robes
13 Removing
14 Classic Milton Bradley war game
16 Away and in trouble, initially
17 Martin ____, all-metal Army Air Corps bomber: 2 wds.
21 Johns in Britain: abbr.
23 College year div.
25 Feel sorry about
26 Tulsa sch. named for a televangelist
27 That objeto
28 Admiral's org.
29 Karel Capek robot play: inits.
30 Prefix with pressure
31 Lincoln center?
32 Commemorate, as the Sabbath
34 Ural River city
36 Trance-inducing practice
40 Bag
43 Some community bldgs.
44 The same, in Saint-Malo
45 August, in Angoulême
46 Computer ____
47 Hosp. staffers

Down

1 Certain Nashville trophies, for short
2 Dagger handle
3 Small opening (in a wall) for firing through
4 Further shorten, maybe
5 Slate, for example
6 Singer Dylan
7 ____ Lilly pharmaceuticals
8 Big box: abbr.
9 Kind of team
13 Magnifier of distant objects
15 Words repeated at the start of the "Sailor's Song": 2 wds.
18 Roadside service station: 2 wds.
19 Suffix with chant or mass
20 Endangered goose
21 Get the job done
22 Mötley ____ (Nikki Sixx's band)
24 Bewail
33 ____ Vance, S.S. Van Dine sleuth
35 Megalopolis with about 30 million people, for short
37 North Sea feeder
38 Keith Urban's "Whenever ____": 2 wds.
39 High fliers, initially
40 Letter that's a symbol of victory
41 Farmer's field: abbr.
42 Domestic deity in ancient Rome

103

96

Across

1 Hint
5 Dashiell Hammett terrier
9 Brute
10 Employers
12 Arrange (a situation)
14 A day in Madrid
15 Mediterranean isl.
16 Afrique du ____
17 Slalom curve
18 Large mass of frozen water
20 City in southern King County, Washington
22 Lily family perennial
23 "____ Shoes" (2005 Cameron Diaz movie): 2 wds.
25 Consign to the underworld
28 Chronological accounts of events
32 Wild asses
34 Kind of center: abbr.
35 Published
36 Popular wine, for short
37 Pit stuff
38 This or that
41 Singer Luft
42 View for a further time
43 Flits about
44 Initial response team, initially

Down

1 Color of ripe cherries
2 Una familia residence: 2 wds.
3 Seat, slangily
4 Dry summer wind of the Mediterranean
5 "Other" in France
6 Lat. or Lith., once
7 Prickly plant
8 Italian conductor Toscanini
9 Augurs
11 Grasslike marsh plant
13 Sugar substitute
19 Farm building
21 ____-a-ling
24 Trap
25 Famed Miami country club
26 Non-digital clock
27 "Om," e.g.
29 Creative person
30 Foliage
31 Loose stones on a mountain
33 Pound and Klein
39 Discontinue
40 Pro ____ (for now)

97

Across

1 Leave in, to an editor
5 Going back, like the tide
11 Up ___ good: 2 wds.
12 High schooler
13 Snake, for one
14 Rope for leading an animal
15 500,000 copies sold in the U.S., e.g.: 2 wds.
17 "Vive ___!": 2 wds.
18 Battle of the ___
21 Mushroom-cloud creator: abbr., 2 wds.
25 ___ de mer (seasickness)
26 Here, in Spain
27 Still in play
30 King in "Conan the Barbarian"
32 Idiotic
34 Individually: 4 wds.
39 Technique used in sports broadcasting: hyph.
40 Eurasia-dividing range
41 Sheikh's bevy: var.
42 Color of rosé wine
43 Eagerly and enthusiastically
44 IRS identifiers

Down

1 Party type
2 "___ the mornin'!": 2 wds.
3 Organic compound suffix
4 Walk with short feeble steps
5 Old anesthetic
6 Guiding light
7 City in southeastern Wisconsin
8 Like some verbs: abbr.
9 Grant basis
10 Dog's warning
16 Court matter
18 Diminutive, in Dundee
19 Suffix with ether or id
20 41, in old Rome
22 Place for a plug
23 School subj.
24 Inactive U.S.A.F. org.
28 Watched
29 Crown covering
30 Stop ___ dime: 2 wds.
31 Frame jobs: hyph.
33 Tiny thing, old-style
34 King Harald's predecessor
35 Seaweed, in sushi bars
36 Spring bloom
37 "Buddenbrooks" author
38 Lodge members
39 "___ Na Na" (1970s musical series)

98

Across

1 Tendril
5 New members of society
9 Scaled: 2 wds.
11 Doomsayer's sign
12 Humiliator
13 "___-Di, ___-Da" (Beatles song): 2 wds.
14 Like crudités
15 Get everyone back together
17 Dash a liquid against
19 T-shirt sizes: abbr.
20 Uncontrollable desire to set fire to things
22 Develop
23 Neck of land
27 Tape format, initially
28 Breakfast foods
30 Artist who married John Lennon: 2 wds.
32 Small island in a river
33 Name part: abbr.
34 Chilled
36 Verne skipper
37 Patriot Allen and author Canin
38 Mil. aides
39 In such a manner that: 2 wds.

Down

1 CrazyEgg, e.g.: 2 wds.
2 Sorta: 3 wds.
3 OH and OK, e.g.
4 Island in the Caribbean: 2 wds.
5 Dutch or French follower
6 Blood clots
7 Caviar source
8 Ginger treats
9 Periods of conflict
10 High status importance: hyph.
16 Fundamental
18 ___ Van Huong, Vietnamese Prime Minister 1964–65
21 ___ Galerie (Manhattan art museum)
23 Calls
24 Igloo dweller
25 Second smallest Teletubby: hyph.
26 Martians and such
27 Contending
29 Norms: abbr.
31 Western Indians
35 "So that's your game!"

99

Across

1 Zoom like an eagle
5 "I Am a ___ Constant Sorrow," folk song: 2 wds.
10 Keen about
11 Lighthearted and cheerful
12 Front half of a side of meat
14 Org. that restricts liquids on flights
15 "___ of God" (Jane Fonda movie)
16 A.C. measure
17 Bore
20 Open
23 Four: prefix
24 Mementoes
26 Statistician's middle
27 Member of the Field Artillery in the Civil War
28 Jewish org. founded in 1913
29 "Oy ___!" (cry of dismay)
30 Three-star V.I.P.: abbr., 2 wds.
33 Moon vehicle, for short
36 Policy of extending a country's power
39 Like hot goods
40 Potent prefix
41 Eucharist greetings
42 Alpine animal

Down

1 Remove particles from
2 Yoko and family
3 Razor brand since 1977
4 Fish eggs
5 Express regret
6 Farm measurement
7 Kernel's covering
8 Number of even primes
9 Four before LBJ
11 It carries blood from the head: 2 wds.
13 Persian Gulf nation
16 Air: 2 wds.
18 "It's ___!" ("No-one wins!"): 2 wds.
19 Pain in the neck
20 Islamic community
21 Require
22 Disease eradicated in the 1970s
23 Neatly arranged
25 "It's ___ Hard Day's Night" (Beatles song): 2 wds.
31 Distant: prefix
32 College srs. may sit for them
33 Large branch of a tree
34 Lord's worker
35 2009, to Caesar
36 Initially, you'll need one to get online
37 Underground letters
38 Law, in Le Havre

100

Across

1. "This ___ sudden!": 2 wds.
5. Japanese fish delicacy
9. Angler's basket
10. Hole ___: 2 wds.
12. Machine for turning metal into sheets: 2 wds.
14. Canadian public filmmaking org., initially
15. Dash
16. "Regnava ___ silenzio" (aria from "Lucia di Lammermoor")
17. Settler's building material
18. Pitching star
19. Dept. store merchandise
20. Snick or ___
22. Door opener
24. Poet, in Old England
26. Snow-___ (winter vehicle brand)
28. Some shoe widths
30. Long
32. Verizon, for one, initially
34. Famous mummy, for short
36. ___ Mitchell (Ed from "Good Burger")
37. Something to pick
38. School whose mascot is Wild E. Cat: inits.
39. Uncompressed audio format
40. Survey, using trigonometry
43. Actress Téa
44. Wounds by piercing
45. Irish singer
46. Baghdad's ___ City

Down

1. T-shirt decals: hyph.
2. View favorable to the person who holds it: hyph.
3. Fleur de ___ (French sea salt)
4. 1964 AL Rookie of the Year Tony
5. "It's a ___ of your imagination"
6. Coll. whose mascot is the Lobo
7. Regressing: 2 wds.
8. Lacking a guide
9. Go to the other side of the street
11. Some bends
13. Short cut?
21. Inits. in the classifieds
23. Old Danish coin
25. Plant with colorful, funnel-shaped flowers
27. Crook
29. "Song ___ Blue"
31. Little people
32. Worldwide: abbr.
33. "No ___ Bob!"
35. Enforcers for the mob
41. "___ luck?"
42. Voodoo spirits

101

Across

1. Like mountains
6. Restaurant options
10. Stocking stuff
11. "Put me in that category": 2 wds.
13. When some go to bed: 2 wds.
14. "Oliver Twist" character
15. Very fast animal
17. Bar opener?
18. Ending for beef or bump
19. Bigger than med.
20. Seventh-century date
21. Bond classic: 2 wds.
23. "____ dead!" (worried person's words): 3 wds.
25. One-time TV workers' union
27. Via ship or boat, e.g.: 2 wds.
29. Prefix with graphic
33. Gave de ____, French river
34. Rd. or hwy.
36. H.S. class
37. Comcast e.g., initially
38. Health-check
40. Soda selection
42. Overact
43. Merchant Yale
44. Lowest point
45. Polite reply from a ranch hand: 2 wds.
46. Bygone blades

Down

1. Tranquil
2. Choice word
3. Backward
4. Swiss abstract artist
5. Film directed by and starring Barbra Streisand
6. Perceive words incorrectly
7. Former London music label letters
8. Retirement community restriction: 2 wds.
9. Maintainer of the World Heritage List
12. Class for foreigners, initially
16. Stir
22. Rio Treaty implementer, initially
24. It follows April in Paris
26. Radioactive metal discovered in 1953
27. In a dispicable way
28. Modern affluent sort (acronym)
30. Figure out
31. Dead even: 3 wds.
32. Impertinent types
33. Tube
35. Paradises
39. Single-named supermodel
41. "Pipe down!" sounds

102

Across

1 Somewhat, in music
5 Walk unsteadily
11 Ones in Madrid
12 Yellow-flowered daisies
13 One of 12 popes
14 Cease trying: 2 wds.
15 From side to side, briefly
16 "___ but known…": 2 wds.
17 Son of Ramses II
19 Actress Kemper in "Unbreakable Kimmy Schmidt"
23 Federal warning system activated by FEMA
24 Painted Desert feature
25 Dr. Frankenstein's assistant, and namesakes
27 Got together: 2 wds.
28 Dull sound
29 Hammer-___ (guitar playing techniques)
30 Usher's beat
32 Pope who persuaded Attila not to attack Rome: 2 wds.
35 Cancels
37 Sculler's need
38 Wood louse: 2 wds.
41 1990s Senate majority leader
42 ___ dragon (monitor lizard)
43 "Freejack"'s Morales
44 Classical guitarist Segovia
45 City on the Moselle

Down

1 Chrysalises
2 In reserve: 2 wds.
3 Gracious
4 C.I.A. predecessor
5 Attire for an ancient Roman
6 Nitrous ___ (laughing gas)
7 Reckless mischief
8 Make hair a different color
9 Romanian monetary unit
10 Subject of a psych. experiment
16 Leak indicator
18 Heavy manual work as a punishment: 2 wds.
20 Sets free: 2 wds.
21 Cyclones' sch.
22 "The Murders in the Rue Morgue" author's monogram
25 Give ___ go: 2 wds.
26 Alphabetical sequence
27 What a rolling stone doesn't gather
31 Give forth
33 Erode: 2 wds.
34 AL home run leader of 2006
36 Psyche parts
38 Calypso kin
39 Suffix with ball or bass
40 Generally vague category of arms, initially
41 Moon vehicle, for short

103

Across

1 Cartoon "devil," briefly
4 Long ____
7 ____ Pepper
10 Bolivian president Morales
11 Weapon
12 "Ben-____" (1880 novel)
13 Heir to a will
15 (They) exist
16 Yvette's evening
17 Off-color
19 Analyze, in a way
21 Reproductive cell
24 Censorship-fighting org.
28 New York county
29 Old laborers
30 Cuddle and kiss in London
31 Spanish royal ladies
32 "____ Amarillo" (1951 movie starring Roy Rogers): 2 wds.
34 Completely: 2 wds.
37 Bring in
41 Jack of "Barney Miller"
42 Force into some kind of situation
44 Campus wall cover
45 R.F.C.'s successor
46 Actor Hakeem ____-Kazim of "24"
47 Prof. helpers
48 Work with a shuttle
49 Tel Aviv's country: abbr.

Down

1 Bus. card data
2 Chevrolet subcompact car
3 King of Albania, 1928–39: 2 wds.
4 F.B.I. employee: abbr.
5 "C'est la ____"
6 "____ not amused!": 2 wds.
7 Former center O'Neal, casually
8 Master
9 Forest unit
14 Pianist's challenge
18 Shoreline inhabitant
20 Words before premium or price: 2 wds.
21 Fast sports cars, for short
22 French department and river
23 Bossy's call
25 BBC World alternative
26 Gamboler's spot
27 Letters at sea
29 It can be shocking
31 Floor-cleaning robot
33 Atom bomb trial: abbr., 2 wds.
34 "____ any wonder?": 2 wds.
35 Astronomer's sighting
36 Playthings
38 Japanese golfer Isao ____
39 Narrow inlets
40 Red or Brave, for short
43 Baseball club

104

Across

1 007 creator Fleming
4 Cadets' sch.
8 Little, in Lyons
9 Depart hurriedly, in slang
13 Summer hrs. in Albany
14 Lummox
15 Prehistoric tombs
17 "Serpico" director Sidney
18 Jai ___ (game similar to pelota)
19 Number indivisible by another
20 Argentinian monetary unit
23 ___-compete agreement
24 Investigate: 2 wds.
26 Bolt for holding a machine part in place
28 Travels past (on horseback, e.g.): 2 wds.
31 Awakened
33 Final club at Harvard University
34 Fracas
35 ___ of beans (thing of little value): 2 wds.
36 Paid (a debt), slangily: 2 wds.
38 ___ code (5- or 9-digit number)
39 Final thing: 2 wds.
40 Zuider ___
41 ___ about (legalistic phrase): 2 wds.
42 Continent, briefly

Down

1 Medicinal syrup
2 Ancient Roman magistrate
3 Essentials, so to speak: 3 wds.
4 Snail-mail system, initially
5 Reggae's forerunner
6 Wheel-powering reservoir
7 River in S.W. France
10 Rival of Little Caesars: 2 wds.
11 Ski resort in Vermont
12 Belonging to a cereal class
16 Evergreen shrub
21 Saw eye to eye: 2 wds.
22 Seven, to Cicero
25 John ___, Connie Sellecca's spouse
26 President Nasser
27 "The Faerie Queene" character
29 Conviction
30 Barker
32 Manage: 2 wds.
35 Impressionist
37 One, in Mexico

105

Across

1 Dolores ____ Rio
4 N.H.L. Hall-of-Famer since 1979
7 Mr. Manning
8 Shift
13 Picnickers run races in them: 2 wds.
15 Makes a choice
16 Thoroughfare
17 TV actress Ward
18 Certain école
19 Christian recluse
22 U.S. 101, e.g.: abbr.
23 Smoothness
25 "I don't wanna hear it!," initially
27 Disarrange, in a way
30 Chinese province
32 Novel of the South Seas
33 Actress Bergman
35 Behold, in old Rome
36 Run-down cafe, in slang: 2 wds.
38 Adrenaline, e.g.
39 "____ don't!" (denial): 2 wds.
40 Nintendo's Super ____
41 H.S. subject

Down

1 Boot the dictator
2 One who runs off to wed
3 Digit farthest from the thumb: 2 wds.
4 U.N. Day mo.
5 Greek letters
6 Constantly in motion
9 Pietà figure
10 Hot weather treat: 3 wds.
11 Shooting game
12 Cosmetician Lauder
14 "Ditto": 3 wds.
20 Together: 2 wds.
21 Half a score
24 South African veranda
25 Common stocking height
26 H.H. ____ (Saki)
28 Chrysalis
29 Chekov player on "Star Trek"
31 "Sabre Dance" composer Khachaturian
34 Newton fraction
37 French possessive

106

Across

1 "Jack Sprat could ____ fat…": 2 wds.

6 Sporty Italian cars, for short

11 Pianist Peter and family

12 Donkey used as a pack animal

13 Overbearingly self-assertive

14 Finale

15 Term for some criminals

16 Absorb (liquid) with a cloth: 2 wds.

17 Clumsy fool

18 Penn, host of "Superhuman"

19 Last of 26

20 Like some bow ties: hyph.

22 Encircle

23 Mexican card game similar to rummy

25 Book after Proverbs: abbr.

27 One who leaves to live abroad

30 Thanksgiving follower: abbr.

31 She-bear: Sp.

32 Edgar Allan ____, writer

33 Way in which a something is set out

35 Fossil fuel

36 Attraction near Orlando

37 Spyri heroine

38 Fine net used for veils

39 Navel type, slangily

40 Dueling weapons

41 Load carrier

Down

1 All together: 2 wds.

2 Above the ground

3 Road junction with a central island: 2 wds.

4 It smells

5 ____Kosh B'gosh (clothing brand)

6 Bubbling on the stove

7 Bulge or protuberance

8 Temperature below which a liquid turns into a solid: 2 wds.

9 Polemicist

10 Lathered

16 Most pale or weak

18 "Rock and Roll, Hoochie ____" (1970s hit)

21 Rep. or Dem., e.g.

22 Cantonese dish

24 Nashville-based awards org.

25 Decadent, degenerate

26 Come to notice unexpectedly: 2 wds.

28 Person who handles equipment for traveling bands

29 More slippery

31 "Bellefleur" author

34 Blemish

35 Prefix for bite or taph

37 Smashing success

107

Across

1 ____ Nui (Easter Island)

5 Cartagena currency, once

11 "Chacun ____ goÛt": 2 wds.

12 Egg container

13 Mo.-end document

14 Arizona tourist locale

15 Gas conveyor

17 Work without ____ (be daring): 2 wds.

18 Gets an ____ effort: 2 wds.

22 Insanity

25 Spawn

26 Bar

27 Held on tightly

29 ____ de vie

30 Disbeliever

32 Some community bldgs.

34 Hit flies

35 Touched up

39 Common Russian name

42 Bunuel collaborator

43 Guide

44 ____ out a draw (narrowly avoids defeat)

45 "Who ____?"

46 CDs and LPs

Down

1 Grate harshly

2 Italian wine center

3 Madame de ____, mistress of Louis XV

4 Feeler

5 Assumes for the sake of argument

6 Composed

7 Part of a single or LP: 2 wds.

8 That, in Toledo

9 Get darker

10 Here, in Mexico

16 One-eyed "Futurama" character

19 Nutcase

20 Suffixes with ball and bass

21 Col.'s command

22 Approx. camera flash duration: 2 wds.

23 "I Had ____ When I Came In" (old Irish tune): 2 wds.

24 Upside-down e

28 Youth beloved of Hero

31 Souvenir item: hyph.

33 Fourth canonical hours of prayer

36 Gas used in lasers

37 A.C. or D.C., e.g.

38 Criticize, slangily

39 Makers of Athlon, Duron and Sempron processors, initially

40 ____ Getz ("Lethal Weapon 2" role for Joe Pesci)

41 One way to go, initially

108

Across

1 Gets larger
6 Bites like a beaver
11 Bandleader's directive: 2 wds.
12 Gulf of Aqaba port
13 Class of organic nitrogen compounds
14 Sporty Ford model, familiarly: hyph.
15 Hare found in open country
17 Invalidate
18 Strong fiber
21 Group of major industrialized countries: 2 wds.
25 Suffix with cap or coy
26 Purchase
27 Element or evolution ending
28 Beginning stage of a study: 2 wds.
30 Helper: abbr.
31 Race that includes Odin, Thor, and Balder
33 Relocating of a company to a country with lower costs
38 Bride's acquisition: hyph.
39 He can sometimes be found near Wenda or Wizard Whitebeard
40 Actress Kate of "Dynasty"
41 Lend ___ (listen): 2 wds.
42 Dance track, often
43 Buffy's weapon

Down

1 Letters after F
2 Terza ___ (Italian verse form)
3 Suffix with psych-
4 Visually flirt: 2 wds.
5 Harsh
6 Begin work: 2 wds.
7 Tiny bit of food
8 "Others" in a Latin phrase
9 Dermal development
10 Criterion: abbr.
16 Torture
18 Offshoot of jazz
19 Part of NCAA: abbr.
20 Bering, for one
22 Anatomical vessel or duct
23 Hosp. units
24 W.S.J. rival
26 It's used to make honeycombs
29 Game expedition
30 Out-and-out
32 Siouan speakers
33 Tab grabber's words: 2 wds.
34 Humbug
35 Parts of intestines
36 State whose capital is Bismarck: abbr., 2 wds.
37 Reason for an R rating
38 Ending for super or infer

109

Across

1 Actress Tierney
6 Mil. officer's charge
9 Sayers detective
10 Fragrant garland
11 Stir fry veggies: 2 wds.
13 Protective covers
14 Tire of France?
15 Goad
16 Some sharks
17 U.S.N.A. graduate, briefly
18 Vega's constellation: 2 wds.
20 Salad green
21 "Here lies..." statement
24 MIT, for one
27 Cheerful and lively
28 Greek pastry dough
29 "Jacques ___ is Alive and Well..."
30 Original
32 Artificially produced radioactive element
34 Female in the forest
35 Stands for paintings
36 Old protest grp.
37 ___ la paix: 2 wds.

Down

1 Algonquian tribe
2 Reply to a playground insult: 2 wds.
3 W.W. II power
4 Exercise units, briefly
5 Historic Scottish county
6 Awkwardly solid and outdated
7 Shooting star
8 Something to fall into
9 Linda Ronstadt album of 1998: 2 wds.
11 Innocent
12 Milky gemstones
16 Grid
18 Cafeteria need
19 Wise
20 "Save" shortcut on some computers: abbr., 2 wds.
21 Puts (inside)
22 Era
23 Castle and Rich
24 Wise as an owl, e.g.
25 Santa ___
26 "Workaholics" costar Anders
28 Slapped by a judge?
30 ___ de soie (silk cloth)
31 Go up
33 Thrice, in prescriptions

110

Across

1 Corporate raider Carl
6 MGM co-founder
10 "Cat's Eye" author Margaret
12 Wagner's goddess of wisdom and earth
13 Common condiment: 2 wds.
15 Bother incessantly: 2 wds.
16 Move stealthily
19 ____ snag (got stuck): 2 wds.
22 Trinidadian musician and bandleader Edmundo
23 Numbers puzzle in the paper
25 Instrument for measuring temperature
28 Nearly
29 Part of a line, in geometry: abbr.
30 Origin
31 Demand from a creditor: 2 wds.
33 Mineral used as a flux
35 Hard-working
41 Dedicated by the auth.
42 Pass, like time
43 Violin part
44 Nicholas Gage best seller

Down

1 Cole Porter's "____ Loved": 2 wds.
2 Windy City rail inits.
3 Shoemaker's hole maker
4 Property to buy in Monopoly
5 "Vertigo" actress
6 Dangerous ocean current: 2 wds.
7 Common e-mail address ending
8 Grant-giving agency, initially
9 World ____ I
11 Morse code click
14 Poet laureate ____ Tate
16 Sp. girl
17 Big name in department stores
18 1972 Bill Withers hit: 2 wds.
20 Hotsy-____
21 Defensive tackle Spence of the NFL
23 Boozehound
24 Egg on
26 Male of a small species of deer
27 Windows precursor: hyph.
31 "Je ____" ("I speak" in French)
32 Having a line of symmetry
34 GPS result
35 "Am ____ trouble?": 2 wds.
36 Navigator's dir.
37 Decoration for heroism, initially
38 Expose, poetically
39 CPO's outfit
40 Six, to Italians

111

Across

1. Indonesian outriggers
6. Modern-day tablets
11. Dirt
12. "I won't take ___ an answer": 2 wds.
13. Wind danger
14. Terra ___
15. Bedroom sharers, maybe
17. Rejections
18. Only mediocre: 3 wds.
21. Award bestowed by Queen Eliz.
22. 100 kopeks in Russia
26. Wavy-patterned fabric
29. "Lohengrin," e.g.
30. Conger or moray: 2 wds.
32. Words of rejection
33. Often
36. Spreadable French cheese
39. Teddy bear manufacturer
40. Journal
42. Cupcake topper
45. Totaled: 2 wds.
46. Charlton Heston title role: 2 wds.
47. Type of jar
48. Heads in Paris

Down

1. Letter abbr.
2. Professional wrestling promotion letters
3. Trilogy of Greek tragedies written by Aeschylus
4. Diarist Nin
5. Kevin who played a small-screen Hercules
6. Foot soldiers: abbr.
7. Emphasize: 2 wds.
8. Bushy hairstyle
9. Capitol feature
10. Spanish ladies, briefly
16. NASDAQ unit, shortly
18. ___ de plume (literary aliases)
19. Slender reed
20. Queenside castle, in chess notation
23. "Béatrice et ___" (Berlioz opera)
24. "Mission Earth" series author Hubbard: 2 wds.
25. West's bridge partner
27. Cite: 2 wds.
28. Poetic adverb
31. Journey part
34. Peaceful
35. "I give up!"
36. Real estate ad abbr.
37. Fighter of pirates, initially
38. Fleming and Ziering
41. Thither
43. Never, in Berlin
44. Mdse.

112

Across

1 Large stringed instrument
8 Hoops org.
11 Propriety in conduct and manners
12 Dr. Seuss's Sam-___: 2 wds.
13 ___ of God (Attila the Hun)
14 Medicare minders, initially
15 Grp. directed by Andris Nelsons
16 Actor Dullea
17 Blue shade
20 Famous chimney visitor, briefly: 2 wds.
22 Give it a rest?: 2 wds.
24 Town in Ontario
25 Comets and Montereys, to car collectors: abbr.
29 Uniformity
31 Comment said with shrugged shoulders: 2 wds.
34 Alike: Fr.
35 Former king of Saudi Arabia
36 Seabird: var.
38 Explorer Johnson
39 Puzzles
43 Moldovan monetary unit
44 Preordain
45 High-speed hookup, for short
46 Engraving with acid

Down

1 Docs
2 N.R.C. predecessor
3 Army figure, for short
4 Bassoon, e.g.: 2 wds.
5 "The Pearl of ___ Island" (Harriet Beecher Stowe novel)
6 Dracula portrayer
7 Gallic soul
8 Japanese-American group
9 Computer language acronym
10 Leave ___ on (influence): 2 wds.
16 Extending halfway down the leg: hyph.
17 Downed a sub, say
18 Ending with exter or inter
19 Doubled, a Dixie Cups oldie about New Orleans
21 Rating for "South Park," initially: hyph.
23 Internet explanation pages, initially
26 Fix, as an election
27 Windy City rail system letters
28 Word pt.
30 Online newsgroup system
31 Poker player's declaration: 2 wds.
32 Krypton and xenon, e.g.
33 DIY mover's rental: hyph.
37 Computer acronym
39 Ethnic group of Vietnam
40 1002, to Nero
41 Former Texas governor Richards
42 Circle pt.

113

Across

1 Japanese poem in three lines

6 Extra notes at the end of a letter, initially

9 Princess Leia ___

11 "The Lion King" lioness

12 Unexcitable

13 Abba ___ of politics

14 Weigh

16 Speak in a low voice

18 Its symbol is Pb

19 Three-legged ornamental table

23 Boy's toy: 2 wds.

25 Hebrew letter: var.

26 "Stolen Innocence" novelist Wall

28 General ___ Chicken (Chinese menu dish)

29 Oil used as an insect repellent

31 Escalate, intensify

34 Colloquial denial

35 Charge

39 Suffix for assist or resist

40 Spirals around a support, as a plant

41 NYC to Bermuda dir.

42 TV comedian Bob

Down

1 O.T. book after Dan.

2 Picasso's field

3 Billy Joel's "___ to Extremes": 2 wds.

4 Constantly changing pattern of objects

5 Insts. of higher learning

6 Sunblock ingredient, initially

7 Thin strip

8 Well-balanced

10 Go with the flow

11 Old term for a nervous breakdown

15 Informal language used on the internet

16 "Oppression and Liberty" author Simone

17 Muslim pilgrim

18 Big, for short

20 El ___, Texas

21 Skunk's defense

22 "Sirree" preceder

24 Genesis man

27 Circuit

30 They turn up in the country

31 Genetic molecules, initially

32 Multiple millennia

33 12 in Tijuana

36 Gerund's end

37 Alphabet's end

38 Repair shop fig.

114

Across

1 Reasoned judgement
6 Bobby Darin's label until 1963
10 Greek twenty prefix
11 1920s Olympics star from Finland
13 Creamed processed meat served on toast: 2 wds.
15 Farm layer
16 Degree for a Canadian att.
17 Word on the option key on a Mac keyboard
18 "___: Deadliest Roads" (reality TV series)
19 Nondiscriminating hirer in help wanted ads, initially
20 Just so-so
21 "Cell" starts with one: 2 wds.
23 City near Padua
24 Pressurized garment worn by airmen: hyph.
26 File folder features
29 Hebrew letter: var.
32 Everything
33 Hodges of baseball lore
34 They're between ems and ohs
36 "Strange Magic" band letters
37 Mauna ___, Hawaii
38 El stop: abbr.
39 Flower worn on the lapel of a tuxedo
42 Name on a title
43 More terrible
44 Hang around
45 In place

Down

1 Chinese fruit (var.)
2 Earthy yellows
3 Discuss, as a topic: 2 wds.
4 CenturyLink, for example: inits.
5 Coated oral tablets
6 "Eat, drink, ___ merry!": 2 wds.
7 Spa spot
8 Routs, slangily
9 Brunch fare
12 "___ cap fits, wear it": 2 wds.
14 Skill of clear and expressive speech
22 3-pointers, in football: inits.
23 O'Hare announcement, initially
25 Cruise stops
26 1990s exercise fad: 2 wds.
27 Lets
28 Mel of the NFL Hall of Fame
30 Leave alone
31 Main dish on a menu
33 State of high honor
35 A Bergen puppet
40 Boston ___ Party
41 Three, in ancient Rome

115

Across

1 Bird venerated by ancient Egyptians
5 Labors
10 Trig. function
11 Rock used to armor shorelines
12 Scandinavian epic
13 Immunological disorder
14 Synchronized swimmer Tracie, who won three Olympic medals
15 Skye of "River's Edge"
16 Crow
18 Some desktops, for short
21 Containing little excess
23 Set (down)
24 First ___
25 Prefix with propyl
27 Part of Q & A, briefly
28 Former Facebook rival, initially
29 Educe
31 Org. that gives out 9-digit IDs
32 "Gene Simmons Family Jewels" channel: 3 wds.
33 Metallica drummer Ulrich
35 "The law is ___..." (Dickens): 2 wds.
38 Nobleman, briefly
40 I-beam relative: hyph.
41 Small disk on a garment
42 Roman "olive"
43 Foam opener
44 Meeting: abbr.

Down

1 Body passage
2 "Mama's Gun" singer Erykah
3 Uniqueness
4 Captain Marvel's exclamation
5 Seat of Ward County, N.D.
6 In full bloom
7 Without possible substitute
8 Fall behind
9 Acquire intelligence
11 Annual period of wet weather: 2 wds.
17 News inits.
19 "Would you allow me...?": 2 wds.
20 Network: abbr.
21 Some srs. take them
22 "Rock and Roll All Nite" band
26 Canadian TV channel, initially
30 Some spuds
32 ___-Detoo, 2003 Robot Hall of Fame inductee
34 Study of celestial bodies, briefly
36 Manuscript encs.
37 Mrs.'s counterparts, in Mexico
38 Stomach six-pack, shortly
39 Furrow

116

Across

1 Command to an attack dog: 2 wds.
6 Lat., Rus., and Ukr., once
10 Part of an induction motor
12 Rapa Nui carvings
13 Philippic
14 Checkers' bars, initially
15 Like non-oyster months: hyph.
17 Peggy Lee's "___ a Tramp"
18 Star Wars, initially
20 French thank-you
22 Feudal land
24 Ford of fashion
27 Jeopardy
29 Corey Feldman's former spouse
30 House for two families
32 Neutral color
33 Basketball Hall of Famer Thomas
35 One of L.B.J.'s beagles
36 Whiner
38 Blessing preceder
40 Hammock holder
42 Brit. political party, colloquially
45 Opening for a coin
46 Small weights
47 Create social or emotional ties
48 Baseball's Little Colonel

Down

1 Arrival at Heathrow, initially
2 "Is ___?": 2 wds.
3 Bird trained to take messages: 2 wds.
4 And others: Lat.: 2 wds.
5 Data transmitter
6 Home of the Mustangs, initially
7 William Styron novel: 2 wds.
8 Gallop
9 Snake sound
11 Take in again
16 Hindu titles
18 Org. in TV's "Monk"
19 "Mon ___!"
21 Game with Mr. Boddy
23 Son, in Somme
25 Green land
26 Prefix with -algia
28 "Star Wars" figure
31 Knife brand: hyph.
34 Crucial moment, militarily: hyph.
36 Crash investigating agcy.
37 Woody Guthrie's son
39 Writer Sarah ___ Jewett
41 Approx. takeoff hr.
43 Some Caltech grads, for short
44 Tampa to Miami dir.

117

Across

1 Fire residue

4 Youngest world chess champion before Kasparov

7 "All-American Girl" Margaret

8 Punish with an arbitrary penalty

12 Poetic contraction

13 Make imperfect

15 Boston Red Sox song covered by the Dropkick Murphys

17 Football's Tarkenton

18 "Dedicated to the ___ Love" (hit for The Mamas & the Papas): 2 wds.

19 Monies owed

20 Framework

23 Suffix with lact-

24 Soprano Swenson: 2 wds.

26 "It just came to me!"

28 Securely fastens again

31 "I Am Woman" singer Helen

33 ___ & Chandon, champagne

34 Toyota hybrids

35 Pick-up expert: abbr.

37 Native New Yorkers

39 Skating champion Midori

40 Exotic pet

41 Finnish-American actress and dancer Taina

42 Summer clock setting, initially

43 Witness

Down

1 Colorless ketone

2 Singer Easton

3 Hard and shrewd bargaining: hyph.

4 Rikki-tikki-___

5 Frenchman's flame

6 Not the best service

9 Abundant

10 Exact replicas: 2 wds.

11 Les ___-Unis

14 Start of Massachusetts' motto

16 In ___ (as found)

19 "Agreed!"

21 "It's my best effort": 2 wds.

22 "The Motorcycle Diaries" guy

25 Norton Sound city

26 Early Dadaist works

27 "Ready or not, ___ come!": 2 wds.

29 Water boiler

30 Dimwit

32 God, to a garçon

35 Okla. neighbor

36 Future ABA member's hurdle

38 Knave

118

Across

1 Old expletive
5 Holiest city, in Islam
10 Company whose logo is four rings
11 Edible clam
12 Cheer starter
13 Last month
14 Garden with a snake
15 Wed economically
16 Baseball great Banks
18 Where Kazakhstan was, initially
20 Nashville's st.
21 Russian pop duo
22 Prefix with log or leptic
24 Fish often batter-dipped
26 It goes with neither
27 Like some Fr. nouns
29 Having a liking for
31 French tire
32 Reagan's second Attorney General
34 More than sufficient
36 Former Chinese monetary unit
38 Chilled drink: 2 wds.
39 French girl, briefly
40 Harmless
41 "___ of Variations" (Frank O'Connor short story collection): 2 wds.
42 San ___ (California county)
43 Japan's first capital

Down

1 Icicle's locale
2 Lead
3 Public promotion of a product
4 California senator Feinstein
5 Think (over)
6 Dine away from home: 2 wds.
7 Spicy Tex-Mex snack: 3 wds.
8 Totals: 2 wds.
9 Back when
11 Leona Helmsley's nickname, with "The": 3 wds.
17 Monthly business magazine
19 Major river flowing through Belgium, Germany, and the Netherlands
22 Tiberius's title, briefly
23 Nostrum
25 Anonymous John
28 Final game in a trophy competition: 2 wds.
30 Court figure
33 Conger catcher
35 Building block brand
37 "I ___ Song Go Out of My Heart" (Duke Ellington song): 2 wds.
38 "Think" company

119

Across

1 Look
5 Moniker for Mussolini: 2 wds.
11 Evangelical Roberts
12 Warm-blooded creature
13 Words on a monument, briefly
14 In a formal, proper manner
15 Fervent supporter of a person or institution
17 Receiver Collinsworth or Carter
18 Former WBA world champion Brandon
22 Marked by great enthusiasm: hyph.
24 Chichén ___ (Mayan city)
25 ___ standstill: 2 wds.
26 Tiny, in Edinburgh
27 Word before gras
29 Baseball family name
32 Course
33 Fullness of flavor
34 Extremely idealistic
38 Laughable
41 Coach Houston
42 Digestive enzyme
43 1982 Disney film
44 Seedy, disreputable
45 Lennon's in-laws

Down

1 Dirt
2 Cube creator Rubik
3 Large and comfortable seat: 2 wds.
4 Celtics head coach after Chris Ford: inits., 2 wds.
5 Like a mischievous child
6 Unseen "Mary Tyler Moore Show" character
7 One of the Brothers Karamazov
8 "Lemme think…"
9 "Silent" president, familiarly
10 Tarzan portrayer Ron
16 "Weetzie Bat" author Francesca ___ Block
19 Hit song for Diana Ross: 3 wds.
20 "___ of Oz" (L. Frank Baum novel)
21 Coal-rich German region
22 Huck and Jim's escape vehicle
23 Put ___ in (test the water): 2 wds.
28 Typesetter's unit: 2 wds.
29 Bore
30 Bagel topping
31 Tooth: prefix
35 Bears: Lat.
36 "Was ___ harsh?": 2 wds.
37 Egg holders: abbr.
38 Smith and Gore
39 Life, briefly
40 Apr. season

120

Across

1 "___ Like Mine" (Bow Wow song)
8 Seventh-century date
11 Metal named for an animal: 2 wds.
12 Commercial suffix with Rock-
13 Planet seen at sunset: 2 wds.
15 ___ lawyer (gets legal advice): 2 wds.
16 "___ luck!" ("Knock 'em dead!")
17 Hamilton and Brown
19 "Pygmalion" writer's monogram
22 Election loser: hyph.
24 Want ad. initials
25 Fed. medical org.
26 Environmentalist's prefix
27 Paving material
29 8½" x 11" paper size: abbr.
30 Comment after the bell: 2 wds.
32 Former Delta rival
33 Clotho, Lachesis, and Atropos
37 "New Hampshire" poet: 2 wds.
39 Void, in Vichy
40 East, in Ecuador
41 Somme summer
42 Act without restraint: 2 wds.

Down

1 Roman goddess of hope
2 Bee's home
3 Molding
4 Dentist's direction
5 Experimentation: 3 wds.
6 Particle that's emitted
7 Breakfast food named for a European country: 2 wds.
8 Small plover of the tundra
9 Person displaying impressive style: 2 wds.
10 Superman's mother
14 Prefix with graph or gram
18 Cover
19 Marvel
20 Defeats, as for a part in a play: 2 wds.
21 Friendly and outgoing
23 Easter preceder?
28 Girlfriend, in France
31 Cutter
32 Vase, in Versailles
34 Nobelist Morrison
35 Last word of Missouri's motto
36 Editor's "let it stand"
38 Capote, to friends

121

Across

1. Italian "thing"
5. Take it all off
10. Gives a darn
11. Link: 2 wds.
12. Nap
13. Nixon VP who resigned
14. Confidence in own's own worth or abilities: hyph.
16. Type of ear or tube
17. Mgr.'s aide
20. "Use Me" novelist Schappell
24. Classification system for blood
25. "Oy ___!"
26. "The Fall of the House of Usher" author's monogram
27. Ending for fund or fire
29. House in Honduras
30. Full of wonder: 2 wds.
32. Hospital for recuperation
37. Jockey's wear
38. Raison ___
39. Gluck's "___ ed Euridice"
40. Lets up
41. Discover
42. Bump off

Down

1. "Providence" actress Paula
2. Hurler Hershiser
3. Deem appropriate: 2 wds.
4. Ski resort
5. Grand in size or appearance
6. German W.W. II tank: 2 wds.
7. Mathematician Descartes
8. News squib
9. Comic book punch sound
10. Authors Lewis and Forester, initially
15. Smile in a contemptuous way: 2 wds.
17. River to the Rhine
18. Govt. agency once headed by Karen Mills
19. "___ gather": 2 wds.
21. Q.E. 2 setting
22. European carrier letters
23. Shrinks' org.
25. Deer meat
28. Tricky pitch
29. Breakfast food
31. Walks through water
32. Be the father, in the Bible
33. Italian car, briefly
34. "___ Heartache" (Bonnie Tyler song): 2 wds.
35. Harold ___, Nobel Prize for Chemistry winner (1934)
36. ___ amis
37. Staff note after fa

122

Across

1. "___ the Fall" (Miller drama)
6. Adrien ___ skin care products
11. Architect of the Guggenheim Museum in Bilbao
12. "Bleeding Love" singer Lewis
13. Spa brand
14. "What ___ You" (Reba McEntire album): 2 wds.
15. Irregular
17. Lennon's in-laws
18. Kind of dealer
19. Chipper
21. Mine, in Italy
22. Rigging supporter
25. Nile viper
26. Prefix with center or cure
27. FDR home loan org.
28. Some garden flowers
30. Joanne of "Red River"
31. Initial stake
32. Hurdle for some univ. seniors
33. Singer/songwriter Hyman
35. Place for a massage
37. Swedish seaport on the Baltic
39. Brockovich and Moran
41. Eagles and double eagles
42. Puts (potatoes, e.g.) through a sieve
43. How some music is sold: 2 wds.
44. It's sometimes sprained

Down

1. Ottoman officer
2. Febrile
3. Celluloid, e.g.
4. Hungarian mathematician Paul
5. Hand-woven rugs
6. Son-in-law of Mohammad
7. Go straight
8. How to follow a hyperlink, using a cursor and mouse: 3 wds.
9. Opposite of exo-
10. Girl of Glasgow
16. Heroic poems
18. Traveler's need: 2 wds.
20. Certain Prot.
22. Send a message to, over the phone
23. Fragments of a bomb
24. Lacking slackness
29. Readily available: 2 wds.
32. County north of San Francisco
33. Longtime Magic 8 Ball maker
34. "The heat ___!": 2 wds.
36. "This is the End" costar Michael
38. Grad. degree
40. Atlanta to Tampa dir.

123

Across

1 Hectic hosp. sections
4 Hydromassage facility
7 P.D. alert
10 Mouse's larger relative
11 Make a mistake
12 Sargasso or Salton
13 Plane pilot's emergency system: 2 wds.
16 Boxer Max
17 Meeting of members of a political party
18 Got out of bed: 2 wds.
20 Changes to suit a new purpose
22 Hit hard
26 Fix
27 End of a cigarette
29 ____ Z: 2 wds.
30 Beach drinks, maybe
32 Petty potentate
34 Agreement made before marriage: abbr.
36 Cream-filled pastry
39 Hits head-on
42 Greeting on meeting late in the day: 2 wds.
44 Part of Q & A, briefly
45 Waikiki wear
46 It's a real mesh
47 Primus leader Claypool
48 AARP members, briefly
49 Company symbols, briefly

Down

1 Holiday eve in Jerusalem
2 Hindu prince
3 Low-cost sea fare
4 Get firm
5 Writ deliverer: 2 wds.
6 Chilean pianist Claudio
7 "Hold on ____!": 2 wds.
8 ____ de soie (silk cloth)
9 Cuckoo
14 Clip
15 Banquets
19 Short stop?
20 Former Notre Dame coach Parseghian
21 Carried out
23 Tribal decoration before battle: 2 wds.
24 ____ minimum: 2 wds.
25 Apex
28 Qin dynasty follower
31 W.W. I French biplane
33 Go bad
35 They're 100 sen in Cambodia
36 Alike: Fr.
37 "Cup or ____?" (ice cream parlor question)
38 Standings setback
40 Memory: prefix
41 Mil. ranks
43 Frozen water, in Berlin

124

Across

1 UPS unit, briefly
4 Shiba ____, Japanese breed of dog
7 ____-ha
8 Greek letters
9 Army E-3, initially
12 Score a touchdown rushing the ball: 3 wds.
14 Archival file format, initially
15 Seat of Marion County, Fla.
16 Ex-model Gabrielle
18 One of Satan's nations, in the Bible
19 Hold back
20 Pilothouse letters
21 Jake ____, boxer nicknamed "The Bronx Bull"
24 Not in a quiet way
26 Muesli relative
28 Big Ten sch.
31 Psychohistorian Seldon of Isaac Asimov's "Foundation" books
32 Utah's Senator Hatch
34 Michael ____, former president of the Walt Disney Company
36 Does some yardwork
37 Irish or North
38 Stiff hair
40 C&W channel
41 French department and river
42 Kind of service
43 Dusting item
44 Big initials in fashion

Down

1 Silvery metallic compound
2 Colorful bird
3 One whose age is in the nineties
4 Design engraved into a material
5 Rapa ____ (Easter Island)
6 Natl. Guard counterpart
9 "____ Princess" (kids' board game): 2 wds.
10 Aspect
11 Espresso foam
13 U.N. agcy. concerned with working conditions
17 Class for foreigners, for short
22 Deaf person's communication letters
23 Catcalling
25 "Step ____!": 2 wds.
26 Haunting presence
27 Poe's "The ____"
29 Sashays
30 Declassify
33 Thing: Lat.
35 Construction piece shaped like the last letter of the alphabet: hyph.
39 Narrow inlet

125

Across

1 Obi
5 Bar
11 Dip ____ in (test): 2 wds.
12 Upright slabs of antiquity
13 Forgoing personal pleasures: hyph.
15 Computer add-on?
16 W.W. II arena
17 Argentine aunt
18 Prestige
20 QB's misfire
21 Cake finisher
23 ____-Anne-de-Beaupré (Quebec)
24 Donnybrook
27 ____ miss (randomly): 2 wds.
29 River that forms part of the Paraguay-Brazil border
30 "Somethin' Stupid," for one
32 "____ for iceberg": 2 wds.
33 Medicinal infusion, such as sweetened barley water
37 Mil. titles
38 Blood-typing letters
39 "The Killers" costar Gulager
40 Additional dose of a vaccine: 2 wds.
43 Mario Puzo bestseller
44 ____ milk
45 Struck off, in a way: 2 wds.
46 Like child's play

Down

1 MS. enclosures
2 "This is ____" (radio line): 2 wds.
3 Church platform
4 Playboy founder, for short
5 Dangerous fly
6 "____ extra cost!": 2 wds.
7 "Oy ____!"
8 One who believes in rule by a select group
9 Collided with: 2 wds.
10 Veto, for example
14 Mild expletive
19 No-win situation?
22 Isocrates, for one
24 Storage file for e-mails
25 Archetype
26 Caught with a noosed rope
28 "Is ____?": 2 wds.
31 Happy, cheerful
34 "Long Island" sound
35 Healing plants
36 Insane, slangily
38 One of the Near Islands
41 Full house sign, for short
42 Deem appropriate

126

Across

1 Involving a 24-hour period, in biology
5 Princess in Woolf's "Orlando"
10 Hindu deity
11 "A Doll's House" author
12 Seemed about to happen, ominously: 2 wds.
15 "You've got mail" ISP
16 "C'est la ___!"
17 Partner of poivre
18 Trapped: 3 wds.
20 Golfer who designed the Oubaai course in South Africa
21 Peppy piano piece
22 Sheet
23 "King of the Hill" town
26 Groucho's "Duck Soup" role
27 Caboose
28 Trinidadian musician and bandleader Edmundo
29 Coral ridges: abbr.
30 Deploying more than once
34 Old hat
35 18th Pres.
36 Classic car make
37 Nice-mannered
40 Boxer Ali
41 Pooch's name
42 Fast speech or story
43 Research facility: abbr.

Down

1 Part of a religious title
2 "How Can ___?" (Freddie Mercury song): 3 wds.
3 ___ Gay (W.W. II plane)
4 Calculus calculation: abbr.
5 Short track opening onto a railroad line
6 Differently-___ (handicapped)
7 Nine-digit no. issuer
8 She
9 "All God's Children Need Traveling Shoes" writer Maya
13 Perrier rival
14 Someone ___ (not yours)
19 ___ Rabbit
22 Bother
23 GPS line
24 Supplies the car with more gas
25 Race climax: 2 wds.
26 Like sandpaper
28 Fasten again (as an envelope)
30 100 kopecks
31 "From Here on OUT" director, Sam ___
32 Requires
33 Beckett no-show
38 52, to Cicero
39 Movie org. with a "100 Years..." series

127

Across

1 Gelatin substitute

5 Stress and trauma, for some

10 Bob, first host of "This Old House"

11 Certain about: 2 wds.

13 Not easily put into words

15 Enzyme suffix

16 L.B.J.'s successor

17 Erie hrs.

18 Papal ambassador to a foreign court

20 102, to Hadrian

21 Further ahead in development

24 Unconscious state

26 Back

27 Narrow street with walls on both sides

29 Overmodest

30 Be plentiful

34 Something to believe in

35 52, to Cicero

36 Rapa ____, native Polynesians of Easter Island

37 State of extreme poverty

40 Muffle, suppress

41 Asphalt

42 Brewery fixtures

43 Railroad buildings, briefly

Down

1 Winged

2 Knife name in TV ads

3 "Hail Caesar!" star Ehrenreich

4 "The Facts of Life" actress

5 Sci-fi writer Isaac

6 "Treasure Island" castaway Ben

7 Prohibition ____

8 "____ of Sunnybrook Farm"

9 Paid fighter

12 Unpleasantly smelly

14 Robinson Crusoe's companion

19 Originated

22 Peninsula between the Persian Gulf and the Red Sea

23 "Because of You" singer: hyph.

24 Near: 2 wds.

25 Port on Puget Sound

27 Compounds capable of turning litmus red

28 Relinquishes a right

31 Eastern Christian

32 New, in Naples

33 Attends a banquet

35 Articulate in a very careful and rhythmic way

38 Coral ridges: abbr.

39 Defaces with rolls?: abbr.

128

Across

1 1930s heavyweight champ Max
5 Department store section
9 "___-Di, ___-Da" (Beatles song): 2 wds.
10 Grave
12 It covers areas not to be painted: 2 wds.
14 "Am ___ believe…?": 2 wds.
15 Sicilian six
16 Subject of a tipster's tip
17 Celtic sea god
18 Wheat covering
19 Boxing promoter D'Amato
20 Wall St. figures
22 It includes pitching changes
24 Catches sight of
26 Trader, historically
28 Kind of shell
32 "Norma ___"
33 Org. that offers the "Canine Good Citizen" program
35 Dernier ___ (the latest thing)
36 Room renter
37 Homily: abbr.
38 Chess champion of 1960–61
39 Weather forecasting
42 Aria from "Un Ballo in Maschera": 2 wds.
43 Caroled
44 Cockeyed
45 Chop ___ (Chinese dish)

Down

1 Panama hat
2 Soak up
3 Great Smoky Mountains deer
4 Mrs. Gorbachev
5 French line of defense
6 Outside: prefix
7 Subtlety
8 State capital of Minnesota: 2 wds.
11 Brain activity records, initially
12 Leon Uris's "___ 18"
13 One from Brooklyn: 2 wds.
21 Fed. support benefit
23 Summer hrs.
25 Dense fog: 2 wds.
26 Sandwich chain
27 Edible seed
29 Prologue follower: 2 wds.
30 Mountainous
31 Too smooth
32 Winter coating
34 Church figure
40 W.W. II map letters
41 Charley ___, "The Art of Hitting .300" author

129

Across

1 Stinging insect
5 Food Network celeb ___ De Laurentiis
10 Climax
11 Encourage
12 Laser-pointer battery, initially
13 All worked up: 3 wds.
14 Show disapproval towards, as a speaker: 2 wds.
16 First TV drama to feature a black actor: 2 wds.
17 Greek hearth goddess
19 Syllable of dismissal
21 "And that's that!": 2 wds.
25 Light starter?
26 Delivery room doctors, for short
27 In place of
28 Release: 2 wds.
30 Kind of approval letters
31 Potsdam Conference attendee
33 Henry VIII's sixth
36 "___ Dream" (Presley album): 3 wds.
39 Slender church spire
41 Major addition?
42 Astronaut Pete, third man to walk on the Moon
43 "___ guys like you for breakfast!": 2 wds.
44 Fixes kitty
45 Bookie's quote

Down

1 Cry from a crib
2 Health food berry
3 Big success: 2 wds.
4 Porridge ingredient
5 Geometry suffix
6 "Four Essays on Liberty" author Berlin
7 Biol. energy sources
8 Adele's "Rolling in the ___"
9 Chichi
11 Extremely angry: 4 wds.
15 Catalog
18 In ___ (per se)
19 Military bases: abbr.
20 Merino mother
22 Settled unconditionally
23 Abacus part
24 Onetime NOW cause
29 Long way (from): 2 wds.
32 Refrain in "Old MacDonald"
33 Some G.I.s
34 Crooked
35 "General Hospital" actress Sofer
37 Not much: 2 wds.
38 Clears
40 Orders

130

Across

1 Place for mil. planes
4 "Harrumph!"
7 Anesthetic used by veterinarians, initially
10 151, to Nero
11 Some aliens
13 Steely: 3 wds.
15 Glorify
16 Has beens, probably: hyph.
17 Annoyance
19 Suffix with planet or paran
21 CBer's "Bad reception": hyph.
25 Hungarian actress: 3 wds.
28 Assent: 2 wds.
29 Ecol. watchdog
30 Beefed
33 Hound's trail
36 Gallic girlfriends
39 Use only one or two fingers to type: hyph.
41 Instrument for measuring electrical current
42 "___ won't!": 2 wds.
43 ___ Day
44 Lambkin's kin
45 Channel owned by Viacom

Down

1 Be sore
2 Linseed oil source
3 Time for cake and candles
4 Jennifer of "The L Word"
5 Mornings, briefly
6 Kicker: 2 wds.
7 Toyota hybrid models
8 Collectible frames
9 "Hey!" in a library
12 Principal ore of lead
14 ER pronouncement
18 Former East German secret police
19 Divisions of a lb.: abbr.
20 "This ___ test...": 2 wds.
22 Following orders
23 Alphabet trio
24 Memorable time
26 Fertilized cell
27 Make saw-toothed
31 Father
32 Title of Japan's Akihito: abbr.
33 Bogus
34 Big cat native to the Americas
35 "Teardrops ___ Guitar" (Taylor Swift song): 2 wds.
37 Financial field, for short
38 Scrape, as the knee
40 Just released

131

Across

1 Adhesive
5 Peaks
9 Boorish
10 "For two," on sheet music: 2 wds.
11 Western movie, slangily: 2 wds.
13 Eared pitcher
14 Caught with a lariat
16 Airport schedule letters
17 Arab name part
18 One-eighty
19 Girl in a Beach Boys song
21 Hawaiian goddess of volcanoes
22 Edmonton hockey player
24 Police radio messages, briefly
27 Made up (for)
31 "The Pride of St. Louis" costar Joanne
32 JKL followers
33 Lyric poem
34 Avian lung extension: 2 wds.
36 As busy as ___: 2 wds.
37 Bonus feature on "You Bet Your Life": 2 wds.
39 Guns N' Roses guitarist Hudson
40 How a fire might glow
41 Arizona city
42 "___ sow, so shall...": 2 wds.

Down

1 Process of increasing in size
2 Rio Grande city
3 Cold War inits.
4 Suffix with Japan
5 Hit lightly, as glass: 2 wds.
6 Prefix with logical
7 Go in search of
8 Conger or moray: 2 wds.
9 Dispel gloom
12 With all things considered: 2 wds.
15 Salon supply
17 Former dictator ___ Amin
20 Taboos
21 Paid performer
23 W.W. II map letters
24 Oklahoma's Pontotoc County seat
25 Excessively respectable
26 Item of furniture for storing clothes
28 "___ Does It Like Me" (Shirley Bassey album)
29 1924 gold medal swimmer
30 Carmen Agra ___, "The Library Dragon" author
32 Former wife of Donald Trump
35 Nasty film
36 Blows away
38 Singing syllable

132

Across

1. Kafka character Gregor
6. Cup
11. Caramel-topped desserts
12. Shred: 2 wds.
13. Settle a bill: 2 wds.
14. Atlanta research university
15. Diversity, contrast
17. Words before an alternative: 2 wds.
18. Compressed data
20. Implored
25. Spreadsheet cell contents
27. Stirs
28. "You're Lucky I Love You" singer Susan
30. Certain coffee table shape
31. 45 rpm record half: hyph.
33. Cooking in a wok, e.g.: hyph.
38. "Would you like ___?" (waitress' question): 2 wds.
39. Fix a knot
40. Corrupt
41. "Alice in Wonderland" tag line: 2 wds.
42. "Beau ___"
43. A dozen dozen

Down

1. Bay Area law enforcement org.
2. Jai ___
3. Cinco de Mayo: 2 wds.
4. Put an end to: 2 wds.
5. Colorado skiing mecca
6. Entranceway employee
7. Paint
8. Universal destruction: abbr.
9. "Absolutely!"
10. Acquire intelligence
16. Fleece
18. Cretan peak
19. Rapper who has feuded with Jay-Z
21. Charles ___, inventor (1800–60)
22. Tongue-lash: 3 wds.
23. She, in Lisbon
24. High-speed Internet inits.
26. Ochlocracy: 2 wds.
29. Letters on a rubber check
32. Like some vbs.
33. Hook underling
34. Addition column
35. ___ the finish: 2 wds.
36. "___ Island" (2008 movie starring Jodie Foster)
37. The Bee ___ (singing group)
38. Student's stat.

133

Across

1 Fiesta Bowl site
6 Scene of W.W.I fighting
11 Less cordial
12 Tennis player John
13 Mexican silverwork center
14 Tender-hearted soul, informally
15 Otto I's realm, for short
16 Poet Siegfried
18 J.F.K. advisory
19 Dr. Seuss's Sam-___: 2 wds.
20 Carpet
21 One who owes
23 Quintillionth: prefix
24 First name in horror
25 Capote onstage
26 Fruity coolers
28 Half-human, half-Betazoid "Star Trek" character Troi
31 101 instructors, briefly
32 Wichita's state, briefly
33 Aviation prefix
34 Dispatches again
36 Twitch
37 Very slightly: 2 wds.
38 Clyster
40 Adventurous tale
41 Prussian lancer
42 TV actress Georgia
43 John of "Miracle on 34th Street"

Down

1 Gave 10% to the church
2 Card game for two
3 Thing that has both good and bad features: 2 wds.
4 Chest muscle, for short
5 Shoreline problem
6 The Divine ___ (Bette Midler nickname): 2 wds.
7 Those, in Guadalajara
8 By bad luck
9 Leave: 2 wds.
10 Sea holly
17 Swiss river
22 Fros' mates
23 Faint constellation next to Scorpius
25 Become nervous or uneasy: 2 wds.
26 Disappear without ___: 2 wds.
27 Evil spirit: var.
28 June honoree
29 American painter of sports scenes
30 Esoteric
32 Prepare to propose
35 Quart ending
39 FDR home loan org.

134

Across

1 Ryan or Kyle on "Another World"

5 Dry, like Spanish wine

9 "This is the End" director Goldberg

10 Antediluvian: hyph.

12 They may be picked

13 Yachtsman Conner

14 Warranty fig.: 2 wds.

16 Eccentric

17 Russian range

21 Dragged, historically

23 Spock's father in "Star Trek"

24 Former federal agency for carriers: inits.

25 Mystery writer Rita ____ Brown

26 SeaWorld star

29 Level

31 Peter and Franco

32 Danger in Iraq, initially

33 Sign up again: hyph.

37 Off the mark

40 Mixed bag

41 Act as a go-between

42 Chrysler Building architect William Van ____

43 Hospital carers, initially

44 Rapper Snoop

Down

1 Bic items

2 1960s–70s singer Sands

3 Police vehicle: 2 wds.

4 Part of a racetrack nearer the center

5 Lady of León

6 Time out of mind

7 151, once

8 Takes too much, briefly

10 Jewish org. founded in 1913

11 Trivial Pursuit edition

15 Do some arithmetic

18 Mammal with a body covered in bony plates

19 Show the way

20 Arcade game, ____-Ball

21 "____ Hers" Pulp album of 1994

22 Hurt sorely

27 "The Naked Ape" author Desmond

28 "____ directed" (medicine alert): 2 wds.

29 Snare

30 Put more bullets in

34 Look at

35 Victory: Ger.

36 Handle food with a metal server

37 Every ounce

38 Little bit of a drink

39 Lay out in the sun

135

Across

1 I.W.W. rival
4 Much flurry
7 "Who cares?"
10 Suffix with mod or nod
11 Cries of revulsion
12 Arles agreement
13 Shades
15 Ending for Japan
16 Head, to Henri
17 Alphabet character
19 Jean of "Bombshell"
21 Turns aside
23 Like JFK
27 Successful job seeker
28 "Peace ___ Time": 2 wds.
29 "Don't ___ word": 2 wds.
30 Enjoying
31 Gone bad
33 Card game also called sevens
36 One, in Bonn
39 Certain linemen: abbr.
40 Resolved (to do): 2 wds.
42 Sure shot
43 G.I. chow
44 Jazz grp.
45 Of a calling: abbr.
46 Pothook shape
47 Kind of poodle

Down

1 Great-___
2 Kind of pipe
3 Having a tough, hard texture
4 Pre-1975 power agcy.
5 Lingers (on), as a subject
6 Bone: prefix
7 Bubbly name
8 Feminine suffix
9 Here, in Hanover
14 Countries of southwestern Asia: 2 wds.
18 Shone like a star
20 Highway: abbr.
21 Cries of surprise
22 By the agency of
24 Words of contradiction: 3 wds.
25 252 wine gallons
26 Big: abbr.
28 Jr.'s Jr.
30 They shun company
32 Luke's mother in "Star Wars"
33 Griff and D's Public Enemy cohort
34 Bobby Darin's label until 1963
35 Tiny fraction of a min.: 2 wds.
37 Biblical peak
38 Abide
41 J.F.K.'s U.N. ambassador

136

Across

1 Hua ___ (Thai beach resort)
4 Sleep ___
7 Self-importance
8 Crab, lobster or shrimp, e.g.
13 1920 science fiction play, initially
14 Fight stopper
15 Alexandra in "Law & Order"
17 Room in Rouen?
18 ___ open road: 2 wds.
19 Observer
20 Product of the imagination
24 End zone scores, for short
25 Disorderly, lawless
27 "The Good Shepherd" org.
29 Dosages similar to pills
32 Medical suffix
34 Robbie who played Cousin Oliver on "The Brady Bunch"
35 Toast in Toulouse
37 Progeny
38 View
40 Prefix with oxide
41 Lot event: 2 wds.
42 "Am ___ trouble?": 2 wds.
43 Hanoi's country, for short
44 Markup language descriptor, initially

Down

1 Concerning this
2 Galapagos critter
3 "Ancient Evenings" author: 2 wds.
4 Father of Cleopatra in Greek mythology
5 India neighbor, briefly
6 Cpls. and others
9 Wings: Lat.
10 Believing in more than one god
11 Feasted one's eyes
12 Batik workers
16 Opposite of exo-
21 Fox competitor
22 Govt. agency founded in 1953, initially
23 Pound sound
26 Some cameras, initially
27 Trig. function
28 "___ Little Prayer" (Aretha Franklin hit): 3 wds.
30 Aggravation, in Yiddish
31 Earthenware beer mugs
33 Figure (out), slangily
36 Compared to
37 Bullet point
39 Suffix with schnozz

137

Across

1. Lovers' quarrels
6. Girder: hyph.
10. Unsaturated alcohol
12. Prefix with -phile
13. Evocative
15. Explorer Cabeza de ___
16. Fish-to-be
17. Concise and pithy observations
21. Shrinking Asian sea
22. Leon Uris novel about a Palestinian family: 2 wds.
25. Phrase of agreement: 3 wds.
27. "Rolling in the Deep" singer
28. Moved forward rapidly
30. Rather: 2 wds.
31. Swing from side to side regularly
33. Army cops, initially
35. Shade of blue
36. "How original!": 3 wds.
41. Tasteless ornamentation
42. Clog: 2 wds.
43. Blunders
44. Barbershop sounds

Down

1. Dungeons & Dragons game co., initials
2. Ore suffix
3. Opposite of masc.
4. Carefree, not serious
5. Submarine machine
6. Ad ___ committee
7. Southernmost city of ancient Palestine
8. ___ mundi
9. Memorization method
11. Allowed
14. Princess in Woolf's "Orlando"
17. "The law is ___..." (Dickens): 2 wds.
18. Play thing
19. Duck-billed dinosaur
20. Award hung on a ribbon
23. Came down
24. Ballet leap
26. They had an empire in South America
29. Gershon and Carano
32. Gives a boost to
33. Homeowner's regular pymt.
34. "___ Lap" (1983 racehorse film)
37. 6-pointers, in football stats
38. The Engineers' sch.
39. Dine
40. Defaces with rolls?: abbr.

138

Across

1 1300, to Caesar
5 Rent out to someone else
11 Manager Felipe
12 Has a hankering for
13 Lovers' quarrel
14 Ancient Roman magistrate
15 "Knight Rider" star's nickname, with "The"
16 Archival file format, initially
17 Cable channel that sometimes shows bowling, for short
19 Take ___ from (learn something): 2 wds.
23 Former New York City mayor Beame
25 Disregard: 2 wds.
27 Right-hand page of a book
29 There's many ___ 'twixt the cup and the lip: 2 wds.
30 Clump, bundle
32 12 meses
33 Cheka successor, initially
34 Biblical kingdom
36 Woman's bio word
38 Where Warhol's "Campbell's Soup Cans" can be seen, briefly
41 Hairsplitter
44 August, in Angoulême
45 College graduates
46 Letters before V
47 Astrological system
48 Wide widths, initially

Down

1 Algebra or trig.
2 Advertising award named for one of the Muses
3 Item of crockery: 2 wds.
4 Shirt pair
5 Gaming guru John
6 Fertilizer
7 Unjust judgments, slangily: 2 wds.
8 Year in Nero's reign
9 Sargasso Sea breeder
10 Canadian market inits.
18 Map
20 Prison, slangily
21 "...'tis a pageant, To keep ___ false gaze" (Othello): 2 wds.
22 Orr colleague, familiarly
23 With the bow, in music
24 Ger. neighbor
26 Tropical root
28 Huge destructive wave
31 Medicine that induces vomiting
35 "Te ___" (Gloria Estefan song)
37 Sicilian city
39 Remote option
40 "Look ___" (Vince Gill hit of 1991): 2 wds.
41 La ___, Bolivia
42 "Shine a Little Love" rock grp.
43 Flop

139

Across

1 Live in a tent
5 Glue
10 State sch. in Athens: 2 wds.
12 "Nashville" costar Blakley
13 Drive
14 Bee's "bite"
15 Kind of cord
17 Like some shows
18 Rubber
20 Slangy suffix
22 No Oscar winner: hyph.
26 Vengeance
29 Backdoor
30 Calculator feature, initially
31 Deplorably bad
34 "Rhoda" costar David
37 Gradually slower, on a score
40 Sit in on, as a class
42 More bashful
43 Children's writer Blyton et al.
44 Funny Youngman
45 Punch spiker
46 Some loaves of bread

Down

1 Dot-___
2 "Just ___, skip and jump": 2 wds.
3 Make less severe
4 Former name of Pune, a city in Maharashtra, India
5 Hesitant sounds
6 Bullet aimed at something with no chance of self-defense
7 "Put a lid ___!": 2 wds.
8 "Hercules" spinoff
9 Vault cracker
11 Caspian feeder
16 Persuader of legislators
19 The Mustangs of the N.C.A.A.
20 Hospital sections, initially
21 Football Hall-of-Famer Dawson
23 Wicked or criminal behavior
24 Quadrennial games org.
25 Epilogue
27 Clint Eastwood TV show
28 Language of Nigeria
32 Water-dwelling creature
33 King Arthur's father
34 Highlander
35 ___ risk: 2 wds.
36 Lyrical
38 Artist Magritte
39 Teetotalers
41 Early role-playing game co., initially

140

Across

1 Grenoble girlfriends
6 Bobby Ray who withdrew a Secretary of Defense bid under Clinton
11 Knife name in TV ads
12 "Cut it out!"
13 One who's done stretches?: hyph.
14 Bone: prefix
15 As ___ the hills: 2 wds.
17 Form 1040 datum
18 AOL alternative
20 Slack-jawed
22 Shopping bag
24 "Spartacus" composer Khachaturian
27 Pseudonym
28 Geneva's river
29 Actress Thompson
30 Computer file container
31 French story
33 "Assault on Wall Street" director Boll
34 Because
36 Submarine-detecting acronym
38 "The Lonely Polygamist" author Brady
40 Markey and Bagnold
43 Musical form
44 Tedium
45 Diciembre follower
46 Actor Seth

Down

1 Era
2 Combine
3 Uncaring, selfish
4 Foreigners' class, briefly
5 Ice cream parlor orders
6 Twenty: prefix
7 Old video game inits.
8 Making very large quantities: hyph.
9 "___ Death" (from Peer Gynt Suite No. 1)
10 Light material
16 FBI worker, for short
18 Budding entrepreneurs, for short
19 Large hall
21 Funnyman Mort
23 "Still Pitching" author Jim
25 Avon anti-aging brand
26 A ___ bagatelle
28 Graceful Eurasian woodland animal: 2 wds.
30 Football three-pointers, initially
32 Finnish architect Alvar ___
34 "Drows'd with the ___ of poppies…": Keats
35 Have an excessive amount, briefly: 2 wds.
37 Words before way or hurry: 2 wds.
39 Celtic sea god
41 Set to arrive
42 Wrath or envy, e.g.

141

Across

1 Those, to José
5 Army members below col.
9 Andy of the comics
10 Gets ready to play (golf): 2 wds.
12 Violinist André
13 Good part of the deal
14 Seagoing backup group, initially
15 "Strangers and Brothers" author: 2 wds.
16 Willy ____ (Roald Dahl character)
18 Actress Kazan
20 Range part: abbr.
23 Danger in Iraq, initially
24 What may follow you
26 Battery buys, initially
27 Rocks at the bar
28 Bet on the first two places in a race
30 Non-gaming hotel on the Las Vegas Strip
31 Young child's word for a cow: 2 wds.
35 Comedic actor Johnson
38 George ____, Romanian composer of the opera "Oedipe"
39 ____ War (1899–1902)
40 Remote, say
41 Marathon
42 Aide-de-camp, briefly
43 Prefix meaning "within"

Down

1 Eggshell's cousin
2 "Je ne ____ quoi"
3 Dentist's request: 2 wds.
4 Encourage: 2 wds.
5 Clutter
6 Speller's phrase: 2 wds.
7 Sport of unarmed combat
8 Belch forth
10 Exhausted, slangily: 2 wds.
11 Early baseball Hall-of-Famer ____ Rixey
17 Vardalos of "My Big Fat Greek Wedding"
18 52, to Hadrian
19 Pre-1975 power agcy.
20 Light cookie made with almonds
21 Tit for ____
22 Decryption org.
25 Metric system prefix
29 Like farmland
30 Sotto ____
31 Phone preceder
32 "Business Goes ____ Usual" (Roberta Flack song): 2 wds.
33 Brit. dictionaries
34 N.C.O. rank
36 Mind
37 Proof word

142

Across

1 Plants related to the iris

6 Dotcom that owns StubHub

10 Spanish blooms

11 Add punch to the punch

12 Filled with a great quantity

13 David of "Rhoda"

14 Handy form of communication letters?

15 Trial lawyer's advice

17 Marlena's son in "Despicable Me"

18 Drugs, briefly

20 Enlarge

22 Virtual meeting of a sort

24 "___ gotta see": 2 wds.

25 Human male

26 Skedaddled

27 Brush off

29 Turkish titles

32 Hangs, in a way: 2 wds.

34 Will Varner's daughter-in-law in "The Long, Hot Summer"

35 Legal scholar's deg.

36 Suffix with cloth or cash

38 Miami Marlins' div.

39 In that case: 2 wds.

41 Continued: 2 wds.

43 Distress

44 Long-plumed herons

45 Former US national soccer team coach Schwarz

46 Whiskey drinks

Down

1 Not open

2 Norwegian explorer (1872–1928): 2 wds.

3 California's Fort ___

4 Soccer centers?

5 Deserves it: 2 wds.

6 Taina of "Les Girls"

7 Shopper who looks at for items at low prices: 2 wds.

8 Squirrel's horde

9 Violinist Menuhin

10 Candle's feature

16 Additional

19 Australian flag features

21 Suffix meaning "eater"

23 Listlessness

27 Flexible strip of wood

28 Lift, so to speak

30 Gives out

31 French composer Saint-___

33 Lap dogs

37 ___ Park, N.Y.

40 ___ the Hero, wizard in "Harry Potter and the Half-Blood Prince"

42 "The ___" (Boston skyscraper, informally)

143

Across

1 Jungle vine: var.
6 Former name of Ulaanbaatar
10 Town on the south shore of Long Island
11 Johnny who pitched with Warren Spahn
12 Boxing, facetiously
14 Ambient music pioneer
15 ___-al-Arab (Iraqi waterway)
16 Shred of waste silk
17 1960s campus grp.
20 Chinese temple
23 Jazz trumpeter Baker
24 Start a tennis match
25 Cry to get the attention of swine
26 Mars: prefix
27 Lofty poetry
28 Ballerina's pivot point
29 Elliptical track
30 Serbian monetary unit
32 Drunk-skunk connection: 2 wds.
35 Patrimony
37 Informal affirmative
38 "Hamlet" courtier
39 Tralee tongue
40 Frisbee maker: hyph.

Down

1 Period of existence
2 "The doctor ___": 2 wds.
3 Further
4 ___-picking
5 Happening
6 Order from a regular
7 Whitewater vessel
8 Feature of many hotels: 2 wds.
9 Reply to a ques.
13 Green-headed pet?
16 De ___ (from the beginning)
18 ___-Lite, group whose albums include "Infinity Within"
19 Problem for an oculist
20 H.S. junior's challenge
21 Dynamic introduction?
22 More avaricious
23 Not nerdy
25 Songbird
27 "Well, Did You ___!" ("High Society" song)
29 ___ air (broadcasting live): 2 wds.
31 Bank offerings, initially
32 Taj Mahal's city
33 Carpenter's wedge
34 Early record label for Bobby Darin and the Beatles
35 "Sayonara!"
36 Like: suffix

144

Across

1 Calf's cry
4 Old nuke org.
7 Where It.'s at
10 Brisk
12 ___ test ("Law & Order" evidence)
13 Express annoyance: 3 wds.
15 ___ ware (Japanese porcelain)
16 Fancy tie
17 Lousy, like a movie: hyph.
19 Atomic
22 Bank acct. report
24 Mil. award
25 Brew "for two"
27 Fed. aid agency
28 Surface-to-surface missile
30 Exaggerate
32 Orthodontic device
34 Old wintergreen-flavored toothpaste
35 One of the family
39 1980s title role for Lee Horsley: 2 wds.
41 European fish
42 Mat that covers only part of a floor: 2 wds.
43 Mr. Beatty
44 Tip for a writer?
45 Some dance records, for short

Down

1 When doubled, a seafood entree
2 Reunion attendee, briefly
3 ___ Romeo (sports car)
4 Versus
5 "Ol' Rockin' ___" (album by Tennessee Ernie Ford)
6 Musical endings
7 Instructor
8 Amorphous
9 Lot
11 "The Greatest Showman" actor Zac
14 Attention-getters
18 "___ Sports" (CBS show): 2 wds.
19 6-point plays, for short
20 Exciting adventure
21 Modeled oneself on
23 "Not a moment ___ soon!"
26 Iggy Pop album of 1999: 2 wds.
29 By ___ of (owing to)
31 Pension plan law, initially
33 "Nuts" cartoonist Wilson
34 Poker player's declaration: 2 wds.
36 To be, to Thérèse
37 Military overthrow
38 Professional people: abbr.
40 "Either he goes, ___ will!": 2 wds.

145

Across

1 It tests the water, initially
4 Transcript stat.
7 Ms. Benaderet
10 TV's "Emerald Point ___"
11 Wick holder: 2 wds.
13 Word with mechanics or significance
15 With "coals," firewalking phrase: 2 wds.
16 Beat
17 Indian yogurt dish
18 Encore telecast
19 Mélange
21 Michigan's biggest city: abbr.
22 Not permanently
26 Pretoria's country letters
27 It means nothing to King Juan Carlos
28 Reply to "Who's there?": 2 wds.
30 Burn
34 ___ Field (baseball park)
35 Region that included Ephesus
36 Venus when seen at dusk: 2 wds.
39 Model
40 ___ funk: 2 wds.
41 Slippery
42 Hosp. areas
43 Places for trials: abbr.

Down

1 TV journalist David
2 City on the Ganges River
3 Popular Japanese beer
4 Act without assistance: 3 wds.
5 Gumshoes, briefly
6 Flier's stat.
7 Rum brand
8 Common temple name
9 Very much
12 Hair critters
14 From bottom ___: 2 wds.
18 Travel indicators: 2 wds.
20 Savings vehicle for later yrs.
22 Skeletal muscle having three origins
23 Summerlike
24 Prowess
25 12th president of the Philippines
29 Ancient weight
31 Monkeyshine
32 Pleasant, attractive
33 Skater Lipinski and others
37 "Here ___ Again" (1987 #1 hit): 2 wds.
38 Common conjunction

146

Across

1. Overseas article
4. Uncle ____ (taxing relative?)
7. Univ. degrees
10. Gain access: 2 wds.
12. "Now I get it!"
13. Sustained burst of applause
14. Gun grp.
15. Trainee
16. "Major" in Munich
17. Ball girl?
19. It might be airtight
21. Gov. assistance to the needy
22. Opposite of hence
23. Chance
29. "Slumdog Millionaire" actor ____ Patel
30. Rx instruction, initially
31. "Frasier" character
34. Attention-getting sounds
36. "This ____ test…": 2 wds.
37. Doctor
39. All in the family
40. Drain diverter: hyph.
43. Country music's ____ Ridge Boys
44. Cap similar to a fez: var.
45. Old home loan org.
46. Bridge guru Culbertson
47. Want ad. initials

Down

1. Italian playwright Betti
2. Carson City's state: abbr.
3. All at once: 3 wds.
4. Like a snicker
5. First part of an encyclopedia, maybe: 3 wds.
6. Earl of Sandwich name
7. Actress Beulah
8. Bushy plant
9. Puppet lady Lewis
11. Slanted: abbr.
17. Grp. once headed by Seiji Ozawa
18. Never-proven mental ability: inits.
20. "Man of a Thousand Faces" Chaney
22. Off-roader's purchase, for short
24. Keats creation
25. Say again or differently
26. "No lie!": 2 wds.
27. Small bird
28. N.F.L. gains
31. Canon rival
32. Basketball Hall of Famer Thomas
33. Sri ____
34. "The Hero of Lake Erie"
35. Letters identifying the four voices in a choir
38. Iranian money
41. Enzyme suffix
42. Saigon soup

147

Across

1. Girder type: hyph.
5. Marlon Brando, by birth
11. Charles Lamb's nom de plume
12. Living dragon
13. Including unappealing features: 3 wds.
15. Cholesterol carrier, for short
16. Film-preserving org.
17. Thor Heyerdahl craft: 2 wds.
18. "How Do Your Children Grow?" host LeShan
19. Place for a nap
20. Item included with many board games
21. Lean
23. Korean soldier, initially
25. Lock
27. Motocross participant
31. Canadian Inc.
33. Edison's middle name
34. Indian P.M., 1991–6
37. Stray
39. Phanerozoic, for instance
40. Pacino and Capone
41. Finished on top
42. Relative of "Oh, no!"
43. Expression of an unfavorable opinion
46. Dispatch boats
47. Parcel (out)
48. Lots
49. Brought up

Down

1. Big name in computers
2. Thin distensible bag
3. Path regularly used by planes: 2 wds.
4. Pied Piper devotee
5. Emeka of the Charlotte Bobcats
6. Watch
7. Makers of Bobcat and Jaguar processors, initially
8. Stockpile
9. Dwight's opponent in 1952 and 1956
10. "It's true": 2 wds.
14. Spider's pouch
22. High-speed Internet inits.
24. "The Jungle Book" snake
26. Cassoulet cooker
28. Meat-chopping tool
29. Call forth
30. Made resentful and angry
32. Edema, old-style
34. Kind of screen
35. Still in the game
36. Easier version indicator, in music
38. Genre of popular music, initially
44. Soundless communication, initially
45. Fed. money overseer

148

Across

1 Area of 640 acres: abbr., 2 wds.
5 Peak or tip: prefix
9 Prefix with surgery or transmitter
10 Additional
11 Expect
12 Underground network
13 "___ Rosenkavalier"
14 Pres. appointee
16 Iowa college
17 "___: Deadliest Roads" (reality TV series)
18 ___ generis (unique)
19 Former Boston Bruin Bobby
20 "___ Death" (from Peer Gynt Suite No. 1)
22 It's a wrap
24 Two-wheeled Asian vehicle
26 Fire remnant
27 URL starter
30 Snow, to Burns
31 ___-di-dah
33 Ample shoe width
34 Submissions to an editor: abbr.
35 Suffix for señor
36 Cable channel with the citizen journalist iReport section
37 "Get me ___ here!"
39 Title for an earl or baron: abbr., 2 wds.
41 Dimin.'s musical opposite
42 Reflecting light
43 The Galloping Gourmet Graham
44 Ballyhoo

Down

1 Rat residences
2 Military procurement officer
3 3D exam
4 Scintillas
5 ___ Z: 2 wds.
6 Piece in a cookie: 2 wds.
7 Ripped again
8 Figure skater Brian
9 Boulanger or Comaneci
10 Goes round the Sun, e.g.
15 Aquatic rodent
21 Bro or sis
23 "Now I get it!"
25 Abdominal cavity
26 Check
28 "Bad reception" in CB radio code: hyph.
29 One-cent coin, informally
30 Painter's protection
32 Grating
38 Dungeons & Dragons game co., initially
40 "Honor ___ father"

149

Across

1 Crumpler who played in the NFL for 10 seasons
5 Alloy of iron and nickel
10 "Children of the Tenements" writer Jacob
11 Money in Nigeria
12 Ground level part of a building: 2 wds.
14 Relating to the stars
15 Conn. neighbor
16 It may be due
20 Stare with the mouth open wide: 2 wds.
23 Blows up, casually
24 Individual
25 Letters indicating price flexibility
26 Hwys.
28 Flips
31 ___ passu (on an equal footing)
32 More, in music
33 Touched up
38 In a compassionate manner
40 Resembling a wild animal
41 Three-dimensional shape
42 Make twisty
43 Flanged girder: hyph.

Down

1 Bulldog barks
2 53, to Cicero
3 Surround
4 Ancient Palestinian
5 Overrun
6 Lioness in "The Lion King"
7 Bluish-purple
8 Spanish hoop
9 Archival file format, initially
13 "___ Little Kindness" (Glen Campbell album): 2 wds.
17 Not quite yet
18 Port's opposite: abbr.
19 General ___ Chicken (Chinese menu dish)
20 Trail mix
21 Architectural pier
22 Jury member
27 ___ Madre
28 Against the odds, as a struggle
29 "Hymne à l'amour" singer Édith
30 Harem guard
34 CSA member, shortly: 2 wds.
35 Heavy stick used as a weapon
36 Isle of exile for Napoleon
37 Henna user
38 Industrial activity: abbr.
39 Hallow ending

150

Across

1 "Indecent Proposal" actress Moore
5 Early late-night name
9 Manner
10 "___ Halfway," Black Eyed Peas single: 2 wds.
12 St. Louis landmark
13 Dads, slangily: 2 wds.
14 Son of Jehoshaphat and king of Ancient Israel
15 Brick-carrying trough
16 "___ Psycho" (song by Midwest rapper Tech N9ne): 3 wds.
18 Garage job
22 Navy vessel
25 "Either she goes, ___ go": 2 wds.
26 Squeeze (out)
27 "Star Wars" project of the 1980s
28 "Clue" suspect: 2 wds.
31 "___ mother used to say": 2 wds.
32 "This ___" (Loggins hit): 2 wds.
33 Unspecified no.
35 Spitting sound
38 Go away at once!: 2 wds.
41 ___ McCray, character in "The Chicago Teddy Bears"
42 Point at which two sides meet
43 Michael ___, German writer of fantasy and children's fiction
44 Church lectures, briefly
45 Bela, in "The Ghost of Frankenstein"

Down

1 Key of Bach's Brandenburg Concerto No. 5: abbr., 2 wds.
2 Dublin's land
3 Device with moving parts
4 Place in a grave
5 Hawk
6 Bank letters
7 Soul, to Solange
8 TV pooch
10 It flows through Amsterdam: 2 wds.
11 Band that sang "Don't Bring Me Down," shortly
17 "That's clear": 2 wds.
19 Causing distress
20 Eliot's "Adam ___"
21 Andrews or Brockovich
22 N.Y.C. institution
23 Goddess represented by a rainbow
24 Brain activity records, initially
29 Boxer Mike and actress Cicely
30 "Believe It or Not" name
34 Compass dir.
36 Disconnect
37 Champagne chiller
38 N.C.A.A. football ranking system
39 Inits. in the classifieds
40 Dog's warning sound

151

Across

1 In the lead
6 "You don't have to tell me twice": 2 wds.
11 William ___, Cherry Peck in "Nip/Tuck"
12 Babes in the woods
13 Sister of Calliope
14 Mix-up in slang
15 Something considered choice to eat
17 Chesspieces, e.g.
18 Like custard
22 Nervous
25 ___ de Nil (pale greenish color)
26 Half a dozen
27 "Stuart Little" author's initials
29 Dream state?
30 Indian near the Platte
31 Frozen french fries brand: hyph.
33 Emmy-winning Thompson
35 Jane in a court case
36 Give up: 2 wds.
41 De ___ (in effect)
44 Pressurized garment worn by astronauts: hyph.
45 Computer notation that predates hexadecimal
46 Make a pass at: 2 wds.
47 Dress to kill, with "up"
48 "Lovergirl" singer ___ Marie

Down

1 Lying, maybe
2 Roll call call
3 Airline to Israel: 2 wds.
4 Popular Nissan
5 Bishopric
6 Words on a monument, briefly
7 West whose albums include "The Life of Pablo"
8 Long or Peeples
9 Not quite right
10 "Warriors" sch.
16 No one in particular
19 One of the Spice Girls
20 "Went," in Scotland
21 Arizona city near the Mexican border
22 GI hangouts, initially
23 Naldi of the Ziegfeld Follies
24 Biblical bk.
28 Shaped by hammering
32 Minuscule: var.
34 Serve in the capacity of: 2 wds.
37 Poly preceder
38 Like kittens
39 Big cat
40 Mount SW of Messina
41 Driving hazard
42 Prefix with pressure
43 Price tag abbr.

152

Across

1 Bedside watch
6 Colorado senator Mark
11 "Who's there?" response: 3 wds.
12 Locale
13 Thin piece of wood used to light a fire: 2 wds.
15 Web address ender
16 Bucks and does
17 Actress Louise
20 "Star Trek: Voyager" character
22 Unclose, to Shelley
23 Become oblivious to one's surroundings: 2 wds.
27 Grammatical mood
29 Peculiar
30 Wii ancestor
31 Half of a 1955 merger, initially
32 Three-hand card game
33 Writer Dinesen
36 Global positioning fig.
38 Succession of good and bad experiences: 3 wds.
43 Damp
44 O. Henry specialty
45 Narc's find
46 Eddie's "Coming to America" role

Down

1 Power to a Roman
2 "Give ____ whirl": 2 wds.
3 Format for compressing image files
4 "____ Darkness" (Johnny Cash song): 3 wds.
5 English professor's deg.
6 Burlington sch.
7 Determined attempt: 2 wds.
8 Advance amount
9 "Life" founder Henry
10 John ____, of TBS's "10 Items or Less"
14 Variety of potato: 2 wds.
17 Pitch
18 "How do ____ this gently?": 2 wds.
19 The Missouri R. forms part of its border
21 Ending with defer or refer
23 Member of the Pueblo people of western New Mexico
24 Farm call
25 Iris holder
26 Exam
28 Male donkey
32 Long-legged wading bird
33 Suffixes in many element names
34 Get a look at
35 Katmandu's continent
37 Sarah McLachlan hit of 1998 (or, backwards, an opera)
39 Ultimate
40 Begone beginning
41 Dir. away from SSW
42 Orchestra: abbr.

153

Across

1 In the company of
5 Mythical fire-breathing monster
11 Golfer Aoki
12 Actress Marilyn
13 Agriculturist Jethro ___
14 "No more, thank you": 2 wds.
15 Sharp piece of wood
17 Board member: abbr.
18 "Autumn Leaves" singer Montand
22 Imbibes: 3 wds.
26 Anglo-Saxon letter in the form of a crossed 'D'
27 Color anew
28 Billy Dee role in "The Empire Strikes Back"
30 First name in Notre Dame football
31 Nuclear structure
33 Jab at
35 Small island
36 Full of twists and turns
41 Forgo
44 Propel with force
45 Citizen of Sana'a
46 "Cup ___" (1970s Don Williams song): 2 wds.
47 Literary postscript
48 London stoolie

Down

1 Mental acuity
2 "The jig ___!": 2 wds.
3 Farfetched
4 Jazz musician Billie
5 Composer Shostakovich
6 "City of Seven Hills"
7 Furious
8 One doz. doz.
9 Queenside castle, in chess notation
10 Dime novelist Buntline
16 Nickname for a San Francisco football team
19 Let out
20 Plant of the arum family
21 Manhattan restaurateur Toots
22 1960s militant Brown, familiarly: 2 wds.
23 Flying start?
24 Neb. neighbor: 2 wds.
25 Braid
29 Follow: 2 wds.
32 Small elongated insect
34 Lucy's friend, on "I Love Lucy"
37 Vintner's prefix
38 "I'm Gonna Wash That Man Right ___ My Hair"
39 Manipulative person
40 "Othello" playwright: abbr.
41 One of two that view
42 Calendar abbr.
43 901, to a Roman

154

Across

1 Chills out
6 Straight muscles
11 Written with a pen, not a pencil: 2 wds.
12 Float ____ (arrange financing): 2 wds.
13 There are five in "The Twelve Days of Christmas": 2 wds.
15 Ocean west of Portugal: abbr.
16 Hair colorer
17 Lady rabbit
18 Meteorologist's comfort meas.
19 Part
21 Fair-hiring agcy.
23 Anatomical pouch
24 Genetic molecules, initially
26 Bulges downward under weight
29 Very softly, in music: abbr.
31 ____ II (razor brand)
33 Lot event: 2 wds.
37 Certain mail letters
38 Time, in Turin
39 One of the Bobbsey Twins
40 Cal. quarter
41 Stain inherited from Adam: 2 wds.
44 Riveter of World War II
45 Free-for-all
46 Expand abnormally
47 Not exactly active

Down

1 Tie up, to stop bleeding
2 Repeat order at the bar
3 Very large indeterminate number
4 Goal
5 Programs, briefly
6 Argon, e.g.: 2 wds.
7 New Haven student
8 ____ Nast
9 Attach: 2 wds.
10 Map feature
14 Comedian Louis and Science Guy Bill
20 Future doc's exam
22 Stadium souvenirs
25 Dog with a long silky coat
27 Karen of "Little House on the Prairie"
28 More mawkish, so to speak
30 Layout
32 Brass instrument played in a band
33 Brewery in Golden, Colorado
34 One-way sign symbol
35 Erect
36 As a friend in France: 2 wds.
42 "Drums Along the Mohawk" hero
43 Cariou of "Blue Bloods"

155

Across

1 "Saturday Night Fever" music
6 Sleeve ends
11 Deprive of courage
12 High hideaway
13 Marine mollusks
14 Projection that prevents slipping
15 Advocate for srs.
16 Lusters
17 Demolition stuff, shortly
18 Address abbr.
19 Cable company that merged with AT&T in 1999
20 Middle eastern currency unit
22 At a particular time
23 Veto
25 It goes with the flow
27 Earlier in time
29 Unclose, to Shelley
30 Poetic contraction
31 "No ___!"
33 Perfect-bound, in bookbinding
35 River that flows through Hamburg
36 ___ Dame Cathedral
37 Plagiarizes
38 Crystal-lined stone
39 ___ Park, N.J.
40 Dog-___
41 "What're ya having?" reply: 2 wds.

Down

1 Gold coin of old
2 Away from the shore
3 Market-savvy sort: 2 wds.
4 Place for a tent
5 Run-___ (some sentences)
6 Hoarder's supply
7 River of Africa
8 It's 15 feet from the hoop, in basketball: hyph., 2 wds.
9 Bridegroom-to-be
10 Becomes established: 2 wds.
16 Secure: 2 wds.
18 Piano piece
21 Gallery-funding gp.
22 Chinese dynasty
24 Change the position of words, letters, etc.: abbr.
25 One of the rooms in the board game Clue
26 Sleep problem, to Brits
28 ___-rouser (instigator)
30 Like some jackets
32 "___ no?": 2 wds.
34 Earth, in Essen
35 Holiday eve in Tel Aviv
37 Nashville-based awards org.

156

Across

1 Psychiatrist's appt.
5 Twelve people in court
11 Cookie often twisted
12 Small eggs
13 Service branch, initially
14 Acceptances
15 Feral feline: 2 wds.
17 Orchestra group
18 Bear or boor follower
21 Word that qualifies another
23 Duck, in German
24 Capital of New Brunswick, Canada
26 Blackens
27 Irish-themed Vegas casino that features a tattoo parlor
28 Part of DOS, briefly
29 Cousin of a mink
30 Academic types
33 Read into, as motives
36 King Harald's father
37 Fairly close: 2 wds.
38 Late dinner hour
39 Stripes' counterparts, in pool
40 1940s–50s All-Star Johnny

Down

1 Kind of chef
2 In the past, in the past
3 Pirates: 2 wds.
4 Guest facilities, perhaps: 2 wds.
5 Psychologist who was a frequent guest of Johnny Carson: 2 wds.
6 Eye parts
7 Corroding sign of disuse
8 They protect QBs
9 Suffix for jambo or kedge
10 Draft board inits.
16 Bygone days
18 Among other things: 2 wds.
19 Ancient colonnade
20 Egg producers
21 PM times: abbr.
22 Squirrel's nest
23 Ranks
25 Analogy words: 2 wds.
29 Group of eight
30 Certain Muslim
31 Eastern royal
32 Cinematographer Nykvist
33 Helpful connections
34 Cow's sound
35 Jim Bakker's club letters

157

Across

1 Have an ____ one's sleeve: 2 wds.
6 European coal area
10 Medicinal plant
11 Indian coin
12 She won the U.S. Open in 1979 and 1981: 2 wds.
14 Razz
15 D.C. United's org.
16 Can. province
17 "Lost" setting: abbr.
18 U.F.O. occupants
19 "____ geht's?" (German "How are you?")
20 House and club/dance music group ____-Lite
22 Former Disney CEO
24 NFL team in Calif.: 2 wds.
26 Words before "friends": 2 wds.
29 Parietal cell secretion
33 The ____ Glove (hot surface mitt)
34 Some guys in rap songs, initially
36 Clandestine maritime org.
37 Gnarls Barkley member ____-Lo
38 Cattle call
39 Roman house god
40 Take your name off the mailing list
43 Unfair putdowns
44 Turkey's Atatürk
45 Label A or B, e.g.
46 Egg producer

Down

1 ____ Lindgren, creator of Pippi Longstocking
2 Ruby
3 Make possible
4 Mom's brother, briefly
5 "Hand over the money!": 2 wds.
6 Lenin's language: abbr.
7 Affluent area in a city
8 Baseball Hall-of-Famer Manush
9 Person who gives a monthly check to a landlord
11 Pasternak's homeland
13 Trusted friends: 2 wds.
21 Loop transports
23 Little, in Leith
25 Mushroom-cloud producers: hyph.
26 Insect that swarms in large numbers
27 In a fair way
28 Gets ready to swing: 2 wds.
30 Mexican state or its capital
31 Joke locale: 3 wds.
32 In an unpleasant way
35 Smashing
41 Suffix for press
42 Gun, as the engine

158

Across

1 Clinic workers, for short
4 Notebook maker
7 Airline inits.
10 Collectible item made in an earlier period
12 "To each ___ own"
13 Pledge money (by law) to a specific purpose
15 "The Optimist's Daughter" author
16 Epic tales
19 Series between K and Q
23 French race car driver Alain
24 Simple question type: 2 wds.
25 Ike's W.W. II milieu
26 "___-haw!"
27 "Obviously!" (slang): 2 wds.
30 Penh lead-in
32 ___ good turn (helps out): 2 wds.
33 "Filthy" funds
34 Roll of tobacco
36 Angry or dissatisfied
42 What a "Wheel of Fortune" contestant might buy: 2 wds.
43 Severe
44 Producer: abbr.
45 Not just my
46 "What ___ care?": 2 wds.

Down

1 ___-jongg
2 Letters after Kirsten Gillibrand's name
3 Big race sponsor, initially
4 Brightness measure: 2 wds.
5 Material used for inlaying furniture
6 In a fitting manner
7 "___ Carter" (Lil Wayne album)
8 1999 Pulitzer Prize-winning play
9 Peer Gynt's mother
11 Siouan speakers
14 Flower cluster
16 Devote, as time
17 "Star Wars" character, informally
18 "As the World Turns" actress Elena
20 "Bye Bye Bye" boy band
21 ___ more (several): 2 wds.
22 Verse, in Paris
28 SOS responders
29 Bob or beehive
30 Less than three-dimensional
31 Wounds
35 Old pro
36 Public works project
37 Like Brahms's Symphony No. 3: 2 wds.
38 Geraint's title
39 Abbr. in many company names
40 Letters that end a kids' song
41 601 in Roman numerals

159

Across

1 Darkest part of a shadow
6 Errand runner, casually
11 "Norwegian Wood" instrument
12 Rio Grande do ___, Brazil
13 Difficult situation
15 One of 100 in D.C.
16 Interest loan fig.
17 Federal warning system, initially
18 Swab analysis site, briefly: 2 wds.
20 Lazy and black-eyed
23 Alone
26 Prefix with cranial or muscular
27 Type of legal action: 2 wds.
28 University mil. group
29 Dutch royal house
30 Plant of the mint family
32 Ref.'s ruling
34 TV channel relaunched as "Versus" in 2006
35 Some coll. degrees
38 Chinese vegetable: 2 wds.
41 "It's ___ against time": 2 wds.
42 Schectman who scored the first basket in the NBA
43 Football's Grier
44 Forty-___ (prospector)

Down

1 FedEx rival
2 Goo
3 Bingo call: 2 wds.
4 Totally cool: abbr.
5 Monteverdi opera
6 Distort
7 "___-Pah-Pah" (song from "Oliver!")
8 City and county of Minnesota
9 1169 erupter
10 Soaks, as flax
14 They prepare tax returns, shortly
18 Austen character
19 No problem at all: 2 wds.
20 Arthur Conan Doyle title
21 Card game with 108 cards
22 Columbus discovery of 1493: 2 wds.
24 Bird's "drumstick"
25 "Take Me Bak ___" (1972 Slade song)
27 Affixes T-shirt designs: 2 wds.
29 Munch Museum site
31 County fair cry
32 Skier's aid: hyph.
33 Brand of corn syrup
35 Rigging pro
36 French silk
37 Suffix with hip
39 Letters accompanying some 2,000-year-old+ dates
40 Chinese philosopher Chu ___

160

Across

1 "Ulalume" poet
4 Another name for the Sun
7 Hems and haws
10 Dawn deity
11 Prefix with light
12 Classic Japanese drama
13 Foul: 2 wds.
15 Certain gambler
17 Seoul's country, initially
18 Insurance giant, for short
19 Tree with lobed leaves
21 Fiber used for matting
24 Crime-busters' grp.
25 N.Y. or Rio, e.g.: abbr.
26 Like the colors in some boxes of crayons: abbr.
29 Pharmaceutical company
31 Swiss river
32 Teacher's deg.
33 Difficult or stubborn
38 Person who keeps a journal
39 Prudhoe Bay product
40 Env. extra
41 Corp., e.g.
42 Hallucinogen's initials
43 Prefix meaning "ten": var.
44 NASDAQ unit, shortly

Down

1 Transport company
2 "Amazing!"
3 Bars
4 Possession that indicates a person's wealth or high social position
5 Boo-boo, to a tot
6 Commuter rail company, initially
7 Pop's kin
8 Acidic humus
9 Extremely astute: 4 wds.
14 "Bless me, Father, ____ have sinned": 2 wds.
16 Member of Cong.
19 Jerry Lewis's telethon org., once
20 1950s political inits.
22 Zoo denizen
23 Paper size: abbr.
27 Wyndham Lewis novel
28 Empties the tub
29 Person making a wager
30 Critic ____ Louise Huxtable
33 Picked out of a lineup, briefly
34 First word of a Dolly Parton hit
35 Function used in arrays
36 Lily, in Lyon
37 Antiquity, in antiquity

161

Across

1 "Me, myself ___": 2 wds.
5 Chutzpah
11 Bookstore sect.
12 Historic city of eastern Brazil
13 It fights for your rights, initially
14 Peanut butter cup brand
15 Big name in meatless burgers
16 Sun. talk
17 Ending with defer or refer
19 Bay or day preceder
23 Bring forward
26 Due + due + due
27 Luau souvenir
28 Codgers' replies
29 Company called "Big Blue"
30 Apprehend
31 Bacterial disease
33 The Daily Beast, e.g.: hyph.
35 Catch, as fly balls
36 German compass point
38 Ad agency award
41 When there's darkness, in a Koestler title: 2 wds.
44 Unyielding
45 Part of FBI
46 Morales of "Jericho"
47 Surround in a sac, anatomically
48 Tiny fraction of a min.: 2 wds.

Down

1 Simple rhyme scheme
2 One-named singer for the 1960s Velvet Underground
3 The sweet life, in Italy: 2 wds.
4 Green animal some keep as a pet
5 Deciduous tree with large leaves: 2 wds.
6 1997 Peter Fonda role
7 Coffin holders
8 Assts. to M.D.s
9 Fish of the carp family
10 KLM rival
18 American media website
20 Fish gelatin
21 Philippine island
22 Basinger and Novak
23 Four-time Pro Bowl tight end Crumpler
24 Believe
25 Job preceder: abbr.
32 German cathedral city
34 Soft and sticky
37 On condition that: 2 wds.
39 "Dies ___"
40 Like poems of praise
41 Honest ___ (Lincoln)
42 Wine holder
43 A.E.C. successor

162

Across

1 In ___ (as found)
5 Dining
11 Scaredy-cat player of 1939
12 Does penance
13 Boxers Muhammad and Laila, for two
14 Masonry finish applied when wet
15 Coins of India
17 Onetime Golden Arches' offering
19 Sweet ___, brand of artificial sweetener: 2 wds.
22 Wall hanging
23 Put off until later
25 Mens ___ (criminal intent)
26 Neighbor of Ala.
27 Kurt Wallander's home town
30 A-list
32 "The Hive" author Camilo José
33 Famous New York City department store
34 "Ciao for now!": hyph.
36 Entry
39 New corp. hires
42 Cooking directions
43 It follows juillet
44 Certain mattresses
45 Laura whose albums include "Walk the Dog and Light the Light"

Down

1 Hearst kidnap grp.
2 Affluent suffix
3 Inferior in quality: 2 wds.
4 Actress Andress
5 Mollify
6 Show up for
7 Make disheveled
8 Part of some co. names
9 Computer giant, initially
10 Mil. aide
16 You get three for an FG
17 Mother of Jesus
18 Dimin.'s opposite
20 Young man who does minor jobs: 2 wds.
21 "The Optimist's Daughter" author
24 Actress Martha, et al.
28 Even though
29 Place for a massage: 2 wds.
30 Diplomat's office: abbr.
31 He's not an expert
35 Mexican men, colloquially
36 Horace's "___ Poetica"
37 Capital of Connecticut?
38 "Up Around the Bend" band, briefly
40 Sound-related prefix
41 Pou ___, standing place

163

Across

1 Just so-so
4 "The Tears ____ Clown" (#1 tune of 1970): 2 wds.
7 Retail estab.
10 Remain where you are: 2 wds.
12 Word on many planes
13 Newspaper
14 Flying start?
15 Insignificant
16 Depletes: 2 wds.
18 At a short distance away from: 2 wds.
20 From that location
22 Sask. neighbor: 2 wds.
26 Stammerer's syllables
27 Feature of a nice hotel
29 Ranch add-on
30 Chief
32 Charm
34 Regarding this point
36 Sever, detach: 2 wds.
39 Slurpee-like drink brand
42 "____ understand it...": 2 wds.
43 Finds a new way to express
45 Palindromic music genre
46 Source of "The True North strong and free!": 2 wds.
47 L.A. hrs.
48 Maximum
49 Cobb of baseball fame et al.

Down

1 Voicemails: abbr.
2 Series ender, shortly: 2 wds.
3 Obscurity
4 ____-in (like some mailing lists)
5 Grammar tense: 2 wds.
6 Boom source, for short: 2 wds.
7 "In a Child's Name" author Peter
8 Lake between Rwanda and the Democratic Republic of the Congo
9 Guilt or round follower
11 Neighbor of Oman
17 Many chiliads
19 Summertime coolers, for short
20 Butter holder
21 Med. care provider
23 Barack Obama, for one
24 Spanish hoop
25 S. ____ (Seoul's country: abbr.)
28 "Wheel of Fortune" buy: 2 wds.
31 Cable choice, briefly
33 Noun-forming suffix
35 "High School Musical" star Zac
36 "Li'l Abner" cartoonist
37 GI hangouts, initially
38 Put a point on, old-style
40 Miniature whirlpool
41 Those girls, to Juanita
44 Comic strip cry

164

Across

1 China neighbor, for short
4 Record store section
7 Extra notes at the end of a letter, initially
10 Alfonso XIII's queen
11 Hearing range
13 Operate simultaneously
15 "Head ___" (Sean Paul song): 2 wds.
16 Mouselike critters
17 School class that teaches cooking, sewing, etc.: abbr., 2 wds.
19 Bartender on "The Simpsons"
21 Arts and ___
25 Snowman's accessory, at times: 2 wds.
28 "What's your hurry?": 2 wds.
29 Summer clock setting, initially
30 Lofty verse
33 Former East German secret police
36 Arctic abode
39 Undeceive
41 Gets the better of: 2 wds.
42 It's past due
43 Jennifer Lien's role in "Star Trek: Voyager"
44 Lash
45 Pay stub abbr.

Down

1 Where an egg might be found
2 Lover of Ares in Greek mythology
3 Leopards' cousins
4 Shorten again, as a skirt
5 Swiss river to the Rhine
6 Aphorism
7 One of the Everly Brothers
8 Keyser ___ ("The Usual Suspects" villain)
9 Holy Fr. women
12 Chocolate treat with white nonpareils: hyph.
14 Gentle sound
18 ___ Lodge
19 Hosts, initially
20 Tic-tac-toe winner
22 Faithfulness
23 Decorates with bathroom tissue, for short
24 Pin down
26 Understanding, technically
27 Flight deck colleague
31 A Uto-Aztecan language
32 Latin abbrs.
33 Neb. neighbor: 2 wds.
34 Former Oakland Raiders coach Mike
35 Enzymes' suffixes
37 ___ cloud (comet-filled region of space)
38 Lacking width and depth: hyph.
40 French pronoun

165

Across

1 Two semesters
5 Some PC ports
9 "It Must Be Magic" singer ___ Marie
10 Banda ___ (Sumatran city)
11 Vandal, e.g.
12 City on the Brazos
13 Make a choice
14 Supply with staff
16 "Citizen Kane" studio, briefly
17 Bear in "The Jungle Book"
19 Orr colleague, familiarly
21 River of Flanders
22 City on the Yangtze
23 "The Other Day ___ Bear" (traditional campfire song): 3 wds.
25 Gasps for breath
27 Loaf
31 Put your name to
32 Flower girl in "Pygmalion"
33 Aviation prefix
34 Round Table address
36 Alien life forms, initially
37 Swimwear designer Gernreich
39 Grape used in Bordeaux wine
41 Real estate ad abbr.
42 Carve, engrave
43 ___ bean
44 Other, in Spain

Down

1 Dr. Seuss title turtle
2 Suffix with musket
3 Prefix with graph or meter
4 ___ avis, unique bird
5 Detroit-based org.
6 Sports shoes manufacturer
7 Summon with a nod or a wave
8 "Get lost!"
9 Spanish savory dishes
11 "___-Dick"
15 Not masc. or fem.
18 Gasket with a circular cross-section: hyph.
20 "___ We Dance?"
22 "Scream" director Craven
24 Everest and Matterhorn, briefly
25 Not genuine
26 Hang on a line, as laundry: hyph.
28 "The Last Don" costar Danny
29 Band whose albums include "Antenna": 2 wds.
30 Down ___ (Maine)
32 Put up, as a building
33 Stock market figures, briefly
35 "___ Tired" (Beatles song): 2 wds.
38 "Baby ___ Star" (Prince song): 2 wds.
40 1920 play that introduced the word "robot," initially

173

166

Across

1 Emperor who shares his name with a salad

7 Civil War inits.

10 Football's Fighting ____

11 A puppet has three

12 "That's good enough for me": 2 wds.

13 River in Spain

14 Something incredibly simple: 2 wds.

16 "Lord of the Rings" baddies

19 Type of medical treatment, intially

20 Former British prime minister

22 "Little ____" (Ibsen play)

26 Summary stanza

27 Cell phone company

28 Strike back

29 Key for Elgar's Symphony No. 1: 2 wds.

30 Colo. neighbor

32 Meter reading

33 Japanese chicken dish

37 ____ Bator (capital of Mongolia)

38 Noisy insect

42 Dept. that works with Sales

43 In layers

44 Bumper sticker letters

45 David, "the sweet psalmist of ____"

Down

1 102, to a Roman

2 Supermodel Carol

3 Corner piece

4 Wealthy: hyph.

5 "The King ____": 2 wds.

6 ____ Janeiro: 2 wds.

7 Island of the south central Philippines

8 Lowly worker

9 Starting from: 2 wds.

11 Coast Guard officer: 2 wds.

15 Extended operatic solo

16 Former Carolina Panthers offensive tackle Michael

17 French politician Jacques ____ Chirac

18 Spanish sparkling white wine

21 Deride: 2 wds.

23 "The Sooner State," briefly

24 One whose pants are on fire

25 Fortune

31 Prefix meaning "night"

33 City in southwestern Arizona

34 ____-Seltzer

35 Karate exercise

36 Reformer Jacob

39 Constellation next to Telescopium

40 River to the North Sea

41 Jewish org. founded in 1913

167

Across

1. Felines
5. Pumpkin seed snack
11. Resort town in the Catskills
12. New Jersey city
13. Poetry ___ (literary competition)
14. Of no use
15. Unmelodious
17. Well-known whale of the 1960s
18. Forensic drama on CBS
21. "___ Irish Rose"
23. "De profundis," for one
25. Salacious glance
26. Unseals, in verse
27. Bancroft and Baxter
29. Argentine V.P. Boudou
30. J.F.K. sight, initially
31. Shout of approval
33. Professional business
36. Michael, in Mexico
39. Sister of Osiris
40. Library desk
41. Extra
42. Tristram Shandy's creator
43. Items included in envs.

Down

1. Threw
2. Org. concerned with rights
3. Ephemeral
4. "Ditto": 2 wds.
5. Preface to a book
6. Really enjoys: 2 wds.
7. Fraternity letters
8. "Letters from ___ Jima" (2006 film)
9. Professor's helpers, initially
10. Word of agreement
16. Vegas head
18. Ornamental covering for a horse
19. Kids take it down hills
20. "___ Excited" (Pointer Sisters hit): 2 wds.
21. "Such a pity!"
22. Uncle ___ (rice brand)
24. At an unfixed moment
28. Shield
29. Pre-1975 power agcy.
32. Actress Berry of "Extant"
33. Burmese sound
34. Round line: abbr.
35. Spanish men, colloquially
36. Hosts, initially
37. "Can ___ least sit down?": 2 wds.
38. Educ. test

168

Across

1. "...___ man with seven wives...": 3 wds.
6. ___-Japanese War
11. Cuts with light
12. Late lunch time: 2 wds.
13. Metal golf clubs
14. Annual celebrations, for short
15. Not pertinent to what is under consideration
17. Donkey in "Winnie the Pooh"
18. Ring: abbr.
20. Julia Sweeney box office bomb of 1994: 2 wds.
24. Prefix with fauna or form
25. Simile center: 2 wds.
26. Queenside castling in chess notations
27. Pennsylvania's ___ Mountains
29. Bigger photos: abbr.
30. Hulled corn used in grits
32. Broker of a utility service
36. Lorena of the LPGA
37. Adult insect
38. Pat down, as for weapons
39. Hides
40. Indian nursemaids
41. Girls in France

Down

1. Tennis champ Nastase
2. "Time wounds all heels" comic
3. Abstruse
4. Insect-eating mammal of Madagascar
5. Examine
6. "Killing Me Softly with His Song" singer Flack
7. Negates
8. Linebacker Junior
9. 1974 Donald Sutherland/Elliott Gould movie
10. Mantra sounds
16. Having a very bad smell
18. Top
19. Literature Nobelist Andric
21. Simple hairstyle
22. MSN competitor
23. Lean-___ (camping structures)
25. Hooded jackets
28. "Gracious me!": 2 wds.
29. White coating
31. "___ up!" ("Uncle!"): 2 wds.
32. Streep's "___ in the Dark": 2 wds.
33. Karmann-___ (sports car)
34. Lothario's look
35. "Friends" guy
36. One ___ kind: 2 wds.

169

Across

1. ___ an der Thaya, Austrian town
4. Hosp. employee, perhaps
7. Hwy. that runs through Williamsburg
10. Able to produce the result intended
13. Concert instruments: 2 wds.
14. Dutch astronomer who proved the galaxy rotates
15. Name in "Nine Stories"
16. Be off base
18. Leeds's river
21. Microorganism that requires oxygen for growth
24. Never say this
25. St. Paul's twin
27. Kooky
28. Public flaps
29. Czech river that is an Elbe tributary
31. Plunk starter?
32. Simple quatrain pattern
34. Whitney and Gray
38. Area in which something exists or lives
41. 1952 musical starring Bette Davis: 2 wds.
42. Crew member
43. Biathlon need
44. Blend

Down

1. Building block
2. Big hair
3. Not nigh
4. ___ Soundsystem, rock band
5. Novel, e.g.: 2 wds.
6. Marine Corps law enforcement agency, initially
7. Constitutionally lazy: hyp.
8. "___ Vadis?"
9. Slalom maneuver
11. Confine
12. Kanye West's "___ God": 3 wds.
17. Some deer
19. "How the Other Half Lives" author Jacob
20. Some M.I.T. grads
21. Helps out
22. Try hard to achieve
23. Sword in the Olympics
25. "Excusez-___!"
26. Sloping road to a highway: hyph.
30. Batters' stats
33. Moves with a curving trajectory
35. Clothes line
36. Years, in old Rome
37. Charon's waterway
38. D.D.E.'s arena
39. They were straight outta Compton
40. Abbr. between a first and last name, maybe

170

Across

1 Flavor
6 Jai alai basket
11 Wing-shaped
12 Express
13 Shocking
14 Money-saving, in product names
15 Dark red legume: 2 wds.
17 "Super!"
18 Dadaist artists Jean and Hans
21 Celtics head coach before Rick Pitino: inits., 2 wds.
25 Memo letters
26 Solidify
27 Place for a manicure or a massage
28 Win back, as trust
30 Have ___ for: 2 wds.
31 Physical stature
33 Extremely rarely: 2 wds.
38 Sean Paul's "Head ___": 2 wds.
39 He sang "Beauty And The Beast" with Celine
40 Place to exchange vows
41 "See what you think!": 2 wds.
42 Piano lesson piece
43 No liability

Down

1 Jonas who tested the polio vaccine on himself
2 To him, to Pierre: 2 wds.
3 "Howdy!" sayer
4 Rubber gaskets: hyph.
5 Actress Winona
6 Object struck in a game of pool: 2 wds.
7 "… and all that jazz," for short: 2 wds.
8 Ancient colonnade
9 Ga. neighbor
10 Spanish hoop
16 Natives of Sana'a
18 Algeria's continent: abbr.
19 Hard liquor choice
20 Pizza order
22 Curaçao clock setting letters
23 Sch. in Troy, N.Y.
24 Oversaw
26 Swiss cheese with small holes
29 Overseas
30 Goof-offs
32 Greek monetary units worth one hundredth of a drachma
33 Electrical unit
34 Words from Caesar: 2 wds.
35 Fortnight's fourteen
36 Village Voice award
37 Social reformer Lucretia (1793–1880)
38 ___-Bo

171

Across

1 Korean autos
5 Experienced leader
10 Pale shades of beige
12 "___ Mio": 2 wds.
13 Frat. whose alumni include Dr. Seuss, briefly
14 Weary cry: 2 wds.
15 Sore spot
17 Young-___ (little tykes)
18 Group of whales
20 Glow
22 Stress may be one
24 Small restaurant
27 Charge: 2 wds.
29 Finland's second-largest city
30 Improved
32 "Modern Maturity" org.
33 Depleted: 2 wds.
35 Trains: abbr.
36 Welcome ___
38 Coffee that won't keep you up
40 Commercial corn chip
42 Massenet opera
45 Hardly friendly
46 View from the Rive Gauche
47 "___ a gun!": 2 wds.
48 K2 and Makalu, briefly

Down

1 Female Ocampa in "Star Trek: Voyager"
2 Here, in Le Havre
3 Line of reasoning
4 Gibberish-talking "SNL" character ___ Forrester
5 Desperate: 3 wds.
6 City in western Kyrgyzstan
7 Dessert made with granola and fruit: 2 wds.
8 SpaceX founder, ___ Musk
9 Composer Rorem and others
11 Pet-lover's org.
16 Tarzan creator's monogram
18 Duds
19 Chills and fever
21 Bones, anatomically
23 "Out of the Cellar" heavy metal band
25 "Signs" costar Culkin
26 "I've made a mistake"
28 Began a round of golf: 2 wds.
31 Wish you could take it back
34 Poll amts.
36 Degs. for playwrights
37 Guthrie with a guitar
39 Interrupter's interjection
41 Extremely
43 Bed-and-breakfast cousin
44 Parisian possessive

172

Across

1 Bruins' sch.
5 Port at the mouth of the Amazon
10 Chapati alternative
11 Like leaning letters
13 Crucially
15 Equinox mo.
16 "___-Pah-Pah" (song from "Oliver!")
17 Mama bear, in Mexico
18 Cheri formerly of "Saturday Night Live"
20 "___ its course": 2 wds.
22 Butterfly's cousin
23 Busybodies
24 "Eeech!"
26 Speak softly
29 Apropos of, in contracts: 2 wds.
33 Tipped rapiers
34 Delicate
35 Barbados clock setting letters
36 That objeto
38 H.S. figure
39 Missile hurled by Jupiter
42 Beethoven specialty
43 Chinook salmon
44 Barbershop quartet member
45 Methods

Down

1 Chattem sleep aid brand
2 Snapped out of it: 2 wds.
3 Small flap on a garment
4 "Is that ___?": 2 wds.
5 ___-Honey (candy bar): hyph.
6 Lightweight open-weave fabric
7 Linked-computers acronym
8 Matador's opponent: 2 wds.
9 "It Was Almost Like a Song" singer Ronnie
12 Blue-green hues
14 Louis XIV, e.g.
19 Be similar in end sound, e.g. cat and mat
21 "___, With Love" (1967): 2 wds.
23 Growing season: abbr.
25 "That was my habit once": 3 wds.
26 Butchers' offerings
27 Outcome
28 Alter the pitch of (an instrument)
30 City on the southern coast of Honshu, Japan
31 "Believe It or Not" name
32 Makes jubilant
34 "Look ___ the union label"
37 Cook quickly
40 Palindromic woman's name
41 Incidentally, initially

173

Across

1 Actor Alan
5 Big cheese in Bengal
10 Island the Greeks call Kérkira
12 Piano practice piece
13 With intense feeling
15 Burns's "Tam o' Shanter" for one
16 Binds
17 Ship's commander, briefly
19 More gelid
21 Do-re-mi?
22 Pro ___ (for now)
23 ___ diem
26 Minuscule, slangily
30 Biblical craft
32 Mama bear, in Madrid
33 Rush
35 Grocery label amt.: 2 wds.
36 Gp. that opposes greyhound racing
37 Pasta sauce brand
39 Warnings about things that fail to happen: 2 wds.
43 Antigone's cruel uncle
44 Baseball's Martinez and others
45 Fashion sense
46 Sugar suffixes

Down

1 Part of a royal flush
2 Award worn between the DSSM and the DFC
3 Glass tube with a rubber bulb at one end
4 ___ Alps, Minnesota ski resort
5 "___ and Stimpy"
6 "One Day ___" 1970s–80s CBS sitcom: 3 wds.
7 "Mary Poppins" star Andrews
8 Freud contemporary
9 Attention-getting shouts
11 Quick turnaround, slangily
14 Forget
17 LX quintupled
18 Palindromic heroine of "The Piano"
20 Certain semicircle
24 Sunshade
25 Miss the mark
27 City traffic sign: 2 wds.
28 Direction for navigators, initially
29 China's Sun ___-sen
31 Davis who wrote the "Just One Night" trilogy
33 Coward's lack
34 Six-time All-Star second baseman Chase ___
35 Whodunit author Marsh
36 Some G.I.s
38 Key abbr.
40 From Okla. City to Tulsa
41 Duff Beer vendor
42 "Boo-o-o!"

174

Across

1 Veterinary anesthetic, initially
4 Masseur's employer
7 Sports org. officially formed in February 1995
10 Former Mideast inits.
11 Slip
12 Letters that end "Old MacDonald Had a Farm"
13 Seal's limb
15 Blakey of "Birth Day Live!"
16 Sooty deposits
17 Bra specification: 2 wds.
18 Run up ___: 2 wds.
19 ___ Tzu (toy dog)
21 Automobiles
22 Two dots over a vowel, in German
25 Suffix with rapid or rational
26 Partner of plata
27 Big inits. in news
28 Withdraw
30 "Laura" director Preminger
31 Blood type, briefly: 2 wds.
32 Court helper: hyph.
33 Digestion aid
35 Attorney-___: hyph.
37 "___ Z Mysteries" (kids' series): 2 wds.
38 Journey hit of 1986
40 Data compression format letters
41 Authors' assoc.
42 ___ Mitchell, actor and musician
43 Agcy. concerned with returns
44 Sonnet ending
45 "No more seats," briefly

Down

1 Sta-___ fabric softener
2 School system for Chico and Stanislaus: 2 wds.
3 Cyan and yellow, e.g.: 2 wds.
4 Fall mo.
5 Instrument indicating force of air in a tire: 2 wds.
6 J.F.K. abbr.
7 Financial institutions for commerce: 2 wds.
8 In ___ of (for)
9 Dove or Dial
14 Bars
17 Baby Pickles on "Rugrats"
18 Galatea's love in Greek myth
20 Insurance grp.
23 Inhabitant of a prosperous part of a city
24 2004 Brad Pitt film
26 Laudatory lines
29 Ending for benz
30 "___-Di, ___-Da" (song)
33 Adriatic port
34 ___-TASS Russian news acronym (1992–2014)
36 Former Russian ruler: var.
38 Neighbor of Fin.
39 Roy Wood's band before Wizzard, shortly

175

Across

1 Wanderers
6 Argentinian expanse
11 Running wild
12 Architectural projection
13 "Back ___ Heart" (Olivia Newton-John album): 2 wds.
14 Like a forest of firs
15 Have, in Edinburgh
16 Pliers
18 Crawling critter
19 Letters after Charles Schumer's name
20 ___ gestae (things done: Lat.)
21 Pedal on an electric guitar: hyph.
23 Thompson in "Pollock"
24 Appearing in summer
26 English Lit., e.g.
28 Kingpin
31 Big Ten team, initially
32 "___ Heldenleben" (R. Strauss)
33 Collector's suffix
34 Beat
36 Greek consonant
37 NFL cofounder George
38 Shooter Bernhard known as "The Subway Vigilante"
40 ___ Ré, La Rochelle airport: 2 wds.
41 Lofty stronghold
42 Late bloomer
43 Valentine's Day dozen

Down

1 Horselaugh: hyph.
2 Writer Fallaci
3 Grasp the nettle: 3 wds.
4 "Aah!" accompaniment
5 ___ attention (wait): 2 wds.
6 Field flower with milky sap
7 Have ___ (be torn, as jeans): 2 words
8 Dasani and Ferrarelle, e.g.: 2 wds.
9 Gazed searchingly
10 Actress Milano
17 Curb
22 Financial newspaper, for short
23 Decline
25 Sour-tasting condiment
26 Actress Loren
27 Certain drink orders
29 Dead even: 3 wds.
30 Thin translucent fabrics
32 Anodyne
35 Singer born Helen Adu
39 Antipoverty agcy.

183

176

Across

1 Hip scooter
6 Big drawer?
11 Detached
12 History Channel show that follows loggers in the Pacific Northwest: 2 wds.
13 Top part of a skeleton
14 Last-minute greeting: hyph.
15 Be a vagabond
17 Enzymes' suffixes
18 BBC rival
20 Cable syst.
22 Ancient temple
24 Minors' level: 2 wds.
28 Correlation
30 Group with family ties?: 2 wds.
31 Alaska's first governor, Bill ____
32 Gillette brand
34 Gun owner's grp.
35 Miss Universe pageant attire
38 O.K. Corral surname
40 Crested ridge
42 Bunk
45 Arm bones
46 Borden spokescow
47 Veto
48 "Star Wars" droid Artoo-____

Down

1 "____ in Victor": 2 wds.
2 Great Plains grazer
3 It's not well-pitched: 2 wds.
4 Game with four-foot mallets
5 Supplemental health insurance giant
6 Li'l Abner's Daisy ____
7 Dig for, as artifacts
8 Blake Shelton has won a lot of them: inits.
9 Wrap in waxed cloth
10 Added details
16 Ghastly
18 Monogram unit: abbr.
19 Trig. function
21 Special attention, for short
23 Of meaning in language
25 Pointer
26 Fly with the eagles
27 Actress ____ Magnani
29 Fail to keep
33 Sighed with delight
35 Vestments, e.g.
36 Face-to-face exam
37 "The Things ____ for Love": 2 wds.
39 Actor's goal
41 Apt. feature, in the classifieds
43 Letters that end "Old MacDonald Had a Farm"
44 USN cleric, for short

177

Across

1. Sewing case
5. Current choice?: hyph.
9. Physics lab device, for short
11. Calculus calculations
13. Anatomical dividers
14. Kama ___
15. Part of E.U.: abbr.
16. Reddish-brown
18. Address
20. Apt. ad figure
21. Artist skilled at drawing plans
24. Southern breakfast dish
26. Safari sight, in short
27. Period of economic decline
29. Court fig.
30. Bad-smelling flower?
33. They talk foolishly
36. Stockbroker's steer
37. Hymn writer Reginald
38. Transparent linen
40. Kind of fork
41. Abrade
42. Feign a pass, e.g.
43. Santa ___ (hot winds)

Down

1. Someone ___ (not mine)
2. Entanglement: hyph.
3. Impossible to foretell
4. "Am ___ risk?": 2 wds.
5. "The law is ___..." (Dickens): 2 wds.
6. Superior vineyards
7. Single-mindedness, persistence
8. Teamster
10. Dead body of an animal
12. Declines: 2 wds.
17. Channels 14 through 83, initially
19. Art deco master
22. Adriatic port
23. Air
24. Charts
25. Unoriginal work, informally
28. Letters on old maps
31. Comedian Radner
32. Olympians' blades
34. Furniture wood
35. "Das Lied von der ___"
39. Man-mouse connection: 2 wds.

185

178

Across

1 "___ there, done that!"
5 Dating from: 2 wds.
9 Exit: 2 wds.
11 Substitute: abbr.
12 Pretend to be someone else
14 Narc's org.
15 Docs for women only
16 Prefix for fit or fire
17 Recipe qtys.
19 Fish of the carp family
21 ___ problem with (doesn't care for): 2 wds.
22 Singer Celine and others
23 Mexican city famed for its silverwork
25 Boredom
27 Degs. for attorneys
31 Beseech
32 "The Moor's Account" author Lalami
33 Muldaur's "___ Woman": 2 wds.
34 Danger in Afghanistan, initially
36 Opposite of 'taint
37 State of abeyance: 2 wds.
40 Hebrew name for Uranus
41 Conjectures
42 Till compartment
43 Charles ___, pitching coach for the Angels

Down

1 Go around
2 Help wanted ad letters
3 Continental currency
4 Accident investigating org.
5 "Prince Valiant" character
6 Mariner
7 Science of light
8 Soft tissue of the body
9 Breadth
10 Single-celled animal
13 King in "Conan the Barbarian"
18 City in northeastern India
20 Character in "Alley Oop"
22 511, to Caligula
24 Some German cars
25 "Mr. Majestyk" novelist Leonard
26 "Man with a Plan" costar Kevin
28 Prayer with responses from the congregation
29 Music's Mary J. ___
30 Eds.' requests
31 Ornamental loop
32 Anti-Parkinson's drug: hyph.
35 George Orwell's alma mater
38 Internet protocol, initially
39 Equip (a boat) with sails

179

Across

1. Burkina ___
5. "Ditto!": 3 wds.
10. Biol. energy sources
11. Lounger's robe
12. Sally in "Boston Legal"
13. Cause to feel indignation
14. Bucks
15. To date
16. Lily-Rose ___, daughter of Vanessa Paradis
18. Sultana's chambers
22. Massage: 2 wds.
25. Special gift letters
26. Liqueur flavorer
27. Worrier's worry
29. TV inits.
30. Empty-headedness
32. Boxing prize
34. Overindulgent
35. North Carolina capital: abbr.
37. Girl's name
40. A Gandhi
43. Frog's cousin
44. Design made of small pieces of colored stone
45. Bluefin, for one
46. Long robe worn by Roman women
47. Those things, in Oaxaca

Down

1. Saudi Arabian king
2. Have it to ___: 2 wds.
3. Function on some phones: 2 wds.
4. Hawk relatives
5. Yegg's target
6. "We're ___ see the wizard": 2 wds.
7. Took in
8. Fortify
9. Polit. label
11. Beaver-like animal
17. Before: abbr.
19. Not evergreen
20. At ___ time (prearranged): 2 wds.
21. Nimble
22. Insulting remark
23. A long time ago
24. Osso ___
28. Arched opening in a vault
31. Big name in supplemental insurance
33. Courtroom proceeding
36. Opera solo
38. Lang of Smallville
39. Some prosecutors, initially
40. Chats with, online
41. "She loves me ___"
42. Brit. honor

180

Across

1. Soviet secret police 1946–54: inits.
4. "The Tears ___ Clown" (hit of 1970): 2 wds.
7. Here, in Acapulco
10. Nonprofessional sports grp.
11. Male sheep, in Britain
12. Greek letters
13. A.C.L.U. concerns: abbr.
14. Brian of "Here Come the Warm Jets"
15. General ___'s chicken (Chinese restaurant dish)
16. Takes on again
18. BBC rival
19. Suffer humiliation, casually: 2 wds.
20. ___ polloi
21. Two singers who perform together
22. Popular Nissan
24. Unrestrained
26. Difference in years between people: 2 wds.
28. "___ boy!" ("Nice going!")
31. Hang back
32. Maritime distress signals
34. Hockey's Bobby
35. Bump
36. Granting grp.
37. Suffix with prim or pap
38. Suffix with front
39. Fuel additive letters
40. Neighbor of Alg.
41. Actress Vardalos of "My Big Fat Greek Wedding"
42. "Now I get it!"
43. S.A.T. takers
44. Make bigger, like a photo: abbr.

Down

1. Ruined
2. Rich cake
3. Informal network by which gossip is spread: 2 wds.
4. Cheri formerly of "SNL"
5. Mortuary: 2 wds.
6. Original disciple
7. Medicine used to treat allergies
8. Habit
9. Saint ___, Canadian rock band
17. Luggage attachment: 2 wds.
23. Hebrew letter: var.
25. Decorative belts made of shells
26. Actress Daniella of "Friday Night Lights"
27. Round Table knight
29. Enter, as data: 2 wds.
30. Star-related
33. Long time

181

Across

1 Insect egg case
4 Authors' assn.
7 "___ tu"
8 ___ Toretto, character in "The Fast and the Furious"
11 Persuasion: hyph.
14 Coal-rich German region
15 "Please enter!": 3 wds.
16 Cash register part
17 Berliner's "please"
18 Finnish-American actress and dancer Taina
19 Eternal
21 Vexed
23 Natives of Apia
25 Aegean tourist mecca
28 Necklace feature
29 Chichén ___ (Mayan city)
30 Tethers again
32 Aunts in Madrid
33 Appears more prominent or important than
35 ___ Moines, Ia.
36 Mon. follower
37 Indeed
38 Attack word

Down

1 Church bench
2 Not a copy: abbr.
3 Is out of order
4 Garbage
5 Holy chalice
6 Combines
8 Unblemished find for a book collector: 2 wds.
9 Monogram ltrs.
10 "___ of God" (Jane Fonda movie)
12 Erstwhile MTV countdown program, initially
13 Upholstery fabric
19 Metrical units in prose
20 Geometry suffix
22 Negative reply to a general: 2 wds.
23 Seafood entree
24 Pain reliever brand
26 Conductor Seiji
27 Impudently bold
29 "___ be a pleasure!"
31 Feng ___ (art of placement)
34 N.R.C. predecessor

182

Across

1. Math calculation
5. Capable of: 2 wds.
10. Part of a C.S.A. signature: 2 wds.
11. Prayer
12. Cried
13. Classic Peter Lorre role
14. Not loose
15. Heavyweight boxer "Two ___" Tony Galento
16. Glitzy rock style
18. Chantilly's department
22. Biological groups
24. 1960s civil rights org.
25. Financial planner's recommendation, briefly
26. Scottish skiing surface
28. Winery sight
29. Russian river
31. "___ Man" (movie starring Brendan Fraser)
33. English professor's deg.
34. Sounds of disgust
35. Flat paper container, briefly
37. German "a"
40. Maroon
43. Power stats
44. Friend of Odysseus
45. Actress Chase
46. Moisten with drops of water
47. Wide widths, initially

Down

1. 2012 presidential candidate Gingrich
2. Olive genus
3. Extremely distasteful
4. Grit
5. Jason's craft
6. Keyboard instruments
7. Battlesystem game co., initially
8. Trike rider
9. Start for step or stop
11. Get the better of
17. ___ gratia artis
19. Hidden
20. Read
21. Prefix with derm or therm
22. Fish's breathing organ
23. Part of a famous palindrome attributed to Napoleon: 2 wds.
27. "Brokeback Mountain" director Lee
30. Start of a Christmas carol
32. Dieppe darling
36. Sweet ___, sugar alternative: 2 wds.
38. Adidas rival
39. Those girls, in Guatemala
40. Diplomat's office: abbr.
41. Born, in wedding announcements
42. State between Mi. and Ky.

183

Across

1 Online store for handmade goods
5 Suffix for alien or assassin
10 Scotch ___
11 Einstein or Chagall, e.g.
12 Banda ___ (Sumatran city)
13 TV ad phrase: 2 wds.
14 Aromatic yellowish brown balsam
15 Jet set jet letters
16 Shankar of Indian theater
18 Literary critic and biographer Leon
22 Measurement for the fineness of stockings
24 ___ race: 2 wds.
25 Be a pain
26 Rest time: abbr.
28 Pitchfork-shaped letter
29 Financial columnist Marshall
31 Like some blankets
33 Actress Loughlin
34 ___ O'Grady, Mary in "Eight is Enough"
35 Poli ___ (college field of study)
37 Look over
40 Almost: 2 wds.
43 Locker room supply
44 Lens settings: hyph.
45 "___ girl!"
46 Tiptoed
47 Back

Down

1 South Dakota, to Pierre
2 Food in a shell
3 Cave explorer
4 Violinist Menuhin
5 Javelins, Marlins and Gremlins, initially
6 Self-conscious laugh
7 Starter: abbr.
8 Montana's motto "___ y plata"
9 ___ Brunswick
11 Walter Mosley's sleuth: 2 wds.
17 Loser to H.C.H.
19 Exact copy
20 First word of Massachusetts' motto
21 Reclined
22 Herb of the parsley family
23 Ending for switch or buck
27 Fluffy scarf
30 "Brittle Innings" author Michael
32 GM brand
36 Egyptian Christian
38 Sask. neighbor
39 Duke U. location: 2 wds.
40 Grp. for Packers and Panthers
41 UN member since 1949: abbr.
42 Telecom giant, for short

184

Across

1 Church area
5 Carter-Wallace brand
10 It's hot stuff
12 Pope after John X: 2 wds.
13 French states
14 Weighed down
15 Mute
17 U.N. agency
19 Warty hopper
20 Jenny "The Swedish Nightingale"
22 Determined in advance
26 Disgrace
28 "Parade" composer Erik
29 Insignificant person
31 Crow's-nest call
32 Some sports cars, initially
34 "Of course"
35 Seabird with a massive wingspan
39 "Cybill" creator Chuck
40 Beau
43 Vestibule
44 Make beam
45 Meara and Hathaway
46 Indulge in excessively, for short: 2 wds.

Down

1 Enzyme ending
2 Memorized to the letter
3 Historical region of Croatia
4 ___ perpetua (Idaho's motto)
5 Listening carefully: 2 wds.
6 Genuine article: 2 wds.
7 Took a bus or a train
8 Currier's partner
9 Clamors
11 "___ happens…": 2 wds.
16 Flatfoot
17 Disaster
18 Auxiliary
21 Blue denim
23 Holds a grudge: 2 wds.
24 One, in Weimar
25 Williams and Kennedy
27 Talks indistinctly
30 Rocky peak
33 Hurting
35 Italian sports car, briefly
36 Canadian-dollar image
37 ___ Mawr, Pa.
38 Feat for a novice pilot
41 W.W. II inits.
42 Vintner's prefix

185

Across

1 Eva or Magda
6 Run up
11 Gland-related comb. form
12 Golden, in Granada: 2 wds.
13 Cat's cry: var.
14 Fees levied for the use of roads or bridges
15 Disparagement of something unattainable: 2 wds.
17 Stock market figures
18 Lethargic
22 Original matter of the universe
25 "Thou ___ not kill"
26 City and port in Shiribeshi, Hokkaido, Japan
27 Cashew ___, Brown & Haley candy
28 Like coffee
29 Disinfectant brand
31 Kind of state
36 Head ___ (thorough): 2 wds.
37 North African capital
38 Played a part
39 "Blue Bloods" costar Rob
40 Has a villain's expression
41 Mary Richards' neighbor

Down

1 Pinup's legs
2 "Grazie ___!" (Italian for "Thank God!"): 2 wds.
3 Flame
4 ___ about (approximately): 2 wds.
5 Do without basic comforts, slangily: 2 wds.
6 Badge with a photo on it, for short: 2 wds.
7 Apprentice
8 Deli dish
9 Web page addresses, initially
10 Sigur ___, Icelandic rock band
16 Free
18 Early role-playing game co., initially
19 "So that's it!"
20 Swiss cheese and potato dish
21 Regular theater attendee
23 Previously, in poetry
24 Kid's pie material
26 "Sooner ___" (eventually): 2 wds.
28 Computerized task performer
30 Tournament favorites
31 Viva ___
32 Rear end, slangily
33 Really keen on
34 Fought
35 It: It.
36 Mikhail ___, chess champion of 1960–61

186

Across

1 Med. land
4 2001, to Nero
7 Ruler's length: 2 wds.
9 Season starter?
12 Visits casually: 2 wds.
13 Obie Award winning playwright Will
14 Bears, in old Rome
15 Cry of frustration
16 Miss. neighbor
18 "The Raven" actor Peter and others
20 Variant of backgammon: hyph.
22 Marrakesh's nat.
23 Dorm authority figures, briefly
24 Moo ___ gai pan
27 Mature period of life
30 Respiratory disorder
32 Alençon's department
33 Give
34 ___ Spirit (stealth bomber): 2 wds.
36 Hebrew letter
37 Pause in poetry
40 "___ you sure?"
41 Smelling salts ingredient
42 Father, to Huck Finn
43 "Hawaii Five-0" actor, Daniel ___ Kim

Down

1 Games grp.
2 ___-Cat
3 Financially rewarding
4 Creeping low plant
5 Gulf Coast city: 2 wds.
6 Suffix with inferior or infidel
8 Full of bracken
9 Amusement park attraction: hyph.
10 "Little Sheba" playwright
11 Homer Simpson shouts
15 Missile's path
16 Scottish hat
17 "The Name of the Rose" writer
19 Give the heave-ho
21 Beaten instrument
25 Suffix with ball or buff
26 Pindar work
28 World's largest logistics company, initially
29 "In what way?": 2 wds.
30 Skin conditioner brand
31 Coal-rich German region
35 Sub. in the office
37 Part of some uniforms
38 Small inlet
39 Org. for dentists

187

Across

1 "The Addams Family" cousin
4 Model wood
9 You, abroad
10 Increase
13 Campaign leader
15 Madrid maiden: abbr.
16 Nigerian tribesman
17 Place
19 Distract
22 Communication for the deaf, initially
23 Prefix meaning "common"
24 Reason's partner
26 First words of "Satisfaction": 2 wds.
30 Sales slip: abbr.
32 Ending for inter or exter
33 Couch
36 Fashion illustrator of the 1920s
37 Al Jolson's real first name
38 Like some Fords
40 Using a lot of bad language: hyph.
45 Champion
46 "Am ___ blame?": 2 wds.
47 "___ Forever" (album by The Ataris): 2 wds.
48 Delt. neighbor

Down

1 Follower's suffix
2 Familia member
3 In an abrupt manner
4 Thailand currency
5 Morning music
6 "T" size: abbr.
7 A little Scotch?
8 Whence eagle eyes may watch
11 Wyo. neighbor
12 Harness race gait
14 Wine grade
17 Gibbon of Thailand and Malaysia
18 It's like -like
20 Quick approval: abbr.
21 Of a calling: abbr.
23 Peniston of R&B
25 "The A-Team" actor: 2 wds.
27 Dirigible craft
28 "You Are ___ Alone"
29 One after due
31 First female House Speaker
33 Untouchable?
34 Those, to Carlos
35 Gray with a tinge of brown
36 Erie hrs.
39 Mon. follower
41 First name in horror films
42 Really bad coffee
43 It follows printemps
44 Wyatt's cohort

188

Across

1 Former film brand
5 Tons
11 Hostel, briefly
12 Jitters
13 What to give an attentive waiter: 2 wds.
14 Comic Judy ____, self-described as "The Aphrodite of the Accordion"
15 Black and yellow insect resembling a wasp
17 Crunchy ice cream flavor
18 Spanish ladies, briefly
22 Very attentive: 2 wds.
25 Direction away from WSW
26 Give a hand to
27 Hides
29 1,055 joules, initially
30 Go through hell, as when making a decision
32 "The Brady Bunch" actor Robbie
34 Junction point
35 Busy
39 List ender: 2 wds.
42 "For ____ be Queen o' the May" (Tennyson): 2 wds.
43 Railroad signal flares
44 Operates (a piece of equipment)
45 Matters of taste
46 Fencing sport

Down

1 Wife of Esau
2 Head for: 2 wds.
3 Flighty, superficial
4 Current units
5 "____ lunch": 2 wds.
6 Scott Turow's first book: 2 wds.
7 ____ Cazet, author of the "Minnie and Moo" children's books
8 Charley ____, author of "The Winning Hitter"
9 New York time zone, shortly
10 "Twenty Thousand Leagues Under the ____"
16 Rodeo rope
19 Plan of an area with shading and contour lines: 2 wds.
20 1998 movie with the voices of Jennifer Lopez and Woody Allen
21 Zaire's Mobutu ____ Seko
22 Shortened form, for short
23 French novelist Pierre
24 Measuring utensil
28 Apocalypse: 2 wds.
31 Rock variety
33 Early competitor to Skype
36 Four, in Germany
37 Magazine founder Eric
38 Shake off
39 Two in taffeta
40 River that flows through Mirandela, Portugal
41 Venom source

189

Across

1 Apiece
5 Hand movement in Hindu dancing
10 Aviation org.
11 Parting words: 2 wds.
12 Old Testament mountain
13 Actresses Pompeo and Travolta
14 ___ Tzu
15 Emulated Pinocchio
16 Innocents
18 Lance of justice
21 Trick-taking card game
23 Org. that regulates the use of radioactive materials
24 Est., once
25 New Deal inits.
27 Vietnamese lunar New Year festival
28 More, musically
29 Some potatoes
31 Military intelligence agency, initially
32 Online courtship
33 1980 NFL MVP Brian
35 Minor wound, to a tot
38 Candy company
40 ___ de plume (literary aliases)
41 Cold dessert
42 Cover
43 Grps.
44 "Tickle me" doll

Down

1 One in Westphalia
2 Banda ___ (Indonesian city)
3 Recreational motorboats: 2 wds.
4 Commotion: hyph.
5 Paar's bandleader José
6 Congo river
7 Inveterate, unchanging: hyph.
8 Former White House nickname
9 Hung. neighbor
11 Not needing to be demonstrated, obvious
17 An N.Y.C. subway
19 BlackBerry rival, once
20 Fall times: abbr.
21 Boston Bruins Line
22 "…will smile and take ___" (Steve Winwood lyric): 2 wds.
26 Palindromic female name
30 Directly: 2 wds.
32 Fencing equipment
34 Library ID
36 Muslim holy man
37 Idaho motto starter
38 Johannesburg country, initially
39 One of the Cyclades

190

Across

1 Gets together
6 ____ Alfonsín, former President of Argentina
10 Sailor
11 Danish opera composer, August (1859–1939)
12 Sodden, saturated
14 Ken and Lena
15 Control a motor vehicle
16 Peeled part
17 Lamented
18 Item in a photog.'s file
19 Native of Wichita
20 Framework supporting a roof
21 Equally hard to locate: 2 wds.
23 High-ranking royal: inits.
26 Pope who crowned Charlemagne emperor of the Romans: 2 wds.
27 Architect Mies van der ____
28 Artist Max
29 Gemstone that's also a girl's name
30 They assist senior military officers: hyph.
32 Jeanne ____, French heroine
33 Soy and pesto, e.g.
34 Wooden part of a bed
35 Renaissance Fair instruments

Down

1 South African maize plant
2 Consuming food
3 Change
4 Pitches
5 Kenan Thompson's show, initially
6 Slip
7 Heart condition with chest pain
8 Not level or smooth
9 Put aboard
10 Given under oath
13 Port in eastern Denmark
17 New Zealand timber tree
19 Asian snakes of the cobra family
20 Divide into three parts
21 Above the ground
22 "Any Which Way You Can" costar Locke
23 Bartender of The Drunken Clam on "Family Guy"
24 Moon, spoon, and June, e.g.
25 Lends a hand
26 Goes in front
27 Remove further material from (a movie)
29 Sweetheart
31 Networking letters

191

Across

1 Pituitary hormone, initially
5 Physical toil
10 Scope starter?
11 Herb with bitter minty leaves
12 Dress feature
13 Verdi opera first performed in 1844
14 "Step ___ pets" (popular palindrome): 2 wds.
15 ___ an der Thaya, Austrian town
16 Hug and kiss in Britain
18 Stride
22 Floating leaf on a pond: 2 wds.
25 Snack
26 Four-legged Andean
27 Like some seals
29 It starts in Mar.
30 Warm-up acts: hyph.
32 Freelancers' encs.
34 Part of T.A.E.
35 Professor's aides, for short
37 Hebrew month preceding Yom Kippur
40 Three-legged ornamental table
43 Good news on Wall Street
44 "Calendar Girl" singer
45 Tax IDs
46 Origins
47 To be, to Pierre

Down

1 Facetious "I see": 2 wds.
2 "The Big Lebowski" director
3 Convert from one language to another
4 Word spelled the same but with a different meaning to another
5 Vega's constellation
6 Easy as could be: 2 wds.
7 Jamboree grp.
8 Suffix with cart or drag
9 Upstate N.Y. college
11 Hägar the Horrible's honey
17 Kind of glass
19 Tightrope walker
20 Setting of William the Conqueror's castle
21 Airport guesses, for short
22 Attys.' degrees
23 Role for Ingrid
24 Do business
28 Hostile
31 Cushy school course: 2 wds.
33 March honoree, familiarly: 2 wds.
36 Approvals, slangily: hyph.
38 "Anchors Aweigh" readiness grp.
39 ___-humanité
40 Dungeons & Dragons game co., initially
41 Fair-hiring inits.
42 Toil and trouble

192

Across

1 Piece of door siding
5 Pope of the mid-100s: 2 wds.
10 Letter-shaped fastener: hyph.
12 Arctic dwellers
13 "___ Final Door" (Truman Capote story): 2 wds.
14 Answer to "Are not!": 2 wds.
15 Huge amount
16 Lose consciousness: 2 wds.
18 Most highfalutin'
20 General on some Chinese menus
21 Eagle's nest
22 With it
23 Endure
25 One of the brothers on "Malcolm in the Middle"
27 Delivery vehicle
28 The ileum opens into it
30 South African political party, initially
31 Simple wind instrument
34 Casual tops: hyph.
36 Discouraging words
37 Lend ___ (help): 2 wds.
38 Get the better of
40 Marie Antoinette, e.g.
41 Bristles
42 Guadalajara guy
43 Neighbor of Mo.

Down

1 "___ second!": 2 wds.
2 Dislike more than a little
3 Adirondacks, e.g.: 2 wds.
4 Club alternative: inits.
5 Bone-knitting aids: 2 wds.
6 Brand of pet food
7 Current: 4 wds.
8 Husbands and wives
9 Carbon-14, for one
11 Device used in some interviews: 2 wds.
17 "___ see it...": 2 wds.
19 Danger in Iraq, initially
23 Embodiments
24 Wailing spirit of Irish folklore
26 Continent with Germany and France: abbr.
29 Shock treatment, initially
32 "___ is an island": 2 wds.
33 Tree with quaking leaves
35 "___ Time at All" (Ronnie Milsap single): 2 wds.
39 Abbr. after a name

193

Across

1 Send forth
5 Excoriate
11 Astronaut Slayton
12 Fought
13 Scott Turow novel: 2 wds.
14 Fatty acid salt
15 Italian dictator
17 One-time MTV afternoon show
18 Dye-yielding plant
21 Order of whales and dolphins
25 ___ Lanka (country)
26 Cause of depreciation: 3 wds.
28 Part of TNT
29 Marksman
30 Word seg.
32 Time on end
33 Good ___, charitable sort
38 ___ up (enlivened)
40 Like a foreboding sky
41 Puckered textile finish
42 His and ___
43 "Nothing Compares 2 U" singer O'Connor
44 Hit the bottle

Down

1 Ancient Palestinian land
2 Restaurant handout
3 D.D.E. namesakes
4 Early communications satellite
5 Self-conceited: hyph.
6 City southwest of Bogotá
7 Field of play
8 Basement layout, at times: 2 wds.
9 Worked (up)
10 Dutch city
16 Killer whales
19 "Dies ___"
20 Dashing Dan was in its logo, initially
21 20ths of a ton: abbr.
22 Mysterious: var.
23 Dramatic downturn
24 "___ Into Ocean" (Joan Slonczewski novel): 2 wds.
27 This evening
31 End, as a subscription
34 Tableland
35 Palm product
36 Org. for seniors
37 AMEX or NASDAQ rival
38 Second letter addendum: abbr.
39 Lilly of pharmaceuticals

194

Across

1. 1974 Donald Sutherland/Elliott Gould movie
5. Within one's powers
11. Oak or hickory
12. 20 Questions category
13. Savvy Shields or Betty Cantrell, e.g.: 2 wds.
15. Something just waiting to go off: 2 wds.
16. Enjoying a series of successes: 3 wds.
20. "The Day the Earth Stood Still" star Reeves
24. Dapper
25. Cruel person
26. Jean or Deborah
27. Judges' seats
29. Charter
30. Record label of CeeLo Green
32. Washes and irons (clothes, etc.)
37. Absolute, out-and-out
40. Like guests at home: 2 wds.
41. Peloponnesian portico
42. San Diego State University's team name
43. Corn holder

Down

1. Bank acct. report
2. Toyota hybrids
3. Backwoods affirmative: 2 wds.
4. Mobutu ____ Seko of Zaire
5. Matt of "Jason Bourne"
6. "____, one vote" (old saying about election rights): 2 wds.
7. Mechanical device that operates by compression: hyph.
8. Weight to height ratio, initially
9. Fond du ____, Wisc.
10. Highest note in Guido's scale
14. "____ Ben Adhem" (Leigh Hunt poem)
17. "Cup ____" (1970s Don Williams song): 2 wds.
18. Written communications: abbr.
19. Orpheus' instrument
20. Japanese port city
21. Equal, in Marseilles
22. Gov. Carlson of Minnesota
23. V formation, often
28. Criticism, so to speak
29. Lana of "Smallville"
31. Destroys
33. Short run
34. Latin accusation: 2 wds.
35. Antique autos, initially
36. Pierre's state: abbr., 2 wds.
37. Country south of Can.
38. ____ Percé
39. Crossed one's path

195

Across

1 Ceiling
4 Sun Devils' campus letters
7 Adds up
9 Sixth word of the Gettysburg address
12 Flat takers
13 Modern: Ger.
14 Former unit of currency in Peru
15 Absentee
17 French coin, once
19 Greek promenade
20 Mattress problem
21 Building site requirement: 2 wds.
24 Kill as a political act
26 Word in a Captain and Tennille title
28 "The Wizard of Oz" studio
31 Duck, in Dortmund
32 Daunt
34 Largest U.S. state
37 Missouri's ally, once
38 President pro ___
39 Chipping tool: 2 wds.
41 Indy sponsor, initially
42 Glazed, salted biscuit
43 Neighbor of Isr.
44 Suffix with arch or art

Down

1 Muslim rulers: var.
2 Sun god of Ancient Egypt: hyph.
3 Token that mailing fees have been paid: 2 wds.
4 Actress Sue ___ Langdon
5 Editorial mark
6 Nation disbanded in 1991, briefly
8 "We'll be there: count ___!": 2 wds.
9 Curse or declare to be evil
10 Italian seaport
11 ___ the elbows (poor): 2 wds.
16 DOT, alternatively
18 Chastity's mother
22 Here, in Uruguay
23 Road grooves
25 Some Jaguars
26 Supermarket section
27 Available, as a room
29 Worker with an apron
30 In a humble manner
33 Egyptian Christian
35 ___ Bay, neighborhood in the borough of Manhattan
36 "___ From Within" (2014 horror movie): 2 wds.
40 Suffix with musket or market

196

Across

1. Fast-swimming shark
5. J.M. Barrie's buccaneer
9. "Let's go!," for short
10. Ramp
11. Like everyday talk
13. Person who is the center of attention
14. Nutty ____ fruitcake: 2 wds.
15. Start of Edison's signature
19. Female follower of Bacchus in Ancient Greece
22. Casual agreements
23. Semiconductor company based in Sunnyvale: inits.
24. Code word
25. Okinawa port
27. Assent: 2 wds.
30. Pt. of PGA
31. Suffix with scap or spat
32. Marlon Brando role: 2 wds.
37. Branch of medicine
39. Teen soap opera series: 2 wds.
40. Grandson of Jacob and Leah
41. "What time ____?": 2 wds.
42. Milldam

Down

1. 1300, in old Rome
2. Former name of Xiamen
3. City on the Rhein
4. Being borrowed: 2 wds.
5. Speak indistinctly
6. One of two roughly equal parts
7. Govt. watchdog
8. Sushi offering
10. Div. of a platoon
12. Northern Greece peak
16. "Boston Common" costar Burress
17. Bee's charge on "The Andy Griffith Show"
18. Some J.F.K. arrivals
19. "Every ____ King" (autobiography of Huey Long): 2 wds.
20. Latin trio center
21. Old English letters
26. Peace Nobelist Sakharov
27. Shrub that causes dermatitis
28. Oceans: 2 wds.
29. Garden flower
33. Violent public disturbance
34. Mozart's "____ kleine Nachtmusik"
35. Antioxidant-rich berry
36. Grp. that may be deployed
37. Volkswagen Golf model
38. Hesitant syllables

197

Across

1 Rajahs' wives
6 Metaphor
11 Brouhaha
12 Send, as for treatment
13 Cheney and Colfax, slangily
14 Atlanta Tennis Championship winner in 2013 and 2014
15 Volume for people visiting a foreign country: 2 wds.
17 Better for the experience
18 Is unable to
21 Anklebones
25 Major Calif. airport
26 "Regnava ___ silenzio" (aria from "Lucia di Lammermoor")
28 Summer hrs. in Wyoming
29 Galatea's love in Greek myth
31 In an obscene manner
33 Cannes award the ___ d'Or
35 Long grueling walk: 2 wds.
40 Miniseries opener?: 2 wds.
41 Ex of "the Donald"
42 Concert hall
43 Arid part of Israel
44 Amiens is its capital
45 "On the Record" host Van Susteren

Down

1 Reply in letters
2 Banda ___ (Sumatran city)
3 Not e'en once
4 Hocked: 2 wds.
5 Musical performance for a recording
6 Cheyenne or Cherokee
7 Turn (to)
8 "River ___ Return" Western directed by Otto Preminger: 2 wds.
9 Look-see
10 Flub
16 Costar of Bea, Betty, and Rue on "The Golden Girls"
18 Jefferson Davis's org.
19 Patriots' grp.
20 "There's ___ in 'team'": 2 wds.
22 Makers of Athlon, Duron and Sempron processors, initially
23 Cholesterol carrier, for short
24 Suffix with acid or fluid
27 Arctic vole
30 Saliva, spittle
32 Craftsman who makes cloth
34 "___ to Kill" (John Grisham novel): 2 wds.
35 "Hair" co-author James
36 Utah city
37 ___ Against the Machine (rock-rap group)
38 Tech. product reviews website
39 2002 US election law, briefly
40 Where to send letters, initially

198

Across

1 Author Marsh
6 Natives of Belgrade
11 John Hiatt song "When ___": 2 wds.
12 Town in Ontario
13 Words of wisdom
14 Not shy
15 Dictionary abbr.
17 Store that sells Swedish meatballs
18 PTA concern
20 Society newcomer: abbr.
22 Group of schools in one area, for short
23 Leonardo, Raphael, Michelangelo and Donatello, initially
25 English act of 1715
27 Newsstand
29 Conundrum
32 Meat from a pig
34 1300, to Nero
35 "No great shakes"
37 Ancient Egyptian priest
39 Spanish diminutive
40 Angler's need: 2 wds.
42 Get one's dander up
44 Cop, in Cornwall
46 High-IQ group
49 Ancient Roman magistrate
50 In need of a scratch
51 Let
52 Back

Down

1 Meteorological society, initially
2 H.S. proficiency exam
3 Irrational fear of spiders
4 "Othello" villain
5 Interminably: 2 wds.
6 Popular Indian snack food
7 Race met by the Time Traveller
8 Complex, detailed or confusing thing, slangily: 2 wds.
9 "… among the green ___": Burns
10 Cold vegetable dish
16 O.T. bk.
18 OTC offering
19 Year in Edward the Elder's reign
21 Marcel Marceau character
24 Nian Rebellion general
26 Dutch "uncle"
28 ___-One (rapper who guested on R.E.M.'s "Radio Song")
30 Shock treatment, initially
31 VCR maker
33 "Plop" preceder
35 "The Whistling Shadow" author Seeley
36 Cut into
38 Weddell, Rogers and others
41 Some RBI producers: abbr.
43 Riga native
45 "___-haw!"
47 NYSE purchase: abbr.
48 Author Rand

199

Across

1 Voodoo priestess
6 Bottom line
9 Change gradually
11 Biblical peak
12 Remove the pips from
13 Olympic weapon
14 George Lucas movie of 1977: 2 wds.
16 Feeling of unease
19 Book before Neh.
20 Bundle
21 "La Cage aux Folles" Tony winner George
24 Pianist's technical piece
26 Bay Area's San ___ Bridge
27 Fruity-smelling compound
28 Farm soil
29 "___ Had It" (1959 hit)
30 Five of hearts and two of spades, e.g.
31 Official who assists a referee
34 Frequently clicked image
35 "Bewitched" witch
39 Neither masc. nor fem.
40 Youth
41 Classified information?: abbr.
42 Running wild

Down

1 Kind of school: abbr.
2 Many a D.C. road
3 Calendar pages: abbr.
4 Childbirth: 2 wds.
5 British track star Steve
6 Threshing machine, e.g.
7 Over, in Germany
8 ___ Tavern ("The Simpsons" locale)
10 "When Your Child Drives You Crazy" author LeShan
11 One from Wellington, e.g.: 2 wds.
15 Diane of NPR
16 "Float like a butterfly, sting like ___": 2 wds.
17 Washington baseball team, briefly
18 Gummy, sticky
22 Digest digests
23 ___ de plume (literary aliases)
25 "You are" in Spain
30 Cretan port: var.
31 Italian director Wertmüller
32 Coffee variety
33 Fulfilled
36 Clandestine maritime org.
37 Rock's ___ Speedwagon
38 Museum pieces

200

Across

1 Long part of a flower
5 Cabbie's line: 2 wds.
10 1964 AL Rookie of the Year Tony
11 1985 movie starring Kate Nelligan
12 Orange-sized fruit
14 Wool coat owner
15 The Battle Born St.
16 Rapper Tone ___
17 Void, in Vichy
18 Epoch
19 Season of l'année
20 1974 CIA spoof movie
22 "___ easy to fall in love" (1977 lyric): 2 wds.
24 "Stay of Execution" author Stewart
26 Divided
28 L.B.J. in-law
32 Law, in Le Havre
33 Test for a college sr.
35 Abbr. between a first and last name, maybe
36 "Life of Pi" director Lee
37 Laughter syllable
38 Outfield surface
39 Modest, unassuming
42 Be a conservationist
43 Apply (for): 2 wds.
44 Perfume oil
45 Gum or plum

Down

1 Lose velocity: 2 wds.
2 Just at the right moment
3 First family member
4 ___ cum laude
5 Stop one's boat: 2 wds.
6 TV channel relaunched as "Versus" in 2006
7 Norman Vincent's family
8 Altogether: 2 wds.
9 Heiress, perhaps
10 Starts
13 Record-keeper
21 Maglie of baseball fame
23 It follows winter, briefly
25 Device that produces a small flame
26 Poem of 14 lines
27 Eat way more than you should: 2 wds.
29 Like some inspections: hyph.
30 Low-budget film: hyph.
31 Delaware senator (1973–2009)
32 Author ___ Ingalls Wilder
34 Blow up, like Vesuvius
40 Cubs' org.
41 Big ___, Calif.

201

Across

1 Atmosphere
5 Vice president under Jefferson
9 King ___ (Michael Jackson title): 2 wds.
11 Langston Hughes poem: 2 wds.
12 "___ Shoes" (2005 Cameron Diaz movie): 2 wds.
13 Relating to the organ of smell
15 Fall to pieces
16 D followers
18 Ethnic group of Vietnam
19 Part of NCAA: abbr.
20 Rock's ___ Fighters
21 A round of secs.
22 Corrode: 2 wds.
24 "Went," in Edinburgh
25 Roustabout
27 Abounding in shade trees
29 Actress Streep
31 Kung ___ shrimp
32 "___ in alpha": 2 wds.
33 Back-to-school mo.
35 Rep. or Dem., e.g.
36 Way: abbr.
37 Sheepish sound
38 Vodka order, familiarly
40 Couples
42 Campus orgs.
43 "Seascape" playwright
44 Flemish painter Jan van ___
45 Beginner

Down

1 "What Gets Into Us" author Crone
2 Distinguished: 2 wds.
3 Branch of medicine relating to the eye
4 Forest female
5 "Right on the nose!"
6 Hagen of "Reversal of Fortune"
7 Ira Levin novel: 2 wds.
8 Person who sets up equipment for rock concerts
10 Factory-made, as housing
14 Extend credit
17 Bygone company with yellow-roofed kiosks
23 Scotland's Firth of ___
24 Frankfurt's country: abbr.
26 Los Angeles suburb mentioned in Tom Petty's "Free Fallin'"
27 Actor Omar
28 Chinese philosopher: hyph.
30 President, say
32 Take ___ (chance it): 2 wds.
34 Leisurely walk
39 Resinous deposit
41 Last, for short

202

Across

1 Brynner who played Rameses in "The Ten Commandments"
4 Masefield play "The Tragedy of ___"
7 Some scale tones
10 Rio de___
11 Fiji to Samoa dir.
12 Letters after Kirsten Gillibrand's name
13 Neat and tidy
16 Astronomer Tycho
17 Cartoon Mr.
20 Raggedy-edged
24 Sitcom based in Harlem, "___ Andy": 2 wds.
25 Hall of Famer Sandberg et al.
26 Nashville to St. Louis dir.
27 Timely
28 Composer Alexander
31 Indian side dish
33 "… a poem lovely as ___" (Kilmer): 2 wds.
34 Pound and Klein
35 ___ Picchu
37 Brief periods of study
43 One ___ million: 2 wds.
44 Spike TV, once
45 Hoppy pub quaff, shortly
46 ___-de-sac (blind alley)
47 Part: abbr.
48 W.W. II craft letters

Down

1 "___ bet your bottom dollar"
2 Pedestal display
3 Site: abbr.
4 Synapse neighbor
5 Stage org.
6 Infernal
7 He served four terms, initially
8 "Wheel of Fortune" request: 2 wds.
9 Cartoonist Hoff
14 Deals on Wall Street, initially
15 Spooky: var.
17 Style of Japanese comics
18 Reply to a playground insult: 2 wds.
19 One of the Champions
21 Station sign: 2 wds.
22 Dividing membranes
23 Part of a Spanish 101 conjugation
29 Half in front?
30 Shows stimulation
31 Moved the picture to a different room, e.g.
32 Cote d'___
36 Construction site sight
37 Boom box abbr.
38 Shiba ___, Japanese breed of dog
39 Ending with exter or inter
40 Part of R.S.V.P.
41 Pre-album collectibles, for short
42 Used the sofa

203

Across

1 "___ in Toyland"
6 Charge
10 Not a child
11 OPEC V.I.P.: var.
13 Large bird with yellow-tipped head feathers: 2 wds.
15 Miracle-___
16 Fine and dandy: hyph.
17 Pinch
18 Entail
20 Chemical ending
21 Those things, in Tijuana
22 All at the same time: 2 wds.
24 Broom ___ (comics witch)
26 Label again, as a computer file
29 Letters for distributing news to Web users
33 Legal org.
34 Kind of case
36 N. ___ (Pyongyang's country): abbr.
37 Sports car of old, initially
38 Divested
39 Loud and shrill: hyph.
42 Ancient colonnades
43 Monte Cristo, par exemple
44 Like the beginning of triathlons
45 Some needles, briefly

Down

1 Plastic "zip-loc" container
2 Bejewels
3 Manufacturer of watches
4 "Ragtime" author's monogram
5 Boost
6 Saturday and Sunday
7 Doctors' org.
8 Of a year in a reign
9 Presidential middle name
12 Medieval musical instrument
14 Short romantic book
19 Labor Dept. div.
23 Vamp Theda
25 Early 20th-century poetry movement
26 Garden tools
27 W.W. II torpedo ships: hyph.
28 Intolerant
30 Be parsimonious
31 "Way of the gods," literally
32 Marsh plants
35 Tallow-soaked cloth on a pole, used for lighting
40 Gave de ___, French river
41 Demure

204

Across

1 Ger. neighbor
4 Annuls
9 Chemical endings
11 Female follower of Bacchus in Ancient Greece
12 "Bring Me Your Love" singers ___-Lite
13 "Non-Stop" author Brian
14 A teacher administers it: 2 wds.
16 1984–88 skating gold medalist Katarina
17 Potent or penitent ending
20 They have pull
23 Multigenerational story
24 Up ___ (cornered): 2 wds.
25 Baseball's Babe and others
26 Kind of lighting
27 ___ corpus (protection against illegal imprisonment)
28 It replaced CQD
29 Frat party containers
30 Sagittarius and Leo, e.g.: 2 wds.
35 Elizabeth George ___, "Calico Captive" author
37 Little fight
38 Shearer and Talmadge
39 Cassette contents
40 Football Hall-of-Famer Merlin
41 Patsy

Down

1 President's confidante
2 French ones
3 Gets an eyeful of
4 Hotel employee
5 Brit. dictionaries
6 Get going
7 Perp prosecutors, shortly
8 Old activist org.
10 Ocean plant
11 Damon and LeBlanc
15 "Egad!"
18 Turkish honorific
19 Bonny one
20 Loud hits
21 "Me as well": 2 wds.
22 Ratfinks
23 Support oneself
25 Riches preceder, sometimes
27 Start of a toast
29 The K in DKNY
31 Gentle
32 Acad. values
33 Sonoma neighbor
34 Choreography move
35 Hostess's ___ Balls
36 D.C. type

205

Across

1 Hang ominously on the horizon

5 Faculty

10 ____-European

11 Get mad, casually: 2 wds.

12 "____ Kampf"

13 Vehicle for carrying liquid

14 Start suddenly (as a fight): 2 wds.

16 1957 Physics Nobelist Tsung-____ Lee

17 Mideast capital: var.

21 Thug

25 It's not quite lge.

26 Prepare a plane for winter takeoff: hyph.

27 More than fervent

29 Cape ____

30 Backscratch, politically

32 Discipline with poses

34 Seize

35 Sausage topped by stew: 2 wds.

40 Corporate asset replacement calculation: 2 wds.

43 Member of the arum family

44 Not learned after birth

45 Mr. 'iggins

46 Mother-of-pearl

47 Civil rights figure Parks

Down

1 Arm or leg

2 Doozy

3 Cartoon dog

4 Believer in the philosopy of Leibniz

5 Linebacker Junior

6 Campsite sights

7 "Raiders of the Lost ____"

8 Honorarium

9 HST predecessor

11 Barfly's perch

15 Superman's name on Krypton: hyph.

18 Early pulpit

19 "Sweet Caroline" singer Diamond

20 Extra: abbr.

21 Down Under greeting

22 Wine: prefix

23 Wrestlers' location

24 Wild sheep of Asia

28 Judge

31 Bagel choice

33 Movie star

36 Engage

37 "Another World" actress Linda

38 "The Pearl of ____ Island" (Harriet Beecher Stowe novel)

39 "The Clothed Maja" painter

40 Dynasty during which much of the Great Wall of China was built

41 Biology class, initially

42 2 letters on a phone?

206

Across

1 Hit
5 Obsessed with, slangily
11 Wild ox of Sulawesi
12 Old-style form of transport
13 Lang. of Israel
14 Names of books
15 Stockholm resident
17 Suffix denoting a sugar
18 Spread, as lotion: 2 wds.
20 Day the Last Supper took place: abbr.
23 Instrument used in an attack
25 Formal requirement
26 Art, to Tacitus
27 Hunting rights org.
29 Schubert's "The ___-King"
30 "Danny Boy" actor Stephen
31 New York's ___ Stadium
33 Lunchbox fave
34 Onetime president of Argentina
35 Road reversal, familiarly
37 "Who's Who" group
40 Abduct
43 Flush
44 John Irving hero: inits., 2 wds.
45 Mobutu ___ Seko of Zaire
46 Surgical holders
47 High fliers, initially

Down

1 Comments heard often by Bob Cratchit
2 De novo
3 Not wasted at all: 4 wds.
4 Desperate: 2 wds.
5 On a roll
6 Thessalian king
7 Statistician's figs.
8 Thin steel blades used by artists: 2 wds.
9 "___ on my bed my limbs I lay" (Coleridge)
10 "The shakes," initially
16 Black, to Blake

19 Deli specification: 2 wds.
21 Put in a position
22 River to the Ubangi
23 Distort
24 Jewish eve
28 Bern's river
32 Equally: 2 wds.
34 Rush drummer Neil
36 Put ___ offer: 2 wds.
38 Reason to cram
39 Chemical endings
40 Chess pieces that make L-shaped moves: abbr.
41 Ending for classic or violin
42 Second letter addendum, initially

207

Across

1 Overripe fruit problem
5 Prefix with logical
10 When repeated twice, a "Seinfeld" catchphrase
11 Seventh planet from the Sun
13 Think out (a plan) beforehand
15 Put on television
16 European sports car, briefly
17 Jack's "On the Road" alter ego
18 Large number
21 Suffix with hip or quip
23 Bill of PBS
24 Jewish community orgs.
26 Papal ambassador to a foreign court
29 Over yonder, to a whaler
33 City on the Susquehanna
35 Harem room
36 Comb. form denoting flow
37 Capital on the Red River
39 Legendary Mississippi bluesman: 2 wds.
42 Angioplasty target
43 "Understood": 2 wds.
44 Headless and limbless sculpture
45 Dino flyer's prefix

Down

1 Circumvent
2 Rope used for tethering
3 1926 Channel swimmer
4 Not wild
5 Afrique du ___
6 "... ___ quit!": 2 wds.
7 Substance that accelerates a chemical reaction
8 Caught ___ (being dishonest): 3 wds.
9 Aiming to get: 2 wds.
12 Hannity and Penn
14 Harvard deg.
19 Dog days declaration: 2 wds.
20 Mauna ___
22 1994 Grammy co-winner for "Talking Timbuktu": 2 wds.
25 Not max.
26 "Goodbye, ___ Jean" (movie starring Misty Rowe)
27 O.K.
28 Have no choice in the matter: 2 wds.
30 "I am telling you the truth"
31 "Call of the Flesh" costar Renée
32 Ending for curtain
34 "Now I get it!"
38 Eagerly expectant
40 Soph. and jr.
41 Neb. neighbor

208

Across

1 Tepee
7 Petits ____ (little peas)
11 Former Miami Marlins outfielder Suzuki
12 Tachometer readings, initially
13 Do something perfectly, so to speak: 2 wds.
14 Platte River tribe
15 Mideast carrier: 2 wds.
16 Magazine magnate, familiarly
18 Town in Tennessee
21 Greek portico
25 Encore performances
27 Successor
29 1887 Verdi opera
30 Irish isles
31 Verdi aria sung by Renato: 2 wds.
32 Diarist Anaïs
33 Hollywood fail
37 Gumbo pod
40 Sister of Calliope
42 Navy commando
43 Type of pasta
44 Like some airports: abbr.
45 Start of a pirate's chant: 3 wds.

Down

1 ____ list
2 Suffix with poet or paradox
3 Karmann-____ (sports car)
4 Conscious choice and decision
5 Vince's agent, on "Entourage"
6 Homeland: 2 wds.
7 As a matter of politeness: 2 wds.
8 Make a decision
9 "What I think," online
10 Draft org.
17 Robert ____: 2 wds.
19 Sorrowful sort
20 Karenina of literature
21 Theater sign, initially
22 Head, to Henri
23 Letters above 0
24 Generally: 3 wds.
26 Amtrak stop: abbr.
28 Prefix meaning "height"
33 Large container for water
34 Gallimaufry
35 Ho Chi ____ City (former name for Saigon)
36 "See Dad Run" star Scott
37 Short-lived government agency formed in 2001, initially
38 Grasp
39 Snitch
41 Boo or yoo follower

209

Across

1 Missile fired from a mobile launcher

5 Freelancers' encs.

10 Kind of society

12 City on the Yangtze

13 Jack of "The Great Dictator"

14 Prince Valiant's princess

15 Furniture with compartments for pens and paper: 2 wds.

17 CPO's group

18 Schnauzer or Rottweiler

19 Never, in Berlin

20 Prefix with cab

22 Canadian pop duo ___ and Sara

24 Sort

26 Hawaiian porch

28 Initial response team, initially

32 SPAR's counterpart

33 Toshiba competitor, initially

35 "Just as I thought!"

36 "The Adventures of ___ Finn," Mark Twain novel

39 ___-Detoo, 2003 Robot Hall of Fame inductee

40 Water under the "ponte"

41 160 ounces: abbr., 2 wds.

42 "King Cotton" composer

43 Deserted

44 Belgium neighbor: abbr.

Down

1 Arrive for an appointment: 2 wds.

2 Rough

3 Mean, inconsiderate

4 "Go ahead!": 2 wds.

5 Bravado

6 Old, in Aberdeen

7 TV's "Queen of the Jungle"

8 Dines at home: 2 wds.

9 Chinese zodiac creature

11 Senator Harry or actor Tim

16 Mean: 2 wds.

21 Engine part: abbr.

23 A thousand dollars, slangily

25 Ring locale

26 Aromatic shrub related to the bay

27 Bank info: abbr., 2 wds.

29 Brand name

30 Shove

31 Doctor's request: 2 wds.

32 "___ Fool Believes" (1979 #1 hit): 2 wds.

34 Desert garments

37 City on the Rhein

38 Subj. for an M.B.A.

210

Across

1 Cape ____ (westernmost point of mainland Europe)
5 Convention label: 2 wds.
10 Those, in Guadalajara
11 To a great extent
12 Molded frame round a door
14 Water____ (flosser)
15 Around
16 Young fish prepared for cooking
18 Violinist Leopold
22 "The Flowering Peach" playwright
24 Aid group, often: initials
25 Play hard to get
27 Bridge support
29 Word before room or center: abbr.
30 They're calling, in "Danny Boy"
32 Radio talk show host Diane
34 Native range horse
37 French God
39 Solothurn's river
40 Spicy vegetable relish
43 Assumed name user, briefly
44 "Something ____ Again" Chris DeBurgh
45 "The Nightmare Room" author R. L. ____
46 Swedish floor coverings

Down

1 Brings in
2 "Hamlet" fop
3 Nocturnal insect, a domestic pest
4 Flue residue
5 Brightness measure: 2 wds.
6 ____ mater (brain membrane)
7 It may be fit for a queen
8 Off-road goer, briefly
9 Thou
13 Completely committed: 2 wds.
17 Funny
19 To a remarkable degree
20 Latin abbrs.
21 Icelandic band Sigur ____
23 State capital of Minnesota: 2 wds.
25 "To ____ is human…"
26 Churchill's sign
28 Actor Fernando of "The French Connection"
31 Cooling-off period: 2 wds.
33 1701, to Cicero
35 Mexican restaurant condiment
36 Northern Indians
38 Image on a desktop
40 Certain detectives, initially
41 QB's misfire
42 Ending for cloth or bombard

211

Across

1 Menlo Park middle name
5 Symbol of authority
10 Subatomic particle
11 ___ a kitten: 2 wds.
12 Toyota hybrid models
13 Family singers' surname
14 Milk: prefix
15 Johannesburg country, initially
16 Land of the leprechauns
18 Hair removal brand
22 Bed skirt
25 Queens airport, initially
26 "When Will ___ Loved" (Everly Brothers hit of 1960): 2 wds.
27 Classic 1950 film noir movie remade in 1988: inits.
28 Hold out one's paw
29 Change the position of words, letters, etc.: abbr.
30 Remove (a need for)
32 "The law is ___..." (Dickens): 2 wds.
34 Vegetable fuel
35 Yellowfin, on Hawaiian menus
37 Some scans, initially
40 Mistake that leads to confusion
43 Coloring
44 Digit
45 Bone in comb. form
46 Lester ___, Earl Scruggs's partner
47 Medical suffix

Down

1 Kitchen item: abbr.
2 Old Italian coin
3 Not able to speak
4 "Peer Gynt" dancer
5 Kiss, slangily
6 One's true self in Hinduism
7 "Gloria in excelsis ___"
8 Started, poetically
9 Group of schools in one area, for short
11 Snowman's accessory, at times: 2 wds.
17 Prefix with European
19 Bird in "The Rime of the Ancient Mariner"
20 "By the Time ___ to Phoenix": 2 wds.
21 Extreme anger
22 IRS program, initially
23 "East of Eden" siren
24 Icicle spot
31 "Likewise!": 3 wds.
33 Parisian toast
36 Offended
38 Former unit of currency in Peru
39 Notices
40 Very loud, to a composer
41 Sunflower product
42 Sch. in Athens or its bulldog mascot

212

Across

1 Bambi's aunt
4 Action on Wall St.
7 Cabinet dept.
10 Research facility: abbr.
11 Where to find It.
12 Alternative rock genre
13 In any place that, old-style
16 Tribute to a deceased person
17 Feathered missile
18 Spread
19 Et ___ (and other men)
20 Alaskan breed of dog
23 Period of the past
26 IBM competitor
27 Federal warning system activated by FEMA
28 Live in a dull, inactive, unchallenging way
31 Sent some cybernotes, briefly
32 "If ___ Myself" (OneRepublic song): 2 wds.
36 Short ___ (Monopoly property)
37 Prepared to fight: 2 wds.
38 Surrender of a person from one country to another
40 "Tell ___ Mama" (2009 Norah Jones song)
41 Little bit, in French
42 Barely make, with "out"
43 Ice cream maker Joseph
44 School of thought
45 Bandleader Brown

Down

1 Cary of "The Art of More"
2 Micah's follower
3 White poplar
4 Oscar winner for "Shampoo": 2 wds.
5 Industrious
6 Guadalajara gold
7 Reduce the worth of
8 Retired female college professor
9 The Roaring ___ (strong westerly winds)
14 Be itinerant
15 Red-coated cheese
21 Grazing expanse
22 Radioactive metallic element
23 Stare superstitiously thought to cause harm: 2 wds.
24 Made a new version in the sound studio
25 Go-between's business
29 "Someone Like You" singer Linda
30 Gulf of Aqaba resort: var.
33 Cantilevered window
34 Puff on a cigar
35 Old laborers
37 Day to remember
39 Energy trade organization, initially

213

Across

1. 1981 Stephen King thriller
5. Kudrow and Bonet
10. "___ Ben Adhem" (Leigh Hunt poem)
11. "Johnny B. ___"
12. New England dish: 2 wds.
15. "Seascape" playwright
16. Ontario natives
17. Suffix with social
18. Inflection of the voice
21. Lat., Rus., and Ukr., once
23. ___ case scenario
24. Saw
26. Protective covering
28. Baseball stats
32. Protective care or guardianship
34. Command level: abbr.
35. Jug handle, in archeology
36. It's a gas
38. The "___" (epic in Hindu literature)
41. ___ K., "16 Tons of Monkeys" singer
42. Cook's cooker
43. Military camp (Fr.)
44. Watered-down

Down

1. French coastal town
2. Horseshoe-shaped fasteners: hyph.
3. Wholesaler
4. Any of three English rivers
5. Clothing label, briefly
6. Ending for super or inter
7. He performs magic
8. Prettifies
9. Pick
13. Shamus
14. Area away from the wind
19. Bestow upon
20. Tail tirelessly
22. California's ___ winds: 2 wds.
25. ___ gratias
26. Crescent-shaped
27. Doesn't work anymore, informally: 2 wds.
29. Act appropriately
30. Summer cooler: 2 wds.
31. Got smaller
32. Video maker, for short
33. Assent word
37. Believe, old-style
39. Marcel Marceau character
40. Ground breaker

214

Across

1 Cry and cry
4 Surgeon's knife
11 N.Y.C. airport
12 Christopher Robin's father: inits., 2 wds.
13 Defect in the eye
15 ___'Pea (Popeye's charge)
16 Delighted sound
17 Prefix with sphere
19 Win back, as trust
22 Specter
24 Monopoly railroad: 3 wds.
25 Alphabet intro
29 Surround
31 Extent of a surface: 2 wds.
34 A little of this and a little of that
35 Eggy Christmas drink
36 ___ Pet (novelty item)
38 Protector on the racetrack: 2 wds.
43 Speaker
44 Where cops work, initially
45 "Sorry ___ Be the Hardest Word" (Elton John song): 2 wds.
46 Word in many Brazilian city names

Down

1 Hearst kidnap grp.
2 Old-school tough guys in rap songs, initially
3 Certain baseball player
4 Wise guy
5 Picture taker
6 Physicians' org.
7 Plastered
8 Groove or fold
9 David of CNN
10 Lousy car, slangily
14 "___ what would happen if...": 2 wds.
17 Police alert, for short
18 "___ Carter" (Lil Wayne album)
20 Morales who played Richie Valens' half-brother
21 Involve in difficulties, conflict or intrigue
23 Editorial concern
26 Aids in joining: hyph.
27 551, to Cicero
28 Want ad. initials
30 Flat capsule enclosing a dose of medicine
31 Certain ear bone
32 Opposite of sur
33 Tiny type size
37 Deli offering
39 Two qtrs.
40 Time-card abbr.
41 Voting integrity org.
42 General on a Chinese menu

215

Across

1. China's Zhou ____
6. Longtime Syrian president
11. Specialized investment orgs.
12. English homework list, for short
13. On the surface
15. Chemical compound suffix
16. Prefix with sac
17. Savings acct. accrual
19. Minnesota's St. ____ College
23. Orange munchies
27. "How was ____ know?": 2 wds.
28. Edward, Bill and Norman
29. Question asked twice in Matthew Chapter 26: 3 wds.
31. Final: abbr.
32. Dance similar to the foxtrot
34. Spill the beans
36. Unit of radio frequency: abbr.
37. Road reversal, familiarly
39. Friends in France
43. In consequence
47. Dallas suburb
48. Against a thing, legally: 2 wds.
49. "Loot" playwright Joe
50. High homes

Down

1. Scottish Gaelic
2. Nine in Berlin
3. Certain surgery, for short
4. Artist's workroom
5. Neighbor of Leb.
6. Old Hebrew month
7. Prefix with linguistics
8. ____-fi (literary genre)
9. Battery type, initially
10. Two-bagger: abbr.
14. Picture, commercially
18. Fed. accident investigators
20. 53, to Caesar
21. Memo abbr.
22. Word before gras
23. Association
24. Alternative to high water
25. "I'm so hungry, I could ____ horse!": 2 wds.
26. Long, deep breath
30. Journey hit of 1986
33. ____ out a living (scraped by)
35. Good, in Genoa
38. It gets wrinkles out of clothes
40. Supervisors, briefly
41. "____ a Song Go Out of My Heart" (Duke Ellington hit): 2 wds.
42. Mozart's No. 1 through No. 41, briefly
43. V-mail address, for short
44. Stain removal product, initially
45. Clawer
46. "Whom have ____ heaven but you?" Psalms 73:25: 2 wds.

216

Across

1 Start with boy or girl

5 "Glengarry Glen Ross" star

11 T.A.'s boss

12 "Same here!": 3 wds.

13 Bull: prefix

14 Hanson hit

15 Doodler's aid: 2 wds.

17 Winnie-the-Pooh's creator

18 Go back on a deal

21 "Schindler's ___"

25 It may finish second

26 Stan who created Spider-Man

27 "Need You Tonight" band

29 Mayim who played TV's "Blossom"

32 Continental currency

34 Eloquent

39 Soon: 3 wds.

40 Verb for Tweety

41 Choir section

42 Czech river that is an Elbe tributary

43 Mystery-crime movie of 2000, starring Emily Watson

44 Doesn't fold

Down

1 Many N.Y.C. homes

2 Ford Explorer Sport ___

3 Go on the road

4 Design for a mountain cabin: hyph.

5 Inflamed spot on the skin

6 Jingle creator

7 Drive

8 "Could ___ Magic" (Barry Manilow song): 2 wds.

9 Koh-i- ___ (famed diamond)

10 Alley-___

16 Animal that provides bacon

18 Style of music, a fusion of Arabic and Western elements

19 South extension

20 Greek goddess of night

22 Harm

23 Tre + tre

24 William Shatner title drug

28 Thresher shark: 2 wds.

29 Window-shop

30 Ending for excels or exter

31 The way things currently stand: 3 wds.

33 Holding areas for babies-to-be

34 Dilly

35 Indian princess

36 Four six-packs

37 Bide-___, golf course founded by Chandler Harper in Portsmouth, VA: hyph.

38 Written communications: abbr.

39 Old inits. in tele-communications

217

Across

1 Club music genre
7 Senior citizen, to a Brit.
10 Naismith Memorial Basketball Hall-of-Famer John
11 Schoolyard comeback: 2 wds.
12 Grassy plains of Argentina
13 "Push th' Little Daisies" band
14 Bearing
16 Lord's mate
19 Military intelligence agency, initially
20 Plant also known as bugleweed
22 Make laws
26 ___ Circus (where St. Peter was crucified)
27 Set up: abbr.
28 "The Baron in the Trees" author Calvino
29 Saliva, phlegm and mucus, e.g.
30 Egypt and Syria, from 1958 to 1961: inits.
32 Elbe feeder
33 Perfectionist
37 Informer, informally
38 Said "ne'er," e.g.
42 Gambit
43 County in northwestern California
44 ___ point
45 Register: 2 wds.

Down

1 Start to fall
2 Spanish pronoun
3 Engine part
4 Carefree and casual
5 Home of four ACC teams: abbr., 2 wds.
6 Bone: prefix
7 Augury
8 "Hey, wait ___!": 2 wds.
9 Corn ___
11 Arousing a feeling of wonder: hyph.
15 Dirks of yore
16 It's heaven, in Hawaii
17 "I'm leaving on ___ plane...": 2 wds.
18 ___ mater (brain membrane)
21 Drenched
23 "Look ___" (Vince Gill hit of 1991): 2 wds.
24 "The Monuments Men" costar Blanchett
25 Skier's transport: hyph.
31 Like non-oyster months: hyph.
33 Bay Area law enforcement org.
34 One of a Scrabble set's 100
35 "___ Pronounce You Chuck and Larry" (2007 movie): 2 wds.
36 Race met by the Time Traveller
39 Draper of "Mad Men"
40 Easily tamed bird
41 Touch lightly on the water

218

Across

1 Hebrew letter
6 Long cut
10 One-eighty: hyph.
11 False name
13 Swiss city
14 Greek letter after rho
15 Pueblo hrs.
16 Virgin Islands clock setting: inits.
18 Pen point
19 "Lord, is ___?": Matthew: 2 wds.
20 Suffix with cash
21 Ore suffix
22 Memphis's st.
24 Hold opposing views
26 Japanese grill
28 One who takes spoils
30 Electricity letters: hyph.
33 Canadian public filmmaking organization letters
34 Recording device, briefly
36 Ireland's ___ Lingus
37 "Weird Al" Yankovic movie
38 Mex. neighbor
39 Tampa to Jacksonville dir.
40 Fools, slangily
42 "___ this time" ("maybe later"): 2 wds.
44 Eliminate
45 Nita of old film
46 Novelist Bagnold
47 Indo-European

Down

1 Give in
2 "___ of Honey" (Shelagh Delaney play): 2 wds.
3 "Rain Man" star: 2 wds.
4 Domain of Otto I, initially
5 China's Zhou ___
6 Relating to the stomach
7 Boxing biopic
8 To an important degree
9 Descendant of Noah's son
12 Cavalryman
17 "When You Are Engulfed in Flames" humorist David
23 Small carp
25 Loan overseer, initially
27 Filled with bewilderment
28 "To a ___" poem by Robert Burns
29 Ready to be engaged: 2 wds.
31 "You're welcome," in Brazil: 2 wds.
32 Blockhead
35 Tropical plant with straplike leaves
41 Pressure meas.
43 Crew tool

219

Across

1 Five Pillars religion
6 Cry of frustration
11 Fictional town that was home to Charley Weaver, briefly: 2 wds.
12 Religious song
13 Pond growth
14 Monteverdi opera
15 Gather together
17 Former Disney CEO
18 Ending for switch
20 Profoundly
24 Sch. in Detroit
25 Extra pds. of tied games
26 Bear, in Spain
27 Spicy condiment
29 Prefix with metric or phone
30 Grand Prix site: 2 wds.
32 Amusement or sport
36 Alpine state of western Austria
37 Coffee shop order
38 Large lemur of Madagascar
39 Sects
40 Singer Rimes
41 They can be licked

Down

1 Innovative Apple computer
2 Normandy town nearly destroyed in 1944: 2 wds.
3 Woody
4 Slowly, in musical tempo
5 Fort ___, Fla.
6 Orbital extremes
7 Equally hard to locate: 2 wds.
8 Vessel made of wooden planks
9 Hilarity
10 Med. plan
16 Apocalypse: 2 wds.
18 "Yuck!"
19 Cape Town country, initially
21 Flavored ice on a stick
22 Mil. transport
23 "Hoo" preceder
25 City southwest of Cleveland, Ohio
28 ___ A&M, Mississippi college
29 Doing shows, as a band: 2 wds.
31 Auto repair chain, initially
32 Sandberg of baseball
33 "Ring Cycle" goddess
34 "___ be in England" (Browning): 2 wds.
35 River of northwestern British Columbia
36 Up to, for short

220

Across

1. "May the ___ be with you" ("Star Wars")
6. It may be cracked
11. Windows font
12. Teacher in a temple
13. Chief port of Argentina: 2 wds.
15. Antibiotic target, in short
16. ___ Mae Brown, character in the movie "Ghost"
17. Ocean west of Portugal: abbr.
19. Light blue shade
21. Killer and bodysnatcher Ed
23. After the current act: 2 wds.
27. Needless
29. Causes to go into a rage
30. Cardinal O'Connor's successor
31. New years in Vietnam
33. Soapmaker's ingredient
34. Yellowfin tuna
37. 1980s attorney general
39. Space into which an area is subdivided
43. Make ___-ditch effort: 2 wds.
44. 2003 OutKast chart-topper: 2 wds.
45. Cup in Cannes
46. Clean the floor

Down

1. Awesome
2. Sch. in Tulsa, Oklahoma
3. Dry white wine
4. Doesn't have what it takes
5. Picturesque Ontario gorge town
6. Reviews of an event: hyph.
7. Japanese affirmative
8. Saragossa's river
9. Tucked in
10. "___ great pity" ("Alas"): 2 wds.
14. Take forcible possession of, confiscate
17. Lago contents
18. Ky. neighbor
20. "As I Lay Dying" father
22. Former hair removal product
24. Acuity: 2 wds.
25. CAT scan ancestor: hyph.
26. "Cagney & Lacey" actress Daly
28. Burn, at the end
32. Actor Green and author Godin
34. "___ may look on a king": 2 wds.
35. Granada greeting
36. "___ hungry as a horse": 2 wds.
38. Old World duck
40. Ltr. addenda
41. Bill of kidvid fame
42. Pub fixture

221

Across

1 Churchill Downs event
6 "Für ____" (Beethoven work)
11 Organic compounds
12 Coolers of drinks
13 Grant made to a student
15 Lower corner of a sail
16 Female hare
17 Sock grouping
19 Some flashlight batteries
22 Strip that divides a highway
25 Old Fords, sometimes
26 One who commits an illegal act
28 "The Morning Watch" author
29 "Dallas" family
30 Happy ____ lark: 2 wds.
31 ____ Gailey of "Miracle on 34th Street"
32 1,051, to Nero
33 Resort town northwest of Los Angeles
37 Heedful of potential consequences
41 Shady sort
42 Handle: 2 wds.
43 "The Party's Over" composer Jule
44 Infamous energy company

Down

1 Fam. tree member
2 Bottom-of-letter abbr.
3 Architect Mies van der ____
4 Tube through which darts can be shot by puffing
5 Designer monogram under the Gucci label
6 It may get you to first base
7 Get checkmated
8 Self-identification in Stuttgart
9 Aspen runner
10 Creepy claim, initially
14 Temporarily: 2 wds.
18 Tooth-doctors' org.
19 Abbr. before a name on an envelope
20 "Me and You and ____ Named Boo" (Lobo song): 2 wds.
21 Pol. divisions prior to 1991
22 Film rating org.
23 Instrument used to examine the brain, initially
24 "Shades of Blue" actress de Matteo
25 Exposed: 2 wds.
27 "Concord Hymn" writer's monogram
31 Stroke of luck
32 Shoe seller Thom
34 Hoot
35 Part of a Spanish play
36 "Let's Get ____" (Marvin Gaye song): 2 wds.
37 Markup language descriptor, initially
38 Bank acct. entry
39 "Curious George" author
40 Carlsbad to San Diego dir.

222

Across

1 Actor Eric
5 Sound's partner
9 Stone fruit
11 Blue cartoon figure
13 Month for fools?
14 Skin woe
15 "May I help you?"
16 Publishing execs.
18 CPR expert
19 Arctic transport
21 Musical dir.
22 Restore control, say
25 Retreats
27 Hunt in Hollywood
28 Very inexpensive: 2 wds.
30 Old English letter
31 Crazy Horse, for one
34 Like a fox
35 Prefix with footprint
36 ____ Al Khaimah (one of the United Arab Emirates)
37 Against the clock
39 "____ well": 2 wds.
41 Hostile force
42 "A Confederacy of Dunces" author
43 Mil. aides
44 What the suspicious may smell: 2 wds.

Down

1 Times to give gifts, briefly
2 Adrien ____ skin care products
3 Verses for children: 2 wds.
4 Set of functions in computing, initially
5 Fast jets, for short
6 Bordeaux beau
7 Mortuary: 2 wds.
8 Recluse
10 Mournful
12 Make stout
17 Lion's house
20 Lifter's shoulder muscle, briefly
23 Nanny, for one: 2 wds.
24 Pond duck
25 Holiday song title starter
26 Walking obliquely, in a timid way
29 Ad ____ committee
32 "The Moor's Account" author Lalami
33 It's a plus
35 Brand that has Dibs
38 Sensitive and melodramatic, in slang
40 Mauna ____, Hawaii

223

Across

1 Northern Greece peak
5 Stuck down with glue
11 Flower: Sp.
12 Be plentiful
13 It's softer than gypsum
14 Lets go
15 "Alas!": 2 wds.
17 Wigwam
19 Closing bars
22 Business
23 Newly-weaned pig
25 He played in 657 regular NHL games
26 Lennon's Yoko
27 Actress Annie
30 "No mas!" boxer
32 Contact the host, in letters
33 China's Zhou ___
34 Not so fast
36 "You're in for ___!": 2 wds.
39 ___ and aahs
42 Chinese philosopher: hyph.
43 Corp. money execs
44 "Memoirs of a ___"
45 "Finger Lickin' Good" restaurants, initially

Down

1 Frequently, to Poe
2 Patty Hearst's captors, initially
3 Monologues, e.g.: 2 wds.
4 Like some eyebrows
5 Severe blow
6 Horseshoe-shaped fasteners: hyph.
7 Do-re-mi
8 Juilliard subj.
9 Denver to Detroit dir.
10 Drillmaster, initially?
16 Like a bairn
17 Corvette design detail: hyph.
18 Trial's partner
20 With insufficient resources: 2 wds.
21 Yemen's capital
24 Kukoc of the Bulls
28 Couch potatoes' fixations: 2 wds.
29 Ostentation
30 It might get your feet wet
31 Use a key on a door
35 "Cup ___" (1970s Don Williams song): 2 wds.
36 H.S. class
37 Menlo Park monogram
38 King of France
40 Ad ___
41 Draft board inits.

224

Across

1 Curio
6 Muslim community
10 Grossman and Campbell
12 Ed.'s requests
13 "A Walk in the Woods" author Bill
14 Fraction of a min.: 2 wds.
15 Kind of welder
16 Talk and talk
18 Southwest campus, initially
19 Discern
20 Orbital extremes
22 North Sea feeder
24 Humdingers
25 Adjusts, in a way
27 Beat
28 Ste. Jeanne ____
31 Deteriorate, slangily: 3 wds.
33 Road crew goo
34 ____ Tae-woo, 6th president of S. Korea
35 Major Calif. airport
36 Big blackbird
37 Yankee or Angel, for short
39 Beginning bits
41 Prefix with watt
42 Ally: 2 wds.
43 Addie's husband in "As I Lay Dying"
44 Pulverulent

Down

1 Trying to get home, perhaps: 2 wds.
2 Cask
3 Psychologist who was a frequent guest of Johnny Carson: 2 wds.
4 Printers' widths
5 Pennsylvania county
6 Service arm, initially
7 High-ranking naval officers: 3 wds.
8 "I hate those ____ to pieces!" (Mr. Jinks, re Pixie and Dixie)
9 Fungal spore sac
11 "Pull yourself together!": 4 wds.
17 City where Beethoven was born
21 Turned right
23 Architect Saarinen who designed the TWA Flight Center at JFK
26 Sugar amts.
27 Fleeced
29 Became no longer valid: 2 wds.
30 Like well-fried bacon
31 Persona non ____
32 ____ down (muted)
38 Sally Field's "Norma ____"
40 Fraternity letter

225

Across

1 Pickles brand with a stork logo
7 Philippine island
11 More spacious and well-ventilated
12 Math function
13 Martin of "Ed Wood"
14 Old Fords, sometimes
15 Spoon-bender Geller
16 Princeton mascot
18 Spanish men, colloquially
20 Hunting expedition
23 Gibberish-talking "SNL" character ____ Forrester
25 "Major" in Munich
26 Deciding factor
30 The old college cheer
31 "____ Too Proud to Beg" (1966 song)
32 Buries
34 Christmas season purchases
38 Lodge member
40 Head piece
41 Kind of salad that's also a baseball great
43 Undisturbed: 2 wds.
45 Early smartphone
46 Car driven when yours is in service
47 Agency responsible for highways, initially
48 Media baron Carver in "Tomorrow Never Dies"

Down

1 Worth
2 They don't tell the truth
3 Golfer Palmer
4 "____ and Nancy"
5 "____ Your Skin" (1964 cult horror film): 2 wds.
6 Computer-guided weapon: 2 wds.
7 Symbol for a viola player: 2 wds.
8 "Virtuous" costar Erik
9 Alphabet trio
10 Sounds of hesitation
17 "(I've Got a ____) Kalamazoo" (1942 Glenn Miller hit): 2 wds
19 Wichita to Tulsa dir.
21 Sprint
22 N.Y.C. subway line
24 Heavens: prefix
26 Soft & ____ deodorant
27 Suffix with Jacob
28 ____ a ride (hitched)
29 Greatest possible
33 Iron man?
35 Drupes (of a raspberry, e.g.)
36 San ____
37 Jet
39 Compound common in crosswords
41 Jack Bauer's org. in "24"
42 Surgery sites, initially
44 Actor Mineo of "Rebel Without a Cause"

226

Across

1 Houston MLBer, for short
5 Centerpins on which wheels revolve
10 Overflow (with)
11 Short ____, rapid and curt dismissal
12 ____ Soule, TV animation voice of Batman from 1968 to 1984
13 Form a link (with)
14 Bitterness of tone or manner
16 Scenic-view spot
17 Uncomfortable position: 2 wds.
21 On the diamond, one bounce: 2 wds.
23 Some G.I.s
24 Radii neighbors
26 Allude (to)
27 Symptom
28 Hack
29 Annoying person
31 Tom Clancy subj.
34 Providing (food and drink)
36 King who tried to hold back the tide
39 One Saarinen
40 Arts & ____ (summer camp activity)
41 Blood type, for short: 2 wds.
42 Pocahontas's husband
43 Sphere starter

Down

1 Brown fur
2 Phone service
3 Place in a different order
4 It means everything
5 "Can't you take ____?": 2 wds.
6 Glasses that supposedly let you see through walls: hyph., 2 wds.
7 52, in Ancient Rome
8 Two in an office
9 Start of many Quebec place names
11 Single-master
15 Units now called siemens
18 Functioning competently
19 Phenom
20 Battlesystem game co., initially
22 Shackle (a prisoner's wrists)
24 "Anchors Aweigh" gp.
25 Stretch the truth
26 Not often found
28 Heads of France?
30 Caffè ____
32 Like some legal proceedings: 2 wds.
33 Disco era phrase: hyph., 2 wds.
35 Country music's McEntire
36 "Who'll Stop the Rain" band
37 Nigerian native
38 Ending with mater or pater

227

Across

1. Foot: prefix
5. Soup scoop
10. Espresso topping
12. Awards since 1956
13. The P in PBR
14. Unsophisticated
15. Storm heading, initially
16. Swenson of "Benson"
18. "___ I can help it!": 2 wds.
20. O.R. personnel
23. Statement from the witness stand
25. Linking verb
27. Condiment container
29. Some apples
30. Intense shock
32. Hazy history
33. Country in Eur.
34. Inhabitants of Asgard in Norse myth
36. German river
37. Hosts, initially
40. Welsh dog
43. "You Only Live ___" (1967)
45. Maze wall, sometimes
46. Impressive mark: 2 wds.
47. TV journalist David
48. Mountains crossed by Hannibal

Down

1. Some health professionals, initially
2. Periods
3. Market investment
4. Facebook exchanges, for short
5. Yearn: 2 wds.
6. Org. for dealers in rare books
7. 502, to Nero
8. Bulgarian monetary unit
9. Ending for Vietnam or Siam
11. Going ___ (fighting): 2 wds.
17. Actor Cage, informally
19. NFL star Michael who was the basis for the movie "The Blind Side"
20. Where gossip is spread: 2 wds.
21. Red or Brave, for short
22. Ed.'s request, initially
23. "I Ain't Marching Anymore" singer
24. In ranks
26. ___-sci (coll. major)
28. More sycophantic
31. Riddle-me-___ (rhyme)
35. Mex. miss
36. Waffle grabbed in ads
38. Bra size: 2 wds.
39. Legis. meeting
40. Compadre of Fidel
41. Wine: prefix
42. Tpks.
44. Depression-era inits.

228

Across

1 Marking in violin music: 2 wds.
6 "Get lost!"
11 One of the official languages of India
12 Odes, sonnets, etc.
13 Piercing
15 Haw preceder
16 TV adjustment: abbr.
17 Keanu's role in "The Matrix"
18 Antipollution org.
19 Cumbersome
21 Soaks, as hemp
23 ___ & AJ (teen pop band)
24 Go through volumes
26 Duck, in Germany
29 Church title, for short
31 Doctor's prefix with -ologist
33 Attacks, in a way
37 Dashboard inits.
38 One-eighty
39 Joan of ___
40 Honor society letter
41 It summons help in an emergency: 2 wds.
44 Put up
45 Taco ___, Tex-Mex fast food chain
46 Major food service company
47 Actors Devine and Buckley

Down

1 Burrowing rodent
2 Car mechanic's wheeled board
3 Like a gridiron
4 One of two viewers
5 Jazz pianist Hines
6 Glitter
7 Simple bed
8 Letizia, por ejemplo
9 "Up" actor Ed
10 Expression of dismay: 2 wds.
14 Closest seats to the stage, often: 2 wds.
20 Ed or Keenan of film
22 1986 #1 hit for Starship
25 Actual
27 Beguiled
28 Quality of being pleasing to the ear
30 Kill or cure, e.g.
32 Thick-skinned ungulates, for short
33 Building managers, slangily
34 About to weep
35 Hall of Famer Sandberg et al.
36 Diver's gear
42 One-time truckers' watchdog, initially
43 Wine holder

229

Across

1 Embodiment of gentleness
5 Mixed with foreign matter, adulterated
11 Latin hymn "Dies ___"
12 Fixed sock holes
13 Overly developed, like a weightlifer: hyph.
15 Four Holy Roman emperors
16 Melville tale
17 Calendar string, initially
20 2002 Literature Nobelist Kertész
23 Mary-Kate and Ashley
27 Middle grade
28 Florida N.F.L.er
29 Poll no.
30 100 agorot
32 Early fiddle
33 Fund
35 Have ___, imbibe: 2 wds.
38 Over your head
42 Inertial force
45 Fastens laces again
46 Silver-tongued
47 Musically keyless
48 Ward of "The Fugitive"

Down

1 Car with a bar
2 In ___ (following a tedious routine): 2 wds.
3 Crow's-nest support
4 Turn into
5 European fish
6 Queen of the fairies
7 Trial photographic prints
8 Coin word
9 Clinton Cabinet member
10 Edible corm of the taro
14 W.W. II beach assault vehicle
18 "___ you believe it?"
19 Warm bedside manner, initially
20 Suffix for poet or robot
21 "Who cares?"
22 Suffix for chicka or campo
24 Prefix with log or leptic
25 Army fig.
26 Super Bowl XXXIV winners, initially
28 London's Big ___
31 Confine: 2 wds.
32 Beetle cars, familiarly: 2 wds.
34 Butterfingers
35 Vehicle hire organization, initially
36 Depilatory brand, once
37 Absorbed by
39 Get a lustful eyeful
40 Colorado ski resort
41 Exile isle of fame
43 Stephen of "V for Vendetta"
44 "Lost" setting: abbr.

230

Across

1 Late-night host
5 Benny the Bull, e.g.
11 Fashion model Wek
12 Expression of delight
13 "It's ___ Love": Domino song, 2 wds.
14 Winter Olympics ski course
15 Ireland's ___ Fein
16 Early role-playing game co., initially
17 Summer refresher
19 Rap's ___ Kross
23 Weary with traveling
27 "Gross!"
28 Like falling off a log: 4 wds.
30 Tommy's baby brother on "Rugrats"
31 Carnival treat
32 Castaway's home
34 Sch. in Stillwater
35 104, to Nero
37 ___ La Fume, cartoon skunk
41 Evening party at home
44 Spare tire
45 Shared by two or more parties
46 On or to the left prefix
47 They produce mushroom clouds, briefly: 2 wds.
48 Those things, in Tijuana

Down

1 Potato chip brand
2 Morlock morsels in "The Time Machine"
3 Nine in Nuremberg
4 W.W. II battle site
5 Agatha Christie's output, e.g.: 2 wds.
6 Feels bad
7 Bit of inspiration
8 Sgt.'s inferior
9 Antipoverty agcy. created by LBJ
10 President pro ___
18 Crude bed, to Brits
20 Defaulter's comeuppance: abbr.
21 Cry of triumph: 2 wds.
22 ___'Pea ("Popeye" character)
23 Dry riverbed
24 Unrepaired: 2 wds.
25 Cry
26 Inner cell of an ancient temple
29 Short, confused fight
33 Pale shades of beige
36 "___ men like you for breakfast!": 2 wds.
38 Seine sights
39 Falafel bean
40 Native Nigerians
41 Wee, to Burns
42 Released
43 Suffix with Canaan

231

Across

1 Mideast chief: var.

5 "___ mountain will not come to Mohammad...": 2 wds.

10 Chanel of fashion

11 Not awake

12 Explorer Sport ___ (Ford SUV)

13 Election-return patterns

14 Funny business: hyph.

16 Ribs

17 Botch

19 "The Merry Widow" composer Franz

23 "The Simpsons" bartender

24 Put ___ show: 2 wds.

25 Lees

28 Common shout when you're on TV for a few seconds: 2 wds.

30 Gas rating number

32 Attacked (a target) while swooping down on it: hyph.

36 Ivanhoe's love

37 Johnson of "Laugh-In"

38 More expensive

39 Four: prefix

40 Orgs.

41 Cheese coated in wax

Down

1 Pituitary hormone, initially

2 Former NFL coach Jim

3 "It's too dark in here!": 3 wds.

4 Moved gently from side to side

5 Abba Eban's land

6 Remove blubber from

7 Popular race distance: abbr., 2 wds.

8 Lamarr of film

9 Pre-album collectibles, for short

11 Biol. energy sources

15 Character in Disney's "Mulan"

17 2500, to Nero

18 Ending for super or inter

20 Native

21 Year abroad

22 Hit head-on

26 Rule over

27 Vistas

28 Former Vietnamese coin

29 Fellow con

31 It'll get you to the top of a mountain: hyph.

32 Executes

33 "___ a Teenage Zombie" (movie): 2 wds.

34 Blues great ___ James

35 Skin: suffix

36 Nutritional info.

232

Across

1. Major can maker
6. "Garfield: ___ of Two Kitties": 2 wds.
11. Verb for thou
12. Smut
13. Shift responsibility: 3 wds.
15. Prefix with thermal
16. Longfellow's bell town
17. Cooked
20. Dog breeder's org.
22. Coldplay's "Viva la Vida" producer Brian
23. Precisely
27. Coll. hotshots
29. Opera with the aria "Vissi d'arte"
30. Dominance through threat of punishment
32. Like almost all prime numbers
33. Wedding announcement word
34. What it is in Italy
35. ___ de soie (silk cloth)
38. "La Cage ___ Folles"
40. Easily impressed emotionally
45. Similar to each other
46. County north of the Thames
47. Cup in Cannes
48. Mink cousin

Down

1. Venomous viper
2. "___ note to follow soh...": 2 wds.
3. Baseball great Young et al.
4. Actor Davis
5. Lawyers: abbr.
6. Bruiser
7. Pipe smoker's need
8. In ___ (following a tedious routine): 2 wds.
9. Augmentation: abbr.
10. Instigator of Balder's death
14. Con
17. Credit card problem
18. "Stepped ___ J'z" (Nelly song): 2 wds.
19. Queen who wrote "Leap of Faith"
21. Singer Perry
23. Feudal underling
24. General ___ Chicken (Chinese menu dish)
25. Alternatives to plasma TVs
26. Meaningless talk, slangily
28. NHL team in Vancouver
31. Lowest high tide
34. Get by
35. H.S. exam
36. Lee Remick's role in "The Long, Hot Summer"
37. Sale stipulation: 2 wds.
39. Runnin' ___, 1944 N.C.A.A. basketball champs
41. Letters on some pumps
42. Musicians based in Maryland, initially
43. Grazing spot
44. Phone no. add-on

233

Across

1 Letter before qoph
6 Sunshine on the clock, initially
9 Early even score: hyph.
11 Lingering trace
12 Soak (herbs, etc.) in liquid, to extract flavor
13 Logan of CBS News
14 Filmmaker Buñuel
15 Give the eye: 2 wds.
17 Palindromic fashion mag
18 Public row
19 Regimen
20 Kind of valve in a car
21 Figure skater Brian
23 Result
26 Scraps
30 86 is a high one
31 Hot stuff
32 Next to last syllable of a word
34 Days of ___ (the past)
35 "___ Made to Love Her" (Stevie Wonder song): 2 wds.
36 Home of Lafayette College
38 Weight not charged for
39 Ace a test: 2 wds.
40 Decade divs.
41 Some teachers' degs.

Down

1 Dirty
2 Rings
3 Contaminate
4 Type of search: hyph.
5 Tennis twosome
6 U.S. Capitol's vicinity: 2 wds.
7 Recoiled
8 Perfectly: 3 wds.
10 Reef dweller
11 One way to remove unwanted hair
16 Feudal worker
20 Suffix with guitar or clarinet
22 "That's hilarious!" in textspeak
23 Self-important, arrogant
24 Arms buildup period
25 Submarine detectors
27 Dig like a pig
28 Donut-shaped object
29 Heart implants
33 Famous Downing Street number
37 Winnie-the-Pooh creator's monogram

234

Across

1. ____ Domani (wine brand)
5. Bottom of the ocean
11. Circus crowd's sounds
12. Break into suddenly
13. Pate de foie ____
14. Is frugal
15. Army recruit
17. Actor Stephen of "V for Vendetta"
18. Uses for support: 2 wds.
22. Fill to excess
24. "____ me to your leader"
25. ____ appointment (fix a date): 2 wds.
27. Not true
28. Cooking cavity
29. "Mona ____"
30. Certain outdoor worker
32. Midpoint: abbr.
35. Fabric
37. Descendant of Noah's son
40. Tip-top: hyph.
41. Praying figures
42. Sounds of reproof
43. Strip
44. Suffixes of origin

Down

1. Raring to go
2. Chili con ____
3. Property that defines one's individual nature
4. Skeleton part, in Padua
5. French impressionism pioneer Alfred
6. Some Art Deco works
7. Pieces for Pavarotti, e.g.
8. Hot dog holder
9. FRER competitor
10. Cause of some shaking, initially
16. "Mission Earth" series author Hubbard: 2 wds.
19. Characterized by lust
20. Approves
21. Formerly known as
23. Explosive device: 2 wds.
25. Kind of flour
26. Actress Longoria
27. Just dandy
29. News
31. Dillon and Damon
33. Oncle's wife
34. Like Boston accents, as it were: hyph.
36. Appraise
37. Brick carrier
38. Uris hero
39. Dallas cager, briefly

235

Across

1. Bail out, like a pilot might
6. Soviet prison system
11. Character in David Morrell novels
12. "That's ____ excuse!": 2 wds.
13. Cast out
14. Couric's cohost
15. Big ____
16. Buck
18. Supporter of arms, for short
19. It comes before chi
20. Long time
21. 650, to Caesar
22. Addresses that may be stored in "Favorites," initially
24. Like some cows
26. Fearful of romance: hyph.
28. Slowly (tempo)
30. "Do as I say"
33. Big beer holder
34. Big wine holder
36. "You ____" (Lionel Richie hit)
37. "____ Believer": 2 wds.
38. Some football linemen: abbr.
39. FAA and IATA code for John Wayne Airport
40. Soccer superstar Lionel ____
42. "Omigosh!"
44. Male singer with the lowest voice
45. Atom bomb trial: abbr., 2 wds.
46. Newsman Roger
47. Feline

Down

1. "Are you" in Aragon: 2 wds.
2. Large, spotted feline of tropical America
3. TV chef whose catchphrases include "Bam" and "Kick it up a notch!": 2 wds.
4. Letterman's network letters
5. Sean Paul "Head ____" singer: 2 wds.
6. Lead ore samples
7. Diminutive suffix
8. Clothes hamper: 2 wds.
9. Punish with an arbitrary penalty
10. 1970s White House name
17. Detect as if by smelling: 2 wds.
23. Saturate, in dialect
25. Comedienne Margaret
27. Expression of hatred
28. Like some arms
29. Cheapen
31. Cyclotron inventor ____ Lawrence
32. Frothy
35. "I Want You Back" boy band
41. Fed. assistance program
43. "Give ____ rest!": 2 wds.

243

236

Across

1 Box spring supporters
6 House: Sp.
10 Cabbies
11 Holds back
13 Big name in computer printers
14 Name on a tube of Beyond Paradise
15 Record producer Brian
16 "___ in alpha": 2 wds.
18 Grandma: Ger.
19 "Buena Vista Social Club" director Wenders
20 Sets of two, briefly
21 "Delta of Venus" writer
22 North Sea port
24 Fundraising grps.
25 Suffix with aster or human
26 Infant's cry
27 Disney dog
29 Cut-price events
31 Toothpaste tube palindrome
32 Court figures, initially
33 ___ de lance (pit viper)
35 It isn't gross
36 Play subdivision
37 Outer: prefix
38 Perp's story
40 Hindu princesses
42 It may be blocked when you have a cold
43 Person with a mike
44 Like some batters
45 Apprehensive

Down

1 Nag
2 Actress Kazan
3 Providing lodging for
4 W.B.A. ref's decision
5 Like some curves: hyph.
6 Salad ingredient
7 1950s election monogram
8 Avoid commitment: 4 wds.
9 Blood problem
12 Astin and Lennon
17 Prince Valiant's son
23 Handyman's letters
24 Mac
26 Idler
27 Turner and others
28 Penguin of Antarctica
29 Midwest Indian
30 More physically alluring
32 Part of a simple bouquet
34 Olympic snowboarder Fletcher
39 Insect
41 Gallic soul

237

Across

1 Degree for a future C.E.O.
4 ___-Foy, Que.
7 IRS return datum
10 Strongboxes
12 Additionally
13 Nightclub type
14 Court figure: abbr.
15 Nick at ___
16 Charles, for one
17 Abstain from: 2 wds.
20 Photographer's ratio: hyph.
22 "Buona ___" (Italian greeting)
23 Okinawa port
24 Facial expression
28 Non-profit, voluntary citizens' groups, initially
29 ___ Dullea, David Bowman in "2001: A Space Odyssey"
30 Mexican food, sometimes
32 Less
33 "Gross!"
34 Country that borders Ecuador
36 South Korea's Roh ___ Woo
37 With skill
41 Oklahoma Indian
42 Some potatoes
43 Stimpy's cartoon partner
44 Command level: abbr.
45 Bygone MTV show

Down

1 Abbr. on top of some e-mails
2 Gaudy scarf
3 Military fliers locale, initially
4 Prefix with comic
5 Old waste allowance
6 Gloria of pop
7 Go back to square one: 2 wds.
8 Likewise: 2 wds.
9 Stiff penalty?: 2 wds.
11 Lively Spanish dance for two
17 Presidential advisory gp.
18 Antipoverty agcy.
19 Brit. police officer's stick
21 Radical reorganizations: hyph.
23 Pioneering game console, for short
25 Left over: 2 wds.
26 Inc., overseas
27 Wander
30 Coach
31 Marble material
32 Just harvested
35 P.T.A. concern: abbr.
38 Vietnamese New Year
39 A or B, e.g.: abbr.
40 Inits. on a bottle of Parisienne

238

Across

1 Early baseball Hall-of-Famer ___ Rixey
5 Classify
11 Decree
12 Chinese-American virtuoso cellist: hyph., 2 wds.
13 "Click ___ ticket" (NHTSA campaign): 2 wds.
14 Edible nut
15 Kind of truck
16 King of Kings
17 Flip one's lid?
19 Variety of poisonous snake
23 W.W. II org. 1941–7
24 Campaign sign word
25 Afrikaners' village
27 Classes
28 Port in southeast Iraq
30 Letter that appears twice in the Schrödinger equation
31 Eddie's "Coming to America" role
32 Refine
35 Al of Dixieland
37 "I thought this'd be helpful," briefly
38 Relinquish
41 Actress Ryan of "General Hospital"
42 At the very moment when: 2 wds.
43 Germany's ___ Valley
44 Abounding in trees
45 Hosp. staffers

Down

1 Verdi aria sung by Renato: 2 wds.
2 Feign: 2 wds.
3 Farm worker
4 Gas: prefix
5 Indian nanny
6 Comfort
7 System of emblematic representations
8 Tic-tac-toe line
9 Ford's predecessor, initially
10 Wee bit
16 ___ crossroads: 2 wds.
18 Anticipate with dread or anxiety
20 Plan of an area with shading and contour lines: 2 wds.
21 Comic strip cry
22 U.S.N. officers
25 Trading under the name of, initially
26 Desk wood
29 1000, 500 and 3000UX, e.g.
30 Nev. clock setting
33 "Crossbow" star Will
34 Levels
36 Far from bleak
38 Handful
39 Ab ___ (from day one)
40 Old Olds
41 New American's course letters

239

Across

1. Full of too much energy
6. Martini's partner
11. Saint in Brazil
12. Before
13. State fruit of Idaho
15. Honors word
16. Drunk ___ skunk: 2 wds.
17. Explorer John
19. North Dakota city
21. Like an ignited dessert
23. Feature of blue jeans or a baseball
26. ___ Argento, Italian film director, producer and screenwriter
27. Beatles' "Eleanor ___"
28. Stitches
29. "Are you sure?" reply: 3 wds.
30. Frank ___, New York Sportswriter of the Year in 2015
32. Islet
33. Starter: abbr.
35. Late "Queen of Salsa" ___ Cruz
37. "Boogie Woogie Bugle Boy" singer: 2 wds.
41. End of ___: 2 wds.
42. International Tennis Hall-of-Famer Monica
43. Show shown again on TV
44. Is forbidden to

Down

1. Dash inits.
2. Sports org. for nonprofessionals
3. Long period of darkness and extreme cold scientists predict would follow a full-scale atomic war
4. Actress Chase
5. Peter Falk role
6. Salsa singer Blades
7. First or second number in the Fibonacci sequence
8. In a calculated manner
9. Business letter addressees
10. ___ Prigogine, Nobel Prize-winning physicist
14. 1982 Plimpton best seller
17. Country addresses, for short
18. Wings of an insect
20. Medical suffix
22. Be absent from
24. Quatrain rhyme scheme, sometimes
25. "Goodness gracious!": 2 wds.
27. Sober outlook
29. Source of all matter
31. Bounding main
33. Bridge support: hyph.
34. "Blazing Saddles" actor Wilder
36. Cranial bulb?
38. Jay Presson Allen play of 1989
39. Velvet add-on
40. Q trailers

240

Across

1 Syrian leader
6 Dustin Hoffman role of 1969
11 "New Rules" comic
12 Go in
13 Cape Cod town
14 Golden, in Guanajuato: 2 wds.
15 ___ Hulka ("Stripes" role)
16 Use
18 One of ten for a bowler
19 Megalithic tomb
22 Like hot goods
24 Pair at sea
28 Unused to: 2 wds.
29 George Eliot miser Marner
30 "Portland, Oregon" singer Loretta
31 Don't hurry: 2 wds.
32 Diner-style restaurant chain
34 Video recorder, for short
37 River in northeastern Portugal
38 Cable giant, once: inits.
41 Helps in crime
43 Actress Patricia et al.
45 A ___ santé
46 Folk rocker ___ Curtis
47 Popular snack cake: 2 wds.
48 Professeur's charge

Down

1 Quantities: abbr.
2 Puppeteer Tony
3 Closure of a factory or system
4 ___ Lingus (Irish airline)
5 Minute amount of liquid
6 Color anew
7 Hydrocarbon suffix
8 Sporty car roof: hyph.
9 Bandar ___ Begawan (Brunei's capital)
10 "Off ___?": 2 wds.
17 IJK followers
20 Warner ___, Dr. Fu Manchu actor
21 Cacophonous
22 Eddie Murphy's old TV show, briefly
23 "The Daughter of Time" writer Josephine
25 "Are you in good hands?" insurance company
26 Dileep who played Yusuf in "Inception"
27 NNE's opposite
29 Voice
31 African antelope
33 Bibliographical abbr.: 2 wds.
34 Cleveland basketball team, for short
35 "___ Ben Adhem" (Leigh Hunt poem)
36 City on the Moselle
39 154, in Ancient Rome
40 Words of understanding: 2 wds.
42 Put to the test
44 Suffix with ether or id

241

Across

1 "The Incredible Flutist" composer Walter

7 Passbook abbr.

10 Honor

11 Honeybunch

12 Pants that reach only to the thighs

13 Prefix with pod or pus

14 Kind of file: abbr.

15 Stock exchange in Paris

17 India.____, singer of "Little Things"

18 Letter-shaped girder: hyph.

19 It builds interest

20 Lace with a square mesh

21 From head ____ (completely): 2 wds.

23 Put ____ to (finish): 2 wds.

25 Huff and puff

29 "32 Flavors" singer Davis

30 Vigoda and Saperstein

31 Blues singer Barton: 2 wds.

33 Dissolute man

34 MIT grad, perh.

35 Fun park car: hyph.

37 Grayish

38 "Carmen" and "La Traviata"

39 Negating word

40 Horse rider's seat

Down

1 Computer language

2 Miami Marlins outfielder Suzuki

3 Scum formed on molten metals

4 Celebration of a 300th anniversary

5 Choose

6 Crash investigating agcy.

7 Dictate

8 Bothers persistently: 2 wds.

9 Intro to a book

11 Left one's car alongside another: hyph.

16 Akron's home

20 Flower delivery letters

22 "Chestnuts roasting ____ open fire...": 2 wds.

23 "The Mysteries of Laura" costar Laz

24 Zilch

26 "All ____!" (conductor's shout)

27 Nerve-related

28 Sleeping sickness carrier

29 "Yond Cassius has ____ and hungry look": 2 wds.

32 Gps. like Rockerfeller Foundation and Save the Children, to the UN

36 ____-Locka, Florida

249

242

Across

1 Biblical measure
6 Crowd together in dirty conditions: 2 wds.
11 Espresso topping
12 Stout
13 Sorrow
15 Squirreled-away item
16 Quote from Homer
17 Reno's st.
19 Brief letter
21 F ___ "foxtrot": 2 wds.
23 Arctic expanse
27 Executive perk: 2 wds.
29 Passage leading from the back of the mouth
30 Kitchen appliance
31 Eyelid ailment
33 "Can ___ now?": 2 wds.
34 Some E.R. cases
37 Belgian battle site
39 Abstemious: hyph.
43 Carlo Levi's "Christ Stopped at ___"
44 Cut
45 Place
46 Shoe-factory employee

Down

1 EKG site
2 Cremains holder
3 Conduct, manner
4 Apple product
5 Strike lightly, as a window pane: 2 wds.
6 Reveal the true nature of: 2 wds.
7 Arabic name preceder
8 Turned right
9 Playground retort: 2 wds.
10 Composer/ TV guy John
14 Original model
17 Illustrator Thomas
18 Bk. of the Bible
20 Inner: prefix
22 Mil. workers
24 Tending to cause hostility
25 Film director Nicolas
26 ___ Domini
28 Large grasshopper
32 Arp collaborator Max
34 Suffix for abnormalities
35 Card balance
36 Gin flavorer
38 Looker
40 Miami's st.
41 Word in wedding notices
42 Watchdog's warning

243

Across

1 William H., author of "Middle C"
5 Master, in Swahili
10 Modern, in Munich
11 Daniel Suarez novel
12 Weaponry
13 Drying stands
14 Ladies' man
16 Whac-___ (arcade game): hyph.
17 Sam Cooke's "That's ___ Quit, I'm Movin' On": 2 wds.
20 Detail of etiquette
22 Alliance that includes Kazakhstan, Kyrgyzstan, etc.
23 Shiba ___, Japanese breed of dog
24 Vs.
26 French soul
27 On the ___ (fleeing the police)
28 Car repair courtesy
30 Busch Stadium letters
31 Department tasked with introducing new products: abbr., 3 wds.
32 For the time being: 2 wds.
36 Needlelike
38 Prefix with phobic and lith
39 Dated: 2 wds.
40 Relieve
41 Boat bottoms
42 "Follow me!," briefly

Down

1 Chew on
2 Designed for flight
3 With the highest academic distinction: 3 wds.
4 Kind of oil
5 Woolen material used for card tables
6 Lived and breathed
7 Traditional social ideals: 2 wds.
8 "___ any drop to drink": Coleridge
9 T or F: abbr.
11 Newspaper Superman's alter ego works at: 2 wds.
15 Say ___ (refuse): 2 wds.
18 News magazine
19 Czech river that is an Elbe tributary
20 Rock and Roll Hall-of-Famer Lofgren
21 ___ the finish: 2 wds.
25 ___ Neuf, bridge across the Seine in Paris
29 Concept pitcher, shortly: 2 wds.
31 ___ Italian Ice, restaurant franchise chain
33 "Charlie and the Chocolate Factory" author
34 Words before "many words": 2 wds.
35 Faucet brand
36 Hunky-dory: hyph.
37 A.L. Central city

244

Across

1 Mid-month date
5 Types: abbr.
8 "Breaking Vegas" star Fierro
10 Partake of
11 Shown past the foyer: 2 wds.
12 Hebrew name for Uranus
13 Russian pop duo
14 Mount ___, Washington
16 "Put ___ writing": 2 wds.
17 Alpha Centauri B, for example: 2 wds.
18 Campus military org.
19 Infamous insider trader Ivan
20 Affirmative reply: 3 wds.
22 My friend, in Montmartre: 2 wds.
25 Botch
29 "I'll Pin ___ on Your Pillow" (Billy Joe Royal song): 2 wds.
30 Madrid mansion
31 Put up a struggle
33 Asian river between China and Russia
34 Salmon sort
35 Inflatable life-saver
37 "___, you noblest English!" (Shakespeare): 2 wds.
38 Cowboy's seat
39 Darn
40 Movie lioness

Down

1 "That makes sense now!": 3 wds.
2 Public condemnation
3 Manning at quarterback
4 Not daughters
5 Purity units, to goldsmiths
6 "Slavonic Dances" composer
7 Entry post
8 Buzzing
9 "Outta sight!"
10 Kathleen Turner movie of 1993: 3 wds.
15 Boxing wins, shortly
19 Meas. taken during a physical
21 "The Girls from ___" (2009 Jeffrey Zaslow bestseller)
22 San ___, city in Texas
23 First day of the year, datewise: hyph.
24 Failure to turn up for a performance: 2 wds.
26 Greek 'L'
27 Everyday
28 Freight carrier
32 Zap with a stun gun
36 Suffix with dictator

245

Across

1 Radio switch: hyph.
5 As a friend, to Françoise: 2 wds.
10 The Big Easy acronym
11 Seat of Dawson County, Texas
13 Semi-transparent
15 Become obstructed
16 Drink in the afternoon
17 Schindler with a list
18 "That angers me!": 2 wds.
20 Horror director Craven
21 Earthy pigment
22 Chocolate bean
24 Eyeglasses, briefly
26 Experiences
29 Pope from 440–461: 2 wds.
30 Piece of pizza
32 Tee off
33 Arranged in a row: 2 wds.
35 Legendary Mississippi bluesman: 2 wds.
37 As a whole: 2 wds.
38 Coffeehouse order
39 "Point-Count Bidding" author Charles
40 Eric Cartwright's nickname on "Bonanza"

Down

1 Honeydew-producing aphid: 2 wds.
2 Inclined to sulk
3 Sides (as of a volcano)
4 Style of Japanese comics
5 Some wings
6 Fashionable brand of apparel
7 Pacer producer, initially
8 "___ in St. Louis" (1944 Garland film): 2 wds.
9 Has almost arrived: 2 wds.
12 Just barely: 2 wds.
14 Father's talk: abbr.
19 Unit of electrical conductance
21 Military training acad.
22 Average grade
23 Church aide
24 Threaded
25 Made an emotional appeal for: 2 wds.
26 Cab Calloway catchphrase: hyph.
27 Popular Hondas
28 Blood poisoning
29 California's ___ Valley
30 Snow, to Burns
31 Lewd character
34 Gloating cry: 2 wds.
36 Dung beetle that drones when flying

246

Across

1 "Dynasty" actress
6 Spin doctor: abbr., 2 wds.
11 Architectural projection
12 Alley Oop's heartthrob
13 Vietnam War massacre site: 2 wds.
14 "The Empire Strikes Back" chronologically: 2 wds.
15 Lilly of Lilly Pharmaceutical
16 Canadian policeman, usually on horseback, familiarly
18 Immune system lymphocyte: hyph.
20 Mosque figure
22 Deny
27 Getaway destination, maybe, for short: 3 wds.
29 Golfer Mediate
30 Female prison officer
32 Architect of St. Paul's, London
33 Alfalfa's sweetheart on "The Little Rascals"
35 Catherine the Great, e.g.
39 Tropical fruit, briefly
42 Destroy or kill, casually: 2 wds.
43 Nonverbal feedback
45 Fancy
46 Greek city-state
47 Adhere
48 Dramatic operatic solo

Down

1 Incompletely
2 Chemical compound
3 Disposed to warfare or hard-line policies
4 Airline to Beirut, initially
5 Gunk
6 Well-liked
7 Horse color
8 "Beetle Bailey" creator Walker
9 Prefix meaning "height"
10 Basilica center
17 Canadian TV channel, initially
19 Mil. head honcho
20 Watson's company
21 Lamb's cry
23 Distressed cry
24 Make jumbled or muddled
25 Pass with flying colors
26 Over there
28 "Orca" actress: 2 wds.
31 Rapper in the supergroup The Firm, once
34 Answers an invitation, initially
35 Old English letters
36 Castle's protection
37 "Bah, humbug!"
38 DOD recruiting program
40 Wisconsin bodysnatcher Ed
41 Greek peak
44 Summer Games gp.

247

The grid:

1	2	3	4	5	■	6	7	8	9	10
11					■	12				
13					■	14				
15				■	16	17		■	18	

Across

1 Cackling carnivore
6 Overthrow plotters
11 Desert watering holes
12 Minnesota Twins Hall-of-Famer Tony
13 Neckerchief
14 Tease: 2 wds.
15 Pretoria's country letters
16 Going
18 Razor brand
19 Back-to-school mo.
20 Musical passage for a virtuoso singer
22 Hot
24 Tech sch.
25 Renting
27 Ill-mannered person
29 Provided in small portions
32 Betrothed
34 Former Vietnamese coin
35 TV show named with initials
36 Chu-___ (legendary Confucian sage)
37 Summer, in Savoy
38 Buckwheat porridge
40 Rubbish
42 Pop great ___ John
43 Pound and Klein
44 Unit used in electromagnetism
45 Address, as a person: 2 wds.

Down

1 Gruff, husky
2 ___ Arafat, Palestinian president 1996–2004
3 Breakout experts
4 Prefix with classic
5 Queens neighborhood
6 Second largest of the Ionian Islands
7 Made like, in cookery: 2 wds.
8 Origin of the universe possibility: 3 wds.
9 Skirts
10 Surgical knife
17 Crews' living quarters on ships, briefly
21 Fluff
23 Prefix with flop
26 Chemical salts
27 St. Thomas à ___ (Archbishop murdered in 1170)
28 Offered for purchase: 2 wds.
30 Erodes: 2 wds.
31 Possible rebuttal in a childish argument: 2 wds.
33 Lake Volta locale
39 Neighbor of Belg. and Ger.
41 Hip hop musician who cofounded Soul Temple Records

248

Across

1 Throw

5 When the clock strikes twelve: 2 wds.

11 Legendary basketball coach Adolph

12 James or Oliver of the Harry Potter movies

13 Collections of things of interest (suffix)

14 Cádiz currency, once

15 Committee sess.

16 In ___ (stuck): 2 wds.

17 Wore: 2 wds.

19 "Quietly Brilliant" phone company letters

22 Ready-to-bake cake blend

24 Laser-pointer battery, initially

25 Dietary supplement: 2 wds.

27 Some explosives, initially

28 System of weights and measures

29 1980s military prog.

30 Magnetic induction unit

31 Evening, in adspeak

32 Ltr. additions

35 Microorganism that requires oxygen for growth

38 Air___ (budget airline until 2014)

39 Twaddle

40 Hand: Sp.

41 Certain recall

42 Skin problem

Down

1 Compress, overcrowd

2 Jemima or Bee

3 ___ bolognese

4 Defaces with rolls?: abbr.

5 More or less

6 N.Y.C.-based international org.: 2 wds.

7 Home in a tree

8 Corrida cry

9 Make up one's mind

10 Govt. code breakers

16 Take ___ view of: 2 wds.

18 One of a Latin trio

19 2007 movie starring John Travolta

20 Anklebones

21 H.S. subject

22 Some soldiers: abbr.

23 Coating

24 Living units: abbr.

26 Modern, to Mahler

30 One who utters wisecracks

31 De ___ (anew)

33 Lacking in Le Mans

34 Arrogant, conceited person, slangily

35 Fleet cmdr.

36 Before, in poetry

37 Basketball hoop

38 "Splatterday" network, initially

249

Across

1. Laugh sound
4. Albany is its cap.
7. Patriot ___
10. Mobile's state: abbr.
11. The ___ Glove ("As Seen on TV" mitt)
12. Hawaii tuna
13. "Treat 'Em Rough" writer
15. Border
16. Jeans magnate Levi
17. Chemistry suffix
18. Laughs heartily: var.
19. ___ and improved
20. Cold dessert
22. Capital near the 60th parallel
23. Very funny joke: hyph.
25. Military sch.
26. Rearward
27. French possessive
28. Old gridiron org.
29. Dark and depressing, as music
30. Rings, in biology
33. ___-Tiki
34. In a cheerful way
35. Palindromic preposition
36. Echidna morsel
37. Palindromic girl's name
38. "___ out!" (ump's call)
39. Scoreboard fig.
40. Mdse.

Down

1. Actors Holbrook and Linden
2. Southernmost town in Israel: var.
3. Journalist who founded the "60 Minutes" program: 2 wds.
4. Peacenik's slogan: 2 wds.
5. French fashion designer (1936–2008): 3 wds.
6. Sun. talks
7. He produced "Fantasy Island" and "Beverly Hills 90210": 2 wds.
8. Gouger
9. Impaired as a result of much use
14. Coated (a surface) roughly
20. Old-school fastener at the roller disco
21. Afresh: 2 wds.
22. Decide on: 2 wds.
24. Postulates
30. "Do I have to draw you ___?": 2 wds.
31. "When I Was ___" ("H.M.S. Pinafore" song): 2 wds.
32. Dict. entries

250

Across

1 Railroad buildings, briefly
5 Actress Blake
11 MGM co-founder
12 Animal-bite worry
13 Word said when performing magic
15 Currency
16 Palais social event, ___ masqué
17 Zen riddles with no solution
18 What Washington couldn't tell: 2 wds.
19 Cardinals' letters
20 Reddish brown color
23 Get ready for a tanning session?: 2 wds.
24 Matures
26 Eagles' org.
29 Hawaii's state bird
30 Gooey campfire goodie
32 Old letter (Ð)
33 Worry: 2 wds.
35 Passing of a law a second time: hyph.
37 Dictator
38 Four-time Pro Bowl tight end Crumpler
39 "___ later": 2 wds.
40 It may be hitched to huskies

Down

1 Casual trousers
2 As well: 2 wds.
3 Type of gymnastics maneuver
4 NFL Hall-of-Famer Lynn
5 "He's ___ Picker" (Irving Berlin song of 1914): 2 wds.
6 Fashioned
7 Lawyer's org.
8 Bite off tiny pieces
9 Wreck
10 What bargain-hunters seek: 2 wds.
14 "A Chorus Line" girl
18 Ernst contemporary
21 TV channel relaunched as "Versus" in 2006
22 Unpolished leather
23 Expose, poetically
24 Fly-by-night?: hyph.
25 "Where are you?" response: 2 wds.
26 Kind of motel, slangily
27 Periphery
28 Rented
29 "Doggone!"
31 Rock's Michelle and Cass
33 Not loco
34 Alcohol-eschewing org. for the ladies
36 Dissenting vote

251

Across

1. Win by ___: 2 wds.
6. Take potshots (at)
11. "The ___ Not For Sale" (Rita Coolidge album)
12. Asia Minor region
13. One with a night job
15. Donkey in Durango
16. King, in Portugal
17. Smallest rise and fall of sea level: 2 wds.
22. Sock pattern
25. Start of a giggle
26. Andrew ___, governor of New York State
27. Largest city of Cattaraugus County, N.Y.
29. Units of weight, briefly
30. Decorous
31. Taking (people) to their seats
34. All-natural food no-no, initially
35. Yank or Seattle Mariner, e.g.
39. Character, individuality
43. Like a lawn in the morn
44. La ___, Argentinian port
45. Gladiator's place
46. "Saving Hope" actor Benjamin

Down

1. Michigan college or its town
2. Ancient Greek temple
3. Indulge in excessively, for short: 2 wds.
4. Thesaurus entry
5. Night school subject, initially
6. Frat. with its HQ at Richmond, VA: abbr.
7. Like a rare baseball game: hyph.
8. Savings accrual: abbr.
9. Epitome of easiness
10. Place for a stud
14. Dies ___ (Requiem Mass part)
18. "Evil Woman" band, for short
19. Part of a list
20. Hand out playing cards
21. Counting-out bit
22. Rights grp.
23. Chafes
24. "Gee!"
27. Vintner's prefix
28. As permitted by law
30. ___ Sleep (mattress retail chain): 2 wds.
32. Buddy who played Jed Clampett
33. Valerie Harper sitcom
36. Teller of stories
37. Suffix with sermon or room
38. Shag rugs from Sweden
39. Smartphone forerunner, initially
40. Ending for puppet or auction
41. "Concord Hymn" writer's monogram
42. Shrinks' org.

252

Across

1 Hotel workers
6 Buffalo hockey player
11 Paste used to fill gaps between tiles
12 Synthetic fiber
13 Plant found on coastal sand dunes: 2 wds.
15 Aunt Bee's boy, in 1960s TV
16 "Give ___ chance!": 2 wds.
17 Title of Japan's Hirohito: abbr.
20 Samsung product, e.g.: abbr., 2 wds.
22 "Come on!"
24 Choose
28 Used embellishment in speech
30 Brand of honey: 2 wds.
31 Dance for juniors, for short
32 2007 state quarter
34 Author Rand
35 Brit. news network
38 Water, in Oaxaca
40 Jim-dandy
45 Divider of wedding guests
46 Musical syllable system: hyph.
47 Awards for dramas, familiarly
48 Government issue: hyph.

Down

1 "Ben-Hur" studio
2 The Altar constellation
3 Ending for sen or jun
4 Spanish peso
5 Kind of infection: abbr.
6 Herbal drink: 2 wds.
7 Itinerary info: abbr.
8 ___ B'rith (Sons of the Covenant)
9 Lie
10 Actress Lanchester of "Mary Poppins"
14 Time of one's life
17 Protection: var.
18 Cafe card
19 Baseball great Rose
21 Some RCA products
23 Indian ox
25 Result of cogitating, sometimes
26 Jacques who directed "The Umbrellas of Cherbourg"
27 ___ chief (mag. boss): 2 wds.
29 New shoots
33 "Back Street" writer Fannie
35 Aviation org.
36 Tampa paper, familiarly
37 Prince, in Biblical Hebrew
39 "This is ___ for Superman!": 2 wds.
41 French key
42 Boxer in "The Rumble in the Jungle"
43 Grey Cup grp.
44 Penn of the "Harold & Kumar" franchise

253

Across

1 Spears for landing fish

6 Old Spanish coin

10 Kansas City university, formerly the College of Saint Teresa

11 "___ Am" (Rick Ross song): 2 wds.

12 Aired again

13 Fibber's confession: 2 wds.

14 Dried fish eaten with curry: 2 wds.

16 Bleated

17 Annoyingly slow

20 French cathedral city

24 ___ Tomé and Principe (African republic)

25 Fuss and bother

26 Menlo Park monogram

27 For the time being: 2 wds.

29 Rare blood type: abbr., 2 wds.

30 Europe-Asia divider

32 Sophisticated good taste

37 Roman hearth goddess

38 Ulan ___, Mongolia

39 "The Fault in Our Stars" costar Elgort

40 Chip away at

41 Be in command of

42 "Shut up!": 2 wds.

Down

1 Dress

2 Chevrolet subcompact car

3 Like some mattresses

4 Having a spare tire, so to speak

5 Yemen's capital

6 Dupe

7 Acid related to gout

8 Stink to high heaven

9 Suffix with fact

11 Cab Calloway's signature line: hyph.

15 Railroad worker

17 Sony handheld device, initially

18 Paddle's cousin

19 "Kitchy-___!"

21 Brit. news network

22 Pearl Bailey's middle name

23 Part of a line: abbr.

25 Type of gymnastics maneuver

28 Growing in small dense clumps

29 Capital of Eritrea

31 Mountain Community of the Tejon Pass, Calif.

32 Russo of "Outbreak"

33 Padua pronoun

34 Harrow's rival

35 Knotty complications

36 Waste compensation

37 Kilmer of "The Saint"

254

Across

1. Not skilled in: 2 wds.
6. Report (as of a gun)
10. Church words
11. "___'s Gold" (1997 movie about a beekeeper)
12. Tales of woe: 2 wds.
14. Presidential monogram
15. Inflexible
16. Buddies
17. "Well, ___-di-dah!"
20. Unrequested browser windows: hyph.
23. River of Africa
24. Thrusting blows
25. "Just supposing…": 2 wds.
26. Melodies
27. Spiritual knowledge
28. Airport-screening org.
29. Greek god of war
30. Largest organ in the body
32. Blood letters
35. Hand-operated character printer
37. Polo alternative
38. ___ buffe (Italian comic operas)
39. Large, flat-topped hill
40. Sought out quickly: 2 wds.

Down

1. Blowout
2. Book following Joel
3. Chapter 11 issue
4. Response: abbr.
5. Some shoe fasteners: hyph.
6. Towns, informally
7. Et ___ (and other men)
8. Unnecessary
9. Some stoves, initially
13. Corn and vegetable, e.g.
16. Bars
18. Jai ___ (ball sport)
19. Attention-getting shouts
20. Jr.'s exam
21. Blues singer Redding
22. Bring to a standstill
23. Roswell sightings, initially
25. Mistaken: 2 wds.
27. Increased in size
29. Estée Lauder company
31. Stock market launches, initially
32. Two fives for ___: 2 wds.
33. Ernie's TV buddy
34. Dessert sandwich
35. "Last Man Standing" actor Allen
36. Pubgoer's choice, for short

262

255

Across

1 Forge worker

6 Ginger cookie

10 African language and ethnic group

11 Paper sections: hyph.

12 New structuring, as of a business: abbr.

13 Spurs

14 Sweet soft red fruit

16 Construction girder: hyph.

17 Liquid high in monounsaturated fatty acids

21 Anthropologist Fossey

24 Stock market statistic

25 Ski run of compacted snow

26 Poker variety

27 Raised deck of a ship, for short

28 Annoying person, slangily

30 Competent, well-skilled

35 Hurts badly

36 More frequently, old-style

37 Sal who co-starred with James Dean

38 Dustin Hoffman role of 1969

39 Private liberal arts university in North Carolina

40 Atom bomb trial: abbr., 2 wds.

Down

1 Pol. divisions prior to 1991

2 Champagne house founder Claude

3 "Like ___ not": 2 wds.

4 World created by Jim Henson for "The Dark Crystal"

5 Very enthusiastic, casually: hyph.

6 Infrequent

7 Narrowly avoided accident: 2 wds.

8 Snail mail sender's info, casually

9 They go below signatures, for short

11 S-shaped curve

15 Four-year coll. deg.

17 Baseball's Young et al.

18 Islet

19 Elementary particle

20 Crones: 2 wds.

22 Natl. League city

23 Once called

25 Buttered, salty snack

27 It comes before Sat.

29 In case it's true: 2 wds.

30 Jack and Jill's item

31 Perseverance motto starter: 2 wds.

32 Suffix with cigar or kitchen

33 Loch ___ monster

34 Certain horse race

35 Mrs. in Paris

256

Across

1. Log roll
5. Fell off
10. Cold drink brand
11. Horde
12. DVR with a smiling television set logo
13. Sneaker brand
14. Attending to the task at hand: 2 wds.
16. Flemish painter Jan van ___
17. Breaks into small sharp fragments
20. Harbors ill feelings toward
21. Air travel safety org.
24. Small island
25. Key abbr.
26. Switch positions
27. Gov. assistance to the needy
28. Positions
30. Given to expressing oneself freely or insistently
32. State bordering Canada, briefly
34. Actress Polo
35. Estevez of "St. Elmo's Fire"
37. Memory: comb. form
40. Down Under soldier
41. "I've Got ___ in Kalamazoo": 2 wds.
42. "Gigi" composer
43. Jet-setters' jets, once

Down

1. It may be boring
2. Here, in France
3. Change radically
4. ___ Brezhnev, Soviet statesman
5. Reds great Roush
6. Bramble
7. Women's one-piece undergarments: 2 wds.
8. Air ___ Lifeteam (air ambulance provider)
9. Dilbert's place
13. Bears witness, in court: 2 wds.
15. Swallow
17. Campus orgs.
18. Parti ___ (prejudice): Fr.
19. Get away
22. Old knife
23. Part of NASDAQ: abbr.
29. Shearer and Talmadge
31. International jurisprudence: 2 wds.
32. Spread
33. "___ Angel": 2 wds.
36. Secure
38. Patronize a diner
39. Toronto F.C.'s org.

257

Across

1 Direction away from NNE
4 Where black is white, briefly
7 Nice season?
8 Neighbor of Wyo.
9 Mixed-breed dog
12 Augusto Pinochet's Chile, e.g.: 2 wds.
15 Volunteer's statement: 2 wds.
16 Flapjack topper: var.
17 Choir voice
18 Truncated, briefly
19 Ensure: 3 wds.
23 Fed. aid agency
24 Rainy season
26 Troublemaker
28 Russian ruler's realm, until 1917
31 Have to have
33 Simba's love, in "The Lion King"
34 "Hamlet" courtier
36 Was sweet (on)
37 Not producing the desired result
39 Took control
40 Sch. in Tulsa, Oklahoma
41 Jarrett of NASCAR
42 Payoff
43 Shine, in ad-speak

Down

1 Early photos
2 1966 U.S. Open champion Fred
3 Having a cheerful disposition
4 One-named singer for the 1960s Velvet Underground
5 Ethnic group of Vietnam
6 William H., author of "The Tunnel"
9 Method used to determine the age of an organic object: 2 wds.
10 Lab item measuring fluid pressure: hyph.
11 Copy, for short
13 Patsy Cline's "____ Pieces": 3 wds.
14 Carrere of "Wayne's World"
20 Toronto's province, for short
21 Habitable artificial satellite, briefly
22 ____ fault: 2 wds.
25 "Believe it ____!": 2 wds.
26 One way to saute: 2 wds.
27 Intermediate, at law
29 British secondary school exam: 2 wds.
30 Got by (with): 2 wds.
32 Distinction, slangily
35 Business execs in charge of accounts, initially
36 Bra specification: 2 wds.
38 Canyon or haban suffix

258

Across

1 Made: abbr.
4 Entirely
7 Org. for dentists
10 That: Sp.
11 Year in Ethelred the Unready's reign
12 River of Venezuela
13 Loss leader?: 2 wds.
14 After a fashion: 2 wds.
16 "Don't look at me!": 2 wds.
18 Baseball's Martinez and others
19 Mooch
21 Arthurian lady
23 Ill-judged
25 Flawed somehow: abbr.
27 They were straight outta Compton
28 Sets of two, briefly
29 Ted Baxter's wife on "The Mary Tyler Moore Show"
32 Former film brand
33 Wagnerian heroine
36 Badge with a photo on it, for short: 2 wds.
38 "Shake ___!" (hurry): 2 wds.
39 Method of painting in opaque pigments
41 "The Ransom of Black Stealth One" author Dean
42 Creature with a queen
43 Flight coordinators, initially
44 Prefix with colonial
45 He had the first billion-view YouTube video
46 Believer's suffix
47 Digital cable and satellite television channel, initially

Down

1 Intends
2 Shooter's setting: hyph.
3 Sign up for battle: 5 wds.
4 ___ , amas, amat
5 Stole tons?: 2 wds.
6 "How to Murder Your Wife" star Virna
7 Executive producer of "The Love Boat": 2 wds.
8 More pretentious, as a painting
9 Dawn deity
15 "The ___ Wrote For You" (2014 movie written by David Kauffman): 2 wds.
17 Overnight accommodation
20 Jets or Sharks, e.g.
22 Drill wielder's qualification, initially
24 Big basins
25 Supermarket with a red oval logo, initially
26 Spheres
30 Pro follower
31 Shelley's "___ Skylark": 2 wds.
34 Some northern Canadians
35 Encourage: 2 wds.
37 Berry in modern diet supplements
39 Store with fashionable ads, with "The"
40 Outside: prefix

259

Across

1. Ad ____
4. Kind of agent: abbr.
7. Letter ender, initially
10. Band with the record for most Top 40 hits without a #1 single, in short
11. Former football coach Parseghian
12. Salt: Fr.
13. Musical dir.
14. Roof supported by columns
16. Black quartz
18. Varieties: abbr.
19. "Majesté" preceder
21. Kardashian and Komando
25. "Ethan Frome" star
27. Hindu titles
28. Having had many birthdays
29. Antioxidant additive, initially
31. ____U
32. 10th-century pope: 2 wds.
34. Dazzling effects
36. Facial outbreak
37. Opening run
38. Genre of popular music, initially
40. Brainless one, slangily
43. Collective farm in Israel
47. Simile center: 2 wds.
48. Here, to Pierre
49. School org.
50. Papeete's island: abbr.
51. Decoration for heroism, initially
52. Health gp. based in Atlanta
53. East ender?

Down

1. Achilles, e.g.
2. Actress Lena
3. Seed leaf (botany)
4. Skip of a stone on water
5. Crushed by grief: hyph.
6. Fat from hogs
7. Next-to-last Greek letter
8. Iron pumper's pride: abbr.
9. ____-mo
15. Sounds of disapproval
17. Crosses (out)
20. Break down
22. Expose (food) to gamma rays
23. Atomizer's output
24. Jet set jets, for short
25. Vincent Lopez's theme song
26. A util.
30. Elvis' motto, initially
33. Word that denotes an action
35. ____ Soundsystem, band fronted by James Murphy
39. "____ Dimittis" (canticle in the Book of Luke)
41. Pre-1917 Russian ruler
42. Newswoman Paula
43. Tease
44. Suffix for graph or gymnast
45. Pen or lighter brand
46. Efron of "That Awkward Moment"

260

Across

1. Letters on a rubber check
4. Enzyme suffix
7. Fight
10. Lucy of "Elementary"
11. Windy City rail system letters
12. Sch. whose mascot is Cy the Cardinal
13. Former name of the cable network Versus, initially
14. Geom. figure
15. Z preceder?: 2 wds.
16. Female superhero: 2 wds.
19. Chihuahua bark
20. Resentment
21. Big name in brewing
23. Make progress: 2 wds.
26. "Ain't happening": hyph.
27. Civil War side, with "the"
28. Southern Iraqi city
30. Blues musician Bonnie
31. "Can ___ least sit down?": 2 wds.
32. Abbr. in company names
33. Flat strip on the neck on a stringed instrument
38. T-shirt label abbr.
39. Sports drink
40. When doubled, a yellow Teletubby
41. Federal warning system activated by FEMA
42. June preceder
43. ___ Soundsystem, band fronted by James Murphy
44. Welfare org.
45. Chicago to Miami dir.
46. River in Somerset

Down

1. Sweet ___ (sugar substitute): 2 wds.
2. Corn storage facility
3. Comic behavior: 2 wds.
4. Swallow
5. Cookbook direction
6. Small elongated insect
7. Directly (opposite)
8. Charles barker
9. "___ giorno!"
17. Dinnerware washer
18. Pizza herb
21. Popular meeting place, in London
22. "I knew it!"
24. Granola bit
25. W.S.J. rival
29. Elite groups: hyph.
30. Cut of beef: 2 wds.
33. Cut out
34. Certain food stores, initially
35. Vitamin bottle info.
36. "The Amazing ___" (game show)
37. Area above a column base, in architecture

261

Across

1 Fuji competitor, once
5 Opera number
9 Educate
11 Kind of mail
12 Boxer Marciano's first name
13 Have ___ for (be perceptive to): 2 wds.
14 Rude person
15 Italian baroque painter Guido
17 "___ New York" (1906 song): 2 wds.
19 ___ Jones
22 Ten-cent coin
24 The very beginning: 2 wds.
26 Order from the leader
28 ___ Foods, grocery store chain
29 Informal and unpretentious
31 Make leg warmers, e.g.
32 Literary inits.
33 Glory
35 D-Day target town: 2 wds.
36 Try to win
39 Seeger, Townshend, and Yarrow
42 Not telling the truth
44 Soviet moon mission series
45 Ivan ___, 1980s tennis champ
46 Scraps of a sort
47 "The Morning Watch" writer James

Down

1 Razor brand
2 Small cars of the 1990s
3 Exact copy
4 Grp. for Panthers and Cavaliers
5 ___-Frid Lyngstad (former member of Abba)
6 Dileep who played Dr. Max Patel in "Avatar"
7 "___ for ice cream": 2 wds.
8 Pub potion
10 Scope starter?
11 Strappy shoe
16 Antiquity, once
18 It holds your head
19 Certain movement of a golf club
20 "Dedicated to the ___ Love" (Shirelles hit): 2 wds.
21 Compass point
22 Nimble
23 Union agreements?: 2 wds.
25 John Lennon's widow
27 Syllables of reproach: 2 wds.
30 Bald Brynner
34 "Mama" speaker
35 Six, in Seville
37 French wave
38 Eye amorously
39 Mideast grp.
40 Austria's continent, briefly
41 Explosive letters in "Angry Birds"
43 Vote of support

262

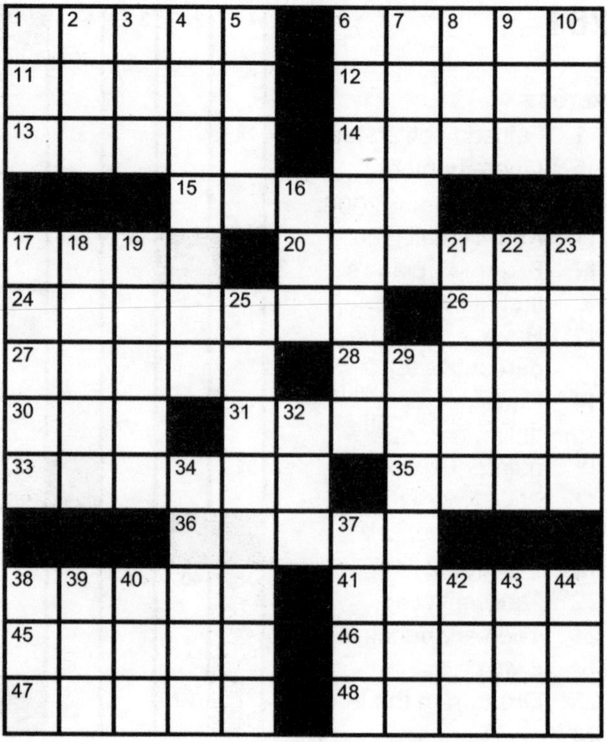

Across

1 Cuban dance
6 Storage disc: hyph.
11 Palestinian party founded by Yasser Arafat
12 ___-Loompa (Roald Dahl creation)
13 Online magazine once owned by Microsoft
14 "Buffalo Stance" singer Cherry
15 Some Apple computers
17 Wall St. figures
20 Brooches, e.g.
24 Transparent, modern-style: hyph.
26 Newspaper worker: abbr.
27 Conn. institution of learning, informally: 2 wds.
28 In an ironically humorous way
30 Wee, so to speak
31 Sofa that converts into a bed
33 Correctly
35 Lucie's brother
36 Laura Petrie's anguished cry: 2 wds.
38 "___ knew Susie like…": 2 wds.
41 Finish second
45 They go on and off the highway
46 Autobahn vehicles
47 Dumpster deposit
48 Depart

Down

1 Certain baseball positions, shortly
2 Suffix with effect
3 N.Y.C. subway inits.
4 Fabric resembling cambric
5 "Could we get started, please…"
6 Bring to a close
7 ___ number on (undermines): 2 wds.
8 Former White House inits.
9 Reveal, poetically
10 Start of a Chinese game
16 To the other side: abbr.
17 Sanctuaries
18 Broadcast again: hyph.
19 Late S.F. attorney Melvin
21 R.E.M. vocalist Michael
22 Mayberry's Goober and Gomer
23 Heidi's creator
25 Classified, slangily: hyph.
29 Another term for "purple": hyph.
32 Paper size: abbr.
34 Oddballs, slangily
37 Iridescent gem
38 N.Y.C. subway line
39 Considerably
40 Singer Sumac
42 Critic ___ Louise Huxtable
43 104 in Rome
44 Suffix with computer

263

Across

1 Famed restaurateur Vincent

6 Band with the 2008 album "Black Ice"

10 Olympic gold medalist, ___ Bolt

11 Forgo

12 State of being without a flaw or defect

14 Summer, in Saint-Tropez

15 Disturb

16 "___ Bowl of Tea" (Wayne Wang movie): 2 wds.

18 Prestigious mil. awards

22 Round up (as livestock)

25 Row producer

26 Biggest artery

27 Pageant winner

29 Louisville Slugger, e.g.

30 Most acidic

32 Old English letters

34 Insect's feeler

35 TV music vendor: hyph. 2 wds.

37 Fed. support benefit

40 It's worthless: 2 wds.

43 Jamaican fruit

44 Congo, formerly

45 Ill-gotten gains

46 City and county in Texas

Down

1 Manager, briefly

2 At ___ time (prearranged): 2 wds.

3 Element of the lanthanide series: 2 wds.

4 Subtraction amt.

5 Krypton, e.g.: 2 wds.

6 Piedmont wine center

7 Infant

8 Pair

9 "Anderson Cooper 360°" channel

13 Shade of black

17 Kitchen pest

19 Type of rug

20 ___ Tavern ("The Simpsons" locale)

21 Enraptured

22 "...did gyre and gimble in the ___" (Carroll)

23 Pike

24 Balance

28 Website address, for short

31 Forthright

33 Top part of a skeleton

36 End-of-the-week letters

38 Sonoran Indian

39 Cruise capitaine's stops

40 Little Labrador

41 Big: abbr.

42 Oil holder

264

Across

1 Peninsula and town in Quebec
6 Rights org.
11 Rap sheet listing
12 ___ Island, Fla.
13 Sandwiches for dessert
14 Spinning
15 Architectural borders
17 Marvin of Motown
18 Team VIPs, shortly
19 K-6: abbr.
21 Roadside rescuers, initially
22 Footstool
25 Part of NATO: abbr.
26 "This ___ surprise!": 2 wds.
27 Egg ___ yung
28 Deems it appropriate (to): 2 wds.
30 Old boat
31 Suffix with narc
32 Ruin
33 Common: prefix
35 Some 1980s Chryslers: 2 wds.
37 Children's author Scott
39 When some have brunch: 2 wds.
41 "Be ___ of" (be intended to help): 2 wds.
42 Intend to
43 Comes down to earth
44 Short-winded

Down

1 Main mail HQ letters
2 Seize, usurp
3 Freetown native: 2 wds.
4 Amalgamates
5 Gaelic tongue
6 "I ___ Man of Constant Sorrow": 2 wds.
7 Three-stripers
8 Active ingredient in baking powder: 3 wds.
9 ___-deucey (backgammon variant)
10 Fish stick?
16 Feeling bad on a boat
18 "Serpico" author
20 Aspiring atty.'s exam
22 LP player: hyph.
23 Gives advice
24 Expensive Japanese beef
29 Unemotional
32 Enjoy the tub
33 Cobra's configuration
34 ___ St. Vincent Millay
36 Play group
38 Mormon letters
40 Nationals grp.

265

Across

1 Soaks, as hemp
5 Hard white fat used in cooking
9 Remote
11 "They'll Do It Every Time" comic strip creator Jimmy
12 Direct-marketed knife brand
13 Make a full confession: 2 wds.
14 Tag on some American-made items: 2 wds.
16 Lass
17 Elephant keeper, in India
21 Traveler's need: 2 wds.
25 Several kings of Norway
26 Critical times: hyph.
27 Flesh of a cow used as food
28 Baudelaire's forte
29 Rani's wear
31 Oil used as an insect repellent
37 ___ bean (source of chocolate)
38 Throng
39 Saint for whom Chile's capital is named
40 Encircle as a military tactic
41 Actress Hathaway
42 U.K. honorees

Down

1 Alternative to Mario Batali
2 Tiger Woods's ex
3 Ms. Morrison, novelist
4 Fair: hyph.
5 Carpenter's need, at times: 2 wds.
6 The ___ Reader (magazine)
7 12th month of the Jewish civil year
8 Best
10 Parasitic plant
11 Frost
15 Fired up
17 Mafia
18 Oktoberfest drink
19 "Some ___ meat and canna eat": Burns
20 Not visible to a theater audience
22 Spare key hider
23 Firth of Clyde port
24 "Gentleman" singer
26 Behavior
28 Master
30 Suffix with buck
31 Brother of Abel
32 Volunteer's words: 2 wds.
33 Country singer Church
34 Singer Lisa who launched her own Eyewear Collection
35 Olympic sled
36 Copies
37 Windy City rail system letters

266

Across

1 Tandoor oven products
6 Fat flier
11 Holding
12 Back porch on "The Golden Girls," named for a Hawaiian island
13 Failure in the supply of electricity: 2 wds.
15 "Bambi" character
16 Hello or goodbye
17 Time off, initially
18 British title
19 French possessive
20 Org. until 1993
21 Love on the Champs-Élysées
23 Blanchett of "Manifesto"
24 LIII x L
26 Line of clothing?
29 Busts
32 "Les Girls" actress Taina
33 South American three-toed sloths
34 Syndicate
36 Ike's command in W.W. II
37 Pipe material, for short
38 Pier gp.
39 Strong wind, especially in New England
42 Shiraz native
43 Hoist again, as a sail
44 Incessantly: 2 wds.
45 Walk ___ in someone else's shoes: 2 wds.

Down

1 Scruffs
2 Saint ___, Canadian rock band
3 Teaming, like angry bees
4 Born: Fr.
5 Layer of rock in the ground
6 B.B. King's musical genre
7 California's largest newspaper, for short
8 Extent-wise: 2 wds.
9 It's attractive on the fridge
10 Puncture
14 State of excessive activity
22 New age chant
23 151, in Roman numerals
25 Purgative made from buckthorn bark
26 Shown past the foyer: 2 wds.
27 Corrida quarry: 2 wds.
28 Ancient meeting places
30 Composer Shostakovich
31 Cirque du ___
33 Apple orchard pest
35 Boat with a flat bottom
40 Spike TV, once
41 College year div.

267

Across

1 Used a surgical beam
6 Certain musical symbol: 2 wds.
11 Prefix for clast or graphic
12 "Space Invaders" maker
13 Pianist Peter and family
14 Family member, after a wedding: hyph.
15 Tight-fitting necklace
17 Southern pronoun
18 Meet, as expectations: 2 wds.
20 Xs to the Greeks
22 Maltreater
26 Put on the line
27 Logical operators
28 Polite shorthand abbr.
29 Shedding tears
31 "___ Rose" (song from "The Music Man")
32 Brain cell
34 Big name in video games
37 "Winnie the Pooh" character
40 Last-minute greeting: hyph.
42 Bulgaria's capital
43 Kris Kristofferson hit: 2 wds.
44 Some Italian cars, for short
45 Atom bomb trial: abbr., 2 wds.
46 Attended: 2 wds.

Down

1 "The Mod Squad" role
2 Banda ___ (Sumatran city)
3 Female students' org.
4 Edible Japanese mushrooms
5 Gives medicine to
6 Volkswagen hatchback
7 "___ Hear Me?" (David Bowie song): 2 wds.
8 Jaime Murray, on "Dexter"
9 Common Latin abbr.: 2 wds.
10 Barnyard bird
16 Take up again, as a case
19 SuperStation initials
20 Toronto media inits.
21 Self starter?
23 Incidental results of larger projects
24 "Ragtime" author's monogram
25 Cape Town country, initially
27 Lunch hour
30 Dire Straits: "Brothers ___": 2 wds.
31 New Orleans university
33 Shorten a plank
34 Tailor-made
35 Rhinelander's "real"
36 Marvin who sang "What's Going On"
38 Org. that sues pirates
39 Orient
41 Sleuth: abbr.

268

Across

1 Chasers
6 Miss ___ (TV psychic)
10 Hubbubs: hyph.
12 Light
13 With money: 2 wds.
14 Long
15 Brightness measure: 2 wds.
17 ___ Khan
19 911 respondent, initially
20 Decorates with bathroom tissue, for short
23 Kind of battery
25 "The Fountainhead" character Howard
27 R.E.M. vocalist Michael
28 "Seascape" playwright
29 Women's rights activist Bella
30 ___ spirits (depressed): 2 wds.
31 Hair colorer
32 Kind of order
34 Pre-album collectibles, for short
35 Shun
37 Hospital supplies
40 "___ that" (the text runs thus): 2 wds.
43 Practice in the ring
44 Beam of natural light
45 "Rooty Tooty Fresh 'N Fruity" chain
46 Equals

Down

1 Greek F
2 Suffix with gall or harp
3 Mix with other people
4 Former Miami Heat star, familiarly
5 Annual candy treats: 2 wds.
6 Police officer ranking below a chief: abbr.
7 52, to Cicero
8 South extension
9 "___ Como Va" (Santana song)
11 Traditional ancestor of the Semites
16 Trustworthy: 2 wds.
17 Longtime Syrian president
18 Managed with difficulty: 2 wds.
20 Articles such as dishes, glasses, etc.
21 Tranquilizing injection before surgery: hyph.
22 Depicts with bias
24 Mountain god in Incan mythology
26 Canadian TV channel
33 Galatea's love in Greek myth
35 Holliday's O.K. Corral ally
36 Anglo-Saxon slave
37 Gov. assistance to the needy
38 Bible book before Phil.
39 "Drag Me to Hell" costar Dileep
41 Tasha ___, Denise Crosby's "Star Trek" role
42 The S in iOS, briefly

269

Across

1 She was Adrian in "Rocky"
6 "It's a Wonderful Life" director Frank
11 Summer ermine
12 James ___ Garfield
13 It's served with fish sticks: 2 wds.
15 Road map abbr.
16 Bugs Bunny's catchphrase: "What's up, ___?"
17 Place to study
18 "___ Lang Syne"
20 Some field workers
22 Make ready, briefly
23 Tulsa sch. named for a televangelist
24 Expertise
26 Lock horns
30 Quick turnaround, slangily
32 McEwan and Somerhalder
33 Kind of ticket
36 Loose earth
37 Party animal?
38 Utmost
40 "Nope"
41 Not working
44 Hayworth and Moreno
45 Dogma
46 Marsh growth
47 Birdie beater

Down

1 Some shoe fasteners: hyph.
2 First president of the Turkish republic
3 Siren of German legend
4 "Ten thousand saw ___ a glance" (Wordsworth): 2 wds.
5 Some: 2 wds.
6 Californian buckthorn
7 Legal letters
8 Easily offended sort
9 Track competitor
10 Words of agreement
14 "___ Cop" 1987 movie
19 Low grade: 2 wds.
21 Glaringly vivid and graphic
25 She's one of the pride
27 Putting on, as weight
28 Come apart
29 Artsy one
31 ___'acte (intermission)
33 Bake, as eggs
34 First word of a counting rhyme
35 Make ___ of (mentally highlight): 2 wds.
39 Detest
42 Hip home
43 Some like it hot

270

Across

1 Center of egocentricity
5 "Oxford Blues" star, 1984
9 New Balance competitor
10 Fruit with a sweet pulpy flesh
11 Directions word
12 Darrin's chief antagonist on "Bewitched"
14 Chemistry suffix
15 Spanish 101 verb
16 Take off
17 Storage file for e-mails
19 Day-___
20 Has almost arrived: 2 wds.
21 Shiny on top?
22 Don't move: 2 wds.
24 Hussy
26 Drive-in employee
29 Donne's "done"
30 Z's
31 Org. for Brendan Steele
32 Bag thickness
33 Q trailers
34 Have a psychological problem about, slangily: 2 wds.
36 In ___ (undisturbed)
37 Cake decorators
38 Nash's "The ___ lama...": hyph.
39 Soft ball material
40 Taj Mahal city

Down

1 Highly-seasoned sausage
2 "... ___ we speak": 2 wds.
3 Policy that pays out on death: 2 wds.
4 Portly plus
5 Big name in bone china
6 Like the farmer MacDonald
7 Indulgence in dreamy imagining
8 Register
10 ROM in some computers: 2 wds.
13 Like two peas in ___: 2 wds.
15 Rhyme scheme pattern
18 Baltic resident
21 Songwriter Bacharach
23 Simon or Williams
24 Campus figure, briefly
25 Writer born Ursula Kroeber
27 Edible shellfish
28 Singer Clark
30 Cartoon figure from Belgium
35 Frankfurt's country: abbr.
36 "___ man walks into a bar...": 2 wds.

271

Across

1 Put to shame

6 "Infestation" rock group

10 Plural seen in geometry textbooks

11 Intro to a book

13 Big name in astrology

14 ___ Park (Thomas Edison's home)

15 Rocket interceptor, briefly

16 Some music purchases, for short

18 Patriotic org.

19 Opponents

21 "___ Got a Crush on You" (Gershwin song)

22 Last Supper question: 3 wds.

24 Sue Grafton's "___ for Lawless": 2 wds.

25 Chengchow's province

27 Burst of artillery

29 Psychiatrists' org.

30 Garden statue, sometimes

32 1968 battle period

33 Liquid used as an antifreeze

36 Black cuckoo

37 Tree that yields dark red timber

38 TNT part

39 Dodger Pee Wee

41 Texas hometown of Gene Autry

43 Like some vbs.

44 Jazz trumpeter Ziggy

45 Offenses

46 Pop singer Taylor

Down

1 Clamorous

2 Thumper's pal

3 First kicker to play in five Super Bowls (winning four of them): 2 wds.

4 Madam's mate

5 Subservient

6 Dashboard measures, for short

7 Exist

8 Certain surgical operation

9 City in Israel: 2 wds.

12 To a greater degree: 2 wds.

17 "Hey, you!"

20 Palindromic man's name

23 Remote

25 Howard Hawks movie of 1962

26 Series starters

28 Grant or Tan

31 First president of South Vietnam, ___ Dinh Diem

34 Kidney, e.g.

35 Radio host Hansen

37 Beer barrels

40 Clinton, e.g.: abbr.

42 Pier gp.

272

Across

1 Radiant look
5 Sarcophagus lid
9 European sports car, briefly
10 Fighting force
12 Having many famous performers (as a movie): hyph.
14 Senior citizen, to a Brit.
15 Mouse catcher
16 "Assault on Wall Street" director Boll
17 Imbibes: 3 wds.
19 Long time: abbr.
20 Nash's "The ___ lama...": hyph.
21 Noble horses
23 Broadway actress Joslyn
25 Low-altitude clouds
28 Icicle site
32 Wide shoe width
33 Going round and round: 3 wds.
35 Modern office machines, for short
36 Latin abbrs.
37 Upper left-hand corner key
38 "Jeopardy!" phrase: 3 wds.
41 "Elementary" costar Quinn
42 I.R.A. part: abbr.
43 Facility
44 Us, in France

Down

1 Philippine locale in W.W. II
2 Pass, like time
3 Chad's continent, briefly
4 Star of "The Goodbye Girl"
5 Carves out
6 Young 'un
7 Advance evidence for
8 Like tea
11 Paradises
12 Area of NYC
13 Rotations
18 Jessica of "Dark Angel"
22 Cavefish's functionless parts
24 ___ Lantier, central character in Émile Zola's "Germinal"
25 Dividing membranes
26 Geek Squad member
27 Los Angeles suburb mentioned in Tom Petty's "Free Fallin'"
29 Quick glance
30 Calls in
31 Items included in envs.
34 It's upstream from Luxor
39 Battery buys, initially
40 Prefix with friendly

273

Across

1. Prima ___ (at first glance)
6. "___ Mio": 2 wds.
11. Switch words: hyph.
12. Slangy denials
13. First name in 1950s politics
14. Annual awards show first hosted by Dennis Miller
15. Prefix for air or Atlantic
16. ___-di-dah (pretentious)
18. Suffix with den or dem
19. Tarzan creator's monogram
20. Green org.
21. "In the Good Old Summertime" lyricist Shields
22. Somersault
24. Land parcel
26. City in western Alaska
28. Make a mess of
30. Black stone
32. Tight
34. "Far out!": abbr.
36. Prefix with sphere
38. Sale tag abbr.
39. Charlemagne's realm, shortly
40. Got the biggest trophy
41. Relative of reggae
42. Do ___ situation: 2 wds.
44. "___ Be," Beatles song: 2 wds.
46. European Union country
47. Dress style: hyph.
48. Seller's counterpart
49. Workout spots, for some, initially

Down

1. Shaving cream applier
2. Fireplace log holder
3. In a callous manner
4. "... ___ woodchuck could chuck wood": 2 wds.
5. www.irs.gov service: hyph.
6. Two quarters: 2 wds.
7. "Send help!," in Morse code
8. Taking immediate advantage, often unethically
9. 1944 battle site
10. City north of Cologne
17. iPhone program
23. K-O connection
25. Michaels and Gore
27. Spectacles
29. Africa's ___ Faso
31. Tic-tac-toe loser letters
33. Hardly soothes
34. Equilateral figure
35. Chilean pianist Claudio
37. Decoration fixed to the surface of something else
43. Manhattan addition
45. Nightmarish street

274

Across

1 Rap group based in Southern Chicago
4 Clodhopper
7 Where: Lat.
10 Starfish feature
11 Clink
13 Country in southwestern Asia: 2 wds.
15 Martinique mountain
16 Issuance from Uncle Sam: hyph.
17 Fergie's namesakes
19 Keep ___ on (control): 2 wds.
21 Give the eye: 2 wds.
25 Task with no hope of success: 2 wds.
27 Use the radio dial: 2 wds.
28 Competes
29 Boring tool
31 Supreme Court justice since 2006
34 Put an ___ (halt): 2 wds.
37 Fail to keep in check: 2 wds.
39 Bud holder?
40 Harem chamber
41 Leave amazed
42 Miner's strike
43 Where to send letters, initially

Down

1 Awestruck response
2 Hillside, to Burns
3 Water-based paint
4 Willow variety
5 Near-Miss. state
6 At a greater distance
7 Central tip of a bivalve shell
8 ___ Din (rabbinical court)
9 Wrath, in Latin hymns
12 Valet, e.g.
14 Undeliverable and unreturnable mail: 2 wds.
18 Coeur d'___, ID
19 Back

20 Baseball's Brock
22 It can fall from the sky
23 Hydrocarbon ending
24 N.F.L. scores
26 Dry wind over the Sahara
30 Pasta with ridges
31 "Dark Angel" star
32 Movie mogul Marcus
33 Fortune teller's words: 2 wds.
35 Chore list header: hyph.
36 Waves, to Pedro
38 Bladed paddle

275

Across

1 Roller derby unit
4 Stage name of rapper John Barnes III
7 5th-century Germanic leader
9 "La Femme Nikita" network
12 Wrongdoing by a public official
14 "___ Psycho?" (song by Midwest rapper Tech N9ne): 3 wds.
15 Brokerage phrase: 2 wds.
16 Milk containers: abbr.
19 Leftover
20 "What ___ thou?"
22 Start of a pirate's chant: hyph.
24 Command level: abbr.
25 Wray of "King Kong"
27 Opposite of masc.
28 What, in France
30 Chemical compound
32 Mom's forte, for short
33 Oaf
34 Jason's sorceress wife
36 Shakespearean villain
39 Camper's need: 2 wds.
42 Spiral: prefix
43 Written language for the blind
44 Havoline competitor
45 Shoe designation

Down

1 ___ Linda, Calif.
2 Burt's "Batman" buddy
3 Person with an insurance contract
4 Letters accompanying some 2,000-year-old+ dates
5 Grazing ground
6 ___ Major (constellation)
8 ___ worse than death: 2 wds.
9 Not beneficial or useful
10 Harmed, injured
11 Gas: prefix
13 "The dog is not ___" (house rule): 2 wds.
17 Worrying bank letters
18 "Blackbeard's Ghost" writer Ben
20 Et ___ (and what follows): abbr.
21 Intensely
23 "Take Me Bak ___" (1972 Slade song)
26 Ming that's not a vase
29 Californian beverage company
31 Louis, in Pisa
34 N.Y.C. sports venue
35 Cop calls, initially
37 Stiff wind
38 S-curve
40 "___: Deadliest Roads" (reality TV series)
41 Short snooze

276

Across

1 Musical pitch
5 Gleaming
11 Biblical name for ancient Syria
12 ____ wait (prepares to ambush): 2 wds.
13 Make a forcefully reproachful protest
15 1986 movie directed by Oliver Stone
16 ____ Arann (Irish carrier)
17 Prefix with plastic
18 Prefix with phobia or polis
19 Old Testament book: abbr.
20 At least: 2 wds.
23 Kind of chair
24 Like some drinks
26 ____ Tomé and Principe (African republic)
29 "____ here"
30 Covers thinly with gold
32 Tulsa sch. named for a televangelist
33 Deluxe
35 Expression of an unfavorable opinion
37 Capacity of many a flash drive, informally: 2 wds.
38 French nut?
39 "____ March hare" (irate): 3 wds.
40 Czech Republic river

Down

1 Herringlike fish
2 Ultimatum words: 2 wds.
3 Superbowl III MVP
4 Chew the scenery
5 In addition
6 ____ Spin (classic toy): 2 wds.
7 "Let ____ Cry" (Hootie & the Blowfish hit)
8 Asimov and Newton
9 All-____ (late study sessions, casually)
10 January, to Mexicans
14 Speechwriter who coined the phrase "Read my lips: no new taxes"
18 Two-time loser to D.D.E.
21 Cockney dwelling
22 Bookkeeper's book
23 Point opposite WSW
24 Canopus's constellation
25 Entertained
26 Worked excessively hard
27 Grown together, in biology
28 Horse handler
29 Sin city
31 Peter and Gordon's "____ Pieces": 3 wds.
33 Like some churches: abbr.
34 Links org. for women
36 Near Eastern honorific

277

Across

1 Vehicle with a meter
4 Cooling units, for short
7 Pale ___ (kind of beer)
8 Mobile's state: abbr.
9 The Cavs, on scoreboards
12 Banishes overseas: 2 wds.
15 Peach or beech
16 Suitable
17 Asian and swine, e.g.
19 Pollution fighting govt. branch
20 Plays for time
22 "High Noon" marshal
24 Games grp.
25 Code breakers' org.
27 White stuff in Edinburgh
28 Makes lace
30 Rope or cable used to tow a ship
32 "Forgot About ___" (1999 rap song)
33 Tombstone name
34 Part of the steering gear of a car: 2 wds.
36 Least little bit
39 Physical or moral ruin
41 L.S.A.T. takers
42 Math subj.
43 Peacock network
44 Welcoming wreath
45 Pipe joint

Down

1 Play group
2 Oriele or Angel, e.g.
3 Woman who gives money to help a cause
4 Small batteries' letters
5 Student's week: 2 wds.
6 Kemo ___
9 NW or NE, for example: 2 wds.
10 Exercise expert, Jack ___
11 Dreyer's partner in ice cream
13 Computer brand
14 Need a bath badly
18 Diminutive suffix
20 Obedience school lesson
21 More sycophantic
23 Musical ability
26 Roadside rescuers, initially
29 Rockefeller Center muralist
31 Official order
34 N.F.L. scores
35 Kind of surgery
37 Soliloquy starter: 2 wds.
38 Suffix with utter or annoy
40 Special effects used in "Avatar," e.g.

278

Across

1. Bohemian
5. Matters of taste
11. "Psycho" actress Miles
12. Absorbed
13. Baltic feeder
14. Chocolate chip, e.g.
15. Skill in hunting, fishing or camping, e.g.
17. Ginnie ___
18. Married ladies of Spain: abbr.
21. It takes four jokers to play it
25. Fripp & ___ ("No Pussyfooting" collaborators)
26. Trim
27. Sling mud at
29. Tsp. or tbsp.
30. Comeback
32. "¿Quién ___?" ("Who knows?")
34. Hair raiser?
35. No longer needed or useful
40. Ancient Greek gathering places
42. "___ Did It Before (Same God)" (Tye Tribbett song): 2 wds.
43. Plovers named for their call
44. Japan's first capital
45. Actresses Estevez and Zellweger
46. Ending for kilo or kisso

Down

1. Acknowledge
2. Completely fix
3. BlackBerry rival, once
4. Outdoor laborer
5. Something only a handful of people know
6. Wild ox of Sulawesi
7. Univ. lecturers
8. Acorn producers
9. Tech. school on the Hudson R.
10. Canonized Fr. woman
16. One checking out a place in planning a crime
19. Biol. subject
20. Bitter
21. Spreadsheet pros, initially
22. First word of the "Aeneid"
23. Rich dark color: hyph.
24. Colorado ski resort
28. Architectural feature
31. "Dunno": 2 wds.
33. Bone-chilling
36. See socially
37. From a remote location
38. Racing org. formed by Wally Parks in 1951
39. Bulls or Bears
40. Truth in Lending no.
41. Plow horse command

279

Across

1 ___ d'oeuvre
5 Anytime: 2 wds.
11 Certain util.
12 Baseballer who played 2,130 consecutive games
13 1935 loser to Braddock
14 Whoever
15 Power to produce the result intended
17 Kind of bean
18 ___-al-Arab (Iraqi waterway)
21 Not reacting
25 Suffix with arbor or app
26 Actress Gardner of "Mogambo"
27 Non-gaming hotel on the Las Vegas Strip
30 Kind of drive: hyph.
32 Newsman Garrick
34 Source of materials to nourish the body
39 Nero or Caligula
40 Boone's nickname
41 Cat of many colors
42 Pierre's brainstorm
43 Having a harsh, high-pitched sound
44 Academy Award winner Blanchett

Down

1 "H.M.S. Pinafore" character
2 Count ___ ("A Series of Unfortunate Events" villain)
3 Coral ___
4 Cast lines
5 "Not ___!"
6 Axioms
7 "Sounds like a good idea!": 2 wds.
8 Camaro ___-Z
9 Wrinkled
10 Bigger than med.
16 Summons: abbr.
18 Wheeled moon vehicle, initially
19 Taken in
20 Taking after: 2 wds.
22 Row
23 Nobel-winning Andric
24 Video recorder, for short
28 Pasternak's homeland
29 Go after
30 100 yrs.
31 Pertaining to the number 2
33 Conductor Anderson
34 Coal-rich German region
35 River to the Ubangi
36 Nothing, in Nicaragua
37 Tech. product reviews website
38 Part of a C.S.A. signature: 2 wds.
39 300, to Nero

280

Across

1 A Musketeer
6 Stogie
11 Hose shade
12 Make used (to): var.
13 Coming beforehand
15 Partially-recognized state of Western Sahara, initially
16 Patriotic society, initially
17 Male hormone
22 Overly: hyph.
25 Reuters rival initials
26 "___ the Earth Move" (Carole King song): 2 wds.
27 Kind of system
29 Gave de ___, river of southwestern France
30 Charge
31 Intimate, cozy
34 Prof's org.
35 Suffix with brain or brawn
39 Singer whose albums include "Pearl": 2 wds.
43 Collectively: 2 wds.
44 Letter-shaped opening in some pistons: hyph.
45 Zellweger of "Bridget Jones's Diary"
46 Connery and Penn

Down

1 Biol. energy sources
2 Scarlett's home
3 Many-___ (multicolored)
4 Run
5 What M or F may indicate
6 Romero of the screen
7 Chap. 1 preceder
8 Visual way of interacting with a computer, initially
9 Edward F. ___, 32nd Governor of Kansas
10 Average: abbr.
14 "___ Anything" ("Oliver!" song): 2 wds.
18 Cambodia's Lon ___
19 Wise guy
20 Like some churches: abbr.
21 Dark time in ads
22 Great Plains home for an Indian: var.
23 The face ___ angel: 2 wds.
24 French egg
27 Buddhist Beastie Boy, initially
28 Put in the shadow
30 Key of Bruckner's Symphony No. 6, briefly: 2 wds.
32 Cat ___ tails (kind of whip): 2 wds.
33 View for a second time
36 Jazz legend Fitzgerald
37 Hill in Jerusalem: var.
38 Some explosives, initially
39 Bump
40 Enzyme suffix
41 No, in Nantes
42 Tiebreakers, briefly

281

Across

1 Chip go-with
4 Jamboree grp.
7 Crew member's implement
8 "Andy Capp" cartoonist Smythe
9 Prefix with bar
12 Long-running U.K. music mag.
13 Adds up
15 "A Day ___ Races": 2 wds.
17 Spanish felines
18 Author of "Pêcheur d'Islande" (1886)
19 Italian artist Guido (1575–1642)
20 Decorative lace mats: var.
24 Riddle-me-___
25 Steals
27 Anthem preposition
29 It may clash with your suit: 2 wds.
32 ___ and terminer
34 ___ Xiaoping, Chinese leader 1978–92
35 Distributes, with "out"
37 Crack
38 Hopping rat of Australia
40 "___ Girls"
41 At all
42 PC maker
43 Pop or op follower
44 Opposite NNW
45 Football positions: abbr.

Down

1 "Blackfire" writer Elizabeth
2 "Me as well!": 3 wds.
3 "___ Princess" (kids' board game): 2 wds.
4 Scottish hillside
5 Theology sch.
6 All excited
9 Between or among stars
10 Pebble
11 Davis of "Grumpy Old Men"
14 Egypt-Syria alliance, 1958–61, initially
16 Seat of Hawaii County
21 Different ending?
22 Prefix with tourism
23 Moo ___ pork
26 Plant of the arum family
27 Half a "Charlie and the Chocolate Factory" character
28 Keep an ___ (watch closely): 2 wds.
30 Flip
31 Gets rid of
33 Royale of old autodom
36 Eastern titles
37 Certain
39 Arch. relative

282

Across

1 Break
4 Burlington sch.
7 Something to chew on
10 95 or 66, e.g.: abbr.
11 Kung ___ shrimp
12 Genetic stuff, for short
13 Neighbor of Russ. and Pol.
14 College life
16 The Crimson Tide, familiarly
18 Wall St. action
19 "I'm so hungry, I could ___ horse!": 2 wds.
21 Straight as ___ (honest): 2 wds.
25 Slippery
28 Big bird
29 Budweiser rival
30 Composer Franz
32 TV's onetime "___ Club"
33 "If you asked me..." follow-up: 3 wds.
35 Play ___ (tennis): 2 wds.
37 Taken in, briefly
38 "Wheel of Fortune" buy: 2 wds.
40 1960s civil rights activist Brown, familiarly: 2 wds.
43 Tall, slim and graceful
47 From left to right: abbr.
48 "Gimme ___!" (start of an Iowa State cheer): 2 wds.
49 Your, in Italy
50 Draw
51 Early 20th-century Chinese president, Sun ___-sen
52 Spring mo.
53 Byrnes of "77 Sunset Strip"

Down

1 Chow
2 Aleutian island
3 Penetrable, porous
4 Work ___ lather: 2 wds.
5 "The Memorandum" playwright Havel
6 Ruth's birthplace
7 Alphabetic trio
8 Albuquerque coll.
9 Chin Ho Kelly in "Hawaii Five-0," Daniel ___ Kim
15 ___ double take: 2 wds.
17 "The law is ___..." (Dickens): 2 wds.
20 South American monkey
22 Lose moisture
23 One-named supermodel
24 Currency in Italy
25 Early baseball Hall-of-Famer ___ Rixey
26 Brewery containers
27 "Or ___!"
31 Per person
34 Prepared, as plans: 2 wds.
36 Chess champion of 1960–61
39 "That's ___ good idea": 2 wds.
41 Type of wit
42 Sentence part, briefly
43 Custom
44 ___ funk: 2 wds.
45 Quite drunk, slangily
46 Shostakovich's "Babi ___" Symphony

283

Across

1. Like some skiing
5. "___ Easy" (Guns n' Roses song): 2 wds.
10. Oslo's country, to natives
12. Christine of "Swing Shift"
13. Belief in a non-interventionist god
14. Thread holder
15. Have
16. Little battery letters
18. Kind of symbol, initially
19. Adjust, in a way
21. Queens airport, initially
22. Lavatory sign: 2 wds.
24. N. ___, 39th state
25. British coins
27. Kind of sole
29. H.S. math
30. Dweeb
32. Sucker
33. Atomic trials of the past, for short: 2 wds.
36. Knight's title
37. 1988 Dennis Quaid remake: inits.
38. Certain numero
39. Prefix with metric or graph
41. Egg cream ingredient
43. Cul ___: 2 wds.
44. It'll give a rise
45. Davis of "Do the Right Thing"
46. Ltr. footnotes

Down

1. Phrase of choice: 2 wds.
2. "My Fair Lady" composer
3. Machine for making books: 2 wds.
4. Latin examples, briefly
5. Ingrid's "Casablanca" role
6. Water source
7. Long strip of material used for carrying a bag: 2 wds.
8. Improvised
9. Cattle food made of the residue of linseeds, etc.
11. Common temple name
17. 1950s election monogram
20. Pop's kin
23. Seventh heaven
25. Fencing thrust
26. May and Stritch
28. Riddle-me-___
31. Palindromic artist
34. Tie up
35. They follow Augs.
37. Spanish 12
40. One month in Montpellier
42. Slangy affirmative

284

Across

1 Do some laps at the pool
5 "The Tragic Comedians" artist Walt
9 One of the O'Neills
10 Slender and elegant
12 Mountains
13 Senseless behavior
14 Hebrew prophet exiled to Babylon
16 Damascus's nation: abbr.
17 Millennium hundredths
22 Have a similar appearance to: 2 wds.
24 ___ terrier
26 Oslo's country, to natives
27 Narrow band in the design of cloth
29 Form of baseball: 3 wds.
30 401, to Nero
33 Free from bacteria, etc.
35 Andy Warhol's field: 2 wds.
39 Slave girl of opera
40 Popular shrub
41 Expensively furnished
42 Sounds of disapproval
43 Any day now

Down

1 Undersides
2 Lightheaded, casually
3 Add an extra layer between two pieces of fabric
4 Camouflage
5 "One Flew Over the Cuckoo's Nest" author Kesey
6 Suffix with form
7 Cellphone co.
8 French marshal in the Napoleonic Wars (1769–1815)
10 Aerodynamic
11 Hard black rubber
15 "It doesn't bother me!": 3 wds.
18 Cockeyed
19 Line leading to a place or point
20 Heart lines, for short
21 Realize
23 Guesstimate phrase: 2 wds.
24 Mil. rank
25 Own, to a Scot
28 Dreadlocked one
31 Child's response to a taunt: 2 wds.
32 Financial mogul Carl
34 Dad
35 Butter amount
36 Bar measures: abbr.
37 Neighbor of China, briefly
38 Singers Green and Jarreau

285

Across

1 Crock
4 1200, in Roman numerals
7 Doubly
10 Cigar residue
11 Help wanted ad letters
12 ___-rock (music genre)
13 "Thar ___ blows!"
14 Internet protocol, initially
15 "Shall I compare thee ___ summer's day" (Shakespeare): 2 wds.
16 Transportation of supplies by plane
18 N.Y.C. sports venue
19 Millionths of a meter
20 Had a taste
21 Vancouver Island native
23 Conn. neighbor
24 "Son of," in Arabic names
25 Ave. intersectors
27 One to beat
28 Coll. whose motto is Vox, Veritas, Vita (Voice, Truth, Life)
29 Dine away from home: 2 wds.
31 And so forth: abbr.
32 Misplay, e.g.
33 Chess champion of 1960–61
34 Lab diagnosis of genetic makeup: inits, 2 wds.
37 Drink cooler
38 Baby Pickles on "Rugrats"
39 Interest on a loan shark's money, casually
40 Highest note in Guido's scale
41 Relative of -ian
42 Center opening
43 Homily: abbr.
44 Hand-___ coordination
45 Whistler, at times: abbr.

Down

1 "Que ___?" (greeting in Spanish)
2 Sumo wrestling move
3 Like some explosive devices
4 Alfalfas' cousins
5 Brotherhood
6 Jai alai basket
7 1995 Val Kilmer movie: 2 wds.
8 "If ___" (Travis Tritt song): 3 wds.
9 Theater scenery, props, etc.: 2 wds.
17 Burning
21 Aspects of polite social behavior
22 Thing that hinders progress
26 Ball Park Franks company: 2 wds.
30 Playpen player
32 "Falcon Crest" actor Albert
35 1980 NFL MVP Brian
36 End-of-the-week letters

286

Across

1 Law enforcement and tax collection agency, initially
4 Weapon for shooting arrows
7 Shade of green
9 Broadcasting inits. since 1970
12 Cheese dish
13 ___ de vie
14 Sugar (pref.)
15 Provide with money
16 Swift
18 Rapper Pablo
19 Hack writer's output
21 Personal ad. spec.
22 Sch. in Tulsa, Oklahoma
23 Scottish expression of surprise
26 Sign, as an agreement: 2 wds.
29 Cattle farm
31 Ready to swing: 2 wds.
32 Melville book of 1847
33 Likewise
34 CPR expert
35 Shine faintly or intermittently
38 Go-___ (1980s band)
39 Carry-on: 2 wds.
40 Porker's pad
41 Some name suffixes

Down

1 Swiss river
2 F.D.R. plan
3 Plants of the borage family: hyph.
4 What a fairy might collect in the night: 2 wds.
5 Like poems of praise
6 Knows, old-style
8 Autograph hound's target: abbr.
9 Some atomic weapons: 2 wds.
10 Glazier's item
11 Crooner Vallee
15 Lawyer's charge
16 Measure of lift, weight, and time, initially
17 Meadow murmur
18 Numerousness
20 Vexation
24 Financial market regulators, initially
25 Selling quickly
27 Staff sgt., e.g.
28 Response at the door: 2 wds.
29 "Two Deaths" director Nicolas
30 Shot, for short
33 Much: 2 wds.
35 Sporty cars, briefly
36 Serving of corn
37 QB protectors

287

Across

1 Debtor's woe, shortly
5 El ___
9 One of the Sox, e.g.
10 One who hears "You've got mail!"
11 Duck's home
12 Labeled
13 Corrosion-resistant metal
15 Flew
16 "Pronto!": inits.
20 Removed the pits from
22 Prompt
23 Gave de ___, river of southwestern France
24 551, to Caesar
26 Hydrocarbon suffix
27 Etched: abbr.
29 Artificial
31 Lt. Kojak
32 Sierra Club founder John
33 Captain's order before sailing: 2 wds.
37 Lingo
40 Anderson and Bowersox
41 "Still ___" (Boney M song_: 2 wds.
42 Hightails it
43 Tolerate
44 Big ice cream brand

Down

1 Bewitched
2 Simple sci-fi race
3 Apartment on the top floor of a building
4 Decree
5 Shearer and Talmadge
6 Classification or type
7 Born, in society pages
8 Former fort on Monterey Bay
10 Track and field org.
12 Intermediary
14 Essential
17 Lead
18 Family circle member
19 D.C. leader
20 Roasting rod
21 Trig. function
25 "Who Can ___ To" (2014 musical movie): 2 wds.
28 Mountain lion
30 Tool used for cutting grain
34 Place for peas
35 "The Last Thing ___ Mind" (Tom Paxton song): 2 wds.
36 Automatic updates from favorite websites, initially
37 Triangular sail
38 Parisian soul
39 Cape Town's home letters

288

Across

1 King, in Hindi
5 Absolute
10 Composer Khachaturian
11 Meager
12 Follower of Hitler
13 Covers with soil
14 Chichén ___ (Mayan city)
15 GPS result
16 Girder: hyph.
18 Award given by a cable sports station, initially
22 Tetley tidbit: 2 wds.
25 Propyl suffix
26 ___ child
27 Alexandra in "Law & Order"
29 Technology that uses polarized light, initially
30 Rare earth element
32 Throw away
34 Newbie
35 Med. plan
37 Fluidly flippant
40 "Accept the facts!": 2 wds.
43 Em, to Dorothy
44 "Ripe" life stage: 2 wds.
45 Fork prong
46 Observers
47 Eat to excess, shortly: 2 wds.

Down

1 Delhi princess
2 Lillian Jackson Braun's "The Cat Who Smelled ___": 2 wds.
3 Exuberant gesture with splayed fingers: 2 wds.
4 Friendly
5 Card game for three
6 Successful job seeker
7 CPR giver
8 Book after Galatians: abbr.
9 Trains: abbr.
11 Sawlike organ
17 Ethereal
19 Not quite solid
20 Tire, in Paris
21 Backwoods affirmative: 2 wds.
22 Lean
23 Old ExxonMobil brand name
24 Greek salad chunks
28 Thank you, in Japan
31 Government bond, for short: hyph.
33 Rid of fleece
36 Planes in "Top Gun"
38 ___ way, shape, or form: 2 wds.
39 Bingo call: 2 wds.
40 Combatant
41 Son of Aga Khan
42 Alphabetical run

289

Across

1 Animal that uses two legs for walking

6 Two in traffic

9 Handle differently?

10 Nod, maybe

11 Sodium ___

13 Maxim

14 "The L Word" actress Daniels

15 "I've Gotta ___" (Sammy Davis Jr. song): 2 wds.

16 Barrio area in S. Calif.: 2 wds.

18 'Fore

19 Leg wrap for soldiers

20 Garage jobs

21 Baseball Hall-of-Famer Manush

23 Airwaves regulator letters

26 Spin around

27 Italian currency, before the euro

28 Black, romantically

29 Bushed

30 Neatness

33 It's spotted in casinos

34 Theraflu alternative

35 Leno's announcer Hall

36 Leaders of the New School debut album, "A Future Without ___": 2 wds.

Down

1 Underwent a change

2 Years old: 2 wds.

3 Take off the peel, as an apple

4 Diplomat's office: abbr.

5 "Gloria in excelsis ___"

6 Game similar to euchre

7 Pointless

8 Beatles song "I've Just ___ Face": 2 wds.

9 Person in the passenger seat

11 Crèche cynosure

12 Crows' homes

16 "I'm Just Wild About Harry" composer, ___ Blake

17 To ___ (perfectly): 2 wds.

19 Former monetary unit of Ireland

20 Eric Cartman's mother on "South Park"

21 Cross-breed

22 Undercut

23 Shoot: 2 wds.

24 Dimin.'s opposite

25 Bounders

26 Crystal-lined rock

27 Fine ravelings of cotton fibers

29 She played Ginger on "Gilligan's Island"

31 Zenith competitor, initially

32 Prune

290

Across

1 Okra
6 Meat skewers
11 Character who said "As God is my witness, I'll never be hungry again."
12 Accept responsibility in a mature way: 2 wds.
13 Surgeon's target
14 Oil supporter
15 Madness
16 Having few stories: hyph.
18 Art on an arm
20 E.T.O. commander
21 Old trucking watchdog gp.
22 Thin
23 Going well, informally: hyph.
26 Gloomy Gus
27 Vietnamese holiday
28 Pier gp.
29 Monk of yore
33 Literary form of Norwegian
36 Ballot abbr.
37 Owing: 2 wds.
38 Bull: prefix
40 North Sea tributary
41 "What the Butler Saw" playwright
42 They come before Octs.
43 Odes, sonnets, etc.

Down

1 "I understand!": 2 wds.
2 Zoe Saldana role
3 "American Buffalo" playwright
4 Dude
5 Fitting on the gunwale of a boat
6 White-crested diving duck
7 Early late-night host
8 Longtime employee, say
9 Day of the week
10 Bad temper
17 Not-yet-mature eggs
19 Jabber?
22 Plenty
23 Papal court: 2 wds.
24 "On the ___," honest or sincere: 3 wds.
25 Working area of a computer screen
26 Brit. term for musical half notes
30 Rinse, as with a solvent
31 Bananarama's "Robert de ___ Waiting"
32 Ivory's counterpart
34 Bump
35 Roger of "Cheers"
39 River of Venezuela

291

Across

1 Large grp. of businesses
5 Decrees
10 Palm product
11 Minority member in India
12 Internet guffaw
13 "Lara Croft: Tomb ___"
14 Tiny insects
16 Singer Turner
17 Speculative, conceptual
20 Games grp.
21 Big galoots
22 Put a match to
23 Perch
24 ___ up (riled)
27 Old atlas initials
28 U.S.N.A. grad.
29 Gab: hyph.
33 Workers' protection org.
34 Jewish month after Av
35 Continues: 2 wds.
37 New Jersey's ___ University
40 Most sick
41 Leavings
42 Seashore
43 Inappropriate in the office, initially

Down

1 Bull's-eye: abbr.
2 Pizarro's quest
3 Mirror
4 Paralyzing disease
5 J.F.K. regulators
6 Eye problem
7 Early form of sonar, initially
8 "Irons in the Fire" singer ___ Marie
9 Of an ecological unit
11 Antecedent
15 Town in western Wisconsin, La ___
17 Up to, in ads
18 ___ polloi (common people)
19 Explosive solid used in detonators
24 Integrative medicine types
25 Bus. letter abbr.
26 "For shame!" noise
27 Decrees
29 Of a Hindu discipline
30 Play ___ (perform alone): 2 wds.
31 Pincerlike claw
32 Territory in northwestern Canada
36 Dortmund direction
38 Raiding grp.
39 Three compass points, initially

292

Across

1. Former football quarterback Brian
5. Sound of high-pitched laughter: 2 wds.
11. ___ about (lawyer's phrase): 2 wds.
12. Add
13. "A friend to honesty and ___ to crime" (Allan Pinkerton): 2 wds.
14. Model anew
15. "Munky" Shaffer's band
16. Rock band ___ Speedwagon
17. Slow to react
19. Sporty car roof: hyph.
23. Concept of great significance
26. ___ provençale: 2 wds.
27. Plains dweller
28. Afternoon gathering
29. Place for trash
30. Sta-___ fabric softener
31. Author taught by H.G. Wells: inits., 2 wds.
33. Instrument in the painting "Spirit of '76"
35. Zaire's Mobutu ___ Seko
36. The Pathet ___ (political movement)
38. Hydrating cream brand
41. Where Memphis is, gazetteer-style: 2 wds.
44. Seductive spy ___ Hari
45. Warbling Warwick
46. Professor 'iggins, to Eliza
47. Bracing coastal atmosphere: 2 wds.
48. Nutritional info. letters

Down

1. Saturate
2. Compressed data?
3. With insufficient money: 2 wds.
4. Before the present: 2 wds.
5. Co-founding journalist of "60 Minutes": 2 wds.
6. Rapier relative
7. Attraction near Orlando
8. "Hath ___ sister?" (Shakespeare): 2 wds.
9. Two of ninety?
10. Summer clock setting, initially
18. "You've ___ Friend" (James Taylor/Carole King song): 2 wds.
20. Plateau
21. Hollywood's Ken or Lena
22. Piece of glass in a window
23. Head, in Hamburg
24. Place for pins
25. Title for Judi Dench
32. Chemical cousin
34. "Mefistofele" role
37. Years, to Cicero
39. Razor name
40. Childish cheers
41. 1960s grp.
42. "___ geht's?" (German "How are you?")
43. ___ T: 2 wds.

293

Across

1 Hoodoo
6 9-3 Aero Sedan maker
10 "You ___ Beautiful" (Cocker hit of 1975): 2 wds.
11 Zoe Saldana role, Nyota ___
12 ___ boom
13 Absent: 2 wds.
14 Raw material sent to some textile plants
16 New Zealander
17 1995 earthquake city
20 Animal dandruff
24 Islet
25 Initially, a psychic gift
26 ___ y plata (Montana's state motto, meaning "gold and silver")
27 "Haven't a clue": 2 wds.
29 Brute
30 "___ as I'm concerned...": 2 wds.
32 Patron, sponsor
37 Bluebird genus
38 Dalai Lama's city
39 Newsman Roger
40 Blotto
41 Frequent site of spectacles
42 Spreads

Down

1 Like some nouns: abbr.
2 Slangy ending for buck
3 Mannerly man, briefly
4 "Am I to blame?": 3 wds.
5 Après-ski drink
6 Person certain to succeed: hyph.
7 Car
8 "Sea" whose name means "sea of islands"
9 Hanger-on?
11 Open, in a way
15 Dozes: 2 wds.
17 Trombonist Winding
18 Suffix with human
19 1,055 joules, initially
21 Follow
22 Foul up
23 Old World deer
25 Stamp, as a document
28 Kids' caretaker: var.
29 Source of litmus
31 Finnish architect Alvar ___
32 Former capital of Moravia
33 Some shoe sizes
34 Bind
35 ___ buco
36 Some stingers
37 Accelerator bit

294

Across

1 SoCal law force, initially
5 Large convex molding
10 Crucifix letters
11 In need of immediate action
12 Cow calls
13 (If) required: 2 wds.
14 Not working: 2 wds.
16 Lee Remick's role in "The Long, Hot Summer"
17 IRS identifiers
21 Discharge waste
24 Kenan's Nickelodeon pal, once
25 Defeats thoroughly
26 Egypt's capital
28 Have some food
29 Con: 2 wds.
31 Sandwich choices
33 Olive genus
34 Tropical shrub with large, colorful flowers
38 Iron-rich mountain range
41 State south of Kans.
42 Follower of Dionysus in Ancient Greece
43 Literally, "numbered"
44 Proclamation reader of old
45 Letters from Greece

Down

1 Cadillac One, for one: abbr.
2 Before long
3 Bring a criminal action against
4 Destroy the peace of
5 Long hike
6 Double-S curves
7 One of the primary colors
8 Canadian sch. with campuses in Fredericton and Saint John
9 ___ Jeanne d'Arc
11 Eastern church member
15 Like May through August, letterwise: hyph.
18 Parka worn while on the piste: 2 wds.
19 Fiddler of Rome
20 Messy dresser
21 "Jekyll & Hyde" actress Linda
22 Internal scan: hyph.
23 Dangerous bacteria: 2 wds.
27 Spectacular
30 Bridge abstention: 2 wds.
32 "Primer" director and costar Carruth
35 Building beam: hyph.
36 Outer arm bone
37 Mailing courtesies, initially
38 2100, to Caesar
39 Q-Tip target
40 Six in Siena

295

Across

1 Has a yen
6 Is wearing: 2 wds.
11 Car company that makes the Volt, briefly
12 City of northeastern Italy
13 "Nine" star Sophia
14 College in Atherton, California
15 Where a plane may be seen: 4 wds.
17 Weekend wear: hyph.
18 "I'm outta here!"
20 Croix de ___, French military decoration
24 Implore
25 "Quiet down!" sounds
26 Long swimmer
27 Cookie fillings
29 Matter in the Big Bang theory
30 Summer cooler: 2 wds.
32 Certain shirt fastening: 2 wds.
36 Disputed islands in the East China Sea
37 Last Supper question: 3 wds.
38 "___ to Be You"
39 Plains tribe
40 Mine excavation
41 Conductor Dohnányi et al.

Down

1 Rights monitoring org.
2 Hack
3 Birthright
4 Be that as it may: 2 wds.
5 Techno instrument, for short
6 Bone extending from the shoulder to the elbow
7 Latin carol opener
8 Make, as a putt
9 Kind of child
10 ___-Impressionism (art movement)
16 Bounding main: 2 wds.
18 Toronto media inits.
19 Ending for beef or bump
21 Sister or uncle, e.g.
22 Suffix for chicka or campo
23 Word after Dutch or American
25 Shut off
28 "(There's) No Gettin' Over Me" singer Ronnie
29 Base words?: 2 wds.
31 Tot's wheels, casually
32 Suffragist Carrie Chapman ___
33 Roman emperor defeated by Vitellius
34 "The Joshua Tree" band: 2 wds.
35 Portuguese navigator, Bartolomeu ___
36 Prefix for conduct or construct

296

Across

1. Refuel: 2 wds.
6. Expand
11. Old saying
12. Patsy Cline's "___ Pieces": 3 wds.
13. Picnickers run races in them: 2 wds.
15. Latin examples, briefly
16. Different ending?
17. Bean cover
18. Complete
20. Mel, singer nicknamed "The Velvet Fog"
23. Sheba, today
27. New Balance competitor
28. Race, in Oaxaca
29. Stand of trees
31. Pungent Indian dish
32. "McSorley's Bar" painter
34. Jackie's "O"
37. Co. that produced "Hill Street Blues"
38. One day in Spain
41. Interlacing strips of metal, etc.
44. Bake in a shallow dish
45. Talk show host Lake
46. ___ vincit amor
47. "I can't believe I ___ much!": 2 wds.

Down

1. Awe-struck expression
2. "I Wouldn't Treat ___" (Bobby Bland song): 2 wds.
3. Some srs. take them
4. Home of the Bulldogs, initially
5. Small size
6. French impressionism pioneer Alfred
7. Club discussed in clubhouses: inits.
8. ___ Lomond, Scotland
9. Aleutian island
10. Royals manager Ned
14. Fodder grain
18. New England sch., home of the Minutemen: 2 wds.
19. Stale air fare
20. Center X or O
21. Ab ___ (from the beginning)
22. Dead letters?
24. Make a dent
25. Book before Neh.
26. Congressional "no" vote
30. Mark Twain's New York hometown
31. Exposure unit?
33. Stock page heading, initially
34. "The Sun ___ Rises"
35. Chicago mayor ___ Emanuel
36. "Put ___ writing": 2 wds.
38. River in southeast Brazil
39. Rubs the wrong way
40. Sony co-founder Morita
42. Angular head?
43. Dorothy Parker quality

297

Across

1 Cell phone need
7 Some transmittable files, initially
11 Excite
12 Bar mitzvah dance
13 Traditional healer: 2 wds.
15 Financial regulators, initially
16 $1,000 bill, slangily: 2 wds.
17 Part of NCAA: abbr.
19 Dramatic work for the stage
21 102, to a Roman
22 Like some old-fashioned lamps: hyph.
26 It may be smoked
27 "Here ___ Again" (1987 #1 hit): 2 wds.
28 Grandma, to Germans
29 Gave it a try: 3 wds.
31 "Cougars" sch.
32 "Tell ___ secrets…": 2 wds.
34 Knows, old-style
35 Band of eight
38 Troop grp.
40 Having a good effect on the body or mind
44 "___ Dies" (William Byrd motet)
45 Italian province in the Lombardy region
46 Tab grabber's words: 2 wds.
47 Five times six

Down

1 Sean Penn title role of 2001
2 Indignation
3 Infant sponsored by an adult at baptism
4 One night in Paris
5 Music industry assoc.
6 Neckpiece
7 Group derived from benzene
8 "___ arigato" ("Thanks a lot" in Japanese)
9 Band of brothers?
10 Not nuts
14 Whodunit author Marsh
17 Banda ___ (Indonesian city)
18 "___ Yellow Ribbon..." (song): 2 wds.
20 Access the Web
23 Level of tide at its ebb: 2 wds.
24 The Pointer Sisters' "___ Excited": 2 wds.
25 Stretched
27 "Boy, Did ___ Wrong Number!" (Bob Hope movie): 3 wds.
30 Punish with an arbitrary penalty
33 Black magic
35 Roman emperor defeated by Vitellius
36 "Keeper of the Keys" detective Charlie
37 Overflow (with)
39 Katie Holmes's daughter
41 Cpl.'s inferior
42 Suffix with capital or copy
43 Ron ("The Penguin") of the 1980s Cubs

298

Across

1 Close, as a race
6 Pelagic soarers
11 Draft holder
12 Full of vigor
13 Having complete authority: hyph.
15 "Kidnapped" monogram
16 Dress up, with "out"
17 Actor Wheaton
18 Round after the quarters
20 Thompson in "Pollock"
23 Sounds some approval from a distance: 2 wds.
27 Large stringed instrument
29 Straighten out
30 Rogers and Cohn
31 Classic Ford: hyph.
33 Do-say connection: 2 wds.
36 When doubled, a 1965 Dixie Cups song
37 Fed. property overseer
40 Award-winning novel by Tatjana Soli, "The ___": 2 wds.
43 Oldsmobile model
44 Storied Butler
45 Evil one
46 Former file-sharing site

Down

1 Ruler opposed by the Bolsheviks
2 "___ all come out in the wash"
3 Reacts to pectin
4 Body part
5 U.S. security: hyph.
6 Wistfully mournful
7 Major river flowing through Belgium, Germany, and the Netherlands
8 "Don't let your boss catch you watching this" initials
9 It may have pins and needles
10 Word seg.
14 Resembling a female
18 French toast
19 Dig discovery: var.
20 "Law & Order: ___": inits.
21 Department of eastern France
22 Elmer, to Bugs
24 ___-mo replay
25 Prince ___ Khan
26 Fros' mates
28 "Crying" singer
32 Ted ___, Chevy Chase's role on "Chuck"
33 "Sing me a Song of ___ that is Gone" (R. L. Stevenson poem): 2 wds.
34 Undivided
35 Particular
37 Disgruntled word
38 Miss in Uruguay: abbr.
39 Nick and Nora's pet
41 Prefix for logical
42 "___ Carter" (Lil Wayne album)

299

Across

1 Resembling wings
6 Scrumptious
11 Cowboy contest
12 It may be dramatic
13 Group of 13
14 Equipment for the game of jai alai
15 Iota
16 President after F.D.R.
17 Butler of fiction
19 Norm: abbr.
22 Injured (a muscle) again
24 Gold: Sp.
25 Dictator Amin
26 It has springs
28 Relatives, slangily
29 Suffix meaning "recipients of an action"
30 Hire
32 Suffix with script or press
33 Desert in southern Israel
34 West of Hollywood
36 As a friend in France: 2 wds.
39 Former "SNL" star Cheri
41 Like some apartments
42 Synthetic fabric
43 Not smooth
44 Hayworth and Moreno
45 Carvey and Rohrabacher

Down

1 Parts of the circumference of a circle
2 Aerial maneuver
3 Notice publicizing a product
4 Bounce back again: hyph.
5 Industrial city north of the Bronx
6 Big, fancy boat
7 Brings into play
8 2001 Anjelica Huston miniseries, with "The": 3 wds.
9 Summer hrs. in Albuquerque
10 Approval vote
18 Sioux shelter
20 "Antony and Cleopatra," e.g.: abbr.
21 Volcano feature
22 André ___, Dutch violinist and conductor
23 German river
27 Infuriated
31 Family subdivisions
33 Sedaka and Armstrong
35 Environs
37 High flat area
38 Suffix with social or suburban
39 Galley tool
40 Prefix with hedron

300

Across

1 Cry of frustration
5 Makes stupid with infatuation
11 Sandwich retailer
12 "God shed his grace ___" ("America the Beautiful"): 2 wds.
13 Dwarf buffalo
14 More lean and sinewy
15 Jeer
16 When doubled, a Teletubby
17 Relating to a city or town
22 "Missing You" singer Peabo
24 Lioness in "The Lion King"
25 Fire fodder
26 Big sweater size, briefly
28 Canterbury can
29 Guayaquil's country, briefly
31 Greenish-yellow hue
33 Item of bathroom linen
35 Suffix with resident
36 "___ the mornin'!": 2 wds.
39 Served in blazing liquor
42 Dwell
43 Equine, to a kid
44 Play to ___, draw: 2 wds.
45 Wedding places
46 Hardy heroine

Down

1 First wife of Lamech
2 City near Tahoe
3 Habitually sullen person, slangily: 2 wds.
4 Break
5 Places for splits and spares: 2 wds.
6 "Giant Brain" computer
7 Exert much effort
8 "___ believe in yesterday": 2 wds.
9 Souvenir shirt
10 To be, to Bolivians
18 Cambodian leader of the 1970s
19 Ross Perot's running-mate of 1996: 2 wds.
20 Others, to Octavian
21 Actress Turner
22 Howled, as the wind
23 ___ Thins, Brown & Haley candy
27 Prefix with system
30 Buddhist principle of nonviolence
32 Besides: 2 wds.
34 Tossing the ___, Scottish sport
37 Parti ___ (prejudice): Fr.
38 Exposes, poetically
39 Loan overseer, initially
40 On-line guffaw
41 Painter's field

301

Across

1 Doesn't relinquish
6 Has fun in the wintertime
11 Natural cavities or hollows in a bone
12 Silent
13 Ban alternative
14 Having land
15 Hang in there: 3 wds.
17 Bony
18 Like some stocks, initially
19 Gives voice to
23 Compote fruit
26 Conger catcher
27 Grown together, in biology
29 "As I see it," online
30 Period in human development: 2 wds.
33 Do it as soon as possible: 3 wds.
36 Part of a single or LP: 2 wds.
37 Bar mitzvah figure
38 Aimée of "La Dolce Vita"
39 "Manhattan Murder Mystery" director
40 Plays energetically
41 Caterpillar competitor

Down

1 Southpaw Enterprises, Inc. founder Jim
2 Deep-seated
3 Ancient Italian
4 Overly proper types
5 18th letter of the Hebrew alphabet
6 Law passed by a legislative body
7 Clothing company with a crocodile logo
8 Eggshell
9 Health regimen
10 Most-used edition: abbr.
16 Debt letters
18 W.W. II agcy. 1941–7
20 Qualified
21 Don't forget
22 B'way posting
24 Boost: 2 wds.
25 Narrow markings of a different color
28 Quite a while
31 U.S./Canada security acronym
32 "Thereby hangs ___": 2 wds.
33 Prefix with type
34 Former NBA star Lamar
35 Mozart's "___ kleine Nachtmusik"
36 Patriotic org.

302

Across

1 Lower oneself
6 Theologian Kierkegaard
11 Declaim
12 Belief
13 Brief periods of study
15 Old spy grp.
16 Bygone daily MTV series, informally
17 Essay
18 "The Prince and the ___"
20 Kid-lit elephant
23 U.S. security: hyph.
26 Shuffle, e.g.
27 Highway
28 Narrative
30 Kid's call
31 Continue to do: 2 wds.
33 Like some stocks, for short
35 Banquet
36 "Think" company
39 Voluntarily brought on: hyph.
42 Nigerian language
43 Girls, in Grenoble
44 Photo-filled book
45 French cup

Down

1 "___ arigato" ("Thanks a lot" in Japanese)
2 Twin sister of Ares
3 Fleming and Ziering
4 Volkswagen model
5 Sugary plant fulid
6 Carve
7 Eight-time Norris Trophy winner
8 Public toilet
9 W. German river
10 Like a busybody
14 Sch. in Tulsa, Oklahoma
18 Junipero Serra, for one
19 "___: The Smartest Guys in the Room" (2006 documentary)
20 Twice
21 Quick
22 Org. that sells novels to members: 2 wds.
24 Skye cap
25 Big name in ice cream
29 Retort to "No, you're not!": 3 wds.
30 Endearingly sweet little child
32 "The Little Drummer Boy" syllable
33 Dept. of Labor division
34 Cousin of a canvasback
36 There are many in the Pacific Ocean: abbr.
37 Honey producers
38 Catalog things: abbr.
40 Home of the Seminoles, initially
41 Pay back?

303

Across

1 Enter all at once: 2 wds.

7 Nashville-based awards org.

10 Absence of the sense of smell

12 Newman title role of 1963

13 Union negotiator: 2 wds.

15 "___ Kröger" (novella by Thomas Mann)

16 Sam ___, director of "Oz the Great and Powerful"

17 Big name in frozen drinks

18 Wife, slangily

19 The Willis Tower, e.g.

21 The works

22 Sixty, old-style

29 Complain

30 "O, my love is like ___...," Burns: 2 wds.

31 First name in hotels

32 Rapper who starred in "The Wash": 2 wds.

33 Rates insufficiently highly

35 Cable company that merged with AT&T in 1999

36 Mesdames, in Mexico

37 Every other hurricane

38 Los Angeles suburb mentioned in Tom Petty's "Free Fallin'"

Down

1 Aniseed-flavored aperitif

2 Owing money: 2 wds.

3 "___ Toons" (cartoon series)

4 Detects

5 "___ Lonesome I Could Cry": 2 wds.

6 Trivial criticism

7 Chair in Cherbourg

8 Make remarks or noises under one's breath

9 ___ Ababa

11 Gymnastics maneuvers

14 Hornet's cousin

18 Bobbettes song that begins "One, two, three": 2 wds.

20 Vegas venue, ___ Palace

22 Channel

23 Certain sweatshirt

24 Mysterious character

25 Guitarist Santana

26 Dung

27 Go back to the book

28 Ancient city in upper Mesopotamia

29 Supplies to excess

32 Comedian ___ Cook

34 Burlington's locale, briefly

304

Across

1. Computer command
5. Ending for evan or lumin
9. Patsy's "Absolutely Fabulous" pal
11. Makes high-pitched whiny noises
12. Prefix meaning "straight"
13. Chance for a hit: 2 wds.
14. Bad result for a QB
15. Print anew
17. Liveried servant
19. Battlesystem game co., initially
20. Actress Meg and pitcher Nolan
21. J.F.K.'s U.N. ambassador
22. Cracked-ice drink
23. Egg holders: abbr.
25. Expanse of salt water
26. Rainbow or lake, e.g.
28. Middle X or O
29. Sells in small quantities
32. Nazareth native
34. Good credit rating letters
35. Messy substances
36. Nick of "Cape Fear"
38. Tablelands
39. Greek physician and anatomist (129–199)
40. Aide: abbr.
41. Dict. entries

Down

1. I part, at times
2. Gland: prefix
3. Brit. military award: 2 wds.
4. Beechbone in "The Lord of the Rings," e.g.
5. Food
6. For the most part
7. Contract provisos
8. Organic compounds
10. Inflatable sleeping surface: 2 wds.
11. Wooden paneling
16. Suffix with Euclid
18. Cobb of baseball fame et al.
22. Disease causing a red rash
24. Douro river tributary
25. Mark of disgrace
27. Islam, for one: abbr.
30. Get nearer to the end of the day
31. "The Carnival of the Animals" composer Saint-____
33. Get ____ on the back (be praised): 2 wds.
37. Alliance created in 1948, initially

305

Across

1. Hostess brand: 2 wds.
6. ___ Picchu, Inca town
11. Aspen visitor, usually
12. Thundering
13. ___-car: hyph.
14. "The Empire Strikes Back" director, ___ Kershner
15. Phoenix to Tucson dir.
16. Make lace
18. Latin abbrs.
19. Above ground level
21. Involving both hearing and sight
26. Vladimir Nabokov book of 1957
27. Women's golf org.
28. At a time when hunting is illegal: 3 wds.
32. Steady flow
33. "Lord, is ___?" (Last Supper question): 2 wds.
35. Financing letters
36. Suffix with bull or bear
39. Nearly under the knife, in announcements: hyph.
41. Native American of California and Nevada
43. Online administrator, briefly: 2 wds.
44. Original "Battlestar Galactica" commander
45. Words Alice read on a cake: 2 wds.
46. Canon rival

Down

1. Lat. and Lith., once
2. They're picked by some Hawaiians
3. Fan mag.
4. Still
5. Difference between market value and replacement value: 2 wds.
6. Drink with an umbrella: 2 wds.
7. Airport monitor abbr.
8. Attempts to conceal mistakes: hyph.
9. Reagan's AI
10. Coffee dispensers
17. "Then" and "there," for example: abbr.
19. North Dakota city
20. Muhammad's religion
21. G.I.'s address
22. Burma's first prime minister: 2 wds.
23. Most scatterbrained, slangily
24. Previously
25. Office computer link, initially
29. Ice cream parlor order
30. Fall mo.
31. Swab target
33. ___ dixit, unsupported assertion
34. "___ Little Tenderness": 2 wds.
36. River in Bavaria
37. Unlikable guy: var.
38. Big put-on
40. Byname for South Africa's Paul Kruger ("Uncle")
42. Summer drink

313

306

Across

1 Blue Triangle org.
5 Strict limit to customers: 2 wds.
11 Former Israeli prime minister Olmert
12 Pumpkin seed snack
13 Songs for one
14 Disney head until 2005
15 Floor covering of coarse fabric
17 In reality: 2 wds.
22 Big name in skin care products
26 Diversion
27 Tears apart
28 "Golden Boy" playwright
29 Greek goddess who bore the Cyclopes
30 Stuck: 3 wds.
31 The Devil, slangily: 2 wds.
33 Lower someone's spirits
38 Person given to spreading rumors
42 "Gimme a break!," briefly
43 Tastelessly affected: hyph.
44 "I ___ pleased…": 2 wds.
45 Set up tents, e.g.
46 9-3 Aero Sedan maker

Down

1 Backwoods affirmative: 2 wds.
2 "Hold it right there!"
3 System of religious belief
4 Mine entrance
5 Not completely turned off by: 2 wds.
6 Horsy "hello"
7 Some music purchases, for short
8 Hold down
9 Somme time
10 Computer file format, initially
16 McEwan and Somerhalder
18 "Das Rheingold" goddess
19 Actor Mischa or violinist Leopold
20 Letters after Q
21 Try out
22 Fleece-bearing craft
23 Wiener schnitzel meat
24 Home of Phillips University
25 Gross of "Free Spirit"
28 Peeling potatoes, perhaps: 2 wds.
30 Colorful summer treat: 2 wds.
32 Expression
34 Some dishes on rooftops, initially
35 Austen novel
36 Slammin' Sammy
37 Too-good type
38 AT&T competitor
39 Suffix with lag or lamp
40 Coll. major
41 Union ___: abbr.

307

Across

1 It's got plenty of twenties, initially

4 Hip hop group, Run-___

7 Lauderdale and Knox, e.g.: abbr.

10 Victoria's Secret product

11 Advert ending?

12 Rome's ___ Pacis

13 Expression of mild annoyance

16 What is more

17 Song on Sunday morning

18 Gross dinner sound

20 Blow up

22 Sailor

24 Condition of regular, proper management

27 Claim again

28 Kind of print, briefly

29 Mathematician who introduced the symbol e for the base of natural logarithms

33 Chalon-sur-___, city SSW of Dijon

35 "That's ___"

36 Basically

38 Pool accessory

39 "The Name of the Rose" author Umberto ___

40 Menlo Park inits.

41 Vietnam holiday

42 Baton Rouge campus, initially

43 Rd. crossers

Down

1 Old Jewish scholars

2 Deliberately inflammatory poster on message boards

3 Disputed islands in the East China Sea

4 Go out

5 Letters on a new car window

6 Halt shooting

7 Bomb

8 Blast furnace apparatuses

9 ___ Diego

14 Farrier's need

15 Large hairy tropical spider

19 Staff

21 ___-80 (old computer)

23 Pale ___

24 The Magic, on some scoreboards

25 Print anew

26 Computer program input: 2 wds.

30 Airs

31 Black key: 2 wds.

32 Last name that means "kings" in Spanish

34 List enders, briefly

36 Shock treatment, initially

37 Letters for debtors

308

Across

1 Subject
6 Hole that an anchor rope passes through
11 Wipe out on a wave, in surfing lingo: 2 wds.
12 ___ alcohol
13 Small musical interval: hyph.
15 German city on the Danube
16 ___ poetica
17 Monarch: abbr.
18 "___ that obvious?": 2 wds.
20 Take out of cipher
22 Italian director Wertmüller
23 "Hold On Tight" group letters
24 Regarding
26 "Don't Cry ___ Argentina" ("Evita" song): 2 wds.
30 More than months: abbr.
32 Indian bread
33 Cause to leave the tracks
36 Shelter grp.
37 River of Venezuela
38 Poet laureate before Southey
40 U.S.A.F. weapon
41 All the world (Fr.): 3 wds.
44 Davis, Mrs. Arable in "Charlotte's Web"
45 Bar order (with "the")
46 Betty Ford Clinic treatment, for short
47 Wedges

Down

1 Liquor made from an agave
2 Arrests, so to speak: 2 wds.
3 Fabric with an open mesh
4 Peace, in Russia
5 Rock and Roll Hall-of-Famer James
6 Feminine pronoun
7 Lawyer: abbr.
8 "___ loves believes the impossible," Elizabeth Barrett Browning: 2 wds.
9 Church assembly
10 Pupil, in Paris
14 Earth, in Berlin
19 Roberts of "That '70s Show"
21 Bandit-faced critters
25 Building divided into three residences
27 Easter Island, to natives: 2 wds.
28 Paving material
29 Colors pottery, perhaps
31 Leonard ___ (Roy Rogers)
33 Went out with
34 Uneven
35 Throw out of bed
39 Birds found on Australian ranches
42 Pedro's uncle
43 City in western Kyrgyzstan

309

Across

1 Steal, slangily
6 1983 movie with Adam Baldwin and Mr. T: 2 wds.
11 Stomach woe
12 She answered to Captain Kirk
13 Siamese fighting fish
14 Small finch
15 Put back
17 Leave in a hurry
18 W.B.A. stats.
20 Call used to attract attention: hyph.
24 Sullivan Award org.
25 Econ. figure
26 Little crawler
27 Corrida quarry: 2 wds.
29 Netman Nastase
30 Remove oneself from, as a bus: 2 wds.
32 Aromatic herb used medicinally
35 Company with orange-and-white trucks: hyph.
36 Breezing through the test
38 Molds and mushrooms, e.g.
39 Campaign issue of 1992, initially
40 Nash of note
41 Like some gases

Down

1 Hero, briefly
2 Marlin or Cardinal, e.g.
3 Performed, as if in a play: 2 wds.
4 Binds anew
5 Swiss currency
6 Maid's prop: 2 wds.
7 Not top-of-the-line
8 Short
9 Racer Luyendyk
10 Prohibition
16 Decline: 3 wds.
18 Menlo Park initials
19 Penn of the "Harold & Kumar" films
21 Measure of radioactive decay
22 Covert maritime org.
23 Suffix with den or dem
25 Imaginary, mischievous creature
28 Model railroad scale: hyph.
29 Conditional promise: 3 wds.
31 Muscat resident
32 Drink in large gulps, slangily
33 Group of cards
34 ___'acte (intermission)
35 Spaceship, maybe: inits.
37 Gangster's sidearm

310

Across

1 Vietnam Memorial designer
4 Some Heisman Trophy winners, initially
7 "____ job's worth doing...": 2 wds.
8 Dr. J's first pro league
9 S. ____ (Seoul's country): abbr.
12 "Kill Bill" tutor Pai ____
13 Soup eater's square
15 "Twelfth Night" character
17 Corporate department
18 Mary-Kate and Ashley
20 N.Y.C. gallery
21 Remove from sight: 2 wds.
23 Prefix with chloride
25 Prefix with cone
26 Years, to Yves
27 Providing opposition
30 Choice words: 2 wds.
31 Magazine worker
34 Orchestra instrument
36 Bonehead
37 Attainable: 2 wds.
39 Library ref.
40 1950s presidential race inits.
41 Major Calif. airport
42 Sch. in Athens or its bulldog mascot
43 Farm mother
44 Jogged

Down

1 Dance done with a stick
2 "____ It" (Moby song): 2 wds.
3 Tool used for manicure: 2 wds.
4 Daredevil's trait
5 Four-year coll. deg.
6 "Do the Right Thing" setting
9 Measure of electrical energy use in 60 minutes: hyph.
10 Kind of show: hyph.
11 Puts another way
14 "Slaves of New York" author Janowitz
16 Goofy collectible, say
19 Henri's health
22 Touring entertainment
23 Information of little importance
24 Improve or perfect, polish
28 Professional sportswriter and boxing expert Kevin
29 CNN correspondent Robertson
32 Last Greek letter
33 Flying monster of film
35 "The law is ____..." (Dickens): 2 wds.
38 Accounts head, for short

311

Across

1. Barbecue-flavored sandwich
6. Nautical direction
11. "32 Flavors" singer Davis
12. Dubya associate Rice
13. Physical or moral ruin
15. Suffix with persist
16. PC "brain"
17. ___-Caps (Nestle candy)
18. Polar coverings: 2 wds.
20. When doubled, a yellow Teletubby
21. World created by Jim Henson for the movie "The Dark Crystal"
22. Introduce gently: 2 wds.
24. "Save" shortcut on some computers: abbr., 2 wds.
26. "There was ___ at the inn": 2 wds.
29. Become stuck (with "onto")
33. Cockney dwelling
34. City in Indiana, on Lake Michigan
36. Suffix with professor
37. Govt. prog. since 1974
38. Goon's gun
39. Bitter or critical way of speaking: 2 wds.
42. "... His wife could ___ lean": 2 wds.
43. Muralist Rivera
44. Comic strip dog
45. Rear-___

Down

1. Succeeded: 2 wds.
2. Hold tight
3. Pattern of scanning lines on a monitor
4. Bankbook abbr.
5. Barcelona boat
6. Formal charge of wrongdoing
7. Type of fly
8. Isolate
9. Another name for God
10. Ancient Aegean civilization
14. Highest in rank or place
19. Incorrect: prefix
23. E-5 in the U.S.A.F.
25. Most coveted position: 2 wds.
26. Snap, crackle, and pop
27. President Ford, for one
28. Pertain
30. Fell behind
31. Toy train scale: hyph.
32. Heavenly streaker
35. ___ la Plata: 2 wds.
40. Genre of popular music, initially
41. "Delta of Venus" writer

312

Across

1 Baptism or bris
5 ____ Qs: 2 wds.
10 Heaps: 2 wds.
11 Talk evasively
12 Heaven
13 Hawthorne's Mistress Prynne
14 Graceful deerlike animal
16 Dutch painter Frans
17 Bar order, with "the"
21 Common postgrad degs.
23 Mem. of the A.B.A.
25 Affirmative action
26 Ranch add-on
27 Measure of conductance
28 Its cap. is Buenos Aires
29 Group of whales
30 ____ Lingus
31 Place
32 "The ____ Love" (R.E.M. song): 2 wds.
34 Swedish tennis player Björn
36 Unfinished business: 2 wds.
40 Soft touch
43 "____ sow, so shall...": 2 wds.
44 Muscat residents
45 Role played by Clarence Williams III in "The Mod Squad"
46 Pitney's partner
47 ____ Clinic

Down

1 La ____ (Mexican-American culture)
2 Raking ____ (getting rich): 2 wds.
3 Temptingly tasty
4 Nine: prefix
5 Chick's word
6 MS. enclosures
7 Puerto Rico clock setting, initially
8 Formerly
9 Middleman: abbr.
11 Tony Danza sitcom: 3 wds.
15 Beast from Peru
18 Inability to feel pain
19 Seahawks head coach Jim
20 High-strung
21 "Let ____!": 2 wds.
22 Irish isles
24 Pamplona runners
33 Graff of "Mr. Belvedere"
35 Domain
37 Medical suffix
38 Biggest city in the U.S.A., initially: 2 wds.
39 Art ____ (design style seen in South Beach)
40 Part of an ear
41 Latin I word
42 Green

313

Across

1 "When I Was ____" ("H.M.S. Pinafore" song): 2 wds.
5 "Get Smart" actor Don
10 Main stem of a tree
11 Baby's garment
12 Musical notes
13 Austrian city
14 Flower part
16 Jewish org. founded in 1913
17 Cedar native to the Himalayas
18 Fork cash over to
19 Outlawed
21 "The Spanish Tragedy" dramatist
22 "How Can ____ Sure?" (hit of 1967): 2 wds.
23 Himalayan peak
26 Alley Oop, for one
28 Department of eastern France
31 Go back
32 Sellout sign letters
33 Chicken piece
34 Words before "friends": 2 wds.
36 Italian director Wertmüller
38 Sign up
39 Don Juan's mother
40 Garden hassles
41 Farmer's prefix

Down

1 Stomach "six-pack," shortly
2 In a relaxed manner, not rigid
3 In sum
4 "The Crimes of Love" author Marquis ____: 2 wds.
5 Have ____ (be connected): 2 wds.
6 Sandra ____ of "Gidget"
7 Simple as ABC: 2 wds.
8 "I don't ____ bit!": 2 wds.
9 Mattress brand
11 At someone's mercy: 3 wds.
15 Wizardry
17 Hägar creator Browne
20 Flood embankment
23 Comical
24 Associate
25 Roadhouse
27 List shortener: 2 wds.
28 Large quantity: 2 wds.
29 Castle of dance
30 Dame's introduction?
33 Oil meas.
35 Lay turf
37 Kind of dye

314

Across

1 Engender
6 Make-or-break times: hyph.
11 Ancient earthenware pot
12 "___ Go Again" (Whitesnake song): 2 wds.
13 Niece in Barber's opera Vanessa
14 Lac ___ (Lake Geneva)
15 Bruce or Laura of Hollywood
17 "___ the cah on Hahvahd yahd"
18 Stand
20 Positive moves
22 It may fill a niche
23 "So soon?"
27 Maj.'s superior: 2 wds.
29 Reply to "You are not!": 3 wds.
30 Oktoberfest sight: 2 wds.
32 Neighbor of Arg. and Parag.
33 Sequent suffix
34 Ural River city
35 Manufactured
38 Data, for short
40 Light sandal
42 And the following, briefly: 2 wds.
45 2018 movie starring John Travolta and Kelly Preston
46 Video game designer Sid
47 Olympians' blades
48 Certain exams

Down

1 Letters used (by some) for dates
2 Misplay, e.g.
3 Counsel, direction
4 Glacial ridge
5 Hightail it
6 FedEx competitor
7 Relating to the lowest parts of the ocean: 2 wds.
8 First word of Virgil's "Aeneid"
9 Bit of a Beatles refrain
10 Plummet
16 None, in Nimes
18 Gardener's purchase
19 Art deco illustrator
21 Bluenose
23 ____-Seltzer
24 Food of the gods (myth.)
25 Brit. awards
26 Central part of an egg
28 Cuban region from the Spanish for "East"
31 Michigan's ___ Broad College of Business
34 More frequently, old-style
35 Homeowner's regular pymt.
36 On the diamond, one bounce: 2 wds.
37 Give a ton of affection to, with "on"
39 Nautilus captain
41 Infantrymen, initially
43 Seafood selection
44 Alphabet trio

315

Across

1 Big name in fruit juices
6 Alexander or Odom
11 "Life's a journey, not ___": 2 wds.
12 Make ___ (go, in chess): 2 wds.
13 Not working full-time: hyph.
15 Liberal arts college in Cedar Rapids
16 Demolitionist's supply letters
17 Constellation near Norma
18 Bob of "Full House"
20 Frasier's brother
23 Kind of battery
27 Bibliography abbr.: 2 wds.
28 Close up tightly
29 Form of Spanish "to be"
31 Whoville creator
32 "___ Romance" (Tristan Garcia novel): 2 wds.
34 Identity
37 Ending with mater or pater
38 Markup language descriptor, initially
41 Surpass all others: 3 wds.
44 Around
45 Apple drink
46 Hitches
47 Shocks with a device

Down

1 Gender abbr.
2 Cookie with its name printed on it
3 Not feral
4 Cable company that merged with AT&T in 1999
5 Certain mattresses
6 Coffee bar choices
7 Friend of Francois
8 Verse measure
9 Say for sure
10 Stigma borne by Nathaniel Hawthorne's Hester Prynne: 2 wds.
14 H.S. requirement
18 Biblical musical direction
19 "Out ___" (Lemmon/Matthau romcom): 2 wds.
20 French born?
21 "___ no problem!"
22 Back muscle, for short
24 Romanian monetary unit
25 Small batteries' letters
26 Monogram of Hyde's creator
30 Yule decorations
31 Blue-ribbon
33 Island where Brando lived: abbr.
34 List enders, briefly
35 Increase
36 Gumbo need
38 Heels
39 "I Wish" rapper ___-Lo
40 Sabbath discourses, in short
42 Heartbeat monitor letters
43 Snoop gp.

316

Across

1 Grammatical case: abbr.
4 Broadcast inits.
7 Leftist president Morales
8 Traffic-stopping org.
9 Canadian attorney's deg.
12 Science of artillery
14 "___ Como Va" (Santana song)
15 Thomas ___ Edison
16 Bug that forms large swarms
18 Parting words: 2 wds.
20 Double-curved molding
21 Big animals of Tibet
22 Applies
23 Minimalist composer who uses the pseudonym CSJ Bofop
25 Mil. award
27 Presidential inits.
28 New York transport system, initially
30 "Make ___": 2 wds.
32 "Could ___ I'm Falling in Love" (The Spinners song): 2 wds.
33 Criminal conspiracy of silence
36 Land of Saabs and ABBA
38 Sainted pope called "the Great": 2 wds.
39 The "S" of R.S.V.P.
40 Aids in joining: hyph.
42 Big inits. in long-distance
43 Granola morsel
44 Soundless communication syst.
45 CD predecessors
46 12/31, initially

Down

1 "Ocean's Eleven" setting, familiarly
2 Immature seed
3 Mechanism for transporting goods in the process of manufacture: 2 wds.
4 Sports-drink suffix
5 Ammunition for a toy gun: 2 wds.
6 Hoosier pol. name
9 Person who loads and unloads ships
10 French secondary schools
11 Bidding
13 Bottled spring water brand
17 Letters of credit?
19 Accepted
23 "Aeneid" queen (alias Dido)
24 Birdbrain
26 Old TV production co.
29 Lobsterlike
31 Ward on TV
34 ___-turvy
35 Many an airline seat request
37 Biol. branch
41 Mil. titles

317

Across

1 Children's author Rabe
5 City north of San Francisco, San ___
11 Orchestra tuner
12 Words intended to intimidate: 2 wds.
13 Work from home via a computer link
15 Ravage
16 Manage to get, with "out"
17 Mal de ___
18 One of the Brothers Karamazov
20 "___ Ruled The World": 2 wds.
21 "Bring Me Your Love" singers ___-Lite
23 Indian bread
24 It can follow vice
27 Sturm und ___
29 Hoppy glassful, for short
30 Italian lake
32 Small intake
33 Visited: 2 wds.
37 Govt. employee
38 Narrow waterway: abbr.
39 "___ want a hula hoop..." (Chipmunks): 2 wds.
40 Come to nothing (as a plan): 4 wds.
43 Opera singer Caruso
44 Asia's shrinking ___ Sea
45 Playground equipment
46 Half a tetrad

Down

1 Did a caddie's job
2 Construction site sight: hyph.
3 Maestro Georg
4 Part of a bray
5 Novice
6 Danish fighting force
7 Opposite of masc.
8 Main constituent of sapphire
9 Singer Gloria
10 Ogling
14 Breakfast food
19 Football scores: abbr.
22 Whodunit awards
24 Facial expressions
25 Inferior imitator
26 Ecstasy
28 Data storage site, initially
31 Urgent infomercial line: 2 wds.
34 Atlanta university
35 Fertile valley of central Lebanon
36 Stockbroker's statistic
38 Vittorio De ___
41 Some detectives, initially
42 Magazine of Fold-In fame

318

Across

1 Nursery program, briefly: hyph.
5 Words on a Renault 5: 2 wds.
10 Son of Jacob and Leah
11 Mammals native to China
12 Aid's partner
13 They're pulled on a dairy farm
14 Ale holders
16 Canvas
17 "Ignorance ___ excuse!": 2 wds.
21 Savage
23 Roof design on some sports cars: hyph.
24 House vote
25 Oolong, for one
27 Stretch of turbulent water
28 Letters identifying a combination of voices (music)
30 Goes along with
32 Greek theaters
33 North Carolina university
34 Commercial deficit: 2 wds.
38 Cast off from the dock
41 Cut-price event
42 "Now I've ___ all": 2 wds.
43 1960s militant Brown, familiarly: 2 wds.
44 Cheese with large holes
45 "What ___ mind reader?": 3 wds.

Down

1 ___ du jour
2 Sitcom with a country star
3 Turn out in the end
4 Candy bar in a red wrapper
5 "Shane" star
6 Calls things off: 2 wds.
7 Alphabetical run
8 Solothurn's river
9 Certain Internet feed
11 Military decoration: 2 wds.
15 Like ___ in a trap: 2 wds.
18 Bully: hyph.
19 Pinot ___ (type of wine)
20 First and last, e.g.: abbr.
21 "And time goes ___ slowly" (Righteous Brothers lyric): 2 wds.
22 Go through
26 Old, in Scotland
29 Marching band sticks
31 TV series starring Brandy Norwood
35 French kings
36 Jai ___ (ball game)
37 Salt-n-___, "None of Your Business" singers
38 Letters on warships
39 ___ Mexico
40 "Kill Bill" tutor Pai ___

319

Across

1. "Summer in the City" group The ___ Spoonful
6. "Fiddle-___!": hyph.
11. Samuel on the Supreme Court
12. New England sch., home of the Minutemen: 2 wds.
13. Make free from vermin, as the Pied Piper did
14. Sacrifices, in baseball
15. Fireplace piece
16. Scottish novelist Josephine
18. Born, in the society column
19. Pharmaceutical tycoon Lilly
20. "Michael Collins" actor Stephen
21. Long
22. Viral disease of the tropics that causes fever
24. Rocket destroyer, initially
25. Chemical ending
26. Poverty-fighting grp.
27. Skip of a stone on water
28. Potbelly
31. French pronoun
32. Right away, initially
33. South American macaw
34. Jaguars' org.
35. Midwest inst.
36. Residential neighborhood: abbr.
37. One of four archangels
39. Duck
41. Brave
42. Castor-oil plant toxin
43. Online administrator, briefly: 2 wds.
44. British 1980 Olympic gold medalist Steve

Down

1. Distributed generously
2. Spanish chant: 2 wds.
3. Philip Morris brand: 2 wds.
4. "Give ___ whirl": 2 wds.
5. "It's a lie!": 2 wds.
6. Former presidential nickname
7. Ostrich look-alike
8. Child star of "The Partridge Family": 2 wds.
9. Respect
10. Folkwang Museum site
17. Wide size
23. Econ. yardstick
24. First Fiesta Bowl winner, initially
26. Cattle driver
27. Bear the expenses of
28. Peace-keeping bodies, initially
29. Accounting entry
30. Ain't got
31. Lies close and warm
32. Hydra or coral
38. Fair hiring letters, for short
40. Actress Tyler

327

320

Across

1 Explorer, Safari, and Navigator, e.g.
5 "Green ___" (1960s sitcom)
10 Light ___ (floaty): 2 wds.
12 Heavy sound of impact
13 Front of a manuscript leaf
14 Parasitic insect
15 ___ Darya (river of central Asia)
16 Move (goods) illegally
18 Fix, as a male cat
20 Pillbox, e.g.
21 Conductor Zubin
23 Old greeting
24 Lake of talk TV
26 Lid or lip application
28 Blow-up: abbr.
29 Went white
31 Ethnic group of Vietnam
32 Start over with pad and pencil
35 Fit the requirements
38 "Strange Magic" band, for short
39 Relating to one of the arm bones
40 Duck
42 "Boy, Did ___ Wrong Number!" (1966 movie): 3 wds.
43 Flip of a hit single: 2 wds.
44 Fathers, to Pierre
45 "9 1/2 Weeks" director Adrian

Down

1 ___ Wrap (plastic wrap brand)
2 1972 Bill Withers hit: 2 wds.
3 Dirt Devil, e.g.: 2 wds.
4 Get benched
5 First Amendment lobbyists, for short
6 Blockage
7 Simple but adequate: 3 wds.
8 Put in irons
9 Biting fly, slangily
11 Fruit used to make tea and jelly
17 1980s TV star who hosted a reality show called "I Pity the Fool": 2 wds.
19 William Shatner title drug
22 Spellbound: 2 wds.
24 Provide with new supplies
25 Pander to
27 Danger in Afghanistan, initially
30 Boxer's bellow
33 Mayflower Compact signer
34 "___ unto him who ...": 2 wds.
36 After curfew
37 401(k) cousins, briefly
41 Cruella de ___, 101 Dalmatians antagonist

321

Across

1 "With ___ breath" (in great suspense)
6 Dry, in Spain
10 "That's ___ excuse!": 2 wds.
11 A little lower?
12 Calaba tree: 2 wds.
14 Head exam letters
15 Press down
16 Old English letters
18 Lacking in Le Mans
22 Places for music storage: 2 wds.
25 Inebriated
26 Indian vegetable dish
27 Thin and ugly old woman
29 Room offerer
30 Mark to indicate a direction
32 Overripe fruit problem
34 AvtoVAZ car brand
35 ___ dawn: 2 wds.
37 Certain corp. takeover
40 Receiver that displays broadcast images
43 Car rod
44 Newswoman Roberts
45 Hinds
46 "A Passage to India" heroine

Down

1 Despicable
2 Wings
3 Shade of orange
4 CPR specialist
5 Poisonous toadstool: 2 wds.
6 Con man's setup
7 Brothers of the Wild West
8 151, to Caesar
9 "The Tears ___ Clown" (hit of 1970): 2 wds.
13 Halloween disguise
17 High-tech recording medium, initially
19 Similar: 3 wds.
20 Baseball field number
21 Ending for young or old
22 Cradle alternative
23 Boone's nickname
24 Type of neuralgia that affects the hips
28 Boxing match div.
31 Norwegian king
33 Gown fabric
36 Pepper has three
38 Get good and steamed
39 Unbeatable rating: hyph.
40 Wee one
41 Prefix with skeleton
42 Lay down the lawn

322

Across

1 Idled
4 France's high-speed rail service, initially
7 Aviation prefix
8 Mouths, anatomically
9 "There but for the grace of God ___": 2 wds.
12 Uncle, in Madrid
13 Hole in the head?
15 Not mine
17 Mythical cave-dweller
18 Erase: 2 wds.
20 Org. involved in the Scopes Trial
21 Written communications: abbr.
22 Tres y tres
23 Drop in on
25 Scratch (out)
27 MapQuest offering: abbr.
28 Danish fighting force
30 "Climb ___ Mountain" (song from "The Sound of Music")
32 88 days, on Mercury
33 Believers in a nonintervening god
36 Cock-a-hoop
38 Area of South Africa, KwaZulu-___
39 Corroded: 2 wds.
41 "Awesome!"
42 "Ben-___" (1880 novel)
43 ___-Ray discs
44 Lobster coral

45 Memorize lines and hit the stage
46 Clairvoyant's ability, initially

Down

1 Debaucher
2 Second-grade sequence, initially
3 Rabble-rouser
4 Shaved crown of a monk's head
5 Miracle ___
6 Brobdingnagian
9 Where to buy food and household supplies: 2 wds.
10 Like some old lamps: hyph.
11 Treat cruelly: hyph.

14 They often precede las
16 Decay
19 Expressed disapproval
23 Dentist's request: 2 wds.
24 "Are you" in Spain: 2 wds.
26 Equalize: 2 wds.
29 "... ___ saw Elba": 2 wds.
31 Estuary
34 Daedalus' nephew
35 "The sweetest gift of heaven": Virgil
37 Ladies' sports org.
40 RN's forte

323

Across

1 All-Star reliever Nen
5 Minor
11 "Song of the South" song syllables
12 Mame, for one
13 Robt. E. Lee, e.g.
14 Cooking in an oven
15 Breaks off (a legal case, e.g.)
17 Popular terrier
20 Monte Cristo, par exemple
22 Vinegar: prefix
24 Kimono tie
25 Dance specialty
26 Small, ring-shaped cake
29 Attention-getting sounds
31 Engagement, old-style
33 Short and plump: hyph.
36 Cassava
39 Skin feature
40 Isolate
41 Those, in Mexico
42 Not fit for kids, as a movie: 2 wds.
43 Ding

Down

1 Indian music
2 Took way too much: abbr.
3 Banneker and Britten
4 Wisconsin city or its college
5 New York hockey player
6 Angola's capital
7 Octopus organ: hyph.
8 Volkswagen Golf model
9 Hua ____ (Thai beach resort)
10 Unshorn sheep
16 Suffix for press
18 Releases: 2 wds.
19 L'____ de catastrophe naturelle
20 Trawler's catch
21 Reed section member
23 Photo ____ (camera sessions, for short)
27 Revolt
28 Past it: 2 wds.
29 "Gangnam Style" rapper
30 Drained, as energy
32 Stomach issue
34 Author ____ Hubbard: 2 wds.
35 Past time, briefly
36 Debussy's "La ____"
37 "People of Earth" costar Gasteyer
38 Louse-to-be

324

Across

1 Range
6 American capital, initially
9 Wraps
10 D.C. school
11 Singer who wrote "From This Moment On": 2 wds.
13 Batty
14 The Lone Ranger's Silver
15 To him in Hainaut: 2 wds.
16 Moors (a ship)
17 "Went," in Glasgow
18 All-Star second baseman Chase
19 Went wrong
21 "Knight, Death and the Devil" engraver Albrecht
23 Extent
27 Comes to
28 Mother of the Valkyries
29 Ratio words: 2 wds.
30 Bunch
31 Grocery store section: 2 wds.
33 Outback bird
34 "I'll do anything!": 2 wds.
35 "Deck the Halls" contraction
36 Verb for thou

Down

1 ___ of Liberty
2 Careful not to inconvenience others
3 Miscellany
4 Stew morsel
5 Dilettante
6 Classic Peter Lorre role
7 Like a rustling skirt, perhaps
8 Beach sights
9 Football Hall-of-Famer Don
11 Stocking trouble
12 Professional championship for major league baseball
16 Raymond and Aaron
20 Gives again, temporarily
21 First notes of the scale: 3 wds.
22 Womb
24 Oktoberfest toast
25 Mature
26 Rabbit punch target
27 "Be silent," in a score
30 No longer fresh
32 "___ note to follow soh...": 2 wds.

325

Across

1 "Call of Cthulhu," e.g.
4 Like the letter Z: abbr.
7 Pol. union of 1958
8 Distant: 2 wds.
12 Letters accompanying some 2,000-year-old+ dates
13 Where a bird may perch: 3 wds.
15 Come together
17 Of nests
18 Russian pop duo
19 Rock garden flower
20 "Just ___" (Linda Ronstadt album): 2 wds.
23 The Mormons' letters
24 Highest in excellence
26 Kitty
28 Milkmaid's measure
31 Chump
33 Cut with light
34 Starts in fright
35 Gives up
36 Unsteady
38 "CSI" sample
39 Guru's headquarters
40 Race part
41 Any car, affectionately
42 Summer on the Riviera

Down

1 Flexible tempo
2 Classic arcade game: hyph.
3 Top tunes of an era: 2 wds.
4 Initially, they travel very long distances
5 Office computer system, initially
6 African republic until 1994
9 Kid's boo-boo
10 Trivial matters: hyph.
11 Deliberate trickery intended to gain an advantage
14 Shade trees
16 "Star Trek" role
21 Adversaries
22 Mouths, anatomically
25 Grenoble girl, briefly
26 Call to attention
27 Lorena of the LPGA
29 Newsgroup source
30 Alain-René ___, "Gil Blas" writer
32 One of the Wu-Tang Clan rappers, for short
35 Inflorescence
37 Stadium cheer

326

Across

1 Massenet opera: 2 wds.
6 Conduits used to convey water
11 Mushroom used in Japanese cooking
12 Lowest deck
13 Blemished
14 "The Power of Positive Thinking" author Norman Vincent ___
15 Refusals
16 Hems and haws
18 Never, in Germany
19 Valved brass instrument
21 Guess as to takeoff, initially
22 Former long-time record label initials
23 Guffaws
25 Back
27 Look over again, as an article
29 Wanted ad letters
31 "Les Girls" actress Taina
32 Quandary
35 Day-___
36 601, to Caesar
37 Heartbeat record, for short
38 Byzantine Emperor from 886 to 912: 2 wds.
40 Inn
42 Excessive
43 "___ Man of Color" (mystery novel by Barbara Hambly): 2 wds.
44 Some hooks
45 Speak biblically

Down

1 Inclined
2 Concert ender, often
3 Food, clothing, etc., intended for direct use: 2 wds.
4 Mike and ___ (candy brand)
5 Renovated: 2 wds.
6 Ariana Grande, e.g.: 2 wds.
7 Miff
8 Math subject: 2 wds.
9 Very early roughly-broken stone implement
10 Makes tracks
17 Musical
20 Diamond spot
24 Conman's victim
26 Fathers
27 Affix anew
28 Actresses Barkin and Burstyn
30 Pageant hosts
33 Beans in a stew
34 Shoelace tip
39 Saturn ___, sport utility vehicle
41 "Portrait ___ Young Man" (Raphael painting): 2 wds.

327

Across

1 Big donors, initially
5 Actress Jessica and others
10 Title for a British prime minister, briefly: 2 wds.
12 Actress Dern
13 Spine-chilling
14 "E pluribus unum," e.g.
15 Part of a golf course
17 Body art, for short
18 Type units
19 Starting place: 2 wds.
21 Letters before U
22 City on the Ganges River
23 Like a cheapskate
26 Spanish-American prairie
27 Some guys in rap songs, initially
30 Cut up for analysis
32 Prefix for logical
33 Last, for short
34 Serving as an essential component
36 Playwright Jones
38 Part of São Paulo
39 "Guys and Dolls" song: 2 wds.
40 Pitch
41 Olympic Games weapons
42 Neuter

Down

1 Go for
2 Elite groups: hyph.
3 Yuletide decoration: 2 wds.
4 Evening, in France
5 Not just operating seasonally: hyph.
6 "___ note to follow soh…": 2 wds.
7 "Shut up!": 3 wds.
8 National Carrier of Afghanistan
9 Health, in Paris
11 The latest buzz
16 Calm: 2 wds.
20 Jim Bakker's club letters
24 Quick online communiqués: inits.
25 Biological classification
26 Accumulate: 2 wds.
28 Highest quality: 2 wds.
29 Exclusively
30 Dark red edible seaweed
31 Blows up, casually
35 Jar contents in a coffeehouse
37 Cockney residence

328

Across

1 Elvis Presley hit "In the ___"
7 Sports franchise est. in 1983
11 Cavalry member
12 Earth goddess
13 Spring rain: 2 wds.
15 R.R. stop
16 Squeeze
17 Italian monk
18 Prince album "___ the Times": 2 wds.
20 Parisian cops, slangily
22 Middling mark
23 Alabama, Alaska or Arizona
24 Person's "equator"
26 Café cup
28 Inactive U.S.A.F. org.
31 Annual awards show first hosted by Dennis Miller
32 Piano part
34 Former name of FandangoNow: hyph
35 "___ was saying ...": 2 wds.
37 Brit. award
38 Abandon an activity or venture: 3 wds.
41 Colleague of Dashiell
42 Clout
43 Heroic poem
44 Guinea pig

Down

1 Tumbler
2 Relating to touch
3 Madden
4 Cable giant, once: inits.
5 Prefix with logical
6 Ural River city
7 "The Fugitive" playwright Betti
8 Considered it correct (to do): 2 wds.
9 Like some competitors
10 "___ Theme" (tune from "Doctor Zhivago")
14 Tests by lifting
19 Full of current events, like a website
21 Starbucks order
23 German pronoun
25 Very, in music
26 John Irving hero: inits., 2 wds.
27 Moon-landing name
29 Person dependent on a drug
30 Building with thick walls and battlements
31 Host
32 Arouse, as anger
33 Also-ran
36 Bank acct. report
39 Aix-___-Bains (French commune)
40 Letters on aircraft carriers

329

Across

1 First glance
7 Spanish bear
10 No-nos
11 "Deutschland ___ Alles"
12 As a whole: 2 wds.
13 "King David" star
14 Excessive adherence to the law
16 Cash in Kashmir
19 Free city to the east of Westeros in "Game of Thrones"
20 Cricket periods
21 Rewrite for a film, say
24 Long times to live: abbr.
25 Ones in Spain
26 "Amerika" author
28 Billy Davis Jr.'s singing partner Marilyn
29 North Carolina city: abbr.
30 Soccer star Michelle
31 Survey of voters as they leave a voting place: 2 wds.
34 ___-Ball (arcade game)
35 Asian island
39 Be inclined
40 Pay no heed to
41 Part of the Apocrypha: abbr.
42 Basketballers, slangily

Down

1 Had a little lamb
2 Criticize harshly
3 Kander's "Cabaret" collaborator
4 Traveled on wheels, in a way: hyph.
5 Aussie shouts
6 Shore patrol grp.
7 Deferential respect
8 Sun. talks
9 City just south of Timpanogos Cave National Monument
11 Cygnet in a tale by Hans Christian Andersen: 2 wds.
15 Pie ___ mode: 2 wds.
16 Scissors beater, in a game
17 Eye layer
18 Pal one writes to: 2 wds.
22 Impoverished
23 General ___ Chicken (Chinese menu dish)
27 Weisshorn, e.g.
28 Port city and resort of southern Spain
31 Punta del ___, Uruguay
32 Classic Jags
33 Auricular
36 Misery
37 Music sheet abbr.
38 Console for playing Super Mario Bros., initially

330

Across

1 Religious offshoot
5 Shepherdess in "As You Like It"
10 Will figure
11 Aftershock
12 "Mater" intro
13 Installing cables
14 Monthly women's lifestyle magazine: 2 wds.
16 Rigid bracelet
17 "Am not!" retort: 2 wds.
19 Port in southern Sweden
23 Breathtaking beast?
24 Real-time Internet communications, for short
25 ___ Park (Thomas Edison's home)
28 Unusual object
30 Halogen salt
32 Totino's product: 2 wds.
36 Hold back
37 Menial laborer
38 Extent of a surface: 2 wds.
39 What a colon means, in a ratio: 2 wds.
40 Short time off: abbr., 3 wds.
41 Beleaguered exec.'s need

Down

1 Burn
2 River of Africa
3 Stew ingredient: 2 wds.
4 Musical syllables: hyph.
5 In a formal, proper manner
6 Virus that causes shingles
7 Actor Jannings
8 Paleontologist's discovery
9 Piece of work?
11 Bud holder
15 ___-Caps (candy)
17 Rocket interceptor, briefly
18 Lobster eggs
20 Indefatigable
21 "Where ___?": 2 wds.
22 Brit. honor
26 Chameleon, for one
27 More slippery and gooey
28 Saturn, for one
29 An ideally perfect place
31 Comic Carvey
32 Clinton cabinet member Federico
33 "I'll consider ___ honor": 2 wds.
34 Loads
35 Arrogant, conceited person, slangily
36 Board member, briefly

331

Across

1 Wood strips
6 Pie chart amts.
10 Apocryphal archangel
11 Literary T. S. or George
12 Yemen's capital
13 Sought out quickly: 2 wds.
14 Carpenter's table
16 Blunt and to the point
17 Rachel's elder sister in the Bible
20 Furthermore: 2 wds.
24 Skillful, facetiously
25 "Law & Order: ___" (police drama series), initially
26 Sch. founded by Thomas Jefferson
27 Vowel sound in "puzzle": 2 wds.
29 Key of Mozart's Violin Concerto No. 4: abbr., 2 wds.
30 Pointer on a sign
32 Trapeze artist
36 Ancient Mexican
37 Luminous
39 Split
40 "Scared Famous" network: hyph.
41 Well-ventilated
42 Game show host Ben

Down

1 Light units: abbr.
2 Get ___ deal: 2 wds.
3 Baseball's Martinez
4 Floor of a fireplace
5 Quench
6 Earth, for one
7 Abbr. akin to POTUS: hyph.
8 Late cartoonist Alex
9 Pou ___, basis of operation
11 "Are you" in Spain: 2 wds.
15 Brilliant or daring display
17 Guitar pioneer ___ Paul
18 Letter from St. Paul: abbr.
19 "___ Z Mysteries" (kids' book series): 2 wds.
21 Sing with closed lips
22 Palindromic rock video award
23 Atlantic City casino, with "The"
25 Unbending
28 Become less dense
29 President Eisenhower
31 Names on King Harald V's family tree
32 Sheryl Crow's "___ Wanna Do": 2 wds.
33 E.R. part, briefly
34 Gin flavor
35 "Tar Baby" author Morrison
36 Peruvian wood sorrel
38 Cyst

332

Across

1. At a great distance
8. Deg. earned after years in a studio
11. How cars with good brakes are said to stop: 3 wds.
12. Suffix with hotel
13. Bar on "Three's Company" (with "The"): 2 wds.
15. Stage after zygote
16. Site of a 1944 Allies breakthrough: 2 wds.
17. Chinese city on the Wei, old-style
18. "Here's to you!" in Denmark
19. Game requiring no equipment
20. Catch sight of
22. "Bad, Bad Leroy Brown" singer
23. It may be motorized: 2 wds.
26. Chair part
29. Replacement for a tooth cusp
30. Org. for dealers in rare books
31. One-___ (baseball cousin): hyph.
32. In the thick of
34. Fall down dead, slangily: 3 wds.
36. Relative of -ian
37. Shackle
38. H.S. alternative
39. Checked in growth

Down

1. Ranger's place
2. Blood condition
3. Hodgepodge
4. Give ___ (care): 2 wds
5. Cunning
6. Early pulpit
7. "___-haw!"
8. Main tent in a circus: 2 wds.
9. Guys
10. Part of the iris bordering the pupil
14. "___ if I care!": 2 wds.
18. Twisted
20. English poet Thomas (1716–71)
21. ___ cit.
22. Jalopy
23. "Your Feet's ___" (hit for Fats Waller): 2 wds.
24. Stir up
25. Jubilant
26. Kidnap
27. Take to the ground, in the hills
28. Tangled
30. "Elementary" costar Quinn
32. "___ in Time," 3D platform game: 2 wds.
33. Computer offering
35. Brand names, briefly

333

Across

1 Alphabet trio

4 Instruments that kill or injure many people, initially

7 Benchmark: abbr.

10 Wanted ad letters

11 "Lord, is ___?": 2 wds.

12 Crying syllable

13 Pence, to Trump: 2 wds.

16 Prefix with plasm

17 Wounds

18 "Tommy" rockers: 2 wds.

21 Thus, in Turin

22 Warner Music Group record label

24 Letter after mem

25 For a song: 2 wds.

28 R.S.V.P. part

29 Kitty

30 Distant: prefix

32 Roll-call list

36 Not level

38 First word of the "Aeneid"

39 Trivial conversation: hyph.

42 "Either you do it, ___ will!": 2 wds.

43 Watch number, initially

44 Match, as a bet

45 Newspaper known as the Gray Lady, for short

46 Neutral color

47 Not him

Down

1 Prince's "Raspberry ___"

2 Cushion site

3 Al ___ (not too soft)

4 Home video game console

5 Mont Blanc, for short

6 Uses a spade

7 "My ___" (#1 hit for the Knack)

8 Adds together: 2 wds.

9 Kills, slangily: 2 wds.

14 "I Dreamed There Was ___" (Eagles instrumental): 2 wds.

15 Soft shoe, shortly

19 Letters before "://"

20 Arise

23 Pretentious phrase of emphasis: 2 wds.

25 Like some supplements

26 Not allowed by law

27 Op-ed offering

28 Decide not to quit: 2 wds.

31 Logo of the Hartford

33 Make a shambles of

34 Host the event

35 Person gathering leaves

37 Send a quick message to

40 Aunt: Sp.

41 Feminine force

334

Across

1 Bana and Benét
6 Barely beats
11 "___ enter": 2 wds.
12 Held up
13 Easy type of question: 2 wds.
14 Boyfriends
15 Award-winning Indian movie star, ___ Kiran
17 Bain de Soleil nos.
18 After-bath wear
20 Facility
22 Bachelor's last words: 2 wds.
23 Gradual absorption
26 Sun. speech
27 1002, in Roman numerals
28 "I'm surprised" in Scotland
29 Modulation of the voice
31 It might be waived
32 Ornamental plant
33 20ths of a ton: abbr.
34 "___ Dimittis" (canticle in the Book of Luke)
36 Neet rival
38 Do-it-yourselfer's van: hyph.
40 Keep away from
43 Untrue: 2 wds.
44 Apply a fresh coat of pitch
45 You might sleep on it
46 Catchall category

Down

1 Joseph ___, who lent his name to ice cream
2 Fish-to-be
3 Disobedient to orders
4 "___ Nast Traveler"
5 Ancient colonnade
6 Drop
7 Possible rebuttal in a childish argument: 2 wds.
8 Henry Fonda film of 1940, with "The": 3 wds.
9 Sufficient, informally
10 Psychiatrist's appt.
16 Optimist's phrase: 3 wds.
18 Computer architecture, initially
19 Ancient theaters
21 Pure Prairie League hit ballad
23 Old Dodge
24 "Rhyme Pays" rapper: hyph.
25 Cows and sows
30 "The dog ate my homework," e.g.
33 Cat-like mammal
34 Holy women
35 "Looks like trouble!": hyph.
37 Prefix with gramme
39 Film studio
41 Jin-Soo Kwon in "Lost" actor, Daniel ___ Kim
42 Take a wrong turn

335

Across

1 "___ Yankees"
5 Andean ruminant
10 Org. that sues pirates
11 ___ Linda, CA (Nixon Library site)
12 ___ and sciences
13 Hannibal ___, character in "The Silence of the Lambs"
14 Admiral Richard ___, first to fly over the South Pole
15 "This ___ joke, right?": 2 wds.
16 Frost's foot, perhaps
18 "___ of Duty"
22 Not translucent
24 Feminine suffix
25 Fold or mutilate
26 Soviet mil. intelligence org.
28 Up to, in ads
29 Depositor's holding: abbr.
31 Be that as it may
33 Fan sounds
34 "___-Team": 2 wds.
35 Links prop
37 It touches the Pacific O.
40 Burned brightly
43 Gds.: abbr.
44 Kind of cross
45 Help
46 Some police dogs, briefly
47 Moscow turndown

Down

1 Boring, colorwise
2 Delicate
3 Female head of a household
4 NYSE rival
5 Caustic cleaners
6 Sniff out
7 Frick collection
8 Two-year degree type
9 Rhine feeder
13 Set free
17 Coffee holder
19 To all appearances
20 Federal agency, initially
21 Depend (on)
22 "ER" actor Epps
23 Cousin of an agouti
27 Granite State sch.
30 Letter-shaped band on a shoe: hyph.
32 "Star Trek" rank
36 Otters eat them
38 Salinger's "love-and-squalor" girl
39 Exploit
40 Measure of lift v. weight, initially
41 ___-di-dah
42 Bananas

336

Across

1. Big cat in Caen
6. Government bond, for short: hyph.
11. Harder to locate
12. Fowl pole
13. Bagnold & Blyton
14. "Leave me alone!": 2 wds.
15. Bars
17. Church area
19. One who eats no meat, briefly
23. Bribed
25. Young-___
26. "___ Wiedersehen!"
27. Tax-deferment plan, for short
28. ____ and buts, objections
29. Nigerian ethnic group
30. Sea of ____, Israel
32. Rowing (a boat)
34. Certain cameras: inits.
35. Elizabeth George ____, author of "The Bronze Bow"
37. Hemispherical home
40. Nomad's transport
43. Board
44. Wife in "Arrowsmith"
45. Brown ermine
46. Extremist

Down

1. Roman trio
2. 2004 Edgar award winner Rankin
3. Mourn: 2 wds.
4. View from Jeddah: 2 wds.
5. Formerly, once
6. Having three feet
7. Food label phrase: 2 wds.
8. "____-Pah-Pah" (song from "Oliver!")
9. Org. doing pat-downs
10. ATL advisory
16. Extra
17. Marsh of mystery
18. Curacao neighbor
20. Diving bird of the auk family
21. Logically reason
22. Ogee shapes
24. Roadside pointer
31. Neighbor of Lebanon and Egypt
33. Frank ____, New York Sportswriter of the Year in 2015
36. Rights org.
37. Chats online with, briefly
38. Perceive
39. Neighbor of a Vietnamese
41. Lapse, perhaps
42. "____ note to follow soh...": 2 wds.

337

Across

1 Milk and espresso coffee drinks

7 Org. whose first endorsed presidential candidate was Ronald Reagan

10 Opera by Jules Massenet

11 Graze

12 Female prison officer

13 100 céntimos in Peru, once

14 Type of pocket knife

16 "What ___!" ("How hilarious!"): 2 wds.

17 Mazda Sassou, notably: hyph.

20 Remorseful

24 Vice president Joe

26 45th President

27 Rio ___, Mexican river

29 ___ Van Huong, Vietnamese Prime Minister 1964–65

30 Second part of a stage production: 2 wds.

32 Explorer with a Colorado peak named after him: 2 wds.

38 W.W. II server

39 Small woods

40 Anglo-Saxon slave

41 Tolls (a bell)

42 "Let's call ___ night": 2 wds.

43 Chill

Down

1 Hits hard

2 Get ___ deal: 2 wds.

3 South American monkey with a long tail

4 Condiment eaten with fish: 2 wds.

5 Cain's eldest son

6 Portuguese Mr.

7 1980s German pop star

8 No longer working: abbr.

9 Straight as ___ (honest): 2 wds.

11 Like some cigars: hyph.

15 Attack

17 Consumer protection org.

18 Spy org.

19 Jewish org. founded in 1913

21 Beaver's coat

22 Thurman of "Batman and Robin"

23 Hosp. employee

25 Salt, to a chemist

28 Amasses a supply of

31 Hole ___, ace golf shot: 2 wds.

32 Two, in the Tyrol

33 How Phileas Fogg traveled

34 "Lone Survivor" costar Eric

35 Actress Fisher, Rebel Alley in "Arrested Development"

36 Fish that has just spawned

37 In ___ (existing)

338

Across

1 Some services
7 Cornfield raider
11 Lowlife
12 Assists
13 Ancient tombstones
14 Load
15 Top off
17 One learning to walk
19 Small river fish
20 Gets rid of
24 Five Norse kings
26 "___ Marriage" (Steven King novella): 2 wds.
27 Elaborate cake
29 Initials on a cross
30 Consultant
32 Give for safekeeping
34 Deanna ___, Marina Sirtis's "Star Trek" role
35 Eye with intent: 2 wds.
39 Lots and lots: 2 wds.
40 Microorganism that requires oxygen for growth
41 Mao's successor
42 Industrial city in eastern Pennsylvania

Down

1 Prefix for alignment or match
2 Insect that lives in a colony
3 U-turn from NNW
4 Futile: hyph.
5 Last-minute greeting: hyph.
6 North Dakota county
7 Machines at checkouts: 2 wds.
8 Bar mitzvah, e.g.
9 Eat to excess, shortly: 2 wds.
10 Samoa to Fiji dir.
16 Big name in games
17 100 sene in Samoa
18 One-___ (kids' game): hyph.
19 Tail
21 "Dove ___" (Mozart aria)
22 Fraction of an atmosphere
23 Military inits.
25 Partially-recognized state of Western Sahara, initially
28 Anatomical flaps
31 "___ Darkness" (Johnny Cash song): 3 wds.
32 One-named costume designer
33 High time?
34 Small fry
36 Hogwash
37 Three blood groups
38 Decimal system base

339

Across

1 Bikini parts
5 Mitterrand's successor
11 Come-on
12 "The Human Condition" author Arendt
13 2000 presidential candidate Keyes
14 Like good meat: 2 wds.
15 Hats, helmets, e.g.
17 Ben Gurion Airport's former name
18 Calyx part
22 "Don't Get Me Started" singer Rhett
24 River joining the Rhone
25 Pen name
26 Actor Chaney or Chaney, Jr.
27 Second-grade sequence, initially
30 Holy person
32 Casual language
33 Frequently, in poems
34 On the payroll
38 Covet
41 Official proceedings
42 One-named folk singer
43 Former golf announcer Dave
44 Zonked out
45 Monthly util. bill

Down

1 Ho-hum
2 Bug
3 Actress (Melissa Agretti on "Falcon Crest"): 2 wds.
4 Forward, as email: 2 wds.
5 Cr. transaction
6 Ride, so to speak
7 Extent of a surface: 2 wds.
8 Wrestling match div.
9 Dental org.
10 Dance step
16 Dept. store stuff
19 Kind of party
20 Any minute
21 Ash Wednesday begins it
22 Desert garments
23 Richard who played Jaws in "The Spy Who Loved Me"
28 Kind of inspection: hyph.
29 Lorre's "Casablanca" role
30 Insurance assessors' org.: inits.
31 Design for a mountain cabin: hyph.
35 Bound upward
36 French existentialist's word
37 Ste. Jeanne ____
38 1950 film noir classic: inits.
39 TV's Norton and Grimley
40 Salt, in Strasbourg

340

Across

1 Spoonful of soup, say: 2 wds.
7 ___-jongg
10 Magical drink
11 "The Lion King" character
12 Baking soda, familiarly: abbr.
13 "What's going ___ your mind?": 2 wds.
14 Dairy worker
16 Head of Hainaut?
19 Rock deposit
20 Endings for gran and can
21 Agree
25 Traveler's stop
27 Music-staff sign: 2 wds.
28 Casual eatery
30 1953 Mel Ferrer musical
31 Came out on top
32 Copied
33 Most powerful or influential
37 Deck crew's boss, briefly
38 Move up and down repeatedly
42 Fireplace fuel
43 Courtyard
44 Dividend earner: abbr.
45 Attends: 2 wds.

Down

1 Police radio message, initially
2 Parisian pronoun
3 Takeoff and landing overseers, initially
4 Chang and Eng, e.g.
5 3-D figures
6 As a whole: 2 wds.
7 "Every ___ King" (autobiography of Huey Long, Governor of Louisiana): 2 wds.
8 Others, to Ovid
9 Full house, e.g.
11 System of names used in a particular specialist field
15 Ray of fast food
16 Mausoleum
17 Morlock morsels in "The Time Machine"
18 Makes lace
22 Hair holder
23 River through Congo
24 Chip in passports, initially
26 Scientologist founder Hubbard: 2 wds.
29 Obsessing, slangily: 3 wds.
33 Sluggers' hits: abbr.
34 Expression of amazement
35 Catholic title, for short
36 Say ___ (deny): 2 wds.
39 Third largest city in Serbia
40 Injured
41 Depressing and introspective, like music

341

Across

1 Kind of yoga
6 Future attys.' exams
11 Watery discharge
12 180-degree reversal: hyph.
13 Port at the northern tip of the Red Sea
14 ___ Hawkins dance
15 Nobel Prize category: abbr.
17 "Oh, no!"
18 2100, in old Rome
20 Big ref. works, for short
22 Heartbeat sound, pit-___: hyph.
24 Abrasive lava
28 Could be reached at the office: 2 wds.
30 Comedians Carvey and Gould
31 Drum sound: hyph.
33 Bra size: 2 wds.
34 Best performers in a sport, initially
36 Former name of the cable network Versus, initially
37 Of Mars (comb. form)
40 Plant part
42 Pompous walk
44 Actresses Bennett and Kruger
47 Tiny, slangily
48 Copy
49 Chuckleheads
50 Rapper ___ West

Down

1 It ended in 1806: inits.
2 Yellowfin tuna variety
3 Air
4 Anti-Red gp., once
5 Answer to "Are not!": 2 wds.
6 Light units: abbr.
7 Holds a grudge: 2 wds.
8 Autobahn auto
9 Vacation
10 Olden dagger
16 Landlocked country in the Himalayas, briefly
18 Bryn ___, college in Pennsylvania
19 Gp. that gives out PG-13s and NC-17s
21 Fizzling firecracker
23 Small songbird
25 Shared, like a characteristic: 2 wds.
26 Woman's close-fitting headdress
27 "SportsCenter" channel, initially
29 Part of U.S.N.A.: abbr.
32 Defaces with rolls?: abbr.
35 Orderly pile
37 Completely lost
38 Ways to go?: abbr.
39 Coastal raptors
41 "The Intimate ___" (1990 jazz album)
43 Cobb of baseball fame et al.
45 One or more
46 "Get the picture?"

342

Across

1. Bubbling over
6. Exams for future attys.
11. ___ Bay, inlet of the Gulf of Maine
12. Pale shades of beige
13. Goodbye, in Grenoble
14. "I almost forgot!": 2 wds.
15. Miniature whirlwinds: 2 wds.
17. Holders for needles and pins
18. Domestic: 2 wds.
21. Time periods, briefly
25. Medical care grp.
26. Suffix with Ecuador
28. Bona ___ (goddess also called Fauna)
29. Res ___ loquitur (law)
31. Sound powers of mind
33. R.E.M. lead
35. Bad-tempered: hyph.
40. Barrel race locale
41. Grammarian's "Who's there?" reply: 3 wds.
42. Available, as an apartment
43. Track events
44. Canadian peninsula
45. Shoreline birds

Down

1. Part of U.S.N.A.: abbr.
2. "On & On" singer Erykah
3. Medical suffix
4. Drink flavored with lemon: 2 wds.
5. It may clash with the rest of the suit: 2 wds.
6. Pope before Stephen VII: 2 wds.
7. Division caused by differences in belief
8. Chemical ending
9. Election day: abbr.
10. Barbecue sound
16. One of the three superpowers in "Nineteen Eighty-Four"
18. Tuna of the Pacific
19. Ref.'s cousin
20. Not neg.
22. ___ Amin
23. Realize
24. Put into words
27. Kindergarten rest period: 2 wds.
30. In a slumber
32. Not feminine or masculine
34. Issuance from Uncle Sam: hyph.
35. New Rochelle college
36. Cholesterol varieties, initially
37. Nothing, in Nimes
38. Renaissance art patron
39. Show no respect for, slangily
40. Persian, e.g.

343

Across

1. Big name in photography, once
5. "One for My Baby" composer
10. Blast with steam
11. Singer Lewis, whose albums include "Spirit"
12. Turkish burden bearer
13. Sheets of ice
14. "SNL" alumna Cheri
15. River isles
16. Small stone
18. Adorn unnecessarily
20. Representation of a person
24. Underground letters
25. Slangy intensifier
26. Classic opener
27. Oregon Indian
29. Brit. decorations
30. Hanson hit
32. Dramatic start?
34. ___-dernier (penultimate: Fr.)
37. Free of impurities
38. Seeker's target
39. It can block the sun
40. River to the Rhone
41. Factions
42. Mock phrase of comprehension: 2 wds.

Down

1. "There's more than one way to skin ___": 2 wds.
2. Match commentators cover it
3. Burned brightly
4. Off-the-cuff: 2 wds.
5. ___ sprouts
6. Assistance given to those in need
7. Sack
8. Chemical suffixes
9. "If I Ruled the World (Imagine That)" rapper
10. Cable network abbreviation
17. Port city in the Amazon delta
18. Big inits. in sports utility vehicles
19. "Make ___ double!": 2 wds.
21. To a high degree, casually
22. Prefix with political
23. Attention getters
25. Family music group (with "The")
28. Two dots over a vowel, in German
29. Opposed to war
31. Coastal Brazilian state
32. Marseilles miss, briefly
33. Civil Rights Act grp.
35. Roman emperor, 54–68 A.D.
36. Three, to Italians
37. Medical amts.

344

Across

1 Dis
5 Natural scientist Charles
11 Chaplin, nee O'Neill
12 Kay Thompson character
13 Father of Cleopatra in Greek mythology
14 Makeup company
15 Dark turquoise color: 2 wds.
17 Actor Neeson
18 Elevated flattop
22 Indicate: 2 wds.
25 Big T-shirt sizes: inits.
26 South African political party, initially
27 "Where did ___ wrong?": 2 wds.
28 Neighbor of Iran: abbr.
29 "There but for the grace of God ___": 2 wds.
30 Refuses
32 Historic times
34 ___ suiter
35 Very small amount of money, slangily: 2 wds.
39 Enter carefully: 2 wds.
42 Cursed
43 Museum and art gallery in Paris (with "The")
44 Suffix with diet or synth
45 Armadas
46 Capone nemesis

Down

1 Linda Ellerbee's "And ___ Goes": 2 wds.
2 Mother ___
3 "Falcon Crest" actress: 2 wds.
4 Former film critic Janet
5 Big name in crossword puzzles: 2 wds.
6 Big surname in baseball
7 Composer/writer Ned
8 Golfer Michelle
9 "That ___ lie!": 2 wds.
10 Classical pianist Anton
16 Bring home?: 2 wds.
19 Speak at length
20 Destroy
21 Acts as the interlocutor
22 Beep
23 ___ about (lawyer's phrase): 2 wds.
24 Evergreen Californian shrub
31 Drenched
33 Martin of Hollywood
36 Trumpet legend Al
37 Dr.'s orders
38 Items included in envs.
39 Little helper at Christmas
40 Internet company that merged with Time Warner in 2000
41 Good name for a lawyer?

345

Across

1 Gesture with the shoulders
6 Cornered: 2 wds.
11 Loyal subject
12 Indian vegetable dish
13 Mix up
14 Composer Bruckner
15 Not often: 2 wds.
17 Danish city, the birthplace of Hans Christian Andersen
18 Hindu title of respect
20 ____ forte (loudly throughout, in music)
24 "Emeril" actor Robert
26 Bubbly
27 Phonetic alphabet letter
29 NYSE banner events
30 Violet flowers
32 Cooking in a wok, e.g.: hyph.
36 Paris bisector
37 Marilyn, lead female vocalist in The 5th Dimension
38 Hunger pains
39 Stan's pal
40 Dental ____
41 Movie holders

Down

1 Bulgar or Croat
2 ____ and seek
3 Restaurant chain founded in 1969: 2 wds.
4 They may become swans: 2 wds.
5 Hissing honkers
6 Asian saltwater lake: 2 wds.
7 Vehicle for two: 2 wds.
8 ____-Honey (Mary Jane candy alternative): hyph.
9 Kind of bomb
10 "____ Can Cook"
16 Lt.'s inferior
18 Obtain for payment
19 Former Notre Dame coach Parseghian
21 Flavored ice on a stick
22 ____ de Janeiro (2016 Olympics host city)
23 Golfer who won the U.S. Open in 1994 and 1997
25 Barbara Hutton, e.g.
28 North Pole dweller
31 Hard suit
32 Make tight
33 Baseballer Martinez
34 Shred of waste wool
35 Departs
36 Tanning lotion letters

346

Across

1 Home made of twigs
5 Essence
9 Fictional futuristic race
10 Rushing sound
12 Sign on for another tour: hyph.
13 "___ Called Bear" 2015 family movie: 2 wds.
14 Idol: 2 wds.
16 "Psycho" setting
17 Prefix with grammatic
20 Shade of purple
22 Prod: 2 wds.
24 Start of North Carolina's motto
25 WWW addresses
26 Bake in individual dishes, as eggs
28 "Old MacDonald" letters
29 Post-Manhattan Project org.
30 Gradual start?: 2 wds.
32 Severe recurring headache
35 Take back, as words
38 Breakfast-eating area
39 Universe
40 Attractive
41 "As I Lay Dying" father
42 Those, to Juan

Down

1 Toy ball material
2 Home of Zeno
3 Aretha Franklin's genre: 2 wds.
4 Capsizes: 2 wds.
5 "As ___ as gold"
6 Ending for excels or poster
7 Onetime lottery org.
8 Word in many movie titles
10 Wise one
11 ___ Foods
15 Summer, in Paris
17 Conspicuously and outrageously bad
18 ___-sci (coll. major)
19 ___ far as: 2 wds.
20 Land form with a flat top
21 Arthur who often raised a racket
23 Counseling
27 Thick-skinned ungulate, briefly
28 Muff
31 PR people: abbr.
32 Rosalind Russell role
33 Say ___ (turn down): 2 wds.
34 ___ out a win
35 They used to produce Victrolas, briefly
36 Archean, for instance
37 Authors Lewis and Forester, initially

347

Across

1 Eskimo knife
4 In lieu of
7 ___ Proudfoot (cousin of Bilbo Baggins)
10 Pope
12 Juice, in gambling: abbr.
13 Bits of inside information: 2 wds.
14 Extreme
15 At some point in the future: 2 wds.
16 Village in Tolkien's Middle-earth
17 Madrid donkey
18 "A Midsummer Night's Dream" role
20 Loose-fitting Hawaiian dresses
21 Despicable
24 Shipping hazard
25 City west of Venezia
26 Radames' love, in opera
30 Sixth Jewish month
31 Textile fiber
33 Tease
34 "Here's the answer!": 3 wds.
35 Ike's command, initially
36 Harpsichord
37 Scandinavian god of battle
38 North Yorkshire river
39 Dict. listing

Down

1 ___ point (just so far): 3 wds.
2 Butcher shop cuts
3 Let out, as hogs
4 Sepp Blatter's org., once
5 Crazy, slangily: 3 wds.
6 Baseball number nines, briefly
7 Invade in great numbers
8 Eat at a restaurant: 2 wds.
9 Nash and others
11 List heading: hyph.
16 "Let It ___" (Everly Brothers hit): 2 wds.
19 Town, informally
20 Producer of faucets and fixtures
21 Gaviscon target
22 Dwell on
23 Girder: hyph.
24 Hostel, in Anatolia
26 From ___ (slight progress): 3 wds.
27 "___ a dark and stormy night…": 2 wds.
28 Small ornamental mat
29 Dramatist Chekhov
32 "Take a Chance ___" (Abba song): 2 wds.
34 "ER" setting

348

Across

1 Carbo-loader's fare, slangily
5 Widespread
9 Silas of the Continental Congress
10 Class for foreigners, for short
11 To an extreme degree
14 Suffix with sinus
15 "La Marseillaise" is one
16 100 yrs.
17 It can be added to impress or effect
18 South African political party, initially
19 Part of Minnesota's state motto
21 "___ small world": 2 wds.
22 Style of Japanese comics
24 Mounties' acronym
27 Organized society
31 Chit in a pot, initially
32 2,000 pounds
33 Refinable rock
34 Respond
36 Slow Churned ice cream
37 Favorable reception
39 Title role for Fonda
40 "All bark ___ bite…": 2 wds.
41 Actor Auberjonois
42 Actress Marsh and others

Down

1 Group of six
2 "Scarface" star Al
3 Ones in Paris
4 Barely passing grade
5 Marie Antoinette, par exemple
6 Fails to be
7 "Slow Ride" band
8 Actresses Foley and Cleghorne
9 Remove the frost from: hyph.
12 One of the Quad Cities
13 Campy dance hit of 1978
17 Pier gp.
20 Mischievous one
21 Confident ending?
23 Geometry suffix
24 Gp. against file-sharing
25 See eye to eye
26 Clout
28 Potassium ___ (compound used in photography)
29 Fitting room activities: 2 wds.
30 Like "20 Questions" answers: 2 wds.
32 Portable conical tent
35 "La Cucaracha" band
36 Sicilian spouter
38 Way to shoot down a plane, initially

349

Across

1. Impudent
6. A Gabor sister
11. To some small degree: 2 wds.
12. Staggering
13. Capital of Yemen
14. Lifted
15. Cone-shaped heaters
17. Brit. bombers
18. Down with, in Dieppe: 2 wds.
20. An earth sci.
22. Tablet
23. Scholarly person
26. Harriet Beecher ___
28. Figure skater Cohen
29. One who gets away
31. Couples, briefly
32. Big name in skin care
33. Peter who wrote "The Valachi Papers"
34. Taxpayer's ID
36. Put back to zero
38. Fish in a Cleese film
40. Kind of yoga
43. Of ___ (somewhat): 2 wds.
44. Like a World Cup crowd
45. Clipped
46. Hunky-dory

Down

1. KLM competitor
2. Doc bloc, initially
3. "Nothing Compares 2 U" singer: 2 wds.
4. TDs and interceptions
5. Give birth to a lamb, old-style
6. Rubber
7. Oils and such
8. "A pint of sweat will save a gallon of blood" speaker: 3 wds.
9. Crème ___ crème: 2 wds.
10. It precedes beth
16. Insurance co. employee
18. Cathedral area
19. Halloween decorations
21. Quarters for Fatima et al.
23. Divide
24. Racing org. formed by Wally Parks in 1951
25. U.S.S.R. news agency
27. Opening of a retail store?
30. It may be blue
33. Jerry Stiller's spouse Anne
34. Kind of team
35. Freelancer's encl.
37. Spawning fish
39. E.R. figures: abbr.
41. Ate
42. It may finish second

357

350

Across

1 Queen's counterpart
5 Opera opener: 2 wds.
9 Misses
11 Brit. Airways, once
12 Hypothetical medicine with wonderful properties: 2 wds.
15 Texted three-letter acronym
16 Modernist style of the 1920s and 1930s: 2 wds.
17 City east of Ft. Worth, Tex.
18 Dorm authority figures, briefly
19 Subject of a tipster's tip
20 What a hopper uses: 2 wds.
22 Biol. energy sources
23 Online courtship
25 Wall St. figures
28 Squabble
32 Tappan ___ Bridge
33 Dot-___ (internet company)
34 Friend of the French
35 Blend additional sounds onto a recording
37 Perjure
38 Planes may create them: 2 wds.
40 "From ___ You": Beatles: 2 wds.
41 First word of a counting rhyme
42 Inhibited
43 Playwright O'Casey

Down

1 Living dragon
2 "Now ___": bar mitzvah boy's phrase: 3 wds.
3 Trifling complaint
4 Volkswagen Golf model
5 Adjoins
6 Wintry
7 Kind of show
8 Polar covering: 2 wds.
10 One way to run
13 Blow your own horn: 2 wds.
14 Duds
21 Guitar innovator Paul
22 Bygone nuclear agcy.
24 Sound quality
25 Black Sea arm
26 Overhaul
27 Belt clip-on
29 Tiger great Al
30 Iago's wife
31 Candy company
33 Kind of drive: hyph.
36 Menu word
39 Two-time loser to D.D.E.

351

Across

1. It's debatable
6. One-time TV workers' union
11. Defeat
12. Sew up again
13. Feature
14. Nancy Drew's creator Carolyn
15. New structuring, as of a business: abbr.
17. Cloud
18. Educator Horace
19. In ____ land (spacy): 2 wds.
21. Aug. hours in Akron
22. Discharges a gun: 2 wds.
25. Medical research agcy.
26. "Lord, is ____?": 2 wds.
27. Ft. Worth college
28. "Hogan's Heroes" sergeant
30. Charlemagne's realm, shortly
31. Olympian sword
32. Author Jorge ____ Borges
33. Blemish
35. Provide with a new supply of missiles
37. Burton of the new "Star Trek"
39. Green people?
41. Like krypton
42. Laughing
43. Brand of skin care products
44. Antiknock fluid

Down

1. Ending for titan or thor
2. Occurring at irregular intervals
3. State of ecstasy: 2 wds.
4. Kind of jack
5. Dam destroyed by the R.A.F. in 1943
6. Religious artifact supposedly hidden in the Well of Souls
7. Hardly hardy
8. Edwin O'Connor bestseller: 3 wds.
9. Bausch & Lomb saline solution brand
10. Western Hemisphere abbr.
16. Sparkle
18. Division of college athletics
20. Neighbor of Mex.
22. Put in the archives
23. Bitterness
24. Calendar abbr.
29. Moving in the direction of a higher place
32. Words before "on the line": 2 wds.
33. Gymnast's feat
34. He goes "Jaywalking"
36. Peut-____ (maybe, in Marseilles)
38. A.C.L.U. concerns: abbr.
40. Cardinal's insignia, initially

352

Across

1. Peak in ancient Palestine
5. Concentrate
10. Dimin.'s musical opposite
12. Woodwork refinement
13. Pipe holder
14. Lascivious looks
15. Fed. support benefit
16. Greek alphabet ender
18. Skipping, as school: 2 wds.
20. 1960s war zone, briefly
23. Fireplace area
25. Toni Morrison novel
26. Guarded rapiers
27. Fleshy fruit: var.
28. Asta's mistress
29. Lose freshness, shrivel
30. 6-pointers, in football stats
31. Abu ___
32. Capital of Bolivia: 2 wds.
34. ___/IP (Internet connection standard)
37. In ___ (urgently): 2 wds.
39. Band whose albums include "Eliminator": 2 wds.
41. Barrier-breaking speed: 2 wds.
42. Copyists
43. Gomer Pyle, e.g.
44. Mardi ___

Down

1. Sgts., e.g.
2. Blunders
3. Success achieved by a novice: 2 wds.
4. Mama bear, in Madrid
5. Seafood entree
6. A thou, slangily: 2 wds.
7. Fourth out of nine, in baseball: 2 wds.
8. Defunct org. that included Syria, initially
9. The "S" of CBS: abbr.
11. Ten of them make a grand: hyph.
17. Badly: prefix
19. "Cup ___" (1970s Don Williams song): 2 wds.
21. Wings of an insect
22. Bryn ___ College
23. Noun suffix
24. Snake, for one
25. Letters identifying a combination of voices (music)
27. Italian square surrounded by buildings
29. "Huh?"
31. Advanced deg.
33. Court great Arthur
35. "The Last of the Mohicans" girl
36. Ltr. add-ons
37. Former First Daughter Carter
38. P.V. Narasimha ___, 1990s Indian P.M.
40. Result of a balance between the birth and death rates, initially

353

Across

1 Some choir voices
6 St. Teresa of ___
11 Seven-time American League batting champion Rod
12 Red Square man
13 Belonging to thee
14 When some go to bed: 2 wds.
15 Coll. course
16 Angola's continent, shortly
18 "The Conspiracy Against Childhood" author LeShan
19 Biblical floater
20 Two-wheeled ox-drawn cart of old
22 Spangle used to decorate a garment
24 Hockey player Bobby and others
25 Last, for short
26 Press a suit
27 "Did You Ever ___ Lassie?": 2 wds.
29 Pauper, perhaps
32 Straighten out
34 PFC's address
35 Step to the plate
36 Sneezy's colleague
37 "___ Carter" (Lil Wayne album)
38 Portuguese girlfriend
40 Elliptic
42 Alteration of a company's structure, briefly
43 ___ Gras
44 Arm bones
45 "Family Ties" mother

Down

1 Fulfills the function of: 2 wds.
2 Pakistani city
3 It may be hard to answer: 2 wds.
4 Vintner's prefix
5 Agonize: 2 wds.
6 Warning device
7 Animals' doc
8 Having the force of a question
9 German art songs
10 Year by year record of events
17 Merriment
21 Former Oriole slugger Powell
23 ___ Bator
26 Glad-hand
27 Legacy creator
28 Tooth covering
29 Feller
30 Plant pests
31 Band aide
33 Wise words
39 Love, in Eire
41 Kilmer of "Batman Forever"

354

Across

1 Cotillion presentee, for short
4 Bundy and others
7 Efron of "Dirty Grandpa"
10 Actress Merkel
11 ___ Rae-woo, 6th president of S. Korea
12 "I like ___ lot!": 2 wds.
13 The Mormons' letters
14 Airline whose last flight was in 2001, for short
15 Beer belly
16 Cowardly villain, old-style
18 Hydrocarbon ending
19 Confiscate, legally
20 Grp. concerned with genealogy
21 Physiological need to drink
22 "The Wolf Man" Lugosi
23 Uncertain: 2 wds.
25 Deliberate
27 Groups of lions
30 Brand that shows whether you're with child, initially
31 Cicero's forte
32 Year in Vigilius's papacy
33 Officials who examine and suppress certain parts of movies, etc.
34 Slip on
35 Popular sushi fish
36 "Gimme ___!" (rude order)
37 Resinous deposit
38 Soccer's Freddy or Fro
39 Snacked on
40 Summer hrs. in Albany
41 Mil. decoration
42 Prosciutto

Down

1 Sweet and soothing, ironically
2 Page range punctuation mark: 2 wds.
3 Sharon Stone movie: 2 wds.
4 Most highfalutin'
5 Some dieters' choices: hyph., 2 wds.
6 Treat unfairly, in slang
7 Song with the line "Mr. Bluebird's on my shoulder": hyph.
8 Like many Schoenberg compositions
9 Late 1990s Cadillac model
17 Pang
22 U.K. citizens, for short
24 Radioactive metallic element
25 Be a busybody
26 Transfer (files) to a server
28 List of mistakes
29 Modus operandi
31 Set of eight things

355

Across

1 Vending machine items

6 "___ & the Women" (Richard Gere film): 2 wds.

9 Rapper Missy ___

11 Debussy's "La ___"

12 Period working parents devote to their children: 2 wds.

14 Lets out (as animals)

15 Run up ___ (accumulate debt): 2 wds.

16 Composer Stravinsky

17 Danger

18 Fasten

19 Machine driven by a flow of water, gas, etc.

21 Artoo-___ ("Star Wars" droid)

22 Part of the laurel tree used in cooking

25 Knock

28 Liquid part of fat

29 Kemo ___

30 "Histoire de Gil ___ de Santillane"

31 Renée of "The Big Parade"

33 Made-to-order: hyph.

35 School class

36 Classic Father's Day gift: 2 wds.

37 French possessive

38 Café cup

Down

1 Apply hastily: 2 wds.

2 Edmonton NHLer

3 Ruin, slangily: 2 wds.

4 Firm parts: abbr.

5 Pig's home

6 Mendeleev who developed the periodic table

7 Stay

8 High singing voice

9 Give gear to

10 Bangladeshi sarong

13 Exercise regimen: 2 wds.

17 Lecturer, briefly

19 "Smells Like ___ Spirit" (Nirvana hit)

20 Three-time Boston Marathon winner Pippig

21 Minor celebrities: hyph.

22 Ohio university mascot

23 Attractive quality

24 Brewery needs

25 Mineral used in paints

26 Dagger symbols in printed matter

27 Calvin of the PGA

29 Arab markets

31 "___ Psycho?" (Tech N9ne song): 3 wds.

32 Sluggers' hits: abbr.

34 German compass point

356

Across

1. ___ management
6. Diamond game for kids: hyph.
11. "The Art of Living" author
12. Treetop home
13. Date palm locales
14. One-time airline, familiarly: 2 wds.
15. Ancestor in the direct line
17. Beetle's wing case
18. "Bali ___"
19. Sourly, tartly
23. Actor Ed of "Up" and "Elf"
26. Eddie's "Coming to America" role
27. Director Spielberg
29. Bush Sr. once headed it
30. First fictional group to have a #1 hit song (with "The")
33. Fee paid for a nominally free service
36. Ballet position
37. Former European currency
38. Convened again
39. "Find ___ and fill it": 2 wds.
40. Department in SE France
41. Cooking fats

Down

1. For one: 2 wds.
2. Turkey's locale: 2 wds.
3. Fuel derived from petroleum
4. Plaintive piece
5. VCR button
6. Pudding ingredient
7. 1950s social rebel
8. Ligurian Sea feeder
9. Untruthful one
10. Apollo vehicle, initially
16. Gun enthusiasts' org.
18. Consumes
20. One who is false
21. Having plenty of free time
22. Singer Sumac
24. Boxer Holyfield
25. Send a different way
28. A.T.M. maker
31. Label for Muslim meat dealers
32. Skater Slutskaya
33. Groundbreaking inventions?
34. Treater's phrase: 2 wds.
35. Club ___ (resorts)
36. Thurs. follower

357

Across

1 André ___, Dutch violinist and conductor
5 Wild sheep of Asia
10 "This is ___ sudden!": 2 wds.
12 Nary a soul: 2 wds.
13 Handsome: hyph.
15 Service award
16 Kind of instinct
17 Your, in Italy
18 Manifest
19 AAU member, briefly
20 Down
21 Camper's snack
23 Aspartame manufacturer, now part of Pfizer
25 Dried coconut meat
27 Seaport and industrial city in northern Spain
30 Company that sells anti-Road Runner devices
34 In this location: Sp.
35 Ring letters
37 Suffix with Ecuador
38 Freedom, briefly
39 Pieces on a board
40 ___ Lanka
41 Movie actors' auditions: 2 wds.
44 "Blame It on Me" singer Davis
45 Record material
46 Copper or lead
47 Postpaid encl.

Down

1 Shabby
2 Repetitive sounding Philippine city
3 One who runs off to wed
4 GBP alternative
5 One more
6 Korean soldier, initially
7 Thyroid enlargement
8 Every twelve months
9 Emissary
11 Korbut of gymnastics
14 Frank in stating one's opinions
22 Chemical banned by the EPA in 1977
24 Route-finding org.
26 Breakfast food
27 Certain fir
28 Frozen spike
29 Animal in an experiment: 2 wds.
31 Big name in small planes
32 Comical Feldman and Ingels
33 Maroon
36 Airing in prime time, say: 2 wds.
42 Alfonso XIII's queen
43 Ice: Ger.

358

Across

1 "Dumb & Dumber" actress
5 Statue
11 Police officer training school in Plainfield, initially
12 Actress Milano
13 Actresses Martin and Grey
14 Instrument for Segovia
15 Two quarters: 2 wds.
17 Give new strength or energy to
22 "Aha!": 3 wds.
26 Latin phrase for a backstabber: 2 wds.
27 Knotty spot
28 City on the Seine
29 Disturb
30 Frame around a window
31 9Lives product: 2 wds.
33 5th-century Germanic leader
38 French "not me": 2 wds.
42 Scene of Jesus' first miracle
43 First letter of "frank" but not "Frankfurt": 2 wds.
44 Bridger
45 King Arthur's foster brother: 2 wds.
46 Fate

Down

1 Marchetti of football fame
2 Economist Greenspan
3 Russo of "Tin Cup"
4 Ill-considered
5 Young raptor
6 Soft downy substance
7 Memo starter letters
8 Suffix with hobby or lobby
9 Govt. property manager
10 Tasha ____, Denise Crosby's "Star Trek" role
16 Onassis and Emanuel
18 Early models had eight-horsepower engines, initially
19 Place for pins
20 W.W. II weapon
21 Attached by a hook
22 Dedicated by the auth.
23 "Jane ____ Gun" (2015 movie starring Natalie Portman): 2 wds.
24 Change a few things
25 Gang's domain
28 "Hair" co-author James
30 Systemize
32 Character in "Alley Oop"
34 Part of U.S.N.A.: abbr.
35 Beloved, in "Rigoletto"
36 Old ExxonMobil brand name
37 Chicago mayor ____ Emanuel
38 Ltr. additions
39 Pal for Pierre
40 Mediterranean isl.
41 Civil rights monogram

359

Across

1 Enough, in France
6 "___ the night before …"
10 Snow vehicle: hyph.
12 Arrangement holder
13 Sani-Flush alternative: hyph.
14 Explorer Cabeza de ___
15 City of Honshu, Japan
16 Scamp
18 Be unlike
21 Gave up (something): 2 wds.
23 College Park school, home of the Terrapins, initially
26 Race that includes Odin, Thor, and Balder
27 Nicholson Baker story: 3 wds.
29 High-ranking royal: inits.
30 Lacking contact with other people
32 "___ Doctor" (Dr. Dre/ Eminem song): 3 wds.
33 Spanish-language hit song of 1974: 2 wds.
36 ___-Bilt (power tool brand)
39 Single element of speech
40 Actor Brad of "Apt Pupil"
43 Query to Brutus: 2 wds.
44 Mystic, supernatural
45 Taekwondo great, Jhoon ___
46 For rent: 2 wds.

Down

1 Barbera d'___ (popular Italian wine)
2 "The ___ the limit!"
3 Raita, for example: 2 wds.
4 Recede, like tidal waters
5 Menagerie
6 1980s–90s entertainment combo: hyph.
7 Cry from a crib
8 Fungal spore sacs
9 Fox News pundit Hannity
11 Tactic in a game of poker
17 Decline
19 1977 Yaphet role
20 Hungarian money
21 "Well, ___-di-dah!"
22 Gas: prefix
23 Illegitimate
24 Jerry Lewis's telethon org., once
25 Board member: abbr.
28 I.R.S. employee: abbr.
31 Suffix with transmission or toxic
32 Deserves it: 2 wds.
33 The America's Cup trophy, e.g.
34 "Snow White & the Huntsman" co-producer Joe
35 Art deco illustrator
37 First name in mysteries
38 1990s Senate majority leader
41 Outer: prefix
42 Sergeant, e.g.

360

Across

1 "___-pocus!"
6 Hard knocks
10 Old Colgate competitor
11 "A Letter for ___" (Hume Cronyn film)
12 Hymn writer Reginald
13 Corrupt
15 Christina's dad
16 Inc., in Paris
18 Airline to Maastricht, initially
19 Go for the bronze?
20 Org. founded in 1913 by B'nai B'rith
21 "The Children Act" author McEwan
22 So, in Sorrento
24 "Step ___ pets" (animal-friendly palindrome): 2 wds.
25 Pool shot
27 Frat. whose mission statement is "Building Balanced Men": abbr.
28 "You can turn off the alarm now": 2 wds.
29 Unhappy states
30 Footballer Sikahema or footballer Taua
31 Know-how
32 Santa's shouts
35 On ___ own terms
36 Popular fruit drink: hyph.
37 Posting at JFK
38 Game played with three six-sided dice: hyph.
40 Ancient

42 Harold who discovered deuterium in 1932
43 Actor Zac ___
44 Blog feeds, initially
45 Catch, in a way

Down

1 Part of a drum set: hyph.
2 "Euridice" was the first complete one
3 Large motorboats: 2 wds.
4 One, in France
5 Caustic comments
6 Cut at an angle
7 The ___ Glove (hot surface mitt)
8 Scissors with a serrated blade: 2 wds.
9 Admiral's avenue: 2 wds.
14 Quick stretch in "The Alphabet Song"
17 Exiled Amin
23 Alley-___
24 Suffix with fact or aster
25 Kind of duty
26 Non-professional
27 Small bag
29 Man's nickname
31 Nautical greetings
33 Others, in Oaxaca
34 Refuse a request: 2 wds.
39 Guitar star Paul
41 "Son ___ gun!": 2 wds.

361

Across

1 ___ good deed: 2 wds.
4 Classification system for blood
7 Biceps' place
8 It has a lot of chapters, initially
9 Dungeons & Dragons game co., initially
12 Hit without restraint: 2 wds.
14 Oklahoma native
15 Prefix meaning outside
16 Hit-or-miss
18 Criminal organization: 2 wds.
20 Straight as ___ (honest): 2 wds.
21 Spiral: prefix
22 Longtime Magic 8 Ball maker
23 "Come on! Please?": 2 wds.
25 Prefix with syllabic
28 Looks down on
32 "Hopalong Cassidy" actor William
33 Bring to a proper musical pitch: 2 wds.
34 Hoist into the air
36 Biblical mother of Jabal and Jubal
37 But, to a Roman
38 Lean back
40 McBain and McMahon
41 Meadow
42 Horizontally: abbr.
43 Giant of old
44 Confederate general

Down

1 Fourth Hebrew letter: var.
2 Spinach substitute
3 Dutch beer
4 ___ Z: 2 wds.
5 French Quarter tourist spot: 2 wds.
6 Prefix meaning eight
9 Some like it hot
10 Zeno follower
11 Casanova
13 Murder
17 Countrywide
19 Mozart's "L'___ del Cairo"
24 The NCAA's Horned Frogs
25 Obloquy
26 Bicycle with a low-power engine
27 The ___, "Chestnut Mare" group
29 Modern phone feature
30 Shade
31 Field
35 He sang of Alice
39 Jaguar or puma

362

Across

1 Casey who voiced Shaggy in "Scooby-Doo"
6 Early inhabitant of Mexico
11 Greek twenty prefix
12 Nintendo turtle
13 Rapper ___ Shakur
14 Put a lid on
15 Raised area of land
17 Naval port in northern Germany
18 TV franchise that uses songs by The Who for their themes
20 Common Market inits., once
22 Hush-hush govt. group
23 Elbe feeder
25 "I Wouldn't Treat ___" (Bobby Bland song): 2 wds.
27 Ingenious
31 "The Chinese Parrot" hero
32 "___ understand": 2 wds.
33 Mortimer Snerd word
35 Fair hirer's abbr.
37 Cable chihuahua
38 Cupid's counterpart
40 Scratch
42 Newspaper section: abbr.
44 Cutting edge
47 Speed demon
48 Rowed
49 Lulus
50 Side to side measure

Down

1 Collection of items
2 Prefix with men
3 1982 movie that won Meryl Streep an Oscar: 2 wds.
4 Morales of "Mi Familia"
5 Flat diamond
6 Plains city, initially
7 Observe
8 Going ahead: 2 wds.
9 Fencing swords
10 "Cheers" role
16 Hear about: 2 wds.
18 Fig. with 360 degrees
19 Reno to San Diego dir.
21 Atlanta-based public health agcy.
24 "Ruh-___!" (Scooby-Doo phrase)
26 Wine: prefix
28 Ajman's locale, initially
29 "Tunnel Rats" director Boll
30 "Star Trek Beyond" director Justin
33 Golden, in Mexico: 2 wds.
34 Kind of legend or renewal
36 Arm joint
39 Ending for gang or poll
41 Jai ___ (fast-moving sport)
43 Prom committee members: abbr.
45 Largest city in Mich.
46 Old letter (Ð)

363

Across

1 Advance again

7 Omission, as of a syllable

9 Acct. figure

12 Young offenders' institution of old

14 St. crosser

15 British trucks

16 Home of the lion killed by Heracles

18 Finnish architect Alvar ___

19 Alternatives to chapatis

21 French heaven

22 Rock of quartz and mica

24 Suffix with canon or comic

26 Shipping hazards

28 "After the Rain" author, Norma Fox ___

30 Summer music festival site

32 Joints

34 ___ Mae Brown (Whoopi Goldberg's "Ghost" role)

35 Artificially produced radioactive element

37 "Should ___ concerned?": 2 wds.

38 Recurrent rhythmical series, beat

39 Threw things at

Down

1 Played over

2 Natural in craps

3 Henry Luce's picture publication: 2 wds.

4 Bilbao bear

5 Course used by planes: 2 wds.

6 Pitcher Hideo who won the 1996 ESPY Award for Breakthrough Athlete

8 Government record agency, initially

9 Temperature at which liquid turns to vapor: 2 wds.

10 Glacial climber's ridge

11 Janitor's supply

13 Some bullets

17 Like some seals

20 Kinsman, shortly

23 Coast

24 Kennedy Library (Boston) architect: 3 wds.

25 Guyana native

27 Tempt successfully

29 Drilling grp.

31 Labeled

33 One of the tides

36 First word of Dante's "Inferno"

364

Across

1. Demi Moore movie of 1997: inits., 2 wds.
7. South African village
11. Brought out
12. Wine choice
13. Tongue-lashing
14. Words on a monument, briefly
15. Star Wars letters
16. Diminutive, in Dundee
18. Prefix with centric
19. Peak in Greek myth
21. Exist in large numbers
23. Slangy denials
25. Rocky ridge
26. Letter run
27. Sudden uncontrollable attack
28. Provide
30. Dry (off)
33. Indian cotton fabric
35. First word of a Dolly Parton hit
36. Mineral suffix
37. Atlantic City mecca, with "The"
39. Moon's counterpart
40. Actresses Martin and Grey
42. Cosa ___
44. Gp. of musicians
45. Not on the job
46. Modern waltz violinist André
47. Atop a mare

Down

1. Makes progress: 2 wds.
2. Contradictory shout: 3 wds.
3. Legal philosophy
4. Code breakers' org.
5. Beatty and Buntline
6. Swelling from excessive fluid buildup
7. Holy Hindu's title
8. "She sells seashells," for one: 2 wds.
9. Express agreement
10. Convert into intelligible language
17. At the stern
20. Inhabitants of Asgard in Norse myth
22. Hunter in the night sky
24. March honoree, familiarly: 2 wds.
28. Key of Tchaikovsky's Symphony No. 5: 2 wds.
29. Doha denizen
31. Accustoms
32. Eastern Indian
34. Capital of Yemen
38. "The Hunger Games" star Hutcherson
41. Egyptian god of light and air
43. ___-mo replay

365

Across

1 Make a plea
4 Ret. account
7 19th-century literary monogram
10 Land est. in 1948
11 Perceive words incorrectly
13 "The Facts of Life" actress
14 Reverberating
15 Probe: 2 wds.
17 Bancroft and Baxter
18 Detroit Lions footballer Michael
19 Comfy footwear, briefly
20 Habit
22 Do away with
25 "Open wide": 2 wds.
27 "Beyond the Sea" singer, 1960
28 "Rad!"
29 Rare blood type, informally: 2 wds.
30 Playtex item
31 Patty Hearst's kidnap grp.
32 Open, in a way
34 Highly agitated: 2 wds.
37 Near: 2 wds.
39 Outrage
40 Proceeds without restraint: 2 wds.
41 Some guys in rap songs, initially
42 Subjective skill
43 French pronoun
44 Prefix with liberal or conservative

Down

1 "A ____ in the hand"
2 Morales of "NYPD Blue"
3 "Shake You Down" singer: 2 wds.
4 "____ Man" (John Ciardi poem): 3 wds.
5 Guitarist Ocasek
6 Feeling embarrassment
7 Rebirth of a soul in another body
8 Decline
9 CGS units of work
12 Worthy of high respect
16 Golf score of three strokes under par
20 "Idiotest" channel, initially
21 Tooth-doctors' org.
23 Thou, to a frau
24 School subj.
26 Deceivers
31 Mall units
32 Golden State campus letters
33 Red or Brave, for short
35 Driving need
36 Mexican currency
38 Secure an apron

366

Across

1 Not rural
6 "Please have ___": 2 wds.
11 Fearful
12 Part of a chamber orchestra
13 Calculation of length, area, volume, etc.
15 "___ silly question...": 2 wds.
16 Keats and others
17 Single-celled fungus
19 Conceal
22 Performance rights org.
25 Fairground attraction: 2 wds.
28 Legend on ice
29 "It was necessary": 3 wds.
30 "Key to the Highway" pianist Charlie
32 Apprentice
35 Lead-in for sci or grip
39 Had one cigarette after another: hyph.
41 "24K Magic" singer Mars
42 Western capital
43 Some bays
44 "On ___ to know basis": 2 wds.

Down

1 Community of Muslims
2 Some bucks
3 "Nonsense!"
4 Analyst who tests metals
5 Big Apple sch.
6 Certain schs.
7 "... born to ___ right!" (Hamlet): 2 wds.
8 Certain Ivy Leaguers
9 Many: 2 wds.
10 Heavy weights
14 Route or speed limit indicators: 2 wds.
18 Pharmaceutical company ___ Lilly
19 BART stop
20 Lyndon Johnson dog
21 Like some vbs.
22 Place to sleep
23 Ran into
24 U.N. working-conditions agcy.
26 "___ happen?"
27 Whale hunter's weapon
30 Notre Dame's river
31 US national soccer team coach Schwarz et al.
32 S.D.I. concern
33 Drag racing org.
34 Prefix meaning bull
36 Dust Bowl refugee
37 Literally, "injured"
38 Picked out of a lineup, briefly
40 Wharton grad.

367

Across

1 Morse code signal
5 Floating aimlessly
11 Bono's band: 2 wds.
12 Rented
13 Polynesian monolithic statues
14 Puts metal plates on
15 Standards against which things are compared
17 Former capital of Japan
18 Holds tight
21 Primatologist Fossey
25 The Beatles' "___ the Walrus": 2 wds.
26 Pou ___, standing place
27 BlackBerry rival, once
29 Of the stars
32 Online pet food retailer
34 Part of a town that borders a lake, e.g.
39 "Zaira" librettist Felice ___
40 Triumphant cries
41 Unimportant things
42 Taboo act: hyph.
43 Sushi offering: 2 wds.
44 Fight enders, briefly

Down

1 Temporarily unable to speak
2 Dip ___ in (test): 2 wds.
3 Long-necked bird
4 Pulls abruptly or with effort
5 Los ___ National Laboratory
6 Rid of vermin
7 Musket loader
8 Doesn't have a problem, casually: 2 wds.
9 Irons, in Paris
10 Six-pt. plays
16 Triangle part: abbr.
18 Op. ___
19 Domestic deity in ancient Rome
20 Amiens soul
22 Leb. neighbor
23 ___ premium: 2 wds.
24 Lon ___, Khmer Republic president in the 1970s
28 Series of eight musical notes
29 Above the ground
30 Personal ad abbr.
31 Cruel and oppressive ruler
33 World-renowned figure skater Sonja
34 Sported clothes
35 "What ___ mind reader?": 3 wds.
36 "I see now": 2 wds.
37 Certain iPod portable media player
38 General ___ Chicken (Chinese menu dish)
39 Some linemen: abbr.

368

Across

1 Flatfoot
4 4.0 is a perfect one in school, initially
7 Gardner of "The Barefoot Contessa"
8 Chat room initials
9 Opening of a retail store?
12 Cache
14 Teacher's deg.
15 Group of lions
16 "(I've Got a ___) Kalamazoo" (1942 Glenn Miller hit): 2 wds
18 Big name in photography, once
19 Miss ___ (TV psychic)
20 King of France
21 Abated: 2 wds.
24 Write music
26 Container for footwear
28 Maui to Hawaii dir.
31 Lyndon Johnson's younger daughter
32 Substitute: abbr.
33 CivPro students: 2 wds.
35 "California, ___ Come": 2 wds.
36 Posting at SFO or LAX
37 Evacuation of casualties to hospital by plane
39 Taxpayer's ID
40 Final: abbr.
41 "___ tu" (Verdi aria)
42 France's 200 m.p.h. train, initially
43 Largest city in Mich.

Down

1 One of a religious trio
2 Exceed
3 Big wet place
4 Hilarity
5 Kitty
6 Hasn't ___ to stand on: 2 wds.
9 Properly merited or earned
10 Departure
11 Series between K and Q
13 Nutritionist's letters
17 Cards with a letter on them
21 Diplomat's office: abbr.
22 G.I.'s mail drop
23 2007 World Series winner
25 Eye, to Pierre
26 Tart fruits
27 Forest forays
29 Elizabeth George ___, "Calico Captive" author
30 Educe
32 Suffix for jambo or kedge
34 Black mark or stain
35 Samsung product, e.g.: abbr., 2 wds.
38 Taina of "Les Girls"

369

Across

1 Nickname for Adrian Gonzalez of the New York Mets: hyph.
5 Modernize
11 Unadorned
12 Shoe materials
13 Spanish island
14 Spoiled
15 From that time
17 Aromatic herb
18 Gemstone mineral
21 Kind of hose
25 Oldest technological univ. in America
26 Home of the Cox Sch. of Business
27 In a melancholy manner
30 These, in Madrid
32 Before: Fr.
34 Having a bristly coat
39 Serenaded: 2 wds.
40 Echelon
41 Fully informed of: 2 wds.
42 Sacramento's state, casually
43 Small piece of broccoli
44 Door fixture

Down

1 Not much: 2 wds.
2 Deep cut
3 Heraldic border
4 Close at hand
5 "___ directed" (RX instruction): 2 wds.
6 Seabird with a triangular bill
7 In a quick and skillful way
8 "Zip-___-Doo-Dah": hyph.
9 Four: prefix
10 "-ish" alternative
16 Suffix with corn or cochin
18 Realtor's abbr.
19 Pollution-fighting org.
20 Empty (of)
22 Amphibious landing craft, initially
23 Grandma: Ger.
24 Fraternity letters
28 Greater in size
29 "ER" actress Freeman
30 "Bambi" character
31 Knitting loop
33 "What ___!": 2 wds.
34 Cry in despair
35 "You're ___ much trouble!": 2 wds.
36 Fighter of pirates, initially
37 Snakelike fish
38 Faucet trouble
39 Lady in personal ads, initially

370

Across

1 Do roadwork
5 Assignment
9 Early computer
11 Ancient kingdom in Asia
12 ____ firma
13 Like someone from Tehran
14 Unshorn sheep
15 ____ way
17 Inane
19 Freezer cubes
20 Not o'er
21 ____ Cruces
22 High school subj.
23 Some bent pipes
25 Some T.V. sets
26 ____ Boingo, "Weird Science" band
28 Georgia's capital: abbr.
29 Not having been satisfied
32 Wrinkly-skinned dog: 2 wds.
34 Former long-time record label initials
35 Pasta choice
36 Put the kibosh on
38 Actors Robert and Alan
39 Zen paradoxes
40 News feeds for Web users, initially
41 DOT, alternatively

Down

1 ____ di pollo (chicken breasts)
2 "On ____ to know basis": 2 wds.
3 St. Croix and St. Thomas are two: 2 wds.
4 Kernel's quarters
5 By way of, briefly
6 Panhandle city: 2 wds.
7 Native New Yorkers
8 Malay daggers
10 Small, round melons
11 "Everything but the ____": 2 wds.
16 Small island in a river
18 Antipoverty agcy. created by LBJ
22 Seamen's chapels
24 Queens airport, initially
25 One of the Magi: var.
27 Chemistry suffix
30 Alter
31 "Thou ____ blow with thy wind ..." (Exodus 15:10)
33 Cell messenger letters
37 Letters on a chit

371

Across

1. "No, you must!": 2 wds.
8. Cool ____ cucumber: 2 wds.
11. Disperse
12. Songwriters' grp.
13. Resembling a dream
14. Ireland's ____ Lingus
15. Ladder section
16. Life ____ know it: 2 wds.
17. H.S. exam
19. Take stock of
21. Web crawler
22. Unit of money in Albania
23. Kind of preview
26. Ottoman title
30. Lush's sound
32. Middle O of O-O-O
33. Kazakhstan's capital
36. Take a quick look
37. Run a blade through
38. Sign that attracts crowds
40. Geometric fig.
41. Onion that is Georgia's official state vegetable
44. Commercial suffix with Motor
45. Stupidity
46. French possessive
47. Decide mutually: 2 wds.

Down

1. Magazine: abbr.
2. Hosp. section
3. Tell a story
4. Swagger
5. Calif.-Fla. route: 2 wds.
6. "Sniper: Special Ops" costar Steven
7. Bygone MTV show
8. Take down a notch
9. Eurasian ducks
10. The Dartmouth ____ (collegiate a cappella group)
16. "____ silly question...": 2 wds.
17. Ad-free TV network
18. Word in many business names
20. Oct. preceder
24. Melville's beluga hunter
25. Relatives
27. Playing marble
28. "Some ____ meat and canna eat": Burns
29. Gagging sound
31. Housing or outer covering
33. English race place
34. Subway entrance
35. "____ Theme" (song from "Gone With the Wind")
36. 757, e.g.
39. Shebat's successor
41. Passing through
42. Olympic figure skater Midori
43. "The Fountainhead" novelist Rand

372

Across

1. ____-daisy: hyph.
5. Xerox competitor
10. Carbonara or béarnaise
12. Put ____ to (stop): 2 wds.
13. Situation fraught with difficulties: 2 wds.
15. One of a Latin trio
16. Bulgarian monetary unit
17. "It's true!": 4 wds.
21. Church title, for short
22. Prussian pronoun
23. Like Boston accents, as it were: hyph.
26. Wipe out, in surfing lingo: 2 wds.
30. "Bali ____"
32. Actress Merkel
33. One who ekes out a living on poor land: 2 wds.
37. Hugs, symbolically
38. Neatnik's nightmare roommate
39. Practical, realistic: 3 wds.
44. Make-or-break times: hyph.
45. Sleepyhead Jacques
46. Major food service company
47. Heidi of "Project Runway"

Down

1. Show to a seat, informally
2. "The Languages of ____" (Jack Vance novel)
3. Get by
4. Blemished
5. ____ Tafari (Haile Selassie)
6. Room renter
7. Green of soul duo Gnarls Barkley
8. Dawn
9. Sony product, e.g.: abbr., 2 wds.
11. Start of a counting-out rhyme
14. They have sobrinas
17. Like some vbs.
18. ____ Mitchell, actor and musician
19. Road reversal, familiarly
20. Granting grp.
24. NYSE purchase: abbr.
25. Took a load off
27. French Revolution conveyance
28. Chemistry suffix
29. Road crew goo
31. In that case: 2 wds.
33. TV puppet surname
34. Siouan speakers
35. It precedes beth
36. "Masters Without Slaves" author
37. Probability
40. The Big Apple initials
41. General ____'s chicken (Chinese restaurant dish)
42. "____ dat"
43. Skirt's edge

373

Across

1 Underground construction worker
8 Philip Roth's "___, the Fanatic"
11 Boone and Day-Lewis
12 Kid
13 Frozen fruit purée
14 Kind of cozy
15 Change the position of words, letters, etc.: abbr.
16 Reverse, e.g.
17 Feckless
20 Keats and others
22 J. Edgar Hoover used one: abbr.
23 Gallery-funding gp.
24 In ___ (lab-grown)
26 ___ alia
30 Tchaikovsky's "Overture ___ Major": 2 wds.
32 "Mon Oncle" star Jacques
33 Hush-hush org.: 2 wds., abbr.
36 Developer's reference
37 Ural River city
38 Tony-winning Hagen
40 Bunkum
41 Noms de guerre
45 Enzyme ending
46 Places into the custody of: 2 wds.
47 Belarus, once, initially
48 "___ Blonde" (Reese Witherspoon movie)

Down

1 Old activist org.
2 Sound at a spa
3 Storm dir.
4 Fast one: 2 wds.
5 Lang. of Israel
6 Nels of "Little House on the Prairie"
7 Clock std.
8 Credited to noted artist Romain de Tirtoff
9 "___ my mercy all my enemies" ("The Tempest"): 2 wds.
10 Bridge beams: hyph.
16 Bearlike mammal of China: 2 wds.
17 Tyler of "The Lord of the Rings"
18 "Gimme ___!" (start of an Iowa State cheer): 2 wds.
19 Benzoyl peroxide target
21 "Fabien ___ Franchi" (Oscar Wilde poem)
25 Military intelligence agency, initially
27 Youngest world chess champion before Kasparov
28 Fraternity letter
29 Musical dir.
31 Animal populations
33 Hartebeests
34 Computer magnate Perot: 2 wds.
35 Banana oil, for one
39 Grip, as ice cubes
41 Calder Cup org.
42 Socialite's clothing initials
43 E-mail address ending for a general
44 Curve of a ship's hull

374

Across

1 "___ Kick out of You" (song by Cole Porter): 3 wds.
6 Part of Nasdaq: abbr.
11 ___ of (disliking): 2 wds.
12 Italian town in a 1945 Pulitzer-winning novel
13 Ideal existence of carefree prosperity, so to speak: 3 wds.
15 Three-time Burmese prime minister: 2 wds.
16 Packed theater sign, in brief
17 Certain mail letters
18 Number after a period: abbr.
19 Slender tower on a mosque
21 Chekov player on "Star Trek"
23 Instrument for Orpheus
24 "Chicago Hope" Emmy winner
26 ___ Beach, Fla.
29 Stick with a small noose at one end
33 Herring-related fish
35 She, in Lisbon
36 "___ lied!": 2 wds.
37 Not any, in Normandy
38 Employment
39 Offshoot's twin brother ("Transformers"): 2 wds.
42 Undamaged: 2 wds.
43 Patty Hearst's name in the S.L.A.
44 View for a second time
45 Reform Party founder Perot: 2 wds.

Down

1 Fortunate: 2 wds.
2 Discuss, as a topic: 2 wds.
3 Flow or spill forth
4 ___ kwon do
5 Loss of the sense of smell
6 First name in the Bible, alphabetically
7 Star Wars, initially
8 Pay
9 Strict limit to customers: 2 wds.
10 Howler
14 Shockingly unpleasant
20 Others, to Octavian
22 Sweet ___, sugar alternative: 2 wds.
25 ___ Night (January 6)
26 ___ Clements, the "Father of Hillbilly Jazz"
27 "The Golden Goblet" author McGraw
28 Rules as a monarch
30 Tex-Mex music genre
31 Leachman of films
32 ___ corpus (protection against illegal imprisonment)
34 Blown away: 2 wds.
40 Born abroad
41 Gibbon species

375

Across

1 Ballet school handrail
6 Way too weighty
11 A layoff, colloquially: 2 wds.
12 Model Werbowy
13 Combined appliance: hyph.
15 Dresden direction
16 ___ vu
17 Unusual object
19 Follower of Fannie or Ginnie
22 Person: 2 wds.
24 Camper's snack
25 ___ doing (thereby): 2 wds.
26 Foreknowledge
30 "Send help!," initials
31 Memory slip
32 Healthy, in Honduras
33 Work for eds.
36 Reply to a boaster: 3 wds.
40 Sign outside a studio door: 2 wds.
41 Exciting
42 Line to the audience
43 Fills up

Down

1 ___ Spirit (stealth bomber): 2 wds.
2 Moments of understanding
3 Spa treatments: 2 wds.
4 Fan sound
5 Seat in stone for several persons
6 Task around the house: 2 wds.
7 Silents star Theda ___
8 "___ tu" (aria for Renato)
9 Prussian pronoun
10 Organ of hearing
14 Restraint
18 Baseball referees, for short
19 Mixture of dried fruit and suet, baked in a pie
20 Handle, in France
21 It can be bruised or deflated
22 Boundary: comb. form
23 One in Oberammergau
24 Family docs
27 Actress Bloom
28 Fleming and Ziering
29 Ages
32 Cargo platform
34 "Smooth Operator" singer
35 1974 Donald Sutherland/Elliott Gould movie
36 ___ man: 2 wds.
37 Reply: abbr.
38 "Love Story" composer Francis
39 "Made ___ woman" (Genesis 2:22): 2 wds.

376

Across

1 C. in C., shortly
5 Lament
11 Bee or Em
12 Creamsicle color
13 Stick shift option: 2 wds.
15 1990 NBA Finals MVP ____ Thomas
16 Coat with gold
17 My Lord, in Hebrew
20 Red gemstone
22 1984 Cyndi Lauper hit: 2 wds.
26 Map abbr.
27 "Just so it's known...": inits.
28 Bostonians rarely say them
29 Prison, in slang: 2 wds.
31 "There's ____ in the air": 2 wds.
32 Get the champagne ready
34 Way out
37 Capital of Yemen
40 Tudor symbol: 2 wds.
43 Lures
44 Quintillionth: prefix
45 "I was right!": 2 wds.
46 Sea swallow

Down

1 ____ passu (side by side)
2 Regrets
3 Sought after
4 Not shaking or moving
5 Mass. city
6 Word with now or long
7 Lisa and Bart's sister
8 "The ____ Love" (2014 movie): 2 wds.
9 "____ in Calico" (1946 song): 2 wds.
10 Dork
14 Fraternity letter
18 Backstreet Boys rivals
19 Yellowfin tuna
20 Slowing, in mus.
21 Show to a seat, informally
23 Piece of paper money
24 Mouth: prefix
25 Sony handheld device, initially
27 Ardent admirer
30 Large migratory shorebird
31 Turkish mountain
33 ____Kosh B'gosh (kids' clothing company)
34 Cubicle furnishing
35 "Bring It ____ It to Win It" (2007 movie starring Ashley Benson): 2 wds.
36 Grimm beast
38 Stargazing, in college course books: abbr.
39 Seemingly forever?
41 Cecil Campbell, a.k.a. ____ Kamoze
42 Retired flier's letters

377

Across

1 Of the cheekbone
6 Burglar
10 Classic toothpaste brand
11 Prefix with logical
12 Conventional greeting: 2 wds.
14 Like the letter Z: abbr.
15 Egg: prefix
16 Third section in a dictionary
17 Ernie of golf
18 A few: abbr.
19 N.Y.C. subway line
20 Leopold's partner in crime
22 Lasso
24 Item on a chain: 2 wds.
26 Xerox competitor
28 Short pencil
32 J.F.K.'s party: abbr.
33 N.A.S.A. vehicle
35 Blow-up: abbr.
36 Pilot's announcement letters
37 Constellation next to Telescopium
38 Local educ. support group
39 High rollers: 2 wds.
42 W.W. II guns
43 Rank below capt.
44 Architect Saarinen (1910–61)
45 Approvals

Down

1 Michael, in Mexico
2 Artemis's twin
3 Chinese philosopher of long ago: hyph.
4 Furthermore
5 "American Dreams" actress Sarah
6 Ginza gelt
7 Bring out
8 Family subdivisions
9 Fetch, so to speak: 2 wds.
11 Minor details
13 Song that features the line "The Yanks are coming": 2 wds.
21 Lighter brand
23 Holder and RFK, for short
25 Go round and round the course: 2 wds.
26 Stop working
27 Graphics machine
29 Conical tents
30 "That's a lie!"
31 Criticizes harshly or violently
32 "Home Improvement" actress Dunning
34 Hairy-chested
40 ____-Off (windshield cover brand)
41 Funny or ____ (comedy website)

378

Across

1 "Bali ___" (song from "South Pacific")
4 Rest
7 Currency of Japan
8 102, to Caesar
9 Kind of gun
12 Small island in a river
13 Part of the pelvis
15 Auto wheel alignment: hyph.
17 Former CIA director George
18 Excite: 2 wds.
20 Area of 640 acres: abbr., 2 wds.
21 Imperial dynasty of China from the 12th to 3rd century B.C.
22 Diamonds or spades, e.g.
23 Get a conversation going: 3 wds.
26 Substitute: abbr.
27 Highland hats
28 Greek bone
29 Actress Mimieux
32 Tertiary
34 Kuwaitis and Iraqis
35 Indiana native
37 Noisy disturbance
38 RR bldg.
39 One with defib. training
40 Córdoba cry
41 Him, to Henri
42 "Treasure Island" inits.

Down

1 Marriott rival
2 Vowel sequence
3 Forward pass catch in football
4 Dope
5 One of the "Rocky" films
6 Put a point on, old-style
9 Hernán Cortés, for one
10 Iron-poor
11 Teeny
14 City southwest of Birmingham, Alabama
16 Asthmatics' devices
19 Cuckoo
23 Simple soups
24 Filmed the scene again
25 Danish cheese
30 Govt. security: hyph.
31 Old serfs
33 Involving a 24-hour period, in biology
36 Source of low-fat meat

379

Across

1 Soak up the sun
5 How some computer files are stored: 2 wds.
10 Static start?
11 Hoofing it: 2 wds.
12 Chinese leader?
13 Hoi ____
14 Olympics blade
16 To be, to Pierre
17 Celtics head coach between Chris Ford and Rick Pitino: inits., 2 wds.
19 News feeds for Web users, initially
20 ER pronouncement
21 Brand of cat food
23 TV music station letters
24 Fictional govt. agency in "24," initially
25 Govt. prog. since 1974
28 Bust
29 Hua ____ (Thai beach resort)
30 Dresden's river
33 "The Ballad of ____" Tennyson poem
35 10th-century pope: 2 wds.
36 Salt, briefly
37 Mickey's "The Wrestler" costar
39 Oriole or Angel, e.g.
42 Spade-like tool
43 Hostess product: 2 wds.
44 Jazz pianist from Philadelphia, McCoy ____
45 Fed. accident investigators

Down

1 Apt. features
2 Pacific tuna
3 Like some Roman tragedies
4 Super Mario Bros. series turtle-like race
5 Musician Yoko
6 Lions and Bears, e.g.
7 Young male horses
8 "The ____ of Perception," Aldous Huxley novel
9 Pigpens
11 Working
15 Susan Lucci's Emmy role
17 Summer hrs. in Salt Lake City
18 Chaney of horror films
22 Hand gesture in Indian dancing
25 Onion substitute
26 Go astray
27 Feminizing suffix
28 Bring back
30 Horror film locale: abbr., 2 wds.
31 Senator from Vermont
32 Element with atomic number 5
34 Former TWA exec Carl
38 Father's talk: abbr.
40 Hesitant sounds
41 Knock off

380

Across

1 Stomach muscles, for short
4 Cries of pain
7 Student's stat.
10 Toujours ___
11 Mass. neighbor
12 Freelancer's enc.
13 Occupy completely
15 NBC sketch series
16 Went down on the knees
17 "Went," in Scotland
18 Long flexible snout
20 Kind of feeling
21 "___ You in Paris" Michelle Gable novel: 2 wds.
24 Love potion
27 "Remington ___" (1980s show)
28 Kristine L. Svinicki's org.
29 Decorate (a floor) with mosaics
32 French wood
34 Accuracy
35 Tartan cap
36 Resembling swine
38 Summer, in Savoy
39 Prefix for dynamic
40 Umpire's call
41 Buffalo's locale, initially
42 Leb. neighbor
43 Imprecise ordinal

Down

1 Cause of wrinkles
2 Insolvent
3 1987 Prince song and album: 4 wds.
4 Convex molding
5 Best Picture Oscar-winner of 1961: 3 wds.
6 G.R.E. takers
7 Planned murder
8 Wind instrument
9 Money: Ger.
14 Jewish man's title
17 Gerard, Hodges and McDougald
18 Major golf tourneys, initially
19 151, in old Rome
22 Subterranean edible seed or root
23 Pilate's "Behold!"
25 "Cheers" actor Roger
26 They protect QBs
30 Typo, e.g.
31 "Star Trek" captain, Jean-___ Picard
32 Classic Army bomber plane: 2 wds.
33 Like granola
36 Sign of infection
37 Old verb ending

381

Across

1 Turn back
6 Balance sheet item
10 First word of a counting rhyme
11 Race in an H. G. Wells novel
12 Entertainer Gorme
13 Blockhead
15 Residents: suffix
16 Actress Francia of "Bring It On: All or Nothing"
17 "Neither Here ___ There" Bill Bryson book
18 Son of Aga Khan
20 Umpire's shout
21 New Zealand mystery writer Marsh
23 ___ prima (painting technique)
24 Jefferson Memorial feature
26 "Got ___ named Daisy…" (Little Richard lyric): 2 wds.
28 Relative of the beguine
30 Prescription instruction, initially
31 Winter hrs. in L.A.
32 Gardner of "The Night of the Iguana"
34 Rudimentary seed
36 Mideast money
37 Show a show again: hyph.
38 Barcelona basket
39 Hwy. abbrs.
40 Table-like structures in the Southwest
41 Zaire's Mobutu ___ Seko
42 Quick on the uptake

Down

1 Greet and seat: 2 wds.
2 "Ant-Man" director Reed
3 College student
4 "How the Other Half Lives" author Jacob
5 Society column word
6 Denounce publicly
7 "Billie, ___, Lena, Sarah" (compilation jazz album)
8 Rich, spicy stew from Provence
9 Christmas tree garland
14 Martial arts exercise
18 Small island
19 Frowns
22 Yahoo! competitor
23 Gen.'s counterpart
25 Pecan or cashew
26 Suffix with fabric
27 Donors
29 Embodiment
31 By itself: 2 wds.
33 As ___ resort (after all else has been tried): 2 wds.
35 False statements
36 Rod attachment
38 Nashville-based awards org.

382

Across

1 Proper sort
5 Confute
10 Make a long, low trilling sound
11 Flying solo
12 Morbid fear of water
14 That, in Toledo
15 Tiny battery letters
16 College football ranking format: inits.
17 Feature of both colonel and could: 2 wds.
19 Wranglers alternative
20 Less harsh
21 Weight
22 City near Venice
24 "___ want for Christmas…": 2 wds.
27 Of the body's main artery
31 Bill accompanier, initially
32 Modernist style of the 1920s and 1930s: 2 wds.
33 Soprano Sumac
34 "Born on the Bayou" band, familiarly
35 Stop
36 Cool in a crisis: hyph.
39 Bill Withers hit of 1972: 2 wds.
40 Bottomless depth
41 "___ La Mancha" (musical): 2 wds.
42 Wear well

Down

1 Prefix for graphic or logical
2 Diesel who invented an engine named after him
3 Like some verbs: abbr.
4 Complained
5 1986 Indy winner Bobby
6 "Do Ya" rock grp.
7 Mishandle (a ball)
8 Social welfare agency, initially
9 Cups, saucers, etc.: 2 wds.
10 Bobby Fischer's game
13 Male head of a family
18 Pins and needles holder
21 Reindeer gathering
23 Fake: 2 wds.
24 Place of refuge
25 San Diego suburb: 2 wds.
26 Get a rise out of?
28 Pendergrass and Riley
29 Most cold
30 Female students, at one time: hyph.
32 Roman ___ (novel genre): 2 wds.
37 Comedian Philips
38 J.D.'s org.

383

Across

1 School of whales
4 601, to Nero
7 Reg.
10 Prefix with sac
11 MGM motto word
12 Social
13 Fictional character created by David Chase: 2 wds.
16 It comes to a point
17 Ways of operating: abbr.
18 Mountain nymphs in Classical Mythology
20 Tres y tres
22 Former Miami Heat star, familiarly
23 Stage direction for an actress ("alone"): 2 wds.
24 Wall St. action
26 Annoy persistently
28 Less than some
29 Isles
31 Quod ___ faciendum
33 German beer
34 Indian chief
37 ___ major, key of Prokofiev's Piano Concerto No. 1: hyph.
39 Actress Hatcher
40 Stylists, manicurists, et al.
42 An N.Y.C. subway
43 Fleece
44 Slowing, in mus.
45 M.I.T. degrees
46 Company letters
47 Mystery novelist Josephine

Down

1 Reached: 2 wds.
2 French 101 verb
3 Famed pool player Rudolf Walter Wanderone: 2 wds.
4 Courtroom figs.
5 Interrogate in great detail: hyph.
6 2002 Eddie Murphy/Owen Wilson movie: 2 wds.
7 Most recent stage of development: 4 wds.
8 Capable of being stretched
9 1957 Physics Nobelist Tsung-___ Lee
14 "You betcha!"
15 Certain Internet feeds, initially
19 Smidgen
21 Cut
24 Scientist's workplace, shortly
25 National Audubon Society devotees
27 Irish sweetheart
30 "Star Trek" navigator
32 Show opener: 2 wds.
35 Banks of baseball
36 Clouded up
38 Longfellow's bell town
40 Lobster-eaters wear one
41 Toronto media inits.

384

Across

1 Lost no more
6 1993 musical starring Bette Midler
11 "Sunset Blvd." actress Nancy
12 Night light
13 Tall perennial plant with silvery plumes: 2 wds.
15 New Deal org.
16 Even score
17 102, to Hadrian
18 Frequent fliers: 2 wds.
20 Punctuation mark (—): 2 wds.
23 Lake Victoria outlet
26 Owe ___ of gratitude: 2 wds.
27 Pierre Corneille play: 2 wds.
28 W.W. II battle site: 2 wds.
29 Command with authority
30 "A-OK to launch": 3 wds.
32 Military org., briefly
34 AAU member, briefly
35 Swiss river
38 Living: 2 wds.
41 Beaming
42 Ahead by a single point: 2 wds.
43 ___ on thick: 2 wds.
44 Icon unit

Down

1 Fancy dressers
2 Hellos, in Portugal
3 DDE's alma mater
4 Alphabet trio
5 Source of exonerating evidence, at times: inits, 2 wds.
6 Some plums
7 Frank Zappa's "Shut Up 'n Play ___ Guitar"
8 Rehearse
9 Emphatic assent in Spain: 2 wds.
10 "___ am" (answer to "No you're not"): 2 wds.
14 Jedi antagonist in "Star Wars"
18 Neckline ruffle
19 One month in Guadalajara
20 Co. that produces AdvantEdge Protein Bars
21 Summer hrs. in The Rockies
22 Rescue
24 Form of ID: abbr.
25 N.J. summer setting
27 Brighten: 2 wds.
29 Some cassettes, briefly
31 Canonized person
32 Ring up
33 "Young Frankenstein" woman
35 Strong as ___: 2 wds.
36 Adolescent woe
37 Fishing rod attachment
39 Twelve in Roman numerals
40 Prefix with center or cure

385

Across

1 There are many in the Pacific Ocean: abbr.

5 Trademark of Apple Inc.

11 Waxing alternative in the 1980s and 1990s

12 Cereal fruit

13 Compel (someone) to do something

15 "Ditto": 3 wds.

16 Great Western Forum player

17 Rocky prominence

18 Letters on a rubber check

20 Spanish hoop

21 Continental money

23 Tight or amorous embrace

25 Cowboy's hat: hyph.

29 Spinning toy

30 Till fillers

32 North Carolina city, briefly

35 Gridiron official: abbr.

37 Deaf person's communication letters

38 1960–65 United Nations ambassador ___ E. Stevenson

40 Swahili or Zulu language group

42 Contemptibly narrow in outlook: hyph.

44 Juries

45 Music's Snoop

46 Arctic vehicle: hyph.

47 "Picnic" playwright William

Down

1 Present from birth

2 Escorts from a building: 2 wds.

3 John who wrote "Our Kind of Traitor": 2 wds.

4 Kind of cell

5 Collection agcy.

6 As much as fills a bucket

7 ___ run of bad luck: 2 wds.

8 1970 World's Fair site

9 Fertilizer component

10 Month before febrero

14 Transgression

19 Form

22 Windsor's prov.

24 ___ Worm (old Playskool toy)

26 Great ape of Africa

27 Continually: 3 wds.

28 Golden years fund: 2 wds.

31 Gunk

32 Irritates

33 Jingle creator

34 South American prairie

36 D.C. org.

39 Baldwin of "Malice"

41 The Beatles' "___ Love Her": 2 wds.

43 Phoenix hrs.

386

Across

1 Nintendo dinosaur
6 2009 movie starring Rupert Friend
11 What a bank may provide: 2 wds.
12 Skeletor is his archenemy: hyph.
13 Some turns on the road
14 Animal lovers' org.
15 Small songbird
16 Tornado
18 "Peer Gynt" character
20 "The Peruvian Songbird" Sumac
21 They can be collective or common
23 Simple coat hook
24 Vision-related
26 Kentucky Derby contender
28 Slangy turndown
29 Bull: comb. form
31 Poet's palindromic preposition
32 Matthew Beard in the "Our Gang" shorts
35 Like some hooks: hyph.
38 Suffix with serpent
39 "How did ____ thing like that happen?": 3 wds.
40 Mary-Kate or Ashley
42 "Horrible Histories" author Terry
43 Sheds tears
44 "Blame It on the Bossa Nova" singer Gorme
45 Very unpleasant

Down

1 Site of the Allied conference in February 1945
2 Fatty liquid
3 Not so bright: 4 wds.
4 Head cover
5 Give direction
6 Masala ____. tea blended with herbs and spices
7 Long-running toy truck brand
8 Meaningless pledges: 2 wds.
9 Elongated flower clusters
10 All lathered up: 3 wds.
17 Sickly pale
19 French pronoun
22 Termination of operations
24 Single facet: 2 wds.
25 Culinary herb
27 Suffix with direct or deposit
30 "Peer Gynt" character
33 Clumsy
34 Extremely small, casually
36 "The Bell of ____" (Longfellow)
37 Brit. tax system, initially
41 ____ Michele, Rachel of "Glee"

387

Across

1 Zaire's Mobutu ____ Seko
5 Google ____
11 Hip spelling of "cool"
12 Skink, for one
13 Epithet of the mother of Romulus and Remus
14 Loyal subjects
15 Popular adventure game
16 Water____ (flosser)
17 Ball handler?
19 "____ Excited" (Pointer Sisters hit): 2 wds.
23 Scottish skiing surface
25 Be disadvantaged: 2 wds.
27 Cardiff denizens
29 Airborne
30 Live-in helpers from overseas: 2 wds.
32 God, in Italy
33 #1
34 Polite reply from a ranch hand: 2 wds.
36 "____ be my pleasure!"
38 Mug
41 Outfit for baby
44 Pale
45 Pea jacket
46 Upper layer of the Earth's crust
47 Lime Street insurance giant
48 1450, to a Roman

Down

1 Whole alternative
2 Elusive
3 St. Moritz locale: 2 wds.
4 Gladden
5 Elite NFLer: hyph.
6 53 in Roman numerals
7 O.T. book
8 Makeshift windshield cleaner
9 Third numero
10 1960s campus org.
18 Precollege: hyph.
20 Background tune intended to create a particular feeling: 2 wds.
21 Muslim mystic
22 "How to Make an American Quilt" author Whitney ____
23 Applicator
24 Das ____ Testament
26 Enclosure with a MS.
28 Fill a need
31 Actress Winona and others
35 Paroxysm
37 Bound
39 Cousin of a herring
40 Word seg.
41 Florida city, briefly
42 "Regnava ____ silenzio" (aria from "Lucia di Lammermoor")
43 Fair hiring letters, for short

388

Across

1 Diving bird
4 Overhead trains
7 ASCAP alternative
10 Clandestine maritime org.
11 ___ long way toward: 2 wds.
12 Egypt-Syria alliance, 1958–61, initially
13 Boom box button, briefly
14 Volkswagen model
15 Half of sei
16 Hoaxed: 2 wds.
18 Bolivian export
19 Houston baseballer
20 Steak from the short loin: hyph.
22 River in Pennsylvania
24 Mexican ones
25 Bliss
27 "Mamma Mia!" group
29 Skedaddle: 2 wds.
32 "How the Grinch Stole Christmas!" author
34 Historic French town
35 Seventh enlisted army rank, initially
36 Nonresident doctors
38 Apt. feature in ads
39 Hawaiian garland
40 Taoism founder ___-tzu
41 Véronique, for one: abbr.
42 "___-brainer": 2 wds.
43 "There's no ___ T-E-A-M": 2 wds.
44 Fast plane, for short
45 Sweetie
46 Polite request, briefly

Down

1 Of the largest artery
2 Nervous feeling
3 Buy the farm: 3 wds.
4 Christmas quaffs
5 Money in Lesotho
6 Holy man
7 Keep quiet: 3 wds.
8 Miami Dolphins great Dan
9 Dunne and Castle
17 Heathers
21 Hustle and ___
23 Cellphone co.
26 Sale at which people make bids
27 Appraise
28 Is appropriate for
30 Remove with a hammer's claw
31 Model Beckford and actress Cicely
33 Psalms interjection
37 Prefix with phobia

396

389

Across

1. Tailless primate
6. Cut, as lumber
11. Zellweger of "Same King of Different as Me"
12. Tilled land in Texas
13. Softener
14. "Truly": 2 wds.
15. Rapping Dr.
16. J.F.K. search party?
18. Gold units: abbr.
19. Like some stocks, for short
20. She won a Tony for playing Martha in "Who's Afraid of Virginia Woolf?"
21. Android alternative for smartphones
22. Brenda of the comics
24. Architect Saarinen who designed the St. Louis Gateway Arch
25. Existing as an essential characteristic
27. Rikki-tikki-___
29. Babies' fathers
31. Labor group, initially
32. N.R.C. forerunner
33. Band of Renown's Brown
35. Geom. point
36. "Alice" waitress
37. Mauna ___ (Hawaiian volcano)
38. New York county
40. "The Cider House Rules" Oscar winner Michael
42. 100% necessary: 2 wds.
43. Give a hint to: 2 wds.
44. Societal stratum
45. Clubs: abbr.

Down

1. Doctrine
2. Playing card suit
3. Like the Venus flytrap
4. "A Nearly Normal Life" author
5. Trouble
6. Arabian capital
7. River of Venezuela
8. Precursors of cell phones: hyph.
9. Newspaper VIP
10. Possible rebuttal in a childish argument: 2 wds.
17. Baked dessert
23. "Wheel of Fortune" request: 2 wds.
24. Antiquity, in antiquity
26. Former Chrysler boss Lee
27. Minty one-and-a-half calories: 2 wds.
28. Popular Nissan
30. Like guests at home: 2 wds.
32. ___ worse than death: 2 wds.
34. "Danse macabre" composer Saint-___
39. Clock std.
41. Neighbor of It. and Slov.: abbr.

390

Across

1 Fortune
4 Dix and Ticonderoga, e.g.: abbr.
7 Mama bear, in Madrid
10 River that forms part of the Paraguay-Brazil border
11 100 qintars
12 Where black is white, briefly
13 Italian ice cream
15 Cooling units, for short
16 George Sand's "___ et lui"
17 Projecting knob or ridge
19 "Destination Wedding" star Reeves
21 Brook or lake fish
23 Difficult to move because of its size
25 Annual Ashland event, initially
28 B.A. or B.S.
29 French article
30 City west of Milwaukee
33 Song snippet
34 Fish with a net
38 Receipt
40 Shankar of Indian theater
41 Site of a 2015 70th-anniversary memorial service, briefly
42 State of being poorly lit
44 FDR home loan org.
45 Slippery as an ___
46 Sprawl
47 "… she loves me ___"
48 Soft & ___ (Gillette brand)
49 T or F, on exams: abbr.

Down

1 Vezina Trophy winner in 1998, 1999 and 2001
2 iPhone company
3 Abdul of "American Idol"
4 Rapper ___ Rida
5 Popular race distance: abbr., 2 wds.
6 Very close-fitting
7 Winning: 3 wds.
8 Keep away from other people
9 Kennedy and Katzenbach, shortly
14 Dessert ___
18 North Yorkshire river
20 Not certain
22 Athletes Cobb and Warner
24 "Vampire in Brooklyn" director Craven
25 Mouse catcher
26 "Oh yeah?": 2 wds.
27 Winter wrap: 2 wds.
31 White-cassis drink
32 Made ___ for it (escaped quickly): 2 wds.
35 "A Passage to India" heroine
36 Remained at home: 2 wds.
37 Recedes, as a disease
39 Berth place
41 What a keeper may keep
43 1,051, to the Romans

391

Across

1 "Corinne" author Madame de ____
6 Sap
11 Horsefeathers
12 Blakley of "Lightning Over Water"
13 John Singer Sargent, e.g.
15 Holder and RFK, for short
16 Former name of the cable network Versus, initially
17 1860s inits.
18 "Prelude ____ Kiss" (Duke Ellington song): 2 wds.
19 More repulsive, slangily
21 Civil rights org. once led by Stokely Carmichael
23 Five Norse kings
24 Pale
26 Answer to "Are not!": 2 wds.
28 Mobutu ____ Seko of Zaire
32 Cast: 2 wds.
34 "The Fresh Prince of ____-Air"
35 Currency unit: abbr.
36 Look through a scope
37 Suffix with corn or cochin
38 Ask a price that is too low
41 Hyundai car model
42 Edgar ____ Poe
43 Valuable veins
44 Sews shut, in falconry

Down

1 March 17 celebration, for short: 2 wds.
2 Forest bird of South America
3 Lung compartment: 2 wds.
4 Skillful, competent
5 "Everybody Hates Chris" co-creator Ali
6 Corrugation
7 Radioactive
8 Org. awarded the 1965 Nobel Peace Prize
9 Letter abbr.
10 Org. opposed to fur coats
14 Lush
20 McEwan and Somerhalder
22 Women's rights pioneer
25 To the extent that: 3 wds.
26 Football coach Amos ____ Stagg
27 Fused
29 Glenn Miller Orchestra vocalist Ray
30 "Absolution" costar Steven
31 Actresses Barkin and Burstyn
33 Jewish community centers, initially
35 Like some exhausts
39 "____ pales in Heaven the morning star" (Lowell)
40 Pub offering

392

Across

1 Gent
6 Arab boats
11 Suffix for ruin or alter
12 Rays
13 Author Victor and family
14 "This is ___" (radio line): 2 wds.
15 Plates, glasses, and cutlery
17 Harder to grasp
18 Certain street dancer: hyph.
20 Blackens, makes dirty
24 Nashville sch.
25 Dept. of Justice bigwigs
26 Stat. for a pitcher
27 Sushi condiment
29 Corvette design detail: hyph.
30 Au pair: var.
32 Florida football site: 2 wds.
36 Pottery fragment
37 Electrical threads
38 Word after "roger"
39 Sully
40 Warm dry mountain wind: var.
41 Religious splinter groups

Down

1 Saudi king until 2005
2 Small needle case
3 Woody
4 "___ Tunes"
5 Landscape photographer Adams
6 Storage compartments in a desk
7 1962 John Wayne movie
8 River to the Baltic
9 Smart and seasoned
10 Remain unused
16 Support system
18 Incidentally, in texts
19 Big inits. in camping
21 Relating to the atmosphere
22 Canyon or ranch ending
23 Chewing gum source
25 Forsake
28 Old-style leader of revolt
29 Large leg bones
31 Salamanders
32 Birthplace of eight U.S. presidents
33 Rattling sound
34 Departed
35 D-Day carriers, initially
36 Personal ad abbr.

393

Across

1 Rainbow or lake, e.g.

6 Mope

10 Eurasian ryegrass

12 Branch site

13 Without having been viewed beforehand: 2 wds.

15 Onassis and Emanuel

16 Hindu dynasty established in 320 A.D.

19 Cravings

23 "Take Me Bak ___" (1972 Slade song)

24 Not outside

26 State of preoccupation

29 Shrouded

30 Boarding place: abbr.

31 Anger

32 Vast chasm

34 Famous wine of Calabria, Italy

36 Striped serpent: 2 wds.

43 Suffix with webs or works

44 "It Hurts ___," Millie Jackson album: 2 wds.

45 Suffix with decor

46 "Honestly": 2 wds.

Down

1 Bills stats: abbr.

2 Style of music, a fusion of Arabic and Western elements

3 Assn.

4 Flip one's lid?

5 Hedron lead-in

6 John, Paul and George: abbr.

7 North Yorkshire river

8 General in gray

9 Boy toy?

11 Him, to Henri

14 "Bye Bye Bye" boy band

16 Wear the disguise of: 2 wds.

17 "Raw" Crayola hue

18 1990 Oscar winner for "Goodfellas"

20 Mass. setting

21 In need of a muffler

22 Blackens with chimney grime

24 "Can ___ least sit down?": 2 wds.

25 Genetic letters

27 One-time MTV afternoon show

28 Model Gabrielle

32 Flareup of crime?

33 Beat it!

35 Kind of agent, initially

36 Italian actress Scala

37 J.D. holder: abbr.

38 Auto last made in 1936

39 Early role-playing game co., initially

40 Part of some e-mail addresses

41 Pond fish

42 Ethnic group of Vietnam

394

Across

1 Prettify oneself
6 Impassive
8 Lao-___
11 First name in women's tennis
12 Hydrocarbon suffix
13 CPR performer
14 Yoke (oxen) together
16 Scanner brand
19 Boxing brothers Max and Buddy
20 Kind of power
22 Every 12 mos.
23 Smoothness
25 Biblical paradise
27 Rights org. since 1909
29 Watches
31 Bantu language
33 Slow on the ___
35 College dorm. chiefs
36 Ending for sen or jun
37 Unreasonably early or inconvenient
40 Pigpen
41 Campus life
42 Rocker Bob

Down

1 Harbors where people and goods come into the country: 3 wds.
2 Musical dir.
3 Here, elsewhere
4 "The ___ Love" (golden oldie): 2 wds.
5 Backup: 2 wds.
6 Captain Hook's helper
7 Packs (down)
8 Device used in some interviews: 2 wds.
9 Rush-hour hassle
10 Minuscule, informally
15 Opens up for the doctor, perhaps: 2 wds.
17 Brazilian beach resort
18 Bert Bobbsey's twin sister
21 TV dog
24 Big band member, briefly
25 Needle cases, in France
26 Home ___ (store chain)
28 Hymn
30 Gull-like birds
32 "___ sow, so shall...": 2 wds.
34 Suffix with depend or differ
38 Prevent from speaking freely
39 Kind of verse

395

Across

1 Carson predecessor
5 Get rid of
9 ___ Dei, set part of the Christian Mass
11 Label on a pet's collar: 2 wds.
13 Chiefs receiver with 309 yards in a 1985 game
14 Virtual meeting of a sort
15 Bank amenity letters
16 Movie org. with a "100 Years..." series
18 "...___ spacious skies"
19 Humiliation
21 "Fee, Fi, Fo, ___"
22 River that forms most of the China-North Korea border
23 Los Alamos experiments, in headlines: 2 wds.
25 Sing-along of a sort
27 Helix
29 Some seabirds
32 Wine: prefix
33 Largest city in Scotland
35 Part of an office sched.
36 Re printing: abbr.
37 First mate?
38 Video's counterpart
40 Lumber jacket pattern
42 Single-masted boat
43 ___ Corporal
44 Ramblers, Gremlins and Hornets, initially
45 Martin ___, 1930s Army bomber: 2 wds.

Down

1 Office of the pope
2 ___ Awards (annual prizes for mysteries)
3 Major division of the natural world: 2 wds.
4 Toupee, slangily
5 Connect with: 2 wds.
6 Bizarre
7 Noncommissioned army officer: 2 wds.
8 Didn't play: 2 wds.
10 Burn
12 Microbes
17 As the last in a series
20 Cluster bean
24 ___ out a living (barely gets by)
26 Cars with convertible roofs
27 Vedic ritual drinks, once
28 Singer Clark
30 Beginner
31 Neighbor of Norway
34 Freezer or blender, e.g.: abbr.
39 Summer Games gp.
41 Scientific site, briefly

396

Across

1. Altogether: 2 wds.
6. "That's ___!"
11. Kyle ___, time traveler in "The Terminator"
12. "Humble" house
13. 1997 N.L. Rookie of the Year Scott
14. Bullion unit
15. "Caroline in the City" costar Andy
17. QB protectors
18. Attell and Goldstein
20. "Admiral Graf ___" (German cruiser scuttled in 1939)
22. Grammar school basics, for short
23. Fabric edge that prevents unraveling
26. It may be between the seats
28. Prudential rival
29. Feminine
31. Perched
32. ___ spumante (Italian wine)
33. Drag racing governing body: inits.
34. Kind of camera, initially
36. "___ Darkness" (Bonnie "Prince" Billy album): 3 wds.
38. Equate
40. "Little Murders" actor-director
43. ___ citato (in the work cited)
44. Beer mug
45. All-out
46. "The Devil's Disciple" girl

Down

1. Discount rack abbr.
2. Opposite of paleo-
3. Economic situation in which goods are scarce: 2 wds.
4. "___ directed" (medicine alert): 2 wds.
5. Computer display
6. Reasonable treatment: 2 wds.
7. Arab name part
8. Not a big deal, colloquially: 3 wds.
9. "Like ___" (Izzy Stradlin album): 2 wds.
10. "___ go!"
16. Ending for legal or Senegal
18. Get ___ deal: 2 wds.
19. Pizazz
21. Night before
23. Guard
24. Snarl or growl
25. "___ Peach" (The Allman Brothers Band album): 2 wds.
27. Syllables meaning "I forgot the words"
30. Sue Grafton's "___ for Lawless": 2 wds.
33. "Dagnabbit!"
34. Groove
35. Prefix with suction
37. ___ up (pitch more slowly)
39. Long time
41. Roman numeral added to names
42. Vane dir.

397

Across

1 Important man, familiarly: 2 wds.

6 Public fight

11 Foreword, for short

12 Flaps: hyph.

13 Spanish actress Carmen ___

14 The British Museum's ___ Marbles

15 Road curve

16 Vega's constellation: 2 wds.

18 Inch furtively

19 Brief moment in time: 2 wds.

25 1963 Pulitzer-winning biographer Leon

26 South Seas starch

27 Having all sides of the same length

31 Roman love god

32 Limits

35 Fleet member

38 Refuse

39 Power glitch

41 Spine-tingling

42 Deprive of weapons

43 Horton the Elephant creator

44 Jazz pianist Blake

Down

1 What Marcel Marceau did, e.g.

2 Genetic letters

3 A/C units

4 Discount rack abbr.

5 Take part in a fight: 3 wds.

6 "The Emperor of Mars" author Allen

7 Got together

8 Irritable

9 Film ___

10 Anglo-Saxon slave

17 Horse height measurements: abbr.

18 Lung disease caused by inhaling particles of quartz or slate

19 Catch on

20 Speedy, for short

21 Currency of Romania

22 Rower's need

23 Gun owner's org.

24 Currency unit of the U.S.: abbr.

28 Heavy drinkers, slangily

29 Wont

30 Disposable handkerchief

32 Sport ___ (modern vehicles)

33 Sequoia or blue gum

34 Maori war god

35 Chesapeake Bay creature

36 Culture starter

37 "I've Gotta ___" (Sammy Davis Jr. song): 2 wds.

40 Burma's first prime minister: 2 wds.

398

Across

1 Part of a tennis match
4 Enlarge
10 Actress Sedgwick
12 Alphas' opposites
13 Suffix with symbol or satan
14 Consumes: 2 wds.
15 Works hastily or carelessly
17 Indian restaurant order: 2 wds.
23 Another word for the Sun
25 Metal marble
26 Oklahoma natives
28 Picturesque Ontario gorge town
29 Red arsenic
31 End-of-proof letters
32 Unhealthy: 3 wds.
34 Bony
37 Puzzle based on Latin Squares
42 Mercury and Mystics gp.
43 Unwelcome obligations
44 Wood sorrels
45 Rush violently
46 Compass pt.

Down

1 Runners used for gliding over snow
2 Flemish painter Jan van ___
3 Boxcars of cargo
4 Fails to
5 "...then ___ monkey's uncle!": 2 wds.
6 Sanction
7 Grundy and Gilpin, for short
8 Cross-shaped letter
9 Telesthesia, initially
11 ___ mater (literally, "generous mother")
16 Earn $200, in a way: 2 wds.
18 Actors Noah and Wallace
19 Subject in a sem. or a ser.
20 Fluent, elegant language
21 Yorkshire river
22 ___ Sea (highly saline body of water)
23 Fruit of the service tree
24 Traditional dance from Tahiti
27 Hobbit's friend
30 Kindle
33 Oxygen, simply: 2 wds.
35 Down with, in Dieppe: 2 wds.
36 Emit coherent light
37 Fifth note in a musical scale
38 Burma's first P.M.: 2 wds.
39 In the middle of, briefly
40 Düsseldorf direction
41 Kenan's Nickelodeon pal, once

399

Across

1 Short sticks used as weapons

8 Cold War monogram

11 City that is home to Disneyland

12 Snakelike fish

13 Scarce: 3 wds.

15 Kind of flour

16 Other, in Oaxaca

17 "Nothin' ____ Good Time" (1988 hit): 2 wds.

20 Available

22 Have an effect: 2 wds.

24 The ____, "Farther Along" group

25 Crete's highest peak: abbr., 2 wds.

29 Release, exudation

31 Pandemonium

34 Sexologist Shere

35 Defeat heavily in a match

36 ____ snail's pace: 2 wds.

38 Everywhere at the same time

43 Period of 100 yrs.

44 Landing stages for boats

45 Chicago to Indianapolis dir.

46 Unusual

Down

1 Half-____ (coffee mix): abbr.

2 French article

3 Black bird

4 Chocolate company

5 Counting-out word

6 Scorecard listing

7 Laura Bush's alma mater, initially

8 Monies owed

9 Fortune 500 company based in Moline, Ill.

10 Urban fantasy novelist Patricia

14 Peak in the Cascades: 2 wds.

17 Consumer protection agcy.

18 Chase scene maneuver, slangily

19 Pitching choice

21 ____ de plume (literary aliases)

23 West Point, for short

26 Three, to Cicero

27 Point

28 Chemical ending

30 Hostel, in Istanbul

31 Coll. hotshots

32 Designer noted for an innovative series of chairs

33 Dominique of "Poltergeist"

37 Four: prefix

39 Sleep attire, briefly

40 German one

41 Photog.'s item

42 Taoism founder Lao-____

400

Across

1. "La Reine Margot" actress Virna
5. Of ___ (somewhat): 2 wds.
10. Saying: "... full of pains ___ old window": 2 wds.
11. Juicy fruit, such as lemon, orange, etc.
12. Races the engine, briefly
13. Cloverleaf part: hyph.
14. Zwei plus eins
15. Aid group, often: inits.
16. Longshoreman
21. Turn red, perhaps
23. Unsolicited MS., perhaps
24. Cardinals, on scoreboards
25. French painter and sculptor Jean
27. Meas. taken during a physical
28. Sch. periods
30. VCR insert: 2 wds.
32. Exactly the same
34. City, in slang
35. Some corporal punishment
38. Movie critic Joel
41. Blows up, initially
42. One who answers a lot of questions
43. "There's more than one way to skin ___": 2 wds.
44. From Nineveh: abbr.
45. 1987 Costner role

Down

1. Enrich, in a way
2. Czech river that is an Elbe tributary
3. Cuts corners: 2 wds.
4. As found: 2 wds.
5. Basketball star Danny
6. Walked with a purpose
7. ___ pro nobis (pray for us)
8. Bacardi, e.g.
9. Sugar amt.
11. Car with a detachable roof
17. Notable time
18. All in all: 2 wds.
19. Mounties' acronym
20. Nadelman, sculptor of the bronze "Man in the Open Air"
21. Actor Oka of "Heroes"
22. "O, my love is like ___...," Burns: 2 wds.
26. Cable material, initially
29. Tightly
31. Scottish pattern
33. Person who corners others
36. School orgs.
37. Jet-setters' jets, once
38. Getaway
39. Android alternative for smartphones
40. Certain trains

401

Across

1 Letters for distributing news to Web users
5 Addis ___
10 Perfume
12 "Grumpier Old Men" actress Sophia
13 "Pulp Fiction" actor Whitaker
14 Messed up
15 Tenth month: abbr.
16 Underground hip-hop release
18 Mil. person
19 "There ___ tide...": 2 wds.
20 Shostakovich's "Babi ___" Symphony
21 Town NE of Bangor
23 Followers: suffix
24 Make up on the stage: 2 wds.
26 Rank above senior airman, briefly
29 Kofi, formerly of the U.N.
32 Mr. Potato Head piece
33 Mom-and-pop org.?
34 Mason's burden
36 Alphabet City street: 2 wds.
38 Have debts
39 Alignment of an auto's front wheels: hyph.
40 "Let ___!" ("Go ahead!"): 2 wds.
42 "Gee, ___ a stinker?": 2 wds.
43 Italian poet Torquato
44 Dimin.'s opposite
45 Bug repellent brand

Down

1 Element that's tested for in people's basements
2 It may be laid on thick
3 Engine part
4 ___ Antonio
5 "The Downeaster ___" (Billy Joel song)
6 Diamonds used as an abrasive in cutting tools
7 Orderly displays
8 Alert another car with a honk: 2 wds.
9 Physicist Ångström
11 Tell again
17 Set apart
22 Healthful grain
23 "Son of," in Arabic names
25 Shortly: 3 wds.
26 Airport in Washington: hyph.
27 ___-faire
28 "The Third Man" writer Graham
30 Riding, old-style
31 Not at all
33 Language of ancient Carthage
35 Embarkation location
37 Louse eggs
41 Small dollop

402

Across

1 "With this ring, I ___ wed"

5 Fills

10 "___ Cassius has a lean and hungry look" (Shak.)

11 Imminent, old-style

12 Leading female opera singer: 2 wds.

14 Perry Mason creator's initials

15 Mt. Rushmore's state: 2 wds.

16 Leave puzzled

18 Train stops: abbr.

22 RM-81, rocket stage

24 President before JAG

25 Machine powered by electricity

27 Brouhaha

29 "___ tu"

30 Striped cat, in France

32 Ricky Martin's "Livin' La Vida ___"

34 Place for nonresident patients

37 Manhattan neighborhood named for being just above Houston Street

39 Bk. of the Bible

40 Showing indifference or disregard

43 ___ the other: 2 wds.

44 Explorer John and others

45 Bear in India

46 Some cameras, initially

Down

1 Easygoing person: 2 wds.

2 Equine animal

3 Inscrutable

4 Harvard deg.

5 Depress

6 Wild ox of Sulawesi

7 Distance runs: 2 wds.

8 Suffix with Ecuador

9 Spanish surname abbr.

13 State confidently

17 "The Fugitive" playwright Betti

19 Occurring every third year

20 Muscles in a "six-pack," for short

21 That lady

23 People of British extraction, informally

25 Sportscaster Allen

26 Pizarro's prize

28 Dwarf played by Adam Brown in "The Hobbit": 2 wds.

31 Suzuki of baseball

33 "November Criminals" costar Elgort

35 "She's All ___ Had" (Ricky Martin song): 2 wds.

36 Popular board game

38 Melville work

40 Application form letters

41 Actress Claire

42 Grads-to-be, for short

403

Across

1 Took home a trophy
4 "___ bin ein Berliner"
7 South American macaw
8 Tasman ___
9 Govt. agency once headed by Hector Barreto
12 Elev.
13 Awaited King of the Jews
15 Morrison Remick ___, US chief justice 1874–88
17 Elusive hero of children's books
18 Deerlike water buffalo
19 Words of dismay: 2 wds.
20 Boxer's coach
23 Starfleet Academy grad.
24 In pieces
26 Web address, for short
28 With a stuffed-up sound
31 Home on the range
33 Gp. against file-sharing
34 Not suitable
35 Per ___ (yearly)
36 Blasted
38 Novelist Levin
39 Sound caused by a mouse
40 Uppercase aitch lookalike
41 "Yeah" opposite
42 Homily: abbr.
43 Fed. construction overseer

Down

1 Guitar effect: hyph.
2 Bail Prestor ___, "Star Wars" character
3 Biscayne or Bryce Canyon
4 "All You Need ___" (Morrissey song): 2 wds.
5 Copyright letter
6 Argues: 2 wds.
9 Hope, in a bad situation: 2 wds.
10 Former German territory
11 Sailor's greetings
14 Opinion
16 Young 'uns
21 Crescent-shaped windows
22 Alfonso XIII's queen
25 Take home
26 Horseshoe-shaped lab item: hyph.
27 Girl in a Left Banke hit
29 Mrs. George W., et al.
30 Japanese company with three tuning forks as a logo
32 Pollution-fighting branch of govt.
35 Jewish calendar's sixth month
37 Toulouse time

404

Across

1 Year in Leo IX's papacy
4 Worrying bank letters
7 French department and river
8 From ___ Z: 2 wds.
9 Chateau ___ Michelle winery
12 Basketball Hall of Famer Auerbach
13 Came into contact
15 Dizzee Rascal's genre
17 Sorry souls
18 Dedicated by the auth.
19 Elite NFLer: hyph.
20 Coffee-Mate producer
22 Chicken Little's mother, e.g.
23 Daunt by arousing fear in
25 Suffix with spat or spec
27 Cite: 2 wds.
30 "Robinson ___"
32 Suggestions on food labels, initially
33 Shish ___: var.
34 Electrical pioneer
35 Oblong cream puffs
37 Parcel, briefly
38 "Do you get it?"
39 Financial regulators, initially
40 Suffix with Israel
41 Ukr., once
42 Dawn personified

Down

1 Border
2 Cross-rib in vaulting
3 Unable to be destroyed
4 Archibald of the N.B.A.
5 Pou ___, vantage point
6 Type of clover: 2 wds.
9 Lamb and potato dish: 2 wds.
10 Land in Le Havre
11 Pelé's real first name
14 ___-de-sac
16 1205, to Nero
19 "It's ___ country!": 2 wds.
21 Exercises that increase the need for oxygen
24 "If I ___ a Rich Man"
25 F.D.R.'s Interior Secretary
26 "It's ___ against time": 2 wds.
28 Address: 2 wds.
29 Missouri natives
31 Insurance assessors' org.: inits.
34 Russian leader before 1917
36 Some football linemen: abbr.

405

Across

1 Long-snouted browser
6 Fool
11 ___ Kenyatta, Kenyan president
12 "___ the Loneliest Number": 2 wds.
13 Having a folding roof (of a car)
15 Wind speed units: abbr.
16 Famous mag. publisher, familiarly
17 Poetic preposition
18 Beg
20 Water in Barcelona
23 Run
27 Gin and ___
29 "Today" weatherman Al
30 Mountain lion
32 Lustful look
33 Warrior exiled by Alfonso VI: 2 wds.
35 Govt. property manager
38 Mantric mutterings
39 Sch. whose mascot is Willie the Wildcat
42 Without material form or substance
45 "The Teflon Don"
46 Comic strip about a girl in high school
47 Pudgy plus
48 Membranes in eggs of a reptile

Down

1 Fold under
2 Like ___ knife through butter: 2 wds.
3 Groaners
4 Kupcinet or Gotti
5 "Married to the Mob" actress Mercedes
6 Foul: 2 wds.
7 Kamoze of reggae
8 Mount from which Moses saw Canaan
9 Cairo's waterway
10 Belgian river
14 Epitome of thinness
18 "The 100" costar Turco
19 Dickens's Edwin
20 F.A.A. airport service
21 Gunky stuff
22 Palindromic Burmese prime minister: 2 wds.
24 Hosp. test
25 Roger Rabbit frame
26 Italian numero
28 Dieter's measurement
31 Mounties' acronym
34 Island (Italian)
35 Data-entry acronym
36 Nose-in-the-air type
37 Entr'___ (intermission)
39 New Jersey college
40 ___-Flush (former bathroom cleaner)
41 Radius neighbor
43 Periods after a tie, in sports: abbr.
44 Coke's partner

406

Across

1 Goes after: 2 wds.
6 Take-out orders?
11 "She had ___ Presbyterian mind…" (Steinbeck): 2 wds.
12 Bring to bear
13 Join the competition
14 Tennis star Rafael ___
15 "Old MacDonald" refrain
17 From ___ Z: 2 wds.
18 "Himself" to Caesar
20 Bread roll
22 Touch lightly on the water
23 Lennox and Clark
26 "Shall ___?" ("Do you want me to continue?"): 3 wds.
28 Pandemonium
30 Paris's Arc de Triomphe de l'___
32 Shine, in ad-speak
33 Fr. term of address
34 559 in Roman numerals
35 Not down: abbr.
38 Take ___ (get ready to propose): 2 wds.
40 Chin indentation
42 Part of a La Scala opera
45 Church tax
46 Theater entrance hall
47 Boastful surfer, slangily
48 Inflict, as havoc

Down

1 Amateur radio operator
2 Suffix with stock
3 Touchy subject: 2 wds.
4 Doggie of "The Quick Draw McGraw Show"
5 Kind of diagram
6 Speak out against
7 Quintillion: comb. form
8 Mother of Helen
9 Proof word
10 W.W. II battle town: 2 wds.
16 Son of, in Arabic names
18 First name in tyranny
19 Book part
21 Medical research agcy.
23 Lively
24 Close watch: 2 wds.
25 Unassisted numbers
27 Byname for South Africa's Paul Kruger ("Uncle")
29 2007 World Series winner
31 Albanian money unit
34 Ambiance factor
35 Pituitary hormone, initially
36 Madison Avenue award
37 Abbr. after many a general's name
39 "Don't let your boss catch you watching this" letters
41 Mortgage org.
43 Union with a Dropout Prevention center, initially
44 Steven Spielberg title word

407

Across

1 Bowling alley initials
4 Letters used (by some) for dates
7 Spotted wild cat
9 Ghost word
12 Water pipe in a street: 2 wds.
14 William H., author of "A Temple of Texts"
15 He played one of TV's Sopranos
16 From the U.S.: abbr.
18 Verdi opera
20 Equipment for the Red Sox
21 ___ corner (make progress): 2 wds.
22 Winnie-the-Pooh creator's monogram
23 It ended in 1806: inits.
24 Secretive U.S. govt. group
27 Poem of lament
29 Two-bagger: abbr.
30 Kind of citizen
32 Exam for future MDs
33 Elvis's middle name
34 Banda ___ (Sumatran city)
36 Alter (a book) by putting in new material
40 Shindigs
41 Variation of something
42 Maui to Hawaii dir.
43 Shrew

Down

1 Gov. Landon
2 "___ Am Mariah" (Mariah Carey album): 2 wds.
3 Low-grown plants with blue flowers: hyph.
4 Scornful cries
5 Say "I didn't want it anyway!": 3 wds.
6 TV announcer Hall
8 Brandy flavor
9 Device put on a prisoner to prevent escape: 3 wds.
10 Student taking Torts, probably: 2 wds.
11 Other, in Oaxaca
13 Nothing, in Nantes
16 "The ___ Daba Honeymoon"
17 Baby goat sound
19 A card
21 Huxtable boy
25 Maria Contreras-Sweet's organization, initially
26 Cockpit dial: abbr.
28 Grocery store hassle
30 Remarked
31 Symphonic conductor Rapée
32 "Alice" diner
35 Apple leftover
37 Campers, for short
38 Come ___ standstill: 2 wds.
39 He was attached to his brother

408

Across

1 Jordan's Queen ____
5 Californian law agency, initially
9 Half a "Charlie and the Chocolate Factory" character
10 Slave
12 Edible tuber with pinkish flesh: 2 wds.
14 ____ Fein
15 Spinach substitute
16 "You shouldn't have done that": 2 wds.
18 Edgy feeling
21 Business letter abbr.
24 Weak, ineffectual, so to speak: hyph.
27 Queen of the fairies
28 Less authentic
29 Get some air
32 Language family that includes Turkish and Mongolian
34 Sound from a spitter
38 Prepare: 3 wds.
40 Start of a clairvoyant's comment, perhaps: 3 wds.
41 Pasture
42 Formerly, in olden days
43 As recently as

Down

1 "____ get it": 2 wds.
2 Foreboding sign
3 Source of running water: 2 wds.
4 Dirtbag
5 Brief
6 Brine-cured cheeses
7 Slits in a garment
8 Shakespearean verb
9 Org. in old spy stories
11 Stocking's end
13 Inscrutable expression: 2 wds.
17 Detroit-to-Memphis dir.
18 City on the Danube
19 Actress Peeples
20 Antagonize
22 Genealogy word
23 Modern-day back-up, initially
25 Suffix with president
26 Ignored the alarm: 2 wds.
30 Archibald and Thurmond of the NBA Hall of Fame
31 Pair of cymbals mounted one above the other: hyph.
32 "____ was saying…": 2 wds.
33 Suffix with Congo or Benga
35 Former Chinese monetary unit
36 Hideous
37 Danger in Iraq, initially
39 BART stop

409

Across

1 Prince album "___ the Times": 2 wds.
6 Mary Kay competitor Lauder
11 Camille ___, French landscape painter (1796–1875)
12 Pack animal
13 Get together
14 Movies
15 Boot out of the country
17 Participate in a game
18 Acrobatic spring: hyph.
20 CIA pt.
23 "Gimme a break!"
27 Series about the Cohens, Coopers and Nichols: 2 wds.
29 "Band of Gold" singer Payne
30 Links, connections: hyph.
32 Polite rural assent: 2 wds.
33 Chess castles
35 "Come on, be ___!": 2 wds.
38 Put (away)
42 Mischief maker
44 Paris's rival
45 Jeer
46 Period of time
47 Old laborers
48 English 101 subject

Down

1 Hightail it
2 Edward Bulwer-Lytton heroine
3 Film crew member
4 "Under no circumstances!": 4 wds.
5 Cheri in "Inspector Gadget"
6 Little being
7 Course of action leading to disaster: 2 wds.
8 Hard to believe
9 Jane Austen novel
10 Like pie?
16 Defaces with rolls?: abbr.
19 "Weird Al" Yankovic movie
20 Esq. affixer
21 Letters on a phone's 4
22 Third letter
24 Big foot meas.
25 Radical grp. of the 1960s
26 He's radio-active
28 Navy noncom
31 Nine-sound signal
34 Eroded limestone landscape
35 Cathedral recess
36 Brief shots?
37 Neural transmitter
39 Some govt. agents: hyph.
40 Slippery swimmers
41 Handout
43 Traffic twosome

410

Across

1 High school dance, for short
5 Hold responsible
10 "___ Song Go Out of My Heart" (big hit for Duke Ellington): 3 wds.
11 Kind of down
12 Former way of programing a computer: 2 wds.
14 Patient gp.
15 British verb suffix
16 Tropical fruit, in short
17 Cut
19 Sheep
21 Eric Bana's "Star Trek" role
22 Small, cutesy-style
23 Bibliographical abbr.: 2 wds.
25 Like a ballerina
29 Element ending
31 "To ___ and a bone..." (Kipling): 2 wds.
32 Another name for God
35 Olivia of "The Wonder Years"
36 Whole bunch
37 Kauai keepsake
39 Seven, on a sundial
40 "Shrek 2" character voiced by Antonio Banderas: 3 wds.
43 "Please have ___": 2 wds.
44 Poppy product
45 Have another go at
46 Zaire's Mobutu ___ Seko

Down

1 Fall fast
2 "Lise with a Parasol" and "Girl with a Hoop," e.g.
3 Non-Rx, initially
4 When doubled, a seafood entree
5 Plague
6 Form of ID: abbr.
7 Rhett's last words: 2 wds.
8 Get together
9 Hungarian-born mathematician Paul
10 Apple device
13 Foreigners' class, briefly
18 Auto wheel adjustment: hyph.
20 Classic war story
24 Grade of excellence
26 Horse-drawn frame once used to transport loads
27 Regular patron
28 Self-interest
30 Bearing
32 How some stocks are acquired: 2 wds.
33 Drench
34 Attack
38 Nigerian natives
41 Genealogically-based community service organization, initially
42 Expose, poetically

411

Across

1 Word with Loa or Kea
6 The same, in Sevres
11 Org.
12 Belonging to a bottom layer
13 Steal
14 Small African antelope
15 Vigor
17 Immature egg cell
18 Twice
21 Captain's spot
24 Word after Days or Quality
25 "May ___ excused, please?": 2 wds.
26 The U.N.'s Kofi ___ Annan
28 Seat of Stark County, Ohio
31 Bad way to be caught: 3 wds.
33 Ship's funnel
37 ___ Bréhat or Batz: 2 wds.
38 Rank first held by George Washington: abbr., 2 wds.
39 Punt propeller
40 Run away to get married
41 Deep fissure
42 Get the feeling

Down

1 Livestock feed
2 "___ forgive those who...": 2 wds.
3 Govt. news agency, once
4 "You got it": abbr., 2 wds.
5 Colorless ketone
6 Very dark brown timber
7 Round Table knight
8 From my point of view: 4 wds.
9 Places for experiments
10 Peyton's little brother
16 Slick
18 Day: Sp.
19 Hudson Bay prov.
20 Not expected
22 Certain corp. takeover
23 Chess pieces
27 Battery poles
28 A.L. Central city
29 Passages between rows of seats
30 Irritate
32 Women's soccer star Michelle
33 Neatnik's nightmare roommate
34 Torment, old-style
35 Wild edible mushrooms
36 Ace bandage site
37 Beer variety, initially

412

Across

1 Arthur ____ Stadium (NYC tennis locale)
5 Argentine former V.P. Boudou
10 Portico
11 Kind of suit
12 Highway department supply
13 Mathematician Kurt
14 Spar's tip
16 Tikkanen of the NHL
17 Ending for insist
18 Day of the week
20 One-quintillionth: prefix
22 Letter abbr.
23 Some Dodges
25 "____, With Love" (1967): 2 wds.
29 Aurora, to the Greeks
31 Baseball's Tony or Alejandro
32 Able to be heard
36 Computer file format, initially
37 San Antonio to Ft. Worth dir.
38 Brand of chewing gum
40 More extreme
42 Hair salon sound
43 Port town on the coast of the Sea of Japan
44 Old ExxonMobil brand name
45 Fix, as a pool cue
46 Chimney blackener

Down

1 Armand of "The Marrying Man"
2 Begin: 2 wds.
3 Phone button
4 Corrode: 2 wds.
5 Increase
6 Phone six letters
7 Gave a lift to
8 ____ good turn (helps out): 2 wds.
9 Replacement for a tooth cusp
14 Give birth to a lamb, old-style
15 Have second thoughts about
19 Poet, in Old England
21 "The ____ Love" (R.E.M. song): 2 wds.
24 Get less drunk: 2 wds.
26 1973 Al Pacino film
27 Stymied: 3 wds.
28 Pink
30 Utah metropolis, initially
32 Alternative phrase: 2 wds.
33 Join
34 Make free from vermin, like the Pied Piper did
35 "Somebody ____ Guy" (Jocelyn Brown single)
39 ____ way, shape, or form: 2 wds.
41 Verdi's "____ tu"

413

Across

1. Fix firmly
6. Fitzgerald and others
11. Chilled: 2 wds.
12. Muhammad Ali's daughter
13. Bank holdings: abbr.
14. Like some private dets.: hyph.
15. 551, to Nero
16. Saturate, in dialect
18. Ending for velvet
19. Life summary, in short
20. Bon ____
21. Animal in the family
22. Plenty, informally
24. Bryn ____ College
26. Cul ____: 2 wds.
28. Marie's beloved
31. "High Hopes" lyricist
33. Play ____ (tennis): 2 wds.
34. Film-preserving org.
36. W.W. I military group
38. "Gross!" sounds
39. Domestic deity in ancient Rome
40. Camcorder brand letters
41. New Deal inits.
42. Slangy name for an admission ticket
44. Like some forces
46. "____ Had" (Katie Holmes movie): 2 wds.
47. Italian landmark name meaning "three roads"
48. Take the helm
49. "It's ____ World" (2007 drama film): 2 wds.

Down

1. Foundation of a rail track
2. Bend
3. Trouble leading to another that aggravates the first: 2 wds.
4. Outer: prefix
5. Actress Ferrer of "Grey's Anatomy"
6. Melancholy
7. Calif. airport
8. Rescue equipment: 2 wds.
9. "Who's Afraid of Virginia Woolf?" playwright Edward
10. Holy man
17. Saturday morning TV show, initially
23. Airline-regulating org.
25. "____ happen?"
27. Contract to hire or lease transportation
29. Mend, as a rug
30. "I've been framed!": 3 wds.
32. Computer giant, initially
34. Actors Robert and Alan
35. San Andreas ____
37. Sunkist competitor
43. Electrify
45. Dog's bark, in comics

414

Across

1 Became angry: 2 wds.
7 Desert garments
11 At a minimum: 2 wds.
12 "___ Marlene" (W.W. II song)
13 Tightly sealed containers: 2 wds.
15 Skier's transport: hyph.
16 Walkman batteries, e.g.
17 Device with moving parts
21 Japanese vegetable
22 Widows' shares
25 Without atomic weapons: hyph.
28 Nastier, slangily
29 T or F, on exams: abbr.
30 Rough-coated terriers
33 Slowing, in mus.
35 "Victory is mine!": 2 wds.
36 Back and forward motion in a rifle: 2 wds.
41 Palm product
42 Pull out of a contract
43 River that feeds the Ubangi
44 Losing moisture

Down

1 St. leader
2 Mouths, zoologically
3 "Showtime" alternative, for short
4 Impudence
5 Island in the Caribbean
6 Ask for money for helping solve a crime: 3 wds.
7 ___ grecque (cooked in olive oil, lemon juice, etc.): 2 wds.
8 Having two chambers (of a legislative body)
9 ____-Seltzer
10 Puncture sound
14 Earlier in time
17 1936 Pasteur portrayer Paul
18 P.T.A. concern: abbr.
19 Small grey Australian parrot with a yellow-crested head
20 Personal ad abbr.
23 1968 Peace Nobelist Cassin
24 Meeting: abbr.
26 Year in Claudius's reign
27 Hair-raising
31 Carrot cutter
32 Champing at the bit
33 Certain string of letters
34 "___ pastore" (opera by Mozart): 2 wds.
37 Female in the forest
38 Sundial number
39 Canadian TV channel, initially
40 Where black is white, briefly

415

Across

1 Moved with a curving trajectory
6 "___ for Innocent" (Sue Grafton novel): 2 wds.
9 Like some sofas: hyph.
11 Eavesdropping org.
12 St. Matthias, for one
13 Product of two and three
14 Life, in Lisbon
15 Associate authorship with
17 Left the bed
19 Tachometer readings, initially
20 But: Lat.
21 Total despair: 2 wds.
24 Spanish painter, born in Greece (1541–1614): 2 wds.
26 Oneness
27 Head producer for the Wu-Tang Clan
30 Stamp of approval, initially
31 Stuffs
33 Everyday
36 Cadillacs and Chevrolets
37 Initially a disc in the sky
38 Shoulder-length hairdo
40 Woman's counterpart
41 Chicken choice
42 Meara and Hathaway

Down

1 Have big goals
2 Shrub with large clusters of flowers
3 Spanish houses
4 Brand that shows whether you're with child, initially
5 Kind of sandwich
6 Intolerable
7 Self-conscious question: 3 wds.
8 Jazz instruments, informally
9 They go with the flow
10 Clinton, e.g.: abbr.
16 Conf. record
18 Some M.I.T. grads
22 ___ y Plata (Montana's motto)
23 Barnyard ladies
25 Neeson in "Nell"
26 The States, familiarly: 3 wds.
28 Round numbers
29 From Nineveh: abbr.
30 Latin word on U.S. coins
32 ___ the hole: 2 wds.
34 Alert, for short
35 Zhivago's love
39 Geometry suffix

416

Across

1 Big name in servers
4 "Stuart Little" author's initials
7 Childish
9 TV's onetime "____ Club"
12 Third, e.g.
13 Thor Heyerdahl craft: 2 wds.
14 East-west highway in the south: 2 wds.
15 Offscreen friend in "Ernest" films
16 Way in or out
18 Retain in employment: 2 wds.
20 Commercial prefix with vision
21 Ma's instrument
22 Euripides play
23 The Braves, on scoreboards
24 ____-Cat
27 Awards for TV shows
29 Special attention, for short
30 Associate
32 Garden hassle
33 Jack edged him out in the 1980 U.S. Open
34 Cohort of Bolger and Haley
36 Nonexistent
37 Many different kinds of
40 High-speed modem hookup, briefly
41 Cover with a hard surface layer
42 "Top Hat" studio, initially
43 Figure out

Down

1 NASDAQ debut, initially
2 Sticker
3 Heavy object used in physical training: 2 wds.
4 Marxian article
5 Euphemism for a vulgar word: hyph.
6 ____-Bilt (power tool brand)
8 "Stanley & Iris" director Martin
9 Completely devoid of wisdom or good sense
10 Tropical tuber
11 Actor Mark ____-Baker
15 Speed: abbr.
16 Lit up in a car: abbr.
17 A, in Acapulco
19 Building wings
21 Army fatigues, for short
25 Phillies and Braves grp.
26 Need to tidy things away all the time, say: inits.
28 String between L and P
30 Back
31 Medical suffix
32 Blender sound
35 Big name in oil
37 Neighbor of N.H.
38 Consumption
39 Chateau ____ Michelle winery

417

Across

1 Monetary units of Laos
5 Basins for liquid
10 Archipelago part
11 Proposed "fifth taste," which means "savory" in Japanese
12 Gluttony, sloth, etc.: 2 wds.
14 "Red River" actress Joanne
15 Fun house sounds
16 Day or year beginning
18 "Hop ___!": 2 wds.
22 "___ sorry!" (apology): 3 wds.
24 Singer David Thomas's rock group, Pere ___
25 Mideast native
27 Show with Jean-Luc Picard as the "Enterprise" captain, in fan shorthand
29 Olive in the comics
30 Workout spots, for some, initially
32 Programme airer, with "the," slangily
34 Breath-mint, e.g.
37 MIT grad, maybe
39 Magazine: abbr.
40 Practical judgment: 2 wds.
43 Virginia colonist John
44 "Star Wars" lovely
45 Erupts
46 Whitney and Gray

Down

1 Stroller brand
2 Rhone tributary
3 Believable
4 But, to Nero
5 Clientele
6 Russian city on the Irtysh River
7 Midsection
8 K-O connection
9 Cheer starter
13 "The Big Bopper" of the MLB: 2 wds.
17 Smear
19 Surpasses in ability
20 "Son of," in Arabic names
21 Sign of a fish on the line
23 Hollywood awards
25 Open up the floodgates, so to speak
26 Sailor's assent
28 Center X or O
31 Fibber and Molly
33 "Mr. Television"
35 Or, musically
36 "___ directed" (medicine alert): 2 wds.
38 "Don't let your boss catch you watching this" initials
40 Brief time periods
41 "Alley-___!"
42 She, in Lisbon

418

Across

1 Raccoon relative
6 General meaning
10 Maestro Rapée et al.
11 Not unter
12 Falcons linebacker Jones
13 Prefix with economic
15 Without purpose
17 Unbroken series of events
18 Vitamin bottle info.
19 Method
20 67.5 degrees on a compass, initially
21 Baseballers Maglie and Fasano
23 Removed the intestines of
25 "Star Trek: Voyager" character
27 Mas' mates
28 Not like any other
31 ___ vu (tedious familiarity)
34 Father's Day gift giver, perhaps
35 Big name in IT
37 Go bad
38 "The Hulk" director Lee
39 Bring to a destination
41 Spokes
43 Bear
44 "I've ___ Feeling" (Beatles song): 2 wds.
45 Mythical cowboy ___ Bill
46 Olympic runner Zatopek
47 Implanted tube

Down

1 Some conifers
2 Golden Crinkles brand: hyph.
3 Category of living organisms: 2 wds.
4 Cat's-paw
5 "What else ___?": 2 wds.
6 Don fancy clothing, slangily: 2 wds.
7 Ethnic group of Nigeria
8 Branch of the Dept. of Homeland Security: 2 wds.
9 Group of three
14 Without width or depth: hyph.
16 Need some support
22 Et ___ (and the following): abbr.
24 Small amount
26 Ornamental timepiece seen in a garden
28 Reserve soldiers' org.
29 Period of youth
30 Wide shoe spec.
32 "Mitchell" star Baker: 2 wds.
33 Motionless: 2 wds.
36 Applauds
40 Skeptical words: 2 wds.
42 Sam Cooke's "That's ___ Quit, I'm Movin' On": 2 wds.

419

Across

1 Stretch of grassy turf
6 Spring beauty
11 Me as well: 3 wds.
12 High hairstyles
13 Opera highlights
14 Good grade: 2 wds.
15 Projection over the entrance to a theater
17 Sound-related prefix
18 Web letters in orange buttons
22 Like some vows
26 Sighed sounds
27 Abbr. at the top of sheet music
28 Disney deer
29 Plant study: abbr.
30 Altar vow: 2 wds.
31 Paper handkerchiefs
33 Japanese pufferfish delicacy
35 Southwestern Colorado native
36 State of being poorly lit
40 Suzette Haden ___, "The Ozark Trilogy" writer
43 Have ___ (stop standing): 2 wds.
45 "I Want You Back" boy band
46 Mrs. Eisenhower
47 Radio feature
48 "Dallas" family name

Down

1 Medicare minders, initially
2 Apple invader
3 Hit song from Sarah McLachlan
4 Obviously enjoy, as humor: 2 wds.
5 Feeling of mild anxiety
6 Hollow cylinder for transporting liquids
7 ___ crust (elite)
8 "Bad" cholesterol carrier
9 Promise to pay letters
10 Ltr. additions
16 Element #92
19 Elephant Boy of a 1930s film
20 It's about a foot
21 Concordes, e.g.
22 Ingenuous
23 Language of Pakistan
24 ___-rock
25 Family appellation: 2 wds.
32 It has its ups and downs
34 City near Venice
37 Raise: abbr.
38 Big truck
39 Johnny who pitched with Warren Spahn
40 Suffix with differ
41 Maravich's alma mater, for short
42 Med. specialty
44 Unshorn sheep

420

Across

1 Rhett's last words: 2 wds.
6 Filmmaker Joel or Ethan
10 Silky yarn for sweaters
12 Snail mail sender's info, casually
13 Keith Murray album of 1996
14 Sing the praises of
15 ____-Loompa (Roald Dahl creation)
17 Warm and humid (weather)
20 Composer Satie
23 Ab ____ (from the start)
24 Lethargy
26 Instrument played by the wind: 2 wds.
29 How lowlifes operate
30 Political party, briefly
31 Marine mammal
32 Houses, in Spain
34 Actress Meg and pitcher Nolan
36 Singer Celine
39 With the result of: 2 wds.
43 Ending with infer or refer
44 Nourishing drink, especially barley water
45 Saudi Arabian king
46 ____ & Young (accounting firm)

Down

1 Richard Allen's church, initially
2 Crime family head
3 Some sushi tuna
4 Armageddon nation
5 "Star Trek III" director
6 Excessive build-up of mucus in the nose
7 French pope Urban II
8 Dean's e-mail address ender
9 Pullitzer Prize winning paper, briefly
11 Hit hard
16 Hacienda hand, maybe
17 Ancient kingdom east of the Dead Sea
18 Some eye parts
19 Dolt
21 Some Apple computers
22 Where Seoul is
24 Scotland's Firth of ____
25 Dashboard measures, for short
27 Committed to memory
28 In a bad way
32 Bill worth 100 smackers: hyph.
33 Moving around
35 Venom carrier
36 Dict. entry
37 "____ pig's eye!": 2 wds.
38 "Oh my!" in Edinburgh
40 TV buying channel
41 "____ in apple": 2 wds.
42 Palindromic explosive

421

Across

1 Concerning: 2 wds.
6 City in Finland
11 Part of a play
12 Crooning cowboy Gene
13 Container for objects for future discovery: 2 wds.
15 Word analogy snippet: 2 wds.
16 Docking spot
17 Rock's ___ Jovi
19 River that flows through York, England
21 Comparable
23 ___ bowling
27 "Answer: ___ no?": 2 wds.
29 Italian town northwest of Venice
30 Sung a song of praise
32 Mexican men, colloquially
33 Sainted pope called "the Great": 2 wds.
35 Three, in Italy
36 Chevy model
39 Former Major League Baseball pitcher, John "Blue Moon" ___
41 Accompanying, related
45 Relating to one of the arm bones
46 Jazz pianist Evans
47 "The Art of Living" author
48 Captured

Down

1 Barbados clock setting letters
2 Genetics, e.g.: abbr.
3 Advocacy of women's rights
4 Small bills
5 Verso's opposite
6 "The Raven" author's monogram
7 Excited or anxious uncertainty
8 Onomatopoetic derision
9 Shield border
10 Terminer's partner
14 August, in Angoulême
17 Evan ___, 46th Governor of Indiana
18 ___-dokey
20 Swell place?
22 Widespread
24 Stamp to show place and time of mailing
25 Robert who played A.J. Soprano
26 It's between your eyes
28 Riddle-me-___ (rhyme)
31 Goner's fate
34 Dimwit
36 Belle & Sebastian's "For the Price of ___ of Tea": 2 wds.
37 Mouselike farmland pest
38 "___ Burning" (fantasy novel by Shannon Hale)
40 Another, in Argentina
42 Mining metal
43 Never abroad
44 C&W channel

422

Across

1 L.B.J. or J.F.K.
5 Be ___ in the neck: 2 wds.
10 News story's first paragraph
11 Food from heaven
12 Averse to companionship
14 Teachers' grp.
15 Formal affairs, usually
16 "You ___!"
18 Crown
21 Result of a tanker leak: 2 wds.
23 Give birth to
26 Door part
27 Collections of star systems
29 Chicago daily, for short
30 Dark gray cloud
34 Big picture
36 Org. that gives out 9-digit IDs
37 Fee paid for a nominally free service
39 Actress Dickinson
40 Rehan, Lovelace and others
41 African antelope
42 Ward of "Sisters"

Down

1 Emergency strategy: 2 wds.
2 Dancer Jeanmaire
3 Bother: 2 wds.
4 "Star Wars" syst.
5 Unprincipled
6 Designer Rabanne
7 Behavior that is characteristic of beasts
8 Spiraling: 3 wds.
9 Ending with exter or inter
13 Statue with the body of a lion and the head of a man
17 Ninja Turtle's phrase
19 Arrhythmia detector letters
20 Classic Jag
22 1980s pop singer ___ E.
23 Cpl.'s superior
24 Goal on a hole
25 Payment to an ex
28 Extent-wise: 2 wds.
31 Hit single's opposite: hyph.
32 Commonplace
33 Kafka character Gregor
35 Churn
37 Sci-fi character Solo
38 ___ Tafari (Selassie)

423

Across

1 Ship dir. sometimes
4 Rudyard Kipling snake
7 Nutritional fig.
10 Pool hall stick
11 Void, in Versailles
12 Japanese vegetable
13 Worn away by evaporation
15 P, to Plato
16 Dominate
17 "The Maltese Falcon" actor Peter and others
19 Palm variety
21 Brontë's "Jane ___"
22 Outdoor meal, briefly
23 Become hard
26 Discourteous, impolite
28 Compound in fungicides
30 ___ Darya (river of central Asia)
33 On-stage extra, briefly
34 VII nowadays
36 "That's fine!": abbr., 2 wds.
39 Response to Little Red Hen?: 2 wds.
40 Map abbr.
41 Colorado, Kalahari, etc.
43 Shock absorber
44 "The Tell-Tale Heart" author's initials
45 "Hold On Tight" band, to fans
46 Some trial evidence, initially
47 Place to winter

Down

1 Beetle considered divine by Ancient Egyptians
2 Outlying district of a city
3 Having the necessary resources: 2 wds.
4 Chivalrous guy, briefly
5 "The Valley of Horses" writer
6 "Battle Cry" actor ___ Ray
7 Like some rice or ramen noodles: hyph.
8 Cling
9 Make less tight
14 Federal agcy., 1946–75
18 Mortgage again, for short
20 Fungal spore sacs
24 Prescription instruction, initially
25 "Concord Sonata" composer
27 Marlin or Cardinal, e.g.
28 Easy as can be: 2 wds.
29 New, in Naples
31 Pluck
32 Concord
35 Ethyl or acetyl ender
37 Had too much, briefly
38 Noggin
42 Massage locale

424

Across

1 Large sailing vessels
6 U.S. school near Juarez
10 Right hands
11 Shade provider
12 Having a daydream
14 Sounds of understanding
15 "Independence Day" aliens, for short
16 L.A. hrs.
17 British prisons
19 Page number in a book
21 Actor Sanborn of "High School Musical"
22 Girl from a nursery rhyme: 2 wds.
23 Saint Joan ___: 2 wds.
25 Blake's ex-wife in "Dynasty"
28 "Ignorance of the law ___ excuse": 2 wds.
32 Response to a general: 2 wds.
33 Title for a British member of parliament, briefly: 2 wds.
34 "That's disgusting!"
35 "Meeting at Potsdam" author
37 Literary monogram
38 Executive's attire: 3 wds.
41 Name in a Salinger title
42 Styles (someone's hair)
43 Greek roofed colonnade
44 Future attys.' exams

Down

1 Walk nonchalantly
2 Discovers, especially by chance: 2 wds.
3 Ore-___ (frozen food brand)
4 Netanyahu's predecessor in 1996
5 Certain N.C.O.
6 Potato chip brand
7 Three times as many
8 Extremely small: var.
9 Pear-shaped spinning toy: hyph.
13 In reference to: 2 wds.
14 Farm-related: abbr.
18 Pope of April 1605: 2 wds.
20 Footnote abbr.: 2 wds.
22 Undergrad degrees, initially
24 Terra ___ (dry land)
25 Seeds of a flavor similar to licorice
26 Tropical grasshopper
27 ___ pie (chocolate-coated ice cream)
29 Confession to a priest, old-style
30 Or more: 2 wds.
31 Walk-___ (cameo parts)
33 Second tries, casually
36 Business letter abbr.
39 Hot drink
40 Aunt: Sp.

425

Across

1 "What else?"
4 Uncompressed audio format
7 Playwright Akins
8 "Either he goes, ___ will!": 2 wds.
9 410, to Cicero
12 Embassy head: abbr.
13 Related by blood or marriage
15 Hanukkah pancake
17 Holy: prefix
18 Relaxation
19 Lens solution brand
20 Surrounded by
24 S.F. hours
25 Full of elaborate words, as a speech
27 President after USG
29 One way to travel
32 Eye
34 Word on a dollar bill
35 Cone-shaped heaters
37 Port town on the coast of the Sea of Japan
38 Athletic contest with a heavy ball: 2 wds.
40 Spanish-American or Korean
41 Genealogically-based community service organization, initially
42 Show on TV
43 Mil. titles
44 Stephen of the silver screen
45 "___-haw!"

Down

1 Spring bloomer
2 Polite turndown: 2 wds.
3 Monies owed that are not legally recoverable: 3 wds.
4 Responded to the alarm
5 Paul Newman's "Exodus" role
6 City in northern Vietnam
9 Unpleasant insect: hyph.
10 Father-and-daughter Hollywood duo
11 Canceled, in a way: 2 wds.
14 Board member: abbr.
16 ___ Ration, brand for Fido, once: hyph.
21 Obtained
22 Texas-based flyer, initially
23 ___-Mex
26 Laugh-a-minute
27 Like Boston accents, as it were: hyph.
28 Former South African President P.W.
30 Commercial cost, briefly: 2 wds.
31 Stock exchange in Paris
33 Krazy ___
36 Practice boxing
37 Other: Sp.
39 Quick turnaround, slangily

426

Across

1 "There it is!" in France
6 Small dot in the ocean
11 Item on a chain: 2 wds.
12 Kerry Weaver of "ER"
13 Very popular, bought by many people
15 Brickell with the New Bohemians
16 Course list letters
17 Steep descent by an aircraft
22 "Geronimo!" or "Banzai!": 2 wds.
25 Shade of brown
26 Color anew
27 Atom bomb trial: abbr., 2 wds.
29 Constellation near Norma
30 Enter: 2 wds.
31 Like some envelopes
34 French thirst-quencher
35 Emilia's slayer in "Othello"
39 Certain Middle Eastern entertainer: 2 wds.
43 Biblical poem
44 Insurance seller
45 Stiff hairs
46 "Angela's ___" (1996 best seller)

Down

1 Feeling, slangily
2 Had too much, for short
3 "Look no further!": 2 wds.
4 Delay between a stimulus and a response
5 Lynch, Holder and Mukasey, initially
6 "___ Home for Christmas" Disney comedy starring Jonathan Taylor Thomas: 2 wds.
7 Light lunch
8 George Sand's "Elle et ___"
9 Sea eagle
10 Identify
14 Site for crafty entrepreneurs
18 Pay dirt
19 East-west highway in the south: 2 wds.
20 Expansive
21 Prefix meaning "within"
22 Prepare a birthday present
23 Prefix with nautical
24 Vitamin bottle info.
27 "___ did not!": 2 wds.
28 News
30 Tasteless ornamentation
32 "I cannot ___ lie": 2 wds.
33 "Hand over the money!": 2 wds.
36 Banda ___ (Indonesian city)
37 "The French Connection" actor Hackman
38 Table scraps
39 Rate at which computer data is transferred, initially
40 Austin to Houston dir.
41 Long. crosser
42 Bond initial rating from Moody's

427

Across

1 Ski run of compacted snow
6 Winter ___ (flowering plant)
11 Fitzgerald and others
12 "Peggy Sue" singer
13 "That's ___ excuse!": 2 wds.
14 1979 film that won an Oscar for visual effects
15 Falafel bread
16 Counteract
17 Romantic gift: 2 wds.
19 Geom. solid
20 Render harmless
21 Actresses Wray and Bainter
22 Former governor of New York State, Mario ___
24 Son of "Pap" Finn
27 Seasickness symptom
31 Back then
32 Like fans
33 Anticlimax
35 Insult
36 Door sign
37 Wavelike design
38 Far from bungling
39 Awards show host
40 Arabian capital
41 Tot up again

Down

1 Vegetable container: 2 wds.
2 "Fighting" football team
3 Roof tiles
4 Slender type of larch
5 180° from WNW
6 Really annoy
7 Massage deeply
8 "After the Thin Man" costar Landi
9 Soporific
10 ARPs et al.
16 Donny, Marie, Jimmy, et al.
18 Sch. in Tulsa, Oklahoma
21 Golf match between two pairs of players
23 Cultural Revolution leader
24 ___ corpus (law)
25 Idi Amin's nation
26 Joseph of "Love Letters"
28 Glass ingredient
29 Made tough by habitual exposure
30 Concurred
32 Big artery
34 Type of air filter
37 French sea

428

Across

1 Amount in a Brylcreem slogan
4 250, to a Roman
7 Improve one's knowledge of (with "on"): 2 wds.
9 BC Lions' org.
12 Stand
13 It's often over your head
14 Southpaw Enterprises, Inc. founder Jim
15 ___ dire (jurors' examination)
16 "Aha!": 2 wds.
18 Whirring sounds
19 Utmost: 2 wds.
21 Exploit
22 502, in Herod's day
23 Tolkien beast
26 Bipedal: hyph.
29 2000s scandal subject
31 "Grand Canyon Suite" composer Grofé
32 "___ here long?"
33 Numerical prefix
34 Took off
35 Cleansing agent for washing the hair
38 Run-of-the-mill: abbr.
39 Fruit used to make tea and jelly
40 The lady in question
41 Gridiron gains: abbr.

Down

1 Twofold: abbr.
2 Verb for you
3 Go against the rule: 3 wds.
4 Two-timed: 2 wds.
5 Brusque
6 Home care provider, initially
8 Sedate
9 Stage dancing
10 Between the foul lines
11 Written communications: abbr.
15 Try
16 Wildebeest
17 Tiebreakers, briefly
18 Container for books and papers
20 "Buck Rogers" actor Gerard
24 Primary color
25 Alphabet trio
27 Came in first
28 "___ Bodied," Beyoncé song: 2 wds.
29 Zaragoza's river
30 Approach
33 Cry of dismay: hyph.
35 High class?: abbr.
36 It's like -like
37 Photo ___: abbr.

429

Across

1 Qatar's capital
5 Embarrassing mistake
10 One of the nine Muses
12 Love, in Roma
13 Common condiment
15 Sky, in Paris
16 Mil. aide
17 Highway 101 song of 1988: 3 wds.
21 Company V.I.P.
22 Taxi rider
23 Easily bribed
25 "This has me down in the dumps!": 2 wds.
29 Encouraging words: 2 wds.
31 Low digit
32 Curved opening in a wall that is fitted with glass: 2 wds.
34 ER pronouncement
36 Greenish blue
37 Put in a short or concise form
42 Bonkers
43 Old comic actress ____ Janis
44 Bellybutton type
45 "Hamlet" author: abbr.

Down

1 Like L.B.J.
2 Pray, to Publius
3 Idyllically happy and peaceful time
4 Loft
5 Started, in poetry
6 Wilberforce University's affiliated denom.
7 Unclear
8 Brothers
9 One Saarinen
11 Flood
14 ____ Prigogine, Nobel Prize-winning physicist
17 205, in old Rome
18 Suffix for chicka or campo
19 Detailed assessment of a theory
20 Rock band that broke up in 2011
24 Shakespearean hubbub
26 Water-softening agent: 2 wds.
27 Spanish year
28 Mountain ____
30 "____ afraid of that!": 2 wds.
32 Slice of cured meat from a pig
33 Cancels
34 Place for pastrami
35 "____, U of K" (fight song): 2 wds.
38 "Wheel of Fortune" purchase: 2 wds.
39 Plant of the daisy family
40 "Instant Mom" star Mowry-Hardrict
41 Cry in cartoons

430

Across

1 Highway hauler
5 "___ shocked as you are!": 2 wds.
9 Soft downy substance
10 Hang around for
11 Actress Oakes of "CHiPs"
12 "From Beyond" star Ted
13 Duct opening?
14 Reflect a flickering light
16 Japanese computer company, shortly
17 Down in the dumps
18 "Eldorado" rock grp.
19 Actress de Matteo of "Sons of Anarchy"
21 Coming into vogue again
23 Buddy-buddy
25 "What Did ___ Be So Black and Blue?" (Louis Armstrong hit): 3 wds.
27 "A Boy Named Sue" songwriter Silverstein
31 Widow in "Peer Gynt"
32 Sound from a kennel
34 Suffix with pay
35 Copes: 2 wds.
37 Charles le Gros, for one
38 Make changes
39 Arrested: 2 wds.
41 "Really!": 2 wds.
42 1980s attorney general
43 Stock market figures, briefly
44 Art deco master

Down

1 Drool
2 Birth name of Nina Simone
3 Assembled, briefly
4 "___ Over" (Mariah Carey song): 2 wds.
5 Triumphant taunt: 2 wds.
6 Magic ___
7 "Dinner Rush" star Danny
8 Pope from 440–461: 2 wds.
9 Compound leaf of a palm
10 Digressions
15 Military commander with a regional power base
20 Private address, initially
22 Athletes Cobb and Warner
24 "___ of Blackberries," Doris Buchanan Smith novel: 2 wds.
25 Psychoanalyst and neurologist Coriat
26 City of northern Illinois
28 Certain stinger
29 "The Golden Goblet" author McGraw
30 "Rawhide" singer
31 Microwave brand
33 "Wait ___" (Moby album): 2 wds.
36 Like some churches: abbr.
40 ___ Lingus

431

Across

1 Tora ____, Afghanistan
5 Washroom sink fitting: hyph.
10 Enemies
11 Rotten
12 Like ____ in a trap: 2 wds.
13 1900 novel by H. Rider Haggard
14 Stage name of Brian Vaughn Bradley, Jr.
15 Sharjah's locale, initially
16 Potholes
18 Computer fare
22 Keyboard player
25 Professor's degree, shortly
26 Ford rival
27 "Have another slice ____": 2 wds.
29 Math subj.
30 Natives of Apia
32 Critic Rex
34 Earth sci.
35 Barely get by (with "out")
37 Defeats
40 Calcified deposit on the teeth
43 Peat ingredient
44 Ledger column
45 Being ____ Ocean, melodic hardcore band: 2 wds.
46 Make like a trumpet
47 D.C. baseball team

Down

1 Degs. for actors
2 ____ cloud (comet-filled region of space)
3 Put another way
4 Blow away
5 Silents star Negri
6 Attempted
7 Rtes.
8 "____ for apple": 2 wds.
9 Samsung Galaxy, e.g., initially
11 "Green Eggs and Ham" author
17 Aunts in la familia
19 Horse breed with a spotted coat
20 Flimsy
21 Fruity drinks
22 "____ Lap" (1983 film)
23 Woman loved by Hercules
24 Heavy reading?
28 Liveried servant
31 Anxiety and trauma, for some
33 Chill
36 Model Moss or actress Winslet
38 10th- or 11th-graders' exam letters
39 Form 1040 IDs
40 Computer key
41 Soundless communication, initially
42 Cape Town's home letters

432

Across

1 Della's creator
5 Lynx and Liberty gp.
9 Milk products
11 Heavy ___
12 "Old MacDonald" refrain
13 Syrian president Bashar al-___
14 Bite-the-bullet type
16 Explorer's org.
17 Hunt's "___ Ben Adhem"
19 Toujours ___
21 The NBA's Walt Frazier, briefly
22 Reprimand to a pooch: 2 wds.
25 Utter
27 Like ___ (probably): 2 wds.
29 It's self-evident
31 Canyon or ranch ending
32 Johannesburg's country, initially
33 Large knife
34 "Am ___ risk?": 2 wds.
37 Moviedom's Marisa
39 Malcolm-___ Warner of "The Cosby Show"
41 Lingo
44 West whose albums include "Yeezus"
45 Biblical mother of Boaz
46 Like the White Rabbit
47 Some community bldgs.

Down

1 Dutch city
2 Style of music, a fusion of Arabic and Western elements
3 Breaks a journey: 2 wds.
4 Aria from "Un Ballo in Maschera": 2 wds.
5 "Moonrise Kingdom" director Anderson
6 Accident investigating org.
7 Sheep cries
8 "Same Time, Next Year" actor
10 "___-hoo!"
11 Paving material
15 Supermarket with a red oval logo, initially
17 Summertime coolers, for short
18 Thai currency
20 Border-crossing necessities
22 Take offense
23 Kind of stand: hyph.
24 Horror film staple
26 Where Switz. is
28 Turning point?
30 ___ Paulo, Brazil
33 Ridge of ice on a glacier
34 Letters between H and M
35 Battery for small devices, initially
36 Leonardo, Raphael, Michelangelo and Donatello, initially
38 Taint
40 Word of support
42 Paddle
43 Channel that reairs "The Big Bang Theory"

433

Across

1 Et ___ (footnote abbr.)
4 Sphinx riddle answer
7 Feathers
9 Part of the Apocrypha: abbr.
12 Small piece of land: 2 wds.
13 CSI evidence
14 Gets out of bed
15 Got together again
17 Some explosives, initially
18 Fisherman's bait
19 "___ see!": 2 wds.
20 Is present
23 On rough terrain: hyph.
25 Medal giver
27 Bell and Barker
30 Rescue mission, briefly
31 French moonlight: clair de ___
32 1924 Edna Ferber novel: 2 wds.
34 Also, in Alsace
35 "Respondez, ___ vous plait"
36 Person from Anchorage or Juneau
38 Ethnic group of Vietnam
39 Available: 2 wds.
40 From, in Scotland
41 Ice: Ger.

Down

1 Newscast feature
2 Weather phenomenon: 2 wds.
3 Open to doubt
4 Apples, briefly
5 Farmer's area of study: abbr.
6 ___-do-well
8 Fannie ___ (securities)
9 Secretary of State, 1980–81: 2 wds.
10 Mortimer ___, Edgar Bergen dummy
11 Palm fruits
16 Zeno of ___
20 Kenya's continent, for short
21 Italian TV channel
22 Craggy prominence
24 Central points
25 "Siddhartha" author
26 Shaped like an egg
28 Aziz of "Parks and Recreation"
29 Fishing nets
31 Elbow-bender
33 Spear for landing fish
34 Rhine tributary
37 Seat of Wayne County, Utah

434

Across

1 English professor's deg.
5 Be ____, assist: 2 wds.
11 "Bon ___"
12 President ____ (acting head): 2 wds.
13 Albacore in a can
14 Big name in Egyptian kings
15 Johnson of "The Fast and the Furious"
17 Pay attention to
18 The appendix extends from it
22 Drilled into
23 Teatime goody
24 Driver's license info, for short
25 Cost-of-living no.
26 Valerie Harper series
29 Wonder-worker in India, etc.
31 Apothegms
32 Spirited vigor
33 Stupid person, slangily
35 Show submission or fear
38 City of central China: var.
41 Remove goods from a vehicle
42 Head of Haiti
43 Taoism founder: hyph.
44 Opening

Down

1 Vehicle used in amphibious operations, initially
2 Debtor's letters
3 Dangerous state of affairs
4 Party to a financial transaction
5 Venerable Nashville institution
6 Belgian currency, once
7 School class that teaches cooking, etc.: abbr., 2 wds.
8 "The X-Files" extras, initially
9 Bruce of martial arts
10 David Cameron and Theresa May, for two: abbr.
16 Recipe instruction
17 Hullabaloo: hyph.
19 Slender, long-crested Australian parrot
20 Take off a diaper, e.g.
21 Former Israeli P.M.
22 Real estate ad abbr.
27 Refused to: 2 wds.
28 1000, 500 and 3000UX, e.g.
29 Small amount
30 Slates of top celebrities: hyph.
34 Inhabitant of Media
35 ___-de-sac (dead end)
36 Genetic factor, initially
37 U.N. workers' rights grp.
39 Z preceder?: 2 wds.
40 Safety device

435

Across

1 Steers (a yacht) nearer the wind

6 Big name in kitchen foil

11 ___ water (facing trouble): 2 wds.

12 Sound made by a horse

13 "Push Comes to Shove" choreographer

14 "If ___ done when 'tis done…" (Macbeth)

15 Cat, in Catalonia

17 N.A.S.A. vehicle

18 Adds sugar

22 N.C.A.A. tournament division

23 Cufflinks' cousin: hyph.

27 Manufacture in large quantities: hyph.

29 Nova ___ (Canadian province)

30 Make ___ adventure: 2 wds.

31 Available when requested: 2 wds.

33 Anesthetic used by veterinarians, initially

36 Ending for opal or fluor

37 Eagle's claw

39 ___ a customer (sale limit): 2 wds.

43 ___ Torch, national symbol of Tanzania

44 Mushroom-cloud creator: abbr., 2 wds.

45 Bullion unit

46 Bone: prefix

Down

1 Ignited

2 Durham sch.

3 Mortgage org.

4 Doesn't remember that one must: 2 wds.

5 Ireland's patron, for short: 2 wds.

6 San ___, site of the Alamo mission

7 Wallace who wrote "Ben-Hur"

8 Heaven in Le Havre

9 Scary creature

10 Interruption

16 Sets of four

18 Sch. periods

19 W.W. II server

20 Old gas brand

21 Deposits in rivers

24 "You Ain't Nothing ___ Hound Dog" (Presley song): 2 wds.

25 Open ___ of worms: 2 wds.

26 Rip apart

28 Edible tree seed: 2 wds.

32 ___ Lodge (motel chain)

33 Spitting sound, in comics

34 "High Hopes" lyricist

35 Cork

38 Spanish treasure

40 Suffix with confer or contact

41 Literary monogram

42 Midwest tribe member

436

Across

1 Capital of Ghana
6 ____ book (be literate): 2 wds.
11 "____ I might…": 2 wds.
12 Brief stanza
13 Not solid-colored
14 Bloodhound's trail
15 Killjoy
17 Device for removing cherry pits
18 Depressed
20 Glacial period in Earth's history: 2 wds.
24 To be, in Barcelona
25 Jacksonville, for one: abbr.
26 The Monkees' "____ Believer": 2 wds.
27 "America's honey" brand: 2 wds.
29 1960s militant Brown, familiarly: 2 wds.
30 Traveling the streets of the city, perhaps: 3 wds.
32 Deprived area on the outskirts of a city
36 Irritate
37 Convey
38 Area where tennis is played
39 Football Hall-of-Famer Herber
40 Attack: 2 wds.
41 Cuts back on calories

Down

1 Biol. energy sources
2 Los Angeles street gang member
3 Center of attention
4 Emu or rhea, e.g.
5 Italian town northwest of Venice
6 Aretha Franklin's signature song
7 "Play more!"
8 Maintain
9 Mother's admonition
10 Islet
16 Shoot from a hiding place: 2 wds.
18 Some coll. degrees
19 Romania's currency
21 On the wing
22 ABC morning show, for short
23 "The Fall of the House of Usher" author's monogram
25 "Keystone Kops" producer
28 Nigerian civil war site, 1967–70
29 1962 movie directed by Howard Hawks
31 Tropical palmlike plant
32 Sneaker or loafer
33 ____ monde (fashionable society)
34 Official order
35 Politicians Glenn, Gerald and George
36 IV amounts, briefly

437

Across

1 Sound of one hard object hitting another
6 "The Lonely Polygamist" author Brady
11 Braves Hall of Famer, Hank
12 Taboos: hyph.
13 Grin
14 Hägar's pooch
15 Classic dessert: 2 wds.
17 Luggage attachment: 2 wds.
18 British peer of the highest rank
21 Perfect society
25 Bronze ___
26 Outdated
27 Unpredictable phenomenon: hyph.
31 Antarctica's Prince ___ Coast
32 Pundit pieces in a newspaper: hyph.
34 Loop of stretchy material for holding things together: 2 wds.
39 "Love is Strange" costar Marisa
40 Major artery
41 Adjust, as a brooch
42 Scottish pants
43 Mixed: abbr.
44 Scythe handle

Down

1 ___ Grande, city in Arizona
2 Light
3 "What ___" ("That's robbery"): 2 words
4 Herding dog
5 Injured sneakily
6 Oust
7 "Please stay!": 2 wds.
8 Without ___ (dangerously): 2 wds.
9 Brightly-colored Australasian parrot
10 Mil. transport
16 Heat meas.
18 "Tru ___!"
19 Actor Tognazzi of "La Cage aux Folles"
20 Jennifer Lien's role in "Star Trek: Voyager"
22 Campaigner, for short
23 Labor group, initially
24 "Fast" and "slow," for example: abbr.
28 "Amen to that": 3 wds.
29 Put together, as pages in a book
30 ___ Dee River
31 Athlete Harold who won two gold medals at the 1924 Olympics
33 Mild oaths
34 Some bucks
35 Ballpark figures, briefly
36 Department
37 Grocery label amt.: 2 wds.
38 Quick run
39 "The flowers that bloom in the spring, ___ la"

438

Across

1 Trash
7 Nos. on sunscreen bottles
11 Record label founded in 1974
12 River in Africa
13 Item replaced after filling up: 2 wds.
14 Sufficient, in verse
15 Tom Jones's "___ a Lady"
16 Long bones
17 Having a disastrous effect on
19 From Jan. 1
20 Cemetery sights
21 Jack who played Jake in "Big Bad John"
23 Bring back into the mouth after swallowing
27 Autocrat
28 Subj. involving sin, cos, and tan
29 Label that bought Motown, initially
31 Absorbs (knowledge or food)
33 Chocolate source
35 Dept. of Labor watchdog
36 Move in a zigzag fashion
37 Genetic anomaly
39 1952 Winter Olympics site
40 Antarctica's ___ penguin
41 Existed
42 Sci-fi writer Ellison

Down

1 Make fun of
2 Operation with a pencil
3 Angler's need: 2 wds.
4 Decennial govt. activity: 2 wds.
5 East German secret police
6 "The Tell-Tale Heart" author's initials
7 Gibberish-talking "SNL" character ___ Forrester
8 "A League of Their Own" director: 2 wds.
9 Levitate
10 Made clothing
16 Unattractive-sounding fruit
17 Major river flowing through Belgium, Germany, and the Netherlands
18 State of Malaysia, ___ Sembilan
22 One giving evidence
24 "Hair" co-author James
25 Moon of Uranus
26 Latin abbrs.
29 Work with few prospects, slangily
30 Induce
32 Mild cheese
34 Long, long time
37 ___-jongg
38 Sawbuck

439

Across

1. Twins Mary-Kate and Ashley
7. Ltr. addenda
11. Show anger: 2 wds.
12. Hydrox alternative
13. "An American Rhapsody" star Nastassja
14. E. follower
15. Coast-to-coast highway: 2 wds.
16. Plymouth Reliant, e.g.: hyph.
17. Took a load off
19. Snick and ___
21. Here, to Henri
22. Perfectly pitched: 2 wds.
26. Aladdin's hat
27. Chivalrous guy: abbr.
28. At once
29. 2013 movie starring John Wojtowicz: 2 wds.
31. Father's Day gift
32. Bryn ___, college in Pennsylvania
34. Bradley and McMahon
35. 53, in old Rome
38. Dutch artist Frans
40. ___ cloud (comet-filled region of space)
41. Ham actor
44. Special person
45. Astronaut Collins
46. Actor Oka of "Hawaii Five-0"
47. Person who inspires others

Down

1. Where Mork and Mindy honeymooned
2. "South Pacific" prop
3. Make clean and hygienic
4. Formerly, formerly
5. Zaps
6. Machine for making yarn: 2 wds.
7. Sink, as a billiard ball
8. Conf. record
9. Ward of "CSI: NY"
10. Evening, in Paris
17. Use a sieve
18. Banda ___ (Sumatran city)
20. Med. specialty
23. Brand-new
24. Reason to be barred from a bar: 2 wds.
25. Lea females
27. R.V. hookup provider
30. Mendeleev who developed the periodic table
33. Tough silky fiber
35. Rise ominously
36. College in New Rochelle, N.Y.
37. Furies
39. "Damn Yankees" temptress
42. Wide shoe width
43. Time off, initially

440

Across

1 Shine with heat
5 Sporting advantages
10 River that feeds the Ubangi
11 Takes fright
13 Action of writing in shorthand
15 Major Calif. airport
16 When doubled, a Teletubby
17 Some detectives, initially
18 Comic DeGeneres
20 Dimin.'s musical opposite
22 Troughs for washing ores
23 Prefix with magnetic
24 Cut off
26 Verdigris
29 Bator's leader
33 Used runners to travel over snow
34 U.S. security: hyph.
35 Suffix with law or saw
36 Tony Award winner Hagen
38 Courteney on "Friends"
39 One who sees into the future
42 Horse-drawn carriage for two
43 Rat tail?: hyph.
44 ___ doctor (gets medical advice): 2 wds.
45 Prefix with drama

Down

1 Piece of material inset to enlarge a garment
2 Cast: 2 wds.
3 Spanish chant: 2 wds.
4 Common cyst of the skin
5 Links org. for women
6 Otalgia
7 Palindromic woman's name
8 Aquatic songbird that catches food underwater
9 Split caused by differences in opinion
12 Big name in food service
14 Former name of the cable network Versus, initially
19 "The Devil's Disciple" girl
21 Like many a TV series
23 Tenn. power project
25 Long-distance vehicle races
26 Intimidate, with "out"
27 Cub Scout leaders, in the U.K.
28 Albania's capital, in its own language
30 Find, trace
31 Not harmonic, like music
32 Beside: 2 wds.
34 Eastern path
37 Rating for "Game of Thrones," initially: hyph.
40 British verb suffix
41 Thanksgiving serving

441

Across

1 Deserving of
6 Finnish architect Alvar ____
11 Female friends in France
12 Shapeless mass
13 Take one's turn, in board games: 3 wds.
15 "Private Lives" playwright Coward
16 Keep tabs on
17 Atoll of the Marshall Islands
19 Product package abbr.: 2 wds.
23 Postpone
26 Poet's contraction
27 Highly imaginative but unlikely
30 "There's ____ in 'team'": 2 wds.
31 XC in Roman numerals
32 Italian bone
34 Endodontist's degree: abbr.
35 Society page word
37 Md. school
41 Celebration noisemaker
45 German W.W. II craft: hyph.
46 Time on the job
47 Avoid: 2 wds.
48 Adlai's 1956 running mate, ____ Kefauver

Down

1 Caution
2 Novel about its author's experiences on Tahiti
3 Disturb
4 Spill the beans: 2 wds.
5 Old White House inits.
6 ____ Duecey, card game involving gambling
7 "Solo: A Star Wars Story" star Ehrenreich
8 French pronoun
9 "Flix" alternative, for short
10 Reveal, in poetry
14 As provided for in the terms of this document
18 Charlottesville sch.
20 "The Texas Chain Saw Massacre" director Hooper
21 Mark left by a whip
22 Low-ranking card
23 ____-Soviet relations
24 Wellness gps.
25 Certain Prot.
28 1951 "Scrooge" star Alastair
29 Places formally in a position
33 Early year: 2 wds.
36 Prefix denoting outside
38 "SNL" piece
39 Spanish child
40 Cultural doings
41 Good times
42 Nigerian tribesman
43 Flapdoodle
44 Enzyme suffix

442

Across

1 Wile E. Coyote's go-to company

5 Charles ____, "A Tale of Two Cities" character

11 Waste

12 Ancient Semite

13 Milliner's stock

14 Secure, as a seat belt

15 911 responder, initially

16 Procedure that can detect brain tumors: inits.

17 Draft letters

18 ____ Buchner (1907 Chemistry Nobelist)

21 Make less dense or solid

23 Equal, in Marseilles

27 ____ Carkoon ("Return of the Jedi" setting): 2 wds.

28 Spread

29 "____ out?" (choice offered a pet): 2 wds.

30 Farriers

31 Chemical salt

33 Sunny state, for short

36 Atmosphere: prefix

37 Pharmacy chain

40 Garden in which Aristotle taught philosophy

42 Self-proclaimed psychic Miss ____

43 Wind off

44 ____ Woods National Monument

45 Derisive

46 Ending for convert or digest

Down

1 Arthur who won the U.S. Open in 1968

2 Oyster's cousin

3 Be of importance: 2 wds.

4 Brief examples

5 Bear the cost of

6 Light ____ (almost weightless): 2 wds.

7 Web letters in an orange button

8 New Jersey basketball team

9 Hydrocarbon suffixes

10 Longings

16 Botch

19 Golden, in Guadalajara: 2 wds.

20 Train station

21 Tech. school on the Hudson R.

22 Own, to a Scot

24 Group in robes: 2 wds.

25 Rhine feeder

26 Fleur-de-____

28 ____-Pei, dog breed

30 Suitable

32 Couric's cohost

33 Spanish and swine, e.g.

34 City between Boston and Salem

35 Farm measurement

38 Nuptial netting

39 Offended

41 Shoe specification

42 901, to Caesar

443

Across

1 Desert animal with humps
6 Big Indian
11 Something from the oven
12 Elicit
13 Climber's spike
14 Army rank
15 Charles, e.g.
16 Command a horse to turn right
18 ___ Chicago Grill
19 Culpable: 2 wds.
21 "Whom have ___ heaven but you?" Psalms 73:25: 2 wds.
22 Shelley's "___ Skylark": 2 wds.
23 Some W.W. II vessels
24 Causing distress
27 "Swept Away" director Wertmüller
28 Palindromic diarist
29 Dockworker's org.
30 Cousin of the tilde and umlaut
34 One of eight Eng. kings
35 Enzyme ending
36 Common Market letters, once
37 Issue
39 Davit
41 "___ Bulba" (fictional Cossack)
42 From Palmyra: abbr.
43 Colorado county
44 Woman who helped the Israelites capture Jericho

Down

1 "Meet John Doe" director
2 "There's ___ Goin' On" (Sly and the Family Stone album): 2 wds.
3 Recurring theme
4 Genre for The Shins
5 Oppressive stillness of the air
6 Convened anew
7 Oklahoma town
8 System of West African beliefs
9 Monkshood or wolfsbane
10 Birds with long legs
17 Hendrix and May
20 Razor brand since 1977
23 Anderson of "WKRP in Cincinnati"
24 Exploratory oil well
25 Where a bird may perch: 3 wds.
26 Cocktail bar offering
27 Misinforms: 2 wds.
30 Playground retort: 2 wds.
31 Chow checker
32 "Semi-Tough" actress Lotte
33 Sharp
38 Boater's tool
40 Cape Town country, initially

444

Across

1 She answered to Captain Kirk

6 Tic-___ (candies)

10 1960s-style protest: hyph.

11 Body wash brand

12 Tissue lining the alimentary canal

14 High-speed Internet option, initially

15 Girls in France

16 Smashed on a highway, briefly

17 Element #10

20 Forming part of a sentence

24 Anguish

25 ___ la paix: 2 wds.

26 Astound

28 Saturday morning TV show, initially

29 Tired-looking: hyph.

31 Mayfield boy, for short

33 Son of Odin in Norse mythology

34 Acapulco assents: 2 wds.

36 Pan, e.g.

39 Alkaloid plant toxin

41 Young adult

42 Soak

43 "Grinding It Out" subject Ray

44 Homies

Down

1 Previously owned, as a car

2 They're above the thighs

3 Certain Monopoly sq.

4 Slowing, in mus.

5 Big name in brewing

6 Kind of call

7 Roswell crash victim, supposedly

8 Overseas Highway feature

9 Orchestra: abbr.

13 "Essays of ___"

16 Pops

18 Exude

19 Necessity

20 "No ___!" ("Certainly!"): abbr.

21 Scottish philosopher David

22 Enhance the quality of a previously made recording

23 Nobility title

27 Boulogne-sur-___

30 Suffix with diet or synth

32 Small songbird

35 In ___ (harmonious)

36 Barbed remark

37 "Step right ___!": 2 wds.

38 G.P.A. spoilers

39 OTC offering

40 Long-running U.K. music mag.

445

Across

1 Et ____
5 Trees with purplish flowers
11 Beatty and Rorem
12 Joan's "Dynasty" role
13 Some RBI producers: abbr.
14 Main protein in cheese
15 Do another hitch: hyph.
17 Command level: abbr.
18 More frequently
22 "With God ____ witness": 2 wds.
24 Pro ____
25 Humeri attachments
27 Flat, even
28 Safety org.
29 ____ Macbeth
30 Add to the scrapbook: 2 wds.
32 Letters accompanying some 2,000-year-old+ dates
35 Brass
37 German drinking salutation
40 Picnic problem
41 Mexican food served in a husk
42 "By the powers vested ____...": 2 wds.
43 Sterilized (a cat, e.g.)
44 Food Network measures, briefly

Down

1 Auto pioneer Citroën
2 Mountain Community of the Tejon Pass, Calif.
3 The Devil makes work for them: 2 wds.
4 Org.
5 Soothe
6 As ____ resort (after all else has been tried): 2 wds.
7 Bugged
8 "The Shining" prop
9 Game console with a movement-sensing controller
10 Fig. in identity theft
16 Capital of Togo
19 Haricots: 2 wds.
20 Toulouse time
21 North Carolina capital: abbr.
23 "Unfortunately ...": 3 wds.
25 One who might get yelled at by the manager: abbr.
26 When doubled, a yellow Teletubby
27 ____ O'Grady, Mary in "Eight is Enough"
29 Stole
31 Submit taxes online: hyph.
33 Pinch
34 Old serfs
36 Art class feedback session, slangily
37 Mtge. units
38 Drake's forte
39 Grandma, to Germans

446

Across

1 Autumnal drink
6 Pimples, slangily
10 Breathe noisily during sleep
11 Have a hankering
12 Fleshy fruit: var.
13 Song of joy
15 Early Dadaist works
16 Lofty poetry
17 "Melody Maker" alternative, initially
18 Hand-woven rug
19 Gaseous beginning
20 Relieve
22 Woody Guthrie's kid
23 Droplet
25 Degs. for curators
27 Winery process
29 Bard's dusk
30 JKL followers
31 Brits' thank-yous
33 100 mongos in Mongolia
35 Web prog. code
36 "Do, ___..." (song): 2 wds.
37 Kevin who plays Gojun Pye in the "Mythica" series
38 Sacramento's ___ Arena
39 "Delta of Venus" author ___ Nin
40 D-Day carriers, initially
41 It may precede perception

Down

1 Political buff's channel: hyph.
2 Up ___, resisting hotly: 2 wds.
3 Ghostly doubles
4 History chapters
5 VCR button
6 Guitarist Dweezil or actress Moon
7 U.N. flight agency
8 1998 remake in which Lindsay Lohan played twins: 3 wds.
9 Conger, e.g.: 2 wds.
14 Agrippina the Younger's slayer
16 SightLife, for one: 2 wds.
18 Film studio with a thunderbolt logo, initially
21 Pacino and Gore
22 Big boxer
24 "The Inquiry" playwright Betti
25 "I never ___ man I didn't like" (Will Rogers): 2 wds.
26 Absurdly outdated or old-fashioned
28 Opening move in chess
30 Some Surrealist works
32 Unappetizing food or drink
34 Geom. shape
35 Edge
37 Dejected

447

Across

1 Opening run
5 "King of Country" singer George ____
11 Radar's favorite beverage
12 Totally
13 Hole, in France
14 More boiling mad
15 Lacking decency
17 Dehydrates
18 W. hemisphere grp.
21 Crackers
23 ____ couture
25 Others, in Latin
26 Posts: abbr.
27 Johnny ____, "Key Largo" gangster
29 Kiddie lit character Dinsmore
30 Wall St. purchase
31 Play a golf shot that's less than the possible distance: 2 wds.
33 Narrowly defeats: 2 wds.
36 Drivel
39 Retail furniture chain
40 "You're going to love my gift!": 2 wds.
41 Grassy plain in southern Africa: var.
42 For each one
43 Chemical endings

Down

1 Against
2 Grass strip beside a road
3 Oriental tableware implement
4 Substance that causes the body to get rid of excess water
5 Filch
6 Separate the wheat from the chaff
7 Crowd sound
8 Word on the option key on a Mac keyboard
9 Martinique, e.g.
10 Norse war god
16 Suffix with access or audit
18 Candid
19 Abruzzo bell town
20 Mobutu ____ Seko of Zaire
21 Candy buys
22 Gazillions: 2 wds.
24 Characterized by indirect references
28 Famous London theater: 2 wds.
29 Needle hole
32 Striped chalcedony
33 German article
34 Congo river
35 Youngsters, so to speak
36 Insurance assessors' org.: inits.
37 PC program
38 It's made of flowers in Hawaii

448

Across

1 Blemished
6 Bluebird genus
11 Part of an act
12 Peter and Franco
13 Nicholas Gage best seller
14 Dweebs
15 One way to swim
17 Actress in the "Road to..." movies
18 Sentence part: abbr.
20 Exclamation of disapproval: 2 wds.
24 Pennies: abbr.
25 Tortoiseshell, e.g.
26 Swiss river to the Rhine
27 Inventor Nikola and family
29 "The ___ the limit!"
30 Feral
32 Recreational plank on wheels
36 Rhône river feeder
37 Exclamation of pain
38 Humble home
39 Avert (with "off")
40 Disney movie of 1998
41 More timid

Down

1 Enzymes' suffixes
2 251, to Caesar
3 Superfluous
4 Group of nine
5 Religious belief based on reason
6 Confidentially: 2 wds.
7 Bring up to date
8 Estrada of "CHiPs"
9 Musical mark
10 Pack animal
16 As you like it: 2 wds.
18 Poll no.
19 I-95, e.g.: abbr.
21 Subtract: 2 wds.
22 Two cents worth
23 ___-One, stage name of Lawrence Parker
25 College restaurant
28 Angola's capital
29 Unwrinkled
31 Yawning hole
32 "Cobra Woman" costar
33 ___ & the Gang ("Celebration" band)
34 Split
35 Big game
36 Uncle of note

449

Across

1 ___ Palmas, Gran Canaria
4 Kinship
7 Grp. once headed by Seiji Ozawa
10 Egg (pref.)
11 It might result in a TD
12 Klutz
13 Freshly painted
14 Dog track org.
15 Pound sound
16 Handicraft with yarn and a hook
18 ___ Tafari (Selassie)
19 Like ___ (quite possibly): 2 wds.
20 18th letter of the Hebrew alphabet
22 "___ Go" (Abril Lavigne song): 2 wds.
23 Main idea
24 Female chicken
25 Canadian TV channel
26 Locality
28 Fathered, in the Bible
31 ___-yard line (center of a football field)
33 Chevy model
34 Antagonist
35 Served with ice cream: 3 wds.
37 Brit. news network
38 Colorful ornamental fish
39 Port on the Danube
40 VCR remote button, briefly
41 Vintner's prefix
42 Envision
43 G.I. grub
44 Autos nicknamed "Bugs," initially
45 Part of the Apocrypha: abbr.

Down

1 Diet abbreviation: hyph.
2 Reluctant (to)
3 Be undecided: 4 wds.
4 Make taut
5 Legalese heading: 2 wds.
6 French states
7 Place providing lodging: 2 wds.
8 Vaughan, McLachlan and Bernhardt
9 Counterbalance
17 Bobby Womack song "Love Has Finally ___ Last": 2 wds.
21 Radiant
25 Acquires
26 Ratify
27 One causing mayhem
29 Scads
30 Rained heavily
32 Russian comic Smirnoff
36 Name of theater fame

450

Across

1 Priest
5 Offshore sight: 2 wds.
11 I.R.A. part: abbr.
12 Chewed on with the teeth
13 Those on the cutting edge
15 Summer cooler: 2 wds.
16 People mentioned in "The Christmas Song"
21 Sink fitting: hyph.
25 Military camp (Fr.)
26 Certain acid
27 "I cannot tell ___": 2 wds.
28 Appearances
30 More sick
31 Weasel family relative
33 Relating to bears
37 Mole: 2 wds.
42 Online annoyances: hyph.
43 Black-and-white predator
44 With the purpose specified: 3 wds.
45 Grounded item

Down

1 It's lost when you stand up
2 Juice berry
3 1300, in Ancient Rome
4 Golfer's need: 2 wds.
5 Double-S curves
6 Consumption
7 High school subj.
8 "The Rhodora" writer's monogram
9 Occupational suffix
10 Mdse.
14 Dance bit
17 Slanted type: abbr.
18 Enclosed shopping area
19 Mayberry minor
20 Crystal ball user
21 Bicycle accessory
22 Duet plus one
23 Cambodian currency unit
24 Teen outbreak
29 Engrave
30 "___ wrap!": 2 wds.
32 Playground retort: 2 wds.
34 "Young Frankenstein" role
35 Claudius's successor
36 Old ExxonMobil brand name
37 Twin killings, in baseball, initially
38 Hugs, symbolically
39 "Pull ___ chair!": 2 wds.
40 Clear (a table)
41 Piece of body art, briefly

451

Across

1 Turbulent

6 After-dinner drink letters

10 San Francisco's Museo ___ Americano

11 Cary who starred in the 2004 movie "Saw"

13 Others, in Oviedo

14 Seek help from: 2 wds.

15 "Muppets Most Wanted" costar Tina

16 Sewing machine attachments

18 Search engine find, initially

19 Hotel sign

20 Narrow inlet

21 Biblical son of Shem (Genesis 10:22)

23 Hawaiian port

25 Paul ___, Uncle Arthur on "Bewitched"

27 Words on a Renault 5: 2 wds.

30 Hill's opposite

32 Tiptop

33 Quadrennial games org.

35 College URL ending

37 Kick ___ fuss: 2 wds.

38 The ideal man: 2 wds.

40 Kabul coin

41 "Same here": 3 wds.

42 Caribbean island nation

44 Hooded snake

45 Modern pentathlon swords

46 Tiny fraction of a min.: 2 wds.

47 "Air Music" composer Ned

Down

1 Source of energy derived from living matter

2 Downright

3 Chesapeake Bay delicacies: 2 wds.

4 Mahmoud Abbas's org.

5 Mario's dinosaur friend

6 Gilded silver or bronze

7 Urban blight

8 Person who lives in a property they have purchased: hyph.

9 Kind of dish

12 Home run great Sammy

17 Military formation, briefly

22 Labor Day telethon org., once

24 Pastoral place

26 Melancholy

28 Person with a limb loss

29 Sober outlook

31 Old English letter

33 Apple on a desk

34 Director Welles

36 King Arthur's father

39 Hungarian patriot Nagy

43 G.I.'s mail drop

452

Across

1 Prefix with syllabic
5 J. Edgar Hoover employees: 2 wds.
11 Come into view
12 Covered in wool
13 Hold (up)
14 Church passages
15 Racing video game of old: 2 wds.
17 "I ___ you so!"
18 Clean air org.
21 Like some old photos
24 It's not clean
25 Edible marine fishes
26 In ___ (unborn)
27 Prefix with metric or phone
28 Hawk relative
29 Mile High Center architect
30 "Beloved" author Morrison
31 Villain
36 "I wish!": 2 wds.
38 R-rated, maybe
39 Defeatist's word
40 Nose: comb. form
41 Howler
42 Be, at the Forum

Down

1 Hannibal's hurdle
2 Satirical Sahl
3 Crude dude
4 Skin infection
5 Showing little emotion
6 Puppeteer Bil
7 "You're ___ much trouble!": 2 wds.
8 Sea traveler's ailment: 3 wds.
9 Nice time?
10 Super ___ (video game console)
16 Geologic periods
19 24-karat
20 "The dog is not ___" (house rule): 2 wds.
21 Unappetizing stuff
22 Ready to eat
23 Element #51
24 French isl. south of Newfoundland: 2 wds.
26 "Anchors Aweigh" readiness grp.
28 Immature ovum
30 Track set in a table for a router: hyph.
32 "___ Time at All" (Ronnie Milsap single): 2 wds.
33 Contented sighs
34 Mark Harmon series on CBS
35 Newcastle's river
36 Old trucking watchdog gp.
37 U.N. agency

453

Across

1 Battery buys, initially
4 Orange seed
7 Financial regulators, initially
10 Educ. institution
11 Put ___ good word for: 2 wds.
12 Vienna's land: abbr.
13 Not needing to be explained, obvious
16 Traditional dance from Tahiti
17 Pencil topper
18 Black and white vehicle, slangily: 2 wds.
20 African antelope
21 Dog in Oz
23 Divested (of)
24 Someone who makes statements on behalf of a group
27 Part of many Brazilian place names
28 Kind of talk
29 Istanbul native
31 "Leaving already?": 2 wds.
35 Hit
37 Battle site in 1944: 2 wds.
38 Abdominal inflammation
40 Gamboling spot
41 "The Trumpet of the Swan" author's monogram
42 Prefix with duct
43 Dreyer's partner in ice cream
44 Code-breaking grp.
45 Mediterranean isl.

Down

1 Org.
2 Vinegar: prefix
3 Lug: var.
4 Chart type
5 They prefer lower class attitudes: 2 wds.
6 Brace
7 Bard's break
8 Listening: 2 wds.
9 Samba singer ___ Gilberto
14 De ___ (in effect)
15 S. ___ (st. whose capital is Pierre)
19 Golfer Isao ___
22 Capital of Norway
24 Fried quickly in a little fat
25 Depict
26 Argentine professional soccer player
27 Certain gun projectile
30 China's Chiang ___-shek
32 Hahn and Klemperer
33 1964 AL Rookie of the Year Tony
34 Boot camp reply: 2 wds.
36 Coast-to-coast highway: 2 wds.
39 They were straight outta Compton

454

Across

1. Nearly
7. January honoree, for short
10. Rough shelters: hyph.
12. Wine cask
13. Trivial ___ (board game)
14. It may be crushed or cubed
15. ___'acte (intermission)
16. 650, to the Romans
17. Sound heard twice in "ginger": 2 wds.
20. Earthlink transmission: hyph.
22. Faulkner's "___ Lay Dying": 2 wds.
23. ___ in "Oscar": 2 wds.
24. Item of cutlery: 2 wds.
30. Mil. authority
31. Patty Hearst's captors, initially
32. Cover story
35. Entire range
37. Like two peas in a ___
38. Gray, in Grenoble
40. ___ glance: 2 wds.
41. Celebrate
45. Kazakhstan letters, once
46. Wealth and resources of a country
47. ___-Bo
48. Sixteenth of a dollar, slangily

Down

1. Swiss peak
2. 100 bani in Romania
3. Vandalize
4. Dawn
5. Swindled
6. Nothing ___ (simple): 2 wds.
7. Crete's tallest summit: abbr., 2 wds.
8. Susan of "All My Children"
9. Toll
11. Winning or losing run
17. Rest day: abbr.
18. Columbus initials
19. Toned
21. AOL rival
23. City in Valley County, Nebraska
25. Letters in Aretha Franklin's "Respect"
26. New citizen, perhaps
27. Something to believe in
28. Viral malady
29. Partake of
32. Leaders of the New School debut album, "A Future Without ___": 2 wds.
33. Many, informally
34. "___ you!" (challenger's cry): 2 wds.
35. Cartoon soldier: 2 wds.
36. Conjointly: 2 wds.
39. Prefix with angular
42. It packs a charge
43. 901, to Nero
44. Looker

455

Across

1 Vigorous and spirited

5 Part of a magazine

9 Mil. computer built under the code name "Project PX"

11 Walks with heavy steps

13 Slow, musically

14 Ragout of game in a rich sauce

15 Tick off

16 Remainder

18 Made progress: 2 wds.

20 H.S. requirement

21 Satirical cartoonist Peter

22 "Jim Button" author Michael

23 One-time TV workers' union

25 Popular apples

26 Ancient Greek temple

27 Buddhist spiritual teacher

28 "The Nemesis Mission" author Dean

29 Line on a weather map

32 Drink with an olive

35 "How Can ___ Sure?" (hit of 1967): 2 wds.

36 What a comet often has: 2 wds.

37 Simmering: 2 wds.

39 Insolent

40 Nine, in Nayarit

41 Plant of the mint family

42 Requisite

Down

1 Archeologist's find

2 "The End of ___" (John Sergeant Wise book): 2 wds.

3 Old machine for showing movies

4 Early 20th-century Chinese president, Sun ___-sen

5 Ltr. add-ons

6 Jai ___ (fast-moving sport)

7 Fiftieth anniversary of an event: 2 wds.

8 10th-century English king: 2 wds.

10 City in SW California

12 Long-term military tactics

17 Spoons drummer Jim

19 Goofs up

22 Currency introduced on January 1st 1999

23 Brute

24 Zealot

25 Cuisine that mixes different styles

27 Drink that's also a card game

30 Higher than

31 Marry again

33 Great Plains home for an Indian: var.

34 ___ Ulyanov, Vladimir Lenin's father

38 Convent dweller

456

Across

1   ____-bitty (small)
5   Artoo-____ ("Star Wars" droid)
10 Jeff of "Lawnmower Man"
12 Europe-Asia divider
13 Mr. T's group: hyph.
14 Singer Cherry, whose albums include "Buffalo Stance"
15 Addams Family member
17 CSI test subject
18 P.T.A. meeting place: abbr.
20 ____ la Paix, Paris: 2 wds.
22 "East of Eden" siren
24 Average
27 Kind of nut
29 Bridge player's comment: 2 wds.
30 Computer access name: 2 wds.
32 It may be hard to swallow
33 Lawn game: var.
35 Author Lewis et al., initially
36 Sturgeon product
38 Affectionate, slangily
40 "Invisible Cities" writer Calvino
42 "____ do" (turndown): 2 wds.
45 Bookworm, at times
46 Court ____ (legal venue): 2 wds.
47 Attempt
48 Prefix with byte

Down

1   "____ Man Answers" (1962 Bobby Darin song): 2 wds.
2   Machine gun syllable
3   Goldilocks and ____: 3 wds.
4   "Uh-huh"
5   Close, dark prison
6   Hitherto
7   Vehicle for two: 2 wds.
8   Pulitzer-winning author Robert ____ Butler
9   Dept. of Labor arm
11 Giant slain by Odin, thus creating the Earth
16 Sister in a convent
18 "Cobra Woman" costar
19 U.K. honorees
21 Stock market "correction"
23 Prefix with phobia
25 Bothers
26 Cholesterol varieties, initially
28 Tree bearing edible nuts
31 601, in old Rome
34 "Ignorance of the law ____ excuse": 2 wds.
36 Opportune
37 Platte River tribe
39 Easily hurt
41 Rustic locale
43 Swiss river to the Rhine
44 Meteorological society, initially

457

Across

1 Letters on business envelopes

5 Part of N.A.A.C.P.: abbr.

9 Common suffix to Japanese ship names

10 Low area of land between hills

12 A.J. Soprano actor

13 Sparkle

14 Days in Lisbon

15 Fan noise

16 Views

18 "May I ___ favor?": 2 wds.

22 Active during the day

25 Vocalist DiFranco

26 Grant and Elwes

27 Instrument most often played on Sunday

29 A, in French

30 She never reached Howland Island

32 "Over here!"

34 Lyrically written

35 Keen intelligence

37 Battery metal

40 Introduce by force, as laws

43 "___ La La!"

44 Italian liqueur

45 Certain bond, informally

46 Jot

47 Mexican guys

Down

1 Bunched in with

2 Anklebones

3 Treats as precious

4 Baby's room

5 Series opener

6 Certain camera, for short

7 Six, to Italians

8 "All the News That's Fit to Print" paper, for short

10 It can follow vice

11 Hard-rock center: 2 wds.

17 Massachusetts motto opener

19 Acutely insightful and wise

20 Wood knot

21 "___ that the truth"

22 Bra size: 2 wds.

23 Fleming and Ziering

24 Lady's man

28 Horizontal plant stem with shoots above and roots below

31 Great Barrier Island of New Zealand

33 Time in Boston when it's noon in Nicaragua: 2 wds.

36 AOL, e.g.

38 ___ the wiser

39 Xs to Xanthippe

40 Supermarket franchise letters

41 Actor who played Clubber Lang in "Rocky III": 2 wds.

42 Kung ___ chicken

458

Across

1 Orbital point
6 Shot a certain spray at
11 Please, in Potsdam
12 "Blame It on Me" singer Davis
13 Light ___ (almost weightless): 2 wds.
14 Division of McGraw Hill Financial, briefly: 3 wds.
15 Mid.
16 Got in on the deal: 2 wds.
18 River islet
19 Winston Churchill and Tony Blair, for two: abbr.
20 Maker of Rive Gauche, initially
21 Casually cheerful
23 Popeye's ___'Pea
24 Rapper in the supergroup The Firm, once
25 It paves the way
26 Vexes
28 Element #27
31 Tarzan creator's monogram
32 Old-style cry of disgust
33 Muslim saint or holy man
34 Relating to heat
36 Jordan Spieth's org.
37 American chameleon
38 "Find ___ and fill it": 2 wds.
40 Above-board, so to speak
41 Door, in Dieppe
42 Powerful sharks
43 Mexican OKs: 2 wds.

Down

1 1981 Genesis album that's also a rhyme scheme
2 Part of a flower comprising the stigma, style and ovary
3 Sprinter's brace: 2 wds.
4 "Lord, is ___?": 2 wds.
5 Sistine Chapel figures
6 Sail supports
7 Wings: Lat.
8 They cover sweet treats: 2 wds.
9 Ultimate application: 2 wds.
10 Parti-colored
17 "Melody Maker" alternative, initially
22 Prof.'s helpers
23 Rest day: abbr.
25 Protective features on shoes
26 Don't panic: 2 wds.
27 Muse of astronomy
28 102, in Roman numerals
29 "Atmosphères" composer György
30 Swaps
32 Acts nervous
35 Medley
39 "___ won't be afraid" ("Stand by Me" lyric): 2 wds.

459

Across

1 Carrier whose name means "skyward": 2 wds.
5 Across the world
11 "Seven Beauties" director Wertmüller
12 Social behavior issue
13 "___ Your Skin" (1964 cult horror film): 2 wds.
14 Grand Slam part: 2 wds.
15 Growth on the lip
17 Relative of -esque
18 Rank above senior airman, briefly
22 Marked by peace and prosperity
26 Toni Morrison book "___ Baby"
27 Adrien ___ makeup brand
28 Alley Oop's wife
30 TV Chihuahua
31 Blip
33 Sling
35 Org. for Annapolis grads
36 Inherit: 2 wds.
41 Soak up
44 Philistine
45 Strong-arm
46 Mom's brothers, briefly
47 Raise or erect
48 Mobuto Sese ___, Zairean dictator

Down

1 Double-___ (kind of tournament, for short)
2 In place of
3 Literary collections (suffix)
4 Framework
5 Cowboy of the South American pampas
6 Green
7 Relatives of the Missouria
8 Marcel Marceau persona
9 Peer Gynt's mother
10 Letter run
16 Refuges
19 Classical portico
20 Brass
21 Kind of table
22 Romance novelist Neesa
23 Of Mars (comb. form)
24 Hosp. staffers
25 Lasso loop
29 Anthology
32 Quantity
34 Make a goal
37 Boat in "Jaws"
38 Zilch
39 Clock sound
40 Roughly: 2 wds.
41 With a needle: prefix
42 Thwack
43 Sun. delivery

460

Across

1 Railyard denizen
5 Blasé
10 Father of Charlemagne
11 Savory taste sensation produced by glutamates
12 Cosmetic surgery procedure
14 Found a place for
15 Two-time loser to D.D.E.
16 ___ and wherefores
18 Women's ___
21 Revolted: 2 wds.
24 Ward of "Once and Again"
25 Be unbeatable, say: 3 wds.
27 ___ out a living (barely got by)
28 Even (with): 3 wds.
29 Fairbanks-to-Anchorage dir.
30 Watchdog's sound
31 Unpaid
32 Hollywood goodbye
36 Marginal resources for existence
40 "Battlestar Galactica" actor Bodie
41 E'en if
42 Leather strap
43 Combustible pile

Down

1 Snarky laughs
2 Andy Taylor's kid
3 Twining plant with trumpet-shaped flowers
4 Plastic ___ Band
5 Verne who wrote "Twenty Thousand Leagues Under the Sea"
6 Latin 101 verb
7 Court figures, initially
8 CPR pro
9 Home improvement letters
10 MetLife rival, briefly
13 Outmoded communication devices: 2 wds.
17 Shed
18 Entrechat or jeté
19 Chase of "Now, Voyager"
20 1930s boxing champ Max
21 Motorist's choices: abbr.
22 Acorn bearers
23 Corrupt, as results of a test
24 Almost not
26 Old Spanish queen
30 Appearance
31 Brit. decorations
33 Foreword: abbr.
34 Hurt
35 Johnson anti-poverty org.
36 Tosspot
37 Suffix with fib or fist
38 German car letters
39 Bug, in a way

461

Across

1 Took off
5 Graft
11 Nash's "The ___ lama…": hyph.
12 Big test
13 Visiting the White House, e.g.: 2 wds.
14 Latin list shortener: 2 wds.
15 Freelancer's enc.
16 Cigarette's end
17 Bygone daily MTV series, informally
18 Figure
21 Dad's mom
23 "I wasn't expecting you!" lead-in: 2 wds.
27 "Head ___," Sean Paul song : 2 wds.
28 "The Dancing Couple" artist Jan
29 Pursue
30 "___ Butterfly" (Puccini opera)
31 Chekhov's first play
33 Pub order
36 Frozen "wasser"
37 Col. in a profit-and-loss statement
40 "Blithe Spirit" playwright Noël
42 River in Bavaria
43 "True enough, but…": 2 wds.
44 Actress Austin
45 Elsewhere in this contract
46 Car roof feature: hyph.

Down

1 Hi's comic strip wife
2 Sicilian resort
3 United under a central government
4 Nursery schooler's need, for short
5 Infamous insider Ivan
6 "Correct" prefix
7 Harem chamber
8 Target of a military press, briefly
9 Burrow
10 Carrier at J.F.K.: 2 wds.
16 Stridex target
19 Mushroom used in Japanese cooking
20 Stay away from: 2 wds.
21 Sporty cars, briefly
22 Shad delicacy
24 Portly
25 ___ and haw (stall)
26 Actress Balin
28 Minus in Marseille
30 "___ Athens, Ere We Part" (Byron poem)
32 Even-numbered page
33 Banda ___ (Sumatran city)
34 Zero, in tennis
35 Ablutionary vessel
38 Hawaiian tuber
39 Boring one
41 Chemical suffix
42 Addamses' hairy cousin

462

Across

1   ___ Avenue, Manhattan
5   Tale
9   Surgeon's target
10   Bend
12   Ex-Yankee pitcher Hideki
13   Under the sea, poetically
14   Mal de ___ (seasickness)
15   Orbit's closest point
17   Inventor ___ Whitney
18   Ms. ___-Man (video game)
19   Four quarters
20   Word seg.
22   Copies, briefly
24   Underwater bloodsucker
26   Worldwide
28   Sunscreen ingredient acronym
31   Not working any longer: abbr.
32   QB's snap count
34   Degs. for historians and linguists
35   Excess, surplus
37   Man's nickname
38   Dot on a computer screen
39   Now, in Peru
41   As a friend, to Pierre: 2 wds.
42   Protest: hyph.
43   Italian pronoun
44   Ending for kitchen or luncheon

Down

1   Completely
2   Panhandle city: 2 wds.
3   Knock over
4   Big name in German steel
5   Less plentiful
6   BMW rival
7   Singer whose albums include "Rhyme and Reason": 2 wds.
8   Johnson & Johnson subsidiary
9   "Behind the ___" (out of date)
11   Foils
16   Protection against noise
21   "Frankenstein" setting, briefly
23   Dash
25   "The Queen of Gospel" singer Jackson
26   Feel blindly
27   Yankees' president Randy
29   Creator of Peter Pan
30   ___-American
33   Josh
36   Sleep phenomena, initially
40   Popular movie or song

463

Across

1 Twist around
6 String bean's opposite
11 Hair dye
12 John Milton's regent of the Sun
13 Diary writing
14 Treated a lawn, perhaps
15 New Deal pres.
16 French lake
18 Needle part
19 Just barely: 3 wds.
21 Fortune 500 listings: abbr.
22 "There ___ time like the present": 2 wds.
23 Waste: 2 wds.
25 Sci-fi film of 1984
27 Curly-haired "Peanuts" character
29 Letters for distributing news to Web users
32 Hosp. readout
33 Bridge consisting of a series of arches
35 Daniel ___ Kim (Chin Ho Kelly in "Hawaii Five-0")
36 Driver's lic. and others
37 Russian for "peace"
38 Some old Dodge models
40 Michael of R.E.M.
42 Table of contents page, often
43 City in ancient Egypt
44 Toward the back
45 Mariposa lilies

Down

1 J. Edgar Hoover's agcy., once: 2 wds.
2 Actresses Barrie and Hiller
3 Unwillingness to change one's views
4 Time off, initially
5 Clapton hit
6 Point on which a lever pivots
7 "Entourage" role
8 Taking too long (of an action): hyph.
9 "___ later": 2 wds.
10 First born
17 Bomb attack by planes: 2 wds.
20 Table d'___
24 Lyric poet
26 Student's counselor
27 Bogart's snap brim
28 Drill used to shape or enlarge holes
30 Hannibal battler
31 Aggravation
34 Mgrs.' helpers
39 Tropical fan palm
41 Menlo Park inits.

471

464

Across

1 "Canine Good Citizen" org.
4 Heart of a motherboard, briefly
7 "Hilarious," to texters
8 Sailors' assents: var.
9 Band associated with Elvis Presley
12 Father of Odysseus
14 Migratory fish
15 Rio de la ___
16 ___ Lawson, "Sanford and Son" character
18 Harder to find
19 History Muse
20 C.I.A. precursor
21 Tour guide feature: 2 wds.
24 Aromatic gum that smells sweet when burned
26 Sirius: 2 wds.
28 Tsp. or tbsp.
31 "___ Came Back Again" (Johnny Cash song): 2 wds.
32 Bone: prefix
34 From the Netherlands
36 Go one better than
37 Find a purpose for
38 Commences a journey: 2 wds.
40 "___ XING" (street sign)
41 Suffix with labyrinth
42 Online feed, initially
43 Tack on
44 "Hurrah!"

Down

1 Outstanding footballer: hyph.
2 Marsupials of Australia
3 Thinking discerningly and sensibly: hyph.
4 Vision defect
5 Perennial plant of the daisy family
6 Nat. dissolved in 1991
9 Bedtime request: 4 wds.
10 Mike's girlfriend in "Monsters, Inc."
11 Hit a ball weakly
13 A.A.A. suggestion: abbr.
17 Edible roots
22 Stephen of "Danny Boy"
23 Implanted firmly
25 Tiny time period: abbr., 2 wds.
26 Fastened (as a coat): 2 wds.
27 Beneficial: 2 wds.
29 Gorgon killed by Perseus
30 Honey-pie
33 Prefix with "pension"
35 Early Chinese dynasty: var.
39 Conclude

465

Across

1 Cough-syrup ingredient
5 Civil rights promoter, initially
10 Give ___ for one's money: 2 wds.
11 Talk show host Bob
12 Shutter speed setting
13 Member of the Siouan people
14 Loiters
16 Pastor's field: abbr.
17 First letter of "fried" but not "Friday": 2 wds.
19 Its nickname is "Big Blue"
20 Like a duck's feet
22 British prime minister Theresa
23 Family tree word
24 Wall St. purchase
27 Small variety of cucumber
29 Sot's sound
32 Show the ropes to
33 Dir. of half of the clues in this puzzle
34 Kind of room
35 Distributes
37 Behold, to Pilate
40 Spout at the end of a hose
41 Heavy impact sound
42 "___ I might...": 2 wds.
43 Court cry: var.

Down

1 Thing settled in a bar
2 Tulsa sch. named for a televangelist
3 Cradle song
4 Open
5 December drinks
6 Communication for the deaf, initially
7 Video game name
8 Biblical spy
9 Sacred hymn
11 Place to get a hot drink
15 Tag ___ with
17 Certain guy, in personal ads: inits.
18 Lebanese airline, initially
21 Tractor maker
24 Outlined, incomplete in detail
25 Plating material
26 Chivalrous sort, briefly
28 Meet, as expectations: 2 wds.
29 Lacks, in brief
30 Blood of the Greek gods
31 Foolish
34 Salon supplies
36 Head producer for the Wu-Tang Clan
38 Stage signal
39 Asner and Begley

466

Across

1 Poli-___
4 When doubled, a yellow Teletubby
7 Douro river tributary
8 Person used by another to gain an end: 2 wds.
13 Cash cache initials
14 Express strong disapproval
15 ___ much (less): 2 wds.
17 River of Lyons
18 Forehead-slappers' cries
19 Handle
20 Constrict, as a bodily passage
24 Parisian possessive
25 Builds, as an appetite: 2 wds.
27 HTC phone, e.g.
29 Eastern prisons of old
32 Bank
34 Ulan Bator, once
35 Others, in Oaxaca
37 "Wuthering Heights" writer Brontë
38 Thin silk fabric with a printed pattern
40 Mystery novelist Josephine
41 "Apologies": 2 wds.
42 "Able was I ___ I saw Elba" (famous palindrome)
43 Habitable artificial satellite, initially
44 Sheet music markings: abbr.

Down

1 Rises to one's feet
2 Suddenly stop working (as a motor): 2 wds.
3 Beatles hit with nonsense lyrics: 4 wds.
4 Calculator displays
5 Dental org.
6 Biol. energy sources
9 Metal refuse
10 Cowardly, old-style: hyph.
11 Palmer, to his fans
12 Blubbers
16 Donkey, to Domingo
21 Heavenly body
22 Cousin of reggae
23 Perry Mason creator's monogram
26 One word on a dollar bill
27 Univ. workers
28 "Star Wars" droid Artoo-___
30 Leering sorts
31 Agree: 2 wds.
33 Californian county
36 Delhi dress
37 Big ice cream brand
39 Short Line and Reading, in Monopoly: abbr.

467

Across

1 Diner order, for short
4 Hipster
7 It fits in a lock
8 Tempe inst.
9 Captain's heading, initially
12 Item of packaging
14 Future fish
15 Lodging house in Mexico
16 Buzzing
18 What Ritalin treats, for short
19 Admit: 2 wds.
20 "As if!"
21 Set decoration
23 Directs a course: 2 wds.
25 Chiromancer
27 Onetime lottery org.
30 Schindler who had a list
31 Cottontail's tail
32 Deft
33 Let ___, allow a thing to proceed with vigor and force: 2 wds.
34 Go brown in the sun
35 Blow up
37 Coll. major
38 Suffix with Caesar
39 Clever comment
40 Subj. of Scoring Rule 10.04 in baseball
41 Canada's Grand ___ National Historic Park

Down

1 Archer
2 Texas city
3 Disparaging your opponent during a sporting event: 2 wds.
4 ___ Crunch
5 Enzyme suffix
6 What "haw" means to a horse: 2 wds.
9 Pain experienced by an author at times: 2 wds.
10 Polite turndown: 2 wds.
11 Pipsqueak
13 Green bean, for example
17 Prefix with -phile
21 With a more smug smile
22 Authors Lewis and Forester, initially
24 Apple on a desk
25 Mail, in Marseilles
26 Movie lion voiced by Liam Neeson
28 Wooer
29 Tampa neighbor, briefly: 2 wds.
31 Cardinals' letters
33 Sidi ___, Morocco
36 Apprehend

468

Across

1 Stage of development
6 New Zealand author Marsh
11 Long Island airport
12 "___ Evil" (1987 book by Roy Masters): 2 wds.
13 Mushroom caps
14 Big-bearded "Legs" band: 2 wds.
15 List enders, briefly
17 Seeming eternity
18 2002 Literature Nobelist Kertész
20 Primitive house
22 Hang down loosely
23 World's largest food company
26 IRA-establishing legislation
28 Golden, in Guerrero: 2 wds.
30 Dr Pepper alternative: 2 wds.
32 Even's opposite
33 Cape Town country, initially
34 Swedish superstore
35 Tire in Toulouse
38 Alcohol-eschewing org. for the ladies
40 Short and stout
42 Former Defense Secretary Les
45 One of the Astaires
46 "Genius ___ percent inspiration...": 2 wds.
47 Dehydrates
48 Actor Peter, Bill Mulder in "The X-Files"

Down

1 Spot on a domino
2 Animal welfare org., initially
3 Kind of reaction
4 Seven, in Santiago
5 Grand in scope
6 Nice nose?
7 Official journal
8 Quintillionth: prefix
9 Get ___ a good thing: 2 wds.
10 Error message?
16 That cruise ship
18 Somerset suffix
19 "The Arrivals" author Melissa
21 Meat inspection inits.
23 Ancient temple
24 Regard: 2 wds.
25 Mahler's "Das Lied von der ___"
27 Qualm
29 ___ Mae Brown (Whoopi Goldberg's "Ghost" role)
31 It's on the books
34 "___ kind of you to ask": 2 wds.
35 Handheld CPUs
36 Classic art subject
37 Subj. of a 911 call
39 Muslim tribal chief: var.
41 "Sounds good to me"
43 Concert or Carol ending
44 Hoopster's target

469

Across

1 It's sometimes mixed
6 "Dancer in the Dark" star
11 Checkout counter count
12 Steel tool used for engraving
13 Type of firework: 2 wds.
15 Oscar winner Jannings
16 "Ramblin' Rose" singer
17 ___ king: 2 wds.
19 Clump
21 La ___, phenomenon responsible for extreme weather conditions
23 Savage
27 Bright fish
29 Rugged ridge
30 Kind of charge listed on a receipt
32 "Tickle-me" fad of 1996
33 Country just south of the Arctic Circle: abbr.
35 Suffix with adopt or address
36 Litmus reddener
39 "Round and Round" rock band
41 Green pigment present in plants
45 Cheap and showy, as dress
46 Old photo color
47 "___ little silhouetto of a man...": 3 wds.
48 No friend

Down

1 Fallen space station
2 D.D.E.'s command in W.W. II
3 Outward behavior
4 Muslim leader
5 In ___ (agitated): 2 wds.
6 Bus. school degree
7 Particular point in time
8 "Novus ___ Seclorum" on a dollar
9 Streamlet
10 Kind of pad
14 Social group
17 Clothing brand Taylor and TV newswoman Curry
18 In ___ of (replacing)
20 Paris's country: abbr.
22 Remedy
24 Fax forerunner
25 "Don't look ___!": 2 wds.
26 Composer Janácek
28 ___ fly (baseball play, for short)
31 Prefix with graphic
34 Run out
36 Stage opening: 2 wds.
37 Chuck alternative
38 Opera by Umberto Giordano: 2 wds.
40 Now's partner
42 Shag rug made in Sweden
43 Boundary, briefly
44 Produce a clutch

470

Across

1 Greek island off the Turkish coast
7 ___ Francisco Bay
10 "Peter Pan" author
11 "Miami Vice" cop ___ Tubbs
12 "___ Every Word He Said" (Ricky Van Shelton song): 2 wds.
13 Soil: prefix
14 Implied comparison
16 Popular sports car, informally
19 Morse minimum
20 Paint layers
22 Two-time loser to Eisenhower
25 Computer data acronym
26 Explosive experiment: abbr., 2 wds.
27 Model Gabrielle
28 Figure skater Brian
29 Washroom, briefly
30 Have ___ in the matter: 2 wds.
31 New Testament book
35 Internet guffaw
36 Capital of Texas
40 Bar association member: abbr.
41 Operatic passage
42 "You got it!"
43 Red dwarfs: 2 wds.

Down

1 Clean-up hitter's stat., initially
2 "Green Eggs and ___"
3 Smelter input
4 In a theatrical way
5 Article in "Der Spiegel"
6 Rectangular paving stone
7 Blind
8 Prefix with bat or phobia
9 Koh-i-___ diamond
11 High-speed urban railroad: 2 wds.
15 "A Bell for ___" (John Hersey novel)
16 "I Got ___" (George Strait song): 2 wds.
17 Shed
18 Cosmetic operations
21 Strainer
23 Dazed
24 Modest comment: 2 wds.
31 Talk in church
32 Table d'___
33 Thank-you-___
34 Couple's pronoun
37 Come ___ halt: 2 wds.
38 Leb. neighbor
39 Votes against

471

Across

1 Old-school tough guys in rap songs, initially
4 QBs' goals
7 OB/GYNs, e.g.
10 Woman's name that sounds like a month
11 Hustle
12 Covert maritime org.
13 Shrubs similar to rhododendrons
15 Take a nap, so to speak: 4 wds.
17 Bagged beverage
18 Ab ___ (from the beginning)
19 Whopper topper
21 Tulip tissue
24 ___ Diego Chicken
25 DVD player's predecessor
26 Feeling of deep dread
29 Spreads
31 Relative from Rio
32 Distant
33 Way of looking at something: 3 wds.
38 Knitted throws
39 No vote
40 Wildcats' sch.
41 Recipient of Bart's prank calls
42 Ethyl finish
43 Parking place
44 Professional suffix

Down

1 Native Nebraskan
2 ___ Strip (area bordering Egypt and Israel)
3 Thresher shark: 2 wds.
4 2013 movie starring Hugh Jackman: 2 wds.
5 "Gangs of New York" costar
6 Cong. period
7 Leather shoe, for short
8 Paternity identifier, initially
9 Not going anywhere: 2 wds.
14 Duty
16 Firm head, initially
19 "I Married Adventure" autobiographer Johnson
20 Indian restaurant bread
22 "Foucault's Pendulum" author
23 Lady's title
27 Hyperbolic sine
28 Japanese floor covering
29 Compensate for
30 John, for short
33 Beatle McCartney
34 Pass the point ___ return: 2 wds.
35 Yoko and family
36 Suffix with Ecuador
37 English river

472

Across

1 Owing: 2 wds.
6 Credited to noted artist Romain de Tirtoff
11 Brewery in Golden, Colorado
12 "The Wreck of the Mary ___"
13 Igloo dweller
14 Sleeper's woe
15 Miss ___: 2 wds.
17 Scottish capital, briefly
18 "___ do for now"
19 Ancient alphabetic symbol
21 You, abroad
22 Photography pioneer
25 Mom's brother, briefly
26 International charitable grp.
27 Letters used (by some) for dates
28 Outcasts
30 Knock off
31 Fairy tale opener
32 Rabbit tail
33 Trace of smoke
35 Persuades
37 Much, in music
39 They had an empire in South America
41 Frets
42 Leaks
43 Smut
44 Place for a comb

Down

1 Here, in Bordeaux
2 Simple musical composition
3 Betrayer: hyph.
4 Poem by Ralph Waldo Emerson
5 This, in Barcelona
6 Author LeShan
7 Apologize for sinning
8 Vehicle with four pedals: 2 wds.
9 "... ___ saw Elba": 2 wds.
10 Actor Penn
16 Criticizes severely
18 "The game ___!": 2 wds.
20 Service club units, initially
22 Air ___ Lifeteam (air ambulance provider)
23 Charges
24 Nair's former competitor
29 Hocked: 2 wds.
32 More sound
33 Insect in a colony
34 Word analogy phrase: 2 wds.
36 1984–88 skating gold medalist
38 "Seeking" letters in personals
40 Leaky tire sound

473

Across

1 Word used to express sympathy
4 Nepalese peak near Tibet
7 Cow's food
10 Frightened
12 Kin of -like
13 Give a different name to
14 Govt. agency whose official early history is entitled "Controlling the Atom"
15 "A Little Bitty Tear" singer, 1962
16 ___ Isaac Rabi, physicist and Nobel laureate
18 "Odyssey" enchantress
20 Cy Young winner Sparky
21 HBO's "Da ___ G Show"
22 Goo
25 Unjust: 2 wds.
27 Go back
29 Crunched muscles, briefly
32 Connors opponent, once
33 As follows: 2 wds.
35 Butt of jokes
38 In the distance
39 Good buddy
40 Sweet, full-bodied sherry
42 Birmingham to Montgomery dir.
43 Becomes enraged: 2 wds.
44 Sellout indicator, shortly
45 Five-star 1950s monogram

Down

1 Cameroon's continent
2 Small beetle
3 Tavern, slangily: 2 wds.
4 Towards the back, on a ship
5 Afghan monetary units
6 Martinique et Guadeloupe, e.g.
7 Supermodel who married Richard Gere in 1991: 2 wds.
8 Open, in a way
9 Formal order
11 Computer architecture, initially
17 Half court game?
19 Feminine suffix
23 Baseball number nines, briefly
24 Toward dawn
26 Cookie often eaten inside-out
27 Woodworking tools
28 Part of a Spanish 101 conjugation
30 Prejudiced
31 Went boldly
34 Crew units
36 Pastor, broadcaster and author Bob
37 Part of E.M.T.: abbr.
41 Fair-hiring agcy.

481

474

Across

1 Like a yenta
5 Emmanuel ___ (French president)
11 "___ Did It Before (Same God)" (Tye Tribbett song): 2 wds.
12 Andre of tennis
13 Inner sanctuary of a Greek temple
14 All-terrain military vehicle
15 Army recruit
17 "You have a point"
18 Foot offense
22 Disentangle
25 Fripp & ___ ("No Pussyfooting" collaborators)
26 Repress: 2 wds.
27 Violinist's stroke: hyph.
29 Mil. designation
30 Encourage
32 1948 Hitchcock thriller
34 Go wild
35 Ahead of no one, in a competition: 2 wds.
39 Stout, ankle-high shoe
42 Greek 'Gray Sister' who shared an eye and a tooth with Deino and Pemphredo
43 Mena of "American Beauty"
44 Geographical features, for short
45 Breastbones
46 "Ugh!"

Down

1 Prime-time time
2 "Death ___ Expert Witness" (P.D. James novel): 2 wds.
3 Baseball fielding position
4 "Give me an answer right now!": 3 wds.
5 "The Song of the Earth" composer Gustav
6 Shivering fit
7 Small part in a play
8 Bible translation published 1946–57, initially
9 Sugar suffix
10 Never, in German
16 Mrs. Van Houten of "The Simpsons"
19 Young woman making a first social appearance
20 "___ off?": 2 wds.
21 Actress Misty of "Hee Haw"
22 Natl. Guard counterpart
23 One-named singer for the 1960s Velvet Underground
24 Glaringly vivid and graphic
28 Greek astronomer and geographer
31 One of the Muses
33 First name in mystery
36 Make
37 Pop music's 'N___
38 Reggae singer Peter
39 Some coll. degrees
40 Same old, same old
41 The ___ Glove (hot surface mitt)

475

Across

1 Serve in the capacity of: 2 wds.
6 Prefix meaning "numbness"
11 "Futurama" character voiced by Katey Sagal
12 ___ Gay (W.W. II plane)
13 Nancy of "Access Hollywood"
14 Canceled, in a way: 2 wds.
15 Coldest season of the year
17 ___ Ben Bella, first president of Nigeria
18 Chief magistrate of Venice or Genoa, historically
20 One-time Yukon capital, ___ City
25 Kind of whale
27 Meddlesome sort
28 Mill site
30 Interminable time
31 Hanukkah pancake
33 Intelligent anthropoid ape
38 Splotches
39 Frail
40 Misrepresent
41 Hebrew letter: var.
42 Small container with divisions
43 Kurt Wallander's home town

Down

1 Strike ___ blow: 2 wds.
2 100 pesewas in Ghana
3 Person from 13 to 19 years old
4 In full possession of one's mental faculties, so to speak: 2 wds.
5 Beaver State capital
6 Overnight (as a delivery): 2 wds.
7 "___ quote...": 2 wds.
8 Sufficient space
9 Board game with a lead pipe and a rope
10 Mare's morsel
16 River to the Mississippi
18 Welfare org.
19 Elect
21 Liability to failure under pressure or stress
22 Regard as of little value: 2 wds.
23 Oklahoma native
24 Masefield play "The Tragedy of ___"
26 Sweet Madeira wine
29 Treasure hunt need
32 Cheap and showy, as dress
33 Alexandria Quartet book
34 Have in one's hands
35 Footnote abbreviation
36 Old Icelandic literary work
37 Checked out
38 Brit. TV co.

476

Across

1 Ghana's monetary unit
5 Mil. school
9 Chinese cuisine
10 Julio A. ___, 9th and 14th president of Argentina
11 Plant with complex and showy flowers
13 Disgusting substance
14 Horror filmmaker Roth
15 Donald's wife
17 Rep.'s counterpart
18 Suffix for favor and fin
19 Venusians or Martians, e.g.
20 Shrivel to nothing: 2 wds.
23 Good start?: 2 wds.
24 Female theatrical flirt
28 ___ Darya (Asian river)
29 Celtic Neptune
30 Nutritional fig.
32 Young cats
34 Chemical suffix
35 Fashion monthly
36 What we breathe: 2 wds.
38 Wide widths, initially
39 The ___ Brothers ("Shout" singers)
40 Don't believe it
41 Football throw

Down

1 Large migratory shorebird
2 Spanish name for the holm oak
3 Morse T
4 Unique
5 Medieval chest
6 Transparent layer of the eye
7 Quick and penetrating intelligence
8 Pops
9 Works in the garden
12 Preventative measure
16 Taking charge
21 ___ mai (dim sum dish)
22 Lb. or oz.
24 "Horse Heaven" author Jane
25 Pipe through which water can escape
26 Court proceedings
27 Whirlpools
28 Linebacker Ayers of the NFL
31 Ethereal
33 "Intelligence for Your Life" host John
37 What that is in Spain

477

Across

1 Unappetizing food or drink
6 Palacio room
10 Bow (to)
12 ____ the air (uncertain): 2 wds.
13 Title bandit in a Verdi opera
14 Ersatz bed, to Brits
15 Preordained
17 Ball wear
20 Some army recruits, initially
24 High society: 2 wds.
26 Solution present in batteries
28 Fonzie's red-haired pal
29 Yelp of sudden pain
30 ____ Motown
31 Quinine, e.g.
37 Stove or washer, e.g.: abbr.
40 Guard
41 Robbie who played Cousin Oliver on "The Brady Bunch"
42 Informed on, slangily
43 City on the Moselle
44 Hebrew letter: var.

Down

1 Timetable, briefly
2 Knowledge
3 Controls
4 Completions, e.g.
5 ____ soit qui mal y pense
6 Abruptly
7 Mil. address
8 Lily in Lille
9 Years, to Yves
11 Kind of weather-resistant jacket
16 Ending for switch or buck
18 Opthalmic irritation
19 Branch of Zen Buddhism
20 One ____ customer
21 Dart
22 Anatomical cavities
23 Excessive sentimentality in a movie, so to speak
25 ____ England
27 Cash drawer
32 Med. sch. course
33 Some W.W. II vessels
34 Eke ____ living: 2 wds.
35 Really steamed
36 2000s Bengals running back Dorsey
37 Give weapons to
38 Kind of chart
39 Attention-getter

485

478

Across

1 Gray and Candler
5 Weights used in China and East Asia
10 A few
11 Chestnut
12 Disney-owned channel, initially
13 Concoct: 2 wds.
14 Logical and consistent
16 R.N. workplaces
17 Woody and Marjorie's son
21 Restaurant entertainment
24 Eternity, seemingly
25 "What a good boy ___!": 2 wds.
26 Rainbow's shape
27 V.I.P. at the top of a ladder
28 Govt. agency once headed by Steve Preston
29 Rest: 2 wds.
31 Slightest bit
33 "The Cairo affair" author Steinhauer
34 Beanie
38 Top-selling Scotch brand
41 "___ kleine Nachtmusik"
42 "Just like me": 3 wds.
43 TV interviewer who called astronaut "Buzz" Aldrin "Buzz Lightyear": 2 wds.
44 Early inhabitant of Mexico
45 Lairs

Down

1 "Just ___!": 2 wds.
2 Just average: hyph.
3 Cold-blooded creature
4 New York county
5 Divided
6 Longtime comic strip queen
7 One of eight Eng. kings
8 "Turandot" slave
9 Oct. preceder
13 "Don't joke!": 2 wds.
15 Relating to the country
18 Cause to coexist in harmony
19 Movie mogul Marcus
20 "___, U of K" (fight song at the University of Kentucky): 2 wds.
21 The C in J. C. Penney
22 Prefix with valence
23 Immune system lymphocyte: hyph.
30 Remove element 82 from
32 Hebrew letter: var.
35 McDonald's founder Ray
36 Has ___ with (is connected): 2 wds.
37 Gamepieces
38 1957 Physics Nobelist Tsung-___ Lee
39 New U.S. resident's course, initially
40 "The Goalkeeper's Fear of the Penalty" director Wenders

479

Across

1 Eagerly expectant
5 Hindu ascetics
11 C-worthy: hyph.
12 Feature of a Las Vegas "bandit": 2 wds.
13 Baseball's Moises
14 Not genuine
15 Call it quits: 3 wds.
17 What a dog or cat usually has: 2 wds.
18 Ignores: 2 wds.
20 Man's nickname
23 Coll. test
24 Initially a port
26 Bireme implement
27 Back
28 Cuisine style
30 Former U.N. leader U ____
31 Final results of a manufacturing process: 2 wds.
37 Pope who crowned Charlemagne emperor of the Romans: 2 wds.
38 Tatters
39 Eastern Canadian native
40 Give off, as radiation
41 Available for purchase: 2 wds.
42 Coppertone nos.

Down

1 "P.D.Q.!"
2 Cough-syrup ingredient
3 Cut off
4 Young turkeys
5 1982 movie starring Meryl Streep: 2 wds.
6 "Billionaire Boys Club" costar Elgort
7 Bass
8 Cart
9 Pakistani tongue
10 Bad air
16 Popular cologne
18 Queens airport, initially
19 "____ tu"
20 Military training establishment: 2 wds.
21 North Carolina city: abbr.
22 It makes one hot
25 Garrett of "Everybody Loves Raymond"
29 Gets used to
30 ____ offer
31 "St. ____'s Fire"
32 No, to Germans
33 MDs: abbr.
34 A fine cotton
35 Weary workers' cry, for short
36 Retired fliers, for short

480

Across

1 Twaddle
5 Italian ___
8 Soul singer Warwick
10 Pittsburgh Penguins' org.
11 January 1st: 3 wds.
13 Female friend in Florence
14 Pretense
15 Snoop (around)
16 Long journey by sea
18 Chargers' sch.
19 Purify
20 Two-time Masters champ Ben
21 Beehive State native
23 Very quietly, in music: abbr.
26 Less important songs on a pop record: hyph.
27 Belgian singer and composer Jacques (1929–78)
28 Big ref. works, for short
29 Home of the Black Bears
30 Waste: 2 wds.
33 Old style "For shame!"
34 "That's life!": 2 wds.
35 Like 1, 3, 5, 7 or 9
36 "___ Death" (from Peer Gynt Suite No. 1)

Down

1 "Heart of Oak" composer William
2 In good health, draftwise: hyph.
3 Highland fall
4 That lady
5 Cherokee or Chippewa
6 Rush forward in attack
7 2008 Freeride World Champion skier Saugstad
8 Evil spirit
9 "If only!": 2 wds.
11 Half of Mork's catchphrase, on "Mork & Mindy"
12 "I'm just ___!"
16 Gamblers' mecca
17 The face ___ angel: 2 wds.
19 Architect Mies van der ___
20 Verb with thou
21 Computer access name: 2 wds.
22 Arranged neatly and in order
23 Move stealthily
24 Kind of code
25 Stratagem
26 Boisterously funny, familiarly
27 Bonny hillsides
29 "... ___ should grow too fond of it": R. E. Lee: 2 wds.
31 ___ fault (overly): 2 wds.
32 Codgers' replies

481

Across

1 ___ Picchu
6 Show with Jean-Luc Picard as the "Enterprise" captain, in fan shorthand
11 W.W. II torpedo vessel: hyph.
12 "... or I'll eat ___!": 2 wds.
13 Cape Cod town
14 Fencing needs
15 Suffix with Salvador
16 Navigational guidance pillar
18 Courtroom event
20 Cir. midpoint
23 Donkey's cry: hyph.
25 ___-Lite, group whose albums include "Infinity Within"
26 San Rafael's county
27 "Center" starts with one: 2 wds.
28 Camus's birthplace
29 Agreement
30 Boston or N.Y.C., e.g.: abbr.
31 Electrician, at times
32 Hebrew letter: var.
34 Elko-to-Reno dir.
37 "Braxton Family Values" sister
39 Send into ecstasy
41 In its original form, as a movie
42 "Gigi" star Leslie
43 "___ another": 2 wds.
44 Attacked: 2 wds.

Down

1 Apportion (out)
2 Magician's opening
3 Put up a fight in response
4 Laugh sound
5 Aiming for a state in which everything is perfect
6 Inhale an odor
7 Dittography, e.g.
8 From that point onward
9 Scot's denial
10 Fast sports cars, for short
17 Twist about a vertical axis (of a plane)
19 Nose: prefix
21 Four: prefix
22 In-basket stamp: abbr.
23 Managed care grps.
24 Holliday's O.K. Corral ally
25 12 in Toledo
27 Sharp piercing cry
29 Band follower?
31 Ralph of "The Waltons"
33 Bathtub ring gunk
35 Greek promenade
36 Collapsed
37 River that flows through Mirandela, Portugal
38 ICU staffers
40 ___ an der Thaya, Austrian town

482

Across

1 Clean, as a floor: 2 wds.
7 Gets down
11 Turns of phrase
12 Donnybrook
13 Flowering plants of the tropics
14 Roman Catholic prelate, briefly
15 Actor McKellen
16 ___ Lama
17 Title for a retired professor, maybe
20 Psychic power letters
21 Kind of CPU (it uses a "less-is-more" philosophy)
22 Fifth qtrs.
24 Darn it!
29 Football measurements: abbr.
30 French wave
31 Suitable for the occasion
34 Billie ___, stage name of Eleanora Fagan
36 Lima and pinto
38 Post-op stop, initially
39 "A Chorus Line" character
40 Worldwide relief org.
43 Over, in Hanover
44 Bygone money
45 "You've ___ Friend" (James Taylor/Carole King song): 2 wds.
46 City across the Delaware from Philadelphia

Down

1 Madison's state, shortly
2 Dutch city
3 Most small
4 Royal family
5 Salalah resident
6 Letter afterthoughts: inits.
7 "At Wit's End" columnist Bombeck
8 Way to the altar
9 Roman robes
10 Bacon unit
16 Facts and figures
17 Tarzan creator's monogram
18 Kraft drinks brand
19 Chest location
23 Uncomplaining fortitude in suffering
25 Old English letters
26 Caused to occur rapidly
27 Harem chamber
28 Marshal under Napoleon
31 Women's rights activist Bella
32 R&B singer Bryson
33 Be silent, in music
35 Long marking on the surface of a planet
37 Drag racing governing body: inits.
40 It's scanned at checkout: inits.
41 Summer: Fr.
42 Cooler

483

Across

1 Bob of sausage fame
6 Biblical measure
11 Ancient sailing ship
12 Whisky ____, nightclub at 8901 Sunset Boulevard, L.A.: 3 wds.
13 Names of people or places, e.g.: 2 wds.
15 Archipelago unit: abbr.
16 Pince-____ glasses
17 Go-____ (1980s band)
18 Catholicism or Judaism: abbr.
19 "____ Beso" (1962 Paul Anka hit)
20 Charlemagne's domain, initially
21 Leyden relative
23 They may take a few years to mature: hyph.
25 "Hamlet" fop
27 Ray of "GoodFellas"
30 Sonoran Indian
34 Not down: abbr.
35 Three, to Caesar
37 François or Françoise, e.g.
38 Printemps month
39 MSNBC rival
40 Econ. statistic
41 Begin a conversation: 3 wds.
44 "Haven't a clue!"
45 Went sniggling
46 ____ Martin (Bond film car)
47 Color anew

Down

1 Run out
2 Knowledgeable about (with "in")
3 Roman military cloak
4 China neighbor, for short
5 Part of a movie or play
6 Italian ballad
7 "The Inquiry" playwright Betti
8 Accepted as true
9 Brush aside
10 Junks
14 Self-control
22 Wisecrack
24 Military training acad.
26 Attach to: 2 wds.
27 Letter after kappa
28 Son of Daedalus
29 Point in the right direction
31 Decorate with gold, old-style
32 Former Dodgers' baseman nicknamed "The Penguin": 2 wds.
33 Check
36 "Men ____ Life" (Warhol painting): 2 wds.
42 "Wheel of Fortune" request: 2 wds.
43 Shoebox letters

484

Across

1 Count ___, jazz pianist
6 Airwaves regulator letters
9 Beach Boys hit "Help Me, ___"
11 Buck addition
12 Key of Haydn's symphony No. 12: 2 wds.
13 Pianist Peter
14 Lady's title
15 Act to retain one's goods at auction: 2 wds.
17 Decree
19 State of Malaysia, ___ Sembilan
21 TV program in which topics are discussed: 2 wds.
23 Taina of "The 39 Steps"
26 Indicates one's choice, in a way
27 Losing come-out roll in craps
28 Slew
31 One way to go: 2 wds.
32 Church figure
36 "Love is ___ Need" (Mary J. Blige song): 2 wds.
38 Freezer or blender, e.g.: abbr.
39 Overseas carrier: 2 wds.
40 Gift to play with: 2 wds.
42 Modern mall features: inits.
43 John of "Fawlty Towers"
44 Newspaper worker: abbr.
45 Talk to the waiter

Down

1 Ornamental braiding
2 Sportscaster Rashad
3 "Me too!" relative: 3 wds.
4 Deliver via hypodermic
5 Old name for Tokyo
6 Goods carried by a large vehicle
7 Afro-Caribbean hairstyle
8 Lovey-dovey sound
10 Short trader?
11 South American high points
16 Cuttlefish's bag: hyph.
18 C.P.A.'s concern: 2 wds.
20 ___ Jima (Japanese island)
22 Denebola's constellation
23 Draw away from shore
24 Allegiance
25 Old form of lighting: 2 wds.
29 Blabs
30 Person who writes a check
33 Decided
34 Imagine, briefly
35 More sharp
37 Bottom-of-letter abbr.
39 Pack away
41 "Can't Get It Out of My Head" rock gp.

485

Across

1 "___ what you did!": 2 wds.

5 Reflective layers in the eyes

11 "Comin' ___ the Rye"

12 "Black Armor" poet Wylie

13 "It's Impossible" singer

14 Kind of block

15 Nutritious substance that's good for you: 2 wds.

17 Architect Saarinen

18 Spring away from an impact

21 Online store for handicrafts

25 Former U.S.S.R. constituent

26 "___ Z Mysteries" (kids' book series): 2 wds.

27 Prefix with technology

29 Third stomach of a ruminant

32 Ex-president of Argentina

34 Unnavigable

39 Melodic pieces

40 Grease

41 Lab burner namesake

42 "___, U of K" (college fight song): 2 wds.

43 Prefix relating to the intestine

44 Actress Rowlands

Down

1 Desire

2 "If the ___ fits …"

3 First word of Virgil's "Aeneid"

4 Like some sweaters

5 Geek Squad member

6 "Get ___!": 2 wds.

7 Spiced and sweetened flour

8 Prefix with morph

9 Word with web or pigeon

10 J.F.K. abbr.

16 Letters of concern

18 Hair style

19 Semi-soft Canadian cheese

20 Footed vase

22 Professor's helpers, initially

23 Actor Erwin

24 Day in Jerusalem

28 Fight

29 Duke in "Twelfth Night"

30 Twelve make a yr.

31 Kind of recording

33 Anodyne

34 "Who Can ___ To" (2014 musical movie): 2 wds.

35 Make money

36 Spoiler

37 "Dianetics" author Hubbard: 2 wds.

38 Actress Best

39 Honest one

486

Across

1 "The Mystery of ____ Vep" (Charles Ludlam play)
5 Argentinian expanse
10 Some Chryslers
12 ____ flu
13 Hindu loincloth
14 Conducted toward: 2 wds.
15 Poetic contraction
16 Fleet cmdr.
18 Number of weeks per annum
19 Hogwash
21 Room renter
22 Pre-calc course
23 One of Time's 1993 Men of the Year
25 Pass slowly from one color to another
27 Beneficial: 2 wds.
29 251 in Roman numerals
32 Fanatic
33 Roustabout
35 Bureau of the Treasury Dept.
36 Three-time Burmese prime minister: 2 wds.
37 Book before Jeremiah: abbr.
38 Relating to a hair
40 Alexander who won the 2016 Indy 500
42 Breathing
43 Works steadily at (one's trade)
44 Pitch again
45 Anglo-Saxon slave

Down

1 Owing money: 2 wds.
2 Try again
3 Hasty departure at night, to avoid paying rent: 2 wds.
4 Little scurrier
5 Ancient city in Syria
6 St.'s cousin
7 Emotional period in one's 50s: 2 wds.
8 Film that forms on bronze
9 Smear
11 City of central China: var.
17 Expressionless
20 Hideous sort
24 Old record label
26 Siren
27 ____ with (equal to): 3 wds.
28 Vain
30 Let up
31 Texas hold 'em pronouncement: 2 wds.
34 Pat a baby on the back after feeding
39 One of Frank's exes
41 Corrida call

487

Across

1 College Park school, home of the Terrapins, initially
4 Always, poetically
7 Home care provider, initially
10 Former Kansas City Royals batting coach Charley
11 International charitable grp.
12 Bank offering, briefly
13 Grow together
15 French "no"
16 "The Jungle Book" wolfpack leader
17 Verne's captain
18 Streets: abbr.
19 Stripped
21 Bit of success
22 Simple shelter: hyph.
25 Pop's kin
26 Put on
27 Long-snouted fish
28 Compares
30 Units of energy
31 "Holy cow!"
32 Back muscle, familiarly
33 Oxford, e.g.
35 Pale purple
37 "Kitchy-___!" (baby tickler's comment)
38 Arising from the action of the wind
40 Germany's Dortmund-___ Canal
41 African animal
42 Long-running U.K. music mag
43 Irish Sea feeder
44 Hall-of-Famer Mel
45 Aide in the Army, initially

Down

1 Suffix with form
2 Feather, to Yankee Doodle
3 Kids' game played in a circle: 3 wds.
4 Stunting legend Knievel
5 Formation, creation
6 Lobster spawn
7 Art form similar to etching: 2 wds.
8 High school dance
9 Billionth: prefix
14 Legal defendant: abbr.
17 Gp. once headed by Heston, initially
20 ___ Lingus (Irish carrier)
21 ___-de-sac
23 Wrestling duos: 2 wds.
24 Where surgeons work, initially
26 Ques. response
29 Inits. in the classifieds
30 Jewish calendar month
33 TV guide info.
34 Main Web page
36 August, in Amiens
38 At some point in the past
39 Colonial prefix?

488

Across

1 ___ the Hutt, "Star Wars" antagonist
6 Split pulses in Indian cooking: var.
10 Exertion
11 "I love you," in Seville: 2 wds.
12 Mont ___ (French mountain)
13 Related to birds
14 1 followed by 100 zeros
16 Toaster waffle brand
19 Typical dwelling-place
21 Activist
22 Move rapidly
24 Ambulance V.I.P.
25 Put money (on something)
26 ROTC relative
27 Russian chess Grandmaster Alexander
29 Hike, in football
30 Dismal
31 Ethereal
32 Working well together: 2 wds.
34 Superfluous
36 Japanese spitz dog
40 Weapon with a long metal blade
41 "The Last Innocents" author Michael
42 Barista's workplace
43 Bandleader Shaw

Down

1 "Air on the G String" composer's monogram
2 Cobbler's tool
3 "___ sport": 2 wds.
4 City on the Penobscot River
5 Early record label for Bobby Darin and the Beatles
6 Eat hungrily
7 Pellet of precipitation
8 Health grp.
9 Actor Chaney, Jr.
11 Baseball act: hyph.
15 Nestlé candy bar: 2 wds.
16 Noble, in Essen
17 Lose it: 2 wds.
18 Disposes: 3 wds.
20 Dana of "The Sting"
23 Catch a glimpse of
25 Favoring one person or side over another
28 Professor's guarantee
29 Baseman
33 "The Lion King" lioness
34 The Trojans of the N.C.A.A.
35 Early gangsta rap collective inits.
37 "Am ___ risk?": 2 wds.
38 Meteorologist's comfort meas.
39 Sailor's "sure thing!"

489

Across

1 Forte
5 Skin care brand
9 Primo: hyph.
10 Horse coat color
12 Pop
13 Flexible
14 Clotho, Lachesis, and Atropos: 2 wds.
16 "Radio Free Europe" group
17 Make an attempt: give ___: 3 wds.
21 Prefix with centric
23 Foul-smelling
24 Former Portuguese colony in India
25 "The Cask of Amontillado" author
26 Knife name in TV ads
29 Judge tentatively
31 As ___ the hills: 2 wds.
32 Genre of popular music, initially
33 Is a part of: 2 wds.
37 "Hold on!": abbr., 2 wds.
40 Leeds's river
41 Smiths
42 Before long
43 He played one of TV's Sopranos
44 Feminine suffix

Down

1 Hold up
2 Sound of joy
3 Acting in a secret or dishonest way
4 Make unable to hear
5 Major record label, once
6 Brother's title
7 Ring count
8 Flier's stat.
10 San Francisco, for one: abbr.
11 Liquid part of fat
15 "Yo te ___"
18 Disparaging remark
19 Some Pontiacs, shortly
20 Court cry
21 Breakfast item brand name
22 Drudgery
27 Smart one
28 He hit #1 with "Nice & Slow"
29 Dog's warning
30 Discomfort
34 Some GE appliances: abbr.
35 Multivitamin component, often
36 It's protected in Hawaii
37 Govt. agency in Stephen King's "Firestarter," initially
38 The Los Angeles Kings, the Edmonton Oilers, etc.
39 Letters in a help wanted ad

490

Across

1 Mountain range from the Arctic to the Caspian Sea
6 Suffix for abnormalities
10 Pull again, say
11 2002 Olympics venue
12 "It's The Girls!" singer: 2 wds.
14 Bard of boxing
15 Bulgaria's continent, for short
16 Storm heading, initially
17 "Regnava ___ silenzio" (aria from "Lucia di Lammermoor")
18 Aviation counterterrorism agency, initially
19 Suffix with tutor or torrent
20 Gross of "Free Spirit"
22 "Save" shortcut on a PC: abbr., 2 wds.
24 Removed a squeak from
26 Ring
28 First word of the "Aeneid"
32 Thor Heyerdahl craft: 2 wds.
33 Here, in Mexico
35 Federal warning system, initially
36 Med. feeders
37 Interruption
38 Wolf Blitzer's channel
39 Vin Santo or Sauternes, for example: 2 wds.
42 Imposing in size
43 Load carrier
44 Course on insects, for short
45 Guest pieces in a newspaper: hyph.

Down

1 Polished
2 Lurched
3 Emperor who died on his wedding night
4 Good deal
5 Dear
6 Letters on O'Hare-bound luggage
7 Somme sun
8 "… ___ we speak": 2 wds.
9 "New York Magazine" cartoonist Edward
11 Copy illegally
13 Auto with a very powerful engine: 2 wds.
21 "___ won't be afraid" ("Stand by Me" lyric): 2 wds.
23 Nutrition stat.
25 Formed a mental picture of
26 Large underground chamber
27 Greet the villain: 2 wds.
29 Enumerate
30 Having a crew
31 Actor Ed's family
32 Blue ___ Mountains
34 Capable of: 2 wds.
40 ___-Cat (winter vehicle)
41 Doo-___ (1950s music style)

491

Across

1 Hindu dynasty established in 320 A.D.
6 One of the Three Stooges
11 DIY mover's rental: hyph.
12 Game show announcer Johnny
13 Rentable: 2 wds.
14 Charlotte ___
15 Cable choice, in listings
16 Punched-in-the-gut sound
18 "___ who?"
19 Goof
22 Spitz dogs of a Japanese breed
24 Neighbor of Tenn.: 2 wds.
28 Add on
29 Toyota MR2 competitor
30 Suffix with authentic
31 Slight
32 Hunt high and low
34 "Prince Valiant" character
37 Rock's Ocasek
38 PC bailout key
41 Somewhat
43 Fluster
45 Not captured
46 Cornerback Sanders
47 "What was ___ wanted?": 2 wds.
48 Flying fish eaters

Down

1 Courage, informally
2 "This can't be good": hyph.
3 Horse originally bred in the southwestern U.S.
4 Day between Mon. and Wed.
5 Jimmy Dorsey's instrument: 2 wds.
6 Greek island where Prince Philip was born
7 "The Subject Was Roses" director Grosbard
8 Blog feeds, initially
9 Leave in the dust
10 California's Santa ___ Valley
17 It turns out Lts.
20 Brain passages
21 Early supercomputer
22 Small battery size, initially
23 Chivalrous guy: abbr.
25 Redeemed: 2 wds.
26 Part of A.S.T.: abbr.
27 Beam
29 "Love's Labour's Lost" lord
31 It follows Avril
33 Noted Verdi aria: 2 wds.
34 Here, in Honduras
35 Smallest of the litter
36 Former Hungarian premier Imre ___
39 Sour fruit
40 100-year periods, briefly
42 "And your point being…?"
44 The, in Germany

492

Across

1. Spring ____: 2 wds.
6. The king, in Italian: 2 wds.
10. Aid to loading a muzzle
12. 10th-century pope: 2 wds.
13. Happen, become actual fact
15. "Forbidden Fruits" movie director Marc
16. Phrase for the slightly miffed and disappointed: 2 wds.
19. Worker's shout, in brief
22. Very, in Veracruz
23. Pellagra preventer
25. Mode of expression
28. ____ Panza (Don Quixote's sidekick)
29. NYSE purchase: abbr.
30. Former Japanese capital
31. "Peachy!"
33. Bean on the screen
35. Long inventory of people or things: 2 wds.
41. Notice
42. Navy builder
43. Double-____ (kind of tournament, for short)
44. ____ different tune (change one's mind): 2 wds.

Down

1. Shirt part
2. "____ note to follow soh...": 2 wds.
3. CPR pro
4. Palm variety
5. Holy text
6. Against the rules
7. Wahine accessory
8. Cartoonist Chast
9. All Hallow's ____ (another name for Halloween)
11. Home improvement letters
14. Deed: Latin
16. Electrical units
17. City on the Yangtze
18. Actress Loy
20. Twenty: prefix
21. Scrap
23. Prefix with realism
24. Laura who wrote "Stoned Soul Picnic"
26. It stands for something
27. Archeologist's fragment
31. "The Highwayman" poet Alfred
32. Zhou ____, prime minister of China 1949–76
34. Some name suffixes
35. Surname of two signers of the Declaration of Independence
36. Handy form of communication letters?
37. News svc. founded in 1958
38. Arab name part
39. Part of a line: abbr.
40. Picker-upper

493

Across

1 Deli machine
7 Songbird of the bunting family
8 Emulate a kangaroo
11 Oblique
12 In this location: Sp.
13 Old Oldsmobile
14 Garden bush
16 Wheat grown as stock feed
17 Pandora's boxful
18 Future fry
19 "Eureka!": 3 wds.
22 "Mean Girls" costar: 2 wds.
24 Reflexive pronoun
26 Draft board inits.
29 Actress Russo
30 Soprano Lehmann
32 Bathroom fixture
34 Fletcher's product
35 French Guiana's Royale, e.g.
36 Mythological hunter turned into a stag and killed by his own dogs
38 Dungeons & Dragons game co., initially
39 City in central Maryland
40 Where you might see Bermuda and Jamaica on a map

Down

1 Sailor's patron: 2 wds.
2 Elvis song: 3 wds.
3 "If ___ A Carpenter" (Bobby Darin hit): 2 wds.
4 Swimming pool additive
5 Ample shoe width
6 Burgundy and cherry
8 London road noted for private clinics: 2 wds.
9 Eyes
10 Colt 45 producer
11 1930s heavyweight champ Max
15 Bees' hangout
20 Shakespearean prince
21 Divine creative impulse
23 "Uh-huh": 2 wds.
24 Elliptical path
25 Armstrong and Harris
27 Bar seats
28 In stitches
31 "___ Ben Jonson" (inscription on a tomb): 2 wds.
33 Bones of the ankle
37 Hoosegow

494

Across

1 Biblical measure
6 Citadel student
11 Mohawk River city
12 Spanish province or its capital
13 Hold off
14 Dahl, creator of "Fantastic Mr. Fox"
15 It can prevent progress
17 Pet-lover's org.
19 Ring org.
20 Rough rock
21 Possible response to "what happened to the last cookie?": 3 wds.
25 Trouble
26 One or more
27 ____ glance: 2 wds.
28 Wife, slangily
30 Lat., Rus., and Ukr., once
31 Ethnic group of Vietnam
32 Auto about-faces, slangily
33 Football offensive position: 2 wds.
36 Hard rain
37 Building material
40 Sea-fowl dung
41 Covering membranes
42 More even
43 Highly agitated: 2 wds.

Down

1 Cow's chew
2 Tribe for which Salt Lake City's state is named
3 Pair of eyeglasses with two-part lenses
4 Swelling shrinker: 2 wds.
5 Crew members, casually
6 Aquavit flavoring
7 Long-legged shorebird
8 Ring up
9 Fashion periodical
10 Small fry
16 Woman's matching cardigan and pullover sweater
17 Con
18 Toyota hybrids
22 Let go subtly: 2 wds.
23 Modest comment: 2 wds.
24 Soviet news agency
26 IRS employee
29 Moon goddess
30 Ice cream parlor order
33 Disparage
34 ____ de soie (silk cloth)
35 A head
36 ____ Hulka ("Stripes" role)
38 "Breathe" singer Cantrell
39 Clairvoyance, e.g.

495

Across

1 Prefix with scope
6 Lines from the heart?: inits.
9 Online program, informally: 2 wds.
11 Atoll of the Marshall Islands
12 Tooth cover
13 Eight: prefix
14 Debussy piece, "La ___"
15 Disobedient
17 "Gross!" sounds
18 Choice steak
19 Saint-___ (Loire's capital)
20 You can get a charge out of it
23 Diver Louganis
24 Mediterranean capital
26 Anon: 2 wds.
27 Copycat
30 Capital of Georgia
31 Permit
32 Remorseful one
33 Name in the grocery freezer: hyph.
35 Professor's helpers, shortly
36 Signal (a person) with an eyelid: 2 wds.
37 Certain football players, initially
38 Christmas songs

Down

1 "You ___ big time": 2 wds.
2 Extend a subscription
3 Ski tows: hyph.
4 Western omelet ingredient
5 Hunting period: 2 wds.
6 All, without exception: 2 wds.
7 Making an incision
8 Protective sea wall: var.
10 Cornrow
13 Impertinent one
16 Russian space pioneer: 2 wds.
20 Almost real
21 Like some drinks
22 Kind of energy
24 Verging on: 2 wds.
25 Being dragged behind: 2 wds.
27 "Great minds think ___"
28 Foot lever
29 French states
34 River of North Carolina

496

Across

1 1965 PGA champ Dave
5 Bleated
10 Eye part
11 Card game
12 Drugged drink, slangily: 2 wds.
14 Scheduled a slot for: 2 wds.
15 "Quiet down!" sounds
16 Actress Thompson
20 Outcasts
24 Mass. city
25 Greg Evans comic strip
26 Salad green
28 "___ the ramparts ..."
29 Astronaut Deke
31 Actress de Matteo of "The Sopranos"
33 Script ending
34 Pedigree animal of unmixed lineage
39 European epidemic of the 14th century: 2 wds.
41 Fine thread
42 "Como ___ usted?"
43 Port in southern Sweden
44 Actor Julia

Down

1 Producer of "Cordon Rouge" champagne
2 Athletic shoe brand with an arrow in its logo
3 Shipping dept. stamp
4 Earns large sums of money: 2 wds.
5 Characteristic of a male child
6 Radio switch: hyph.
7 Broadway's "___ Irish Rose"
8 Directional ending
9 Cubs play here
13 Patriot Allen and author Canin
17 Assist in crime
18 "Go ahead": 2 wds.
19 Part of N.A.A.C.P.: abbr.
20 Trudge
21 Actor Mischa or violinist Leopold
22 Not cooked very much, like a steak
23 Chicken
27 Microbrewery product: 2 wds.
30 Hid in the shadows
32 "Woman With ___" soap opera: 2 wds.
35 David Geffen School of Medicine site, initially
36 Tabula ___ (blank slate)
37 Accusatory words: 2 wds.
38 Lentil-based Indian dish: var.
39 "Iron John" author Robert ___
40 Lily in Lille

497

Across

1 Move, realtor-style
5 Feature of some people's speech
11 Disagreeable obligation
12 Fast-pitched baseball
13 "___ Anything for Love..." (Meatloaf song): 2 wds.
14 Heavy hammer
15 French law
16 Twofold
17 Leftover
19 Bread served with saag aloo
22 Mode of expression
25 "None for me, thanks": 2 wds.
26 Certain bellybutton
27 Spaced equally apart
29 Grad. degree
30 Arab chieftain: var.
31 Conn Smythe Trophy winners, e.g.
32 Magician's name ending
35 Peninsula between the Persian Gulf and the Red Sea
38 Some submachine guns
39 "Assassination Vacation" writer Sarah
40 Distribute
41 Living: 2 wds.
42 Chick follower?

Down

1 Disquiet
2 Within: prefix
3 Absurd, laughable
4 Bear, in Spain
5 Take for granted
6 Jailhouses, slangily
7 Coca-Cola bottled water brand
8 Former word for former days
9 Opposite of pos.
10 Number after due
16 Small whirlwinds: 2 wds.
18 Indian royal
19 Legally certified, as a contract
20 Opposin'
21 Overseas refusal
22 ___ Piper
23 Mil. command center
24 Guitar forerunner
28 Skewer
31 U.K. honors
33 Evening, informally
34 Words of enlightenment: 2 wds.
35 Prefix with culture
36 Director Howard or former congressman Paul
37 Leave dumbstruck
38 Thurman of "Bel Ami"

498

Across

1. Bucks' mates
5. Actress Cuthbert
11. Southernmost town in Israel: var.
12. Movement
13. Rick's old flame
14. Card game
15. ___ Go, poker tournament with no scheduled starting time: 2 wds.
16. Handle, in France
17. Gymnast's goal
18. Put on clothes
21. Noise from the farm
23. Cathedral area near the ambulatory
24. Gives notice of impending danger
26. ___ Wafers (cookie brand)
27. Clever people
28. "Me, Myself ___" (Beyoncé song): 2 wds.
29. Done by staff members: hyph.
31. Airport search party?
34. Ambulance staffers, for short
35. Biol. energy sources
36. 1972 Jack Lemmon comedy
38. Watch face
39. Some knitted pieces, in Britain
40. Central Sicilian province
41. 1962 movie directed by Howard Hawks
42. Peter and Ray's ghost-busting partner

Down

1. Jefferson was one
2. Lt. Col. North, to friends
3. Compass point at 67.5 degrees: hyph.
4. 1972 Wimbledon winner Smith
5. Go aboard
6. Actor Greene
7. Words that can precede a proverb: 3 wds.
8. Causing violent laughter
9. Slangy motorcycle
10. Hydrocarbon ending
18. Internet protocol, initially
19. Immigrant's course letters
20. Raiding grp.
22. Habitual sleeplessness
24. Major conflict of the 20th century, initially
25. Department of eastern France
26. Austin to Dallas dir.
28. Umbrian hill town
30. Express verbally
32. Joe of "Hill Street Blues"
33. C.S. Lewis's lion
35. Chick's tail?
36. Oberhausen "oh"
37. US radio service, initially

499

Across

1 Cop calls, for short
5 Outfit for baby
11 Onion's kin
12 Inn choice
13 Elastic material from the latex sap of trees: 2 wds.
15 It comes after Feb.
16 Chicago hrs.
17 Urban music genre
18 Methuselah's father
20 Slanted type, casually
22 Mil. workers
23 Earth-friendly prefix
24 For a limited period of time
29 Atoll of the Marshall Islands
30 Golfer Aoki
31 Divert
34 Aesthetic appreciation
35 Own, to a Scot
36 Its H.Q. is the J. Edgar Hoover Building
38 Aviation prefix
39 Sitcom starring Christopher Hewett: 2 wds.
42 Neptune, e.g.: 2 wds.
43 Kyrgyzstan range
44 Shafts shot from bows
45 Riverbed crud

Down

1 Sustenance
2 Voluntary self-punishment
3 Place to sleep
4 Go down a mountain
5 Bobby and Colton
6 Brand with a spinnaker logo
7 Diplomat's office: abbr.
8 Tel Aviv native
9 Best
10 Wild West's Wyatt, Morgan and Virgil
14 German shout
19 TV network created in 1979: hyph.
21 Japanese temple entrance
23 Be off
25 Discharge
26 One hailing from Haifa
27 Sidelong pass
28 Tag line: 2 wds.
31 Protagonist in "The Metamorphosis"
32 HR worker, often
33 Open
34 Be a contender
37 Certain boxer shorts
40 Narcissist's problem
41 Courtroom figs.

500

Across

1 Fancy wheels
5 Joy of daytime TV
10 Academy freshman
12 "Dona Flor and Her Two Husbands" author Jorge
13 Biblical sister city
14 Actress Braga
15 Like films before "The Jazz Singer"
17 Postman's Creed conjunction
18 Call letters?
19 Isabella, por ejemplo
21 Deli breads
23 Hubbubs: hyph.
26 Doughnutlike
28 Food label phrase: 2 wds.
29 Kind of charge listed on a receipt
31 Coffee bean choice
32 Start of a comparison involving a beet: 2 wds.
34 Super Mario Bros. console, for short
35 West end?
37 Come up with
39 Late R&B singer ___ Marie
41 "The Devil Wears ___"
43 Peter and others
44 Like some forest smells
45 Old liquid heaters
46 Miami-___ County

Down

1 Vinyl spinners, for short
2 "I Thought ___" (Miley Cyrus song): 3 wds.
3 Sea between Europe and Africa
4 Ancient Greek coin
5 Projecting part of a fortification
6 Whiny music genre
7 TV character played by Miley Cyrus: 2 wds.
8 "___ piacendo" (Italian for "God willing"): 2 wds.
9 Engine sound
11 Like a 911 call: abbr.
16 Book after Ezra: abbr.
18 College knowledge
20 Cozy corner
22 Prepares to be shot
24 How some drugs are taken: 2 wds.
25 Campus orgs.
27 Buzzard's breakfast?
30 Gen-___ (baby boomer's successor): hyph.
33 "A Faithful Man" costar Lily-Rose
35 Novel extension?
36 Musical interval
38 Dry
40 New Deal agcy.
42 Word of approval

SOLUTIONS

SOLUTIONS

1

```
S W E D I S H ■ S A L
E R N E S T O ■ E S A
V E R M E I L ■ E S C
E N Y O ■ L E V I T Y
■ ■ L E E R A T ■ ■ ■
B E G I N S ■ P N I N
I D O T O ■ D O O N E
Z W E I ■ A I R W A Y
■ S O R B E T ■ ■ ■ ■
C O G N A C ■ R A M S
C T A ■ S O N A N C E
C H G ■ T R O I K A S
L O A ■ A D U L A T E
```

2

```
A S S T S ■ A G A N A
N I C H E ■ O R N O T
S N O R T ■ T O N G A
A N T I T H E S I S ■
■ ■ ■ F E T A S ■ ■ ■
G R A T E S ■ E S A S
A A S ■ ■ ■ ■ ■ A V E
S E E S ■ S P R E A D
■ ■ ■ C H I L I ■ ■ ■
■ A C R O B A T I C S
P A C E R ■ S U N R A
A R L E S ■ M A D A M
S E I N E ■ A L O N E
```

3

```
L E S H ■ ■ D A T E
I N C U R ■ L E A R S
P L E B E ■ O A R E D
■ ■ N R A ■ O N O S ■
■ S T I C K M E N ■ ■
A P O S T L E ■ S R S
P U F ■ I E D ■ P H I
A N A ■ O I L S E E D
■ ■ W I N N A B L E ■
■ T O G A ■ R A L ■
T I M O R ■ G R I P S
S L A T Y ■ E R N S T
A T N O ■ ■ O G P U
```

4

```
A R I S T A ■ I F N I
M O T I O N ■ D O E S
C H O L E S T E R O L
S E R I N ■ S A E N S
■ ■ ■ C A P E L L A ■
U N F A I R ■ S I T N
N O U ■ L A B ■ M A E
H T T P ■ D O U B L Y
■ S U L T A N S ■ ■
M O R A Y ■ F E R D E
T H I N S K I N N E D
N O S E ■ G R E A S E
S T M T ■ S E T S I N
```

5

```
A U D I T   ■   H E E P
E X O T I C   ■ A C R A
R O M A N O   ■ R H E O
O R O N ■ C I D ■
■ ■ ■ ■ O S C A R ■
A B C S ■ N A O M I S
D U A L P U R P O S E
M Y F O O T ■ Y N E Z
■ S E W U P ■ ■
■ ■ P T A ■ O B I E
E R N O ■ L I V E T V
H O C K ■ M E A N I E
S I R E ■ R L E S S
```

6

```
U S M C   ■   M S N B C
H E N R I   ■ C E I B A
O G E E S   ■ R A G O N
H O M E O P A T H Y
■ ■ ■ B E E B
R A I L A T ■ E T U I
R O B E R T P L A N T
S L O T ■ I A T E I T
■ ■ S I S S
■ B I R T H S T O N E
M A R I S ■ E S N E S
G L A D S ■ S P U R T
M I N E O ■ S P F S
```

7

```
C A F E   ■   A C R I D
O L I N ■ A D R A T E
M A R V ■ T O O F A R
O N E I ■ T R S ■
■ B R A I N S T E M
H E R O I C ■ E A S T
E D E N S ■ A X M A N
E D A M ■ O K A P I S
P O K E R G A M E ■
■ N O I ■ I R M A
T H A T L L ■ N E E D
B E F A L L ■ E R L E
S T I L E ■ D S O S
```

8

```
N T S B   ■   P I T T S
H I E R O ■ I C E I T
L A V A L ■ N I L L A
■ E C A S H ■ E E G
G S N ■ S T E E P ■
R A Y E ■ P A T H O S
A L E T A ■ D R O N E
U S A U S A ■ E T I C
■ R I P E N ■ O N T
M A I ■ I F E L L
A L T A R ■ C U E I N
R I C C I ■ K I N T E
G A H A N ■ S S N S
```

SOLUTIONS

9

R	O	R	E	M		A	B	E	D	
E	N	A	M	I		U	R	N	E	
C	U	M	U	L	A	T	I	V	E	
S	S	A		L	E	R	O	I		
			M	I	R	E		R	Y	A
B	O	T	A	N	Y		L	O	E	B
C	L	A	N	G		D	I	N	A	R
A	G	I	N		M	O	E	S	H	A
R	A	L		O	U	R	S			
		C	E	N	T	I		T	D	S
	P	O	C	K	E	T	B	O	O	K
	B	A	T	E		O	L	D	I	E
	A	T	O	Y		S	T	O	N	E

10

S	P	I	E	S				T	M	S
V	A	C	A	T	E		D	E	C	I
E	P	H	R	O	N		I	N	N	E
L	U	I	S		G	A	R	D	E	N
T	A	R	P		S	E	T	A	N	
E	N	O	L		N	I	C	O	L	A
			I	D	E	S	T			
D	U	S	T	U	P		S	N	O	G
O	N	E	T	O		P	A	I	R	
U	P	R	I	S	E		E	U	L	A
B	L	I	N		D	O	E	S	I	N
L	U	N	G		E	X	C	E	E	D
E	G	S				O	H	A	R	E

11

	H	A	L	M	A		L	A	D	
A	N	A	L	O	G	Y		A	R	I
T	A	R	T	A	R	S	A	U	C	E
O	D	E	O	N	S		D	R	A	T
L	I	M	N		R	U	E	D	E	
L	A	S		S	P	E	L	L	E	R
			F	L	E	E	T			
S	O	F	A	R	A	S		G	I	P
U	G	L	I	S			W	E	R	E
B	L	U	R		O	M	A	N	I	S
S	A	F	E	T	Y	F	I	R	S	T
E	L	F		H	E	A	V	E	H	O
T	A	Y		A	S	S	E	S		

12

I	C	I	L	Y		P	L	A	N	E
S	O	F	I	E		A	O	T	E	A
M	I	S	B	E	G	O	T	T	E	N
S	L	O	E		E	L	S			
			R	A	D	I	A	T	O	R
S	T	A	T	U	S			O	O	O
C	A	R	Y	S		O	D	O	R	S
U	R	I		S	M	I	T	T	Y	
D	O	L	D	R	U	M	S			
		A	U	D		H	I	S	S	
P	R	O	V	I	S	I	O	N	A	L
P	A	L	I	N		G	U	T	S	Y
P	S	S	T	S		A	T	R	E	E

SOLUTIONS

13

	T	M	A	N		C	A	P	E	S
B	E	A	D	S		A	T	A	L	E
A	R	R	A	Y		S	E	T	O	N
D	R	I		N	E	A		H	I	S
G	O	S		C	A	B		O	S	O
E	R	A	S		S	A	S	S	E	R
			I	D	E	S	T			
H	A	N	D	E	D		P	E	A	R
O	E	O		P	U	M		E	R	E
T	R	S		R	P	I		L	E	M
T	I	T	L	E		S	P	I	T	E
E	A	R	P	S		S	K	E	E	T
A	L	A	N	S			M	G	R	S	

14

T	U	B	S			T	I	N	E	D
E	N	L	A	I		U	S	A	G	E
P	R	O	B	L	E	M	A	T	I	C
I	O	U		L	V	I		U	S	O
D	L	S		I	E	D		R	E	C
	L	E	A	N	N		G	E	S	T
			T	I	T	A	N			
S	C	A	T		U	N	P	E	G	
H	O	G		A	A	S		N	A	H
A	L	A		M	T	A		D	U	I
P	A	S	T	P	E	R	F	E	C	T
E	D	S	E	L		I	D	A	H	O
D	A	I	S	Y			A	R	O	N

15

L	E	E		R	R	S			
E	L	N	I	N	O	S		B	P	S
S	A	F	F	R	O	N		L	E	U
L	I	R	A		F	S	T	O	P	S
E	N	A	T	E		R	O	S	A	
Y	E	N		L	I	V	E	D	I	N
		C	A	S	S	A	T	T	
A	T	H	W	A	R	T		H	E	B
M	A	I	O		S	L	I	M	E
M	I	S	L	A	Y		A	R	C	A
O	T	E		B	R	O	W	S	E	R
S	O	D		B	L	A	S	T	E	D
		A	Y	R		Y	D	S	

16

Z	A	G	A	T		A	S	P	C	A
S	T	O	L	I		R	E	H	A	B
A	L	L	O	T		M	A	Y	B	E
	D	O	O	D	Y		L	S	T	
F	I	E	F		O	B	O	L		
I	T	N		G	A	R	N	I	S	H
F	E	W	E	R		A	S	S	N	S
I	N	E	X	A	C	T		D	O	I
	D	E	F	S		N	I	T	A	
M	A	D		F	I	N	A	L		
A	L	I	B	I		C	A	L	V	E
R	A	N	A	T		O	C	E	A	N
G	I	G	L	I		S	P	R	I	G

17

T	I	N	H	A	T	■	C	U	P	S
A	D	H	E	R	E	■	O	N	I	T
E	E	L	I	E	R	■	R	O	T	E
■	■	N	O	N	U	R	B	A	N	■
T	R	A	I	L	■	B	A	L	■	■
M	E	L	E	E	■	I	L	I	U	M
A	D	M	■	■	■	■	■	G	S	O
N	A	S	T	Y	■	O	R	E	C	K
■	H	A	R	■	H	E	D	G	E	■
N	E	O	N	S	I	G	N	■	■	■
A	R	U	N	■	N	O	E	S	I	S
N	I	S	I	■	T	S	G	A	R	P
S	E	E	N	■	S	H	E	E	S	H

18

N	E	S	T	■	M	E	S	A	■
U	S	U	A	L	■	A	R	E	C	A
T	H	R	E	E	■	R	O	W	E	R
R	A	R	■	A	R	K	■	I	T	T
I	R	E	■	D	E	K	■	N	O	I
A	P	P	L	■	W	A	G	G	L	E
■	T	A	K	E	A	I	M	■		
O	R	I	A	N	A	■	F	A	R	M
P	O	T	■	O	V	A	■	C	E	O
C	S	I	■	C	E	L	■	H	A	D
I	T	O	O	K	■	I	T	I	S	I
T	R	U	R	O	■	S	O	N	O	F
■	A	S	I	N	■	E	E	N	Y	

19

S	E	D	■	I	M	A	■	C	O	G
T	R	U	■	S	E	V	■	O	P	A
P	E	S	■	I	D	O	■	M	E	L
A	S	T	A	T	I	C	■	M	R	E
U	T	I	L	I	T	A	R	I	A	N
L	U	N	K	■	E	D	E	S	S	A
■	■	H	A	D	R	O	N	S	■	
C	O	O	L	E	R	■	N	I	P	A
E	F	F	I	C	A	C	I	O	U	S
I	N	F	■	I	N	T	E	N	T	S
L	O	M	■	D	E	R	■	E	O	E
E	T	A	■	E	A	L	■	R	U	T
D	E	N	■	D	N	S	■	S	T	S

20

G	O	G	H	■	M	U	T	E	R
I	D	E	O	■	S	I	N	G	E	R
L	I	N	T	■	I	N	E	V	E	R
D	E	T	R	I	T	U	S	■		
■	L	O	W	N	E	C	K	E	D
A	L	E	D	O	■	T	O	A	D	Y
D	A	M	■	■	■	R	E	E	
I	N	A	I	D	■	O	V	A	L	S
N	A	N	N	Y	G	O	A	T	■
■	I	S	O	P	R	E	N	E	
A	V	A	T	A	R	■	I	K	E	A
R	E	W	I	R	E	■	E	I	N	S
B	E	S	O	T	■	D	D	A	Y	

SOLUTIONS

21

22

23

24

25

P	H	O		P	I	N				
C	O	N	C	I	S	E		C	A	R
B	R	E	W	P	U	B		O	D	O
		U	T	E	P		C	M	D	R
D	I	P	S	O		R	E	P	L	Y
U	N	M		R	H	O	D	A		
E	V	A	N	G	E	L	I	C	A	L
	N	E	A	L	E		T	A	G	
A	R	S	O	N		M	A	D	R	E
C	A	H	N		C	O	S	I		
R	P	I		R	I	D	E	S	B	Y
Y	A	P		T	R	E	A	C	L	E
		S	O	L		S	Y	R		

26

F	A	Q	S			A	M	M	O
A	L	U	L	A		S	M	E	A	R
T	I	E	R	S		T	U	T	T	I
I	S	S		H	Y	D	R	A	T	E
M	O	T		O	M	S		M	E	L
A	N	I	T	R	A		H	O	D	S
	O	B	E		N	O	R		
R	E	N	A		C	O	W	P	E	A
E	A	N		K	A	S		H	M	M
B	R	A	V	A	D	O		O	P	P
U	N	I	A	T		A	I	S	L	E
F	E	R	N	S		P	R	I	O	R
F	R	E	E			A	S	Y	E	

27

I	B	E		M	E	A		
S	A	N	D	M	A	N		M	R	E
E	D	G	I	E	S	T		I	A	T
E	U	L	A		T	R	I	S	T	E
	I	N	A	S	E	N	S	E	
H	A	S	A	G	O		U	S	D	A
E	D	H		T	U	T		U	P	A
N	E	H	I		T	W	I	N	G	E
	P	O	T	S	H	O	T	S	
A	T	R	A	C	E		S	H	M	O
O	L	N		R	A	I	N	I	E	R
L	Y	S		O	S	M	O	N	D	S
		D	T	S		E	E	O	

28

B	E	E	F			A	N	G	E	L
A	R	A	L		I	D	I	O	C	Y
R	O	T	E		N	O	N	E	T	S
B	O	A	C		O	R	E	S		
		H	Y	P	N	O	S	I	S	
A	N	T	E	U	P		F	L	A	T
T	O	A		L	O	B		O	M	A
N	A	T	S		R	A	H	W	A	Y
O	M	E	L	E	T	T	E		
		R	E	N	U		R	A	I	L
O	P	T	I	O	N		N	U	M	B
G	O	O	G	L	E		I	D	E	O
S	E	T	H	S		A	I	D	S	

517

SOLUTIONS

29

A	N	C	E	■	■	■	A	P	A	R
L	O	O	N	S	■	T	R	A	L	A
P	R	M	A	N	■	W	O	R	L	D
H	A	P	■	Y	M	A	■	K	I	A
A	I	L	■	D	O	S	S	I	E	R
■	N	I	S	E	I	■	E	N	D	■
■	M	O	R	S	E	L	S	■	■	
■	R	E	N	■	T	A	L	O	S	
S	E	N	O	R	E	S	■	N	E	C
E	D	T	■	A	N	Y	■	S	V	U
L	E	A	N	T	■	A	O	L	E	R
E	A	R	L	E	■	S	N	A	R	L
S	L	Y	E	■	■	E	W	E	S	

30

J	C	T	■	E	M	O	■	I	C	C
P	A	R	A	S	O	L	■	R	O	H
A	M	I	L	A	T	E	■	A	N	O
U	P	P	I	S	H	■	U	N	C	O
L	Y	E	S	■	E	Y	R	I	E	S
■	■	■	C	R	U	S	A	D	E	
N	O	V	O	C	A	I	N	E	■	
V	E	N	I	S	O	N	■	■	■	
E	R	E	S	T	U	■	I	S	P	S
I	D	L	E	■	R	U	N	L	E	T
L	I	E	■	C	A	N	T	A	T	A
E	E	S	■	O	G	I	L	V	I	E
D	R	S	■	R	E	V	■	S	T	L

31

C	U	L	P	■	D	O	O	W	O	P
A	M	E	R	■	O	F	L	A	T	E
S	M	O	O	T	H	F	A	C	E	D
H	A	I	F	A	■	A	S	S	A	I
■	■	A	P	A	L	■	■	■		
D	A	R	N	E	D	■	A	S	E	S
A	F	T	E	R	E	F	F	E	C	T
M	I	E	S	■	L	E	F	T	O	N
■	■	R	A	V	I	■	■	■		
A	M	I	N	E	■	E	N	G	E	L
G	U	N	C	A	R	R	I	A	G	E
A	N	T	I	C	S	■	T	I	E	A
R	O	O	S	T	S	■	Y	A	R	D

32

S	E	W	O	N	■	A	P	H	I	D
E	L	E	N	A	■	L	I	A	N	E
A	L	D	E	N	■	M	T	I	D	A
M	I	D	I	S	■	S	A	L	U	D
U	P	I	N	■	■	P	E	E	S	
S	S	N	■	E	Z	R	A	S	■	
■	E	G	G	B	E	A	T	E	R	
■	S	O	B	E	R	■	L	E	B	
F	A	H	D	■	■	M	A	C	E	
I	L	O	S	E	■	L	I	S	L	E
R	E	W	E	T	■	I	N	S	U	M
S	T	E	N	T	■	N	O	I	S	E
T	A	R	D	E	■	T	R	E	E	R

SOLUTIONS

33

```
C A R B   D O C T O R
C L E O   A L U M N A
S A A B   R E T I E S
  E M B A R G O
    E L H I   F D I C
F A D E I N   F E T A
I L O         F O N
F L U E   R E C E N T
E S T E   E M E R
    N O S I R E E
C E S S N A   I N M E
D E N I A L   S C A M
S E L E N E   E E G S
```

34

```
L A P D   S P A I N
I R A E   A L A N A
C O R N S T A R C H
K N I T T I N G
      A R R   H R A P
B O W T I E S   I L A
A N E E D   T C E L L
B E S   E S P O U S E
S I T H   L E M
      E S O T E R I C
  G A R A G E S A L E
  A R E N A   A R K S
  B A S I N   T E S T
```

35

```
  E M I L   O M S K
E D I N A   A R A C E
T E N T H   M U N R O
N N E   T A R   Y A K
A I R   I N I   S M U
S C A N   A T R I S K
    L O W L A N D
T A W D R Y   S E C T
I M A   E Z R   D R E
P E T   N E A   N O P
O L E I C   R E E C E
F I R T H   E N S U E
F E S T   D O S S
```

36

```
R A P A   A D D S U P
B U R P   D E M O T E
I R O N   A C C R U E
    C O S M O   T R L
F R E E T V   A N E
C H E A P I E
C O D   A N S   T U A
      T A K E O F F
N E T   T E R R O R
E X O   F I R E S
W A S H O E   N I M S
M L C A R R   O O O H
E T A L I I   W N B A
```

SOLUTIONS

37

```
    S T A N   G I P
  A T A S T E   N N E
P R I C K L Y P E A R
I T E R S     O I N K
L O G E   T A R S E S
E O S   H O N E S T
    K U D O S
  C A I M A N   M E A
P A R L E Y   D E L L
O M E N     L E A V E
L E N S G R I N D E R
K O D   E R N I E S
A N T   D R Y S
```

38

```
W I G H T   H E E D S
O T R A S   A M A R E
O S O L E   U P S E T
F S U   L A T   Y A T
S O N   I D E   O M E
    D R O Z   I N O R
  I C E T   S I T N
I D O L   M E S H
M S N   L O C   E S D
G A T   A B U   E P I
L Y R I C   L A Y E R
A N O S E   A S E A T
D O L L Y   R I S K Y
```

39

```
P A S S G O   U S O S
R E T A I N   N C A A
A R A B L E   Z A H N
Y O N   T M I N U S
    D O O W O P
C R I M S O N   S W A
I S N E W   G H E E S
R T S   E L E G A N T
    U G A R T E
W I N N O W   A D M
I T O R   F O R G E S
M A G I   U N P L U G
P L O P   L A M E S T
```

40

```
P D F S   R H E T O R
A B L E   O O L A L A
C L U B   U P S I D E
E S C E   N E E
    T R O D   S O A P
D O U G H T Y   B R R
O N A   O H O   V I I
C O T   H E R O I S M
E N E S   C E N O
    H E L   E U R O
A R T U R O   E S E S
L A C T I C   A L I T
G O B A C K   R Y N E
```

SOLUTIONS

41

O	E	D	S		W	E	B	C	A	M
S	H	I	H		A	T	O	D	D	S
E	S	S	E		R	A	M	R	O	D
		T	E	A	M		B	O	B	O
C	L	U	T	C	H		A	M	E	S
M	I	R		C	E	E	S			
S	U	B	S	T	A	N	T	I	A	L
		S	S	R	S		R	P	I	
G	O	G	H		T	U	C	K	I	N
U	L	N	A		E	E	L	S		
I	S	O	P	O	D		I	O	N	A
R	E	T	E	L	L		O	M	A	R
O	N	E	D	A	Y		S	E	P	S

42

S	T	I	E	B				M	A	W
P	O	R	T	I	O	N		E	R	A
O	N	E	A	C	R	E		D	O	R
O	E	N		Y	T	T	R	I	U	M
F	R	E	N	C	H	T	O	A	S	T
		F	L	O		U	T	A	H	
	R	U	L	E		A	B	E	L	
S	A	N	E		S	I	L			
M	I	C	R	O	C	R	E	D	I	T
A	S	I	S	A	I	D		R	N	A
R	E	V		F	O	R	S	A	K	E
M	R	I		S	N	O	R	K	E	L
Y	S	L			P	I	E	R	S	

43

A	R	G	O		S	I	G	E	P	
D	O	O	N		U	R	I	E	L	
H	U	L	L	A	B	A	L	O	O	
D	E	F	O	R	M	E	D			
			A	N	I		E	N	E	S
G	A	N	N	E	T		D	E	M	O
A	N	O					E	M	I	
E	D	E	R		P	A	L	T	E	R
D	A	L	I		A	S	E			
			N	E	W	S	T	Y	L	E
M	A	G	I	S	T	R	A	T	E	
A	R	E	N	A		I	L	R	E	
W	O	R	S	T		P	U	S	S	

44

S	O	B	A		I	M	A	R	E	T
H	E	A	T		M	O	L	A	R	S
I	N	C	R		P	R	Y	N	N	E
H	O	K	I	N	E	S	S			
		B	U	R	L	E	S	Q	U	E
A	N	I	M	A		L	A	U	R	A
T	I	T					A	D	V	
O	D	E	S	A		V	A	G	U	E
Z	I	R	C	O	N	I	U	M		
		A	R	T	E	R	I	A	L	
S	V	E	L	T	E		O	R	M	E
C	U	T	E	A	S		R	E	A	M
H	E	A	R	S	T		A	S	P	S

SOLUTIONS

45

```
U M S . . E N T O M B
P O E M . M O A N E R
C O P A . E T H A N S
S T U P O R . . . . .
. . L U R I D . H B O
T A C T I L E . E A L
S C H O O L B O A R D
O R E . L A U N D R Y
S E R . E G G E D . .
. . . A S T R U D . .
P H A S E S . O E N O
B A L E R S . N S E C
R E F I N E . . S S S
```

46

```
. . . S L A M . . . .
P I C K U P S . D I L
O D O A C E R . O N O
L I N T . S P I G O T
L E V E E . . N C I S
O D E . L A S C A L A
. . R A M P A R T . .
E N T R O P Y . C R T
R E I N . . A C H O O
I M B E A T . R E A M
C E L . B I Z A R R E
H A E . B R E W S K I
. . . R E E L . . . .
```

47

```
O L A F . . M A D A T
L E N O . S E R I E S
A S T R . W A R A C E
. S E A S I D E . . .
. . N Y E S . S A G A
A B A S E S . T U R F
F A T . P C P . D E R
B R A M . H A S A G O
S O L E . E L E C . .
. . . A S E P T I C .
P O I N T S . T O A N
E N T I R E . L U R E
G A T E S . . E S P Y
```

48

```
H D T V . . . S G T S
A I R E . M I N E O S
N O O R . O M E R T A
A R I M A T H E A . .
. . . O R E O . N H A
F L A U N T . P I E T
L E D T O . J O U S T
E V A H . P E N M A N
W O P . E A S Y . . .
. . T U T T U T T E D
A K I T A S . A U R A
L O V E L Y . I N D S
P R E S . . . L E A H
```

SOLUTIONS

49

A	F	T	R	A		K	C	A	R	S
L	I	E	I	N		E	A	S	E	L
I	D	L	E	S		E	S	S	I	E
N	E	A	L	E		P	S	A	N	D
E	L	M	S			D	I	M	E	S
D	I	O		C	M	O	N			
	O	N	T	H	E	W	I	N	G	
		H	O	R	N		A	O	L	
H	O	M	E	O			U	V	E	A
E	N	I	A	C		G	R	A	S	P
B	E	R	T	H		H	A	H	A	S
E	N	E	R	O		E	L	O	P	E
R	O	D	E	O		E	S	S	E	S

50

B	R	A	G	G		S	W	A	I	N
L	E	G	A	L		I	A	M	S	O
E	V	E	N	I	N	G	S	T	A	R
B	S	S		B	E	N		S	O	W
		O	L	E	A	N				
N	E	R	V	Y		L	E	T	U	P
A	L	A	E			O	O	N	A	
Y	A	L	T	A		S	N	O	U	T
		T	R	O	T	S				
S	L	R		C	D	E		L	A	X
W	E	A	T	H	E	R	C	O	C	K
U	N	D	U	E		O	F	P	I	E
M	O	O	E	D		L	O	E	S	S

51

R	A	C	E		E	D	Y	S	
E	L	O	P	E		B	O	O	T	S
H	U	M	A	N	N	A	T	U	R	E
E	L	I		G	E	N	E	R	I	C
M	A	N	T	R	A		E	A	T	
	G	E	O	R	G		A	T	O	
S	A	F	E	S		R	I	D	E	R
C	R	O		S	P	A	S	M		
A	E	R		I	N	S	Y	N	C	
L	O	W	E	R	E	D		M	O	O
P	L	A	N	E	T	A	R	I	U	M
S	A	R	D	I		M	E	N	S	A
	E	D	E	N		I	D	E	S	

52

N	S	W		C	C	I		B	O	S
A	I	R		O	Y	S	T	E	R	S
S	T	E	A	M	B	O	I	L	E	R
I	N	T	O	T	O		D	S	O	S
		C	L	E	R	G	Y			
I	S	H		G	L	U	E	O	N	
R	U	E	H	L		O	P	A	R	T
V	I	D	E	O	S		S	C	H	
		I	M	E	A	N	T			
E	M	A	G		U	N	C	L	A	D
W	A	S	H	E	R	D	R	Y	E	R
O	N	A	T	E	A	R		M	O	E
K	A	N		E	T	E		E	N	A

523

SOLUTIONS

53

```
S O F T G . . P A I N
R H E I M S . A T I E
S O R D I D . C E N O
. R E N A M E . .
S S E . O K A . I I S
M I T E R . D O N H O
E L O N . . E C O L
L A U D E . A D O P T
L S T . T A N . S E I
. . E S C O R T .
C H E R . I M P U T E
T O Y A . D I M M E D
N E E T . . A S E E D
```

54

```
O A K . M R E . A T C
G M A . A O L . P O L
P E T E R C O Y O T E
U N M A S K . E C H O
. A P H I D S .
P E N . N A N T E S
U N D E R G R O W T H
F O U R T H . I D A
. I S O G O N .
I E S T . R E A C T S
R E Q U I S I T I O N
M E M . R E C . T R A
A S I . E S O . Y A P
```

55

```
I N S P . O C C U R S
H O U R . S O O N E R
O T R A . S Y R U P S
P A V I L I O N .
. E S T A T E C A R
H A Y E D . E T A G E
I D I . N A B
Y E N T L . O P A L S
A N G U I S H E D .
. S E E S P A S T
A L Y S S A . P D A S
R E E L I N . E R N O
A T H E N S . R Y E S
```

56

```
S T M T . E L C I D
T R O O P . K A Z O O
U L T R A . E W E L L
. H O H O S . C A T
I T E . S L O S H .
T A R N . N U T R I A
I N C O G . T E E N S
S K O A L S . S P A Y
. U H U R U . U S E
L M N . E S T A B .
O P T E D . I L L G O
L A R G O . L A I N G
L A Y O N . E C U S
```

SOLUTIONS

57

```
I M P . P C S . . .
N E A . E L E C T E E
A R T . P R E P A R E
C I R C A . P A P A L
A N O A . . . S E S E
B O N S O I R . R E D
. S T A T U R E . .
O M A . F I N I C K Y
H E I S . . . F O I E
Y E N T E . V E R S A
E S T E L L E . D S S
S E S S I O N . E M T
. . E D D . R E Y .
```

58

```
S A N A A . A C T I I
A L E C S . T R I E D
S P I C A . H O R A E
S O N O M A . S E T A
. . M I M I S . .
F O A M . B R E A S T
A L C O A . E X C E L
N E E D T O . A S E C
. . A T E A M . .
U S D T . D E I C E R
S P O I L . T N O T E
M A K O S . N E A T O
A N E N T . A R L E S
```

59

```
E D M . P A R . . .
F A O . D R E . S P F
F I R E F I G H T E R
O M N E S . T A R T E
R O I L . . V O I D
T N N . A T E I N T O
. . G I N S E N G .
A N G L E R S . B M I
P O L I . . T R A C
A B O A T . P A E S E
C I R C U M S P E C T
E D Y . N M I . Z O E
. . E D S . E T A
```

60

```
A R I L S . P A T E N
B O N E T . C O R G I
M E T O O . S K E A N
. H S I A . S A D E
O D E . C A V . S S R
M O S S . R E N U .
M I A T A . R E R I G
. M E Z E . P E K E
M R E . T N T . T O T
T I V O . O H E R .
I F E A R . A D O O R
D L I S T . N I V E N
Y E N T E . T E E N S
```

SOLUTIONS

61

```
D E B S █ U L S T E R
E L A T █ M A L A D Y
P L A I N S P O K E N
P E S C I █ S T A R E
█ █ K L E E █ █ █ █ █
S T A P L E █ J I B E
V I V I A N V A N C E
U P I N █ S I L V E R
█ █ N Y R O █ █ █ █ █
E M P T Y █ T U L I P
D I S I L L U S I O N
O R A T O R █ I B L E
M E T I N G █ E S A U
```

62

```
B A S R A █ D C C A B
P R O E M █ R O O M S
M E A T Y █ I O N I A
█ █ P O L L E E █ █ █
B O B O █ O D E S A █
O H O K █ O U S T E D
A I X █ A S P █ A S I
C O E R C E █ L Y O N
█ U S U A L █ I S P S
█ █ I D Y L L S █ █ █
D O O N E █ P I A N O
X Y L E M █ G E N I C
I L E D E █ A S E E D
```

63

```
B O G L E █ E A S T S
O N Y O U █ N T E S T
M E M O R Y C H I P S
B A N K █ E S O █ █ █
█ A S A S █ L E M A █
A S S E R T S █ L O P
B R I E F █ I D A R E
A A U █ S H O E B O X
A S M Y █ I N N O █ █
█ █ O W L █ T R E X █
Y A C K E T Y Y A C K
O N S E T █ O N T H E
D I A L S █ M E E T S
```

64

```
B O A █ █ E T A S █
O R I B I █ N O L T E
T E R R E S T R I A L
█ █ B E A K █ P A B A
H E A R T I N E S S █
I C S █ M A D █ █ █ █
C H E C K █ B O O E R
█ █ H A Y █ N G O █ █
█ P L A T E G L A S S
U T E S █ G R E W █ █
P R O T A G O N I S T
C A R E T █ K O R E A
█ P A N T █ █ E A L █
```

SOLUTIONS

65

K	L	I	E	G		H	A	U	T	
L	A	R	U	E		M	U	S	H	
U	N	O	R	T	H	O	D	O	X	
M	E	N			S	I	S	I		
		O	O	F		O	K	I	E	
T	E	L	A	V	I	V		I	L	S
W	R	I	T	E		A	R	L	E	S
I	D	O		R	A	N	I	N	T	O
N	A	N	U		U	G	A			
		P	N	E	U		R	A	W	
	L	A	B	O	R	A	T	O	R	Y
	B	P	O	E		R	A	M	I	E
	J	O	W	L		D	R	O	P	S

66

S	P	A	S	M		I	M	I	N	E
T	A	B	O	O		N	O	N	O	S
A	R	R	A	U		A	L	F	R	E
G	R	A	S	S	W	I	D	O	W	
		T	S	A	D	E				
G	I	J	O	E	S		R	O	O	K
O	D	A					H	O	E	
O	I	L	Y		O	S	S	I	F	Y
		E	D	A	T	E				
	D	O	O	R	K	E	E	P	E	R
W	I	L	M	A		N	T	E	S	T
T	R	E	A	T		C	H	A	S	E
S	T	A	N	S		H	E	R	O	S

67

N	K	G	B		S	A	G	G	E	D
G	U	R	U		T	U	F	T	E	D
O	N	O	R		O	T	O	O	L	E
	U	S	U	R	E	R				
	I	N	A	S	M	U	C	H	A	S
E	M	D	E	N		R	E	A	T	A
R	A	H				L	T	D		
E	R	O	S	E		O	F	F	E	R
B	I	G	B	A	D	J	O	H	N	
		A	R	E	O	L	A			
S	T	E	R	N	A		D	R	A	G
H	A	T	R	E	D		E	D	H	S
S	P	O	O	R	S		R	Y	A	N

68

L	L	B	S		S	L	O	U	G	H
I	E	A	T		P	O	P	A	R	T
F	I	L	A		O	A	T	E	R	S
E	A	S	T	S	I	D	E			
		U	A	L		D	A	T	S	
H	O	S	T	E	S	S		M	R	E
A	R	L	E	N		L	I	B	E	L
A	E	R		S	P	A	N	I	E	L
S	O	S	A		R	I	T			
		A	S	O	N	E	M	A	N	
S	A	L	L	O	W		A	U	T	O
T	H	E	T	A	S		R	S	T	U
R	I	B	O	S	E		S	H	A	N

SOLUTIONS

69

S	C	U	B	A			D	A	U	B
N	O	P	R	O	B		O	L	G	A
I	L	L	I	N	I		E	G	A	L
D	O	I		E	R	A	S	E		
E	N	T	E		D	R	A	B	L	Y
		A	S	W	E		R	A	T	
S	U	B	S	T	A	N	D	A	R	D
O	R	L		E	T	A	T			
S	E	A	T	A	C		S	A	W	N
	D	E	L	H	I		M	H	O	
I	N	D	C		E	D	G	E	O	F
A	C	E	H		R	A	M	B	L	E
T	O	R	S			S	C	A	L	E

70

D	A	C	C	A		S	A	A	B	
O	R	A	L	B		E	M	M	Y	S
S	A	Y	A	H		L	A	U	R	A
A	R	E	Y	O	U		T	S	O	S
G	A	N		R	N	S		E	T	S
E	T	N	A		C	L	I	M	E	
	E	M	B	R	A	C	E			
	S	P	I	R	O		I	N	D	S
S	H	E		S	S	E		T	O	I
A	R	P	S		S	L	I	P	O	N
D	O	P	E	S		E	V	A	D	E
R	U	E	R	S		M	A	R	L	A
	D	R	E	W		I	N	K	E	D

71

T	H	I	S	I		I	M	H	O	T
B	U	T	T	S		T	E	A	M	O
A	L	E	U	T		A	T	R	I	P
R	U	M	B	L	E	S	E	A	T	
		B	E	A	C	O	N			
O	A	T	Y		S	A	R	G	E	S
M	N	O				U	R	L		
M	A	N	U	A	L		A	E	R	Y
	E	R	N	E	S	T				
	U	P	S	I	D	E	D	O	W	N
A	L	O	U	S		T	A	N	Y	A
P	E	E	L	E		A	W	O	L	S
B	E	M	A	S		E	N	N	E	A

72

A	N	I	L	S		C	A	N	S	O
N	O	F	E	E		A	H	E	M	S
G	R	O	U	N	D	S	H	E	E	T
I	T	N		N	E	T		D	L	I
N	O	L		A	T	L	A	N	T	A
A	N	Y	A		R	E	I	T	S	
		D	E	I	S	M				
	S	P	A	S	M		S	U	C	H
F	A	I	R	I	E	S		L	O	U
I	S	E		A	N	E		T	N	N
C	H	R	I	S	T	E	N	I	N	G
H	A	R	P	O		R	O	M	E	O
E	Y	E	O	N		S	H	O	R	N

SOLUTIONS

73

I	F	S	O		W	O	W	S	
M	I	T	A		E	R	A	T	O
B	R	U	S	H	S	T	R	O	K	E
A	A	R		E	T	H		M	A	N
D	R	M	A	R	I	O		A	F	T
		C	R	E	D	I	T	O	R
C	A	P	R	I		O	V	A	R	Y
O	N	E	O	N	O	N	E	
L	O	T		G	U	T	S	I	E	R
I	P	A		G	T	I		M	N	O
C	I	R	C	U	L	A	R	S	A	W
	A	D	D	L	E		B	E	M	A
	S	I	L	T		I	T	I	N

74

A	B	A	T		A	F	F	O	R	D
T	I	N	Y		T	U	R	N	E	R
N	E	A	L		F	L	O	S	S	Y
O	N	D	E			L	S	T	
			N	O	R	T	H	R	O	P
	A	D	O	N	A	I		I	K	O
B	O	I	L	E	R	M	A	K	E	R
C	U	S		S	E	E	D	E	D	
S	T	P	I	E	R	R	E	
	A	T	A			L	R	O	N
P	O	T	A	T	O		P	A	C	A
E	C	C	L	E	S		H	D	T	V
A	S	H	O	R	E		I	S	A	Y

75

R	A	R	A		E	C	A	R	D
E	X	A	M		M	O	V	I	E
C	I	R	C	U	M	V	E	N	T
T	O	E		P	E	E	R	
I	M	E	A	N	T		S	D	A	K
		A	R	E	T	O		E	D	E
X	E	R	O	X		C	A	T	E	R
I	R	T		T	U	L	L	E	
N	E	H	I		N	O	P	R	O	B
		M	A	S	C		R	I	A
	D	E	A	T	H	K	N	E	L	L
	L	E	G	T	O		E	N	O	L
	S	N	E	A	D		C	T	N	S

76

A	S	U		A	I	M	
R	M	N		S	D	S		C	R	T
M	O	S		S	E	N	O	R	E	S
P	O	C	O	N	O		L	E	T	A
I	T	I	N			O	N	E	A	D
T	H	E	C	E	L	L		P	R	E
		N	E	X	T	D	A	Y	
A	P	T		T	R	E	A	C	L	E
L	A	I	R	S			A	R	I	A
A	G	F	A		I	S	A	A	C	S
M	A	I	N	M	A	N		W	H	Y
E	N	C		I	G	O		L	E	A
			S	O	B		Y	E	S

529

SOLUTIONS

77

F	E	H	■	I	M	F	■	T	B	A
B	L	A	R	N	E	Y	■	Y	A	N
I	M	P	A	S	S	I	O	N	E	D
■	E	N	T	S	■	S	A	R	I	■
L	I	N	D	A	E	V	A	N	S	■
A	R	N	■	N	D	A	K	■	■	■
A	S	Y	E	T	■	C	A	D	D	Y
■	B	L	O	C	■	I	R	E	■	■
E	A	S	Y	V	I	R	T	U	E	■
A	L	P	E	■	U	N	O	S	■	■
T	R	A	N	S	L	A	T	I	O	N
T	O	I	■	G	E	T	H	E	L	P
S	Y	R	■	T	S	E	■	R	N	R

78

O	C	C	U	R	■	A	C	I	S
J	O	L	S	O	N	■	O	Z	Z	Y
O	D	O	N	T	O	■	L	E	O	N
■	S	A	O	N	E	■	C	D	C
B	Y	E	■	R	O	U	G	H	■
O	E	D	S	■	S	L	U	R	P	S
P	A	C	E	R	■	A	R	E	T	O
P	R	I	M	A	L	■	U	P	U	P
■	R	I	S	E	R	■	U	I	E
H	T	C	■	H	B	O	M	B	■
E	A	U	S	■	E	Y	E	L	E	T
Y	M	I	R	■	C	A	N	I	N	E
S	E	T	A	■	L	E	C	A	R

79

T	A	P	A	S	■	O	Z	M	A
B	A	O	B	A	B	■	C	O	I	L
S	A	L	A	D	A	■	H	O	T	E
P	A	T	■	Y	E	O	M	A	N
■	R	A	M	O	N	A	■
N	I	O	B	I	U	M	■	B	A	D
S	P	O	O	R	■	E	B	O	L	I
W	O	N	■	R	O	S	E	A	T	E
■	F	O	G	H	A	T	■
P	R	I	O	R	I	■	L	O	M
D	A	R	C	■	L	O	Y	O	L	A
F	R	A	U	■	L	E	S	A	G	E
S	A	S	S	■	O	L	D	A	S

80

W	A	S	P	■	S	I	T	E
A	C	C	R	A	■	P	S	H	A	W
T	H	E	O	C	■	F	L	U	T	E
C	O	N	■	R	E	S	E	N	D	S
H	O	T	D	O	G	■	D	I	T
■	O	I	N	G	O	■	E	R	I
D	A	F	F	Y	■	N	O	R	T	E
E	V	A	■	M	S	E	D	S
P	O	W	■	A	R	E	T	H	A
T	W	O	T	O	G	O	■	R	A	F
H	A	M	A	L	■	S	A	U	N	A
S	L	A	K	E	■	E	P	C	O	T
■	S	N	A	G	■	O	K	I	E

SOLUTIONS

81

E	G	G		M	T	A		C	S	S
D	E	E		A	R	S		O	L	E
E	L	N	I	N	O	S		M	E	E
		U	N	G	U	A	R	D	E	D
T	R	I	B	E		Y	U	R	T	S
H	A	N	A		T	E	N			
E	J	E	C	T	O	R	S	E	A	T
		K	I	T		I	T	A	S	
A	R	O	O	M		A	N	I	M	E
P	E	R	F	O	R	A	T	E		
A	N	D		T	A	L	O	N	E	D
R	E	I		H	G	T		N	A	P
T	E	E		Y	E	O		E	R	S

82

C	A	R	P		S	C	O	R	E	
O	D	O	R		A	R	R	A	U	
D	I	C	E	P	L	A	Y	E	R	
A	M	A	D	E	U	S				
			A	R	T	H	O	U	S	E
I	S	I	T	I		C	I	S	T	S
P	O	L	I	O		O	L	D	A	S
S	A	R	O	D		U	S	A	G	E
O	P	E	N	P	O	R	T			
			I	T	S	O	V	E	R	
	S	W	E	E	T	E	N	E	R	S
	F	E	N	C	E		E	T	A	S
	O	S	L	E	R		S	O	T	S

83

E	N	E	M	A		C	H	I	C	K
E	A	S	E	L		H	O	M	E	Y
L	O	A	N	D	B	E	H	O	L	D
S	S	I		E	E	R	O			
			B	R	A	U		L	A	S
		F	A	S	T	B	R	E	A	K
S	H	O	R				O	H	M	Y
C	O	U	N	C	I	L	O	R		
H	D	L		A	S	O	K			
			U	N	L	V		S	A	P
C	O	M	M	I	S	E	R	A	T	E
A	R	S	O	N		T	A	B	O	R
F	L	U	K	E		T	R	U	M	P

84

M	O	N		G	P	S		S	A	P
U	R	O		R	I	A		E	D	A
T	A	R	P	O	N	S		L	O	T
U	N	M	A	S	K	S		F	R	O
A	G	A	S	S	I			R	E	I
L	E	N	T	E	N		R	E	E	S
		C	A	R	G	O	E	S		
P	H	O	S		S	C	A	T	H	E
L	A	U		H	A	D	R	O	N	
E	R	S		B	E	R	E	A	V	E
A	R	I		F	A	I	R	I	E	S
S	O	N		A	R	N		N	R	C
E	W	S		S	S	A		T	S	U

531

SOLUTIONS

85

	I	C	E	D		F	O	P	S	
	N	O	V	I		E	P	E	E	S
O	S	M	A	N		T	E	R	C	E
D	A	M	N		H	A	R	P	E	R
D	N	A		A	O	L		E	D	O
S	E	N	O	R	S		K	N	E	W
		D	R	E	A	D	E	D		
M	E	M	O		N	E	W	I	S	H
U	R	O		S	N	O		C	P	A
S	E	D	A	K	A		D	U	H	S
K	N	U	T	E		T	U	L	I	P
S	O	L	T	I		A	R	A	N	
	W	E	A	N		M	A	R	X	

86

S	T	M	T		S	O	L	I	D	I
A	R	A	N		L	I	O	N	E	L
W	A	R	T	S	A	N	D	A	L	L
I	I	I		I	L	K		L	I	U
I	L	O	I	L	O			I	M	S
			L	E	M	A		N	I	E
J	A	V	A	N		N	Y	E	T	S
U	I	E		T	A	T	U			
J	R	R			A	C	K	A	C	K
I	S	M		O	H	O		F	R	A
T	H	E	A	N	S	W	E	R	I	S
S	I	E	N	N	A		M	E	M	E
U	P	R	O	O	T		T	E	E	M

87

P	E	N	A	L		C	L	A	P	S
A	M	T	H	E		R	O	M	E	O
I	M	S	A	D		E	Y	I	N	G
R	A	B	B	I	T	E	A	R	S	
			N	E	L	L				
B	O	A	S	T	S		I	C	B	M
M	I	N	E	O		T	S	L	O	T
I	D	E	A		T	O	T	E	R	M
		O	D	O	M					
	W	A	T	E	R	F	R	O	N	T
P	A	R	T	I		O	U	T	E	R
G	R	I	E	F		O	D	E	T	O
A	P	E	R	Y		L	E	A	S	T

88

	R	O	G	E	R	S		B	B	B
S	A	R	A	L	E	E		E	R	O
M	I	C	H	A	E	L	J	F	O	X
I	N	H	A	L	F		E	O	N	S
L	O	I	N			B	R	U	T	E
E	N	D		B	O	O	K	L	E	T
			M	A	D	L	Y			
S	N	E	E	R	A	T		E	L	S
W	O	L	D	S		S	M	E	E	
A	L	I	I		K	E	Y	P	A	D
G	E	T	C	R	A	C	K	I	N	G
E	S	E		U	T	T	E	R	L	Y
S	S	S		G	O	O	S	E	Y	

SOLUTIONS

89

G	O	D		A	Y	N		S	U	D
R	O	I	S	T	E	R		P	R	E
U	N	S	U	B	S	C	R	I	B	E
	C	L	A	M		H	R	A	P	
R	E	P	U	T	A	T	I	O	N	
A	T	A		N	A	N				
R	O	D	A	N		R	O	T	H	S
		A	E	R			Y	O	U	
	B	O	R	D	E	R	L	I	N	E
B	E	R	G		L	I	E	N		
E	I	G	H	T	Y	E	I	G	H	T
S	N	A		R	O	L	A	I	D	S
S	S	N		A	N	S		N	L	E

90

	L	O	M	A		A	S	A	P	
H	A	Z	E	L		D	Y	E	R	S
E	C	O	L	E		O	N	R	Y	E
N	U	N		D	A	N	C	I	N	G
I	N	I		O	F	A		A	N	E
E	A	C	H		F	I	L	L	E	R
		A	P	A	S	T				
N	E	R	O	L	I		D	A	C	E
O	R	E		O	R	K		N	A	T
T	E	E	N	T	S	Y		I	S	S
A	S	S	E	T		O	H	T	H	E
S	T	E	V	E		T	A	R	I	Q
	U	S	A	R		O	R	A	N	

91

	L	A	C	E	Y		M	C	D	L
	A	F	I	R	E		C	H	A	O
A	G	E	I	S	M		A	E	R	Y
B	O	W		E	E	O		C	R	O
R	O	B	S		N	I	C	K	E	L
I	N	A	W	E		L	E	O	N	A
		D	E	M		U	L	U		
I	S	A	A	C		P	I	T	O	F
S	E	P	T	E	T		A	T	N	O
S	A	P		E	A	L		I	R	S
U	R	L	S		L	I	T	M	U	S
E	L	E	A		C	L	U	E	S	
R	E	S	T		S	T	A	S	H	

92

	O	C	H	O			B	I	L	L
	F	R	E	D	A		B	R	E	E
C	L	O	R	O	X		A	R	A	N
L	A	W		R	E	M		E	P	A
I	T	N		R	A	G	T	O	P	
P	E	P	S		S	C	A	R	N	E
		R	O	D		E	L	I		
E	P	I	L	O	G		L	E	V	O
B	E	N	D	E	R			V	I	R
E	T	C		R	A	T		A	N	Y
R	T	E	S		S	K	Y	B	O	X
L	I	S	T		P	O	I	L	U	
E	T	S	Y			S	P	E	S	

SOLUTIONS

93

T	O	B	E		M	I	L	S	A	P
E	D	O	M		A	T	E	S	T	S
R	O	M	P		N	E	A	R	L	Y
A	M	B	I		I	N	D			
		P	R	O	F		I	F	H	E
D	A	R	E	M	E		N	L	E	R
I	D	O		S	S	T		O	R	A
D	O	O	M		T	O	B	O	O	T
A	G	F	A		A	G	E	R		
			D	A	T		G	L	O	M
W	A	S	A	B	I		G	A	V	E
A	K	I	M	B	O		A	M	U	R
S	C	R	E	E	N		R	P	M	S

94

A	S	P		A	S	S		C	F	O
G	L	A	C	I	A	L		H	A	B
S	O	L	A	R	P	A	N	E	L	S
	P	E	N	H		T	O	S	S	
			D	E	S	E	R	T	E	D
B	A	N	Y	A	N		A	N	T	E
E	V	E		D	O	H		U	T	A
R	I	A	A		W	E	N	T	O	N
G	A	R	G	O	Y	L	E			
	T	E	E	D		P	R	O	W	
T	R	A	D	I	T	I	O	N	A	L
A	I	S		S	E	N	S	U	A	L
E	X	T		T	A	G		P	C	B

95

C	H	E	R		E	J	E	C	T
M	I	M	E		M	A	L	T	A
A	L	B	S		T	A	K	I	N	G
S	T	R	A	T	E	G	O		
	A	W	O	L		B	T	E	N
W	C	S		S	E	M		R	U	E
O	R	U		E	S	O		U	S	N
R	U	R		A	C	U		C	E	E
K	E	E	P		O	R	S	K	
		H	Y	P	N	O	S	I	S
V	A	L	I	S	E		C	T	R	S
E	G	A	L	E		A	O	U	T
E	R	R	O	R		L	P	N	S

96

	C	L	U	E		A	S	T	A	
B	E	A	S	T		U	S	E	R	S
O	R	C	H	E	S	T	R	A	T	E
D	I	A		S	A	R		S	U	D
E	S	S		I	C	E	B	E	R	G
S	E	A	T	A	C		A	L	O	E
			I	N	H	E	R			
D	A	M	N		A	N	N	A	L	S
O	N	A	G	E	R	S		R	E	C
R	A	N		Z	I	N		T	A	R
A	L	T	E	R	N	A	T	I	V	E
L	O	R	N	A		R	E	S	E	E
	G	A	D	S		E	M	T	S	

534

SOLUTIONS

97

S	T	E	T			E	B	B	I	N	G
T	O	N	O			T	E	E	N	E	R
A	P	O	D			H	A	L	T	E	R
G	O	L	D	R	E	C	O	R	D		
		L	E	R	O	I					
S	E	X	E	S		N	T	E	S	T	
M	A	L					A	C	A		
A	L	I	V	E		O	S	R	I	C	
		I	N	A	N	E					
	O	N	E	A	T	A	T	I	M	E	
S	L	O	W	M	O		U	R	A	L	
H	A	R	E	E	M		P	I	N	K	
A	V	I	D	L	Y		S	S	N	S	

98

	W	I	S	P			D	E	B	S
W	E	N	T	U	P		O	M	E	N
A	B	A	S	E	R		O	B	L	A
R	A	W		R	E	G	R	O	U	P
S	P	A	T	T	E	R		L	G	S
		P	Y	R	O	M	A	N	I	A
		A	R	I	S	E				
	P	E	N	I	N	S	U	L	A	
V	H	S		C	E	R	E	A	L	S
Y	O	K	O	O	N	O		A	I	T
I	N	I	T		C	O	O	L	E	D
N	E	M	O		E	T	H	A	N	S
G	S	O	S			S	O	A	S	

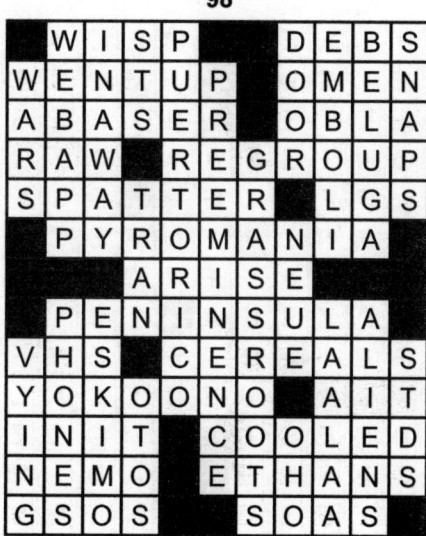

99

S	O	A	R			M	A	N	O	F
I	N	T	O		J	O	C	U	N	D
F	O	R	E	Q	U	A	R	T	E	R
T	S	A		A	G	N	E	S		
		B	T	U			H	A	D	
U	N	S	E	A	L		T	E	T	R
M	E	M	O	R	A	B	I	L	I	A
M	E	A	N		R	E	D	L	E	G
A	D	L		V	E	Y				
		L	T	G	E	N		L	E	M
I	M	P	E	R	I	A	L	I	S	M
S	T	O	L	E	N		O	M	N	I
P	A	X	E	S			I	B	E	X

100

	I	S	S	O		F	U	G	U	
C	R	E	E	L		I	N	O	N	E
R	O	L	L	I	N	G	M	I	L	L
O	N	F		V	I	M		N	E	L
S	O	D		A	C	E		G	D	S
S	N	E	E		K	N	O	B		
	S	C	O	P		T	R	A	C	
		E	E	E	S		A	C	H	E
I	S	P		T	U	T		K	E	L
N	I	T		U	N	H		W	A	V
T	R	I	A	N	G	U	L	A	T	E
L	E	O	N	I		G	O	R	E	S
	E	N	Y	A		S	A	D	R	

SOLUTIONS

101

P	E	A	K	Y		M	E	N	U	
L	I	S	L	E		I	M	O	N	E
A	T	T	E	N		S	I	K	E	S
C	H	E	E	T	A	H		I	S	O
I	E	R		L	G	E		D	C	L
D	R	N	O		I	A	M	S	O	
		A	F	T	R	A				
	B	Y	S	E	A		I	D	I	O
P	A	U		R	T	E		E	N	G
I	S	P		M	E	D	I	C	A	L
P	E	P	S	I		E	M	O	T	E
E	L	I	H	U		N	A	D	I	R
	Y	E	S	M		S	N	E	E	S

102

P	O	C	O		T	O	D	D	L	E
U	N	O	S		O	X	E	Y	E	S
P	I	U	S		G	I	V	E	U	P
A	C	R		H	A	D	I			
S	E	T	H	I		E	L	L	I	E
		E	A	S			M	E	S	A
I	G	O	R	S		M	E	T	U	P
T	H	U	D			O	N	S		
A	I	S	L	E		S	T	L	E	O
		A	X	E	S		O	A	R	
S	O	W	B	U	G		L	O	T	T
K	O	M	O	D	O		E	S	A	I
A	N	D	R	E	S		M	E	T	Z

103

T	A	Z		A	G	O		S	G	T
E	V	O		G	U	N		H	U	R
L	E	G	A	T	E	E		A	R	E
S	O	I	R		R	I	S	Q	U	E
			P	A	R	S	E			
G	A	M	E	T	E		A	C	L	U
T	I	O	G	A		E	S	N	E	S
S	N	O	G		R	E	I	N	A	S
		I	N	O	L	D				
I	N	T	O	T	O		E	A	R	N
S	O	O		E	M	B	R	O	I	L
I	V	Y		S	B	A		K	A	E
T	A	S		T	A	T		I	S	R

104

I	A	N		U	S	M	A			
P	E	U		S	K	I	D	D	O	O
E	D	T		P	A	L	O	O	K	A
C	I	S	T	S		L	U	M	E	T
A	L	A	I		P	R	I	M	E	
C	E	N	T	A	V	O		N	O	N
		D	I	G	I	N	T	O		
G	I	B		R	I	D	E	S	B	Y
A	R	O	S	E		S	P	E	E	
M	E	L	E	E		A	H	I	L	L
A	N	T	E	D	U	P		Z	I	P
L	A	S	T	O	N	E		Z	E	E
		O	N	O	R		A	F	R	

SOLUTIONS

105

D	E	L			O	R	R			
E	L	I		C	H	E	M	I	S	E
P	O	T	A	T	O	S	A	C	K	S
O	P	T	S		S	T	R	E	E	T
S	E	L	A			L	Y	C	E	E
E	R	E	M	I	T	E		R	T	E
		F	I	N	E	S	S	E		
T	M	I		U	N	S	T	A	C	K
H	U	N	A	N			O	M	O	O
I	N	G	R	I	D		E	C	C	E
G	R	E	A	S	Y	S	P	O	O	N
H	O	R	M	O	N	E		N	O	I
			N	E	S		E	N	G	

106

E	A	T	N	O		A	L	F	A	S
N	E	R	O	S		B	U	R	R	O
B	R	A	S	H		O	M	E	G	A
L	I	F	E		W	I	P	E	U	P
O	A	F		K	A	L		Z	E	E
C	L	I	P	O	N		G	I	R	D
		C	O	O	N	C	A	N		
E	C	C	L		E	M	I	G	R	E
F	R	I		O	S	A		P	O	E
F	O	R	M	A	T		C	O	A	L
E	P	C	O	T		H	E	I	D	I
T	U	L	L	E		I	N	N	I	E
E	P	E	E	S		T	O	T	E	R

107

R	A	P	A		P	E	S	E	T	A
A	S	O	N		O	V	I	S	A	C
S	T	M	T		S	E	D	O	N	A
P	I	P	E	L	I	N	E			
		A	N	E	T		A	F	O	R
M	A	D	N	E	S	S		R	O	E
S	H	O	A	L		C	L	U	N	G
E	A	U		A	T	H	E	I	S	T
C	T	R	S		S	W	A	T		
		E	N	H	A	N	C	E	D	
A	L	E	X	E	I		D	A	L	I
M	E	N	T	O	R		E	K	E	S
D	O	E	S	N	T		R	E	C	S

108

G	R	O	W	S		G	N	A	W	S
H	I	T	I	T		E	I	L	A	T
I	M	I	N	E		T	B	I	R	D
J	A	C	K	R	A	B	B	I	T	
			A	N	N	U	L			
B	A	S	T		G	S	E	V	E	N
O	T	E		B	U	Y		A	R	Y
P	H	A	S	E	I		A	S	S	T
			A	E	S	I	R			
	O	F	F	S	H	O	R	I	N	G
I	N	L	A	W		W	A	L	D	O
O	M	A	R	A		A	N	E	A	R
R	E	M	I	X		S	T	A	K	E

537

SOLUTIONS

109

	M	A	U	R	A		C	M	D
	W	I	M	S	E	Y		L	E	I
B	E	A	N	S	P	R	O	U	T	S
A	R	M	O	R	S		P	N	E	U
B	A	I	T			M	A	K	O	S
E	N	S		T	H	E	L	Y	R	E
			C	R	E	S	S			
E	P	I	T	A	P	H		S	C	H
M	E	R	R	Y			F	I	L	O
B	R	E	L		P	R	I	M	A	L
E	I	N	S	T	E	I	N	I	U	M
D	O	E		E	A	S	E	L	S	
S	D	S		R	U	E	D	E		

110

I	C	A	H	N			L	O	E	W
A	T	W	O	O	D		E	R	D	A
M	A	L	T	V	I	N	E	G	A	R
				E	A	T	A	T		
S	K	U	L	K		H	I	T	A	
R	O	S			S	U	D	O	K	U
T	H	E	R	M	O	M	E	T	E	R
A	L	M	O	S	T			S	E	G
	S	E	E	D		P	A	Y	M	E
			B	O	R	A	X			
I	N	D	U	S	T	R	I	O	U	S
I	N	S	C		E	L	A	P	S	E
N	E	C	K			E	L	E	N	I

111

P	R	O	A	S		I	P	A	D	S
P	O	R	N	O		N	O	F	O	R
S	H	E	A	R		F	I	R	M	A
	S	I	B	S		N	O	E	S	
N	O	T	S	O	H	O	T			
O	B	E			R	O	U	B	L	E
M	O	I	R	E		O	P	E	R	A
S	E	A	E	E	L		N	O	S	
		F	R	E	Q	U	E	N	T	
B	R	I	E		G	U	N	D		
D	I	A	R	Y		I	C	I	N	G
R	A	N	T	O		E	L	C	I	D
M	A	S	O	N		T	E	T	E	S

112

M	A	N	D	O	L	A		N	B	A
D	E	C	O	R	U	M		I	A	M
S	C	O	U	R	G	E		S	S	A
			B	S	O		K	E	I	R
A	N	I	L		S	T	N	I	C	K
T	A	K	E	F	I	V	E			
E	L	O	R	A		M	E	R	C	S
		E	Q	U	A	L	I	T	Y	
I	G	U	E	S	S		E	G	A	L
F	A	H	D		E	R	N			
O	S	A		E	N	I	G	M	A	S
L	E	U		D	E	S	T	I	N	E
D	S	L		E	T	C	H	I	N	G

538

SOLUTIONS

113

```
H A I K U . . . P S S
O R G A N A . N A L A
S T O L I D . E B A N
. . . E V A L U A T E
. W H I S P E R . . .
L E A D . T E A P O Y
G I J O E . T S A D E
E L I S S A . T S O S
. . . C A M P H O R .
R E D O U B L E . . .
N O O P . I O N I Z E
A N C E . T W I N E S
S S E . . S A G E T
```

114

```
L O G I C . A T C O .
I C O S A . N U R M I
C H I P P E D B E E F
H E N . L L B . A L T
I R T . E O E . M E H
. S O F T C . E S T E
. . G S U I T . . .
T A B S . T S A D E .
A L L . G I L . E N S
E L O . L O A . S T N
B O U T O N N I E R E
O W N E R . D I R E R
. S T A Y . S I T E D
```

115

```
I B I S . M O I L S
T A N H . R I P R A P
E D D A . A N E R G Y
R U I Z . I O N E .
. V A U N T . P C S
S K I M P Y . L A Y
A I D . I S O . A N S
T S U . E L I C I T
S S A . A A N D E .
. L A R S . A A S S
A R I S T O . H B A R
B U T T O N . O L E A
S T Y R O . S E S S
```

116

```
S I C E M . . S S R S
S T A T O R . M O A I
T I R A D E . U P C S
. . R L E S S . H E S
S D I . M E R C I .
F I E F . E I L E E N
P E R I L . S U S I E
D U P L E X . E C R U
. I S I A H . H E R
N A G . A C H O O .
T R E E . T O R I E S
S L O T . O U N C E S
B O N D . R E E S E
```

SOLUTIONS

117

A	S	H		T	A	L			
C	H	O		A	M	E	R	C	E
E	E	R		V	I	T	I	A	T	E
T	E	S	S	I	E		F	R	A	N
O	N	E	I			D	E	B	T	S
L	A	T	T	I	C	E		O	S	E
		R	U	T	H	A	N	N		
A	H	A		R	E	L	O	C	K	S
R	E	D	D	Y			M	O	E	T
P	R	I	I		K	L	E	P	T	O
S	E	N	E	C	A	S		I	T	O
	I	G	U	A	N	A		E	L	G
			D	S	T		S	E	E	

118

E	G	A	D		M	E	C	C	A
A	U	D	I		Q	U	A	H	O	G
V	I	V	A		U	L	T	I	M	O
E	D	E	N		E	L	O	P	E	
	E	R	N	I	E		U	S	S	R
		T	E	N	N		T	A	T	U
E	P	I		C	O	D		N	O	R
M	A	S	C		F	O	N	D		
P	N	E	U		M	E	E	S	E	
	A	M	P	L	E		T	A	E	L
I	C	E	T	E	A		M	L	L	E
B	E	N	I	G	N		A	S	E	T
M	A	T	E	O			N	A	R	A

119

S	E	E	M		I	L	D	U	C	E
O	R	A	L		M	A	M	M	A	L
I	N	S	C		P	R	I	M	L	Y
L	O	Y	A	L	I	S	T			
		C	R	I	S		R	I	O	S
R	A	H	R	A	H		I	T	Z	A
A	T	A					S	M	A	
F	O	I	E		A	L	O	M	A	R
T	E	R	M		B	O	D	Y		
		Q	U	I	X	O	T	I	C	
A	B	S	U	R	D		N	U	T	T
L	I	P	A	S	E		T	R	O	N
S	O	R	D	I	D		O	N	O	S

120

S	H	O	R	T	I	E		D	C	L
P	I	G	I	R	O	N		O	L	A
E	V	E	N	I	N	G	S	T	A	R
S	E	E	S	A		L	O	T	S	A
			E	L	A	I	N	E	S	
G	B	S		A	L	S	O	R	A	N
E	E	O		N	I	H		E	C	O
M	A	C	A	D	A	M		L	T	R
	T	I	M	E	S	U	P			
U	S	A	I	R		F	A	T	E	S
R	O	B	E	R	T	F	R	O	S	T
N	U	L		O	R	I	E	N	T	E
E	T	E		R	U	N	R	I	O	T

SOLUTIONS

121

	C	O	S	A		S	T	R	I	P
C	A	R	E	S		T	I	E	T	O
S	L	E	E	P		A	G	N	E	W
S	E	L	F	E	S	T	E	E	M	
		I	N	N	E	R				
A	S	S	T		E	L	I	S	S	A
A	B	O		V	E	Y		E	A	P
R	A	I	S	E	R		C	A	S	A
		I	N	A	W	E				
	S	A	N	I	T	A	R	I	U	M
S	I	L	K	S		D	E	T	R	E
O	R	F	E	O		E	A	S	E	S
L	E	A	R	N		S	L	A	Y	

122

A	F	T	E	R		A	R	P	E	L
G	E	H	R	Y		L	E	O	N	A
A	V	E	D	A		I	F	I	T	S
	E	R	O	S	E		O	N	O	S
A	R	M	S		P	E	R	T		
M	I	O		T	O	P	M	A	S	T
A	S	P		E	P	I		N	H	A
P	H	L	O	X	E	S		D	R	U
	A	N	T	E		M	C	A	T	
T	I	S	H		S	C	A	L	P	
Y	S	T	A	D		E	R	I	N	S
C	O	I	N	S		R	I	C	E	S
O	N	C	D	S		A	N	K	L	E

123

E	R	S		S	P	A		A	P	B
R	A	T		E	R	R		S	E	A
E	J	E	C	T	O	R	S	E	A	T
B	A	E	R		C	A	U	C	U	S
		R	O	S	E	U	P			
A	D	A	P	T	S		S	W	A	T
R	I	G		A	S	H		A	T	O
A	D	E	S		S	A	T	R	A	P
		P	R	E	N	U	P			
E	C	L	A	I	R		R	A	M	S
G	O	O	D	E	V	E	N	I	N	G
A	N	S		L	E	I		N	E	T
L	E	S		S	R	S		T	M	S

124

C	T	N		I	N	U				
H	O	O		N	U	S		P	F	C
R	U	N	I	T	I	N		R	A	R
O	C	A	L	A		R	E	E	C	E
M	A	G	O	G		S	T	E	M	
E	N	E		L	A	M	O	T	T	A
	N	O	I	S	I	L	Y			
G	R	A	N	O	L	A		P	S	U
H	A	R	I		O	R	R	I	N	
O	V	I	T	Z		W	E	E	D	S
S	E	A		B	R	I	S	T	L	E
T	N	N		A	I	N		T	E	A
		R	A	G		Y	S	L		

541

125

```
S A S H   T A V E R N
A T O E   S T E L A E
S E L F D E N Y I N G
E S E   E T O   T I A
S T A T U S     I N T
    I C E R   S T E
M E L E E   H I T O R
A P A   D U E T
I I S   P T I S A N
L T S   A B O   C L U
B O O S T E R S H O T
O M E R T A   E W E S
X E D O U T   E A S Y
```

126

```
D I E L   S A S H A
A G N I   I B S E N
L O O M E D L A R G E
A O L   V I E   S E L
I N A B I N D   E L S
    R A G   F L O E
A R L E N   R U F U S
R E A R   R O S
R F S   R E U S I N G
O U T   U S G   R E O
W E L L B E H A V E D
  L A I L A   F I D O
  S P I E L   I N S T
```

127

```
A G A R   A G E R S
V I L A   S U R E O F
I N D E F I N A B L E
A S E   R M N   E D T
N U N C I O   C I I
    A D V A N C E D
  C O M A   R E A R
A L L E Y W A Y
C O Y   A B O U N D
I S M   L I I   N U I
D E P R I V A T I O N
S T I F L E   P A V E
  O A S T S   S T A S
```

128

```
  B A E R   M E N S
  O B L A   A C U T E
M A S K I N G T A P E
I T O   S E I   N A G
L E R   A W N   C U S
A R B S   Y O D E L
    S P O T S
  P L I E R   T A C O
R A E   A K C   C R I
I N N   S E R   T A L
M E T E O R O L O G Y
E R I T U   S A N G
  A L O P   S U E Y
```

SOLUTIONS

129

```
W A S P . . . G I A D A
A C M E . . F O S T E R
A A A A . . I N A P E T
H I S S A T . I S P Y .
. . H E S T I A . . . .
F E H . S O T H E R E .
T W I . O B S . F O R .
S E T F R E E . F D A .
. . A T T L E E . . . .
P A R R . I F I C A N .
F L E C H E . E T T E .
C O N R A D . I E A T .
S P A Y S . . O D D S .
```

130

```
A F B . B A H . P C P .
C L I . E M I G R E S .
H A R D A S N A I L S .
E X T O L . D L I S T .
. . H A S S L E . . . .
O I D . T E N O N E . .
Z S A Z S A G A B O R .
S A Y Y E S . E P A . .
. . G R I P E D . . . .
S P O O R . A M I E S .
H U N T A N D P E C K .
A M M E T E R . N O I .
M A Y . E W E . T N N .
```

131

```
. G L U E . T I P S .
C R A S S . A D U E .
H O R S E O P E R A .
E W E R . N O O S E D
E T D . I B N . U E Y
R H O N D A . P E L E
. O I L E R . . . . .
A P B S . A T O N E D
D R U . M N O . O D E
A I R S A C . A B E E
S E C R E T W O R D .
S A U L . R E D L Y .
Y U M A . A S Y E .
```

132

```
S A M S A . G L A S S
F L A N S . R I P U P
P A Y U P . E M O R Y
D I F F E R E N C E .
. . I F N O T . . . .
I N F O . B E G G E D
D A T U M . R O I L S
A S H T O N . O V A L
. . B S I D E . . . .
S T I R F R Y I N G .
A M E N U . R E T I E
V E N A L . E A T M E
G E S T E . G R O S S
```

133

T	E	M	P	E		M	E	U	S	E
I	C	I	E	R		I	S	N	E	R
T	A	X	C	O		S	O	F	T	Y
H	R	E		S	A	S	S	O	O	N
E	T	D		I	A	M		R	U	G
D	E	B	T	O	R		A	T	T	O
		L	O	N		T	R	U		
A	D	E	S		D	E	A	N	N	A
T	A	S		K	A	N		A	E	R
R	E	S	E	N	D	S		T	I	C
A	M	I	T	E		E	N	E	M	A
C	O	N	T	E		U	H	L	A	N
E	N	G	E	L		P	A	Y	N	E

134

P	E	P	I			S	E	C	O
E	V	A	N		A	G	E	O	L	D
N	I	T	S		D	E	N	N	I	S
S	E	R	I	A	L	N	O		
		O	D	D		U	R	A	L	S
H	A	L	E	D		S	A	R	E	K
I	C	C				M	A	E
S	H	A	M	U		G	R	A	D	E
N	E	R	O	S		I	E	D	
		R	E	E	N	L	I	S	T
A	S	T	R	A	Y		O	L	I	O
L	I	A	I	S	E		A	L	E	N
L	P	N	S			D	O	G	G

135

A	F	L		A	D	O		M	E	H
U	L	E		E	W	S		O	U	I
N	U	A	N	C	E	S		E	S	E
T	E	T	E		L	E	T	T	E	R
		H	A	R	L	O	W		
A	V	E	R	T	S		I	N	T	L
H	I	R	E	E		I	N	O	U	R
S	A	Y	A		L	I	K	I	N	G
		S	P	O	I	L	T		
F	A	N	T	A	N		E	I	N	S
L	T	S		D	E	A	D	S	E	T
A	C	E		M	R	E		N	B	A
V	O	C		E	S	S		T	O	Y

136

H	I	N		I	N	N		
E	G	O		D	E	C	A	P	O	D
R	U	R		A	P	O	L	O	G	Y
E	A	M	E	S		S	A	L	L	E
O	N	A	N			E	Y	E	R
F	A	N	T	A	S	Y		T	D	S
		M	O	B	B	I	S	H	
C	I	A		C	A	P	L	E	T	S
O	S	I	S			R	I	S	T
S	A	L	U	T		I	S	S	U	E
E	Y	E	S	H	O	T		T	R	I
C	A	R	S	A	L	E		I	I	N
		N	A	M		C	S	S

137

T	I	F	F	S			H	B	A	R
S	T	E	R	O	L		O	E	N	O
R	E	M	I	N	I	S	C	E	N	T
			V	A	C	A		R	O	E
A	P	H	O	R	I	S	M	S		
A	R	A	L		T	H	E	H	A	J
S	O	D	O	I		A	D	E	L	E
S	P	R	U	N	G		A	B	I	T
		O	S	C	I	L	L	A	T	E
M	P	S		A	N	I	L			
T	H	A	T	S	A	F	I	R	S	T
G	A	U	D		S	T	O	P	U	P
E	R	R	S			S	N	I	P	S

138

M	C	C	C		S	U	B	L	E	T
A	L	O	U		C	R	A	V	E	S
T	I	F	F		A	E	D	I	L	E
H	O	F	F		R	A	R			
		E	S	P	N		A	C	U	E
A	B	E		L	E	T	P	A	S	S
R	E	C	T	O		A	S	L	I	P
C	L	U	S	T	E	R		A	N	O
O	G	P	U		M	O	A	B		
			N	E	E		M	O	M	A
P	E	D	A	N	T		A	O	U	T
A	L	U	M	N	I		R	S	T	U
Z	O	D	I	A	C		E	E	E	S

139

C	A	M	P			E	P	O	X	Y
O	H	I	O	U		R	O	N	E	E
M	O	T	O	R		S	T	I	N	G
S	P	I	N	A	L		S	T	A	G
		G	A	L	O	S	H			
O	L	A		B	M	O	V	I	E	
R	E	T	R	I	B	U	T	I	O	N
S	N	E	A	K	Y		L	C	D	
		W	O	E	F	U	L			
G	R	O	H		R	I	T	A	R	D
A	U	D	I	T		S	H	I	E	R
E	N	I	D	S		H	E	N	N	Y
L	A	C	E	R		R	Y	E	S	

140

A	M	I	E	S		I	N	M	A	N
G	I	N	S	U		C	E	A	S	E
E	X	C	O	N		O	S	S	E	O
		O	L	D	A	S		S	S	N
M	S	N		A	G	A	S	P		
B	A	S	K	E	T		A	R	A	M
A	L	I	A	S		R	H	O	N	E
S	A	D	A		F	O	L	D	E	R
		E	T	A	G	E		U	W	E
F	O	R		A	S	D	I	C		
U	D	A	L	L		E	N	I	D	S
M	O	T	E	T		E	N	N	U	I
E	N	E	R	O		R	O	G	E	N

SOLUTIONS

141

```
E S O S . . . M A J S
C A P P . T E E S U P
R I E U . U P S I D E
U S N R . C P S N O W
. W O N K A . . . . .
L A I N I E . . M T N
I E D . A R E . A A S
I C E . . E X A C T A
. . . V D A R A . . .
M O O M O O . A R T E
E N E S C U . B O E R
G A D G E T . L O N G
A S S T . . . E N D O
```

142

```
. C R O C I . E B A Y
F L O R E S . L A C E
L O A D E D . G R O H
A S L . S U E . G R U
M E D S . E X P A N D
E D A T E . T H I S I
. M A N . R A N . . .
S P U R N . A G H A S
P I N S U P . E U L A
L L D . I E R . N L E
I F S O . K E P T O N
N E E D . E G R E T S
E R N O . S O U R S .
```

143

```
L I A N E . U R G A
I S L I P . S A I N
F I S T I C U F F S
E N O . S H A T T .
. . N O I L . S D S
P A G O D A . C H E T
S E R V E . S O O E Y
A R E O . E P O P E E
T O E . O V A L . . .
. D I N A R . A S A
. B I R T H R I G H T
. Y E A H . O S R I C
. E R S E . W H A M O
```

144

```
M A A . A E C . E U R
A L L E G R O . D N A
H U F F A N D P U F F
I M A R I . A S C O T
. . . O N E S T A R .
T E E N S Y . S T M T
D S M . T E A . O E O
S C U D . O V E R D O
. A L I G N E R . . .
I P A N A . N I E C E
M A T T H O U S T O N
I D E . A R E A R U G
N E D . N I B . E P S
```

145

```
E P A   G P A   B E A
N A S   O I L L A M P
S T A T I S T I C A L
O N H O T     C A N E
R A I T A   R E R U N
    O L I O   D E T
T E M P O R A R I L Y
R S A   N A D A
I T S M E   S M A R T
C I T I       I O N I A
E V E N I N G S T A R
P A R A G O N   I N A
S L Y   O R S   C T S
```

146

```
U N A   S A M   B S S
G E T I N T O   O H H
O V A T I O N   N R A
    C A D E T   D U R
B E L L E   A L I B I
S S I   A G O
O P P O R T U N I T Y
    D E V   T I D
N I L E S   P S S T S
I S A   T R E A T
K I N   A I R T R A P
O A K   T A R B U S H
N H A   E L Y   E E O
```

147

```
H B A R   O M A H A N
E L I A   K O M O D O
W A R T S A N D A L L
L D L   A F I   R A I
E D A   C O T   D I E
T E N D   R O K
T R E S S   R A C E R
    L T D   A L V A
R A O   E R R   E O N
A L S   W O N   A C K
D I S A P P R O V A L
A V I S O S   M E T E
R E A L T Y   B R E D
```

148

```
  S Q M I   A C R O
N E U R O   O T H E R
A W A I T   R O O T S
D E R   A M B   C O E
I R T   S U I   O R R
A S E S   S T O L E
  R I C K S H A
  E M B E R   H T T P
S N A   L A H   E E E
M S S   I T A   C N N
O U T T A   R T H O N
C R E S C   S H I N Y
K E R R   H Y P E
```

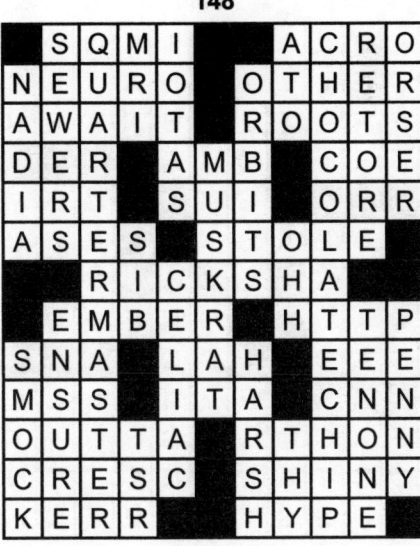

SOLUTIONS

149

```
A L G E ▓ I N V A R ▓
R I I S ▓ N A I R A ▓
F I R S T F L O O R ▓
S I D E R E A L ▓ ▓ ▓
▓ ▓ N Y S ▓ E A S T
G A P E A T ▓ T N T S
O N E ▓ ▓ ▓ O B O
R T E S ▓ U P E N D S
P A R I ▓ P I U ▓
▓ ▓ E N H A N C E D
▓ M E R C I F U L L Y
▓ F E R A L ▓ C U B E
▓ G N A R L ▓ H B A R
```

150

```
D E M I ▓ ▓ ▓ P A A R
M I E N ▓ M E E T M E
A R C H ▓ O L D M E N
J E H U ▓ H O D ▓ ▓ ▓
▓ A M I A ▓ L U B E
M I N E S W E E P E R
O R I ▓ E K E ▓ S D I
M I S T E R G R E E N
A S M Y ▓ I S I T ▓
▓ ▓ S E V ▓ P T U I
B E G O N E ▓ L I N C
C O R N E R ▓ E N D E
S E R S ▓ ▓ Y G O R
```

151

```
A H E A D ▓ I K N O W
B E L L I ▓ N A I F S
E R A T O ▓ S N A F U
D E L I C A C Y ▓ ▓
▓ ▓ M E N ▓ E G G Y
U N E A S Y ▓ E A U
S I X ▓ E B W ▓ R E M
O T O ▓ O R E I D A
S A D A ▓ D O E ▓ ▓
▓ ▓ C R Y U N C L E
F A C T O ▓ G S U I T
O C T A L ▓ H I T O N
G U S S Y ▓ T E E N A
```

152

```
V I G I L ▓ U D A L L
I T I S I ▓ V E N U E
S A F E T Y M A T C H
▓ ▓ E D U ▓ D E E R
T I N A ▓ K E S ▓ ▓
O P E ▓ Z O N E O U T
S U B J U N C T I V E
S T R A N G E ▓ N E S
▓ ▓ C I O ▓ S K A T
I S A K ▓ L A T ▓ ▓
U P S A N D D O W N S
M O I S T ▓ I R O N Y
S T A S H ▓ A K E E M
```

SOLUTIONS

153

W	I	T	H	█	D	R	A	G	O	N
I	S	A	O	█	M	O	N	R	O	E
T	U	L	L	█	I	M	G	O	O	D
S	P	L	I	N	T	E	R	█	█	█
█	█	█	D	I	R	█	Y	V	E	S
H	A	S	A	N	I	P	█	E	D	H
R	E	D	Y	E	█	L	A	N	D	O
A	R	A	█	R	E	A	C	T	O	R
P	O	K	E	█	A	I	T	█	█	█
█	█	█	T	O	R	T	U	O	U	S
E	S	C	H	E	W	█	P	U	S	H
Y	E	M	E	N	I	█	O	T	E	A
E	P	I	L	O	G	█	N	A	R	K

154

L	A	Z	E	S	█	R	E	C	T	I
I	N	I	N	K	█	A	L	O	A	N
G	O	L	D	E	N	R	I	N	G	S
A	T	L	█	D	Y	E	█	D	O	E
T	H	I	█	S	E	G	M	E	N	T
E	E	O	C	█	S	A	C	█	█	█
█	R	N	A	S	█	S	A	G	S	█
█	█	█	P	P	P	█	T	R	A	C
C	A	R	S	A	L	E	█	A	P	O
O	R	A	█	N	A	N	█	S	P	R
O	R	I	G	I	N	A	L	S	I	N
R	O	S	I	E	█	M	E	L	E	E
S	W	E	L	L	█	I	N	E	R	T

155

D	I	S	C	O	█	C	U	F	F	S
U	N	M	A	N	█	A	E	R	I	E
C	L	A	M	S	█	C	L	E	A	T
A	A	R	P	█	S	H	E	E	N	S
T	N	T	█	R	T	E	█	T	C	I
█	D	I	N	A	R	█	W	H	E	N
█	█	N	E	G	A	T	E	R	█	█
L	A	V	A	█	P	R	I	O	R	█
O	P	E	█	T	I	S	█	W	A	Y
U	N	S	E	W	N	█	E	L	B	E
N	O	T	R	E	█	C	R	I	B	S
G	E	O	D	E	█	M	E	N	L	O
E	A	R	E	D	█	A	B	E	E	R

156

S	E	S	S	█	J	U	R	O	R	S
O	R	E	O	█	O	V	U	L	E	S
U	S	A	F	█	Y	E	S	S	E	S
S	T	R	A	Y	C	A	T	█	█	█
█	█	O	B	O	E	S	█	I	S	H
A	D	V	E	R	B	█	E	N	T	E
F	R	E	D	E	R	I	C	T	O	N
T	A	R	S	█	O	S	H	E	A	S
S	Y	S	█	O	T	T	E	R	█	█
█	█	█	S	C	H	O	L	A	R	S
I	M	P	U	T	E	█	O	L	A	V
N	O	T	F	A	R	█	N	I	N	E
S	O	L	I	D	S	█	S	A	I	N

SOLUTIONS

157

A	C	E	U	P		R	U	H	R
S	E	N	N	A		R	U	P	E	E
T	R	A	C	Y	A	U	S	T	I	N
R	I	B		M	L	S		O	N	T
I	S	L		E	T	S		W	I	E
D	E	E	E		E	I	S	N	E	R
		L	A	R	A	M				
L	E	T	S	B	E		A	C	I	D
O	V	E		O	G	S		O	N	I
C	E	E		M	O	O		L	A	R
U	N	S	U	B	S	C	R	I	B	E
S	L	U	R	S		K	E	M	A	L
T	Y	P	E			O	V	A	R	Y

158

M	D	S		I	B	M		T	W	A
A	N	T	I	Q	U	E		H	I	S
H	Y	P	O	T	H	E	C	A	T	E
			W	E	L	T	Y			
S	A	G	A	S		L	M	N	O	P
P	R	O	S	T		Y	E	S	N	O
E	T	O				Y	E	E		
N	O	D	U	H		P	H	N	O	M
D	O	E	S	A		L	U	C	R	E
		C	I	G	A	R				
D	I	S	G	R	U	N	T	L	E	D
A	N	I		D	R	A	S	T	I	C
M	F	R		O	U	R		D	O	I

159

U	M	B	R	A		G	O	F	E	R
S	I	T	A	R		N	O	R	T	E
P	R	E	D	I	C	A	M	E	N	T
S	E	N		A	P	R		E	A	S
		D	N	A	L	A	B			
S	U	S	A	N	S		S	O	L	O
I	N	T	R	A		I	N	R	E	M
R	O	T	C		O	R	A	N	G	E
		H	Y	S	S	O	P			
T	K	O		O	L	N		B	S	S
B	A	M	B	O	O	S	H	O	O	T
A	R	A	C	E		O	S	S	I	E
R	O	S	E	Y		N	I	N	E	R

160

			P	O	E		S	O	L
U	M	S		E	O	S		T	W	I
N	O	H		N	O	T	F	A	I	R
C	R	A	P	S	H	O	O	T	E	R
		R	O	K		P	R	U		
M	A	P	L	E		S	I	S	A	L
D	E	A				S	P	T		
A	S	S	T	D		B	A	Y	E	R
		A	A	R		E	D	M		
I	N	T	R	A	C	T	A	B	L	E
D	I	A	R	I	S	T		O	I	L
E	N	C		N	C	O		L	S	D
D	E	K		S	H	R			

550

SOLUTIONS

161

A	N	D	I		H	U	B	R	I	S
B	I	O	G		O	L	I	N	D	A
A	C	L	U		R	E	E	S	E	S
B	O	C	A		S	E	R			
	E	N	C	E		S	I	C	K	
A	D	V	A	N	C	E		S	E	I
L	E	I		E	H	S		I	B	M
G	E	T		T	E	T	A	N	U	S
E	M	A	G		S	H	A	G		
		O	S	T		C	L	I	O	
A	T	N	O	O	N		H	A	R	D
B	U	R	E	A	U		E	S	A	I
E	N	C	Y	S	T		N	S	E	C

162

S	I	T	U		E	A	T	I	N	G
L	A	H	R		A	T	O	N	E	S
A	L	I	S		S	T	U	C	C	O
	R	U	P	E	E	S				
M	C	D	L	T		N	L	O	W	
A	R	R	A	S		D	E	F	E	R
R	E	A					F	L	A	
Y	S	T	A	D		E	L	I	T	E
	C	E	L	A		M	A	C	Y	S
	B	Y	E	B	Y	E				
A	C	C	E	S	S		M	B	A	S
R	E	C	I	P	E		A	O	U	T
S	E	R	T	A	S		N	Y	R	O

163

M	E	H		O	F	A		M	K	T
S	T	A	Y	P	U	T		A	I	R
G	A	Z	E	T	T	E		A	V	I
S	L	I	M		U	S	E	S	U	P
	N	E	A	R	T	O				
T	H	E	N	C	E		N	D	A	K
U	M	S		S	P	A		E	R	O
B	O	S	S		E	N	A	M	O	R
	H	E	R	E	T	O				
C	U	T	O	F	F		I	C	E	E
A	S	I		R	E	W	O	R	D	S
P	O	P		O	C	A	N	A	D	A
P	S	T		N	T	H		T	Y	S

164

N	E	P		R	A	P		P	S	S
E	N	A		E	A	R	S	H	O	T
S	Y	N	C	H	R	O	N	I	Z	E
T	O	T	O	E		V	O	L	E	S
	H	O	M	E	E	C				
M	O	E		C	R	A	F	T	S	
C	O	R	N	C	O	B	P	I	P	E
S	O	S	O	O	N		D	S	T	
	E	P	O	P	E	E				
S	T	A	S	I		I	G	L	O	O
D	I	S	I	L	L	U	S	I	O	N
A	C	E	S	O	U	T		T	R	E
K	E	S		T	I	E		Y	T	D

SOLUTIONS

165

	Y	E	A	R		U	S	B	S
	T	E	E	N	A		A	C	E	H
M	A	R	R	E	R		W	A	C	O
O	P	T		M	A	N		R	K	O
B	A	L	O	O		E	S	P	O	
Y	S	E	R		W	U	H	A	N	
			I	M	E	T	A			
	P	A	N	T	S		L	A	Z	E
	S	I	G	N		E	L	I	Z	A
A	E	R		S	I	R		E	T	S
R	U	D	I		M	E	R	L	O	T
B	D	R	M		S	C	U	L	P	
S	O	Y	A		O	T	R	O		

166

C	A	E	S	A	R			C	S	A
I	L	L	I	N	I		P	E	E	S
I	T	L	L	D	O		E	B	R	O
			K	I	D	S	T	U	F	F
O	R	C	S		E	C	T			
H	E	A	T	H		E	Y	O	L	F
E	N	V	O	I		N	O	K	I	A
R	E	A	C	T		A	F	L	A	T
			K	A	N		F	A	R	E
Y	A	K	I	T	O	R	I			
U	L	A	N		C	I	C	A	D	A
M	K	T	G		T	I	E	R	E	D
A	A	A			I	S	R	A	E	L

167

C	A	T	S		P	E	P	I	T	A
A	C	R	A		R	A	H	W	A	Y
S	L	A	M		O	T	I	O	S	E
T	U	N	E	L	E	S	S			
		S	H	A	M	U		C	S	I
A	B	I	E	S		P	S	A	L	M
L	E	E	R			O	P	E	S	
A	N	N	E	S		A	M	A	D	O
S	S	T		C	H	E	E	R		
			P	R	A	C	T	I	C	E
M	I	G	U	E	L		I	S	I	S
C	A	R	R	E	L		M	O	R	E
S	T	E	R	N	E		E	N	C	S

168

I	M	E	T	A		R	U	S	S	O
L	A	S	E	S		O	N	E	P	M
I	R	O	N	S		B	D	A	Y	S
E	X	T	R	A	N	E	O	U	S	
		E	E	Y	O	R	E			
C	I	R	C		I	T	S	P	A	T
A	V	I		A	S	A		O	O	O
P	O	C	O	N	O		E	N	L	S
			H	O	M	I	N	Y		
	A	G	G	R	E	G	A	T	O	R
O	C	H	O	A		I	M	A	G	O
F	R	I	S	K		V	E	I	L	S
A	Y	A	H	S		E	L	L	E	S

SOLUTIONS

169

L	A	A		L	P	N		B	Q	E
E	F	F	I	C	A	C	I	O	U	S
G	R	A	N	D	P	I	A	N	O	S
O	O	R	T		E	S	M	E		
			E	R	R		A	I	R	E
	A	E	R	O	B	E		D	I	E
M	I	N	N	E	A	P	O	L	I	S
O	D	D		S	C	E	N	E	S	
I	S	E	R		K	E	R			
		A	B	A	B		A	S	A	S
E	N	V	I	R	O	N	M	E	N	T
T	W	O	S	C	O	M	P	A	N	Y
O	A	R		S	K	I		M	I	X

170

S	A	P	O	R		C	E	S	T	A
A	L	A	R	Y		U	T	T	E	R
L	U	R	I	D		E	C	O	N	O
K	I	D	N	E	Y	B	E	A	N	
			G	R	E	A	T			
A	R	P	S		M	L	C	A	R	R
F	Y	I		G	E	L		S	P	A
R	E	E	A	R	N		I	T	I	N
			B	U	I	L	D			
	V	E	R	Y	S	E	L	D	O	M
T	O	T	O	E		P	E	A	B	O
A	L	T	A	R		T	R	Y	I	T
E	T	U	D	E		A	S	S	E	T

171

K	I	A	S		D	O	Y	E	N
E	C	R	U	S		O	S	O	L	E
S	I	G	E	P		O	H	G	O	D
	U	L	C	E	R		U	N	S
G	A	M		A	R	D	O	R	
A	G	E	R		B	I	S	T	R	O
R	U	N	A	T		E	S	P	O	O
B	E	T	T	E	R		A	A	R	P
	A	T	E	U	P		R	Y	S
M	A	T		D	E	C	A	F	
F	R	I	T	O		T	H	A	I	S
A	L	O	O	F		S	E	I	N	E
S	O	N	O	F		M	T	N	S

172

U	C	L	A		B	E	L	E	M
N	A	A	N		I	T	A	L	I	C
I	M	P	O	R	T	A	N	T	L	Y
S	E	P		O	O	M		O	S	A
O	T	E	R	I		I	T	R	A	N
M	O	T	H		S	N	O	O	P	S
			Y	I	P	E	S			
M	U	R	M	U	R		I	N	R	E
E	P	E	E	S		F	R	A	I	L
A	S	T		E	S	O		G	P	A
T	H	U	N	D	E	R	B	O	L	T
S	O	N	A	T	A		T	Y	E	E
	T	E	N	O	R		W	A	Y	S

SOLUTIONS

173

A	L	D	A			R	A	J	A	H
C	O	R	F	U		E	T	U	D	E
E	M	O	T	I	O	N	A	L	L	Y
		P	O	E	M		T	I	E	S
C	A	P	N		I	C	I	E	R	
C	D	E			T	E	M			
C	A	R	P	E		E	E	N	S	Y
		A	R	K			O	S	A	
	H	U	R	R	Y		N	T	W	T
P	E	T	A		R	A	G	U		
F	A	L	S	E	A	L	A	R	M	S
C	R	E	O	N		T	I	N	O	S
S	T	Y	L	E			O	S	E	S

174

P	C	P		S	P	A		M	L	S
U	A	R		E	R	R		E	I	O
F	L	I	P	P	E	R		R	E	A
	S	M	U	T	S		D	C	U	P
A	T	A	B		S	H	I	H		
C	A	R	S		U	M	L	A	U	T
I	T	Y		O	R	O		N	P	R
S	E	C	E	D	E		O	T	T	O
		O	N	E	G		B	B	O	Y
B	I	L	E		A	T	L	A	W	
A	T	O		S	U	Z	A	N	N	E
R	A	R		W	G	A		K	E	L
I	R	S		E	E	R		S	R	O

175

H	O	B	O	S		P	A	M	P	A
A	R	I	O	T		O	R	I	E	L
W	I	T	H	A		P	I	N	E	Y
H	A	E		N	I	P	P	E	R	S
A	N	T		D	N	Y		R	E	S
W	A	H	W	A	H		S	A	D	A
		E	S	T	I	V	A	L		
S	U	B	J		B	I	G	W	I	G
O	S	U		E	I	N		A	N	A
P	U	L	S	A	T	E		T	A	U
H	A	L	A	S		G	O	E	T	Z
I	L	E	D	E		A	E	R	I	E
A	S	T	E	R		R	O	S	E	S

176

V	E	S	P	A		M	E	C	C	A
A	L	O	O	F		A	X	M	E	N
S	K	U	L	L		E	C	A	R	D
		R	O	A	M		A	S	E	S
I	T	N		C	A	T	V			
N	A	O	S		C	L	A	S	S	A
I	N	T	E	R	A	C	T	I	O	N
T	H	E	M	O	B		E	G	A	N
		A	T	R	A		N	R	A	
G	O	W	N		E	A	R	P		
A	R	E	T	E		H	O	O	E	Y
R	A	D	I	I		E	L	S	I	E
B	L	O	C	K		D	E	T	O	O

SOLUTIONS

177

E	T	U	I			A	C	D	C	
L	I	N	A	C		A	R	E	A	S
S	E	P	T	A		S	U	T	R	A
E	U	R		R	U	S	S	E	T	Y
S	P	E	E	C	H			R	M	S
		D	R	A	F	T	S	M	A	N
G	R	I	T	S		R	H	I	N	O
R	E	C	E	S	S	I	O	N		
A	T	T			S	E	W	A	G	E
P	R	A	T	E	R	S		T	I	P
H	E	B	E	R		T	O	I	L	E
S	A	L	A	D		E	R	O	D	E
	D	E	K	E			A	N	A	S

178

		B	E	E	N		A	S	O	F
W	A	Y	O	U	T		R	E	P	L
I	M	P	E	R	S	O	N	A	T	E
D	E	A		O	B	S		M	I	S
T	B	S	P	S		R	O	A	C	H
H	A	S	A		D	I	O	N	S	
			T	A	X	C	O			
	E	N	N	U	I		L	L	B	S
P	L	E	A	D		L	A	I	L	A
I	M	A		I	E	D		T	I	S
C	O	L	D	S	T	O	R	A	G	E
O	R	O	N		O	P	I	N	E	S
T	E	N	S		N	A	G	Y		

179

F	A	S	O			S	O	A	M	I
A	T	P	S		C	A	F	T	A	N
H	E	E	P		O	F	F	E	N	D
D	E	E	R		Y	E	T			
		D	E	P	P		O	D	A	S
B	O	D	Y	R	U	B		E	S	P
A	N	I	S	E		U	L	C	E	R
R	C	A		V	A	C	U	I	T	Y
B	E	L	T		F	O	N	D		
		R	A	L		E	U	L	A	
I	N	D	I	R	A		T	O	A	D
M	O	S	A	I	C		T	U	N	A
S	T	O	L	A			E	S	A	S

180

M	G	B		O	F	A		A	C	A
A	A	U		T	U	P		N	U	S
R	T	S		E	N	O		T	S	O
R	E	H	I	R	E	S		I	T	N
E	A	T	D	I	R	T		H	O	I
D	U	E	T		A	L	T	I	M	A
		L	A	W	L	E	S	S		
A	G	E	G	A	P		A	T	T	A
L	A	G		M	A	Y	D	A	Y	S
O	R	R		P	R	E	E	M	P	T
N	E	A		U	L	A		I	E	R
S	T	P		M	O	R		N	I	A
O	H	H		S	R	S		E	N	L

SOLUTIONS

181

```
. . . P O D . . .
W G A . E R I . M I A
A R M T W I S T I N G
S A A R . G O O N I N
T I L L . . B I T T E
E L G . A G E L E S S
. . A N N O Y E D .
S A M O A N S . I O S
C L A S P . . I T Z A
R E T I E S . T I A S
O V E R S H A D O W S
D E S . T U E . N A Y
. . . S I C . . .
```

182

```
N O R M . . A P T T O
E L E E . O R I S O N
W E P T . U G A R T E
T A U T . T O N .
. . G L A M . O I S E
G E N E R A . S N C C
I R A . S N A . V A T
L E N A . E N C I N O
L I T D . U G H S .
. . E N V . E I N E
E N I S L E . R B I S
M E N T O R . I L K A
B E D E W . E E E S
```

183

```
E T S Y . . A T I O N
T A P E . E M I G R E
A C E H . A C T N O W
T O L U . S S T .
. U D A Y . E D E L
D E N I E R . R U N A
I R K . S A B . P S I
L O E B . W O O L E N
L O R I . L A N I .
. . S C I . S C A N
N I G H O N . T A L C
F S T O P S . A T T A
C R E P T . . R E A R
```

184

```
A P S E . . A R R I D
S A L S A . L E O V I
E T A T S . L A D E N
. . V O I C E L E S S
F A O . T O A D .
L I N D . P R E S E T
O D I U M . S A T I E
P E A N U T . L A N D
. . G T O S . Y E S
A L B A T R O S S .
L O R R E . R O M E O
F O Y E R . E L A T E
A N N E S . . O D O N
```

SOLUTIONS

185

G	A	B	O	R		I	N	C	U	R
A	D	E	N	O		D	E	O	R	O
M	I	A	O	U		T	O	L	L	S
S	O	U	R	G	R	A	P	E	S	
			H	I	G	H	S			
T	O	R	P	I	D		Y	L	E	M
S	H	A	L	T		O	T	A	R	U
R	O	C	A		B	R	E	W	E	D
	L	Y	S	O	L					
	V	E	G	E	T	A	T	I	V	E
T	O	T	O	E		T	U	N	I	S
A	C	T	E	D		E	S	T	E	S
L	E	E	R	S		R	H	O	D	A

186

I	S	R		M	M	I				
O	N	E	F	O	O	T		M	I	D
C	O	M	E	S	B	Y		E	N	O
	U	R	S	I		A	R	G	H	
T	E	N	N		L	O	R	R	E	S
A	C	E	Y	D	E	U	C	Y		
M	O	R		R	A	S		G	O	O
	A	D	U	L	T	H	O	O	D	
A	S	T	H	M	A		O	R	N	E
F	A	I	L		B	T	W	O		
T	A	V		C	A	E	S	U	R	A
A	R	E		A	M	M	O	N	I	A
			P	A	P		D	A	E	

187

I	T	T		B	A	L	S	A		
S	I	E		A	U	G	M	E	N	T
T	O	R	C	H	B	E	A	R	E	R
	S	R	T	A			I	B	O	
L	I	E	U		D	I	V	E	R	T
A	S	L		C	E	N	O			
R	H	Y	M	E		I	C	A	N	T
		R	C	P	T		I	O	R	
S	E	T	T	E	E		E	R	T	E
A	S	A		L	T	D	S			
F	O	U	L	M	O	U	T	H	E	D
E	S	P	O	U	S	E		I	T	O
	E	N	D	I	S		P	E	C	

188

A	G	F	A		O	O	D	L	E	S
D	O	R	M		U	N	E	A	S	E
A	T	I	P		T	E	N	U	T	A
H	O	V	E	R	F	L	Y			
	O	R	E	O		S	R	A	S	
A	L	L	E	A	R	S		E	N	E
B	O	O	S	T		P	E	L	T	S
B	T	U		A	G	O	N	I	Z	E
R	I	S	T		N	O	D	E		
		E	V	E	N	T	F	U	L	
E	T	A	L	I	I		I	M	T	O
F	U	S	E	E	S		M	A	N	S
S	A	P	O	R	S		E	P	E	E

SOLUTIONS

189

```
E A C H   M U D R A
I C A O S E E Y O U
N E B O E L L E N S
S H I H L I E D
  N A I F S   I T O
E U C H R E   N R C
S S R T V A T E T
P I U   I D A H O S
O N I E D A T E
  S I P E O W I E
R I E S E N N O M S
S O R B E T C O A T
A S S N S   E L M O
```

190

```
  M E E T S   R A U L
S E A M A N   E N N A
W A T E R L O G G E D
O L I N S   D R I V E
R I N D   K E E N E D
N E G   K A N S A N
    T R U S S
  A S R A R E   H R H
L E O I I I   R O H E
E R N S T   B E R Y L
A I D E S D E C A M P
D A R C   S A U C E S
S L A T   L U T E S
```

191

```
A C T H   L A B O R
H O R O H Y S S O P
S E A M E R N A N I
O N N O L A A
  S N O G P A C E
L I L Y P A D E A T
L L A M A E A R E D
D S T L E A D I N S
S A E S A L V A
  T A S E L U L
T E A P O Y R I S E
S E D A K A S S N S
R O O T S   E T R E
```

192

```
J A M B   P I U S I
U B O L T L A P P S
S H U T A A M T O O
T O N P A S S O U T
A R T I E S T T S O
  A E R I E H E P
A B I D E R E E S E
V A N C E C U M
A N C O C A R I N A
T S H I R T S N O S
A H A N D T R U M P
R E I N E S E T A E
S E N O R T E N N
```

SOLUTIONS

193

```
E M I T   S C A T H E
D E K E   W A R R E D
O N E L   O L E A T E
M U S S O L I N I I
      T R L   A N I L
C E T A C E A   S R I
W E A R A N D T E A R
T R I   S H O O T E R
S Y L L   E O N
    S A M A R I T A N
P E P P E D   G R A Y
P L I S S E   H E R S
S I N E A D   T O P E
```

194

```
S P Y S   D O A B L E
T R E E   A N I M A L
M I S S A M E R I C A
T I M E B O M B
        O N A R O L L
K E A N U   N A T T Y
O G R E     K E R R
B A N C S   L E A S E
E L E K T R A
      L A U N D E R S
U N M I T I G A T E D
S E E N I N   S T O A
A Z T E C S   H U S K
```

195

```
C A P   A S U
A M O U N T S   A G O
L E S S E E S   N E U
I N T I   T R U A N T
F R A N C   S T O A
S A G   H A R D H A T
    E X E C U T E
M U S K R A T   M G M
E N T E   S C A R E
A L A S K A   O T O E
T E M   I C E P I C K
S T P   P R E T Z E L
      S Y R   E R Y
```

196

```
M A K O     S M E E
C M O N   S L O P E
C O L L O Q U I A L
C Y N O S U R E
      A S A   T H O S
M A E N A D   Y E P S
A M D       D I T
N A H A   S A Y Y E S
A S S N   U L A
      D R M O R E A U
G E R I A T R I C S
T H E O C   O N A N
I S I T   W E I R
```

SOLUTIONS

197

```
R A N I S   T R O P E
S C E N E   R E F E R
V E E P S   I S N E R
P H R A S E B O O K
    W I S E R
C A N N O T   T A L I
S F O   N E L   M D T
A C I S   L E W D L Y
    P A L M E
  R O U T E M A R C H
P A R T I   I V A N A
O D E U M   N E G E V
S O M M E   G R E T A
```

198

```
N G A I O   S E R B S
W E R A N   E L O R A
A D A G E   V O C A L
  C O N J   I K E A
S C H   D E B   E S D
T M N T   R I O T
K I O S K   P O S E R
  P O R K   M C C C
M E H   S E M   I T A
A R O D   R I L E
B O B B Y   M E N S A
E D I L E   I T C H Y
L E A S E   S T E R N
```

199

```
M A M B O     S U M
E V O L V E   N E B O
D E S E E D   E P E E
    S T A R W A R S
A N G S T   E Z R
B A L E   H E A R N
E T U D E   M A T E O
E S T E R   L O A M
    I V E   C A R D S
L I N E S M A N
I C O N   E N D O R A
N E U T   T E E N E R
A D S     A R I O T
```

200

```
  S T E M   H O P I N
O L I V A   E L E N I
P O M E G R A N A T E
E W E   N E V   L O C
N U L   A G E   E T E
S P Y S   I T S S O
    A L S O P
  S P L I T   R O B B
L O I   G R E   N M I
A N G   H A R   S O D
U N O B T R U S I V E
R E U S E   P U T I N
A T T A R   T R E E
```

SOLUTIONS

201

M	O	O	D			B	U	R	R	
O	F	P	O	P		I	T	O	O	
I	N	H	E	R		N	A	S	A	L
R	O	T		E	F	G		E	D	E
A	T	H		F	O	O		M	I	N
	E	A	T	A	T		G	A	E	D
	L	A	B	O	R	E	R			
E	L	M	Y		M	E	R	Y	L	
P	A	O		A	A	S		S	E	P
P	O	L		R	T	E		B	A	A
S	T	O	L	I		D	U	A	D	S
	S	G	A	S		A	L	B	E	E
	E	Y	C	K			T	Y	R	O

202

Y	U	L		N	A	N		F	A	S
O	R	O		E	N	E		D	N	Y
U	N	C	L	U	T	T	E	R	E	D
			B	R	A	H	E			
M	A	G	O	O		E	R	O	S	E
A	M	O	S	N		R	Y	N	E	S
N	N	W					A	P	T	
G	O	E	H	R		R	A	I	T	A
A	T	R	E	E		E	Z	R	A	S
			M	A	C	H	U			
M	I	N	I	C	O	U	R	S	E	S
I	N	A		T	N	N		I	P	A
C	U	L		S	E	G		L	S	T

203

B	A	B	E	S		W	A	R	D	
A	D	U	L	T		E	M	E	E	R
G	O	L	D	E	N	E	A	G	L	E
G	R	O		A	O	K		N	A	B
I	N	V	O	L	V	E		A	N	E
E	S	A	S		E	N	B	L	O	C
			H	I	L	D	A			
R	E	N	A	M	E		R	S	S	S
A	B	A		A	T	T	A	C	H	E
K	O	R		G	T	O		R	I	D
E	A	R	P	I	E	R	C	I	N	G
S	T	O	A	S		C	O	M	T	E
	S	W	U	M		H	Y	P	O	S

204

A	U	S				V	O	I	D	S
I	N	E	S		M	A	E	N	A	D
D	E	E	E		A	L	D	I	S	S
E	S	S	A	Y	T	E	S	T		
			W	I	T	T		I	A	L
B	I	C	E	P	S		S	A	G	A
A	T	R	E	E		R	U	T	H	S
M	O	O	D		H	A	B	E	A	S
S	O	S		K	E	G	S			
			S	T	A	R	S	I	G	N	S
S	P	E	A	R	E		S	P	A	T
N	O	R	M	A	S		T	A	P	E
O	L	S	E	N				S	A	P

SOLUTIONS

205

```
L O O M . . S T A F F
I N D O . S E E R E D
M E I N . T A N K E R
B R E A K O U T . . .
. . D A O . S A N A
G O R I L L A . M E D
D E I C E . R A B I D
A N N . L O G R O L L
Y O G A . N A B . .
. . C H I L I D O G
Q R A T I O . T A R O
I N B O R N . E N R Y
N A C R E . . R O S A
```

206

```
B A S H . H I P P E D
A N O A . O X C A R T
H E B R . T I T L E S
S W E D E . O S E .
. . R U B O N . T H U
W E A P O N . . T I E
A R S . N R A . E R L
R E A . . Y A N K E E
P B J . P E R O N .
. U I E . E L I T E
K I D N A P . E V E N
T S G A R P . S E S E
S T E N T S . S S T S
```

207

```
B L E T . S O C I O .
Y A D A . U R A N U S
P R E M E D I T A T E
A I R E D . A L F A
S A L . M I L L I O N
S T E R . M O Y E R S
. . Y M H A S . .
N U N C I O . T H A R
O N E O N T A . O D A
R H E O . H A N O I
M U D D Y W A T E R S
A R T E R Y . I S E E
. T O R S O . P T E R
```

208

```
W I G W A M . P O I S
I C H I R O . R P M S
N A I L I T . O T O S
E L A L . H E F .
. . . E L O R A
S T O A . R E R U N S
R E P L A C E M E N T
O T E L L O . A R A N
. E R I T U . .
. . N I N . B O M B
O K R A . T H A L I A
S E A L . R O T I N I
I N T L . Y O H O H O
```

SOLUTIONS

209

S	C	U	D	■	■	S	A	S	E	S
H	O	N	O	R	■	W	U	H	A	N
O	A	K	I	E	■	A	L	E	T	A
W	R	I	T	I	N	G	D	E	S	K
U	S	N	■	D	O	G	■	N	I	E
P	E	D	I	■	T	E	G	A	N	■
■	■	G	E	N	R	E	■	■	■	■
■	L	A	N	A	I	■	E	M	T	S
W	A	C	■	R	C	A	■	A	H	A
H	U	C	K	L	E	B	E	R	R	Y
A	R	T	O	O	■	A	C	Q	U	A
T	E	N	L	B	■	S	O	U	S	A
A	L	O	N	E	■	■	N	E	T	H

210

R	O	C	A	■	I	D	T	A	G
E	S	O	S	■	Q	U	I	T	E
A	R	C	H	I	T	R	A	V	E
P	I	K	■	N	E	A	R	■	■
S	C	R	O	D	S	■	A	U	E	R

R	O	C	A	■	■	I	D	T	A	G
E	S	O	S	■	■	Q	U	I	T	E
A	R	C	H	I	T	R	A	V	E	■
P	I	K	■	N	E	A	R	■	■	■
S	C	R	O	D	S	■	A	U	E	R
■	■	O	D	E	T	S	■	N	G	O
E	V	A	D	E	■	T	R	U	S	S
R	E	C	■	P	I	P	E	S	■	■
R	E	H	M	■	C	A	Y	U	S	E
■	■	D	I	E	U	■	A	A	R	■
P	I	C	C	A	L	I	L	L	I	■
I	N	C	O	G	■	E	L	S	E	■
S	T	I	N	E	■	R	Y	A	S	■

211

A	L	V	A	■	B	A	D	G	E
P	I	O	N	■	C	U	T	E	A	S
P	R	I	I	■	O	S	M	O	N	D
L	A	C	T	■	R	S	A	■	■	■
■	E	R	I	N	■	N	A	I	R	■
V	A	L	A	N	C	E	■	L	G	A
I	B	E	■	D	O	A	■	B	E	G
T	R	S	■	O	B	V	I	A	T	E
A	A	S	S	■	P	E	A	T	■	■
■	■	A	H	I	■	M	R	I	S	■
F	O	U	L	U	P	■	T	O	N	E
F	I	G	U	R	E	■	O	S	T	E
F	L	A	T	T	■	O	S	I	S	■

212

E	N	A	■	L	B	O	■	D	E	F
L	A	B	■	E	U	R	■	E	M	O
W	H	E	R	E	S	O	E	V	E	R
E	U	L	O	G	Y	■	D	A	R	T
S	M	E	A	R	■	A	L	I	I	■
■	■	M	A	L	A	M	U	T	E	■
E	R	A	■	N	E	C	■	E	A	S
V	E	G	E	T	A	T	E	■	■	■
I	M	E	D	■	I	L	O	S	E	■
L	I	N	E	■	I	N	A	R	M	S
E	X	T	R	A	D	I	T	I	O	N
Y	E	R	■	P	E	U	■	E	K	E
E	D	Y	■	I	S	M	■	L	E	S

SOLUTIONS

213

```
C U J O ■ L I S A S ■
A B O U ■ G O O D E ■
L O B S T E R R O L L
A L B E E ■ C R E E ■
I T E ■ C A D E N C E
S S R S ■ W O R S T
■ A D A G E ■
■ L I N E R ■ R B I S
C U S T O D Y ■ E C H
A N S A ■ E T H E R
M A H A B H A R A T A
■ T O N I O ■ O V E N
■ E T A P E ■ W E A K
```

214

```
S O B ■ S C A L P E L
L G A ■ A A M I L N E
A S T I G M A T I S M
■ S W E E ■ C O O
A T M O ■ R E E A R N
P H A N T A S M ■
B A N D O ■ A B C D E
■ E N C I R C L E
I N A R E A ■ O L I O
N O G ■ C H I A ■
C R A S H H E L M E T
U T T E R E R ■ P D S
S E E M S T O ■ S A O
```

215

```
E N L A I ■ A S S A D
R E I T S ■ V O C A B
S U P E R F I C I A L
E N O L ■ O V I ■
■ I N T ■ O L A F
C H E E T O S ■ I T O
L E A R S ■ I S I T I
U L T ■ B E G U I N E
B L A B ■ K H Z
■ U I E ■ A M I S
A C C O R D I N G L Y
P L A N O ■ I N R E M
O R T O N ■ N E S T S
```

216

```
A T T A ■ P A C I N O
P R O F ■ I D O T O O
T A U R ■ M M M B O P
S C R A P P A P E R ■
■ M I L N E ■
R E N E G E ■ L I S T
A R Y ■ L E E
I N X S ■ B I A L I K
■ E U R O S ■
O R A T O R I C A L
I N A F E W ■ T A W T
T E N O R S ■ I S E R
T R I X I E ■ S E E S
```

SOLUTIONS

217

```
T E C H N O . . O A P
I S A A C S . A M S O
P A M P A S . W E E N
. . . P R E S E N C E
L A D Y . O N I .
A J U G A . E N A C T
N E R O S . E S T A B
I T A L O . S P U T A
. . U A R . I S E R
S T I C K L E R . .
F I N K . E L I D E D
P L O Y . S O N O M A
D E W . . S I G N U P
```

218

```
S A D H E . G A S H .
U T U R N . A L I A S
B A S E L . S I G M A
M S T . A S T . N I B
I T I . I E R . I T E
T E N N . D I F F E R
. . H I B A C H I .
L O O T E R . A C D C
O N F . M I C . A E R
U H F . U S A . N N E
S I M P S . N O T A T
E R A S E . N A L D I
. E N I D . A R Y A N
```

219

```
I S L A M . A A R G H
M T I D Y . P S A L M
A L G A E . O R F E O
C O N G R E G A T E .
. E I S N E R . .
E R O O . D E E P L Y
W S U . O T S . O S O
W A S A B I . O P T O
. . L E M A N S .
. R E C R E A T I O N
T Y R O L . M O C H A
I N D R I . C U L T S
L E A N N . O R E O S
```

220

```
F O R C E . W H E A T
A R I A L . R A B B I
B U E N O S A I R E S
. . S T R E P . O D A
A T L . A Q U A . .
G E I N . U P N E X T
U N N E C E S S A R Y
A N G E R S . E G A N
. . T E T S . L Y E
A H I . M E E S E .
C O M P A R T M E N T
A L A S T . H E Y Y A
T A S S E . S W E E P
```

221

D	E	R	B	Y	■	E	L	I	S	E
E	N	O	L	S	■	R	O	C	K	S
S	C	H	O	L	A	R	S	H	I	P
C	L	E	W	■	D	O	E	■	■	■
■	■	P	A	I	R	■	A	A	S	
M	E	D	I	A	N	■	L	T	D	S
P	E	R	P	E	T	R	A	T	O	R
A	G	E	E	■	E	W	I	N	G	S
A	S	A	■	F	R	E	D	■	■	■
■	■	M	L	I	■	O	J	A	I	
C	I	R	C	U	M	S	P	E	C	T
S	N	E	A	K	■	S	E	E	T	O
S	T	Y	N	E	■	E	N	R	O	N

222

B	A	N	A	■	S	A	F	E	■
D	R	U	P	E	■	S	M	U	R	F
A	P	R	I	L	■	T	I	N	E	A
Y	E	S	■	E	D	S	■	E	M	T
S	L	E	D	G	E	■	R	I	T	
■	R	E	I	N	S	T	A	T	E	
A	S	Y	L	A	■	H	E	L	E	N
D	I	R	T	C	H	E	A	P	■	
E	D	H	■	O	G	L	A	L	A	
S	L	Y	■	E	C	O	■	R	A	S
T	I	M	E	D	■	A	L	L	I	S
E	N	E	M	Y	■	T	O	O	L	E
■	G	S	O	S	■	A	R	A	T	

223

O	S	S	A	■	G	U	M	M	E	D
F	L	O	R	■	A	B	O	U	N	D
T	A	L	C	■	L	O	O	S	E	S
■	O	H	W	E	L	L	■			
T	E	P	E	E	■	T	A	P	S	
T	R	A	D	E	■	S	H	O	A	T
O	R	R	■	O	N	O				
P	O	T	T	S	■	D	U	R	A	N
■	R	S	V	P	■	E	N	L	A	I
■	S	L	O	W	L	Y				
A	T	R	E	A	T	■	O	O	H	S
L	A	O	T	S	E	■	C	F	O	S
G	E	I	S	H	A	■	K	F	C	S

224

O	B	J	E	T	■	U	M	M	A
N	A	O	M	I	S	■	S	A	E	S
B	R	Y	S	O	N	■	N	S	E	C
A	R	C	■	G	A	B	■	T	C	U
S	E	E	■	A	P	O	G	E	E	S
E	L	B	E	■	O	N	E	R	S	
■	R	E	T	U	N	E	S			
W	O	R	S	T	■	D	A	R	C	
G	O	T	O	P	O	T	■	T	A	R
R	O	H	■	S	F	O	■	A	N	I
A	L	E	R	■	I	N	T	R	O	S
T	E	R	A	■	T	E	A	M	U	P
A	N	S	E	■	D	U	S	T	Y	

225

```
V L A S I C ■ C E B U
A I R I E R ■ C S C H
L A N D A U ■ L T D S
U R I ■ T I G E R ■
E S E S ■ S A F A R I
■ S U E L ■ D U R
D E T E R M I N A N T
R A H ■ A I N T ■
I N U R N S ■ H A M S
■ M O O S E ■ C A P
C O B B ■ I N S I T U
T R E O ■ L O A N E R
U S D T ■ E L L I O T
```

226

```
S T R O ■ A X L E S
T E E M ■ S H R I F T
O L A N ■ L I A I S E
A C R I M O N Y ■
T O R ■ H O T S E A T
■ A H O P ■ P F C S
U L N A S ■ R E F E R
S I G N ■ T A X I ■
N E E D L E R ■ C I A
■ C A T E R I N G
C A N U T E ■ E E R O
C R A F T S ■ B N E G
R O L F E ■ A T M O
```

227

```
P E D I ■ L A D L E
C R E M A ■ O B I E S
P A B S T ■ N A I V E
S S E ■ I N G A ■
■ N O T I F ■ R N S
O A T H ■ C O P U L A
C R U E T ■ R O M E S
H O R R O R ■ L O R E
S W E ■ A E S I R ■
■ E D E R ■ M C S
C O R G I ■ T W I C E
H E D G E ■ A P L U S
E N S O R ■ A L P S
```

228

```
G C L E F ■ S C R A M
O R I Y A ■ P O E S Y
P E N E T R A T I N G
H E E ■ H O R ■ N E O
E P A ■ A W K W A R D
R E T S ■ A L Y ■
■ R E A D ■ E N T E
R E V ■ N E U R
S T R A F E S ■ M P H
U E Y ■ A R C ■ P H I
P A N I C B U T T O N
E R E C T ■ B U E N O
S Y S C O ■ A N D Y S
```

SOLUTIONS

229

```
L A M B   I M P U R E
I R A E   D A R N E D
M U S C L E B O U N D
O T T O S     O M O O
      M T W T F
I M R E   O L S E N S
C E E   B U C   P C T
S H E K E L   V I O L
      E N D O W
A N I P     A B O V E
C E N T R I F U G A L
R E T I E S   G L I B
A T O N A L   S E L A
```

230

```
L E N O   M A S C O T
A L E K   Y I P P E E
Y O U I   S L A L O M
S I N N   T S R
    A D E   K R I S
W A Y W O R N   E W W
A S E A S Y A S P I E
D I L   S N O C O N E
I S L E   O S U
    C I V   F I F I
S O I R E E   F L A B
M U T U A L   L E V O
A T E S T S   E S A S
```

231

```
A M I R     I F T H E
C O C O   A S L E E P
T R A C   T R E N D S
H A N K Y P A N K Y
    T E A S E S
M I S D O   L E H A R
M O E       O N A
D R E G S   H I M O M
    O C T A N E
    D I V E B O M B E D
R O W E N A   A R T E
D E A R E R   T E T R
A S S N S   E D A M
```

232

```
A L C O A   A T A I L
S A Y S T   P O R N O
P A S S T H E B U C K
    I S O   A T R I
D O N E   A K C
E N O   E X A C T L Y
B M O C S   T O S C A
T Y R A N N Y   O D D
    N E E   E S S A
P E A U   A U X
S U S C E P T I B L E
A L I K E   E S S E X
T A S S E   S T O A T
```

SOLUTIONS

233

S	A	D	H	E				D	S	T
O	N	E	O	N	E		E	C	H	O
I	N	F	U	S	E		L	A	R	A
L	U	I	S		L	E	E	R	A	T
E	L	L	E		S	C	E	N	E	
D	I	E	T		I	N	T	A	K	E
		O	R	S	E	R				
U	P	S	H	O	T		O	R	T	S
P	R	O	O	F		L	O	O	T	
P	E	N	U	L	T		Y	O	R	E
I	W	A	S		E	A	S	T	O	N
T	A	R	E		N	A	I	L	I	T
Y	R	S			M	S	E	D	S	

234

E	C	C	O		S	E	A	B	E	D
A	A	H	S		I	R	R	U	P	T
G	R	A	S		S	T	I	N	T	S
E	N	R	O	L	L	E	E			
R	E	A		R	E	S	T	S	O	N
		C	L	O	Y		T	A	K	E
S	E	T	A	N		F	A	L	S	E
O	V	E	N		L	I	S	A		
Y	A	R	D	M	A	N		C	T	R
			M	A	T	E	R	I	A	L
H	A	M	I	T	E		A	O	N	E
O	R	A	N	T	S		T	U	T	S
D	I	V	E	S	T		E	S	E	S

235

E	J	E	C	T		G	U	L	A	G
R	A	M	B	O		A	L	A	M	E
E	G	E	S	T		L	A	U	E	R
S	U	R		O	N	E		N	R	A
T	A	I		E	O	N		D	C	L
U	R	L	S		S	A	C	R	E	D
		L	O	V	E	S	H	Y		
A	D	A	G	I	O		O	B	E	Y
K	E	G		T	U	N		A	R	E
I	M	A		R	T	S		S	N	A
M	E	S	S	I		Y	I	K	E	S
B	A	S	S	O		N	T	E	S	T
O	N	E	I	L		C	A	T	T	Y

236

S	L	A	T	S		C	A	S	A	
H	A	C	K	S		R	E	I	N	S
R	I	C	O	H		E	S	T	E	E
E	N	O		A	A	S		O	M	A
W	I	M		P	R	S		N	I	N
	E	M	D	E	N		P	T	A	S
	O	I	D		W	A	H			
L	A	D	Y		S	A	L	E	S	
A	D	A		D	A	S		F	E	R
N	E	T		A	C	T		E	X	O
A	L	I	B	I		R	A	N	I	S
S	I	N	U	S		E	M	C	E	E
	E	G	G	Y		L	E	E	R	Y

SOLUTIONS

237

```
B B A . S T E . S S N
C O F F E R S . T O O
C A B A R E T . A T T
. . N I T E . R O I
N O T D O . F S T O P
S E R A . N A H A .
C O U N T E N A N C E
. N G O S . K E I R
T A C O S . F E W E R
U G H . P E R U .
T A E . A D E P T L Y
O T O . R U S S E T S
R E N . E C H . T R L
```

238

```
E P P A . A S S O R T
R U L E . Y O Y O M A
I T O R . A L M O N D
T O W . A H A B .
U N H A T . C O R A L
. O P A . E L E C T
D O R P . I L K S
B A S R A . P S I .
A K E E M . S M E L T
. H I R T . F Y I
F O R E G O . E M M E
E V E N A S . S A A R
W O O D S Y . L P N S
```

239

```
M A N I C . R O S S I
P A U L O . U N T I L
H U C K L E B E R R Y
. L A U D E . A S A
R A E . M I N O T .
F L A M B E . S E A M
D A R I O . R I G B Y
S E W S . Y E S I A M
. I S O L A . C A Y
I G N . C E L I A .
B E T T E M I D L E R
A N E R A . S E L E S
R E R U N . M A Y N T
```

240

```
A S S A D . R A T S O
M A H E R . E N T E R
T R U R O . D E O R O
S G T . P L Y . P I N
. . D O L M E N .
S T O L E N . O A R S
N E W A T . S I L A S
L Y N N . G O S L O W
. D E N N Y S .
C A M . T U A . T C I
A B E T S . N E A L S
V O T R E . C A T I E
S U Z Y Q . E L E V E
```

SOLUTIONS

241

242

243

244

SOLUTIONS

245

A	M	F	M			E	N	A	M	I	
N	O	L	A		L	A	M	E	S	A	
T	R	A	N	S	L	U	C	E	N	T	
C	O	N	G	E	S	T		T	E	A	
O	S	K	A	R		I	M	M	A	D	
W	E	S			O	C	H	E	R		
			C	A	C	A	O				
	S	P	E	C	S			H	A	S	
S	T	L	E	O		S	L	I	C	E	
I	R	E		L	I	N	E	D	U	P	
M	U	D	D	Y	W	A	T	E	R	S	
I	N	T	O	T	O		C	H	A	I	
	G	O	R	E	N		H	O	S	S	

246

S	A	M	M	S		P	R	M	A	N
O	R	I	E	L		O	O	O	L	A
M	Y	L	A	I		P	A	R	T	V
E	L	I		M	O	U	N	T	I	E
			T	C	E	L	L			
I	M	A	M		N	A	Y	S	A	Y
B	A	N	D	B		R	O	C	C	O
M	A	T	R	O	N		W	R	E	N
			D	A	R	L	A			
E	M	P	R	E	S	S		M	G	O
D	O	F	O	R		V	I	B	E	S
H	A	U	T	E		P	O	L	I	S
S	T	I	C	K		S	C	E	N	A

247

H	Y	E	N	A		C	A	B	A	L
O	A	S	E	S		O	L	I	V	A
A	S	C	O	T		R	A	G	O	N
R	S	A		O	F	F		B	I	C
S	E	P		R	O	U	L	A	D	E
E	R	O	T	I	C		I	N	S	T
		L	E	A	S	I	N	G		
B	O	O	R		L	O	T	T	E	D
E	N	G	A	G	E	D		H	A	O
C	S	I		H	S	I		E	T	E
K	A	S	H	A		D	R	O	S	S
E	L	T	O	N		E	Z	R	A	S
T	E	S	L	A		S	A	Y	T	O

248

C	A	S	T		A	T	N	O	O	N
R	U	P	P		P	H	E	L	P	S
A	N	A	S		P	E	S	E	T	A
M	T	G		A	R	U	T			
			H	A	D	O	N		H	T	C
P	R	E	M	I	X		A	A	A	A
V	I	T	A	M	I	N	P	I	L	L
T	N	T	S		M	E	T	R	I	C
S	D	I		G	A	U	S	S		
			N	I	T	E		P	S	S
A	E	R	O	B	E		T	R	A	N
D	R	I	V	E	L		M	A	N	O
M	E	M	O	R	Y		C	Y	S	T

SOLUTIONS

249

H	E	H		N	Y	S		A	C	T
A	L	A		O	V	E		A	H	I
L	A	R	D	N	E	R		R	I	M
S	T	R	A	U	S	S		O	S	E
	Y	U	K	S			N	E	W	
S	O	R	B	E	T		O	S	L	O
K	N	E	E	S	L	A	P	P	E	R
A	C	A	D		A	S	T	E	R	N
T	E	S		U	S	F	L			
E	M	O		A	R	E	O	L	A	S
K	O	N		M	E	R	R	I	L	Y
E	R	E		A	N	T		N	A	N
Y	E	R		P	T	S		G	D	S

250

S	T	A	S		A	M	A	N	D	A
L	O	E	W		R	A	B	I	E	S
A	B	R	A	C	A	D	A	B	R	A
C	O	I	N	A	G	E		B	A	L
K	O	A	N	S			A	L	I	E
S	T	L		S	O	R	R	E	L	
		O	I	L	U	P				
	R	I	P	E	N	S		N	F	L
N	E	N	E			S	M	O	R	E
E	D	H		S	W	E	A	T	I	T
R	E	E	N	A	C	T	M	E	N	T
T	Y	R	A	N	T		A	L	G	E
S	E	E	Y	O	U		S	L	E	D

251

A	N	O	S	E		S	N	I	P	E
L	A	D	Y	S		I	O	N	I	A
M	O	O	N	L	I	G	H	T	E	R
A	S	N	O		R	E	I			
			N	E	A	P	T	I	D	E
A	R	G	Y	L	E		T	E	E	
C	U	O	M	O		O	L	E	A	N
L	B	S		S	E	E	M	L	Y	
U	S	H	E	R	I	N	G			
	B	H	T		A	L	E	R		
P	E	R	S	O	N	A	L	I	T	Y
D	E	W	E	D		P	L	A	T	A
A	R	E	N	A		A	Y	R	E	S

252

M	A	I	D	S		S	A	B	R	E
G	R	O	U	T		A	R	N	E	L
M	A	R	R	A	M	G	R	A	S	S
		O	P	I	E		I	T	A	
E	M	P		H	D	T	V			
G	E	E	Z		D	E	C	I	D	E
I	N	T	E	R	L	A	R	D	E	D
S	U	E	B	E	E		S	E	M	I
		U	T	A	H		A	Y	N	
I	T	N		A	G	U	A			
C	R	A	C	K	E	R	J	A	C	K
A	I	S	L	E		S	O	L	F	A
O	B	I	E	S		T	B	I	L	L

573

SOLUTIONS

253

G	A	F	F	S			D	U	R	O
A	V	I	L	A		H	E	R	E	I
R	E	R	A	N		I	L	I	E	D
B	O	M	B	A	Y	D	U	C	K	
			B	A	A	E	D			
P	O	K	Y		R	H	E	I	M	S
S	A	O		A	D	O		T	A	E
P	R	O	T	E	M		A	N	E	G
			U	R	A	L	S			
	R	E	F	I	N	E	M	E	N	T
V	E	S	T	A		B	A	T	O	R
A	N	S	E	L		E	R	O	D	E
L	E	A	D			C	A	N	I	T

254

B	A	D	A	T		B	A	N	G
A	M	E	N	S		U	L	E	E
S	O	B	S	T	O	R	I	E	S
H	S	T		R	I	G	I	D	
		P	A	L	S		L	A	H
P	O	P	U	P	S		U	E	L	E
S	T	A	B	S		I	F	S	A	Y
A	I	R	S		G	N	O	S	I	S
T	S	A		A	R	E	S		
	L	I	V	E	R		A	B	O
	T	Y	P	E	W	R	I	T	E	R
	I	Z	O	D		O	P	E	R	E
	M	E	S	A		R	A	N	T	O

255

S	M	I	T	H		S	N	A	P
S	O	T	H	O		O	P	E	D	S
R	E	O	R	G		G	O	A	D	S
S	T	R	A	W	B	E	R	R	Y	
			I	B	E	A	M		
C	A	N	O	L	A		D	I	A	N
Y	I	E	L	D		P	I	S	T	E
S	T	U	D		F	O	C	S	L	E
		T	W	I	R	P		
	P	R	O	F	I	C	I	E	N	T
M	A	I	M	S		O	F	T	E	R
M	I	N	E	O		R	A	T	S	O
E	L	O	N		N	T	E	S	T

256

B	I	R	L		E	B	B	E	D
I	C	E	E		D	R	O	V	E
T	I	V	O		A	D	I	D	A	S
	O	N	I	T		E	Y	C	K
S	P	L	I	N	T	E	R	S	
G	R	U	D	G	E	S		T	S	A
A	I	T		E	S	C		O	N	S
S	S	I		S	T	A	N	C	E	S
	O	U	T	S	P	O	K	E	N
M	I	N	N		T	E	R	I
E	M	I	L	I	O		M	N	E	M
A	N	Z	A	C		A	G	A	L
L	O	E	W	E		S	S	T	S

SOLUTIONS

257

S	S	W		N	E	G				
E	T	E		I	D	A		C	U	R
P	O	L	I	C	E	S	T	A	T	E
I	L	L	G	O		S	I	R	U	P
A	L	T	O			A	B	B	R	
S	E	E	T	O	I	T		O	E	O
	M	O	N	S	O	O	N			
I	M	P		T	S	A	R	D	O	M
N	E	E	D		N	A	L	A		
O	S	R	I	C		D	O	T	E	D
I	N	E	F	F	E	C	T	I	V	E
L	E	D		O	R	U		N	E	D
	S	O	P		G	L	O			

258

M	F	D		A	L	L		A	A	E
E	S	O		M	I	I		A	R	O
A	T	A		O	F	S	O	R	T	S
N	O	T	I		T	I	N	O	S	
S	P	O	N	G	E		E	N	I	D
	U	N	A	D	V	I	S	E	D	
I	R	R		N	W	A		P	R	S
G	E	O	R	G	E	T	T	E		
A	G	F	A		I	S	O	L	D	E
	I	D	T	A	G		A	L	E	G
G	O	U	A	C	H	E		I	N	G
A	N	T		A	T	C		N	E	O
P	S	Y		I	S	T		G	S	N

259

H	O	C		D	B	L		P	P	S
E	L	O		A	R	A		S	E	L
R	I	T		P	O	R	T	I	C	O
O	N	Y	X		K	D	S			
		L	E	S	E		K	I	M	S
N	E	E	S	O	N		S	R	I	S
O	L	D		B	H	T		R	S	T
L	E	O	V		E	C	L	A	T	S
A	C	N	E		A	B	C	D		
		R	N	R		D	I	T	Z	
K	I	B	B	U	T	Z		A	S	A
I	C	I		N	E	A		T	A	H
D	S	C		C	D	C		E	R	N

260

N	S	F		A	S	E		D	A	B
L	I	U		C	T	A		I	S	U
O	L	N		C	I	R		A	T	O
W	O	N	D	E	R	W	O	M	A	N
		Y	I	P		I	R	E		
P	A	B	S	T		G	E	T	O	N
U	H	U	H			G	R	A	Y	
B	A	S	R	A		R	A	I	T	T
		I	A	T		I	N	C		
F	I	N	G	E	R	B	O	A	R	D
L	G	E		A	D	E		L	A	A
E	A	S		M	A	Y		L	C	D
D	S	S		S	S	E		Y	E	O

SOLUTIONS

261

A	G	F	A				A	R	I	A
T	E	A	C	H		S	N	A	I	L
R	O	C	C	O		A	N	O	S	E
A	S	S		R	E	N	I			
		I	N	O	L	D		D	O	W
D	I	M	E		D	A	Y	O	N	E
E	D	I	C	T		L	O	W	E	S
F	O	L	K	S	Y		K	N	I	T
T	S	E		K	U	D	O	S		
		S	T	L	O		W	O	O	
P	E	T	E	S		L	Y	I	N	G
L	U	N	I	K		L	E	N	D	L
O	R	T	S				A	G	E	E

262

R	U	M	B	A		C	D	R	O	M
F	A	T	A	H		O	O	M	P	A
S	L	A	T	E		N	E	N	E	H
			I	M	A	C	S			
A	R	B	S		C	L	A	S	P	S
S	E	E	T	H	R	U		T	Y	P
Y	A	L	E	U		D	R	I	L	Y
L	I	L		S	L	E	E	P	E	R
A	R	I	G	H	T		D	E	S	I
		O	H	R	O	B				
I	F	Y	O	U		P	L	A	C	E
R	A	M	P	S		A	U	D	I	S
T	R	A	S	H		L	E	A	V	E

263

S	A	R	D	I		A	C	D	C	
U	S	A	I	N		S	H	U	N	
P	E	R	F	E	C	T	I	O	N	
E	T	E		R	O	I	L			
		E	A	T	A		D	S	M	S
W	R	A	N	G	L	E		H	O	E
A	O	R	T	A		Q	U	E	E	N
B	A	T		S	O	U	R	E	S	T
E	D	H	S		P	A	L	P		
		K	T	E	L		S	S	I	
	P	L	U	G	N	I	C	K	E	L
	U	G	L	I		Z	A	I	R	E
	P	E	L	F		E	N	N	I	S

264

G	A	S	P	E		A	S	C	A	P
P	R	I	O	R		M	A	R	C	O
O	R	E	O	S		A	R	E	E	L
	O	R	L	E	S		G	A	Y	E
M	G	R	S		E	L	E	M		
A	A	A		H	A	S	S	O	C	K
A	T	L		I	S	A		F	O	O
S	E	E	S	F	I	T		T	U	B
		O	T	I	C		B	A	N	E
C	E	N	O		K	C	A	R	S	
O	D	E	L	L		A	T	T	E	N
I	N	A	I	D		S	H	A	L	L
L	A	N	D	S		T	E	R	S	E

265

R	E	T	S				S	U	E	T
A	L	O	O	F		H	A	T	L	O
G	I	N	S	U		O	W	N	U	P
U	N	I	O	N	L	A	B	E	L	
			G	I	R	L				
M	A	H	O	U	T		A	M	A	P
O	L	A	F	S		D	D	A	Y	S
B	E	E	F		P	O	E	T	R	Y
		S	A	R	I					
	C	I	T	R	O	N	E	L	L	A
C	A	C	A	O		G	R	O	U	P
T	I	A	G	O		S	I	E	G	E
A	N	N	E			C	B	E	S	

266

N	A	A	N	S		B	L	I	M	P
A	S	S	E	T		L	A	N	A	I
P	O	W	E	R	O	U	T	A	G	E
E	N	A		A	V	E		R	N	R
S	I	R		T	E	S		E	E	C
	A	M	O	U	R		C	A	T	E
		M	M	D	C	L				
S	E	A	M		R	A	I	D	S	
E	L	G		A	I	S		M	O	B
E	T	O		P	V	C		I	L	A
N	O	R	T	H	E	A	S	T	E	R
I	R	A	N	I		R	E	R	I	G
N	O	E	N	D		A	M	I	L	E

267

L	A	S	E	D		G	C	L	E	F
I	C	O	N	O		T	A	I	T	O
N	E	R	O	S		I	N	L	A	W
C	H	O	K	E	R		Y	A	L	L
		R	I	S	E	T	O			
C	H	I	S		A	B	U	S	E	R
B	E	T		O	R	S		P	L	S
C	R	Y	I	N	G		L	I	D	A
		N	E	U	R	O	N			
S	E	G	A		E	E	Y	O	R	E
E	C	A	R	D		S	O	F	I	A
W	H	Y	M	E		A	L	F	A	S
N	T	E	S	T		W	A	S	A	T

268

P	O	S	S	E		C	L	E	O
H	O	O	H	A	S		A	I	R	Y
I	N	C	A	S	H		P	I	N	E
		I	Q	T	E	S	T			
A	G	A		E	M	T		T	P	S
S	O	L	A	R		R	O	A	R	K
S	T	I	P	E		A	L	B	E	E
A	B	Z	U	G		I	N	L	O	W
D	Y	E		G	A	G		E	P	S
		E	S	C	H	E	W			
S	E	R	A		I	T	S	A	Y	S
S	P	A	R		S	U	N	R	A	Y
I	H	O	P			P	E	E	R	S

SOLUTIONS

269

T	A	L	I	A		C	A	P	R	A
S	T	O	A	T		A	B	R	A	M
T	A	R	T	A	R	S	A	U	C	E
R	T	E		D	O	C		D	E	N
A	U	L	D		B	A	L	E	R	S
P	R	E	P		O	R	U			
S	K	I	L	L		A	R	G	U	E
			U	I	E		I	A	N	S
S	E	A	S	O	N		D	I	R	T
H	E	N		N	T	H		N	A	H
I	N	O	P	E	R	A	T	I	V	E
R	I	T	A	S		T	E	N	E	T
R	E	E	D	S		E	A	G	L	E

270

S	E	L	F			L	O	W	E	
A	V	I	A		M	E	L	O	N	
L	E	F	T		E	N	D	O	R	A
A	N	E		A	M	O		L	O	P
M	A	I	L	B	O	X		G	L	O
I	S	N	E	A	R		B	A	L	D
			S	T	A	Y	P	U	T	
S	L	U	T		C	A	R	H	O	P
O	E	R		S	H	U	T	E	Y	E
P	G	A		M	I	L		R	S	T
H	U	N	G	U	P		S	I	T	U
	I	C	E	R	S		O	N	E	L
	N	E	R	F			A	G	R	A

271

A	B	A	S	H		R	A	T	T	
R	A	D	I	I		P	R	O	E	M
O	M	A	R	R		M	E	N	L	O
A	B	M		E	P	S		S	A	R
R	I	V	A	L	S		I	V	E	
		I	S	I	T	I		L	I	S
H	O	N	A	N		S	A	L	V	O
A	P	A		G	N	O	M	E		
T	E	T		G	L	Y	C	O	L	
A	N	I		K	O	A		T	R	I
R	E	E	S	E		T	I	O	G	A
I	R	R	E	G		E	L	M	A	N
	S	I	N	S		D	A	Y	N	E

272

	B	E	A	M		S	L	A	B	
	A	L	F	A		C	A	D	R	E
S	T	A	R	S	T	U	D	D	E	D
O	A	P		O	W	L		U	W	E
H	A	S	A	N	I	P		C	E	N
O	N	E	L		S	T	E	E	D	S
			B	E	T	S	Y			
S	T	R	A	T	I		E	A	V	E
E	E	E		I	N	A	S	P	I	N
P	C	S		E	G	S		E	S	C
T	H	E	A	N	S	W	E	R	I	S
A	I	D	A	N		A	C	C	T	
	E	A	S	E		N	O	U	S	

SOLUTIONS

273

F	A	C	I	E		O	S	O	L	E
O	N	O	F	F		N	O	P	E	S
A	D	L	A	I		E	S	P	Y	S
M	I	D		L	A	H		O	T	E
E	R	B		E	P	A		R	E	N
R	O	L	L		P	L	A	T		
	N	O	M	E		F	L	U	B	
	O	N	Y	X		S	N	U	G	
R	A	D		E	X	O		I	R	R
H	R	E		W	O	N		S	K	A
O	R	D	I	E		L	E	T	I	T
M	A	L	T	A		A	L	I	N	E
B	U	Y	E	R		Y	M	C	A	S

274

G	B	E		O	A	F		U	B	I
A	R	M		S	L	A	M	M	E	R
S	A	U	D	I	A	R	A	B	I	A
P	E	L	E	E		T	N	O	T	E
	S	A	R	A	H	S				
A	L	I	D		L	E	E	R	A	T
F	O	O	L	S	E	R	R	A	N	D
T	U	N	E	I	N		V	I	E	S
	T	R	E	P	A	N				
A	L	I	T	O		E	N	D	T	O
L	O	S	E	C	O	N	T	R	O	L
B	E	E	R	C	A	N		O	D	A
A	W	E		O	R	E		P	O	S

275

L	A	P		B	L	U				
O	D	O	A	C	E	R		U	S	A
M	A	L	F	E	A	S	A	N	C	E
A	M	I	A		A	T	P	A	R	
	C	T	N	S		O	R	T		
S	A	Y	E	S	T		Y	O	H	O
E	C	H		F	A	Y		F	E	M
Q	U	O	I		H	A	L	I	D	E
	T	L	C		L	O	U	T		
M	E	D	E	A		I	A	G	O	
S	L	E	E	P	I	N	G	B	A	G
G	Y	R		B	R	A	I	L	L	E
	S	T	P		E	E	E			

276

T	O	N	E		A	S	H	I	N	E
A	R	A	M		L	I	E	S	I	N
R	E	M	O	N	S	T	R	A	T	E
P	L	A	T	O	O	N		A	E	R
O	S	T	E	O		A	C	R	O	
N	E	H		N	O	L	E	S	S	
	E	A	M	E	S					
	C	A	N	N	E	D		S	A	O
S	A	M	E		G	I	L	D	S	
O	R	U		E	L	E	G	A	N	T
D	I	S	A	P	P	R	O	V	A	L
O	N	E	G	I	G		T	E	T	E
M	A	D	A	S	A		O	D	E	R

SOLUTIONS

277

```
C A B . A C S . . .
A L E . A L A . C L E
S E N D S A B R O A D
T R E E . S E E M L Y
. F L U S . E P A .
S T A L L S . K A N E
I O C . A C A . S N A
T A T S . H A W S E R
. D R E . E A R P
T I E R O D . I O T A
D E S T R U C T I O N
S R S . A L G . N B C
. . . L E I . T E E
```

278

```
A R T Y . S A P O R S
V E R A . E N R A P T
O D E R . C O O K I E
W O O D C R A F T .
. . M A E . S R A S
C A N A S T A . E N O
P R U N E . S M E A R
A M T . R I P O S T E
S A B E . G E L .
. R E D U N D A N T
A G O R A E . I F H E
P E W I T S . N A R A
R E N E E S . G R A M
```

279

```
H O R S . A T W I L L
E L E C . G E H R I G
B A E R . A N Y O N E
E F F I C I E N C Y .
. . P I N T O .
S H A T T . S T O I C
E A L . . . A V A
V D A R A . C D R O M
. . U T L E Y .
. S U S T E N A N C E
C A E S A R . D A N L
C A L I C O . I D E E
C R E A K Y . C A T E
```

280

```
A T H O S . C I G A R
T A U P E . E N U R E
P R E E X I S T I N G
S A D R . D A R .
. . A N D R O G E N
T O O T O O . U P I
I F E E L . M E R I T
P A U . A C C U S E
I N F O R M A L .
. . N E A . I E S T
J A N I S J O P L I N
A S O N E . T S L O T
R E N E E . S E A N S
```

580

SOLUTIONS

281

```
D I P . B S A . . .
O A R . R E G . I S O
N M E . A M O U N T S
A T T H E . G A T O S
L O T I . . R E N I .
D O Y L I E S . R E E
. . P O A C H E S . .
O E R . L O U D T I E
O Y E R . . D E N G .
M E T E S . S O L V E
P O T O R O O . L E S
A N Y . I B M . A R T
. . S S E . R T S . .
```

282

```
G A P . U V M . C U D
R T E . P A O . D N A
U K R . A C A D E M E
B A M A . L B O . . .
. E A T A . A D I E .
E V A S I V E . E M U
P A B S T . L E H A R
P T L . I D S A Y N O
A S E T . R E C D . .
. A N E . H R A P . .
W I L L O W Y . A C R
A N I . T U A . T I E
Y A T . A P R . E D D
```

283

```
A L P E . I T S S O .
N O R G E . L A H T I
D E I S M . S P O O L
O W N . A A A . U P C
R E T U N E . L G A .
. I N U S E . D A K .
P E N C E . C R E P E
A L G . L O S E R . .
S A P . N T E S T S .
S I R . D O A . T R E
A N E M O . S Y R U P
D E S A C . Y E A S T
O S S I E . P P S S .
```

284

```
S W I M . . K U H N .
O O N A . S V E L T E
L O T S . L U N A C Y
E Z E K I E L . . . .
S Y R . D E C A D E S
. L O O K A L I K E .
C A I R N . N O R G E
P I N S T R I P E . .
O N E O C A T . C D I
. . A S E P T I C . .
P O P A R T . A I D A
A Z A L E A . P O S H
T S K S . . A N O N .
```

SOLUTIONS

285

P	O	T		M	C	C		B	I	S
A	S	H		E	O	E		A	L	T
S	H	E		D	N	S		T	O	A
A	I	R	L	I	F	T		M	S	G
		M	I	C	R	A		A	T	E
N	O	O	T	K	A			N	Y	S
I	B	N		S	T	S		F	O	E
C	S	U			E	A	T	O	U	T
E	T	C		E	R	R	O	R		
T	A	L		D	N	A	T	E	S	T
I	C	E		D	I	L		V	I	G
E	L	A		I	T	E		E	P	I
S	E	R		E	Y	E		R	E	F

286

A	T	F		B	O	W				
A	V	O	C	A	D	O		N	P	R
R	A	R	E	B	I	T		E	A	U
		G	L	Y	C		F	U	N	D
F	L	E	E	T		P	E	T	E	Y
P	O	T	B	O	I	L	E	R		
S	W	M		O	R	U		O	C	H
	E	N	T	E	R	I	N	T	O	
R	A	N	C	H		A	T	B	A	T
O	M	O	O		A	L	S	O		
E	M	T		G	L	I	M	M	E	R
G	O	S		T	O	T	E	B	A	G
		S	T	Y		S	R	S		

287

R	E	P	O			N	I	N	O
A	L	E	R		A	O	L	E	R
P	O	N	D		M	A	R	K	E	D
T	I	T	A	N	I	U	M		
	H	I	E	D		A	S	A	P
S	T	O	N	E	D		S	P	U	R
P	A	U		D	L	I		E	N	E
I	N	S	C		E	R	S	A	T	Z
T	H	E	O		M	U	I	R		
		U	P	A	N	C	H	O	R
J	A	R	G	O	N		K	E	N	S
I	M	S	A	D			L	A	M	S
B	E	A	R			E	D	Y	S

288

R	A	J	A		S	H	E	E	R
A	R	A	M		S	K	I	M	P	Y
N	A	Z	I		E	A	R	T	H	S
I	T	Z	A		R	T	E		
		H	B	A	R		E	S	P	Y
T	E	A	L	E	A	F		E	N	E
I	N	N	E	R		E	A	M	E	S
L	C	D		Y	T	T	R	I	U	M
T	O	S	S		N	A	I	F		
		H	M	O		G	L	I	B
F	A	C	E	I	T		A	U	N	T
O	L	D	A	G	E		T	I	N	E
E	Y	E	R	S			O	D	O	N

582

289

290

```
B I P E D   E F S
  R E N A M E   C U E
B I C A R B O N A T E
A D A G E     E R I N
B E M E   E A S T L A
E R E   P U T T E E
      L U B E S
  H E I N I E   F C C
G Y R A T E   L I R A
E B O N     T I R E D
O R D E R L I N E S S
D I E   C O N T A C
E D D   A P A S T
```

```
G U M B O   S P I T S
O H A R A   M A N U P
T U M O R   E A S E L
I R E   L O W R I S E
T A T T O O     D D E
      I C C   L E A N
  H U N K Y D O R Y
M O P E   T E T
I L A   E S S E N E
N Y N O R S K   L I B
I S D U E   T A U R O
M E U S E   O R T O N
S E P T S   P O E S Y
```

291

292

```
C O R P   F I A T S
T R E O   P A R S E E
R O F L   R A I D E R
    L I C E   T I N A
T H E O R E T I C A L
I O C   O X E S
L I T   S I T   H E T
    U S S R   E N S
Y A C K E T Y Y A C K
O S H A   E L U L
G O E S O N   K E A N
I L L E S T   O R T S
C O A S T   N S F W
```

```
S I P E   H E E H E E
O N O R   A P P E N D
A F O E   R E C A S T
K O R N   R E O
    L O G Y   T T O P
K E Y W O R D   A L A
O T O   T E A   B I N
P U F   A A M I L N E
F I F E   S E S E
    L A O   O L A Y
S W T E N N   M A T A
D I O N N E   E N R Y
S E A A I R   R D A S
```

SOLUTIONS

293

M	A	G	I	C			S	A	A	B
A	R	E	S	O		U	H	U	R	A
S	O	N	I	C		N	O	T	A	T
C	O	T	T	O	N	W	O	O	L	
		M	A	O	R	I				
K	O	B	E		D	A	N	D	E	R
A	I	T		E	S	P		O	R	O
I	D	U	N	N	O		O	G	R	E
		A	S	F	A	R				
	B	E	N	E	F	A	C	T	O	R
I	R	E	N	A		L	H	A	S	A
O	N	E	I	L		T	I	P	S	Y
N	O	S	E			O	L	E	O	S

294

L	A	P	D			T	O	R	U	S
I	N	R	I		U	R	G	E	N	T
M	O	O	S		N	E	E	D	B	E
O	N	S	T	R	I	K	E			
		E	U	L	A		S	S	N	S
E	X	C	R	E	T	E		K	E	L
D	R	U	B	S		C	A	I	R	O
E	A	T		S	N	O	W	J	O	B
R	Y	E	S		O	L	E	A		
			H	I	B	I	S	C	U	S
M	E	S	A	B	I		O	K	L	A
M	A	E	N	A	D		M	E	N	E
C	R	I	E	R			E	T	A	S

295

A	C	H	E	S		H	A	S	O	N
C	H	E	V	Y		U	D	I	N	E
L	O	R	E	N		M	E	N	L	O
U	P	I	N	T	H	E	S	K	Y	
	T	S	H	I	R	T				
C	I	A	O		G	U	E	R	R	E
B	E	G		S	H	S		E	E	L
C	R	E	M	E	S		Y	L	E	M
		I	C	E	T	E	A			
	C	O	L	L	A	R	S	T	U	D
M	A	T	S	U		I	S	I	T	I
I	T	H	A	D		K	I	O	W	A
S	T	O	P	E		E	R	N	O	S

296

G	A	S	U	P		S	P	L	A	Y
A	D	A	G	E		I	G	O	T	O
P	O	T	A	T	O	S	A	C	K	S
E	G	S		I	A	L		H	A	T
		U	T	T	E	R				
T	O	R	M	E		Y	E	M	E	N
A	V	I	A			R	A	Z	A	
C	O	P	S	E		C	U	R	R	Y
		S	L	O	A	N				
A	R	I		M	T	M		D	I	A
L	A	T	T	I	C	E	W	O	R	K
S	H	I	R	R		R	I	C	K	I
O	M	N	I	A		A	T	E	S	O

584

SOLUTIONS

297

S	I	G	N	A	L	■	P	D	F	S
A	R	O	U	S	E	■	H	O	R	A
M	E	D	I	C	I	N	E	M	A	N
■	C	T	A	■	G	N	O	T	E	
A	T	H	■	P	L	A	Y	■		
C	I	I	■	O	I	L	L	I	T	
E	E	L	■	I	G	O	■	O	M	A
H	A	D	A	G	O	■	W	S	U	
■	M	E	N	O	■	W	O	T		
O	C	T	E	T	■	B	S	A	■	
T	H	E	R	A	P	E	U	T	I	C
H	A	E	C	■	V	A	R	E	S	E
O	N	M	E	■	T	H	I	R	T	Y

298

T	I	G	H	T	■	E	R	N	E	S
S	T	E	I	N	■	L	U	S	T	Y
A	L	L	P	O	W	E	R	F	U	L
R	L	S	■	T	O	G	■	W	I	L
■	S	E	M	I	S	■				
S	A	D	A	■	A	A	H	S	A	T
V	I	O	L	O	N	C	E	L	L	O
U	N	C	U	R	L	■	R	O	Y	S
■	T	B	I	R	D	■				
A	S	I	■	I	K	O	■	G	S	A
L	O	T	U	S	E	A	T	E	R	S
A	L	E	R	O	■	R	H	E	T	T
D	E	M	O	N	■	K	A	Z	A	A

299

A	L	A	R	Y	■	Y	U	M	M	Y
R	O	D	E	O	■	A	S	I	D	E
C	O	V	E	N	■	C	E	S	T	A
S	P	E	C	K	■	H	S	T	■	
■	R	H	E	T	T	■	S	T	D	
R	E	T	O	R	E	■	O	R	O	
I	D	I	■	S	P	A	■	F	A	M
E	E	S	■	E	N	G	A	G	E	
U	R	E	■	N	E	G	E	V	■	
■	M	A	E	■	E	N	A	M	I	
O	T	E	R	I	■	R	E	L	E	T
A	R	N	E	L	■	E	R	O	S	E
R	I	T	A	S	■	D	A	N	A	S

300

A	R	G	H	■	B	E	S	O	T	S
D	E	L	I	■	O	N	T	H	E	E
A	N	O	A	■	W	I	R	I	E	R
H	O	O	T	■	L	A	A	■		
■	M	U	N	I	C	I	P	A	L	
B	R	Y	S	O	N	■	N	A	L	A
L	O	G	■	L	G	E	■	T	I	N
E	C	U	A	■	A	C	A	C	I	A
W	A	S	H	C	L	O	T	H	■	
■	I	A	L	■	T	O	P	O		
F	L	A	M	B	E	■	H	A	R	P
H	O	R	S	E	Y	■	A	T	I	E
A	L	T	A	R	S	■	T	E	S	S

SOLUTIONS

301

K	E	E	P	S		S	L	E	D	S
A	N	T	R	A		T	A	C	I	T
A	R	R	I	D		A	C	R	E	D
T	O	U	G	H	I	T	O	U	T	
	O	S	S	E	O	U	S			
O	T	C			U	T	T	E	R	S
P	E	A	R	S		E	E	L	E	R
A	D	N	A	T	E			I	M	O
		I	R	O	N	A	G	E		
	L	O	S	E	N	O	T	I	M	E
S	I	D	E	A		R	A	B	B	I
A	N	O	U	K		A	L	L	E	N
R	O	M	P	S		D	E	E	R	E

302

D	E	I	G	N		S	O	R	E	N
O	R	A	T	E		C	R	E	D	O
M	I	N	I	C	O	U	R	S	E	S
O	S	S		T	R	L		T	R	Y
			P	A	U	P	E	R		
B	A	B	A	R		T	N	O	T	E
I	P	O	D			R	O	A	D	
S	T	O	R	Y		M	O	M	M	Y
		K	E	E	P	O	N			
O	T	C		S	U	P		I	B	M
S	E	L	F	I	M	P	O	S	E	D
H	A	U	S	A		E	L	L	E	S
A	L	B	U	M		T	A	S	S	E

303

P	I	L	E	I	N		C	M	A
A	N	O	S	M	I	A		H	U	D
S	H	O	P	S	T	E	W	A	R	D
T	O	N	I	O		R	A	I	M	I
I	C	E	E		M	I	S	S	U	S
S	K	Y	S	C	R	A	P	E	R	
			A	L	L					
	T	H	R	E	E	S	C	O	R	E
G	R	O	U	S	E		A	R	E	D
L	E	O	N	A		D	R	D	R	E
U	N	D	E	R	V	A	L	U	E	S
T	C	I		S	E	N	O	R	A	S
S	H	E		R	E	S	E	D	A	

304

S	A	V	E			E	S	C	E
E	D	I	N	A		W	A	U	L	S
R	E	C	T	I		A	T	B	A	T
I	N	T		R	E	I	S	S	U	E
F	O	O	T	M	A	N		T	S	R
	R	Y	A	N	S		A	E	S	
	M	I	S	T		C	T	N	S	
S	E	A		T	R	O	U	T		
T	A	C		R	E	T	A	I	L	S
I	S	R	A	E	L	I		A	A	A
G	L	O	P	S		N	O	L	T	E
M	E	S	A	S		G	A	L	E	N
A	S	S	T			S	Y	N	S	

SOLUTIONS

305

S	U	Z	Y	Q		M	A	C	H	U
S	K	I	E	R		A	R	O	A	R
R	E	N	T	A		I	R	V	I	N
S	S	E		T	A	T		E	G	S
			M	I	D	A	I	R		
A	U	D	I	O	V	I	S	U	A	L
P	N	I	N				L	P	G	A
O	U	T	O	F	S	E	A	S	O	N
		S	T	R	E	A	M			
I	T	I		A	P	R		I	S	H
P	R	E	O	P		W	A	S	H	O
S	Y	S	O	P		A	D	A	M	A
E	A	T	M	E		X	E	R	O	X

306

Y	W	C	A		O	N	E	P	E	R
E	H	U	D		P	E	P	I	T	A
S	O	L	I		E	I	S	N	E	R
M	A	T	T	I	N	G				
			A	T	H	E	A	R	T	
A	V	E	E	N	O		R	U	S	E
R	E	N	D	S		O	D	E	T	S
G	A	I	A		I	N	A	R	U	T
O	L	D	N	I	C	K				
			D	E	P	R	E	S	S	
G	O	S	S	I	P		C	M	O	N
T	O	O	T	O	O		A	M	S	O
E	N	C	A	M	P		S	A	A	B

307

A	T	M		D	M	C		F	T	S
B	R	A		I	S	E		A	R	A
B	O	T	H	E	R	A	T	I	O	N
A	L	S	O		P	S	A	L	M	
S	L	U	R	P		E	R	U	P	T
		S	E	A	F	A	R	E	R	
O	R	D	E	R	L	I	N	E	S	S
R	E	A	S	S	E	R	T			
L	I	T	H	O		E	U	L	E	R
	S	A	O	N	E		L	I	F	E
E	S	S	E	N	T	I	A	L	L	Y
C	U	E		E	C	O		T	A	E
T	E	T		L	S	U		S	T	S

308

T	H	E	M	E		H	A	W	S	E
E	A	T	I	T		E	T	H	Y	L
Q	U	A	R	T	E	R	T	O	N	E
U	L	M		A	R	S		S	O	V
I	S	I	T		D	E	C	O	D	E
L	I	N	A		E	L	O			
A	N	E	N	T		F	O	R	M	E
			Y	R	S		N	A	A	N
D	E	R	A	I	L		S	P	C	A
A	R	O		P	Y	E		A	A	M
T	O	U	T	L	E	M	O	N	D	E
E	S	S	I	E		U	S	U	A	L
D	E	T	O	X		S	H	I	M	S

587

309

S	N	A	R	F		D	C	C	A	B
U	L	C	E	R		U	H	U	R	A
B	E	T	T	A		S	E	R	I	N
	R	E	I	N	S	T	A	T	E	
	D	E	C	A	M	P				
T	K	O	S		Y	O	O	H	O	O
A	A	U		G	N	P		A	N	T
E	L	T	O	R	O		I	L	I	E
			G	E	T	O	F	F		
	C	H	A	M	O	M	I	L	E	
U	H	A	U	L		A	C	I	N	G
F	U	N	G	I		N	A	F	T	A
O	G	D	E	N		I	N	E	R	T

310

L	I	N		R	B	S				
I	F	A		A	B	A		K	O	R
M	E	I		S	A	L	T	I	N	E
B	E	L	C	H		S	A	L	E	S
O	L	S	E	N	S		M	O	M	A
		C	L	E	A	R	A	W	A	Y
T	R	I		S	N	O		A	N	S
R	E	S	I	S	T	A	N	T		
I	F	S	O		E	D	I	T	O	R
V	I	O	L	A		S	C	H	M	O
I	N	R	E	A	C	H		O	E	D
A	E	S		S	F	O		U	G	A
		S	O	W		R	A	N		

311

M	C	R	I	B		A	B	E	A	M
A	L	A	N	A		C	O	N	D	I
D	E	S	T	R	U	C	T	I	O	N
E	N	T		C	P	U		S	N	O
I	C	E	C	A	P	S		L	A	A
T	H	R	A		E	A	S	E	I	N
		C	T	R	L	S				
N	O	R	O	O	M		G	L	O	M
O	M	E		P	O	R	T	A	G	E
I	A	L		S	S	I		G	A	T
S	H	A	R	P	T	O	N	G	U	E
E	A	T	N	O		D	I	E	G	O
S	N	E	R	T		E	N	D	E	R

312

R	I	T	E		P	S	A	N	D
A	T	O	N		W	E	A	S	E	L
Z	I	O	N		H	E	S	T	E	R
A	N	T	E	L	O	P	E		
	H	A	L	S		S	A	M	E
M	A	S		A	T	T		N	O	D
E	R	O		M	H	O		A	R	G
G	A	M		A	E	R		L	A	Y
O	N	E	I		B	O	R	G	
	L	O	O	S	E	E	N	D
C	A	R	E	S	S		A	S	Y	E
O	M	A	N	I	S		L	I	N	C
B	O	W	E	S		M	A	Y	O

SOLUTIONS

313

A	L	A	D			A	D	A	M	S
B	O	L	E		O	N	E	S	I	E
S	O	L	S		V	I	E	N	N	A
	S	T	A	M	E	N		A	D	L
D	E	O	D	A	R		P	A	Y	
I	L	L	E	G	A	L				
K	Y	D		I	B	E		A	P	I
			C	A	V	E	M	A	N	
A	I	N			R	E	T	U	R	N
S	R	O		B	R	E	A	S	T	
L	E	T	S	B	E		L	I	N	A
E	N	R	O	L	L		I	N	E	Z
W	E	E	D	S			A	G	R	O

314

B	E	G	E	T		D	D	A	Y	S
C	R	U	S	E		H	E	R	E	I
E	R	I	K	A		L	E	M	A	N
	D	E	R	N		P	A	H	K	
B	E	A	R		U	P	S			
U	R	N		A	L	R	E	A	D	Y
L	T	C	O	L		I	A	M	S	O
B	E	E	R	K	E	G		B	O	L
		I	A	L		O	R	S	K	
M	A	D	E		I	N	F	O		
T	H	O	N	G		E	T	S	E	Q
G	O	T	T	I		M	E	I	E	R
E	P	E	E	S		O	R	A	L	S

315

M	O	T	T	S		L	A	M	A	R
A	R	A	C	E		A	M	O	V	E
S	E	M	I	R	E	T	I	R	E	D
C	O	E		T	N	T		A	R	A
		S	A	G	E	T				
N	I	L	E	S		S	O	L	A	R
E	T	A	L			S	E	A	L	
E	S	T	A	S		S	E	U	S	S
		H	A	T	E	A				
E	G	O		N	A	L		C	S	S
T	A	K	E	T	H	E	C	A	K	E
C	I	R	C	A		C	I	D	E	R
S	N	A	G	S		T	A	S	E	S

316

V	O	C		A	P	B				
E	V	O		D	E	A		L	L	B
G	U	N	N	E	R	Y		O	Y	E
A	L	V	A		C	H	I	N	C	H
S	E	E	Y	O	U		O	G	E	E
		Y	A	K	S		U	S	E	S
E	N	O		D	S	M		H	S	T
L	I	R	R		I	T	S	O		
I	T	B	E		O	M	E	R	T	A
S	W	E	D	E	N		L	E	O	I
S	I	L		C	C	L	A	M	P	S
A	T	T		O	A	T		A	S	L
			L	P	S		N	Y	E	

SOLUTIONS

317

T	I	S	H	■	R	A	F	A	E	L
O	B	O	E	■	O	R	E	L	S	E
T	E	L	E	C	O	M	M	U	T	E
E	A	T	■	E	K	E	■	M	E	R
D	M	I	T	R	I	■	I	F	I	■
■	■	D	E	E	E	■	N	A	N	■
V	E	R	S	A	■	D	R	A	N	G
I	P	A	■	L	A	G	O	■	■	■
S	I	P	■	C	A	M	E	B	Y	■
A	G	T	■	S	T	R	■	M	E	I
G	O	U	P	I	N	S	M	O	K	E
E	N	R	I	C	O	■	A	R	A	L
S	E	E	S	A	W	■	D	Y	A	D

318

P	R	E	K	■	L	E	C	A	R
L	E	V	I	■	P	A	N	D	A	S
A	B	E	T	■	U	D	D	E	R	S
T	A	N	K	A	R	D	S	■	■	■
■	■	T	A	R	P	■	I	S	N	O
B	R	U	T	A	L	■	T	T	O	P
Y	E	A	■	T	E	A	■	R	I	P
S	A	T	B	■	H	U	M	O	R	S
O	D	E	A	■	E	L	O	N	■	■
■	■	■	T	R	A	D	E	G	A	P
U	N	M	O	O	R	■	S	A	L	E
S	E	E	N	I	T	■	H	R	A	P
S	W	I	S	S	■	A	M	I	A

319

L	O	V	I	N	■	D	E	D	E	E
A	L	I	T	O	■	U	M	A	S	S
D	E	R	A	T	■	B	U	N	T	S
L	O	G	■	T	E	Y	■	N	E	E
E	L	I	■	R	E	A	■	Y	E	N
D	E	N	G	U	E	■	A	B	M	■
■	■	I	D	E	■	V	S	O	■	■
■	D	A	P	■	P	A	U	N	C	H
S	E	S	■	P	D	Q	■	A	R	A
N	F	L	■	O	S	U	■	D	E	V
U	R	I	E	L	■	E	L	U	D	E
G	A	M	E	Y	■	R	I	C	I	N
S	Y	S	O	P	■	O	V	E	T	T

320

S	U	V	S	■	A	C	R	E	S
A	S	A	I	R	■	C	L	O	N	K
R	E	C	T	O	■	L	O	U	S	E
A	M	U	■	S	M	U	G	G	L	E
N	E	U	T	E	R	■	H	A	T	■
■	■	M	E	H	T	A	■	A	V	E
R	I	C	K	I	■	L	I	N	E	R
E	N	L	■	P	A	L	E	D	■	■
E	D	E	■	R	E	D	R	A	W	■
Q	U	A	L	I	F	Y	■	E	L	O
U	L	N	A	R	■	E	V	A	D	E
I	G	E	T	A	■	S	I	D	E	B
P	E	R	E	S	■	L	Y	N	E

SOLUTIONS

321

B	A	T	E	D		S	E	C	O	
A	L	A	M	E		C	A	L	F	
S	A	N	T	A	M	A	R	I	A	
E	E	G		T	A	M	P			
	E	D	H	S		S	A	N	S	
C	D	R	A	C	K	S		L	I	T
R	A	I	T	A		C	R	O	N	E
I	N	N		P	O	I	N	T	E	R
B	L	E	T		L	A	D	A		
			U	P	A	T		L	B	O
	T	E	L	E	V	I	S	I	O	N
A	X	L	E		C	O	K	I	E	
	D	O	E	S		A	D	E	L	A

322

S	A	T		T	G	V				
A	E	R		O	R	A		G	O	I
T	I	O		N	O	S	T	R	I	L
Y	O	U	R	S		T	R	O	L	L
R	U	B	O	U	T		A	C	L	U
		L	T	R	S		S	E	I	S
S	E	E		E	K	E		R	T	E
A	R	M	E		E	V	R	Y		
Y	E	A	R		D	E	I	S	T	S
A	S	K	E	W		N	A	T	A	L
A	T	E	I	N	T	O		O	L	E
H	U	R		B	L	U		R	O	E
			A	C	T		E	S	P	

323

R	O	B	B		S	L	I	G	H	T
A	D	E	E		A	U	N	T	I	E
G	E	N	L		B	A	K	I	N	G
A	D	J	O	U	R	N	S			
		A	I	R	E	D	A	L	E	
C	O	M	T	E		A	C	E	T	O
O	B	I					T	A	P	
D	O	N	U	T		P	S	S	T	S
	E	S	P	O	U	S	A	L		
		R	O	L	Y	P	O	L	Y	
M	A	N	I	O	C		P	O	R	E
E	N	I	S	L	E		E	S	O	S
R	A	T	E	D	R		D	E	N	T

324

	S	C	O	P	E		U	S	D	
	S	T	O	L	E	S		G	W	U
S	H	A	N	I	A	T	W	A	I	N
N	U	T	S	O		H	O	R	S	E
A	L	U	I		B	E	R	T	H	S
G	A	E	D		U	T	L	E	Y	
		E	R	R	E	D				
	D	U	R	E	R		S	P	A	N
T	O	T	A	L	S		E	R	D	A
A	R	E	T	O		G	R	O	U	P
C	E	R	E	A	L	A	I	S	L	E
E	M	U		N	A	M	E	I	T	
T	I	S		S	A	Y	S	T		

SOLUTIONS

325

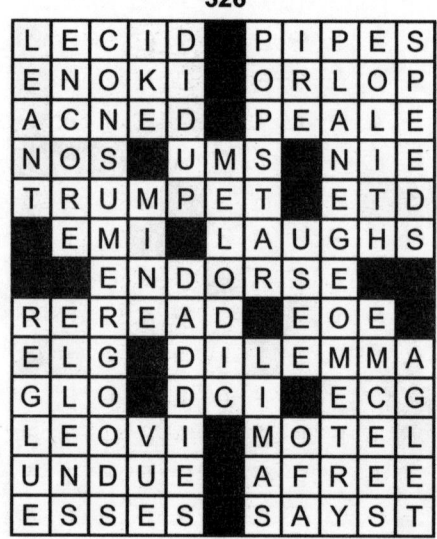

R	P	G		U	L	T			
U	A	R		F	A	R	O	F	F
B	C	E		O	N	A	W	I	R	E
A	M	A	S	S		N	I	D	A	L
T	A	T	U			S	E	D	U	M
O	N	E	L	O	O	K		L	D	S
		S	U	P	R	E	M	E		
P	O	T		P	A	I	L	F	U	L
S	C	H	M	O			L	A	S	E
S	H	I	E	S		C	E	D	E	S
T	O	T	T	E	R	Y		D	N	A
	A	S	H	R	A	M		L	E	G
			S	H	E		E	T	E	

326

L	E	C	I	D		P	I	P	E	S
E	N	O	K	I		O	R	L	O	P
A	C	N	E	D		P	E	A	L	E
N	O	S		U	M	S		N	I	E
T	R	U	M	P	E	T		E	T	D
	E	M	I		L	A	U	G	H	S
		E	N	D	O	R	S	E		
R	E	R	E	A	D		E	O	E	
E	L	G		D	I	L	E	M	M	A
G	L	O		D	C	I		E	C	G
L	E	O	V	I		M	O	T	E	L
U	N	D	U	E		A	F	R	E	E
E	S	S	E	S		S	A	Y	S	T

327

P	A	C	S		A	L	B	A	S
R	T	H	O	N		L	A	U	R	A
E	E	R	I	E		L	A	T	I	N
F	A	I	R	W	A	Y		T	A	T
E	M	S		S	T	E	P	O	N	E
R	S	T		P	A	T	N	A		
	M	I	S	E	R	L	Y		
	P	A	M	P	A		O	G	S
D	I	S	S	E	C	T		U	R	O
U	L	T		C	E	N	T	R	A	L
L	E	R	O	I		T	I	L	D	E
S	U	E	M	E		S	P	I	E	L
E	P	E	E	S		S	P	A	Y

328

G	H	E	T	T	O		U	S	F	L
L	A	N	C	E	R		G	A	I	A
A	P	R	I	L	S	H	O	W	E	R
S	T	A		E	K	E		F	R	A
S	I	G	N	O		F	L	I	C	S
	C	E	E		S	T	A	T	E	
		W	A	I	S	T			
	T	A	S	S	E		T	A	C
E	S	P	Y	S		P	E	D	A	L
M	G	O		A	S	I		D	S	O
C	A	L	L	I	T	Q	U	I	T	S
E	R	L	E		M	U	S	C	L	E
E	P	O	S		T	E	S	T	E	R

SOLUTIONS

329

```
A P E R C U . . O S O
T A B O O S . U B E R
E N B L O C . G E R E
. . . L E G A L I S M
R U P E E . L Y S .
O V E R S . A D A P T
C E N S . . U N O S
K A F K A . M C C O O
. R A L . A K E R S
E X I T P O L L .
S K E E . T A I W A N
T E N D . I G N O R E
E S D . . C A G E R S
```

330

```
C U L T . . P H E B E
H E I R . T R E M O R
A L M A . W I R I N G
R E A L S I M P L E .
. . B A N G L E .
A R E S O . Y S T A D
B O A . . . I M S
M E N L O . C U R I O
. . I O D A T E .
. P I Z Z A R O L L S
D E T A I N . P E O N
I N A R E A . I S T O
R A N D R . A S S T
```

331

```
L A T H S . P C T S
U R I E L . E L I O T
S A N A A . R A N T O
. W O R K B E N C H .
. . T E R S E .
L E A H . A T T H A T
E P T . S V U . U V A
S H O R T U . D M A J
. . A R R O W .
. A E R I A L I S T .
O L M E C . A G L O W
C L E F T . V H O N E
A I R Y . S T E I N
```

332

```
F A R A W A Y . B F A
O N A D I M E . I E R
R E G A L B E A G L E
E M B R Y O . S T L O
S I A N . S K O A L
T A G . G L I M P S E
. . C R O C E .
T I E R A C K . A R M
O N L A Y . A B A A
O C A T . A M I D S T
B I T E T H E D U S T
I T E . M A N A C L E
G E D . S T U N T E D
```

SOLUTIONS

333

B	C	D		W	M	D		S	T	D
E	O	E		I	T	I		H	O	O
R	U	N	N	I	N	G	M	A	T	E
E	C	T	O			S	O	R	E	S
T	H	E	W	H	O		C	O	S	I
			A	T	C	O		N	U	N
	D	I	R	T	C	H	E	A	P	
S	I	L		P	U	S	S			
T	E	L	E		R	O	S	T	E	R
A	T	I	L	T			A	R	M	A
Y	A	C	K	E	T	Y	Y	A	C	K
O	R	I		X	I	I		S	E	E
N	Y	T		T	A	N		H	E	R

334

E	R	I	C	S		E	D	G	E	S
D	O	N	O	T		B	O	R	N	E
Y	E	S	N	O		B	E	A	U	S
	U	D	A	Y			S	P	F	S
R	O	B	E		E	A	S	E		
I	D	O		O	S	M	O	S	I	S
S	E	R		M	I	I		O	C	H
C	A	D	E	N	C	E		F	E	E
		I	X	I	A		C	W	T	S
N	U	N	C		N	A	I	R		
U	H	A	U	L		E	V	A	D	E
N	O	T	S	O		R	E	T	A	R
S	H	E	E	T		O	T	H	E	R

335

D	A	M	N			L	L	A	M	A
R	I	A	A			Y	O	R	B	A
A	R	T	S		L	E	C	T	E	R
B	Y	R	D		I	S	A			
		I	A	M	B		T	O	U	R
O	P	A	Q	U	E		E	U	S	E
M	A	R		G	R	U		T	I	L
A	C	C	T		A	N	Y	W	A	Y
R	A	H	S		T	H	E	A		
		T	E	E		O	R	E	G	
F	L	A	R	E	D		M	D	S	E
P	A	P	A	L			A	L	M	S
S	H	E	P	S			N	Y	E	T

336

T	I	G	R	E		T	N	O	T	E
R	A	R	E	R		R	O	O	S	T
E	N	I	D	S		I	M	M	A	D
		E	S	T	O	P	S			
N	A	V	E		V	E	G	G	I	E
G	R	E	A	S	E	D		U	N	S
A	U	F		I	R	A		I	F	S
I	B	O		G	A	L	I	L	E	E
O	A	R	I	N	G		S	L	R	S
			S	P	E	A	R	E		
I	G	L	O	O		C	A	M	E	L
M	E	A	L	S		L	E	O	R	A
S	T	O	A	T		U	L	T	R	A

SOLUTIONS

337

L	A	T	T	E	S			N	R	A
A	R	I	A	N	E		F	E	E	D
M	A	T	R	O	N		I	N	T	I
S	W	I	T	C	H	B	L	A	D	E
		A	H	O	O	T				
B	C	A	R		R	U	E	F	U	L
B	I	D	E	N		T	R	U	M	P
B	A	L	S	A	S		T	R	A	N
		A	C	T	I	I				
Z	E	B	U	L	O	N	P	I	K	E
W	A	A	C		C	O	P	S	E	S
E	S	N	E		K	N	E	L	L	S
I	T	A			S	E	D	A	T	E

338

M	A	S	S	E	S		C	R	O	W
I	N	S	E	C	T		A	I	D	S
S	T	E	L	A	E		S	T	O	W
			F	R	E	S	H	E	N	
	T	O	D	D	L	E	R			
D	A	C	E		E	G	E	S	T	S
O	L	A	F	S		A	G	O	O	D
G	A	T	E	A	U		I	N	R	I
			A	D	V	I	S	O	R	
	E	N	T	R	U	S	T			
T	R	O	I		L	E	E	R	A	T
A	T	O	N		A	E	R	O	B	E
D	E	N	G		E	A	S	T	O	N

339

B	R	A	S		C	H	I	R	A	C
L	I	N	E		H	A	N	N	A	H
A	L	A	N		G	R	A	D	E	A
H	E	A	D	G	E	A	R			
		L	O	D		S	E	P	A	L
A	K	I	N	S		S	A	O	N	E
B	I	C					L	O	N	
A	E	I	O	U		S	A	I	N	T
S	L	A	N	G		O	F	T		
		S	A	L	A	R	I	E	D	
D	E	S	I	R	E		A	C	T	A
O	D	E	T	T	A		M	A	R	R
A	S	L	E	E	P		E	L	E	C

340

A	T	A	S	T	E			M	A	H
P	O	T	I	O	N		N	A	L	A
B	I	C	A	R	B		O	N	I	N
			M	I	L	K	M	A	I	D
T	E	T	E		O	R	E			
O	L	A	S		C	O	N	C	U	R
M	O	T	E	L		C	C	L	E	F
B	I	S	T	R	O		L	I	L	I
			W	O	N		A	P	E	D
D	O	M	I	N	A	N	T			
B	O	S	N		J	O	U	N	C	E
L	O	G	S		A	T	R	I	U	M
S	H	R			G	O	E	S	T	O

595

SOLUTIONS

341

H	A	T	H	A			L	S	A	T	S
R	H	E	U	M			U	T	U	R	N
E	I	L	A	T			S	A	D	I	E
		E	C	O	N			Y	I	P	E
M	M	C		O	E	D	S				
A	P	A	T			P	U	M	I	C	E
W	A	S	I	N			D	A	N	A	S
R	A	T	T	A	T			D	C	U	P
			M	V	P	S			O	L	N
A	R	E	O			S	T	E	M		
S	T	R	U	T			A	L	M	A	S
E	E	N	S	Y			C	L	O	N	E
A	S	S	E	S			K	A	N	Y	E

342

A	B	O	I	L			L	S	A	T	S
C	A	S	C	O			E	C	R	U	S
A	D	I	E	U			O	H	Y	E	S
D	U	S	T	D	E	V	I	L	S		
			E	T	U	I	S				
A	U	P	A	I	R			M	I	N	S
H	M	O		E	A	N		D	E	A	
I	P	S	A			S	A	N	I	T	Y
			S	T	I	P	E				
		I	L	L	N	A	T	U	R	E	D
R	O	D	E	O			I	T	I	S	I
U	N	L	E	T			M	E	E	T	S
G	A	S	P	E			E	R	N	E	S

343

	A	G	F	A			A	R	L	E	N
S	C	A	L	D			L	E	O	N	A
H	A	M	A	L			F	L	O	E	S
O	T	E	R	I			A	I	T	S	
		P	E	B	B	L	E				
G	I	L	D			E	F	F	I	G	Y
M	T	A		O	L	A		N	E	O	
C	A	Y	U	S	E			D	S	O	S
			M	M	M	B	O	P			
	M	E	L	O			A	V	A	N	T
C	L	E	A	N			H	I	D	E	R
C	L	O	U	D			I	S	E	R	E
S	E	C	T	S			A	H	S	O	

344

S	L	A	M			D	A	R	W	I	N
O	O	N	A			E	L	O	I	S	E
I	D	A	S			L	O	R	E	A	L
T	E	A	L	B	L	U	E				
		L	I	A	M			M	E	S	A
P	O	I	N	T	A	T			X	L	S
A	N	C		I	G	O		P	A	K	
G	O	I		N	A	Y	S	A	Y	S	
E	R	A	S			Z	O	O	T		
			T	H	I	N	D	I	M	E	
E	A	S	E	I	N			D	A	R	N
L	O	U	V	R	E			E	T	I	C
F	L	E	E	T	S			N	E	S	S

SOLUTIONS

345

S	H	R	U	G		A	T	B	A	Y
L	I	E	G	E		R	A	I	T	A
A	D	D	L	E		A	N	T	O	N
V	E	R	Y	S	E	L	D	O	M	
	O	D	E	N	S	E				
B	A	B	U		S	E	M	P	R	E
U	R	I	C	H		A	B	O	I	L
Y	A	N	K	E	E		I	P	O	S
		L	I	L	A	C	S			
	S	T	I	R	F	R	Y	I	N	G
S	E	I	N	E		M	C	C	O	O
P	A	N	G	S		O	L	L	I	E
F	L	O	S	S		R	E	E	L	S

346

N	E	S	T				G	I	S	T
E	L	O	I		S	W	O	O	S	H
R	E	U	P		A	H	O	R	S	E
F	A	L	S	E	G	O	D			
	M	O	T	E	L		E	P	I	
M	A	U	V	E		E	G	G	O	N
E	S	S	E			U	R	L	S	
S	H	I	R	R		E	I	E	I	O
A	E	C		H	A	R	D	G		
	M	I	G	R	A	I	N	E		
R	E	C	A	N	T		N	O	O	K
C	O	S	M	O	S		C	U	T	E
A	N	S	E				E	S	O	S

347

U	L	U		F	O	R		O	D	O
P	O	N	T	I	F	F		V	I	G
T	I	P	O	F	F	S		E	N	D
O	N	E	D	A	Y		B	R	E	E
A	S	N	O		O	B	E	R	O	N
		M	U	U	M	U	U	S		
	A	B	H	O	R	R	E	N	T	
I	C	E	B	E	R	G				
M	I	L	A	N	O		A	I	D	A
A	D	A	R		C	O	T	T	O	N
R	I	B		I	K	N	O	W	I	T
E	T	O		C	E	M	B	A	L	O
T	Y	R		U	R	E		S	Y	N

348

	S	P	U	D		R	I	F	E	
D	E	A	N	E		E	S	O	L	
E	X	C	E	E	D	I	N	G	L	Y
I	T	I	S		A	N	T	H	E	M
C	E	N		I	V	E		A	N	C
E	T	O	I	L	E		I	T	S	A
			M	A	N	G	A			
R	C	M	P		P	O	L	I	T	Y
I	O	U		T	O	N		O	R	E
A	N	S	W	E	R		E	D	Y	S
A	C	C	E	P	T	A	T	I	O	N
	U	L	E	E		A	N	D	N	O
	R	E	N	E		M	A	E	S	

SOLUTIONS

349

S	A	S	S	Y		M	A	G	D	A
A	M	I	T	E		A	R	E	E	L
S	A	N	A	A		S	T	O	L	E
		E	T	N	A	S		R	A	F
A	B	A	S		G	E	O	G		
P	A	D		S	T	U	D	E	N	T
S	T	O	W	E		S	A	S	H	A
E	S	C	A	P	E	E		P	R	S
		O	L	A	Y		M	A	A	S
S	S	N		R	E	S	E	T		
W	A	N	D	A		H	A	T	H	A
A	S	O	R	T		A	R	O	A	R
T	E	R	S	E		D	A	N	D	Y

350

K	I	N	G			A	C	T	I	
O	M	I	T	S		B	O	A	C	
M	A	G	I	C	B	U	L	L	E	T
O	M	G		A	R	T	D	E	C	O
D	A	L		R	A	S		N	A	G
O	N	E	L	E	G		A	T	P	S
			E	D	A	T	E			
A	R	B	S		B	I	C	K	E	R
Z	E	E		C	O	M		A	M	I
O	V	E	R	D	U	B		L	I	E
V	A	P	O	R	T	R	A	I	L	S
	M	E	T	O		E	E	N	I	E
	P	R	I	M			S	E	A	N

351

I	S	S	U	E		A	F	T	R	A
U	P	E	N	D		R	E	H	E	M
M	O	V	I	E		K	E	E	N	E
	R	E	O	R	G		B	L	U	R
M	A	N	N		L	A	L	A		
E	D	T		F	I	R	E	S	A	T
N	I	H		I	T	I		T	C	U
S	C	H	U	L	T	Z		H	R	E
	E	P	E	E		L	U	I	S	
F	L	A	W		R	E	A	R	M	
L	E	V	A	R		T	Y	R	O	S
I	N	E	R	T		R	I	A	N	T
P	O	N	D	S		E	T	H	Y	L

352

N	E	B	O			F	O	C	U	S
C	R	E	S	C		I	N	L	A	Y
O	R	G	A	N		L	E	E	R	S
S	S	I		O	M	E	G	A		
		N	O	T	A	T		N	A	M
M	A	N	T	E	L		S	U	L	A
E	P	E	E	S		P	A	P	A	W
N	O	R	A		W	I	T	H	E	R
T	D	S		D	H	A	B	I		
		L	A	P	A	Z		T	C	P
A	R	U	S	H		Z	Z	T	O	P
M	A	C	H	I		A	P	E	R	S
Y	O	K	E	L			G	R	A	S

SOLUTIONS

353

A	L	T	O	S	■	A	V	I	L	A
C	A	R	E	W	■	L	E	N	I	N
T	H	I	N	E	■	A	T	T	E	N
S	O	C	■	A	F	R	■	E	D	A
A	R	K	■	T	U	M	B	R	E	L
S	E	Q	U	I	N	■	O	R	R	S
■	■	U	L	T	■	W	O	O	■	■
S	E	E	A	■	B	E	G	G	A	R
U	N	S	N	A	R	L	■	A	P	O
B	A	T	■	D	O	C	■	T	H	A
A	M	I	G	A	■	O	V	O	I	D
R	E	O	R	G	■	M	A	R	D	I
U	L	N	A	E	■	E	L	Y	S	E

354

D	E	B	■	A	L	S	■	Z	A	C
U	N	A	■	R	O	H	■	I	T	A
L	D	S	■	T	W	A	■	P	O	T
C	A	I	T	I	F	F	■	A	N	E
E	S	C	H	E	A	T	■	D	A	R
T	H	I	R	S	T	■	B	E	L	A
■	■	N	O	T	S	U	R	E	■	■
M	U	S	E	■	P	R	I	D	E	S
E	P	T	■	O	R	A	T	O	R	Y
D	L	I	■	C	E	N	S	O	R	S
D	O	N	■	T	A	I	■	D	A	T
L	A	C	■	A	D	U	■	A	T	E
E	D	T	■	D	S	M	■	H	A	M

355

■	■	S	O	D	A	S	■	D	R	T
E	L	L	I	O	T	T	■	M	E	R
Q	U	A	L	I	T	Y	T	I	M	E
U	N	P	E	N	S	■	A	T	A	B
I	G	O	R	■	P	E	R	I	L	■
P	I	N	■	T	U	R	B	I	N	E
■	■	D	E	T	O	O	■	■	■	■
B	A	Y	L	E	A	F	■	B	O	P
O	L	E	I	N	■	S	A	B	E	■
B	L	A	S	■	A	D	O	R	E	E
C	U	S	T	O	M	B	U	I	L	T
A	R	T	■	S	I	L	K	T	I	E
T	E	S	■	T	A	S	S	E	■	■

356

A	N	G	E	R	■	T	B	A	L	L
P	E	A	L	E	■	A	E	R	I	E
O	A	S	E	S	■	P	A	N	A	M
P	R	O	G	E	N	I	T	O	R	■
■	E	L	Y	T	R	O	N	■	■	■
H	A	I	■	A	C	I	D	L	Y	■
A	S	N	E	R	■	A	K	E	E	M
S	T	E	V	E	N	■	C	I	A	■
■	■	A	R	C	H	I	E	S	■	■
■	H	O	N	O	R	A	R	I	U	M
F	O	N	D	U	■	L	I	V	R	E
R	E	M	E	T	■	A	N	E	E	D
I	S	E	R	E	■	L	A	R	D	S

SOLUTIONS

357

R	I	E	U	■	A	R	G	A	L
A	L	L	S	O	■	N	O	O	N	E
G	O	O	D	L	O	O	K	I	N	G
T	I	P	■	G	U	T	■	T	U	A
A	L	E	■	A	T	H	■	E	A	T
G	O	R	P	■	S	E	A	R	L	E
■	■	C	O	P	R	A	■
B	I	L	B	A	O	■	A	C	M	E
A	C	A	■	T	K	O	■	E	A	N
L	I	B	■	M	E	N	■	S	R	I
S	C	R	E	E	N	T	E	S	T	S
A	L	A	N	A	■	V	I	N	Y	L
M	E	T	A	L	■	S	A	S	E

358

G	A	R	R	■	E	F	F	I	G	Y
I	L	E	A	■	A	L	Y	S	S	A
N	A	N	S	■	G	U	I	T	A	R
O	N	E	H	A	L	F	■
■	R	E	F	R	E	S	H
I	G	E	T	I	T	■	E	T	T	U
N	O	D	U	S	■	R	O	U	E	N
S	T	I	R	■	C	A	S	I	N	G
C	A	T	F	O	O	D	■
■	O	D	O	A	C	E	R
P	A	S	M	O	I	■	C	A	N	A
S	M	A	L	L	F	■	A	R	C	H
S	I	R	K	A	Y	■	D	O	O	M

359

A	S	S	E	Z	■	■	T	W	A	S
S	K	I	B	O	B	■	V	A	S	E
T	Y	D	B	O	L	■	V	A	C	A
I	S	E	■	U	R	C	H	I	N
■	D	I	F	F	E	R	■
L	A	I	D	O	F	F	■	U	M	D
A	E	S	I	R	■	U	A	N	D	I
H	R	H	■	I	N	S	U	L	A	R
■	I	N	E	E	D	A	■
E	R	E	S	T	U	■	W	E	L
W	O	R	D	■	R	E	N	F	R	O
E	T	T	U	■	O	C	C	U	L	T
R	H	E	E	■	T	O	L	E	T

360

H	O	C	U	S	■	B	O	P	S
I	P	A	N	A	■	E	V	I	E
H	E	B	E	R	■	V	E	N	A	L
A	R	I	■	C	I	E	■	K	L	M
T	A	N	■	A	D	L	■	I	A	N
■	C	O	S	I	■	O	N	N	O
C	A	R	O	M	■	S	I	G	E	P
I	M	U	P	■	B	A	D	S	■
V	A	I	■	A	R	T	■	H	O	S
I	T	S	■	H	I	C	■	E	T	A
C	E	E	L	O	■	H	O	A	R	Y
■	U	R	E	Y	■	E	F	R	O	N
■	R	S	S	S	■	L	A	S	S	O

SOLUTIONS

361

D	O	A		A	B	O			
A	R	M		T	O	C		T	S	R
L	A	S	H	O	U	T		O	T	O
E	C	T	O		R	A	N	D	O	M
T	H	E	M	O	B		A	D	I	E
H	E	L	I	C	O		T	Y	C	O
		C	A	N	T	I				
A	M	B	I		S	C	O	R	N	S
B	O	Y	D		T	U	N	E	U	P
U	P	R	E	A	R		A	D	A	H
S	E	D		R	E	C	L	I	N	E
E	D	S		L	E	A		A	C	R
			O	T	T		L	E	E	

362

K	A	S	E	M		O	L	M	E	C
I	C	O	S	A		K	O	O	P	A
T	U	P	A	C		C	O	V	E	R
	H	I	L	L		K	I	E	L	
C	S	I		E	E	C		N	S	A
I	S	E	R		A	D	O	G		
R	E	S	O	U	R	C	E	F	U	L
	C	H	A	N		N	O	W	I	
D	U	H		E	O	E		R	E	N
E	R	O	S		F	L	A	W		
O	B	I	T	S		B	L	A	D	E
R	A	C	E	R		O	A	R	E	D
O	N	E	R	S		W	I	D	T	H

363

R	E	L	O	A	N					
E	L	I	S	I	O	N		B	A	L
R	E	F	O	R	M	A	T	O	R	Y
A	V	E		L	O	R	R	I	E	S
N	E	M	E	A		A	A	L	T	O
	N	A	A	N	S		C	I	E	L
		G	R	E	I	S	E	N		
I	C	A	L		B	E	R	G	S	
M	A	Z	E	R		A	S	P	E	N
P	R	I	S	O	N	S		O	D	A
E	I	N	S	T	E	I	N	I	U	M
I	B	E		C	A	D	E	N	C	E
			P	E	L	T	E	D		

364

G	I	J	A	N	E		S	T	A	D
E	D	U	C	E	D		R	O	S	E
T	I	R	A	D	E		I	N	S	C
S	D	I		S	M	A		G	E	O
O	S	S	A		A	B	O	U	N	D
N	O	P	E	S		A	R	E	T	E
		R	S	T		F	I	T		
E	Q	U	I	P		T	O	W	E	L
M	A	D	R	A	S		N	I	N	E
I	T	E		T	A	J		S	U	N
N	A	N	S		N	O	S	T	R	A
O	R	C	H		A	S	L	E	E	P
R	I	E	U		A	H	O	R	S	E

SOLUTIONS

365

B	E	G		I	R	A		R	W	E
I	S	R		M	I	S	H	E	A	R
R	A	E		E	C	H	O	I	N	G
D	I	G	A	T		A	N	N	E	S
	O	L	A		M	O	C			
G	A	R	B		E	R	A	S	E	
S	A	Y	A	H		D	A	R	I	N
N	E	A	T	O		B	N	E	G	
	B	R	A		S	L	A			
U	N	B	O	X		H	E	T	U	P
C	L	O	S	E	T	O		I	R	E
L	E	T	S	R	I	P		O	G	S
A	R	T		S	E	S		N	E	O

366

U	R	B	A	N		A	S	E	A	T
M	O	U	S	Y		C	E	L	L	O
M	E	N	S	U	R	A	T	I	O	N
A	S	K	A		O	D	I	S	T	S
			Y	E	A	S	T			
S	H	I	E	L	D			B	M	I
F	E	R	R	I	S	W	H	E	E	L
O	R	R		I	H	A	D	T	O	
	S	E	G	A	R					
I	N	T	E	R	N		P	O	L	I
C	H	A	I	N	S	M	O	K	E	D
B	R	U	N	O		B	O	I	S	E
M	A	R	E	S		A	N	E	E	D

367

D	A	S	H		A	D	R	I	F	T
U	T	W	O		L	E	A	S	E	D
M	O	A	I		A	R	M	O	R	S
B	E	N	C	H	M	A	R	K	S	
			K	Y	O	T	O			
C	L	A	S	P	S		D	I	A	N
I	A	M					S	T	O	
T	R	E	O		A	S	T	R	A	L
			C	H	E	W	Y			
	W	A	T	E	R	F	R	O	N	T
R	O	M	A	N	I		A	H	A	S
T	R	I	V	I	A		N	O	N	O
S	E	A	E	E	L		T	K	O	S

368

C	O	P		G	P	A				
A	V	A		L	O	L		W	A	L
S	E	C	R	E	T	E		E	D	M
P	R	I	D	E		G	A	L	I	N
A	G	F	A			C	L	E	O	
R	O	I		E	A	S	E	D	U	P
		C	O	M	P	O	S	E		
S	H	O	E	B	O	X		S	S	E
L	U	C	I			R	E	P	L	
O	N	E	L	S		H	E	R	E	I
E	T	A		M	E	D	E	V	A	C
S	S	N		U	L	T		E	R	I
			T	G	V		D	E	T

SOLUTIONS

369

A	G	O	N		U	P	D	A	T	E
B	A	R	E		S	U	E	D	E	S
I	S	L	A		E	F	F	E	T	E
T	H	E	R	E	A	F	T	E	R	
			B	A	S	I	L			
B	E	R	Y	L		N	Y	L	O	N
R	P	I					S	M	U	
S	A	D	L	Y		E	S	T	A	S
			A	V	A	N	T			
	W	I	R	E	H	A	I	R	E	D
S	A	N	G	T	O		T	I	E	R
W	I	S	E	T	O		C	A	L	I
F	L	O	R	E	T		H	A	S	P

370

P	A	V	E			T	A	S	K
E	N	I	A	C		K	H	M	E	R
T	E	R	R	A		I	R	A	N	I
T	E	G		N	A	T	U	R	E	S
I	D	I	O	T	I	C		I	C	E
	N	E	A	T	H		L	A	S
	B	I	O	L		E	L	L	S
G	E	S		O	I	N	G	O	
A	T	L		U	N	S	A	T	E	D
S	H	A	R	P	E	I		E	M	I
P	E	N	N	E		N	I	X	E	D
A	L	D	A	S		K	O	A	N	S
R	S	S	S			U	S	D	T

371

I	I	N	S	I	S	T		A	S	A
S	C	A	T	T	E	R		B	M	I
S	U	R	R	E	A	L		A	E	R
		R	U	N	G		A	S	W	E
P	S	A	T		A	S	S	E	S	S
B	O	T		L	E	K			
S	N	E	A	K		P	A	S	H	A
		H	I	C		T	A	C	
A	S	T	A	N	A		P	E	E	K
S	T	A	B		S	A	L	E	
C	I	R		V	I	D	A	L	I	A
O	L	A		I	N	A	N	I	T	Y
T	E	S		A	G	R	E	E	O	N

372

U	P	S	A		R	I	C	O	H
S	A	U	C	E		A	N	E	N	D
H	O	R	N	E	T	S	N	E	S	T
	V	E	N	I		L	E	V
I	K	I	D	Y	O	U	N	O	T
R	E	V		S	I	E			
R	L	E	S	S		E	A	T	I	T
	H	A	I		U	N	A	
	D	I	R	T	F	A	R	M	E	R
O	O	O		S	L	O	B	
D	O	W	N	T	O	E	A	R	T	H
D	D	A	Y	S		F	R	E	R	E
S	Y	S	C	O		K	L	U	M

603

SOLUTIONS

373

S	A	N	D	H	O	G	■	E	L	I
D	A	N	I	E	L	S	■	R	I	B
S	H	E	R	B	E	T	■	T	E	A
■	■	T	R	S	■	G	E	A	R	
L	A	Z	Y	■	O	D	I	S	T	S
I	N	I	T	■	N	E	A	■	■	
V	I	T	R	O	■	I	N	T	E	R
■	I	N	F	■	T	A	T	I		
T	H	E	C	I	A	■	P	L	A	T
O	R	S	K	■	U	T	A	■	■	
R	O	T	■	A	N	O	N	Y	M	S
A	S	E	■	H	A	N	D	S	I	N
S	S	R	■	L	E	G	A	L	L	Y

374

I	G	E	T	A	■	A	S	S	O	C
N	O	F	A	N	■	A	D	A	N	O
L	I	F	E	O	F	R	I	L	E	Y
U	N	U	■	S	R	O	■	A	P	O
C	T	S	■	M	I	N	A	R	E	T
K	O	E	N	I	G	■	L	Y	R	E
■	■	■	L	A	H	T	I	■	■	
V	E	R	O	■	T	W	I	T	C	H
A	L	E	W	I	F	E	■	E	L	A
S	O	I	■	N	U	L	■	J	O	B
S	I	G	N	A	L	F	L	A	R	E
A	S	N	E	W	■	T	A	N	I	A
R	E	S	E	E	■	H	R	O	S	S

375

B	A	R	R	E	■	O	B	E	S	E
T	H	E	A	X	■	D	A	R	I	A
W	A	S	H	E	R	D	R	I	E	R
O	S	T	■	D	E	J	A	■	■	
■	■	C	U	R	I	O	■	M	A	E
■	H	U	M	A	N	B	E	I	N	G
G	O	R	P	■	■	■	I	N	S	O
P	R	E	S	C	I	E	N	C	E	
S	O	S	■	L	A	P	S	E	■	
■	■	S	A	N	O	■	M	S	S	
T	A	L	K	I	S	C	H	E	A	P
O	N	A	I	R	■	H	E	A	D	Y
A	S	I	D	E	■	S	A	T	E	S

376

P	R	E	S	■	B	E	M	O	A	N
A	U	N	T	■	O	R	A	N	G	E
R	E	V	E	R	S	E	G	E	A	R
I	S	I	A	H	■	G	I	L	D	
■	■	A	D	O	N	A	I	■	■	
R	U	B	Y	■	S	H	E	B	O	P
I	S	L	■	F	Y	I	■	A	R	S
T	H	E	C	A	N	■	A	N	I	P
■	■	U	N	C	O	R	K	■	■	
D	O	O	R	■	S	A	N	A	A	
E	N	G	L	I	S	H	R	O	S	E
S	I	R	E	N	S	■	A	T	T	O
K	N	E	W	I	T	■	T	E	R	N

SOLUTIONS

377

```
M A L A R . . Y E G G
I P A N A . T E L E O
G O O D M O R N I N G
U L T . O V I . C E E
E L S . S E V . I R T
L O E B . R I A T A .
. . . I D T A G . . .
. R I C O H . S T U B
D E M . L E M . E N L
E T A . A R A . P T A
B I G S P E N D E R S
B R E N S . L I E U T
E E R O . . Y E S E S
```

378

```
H A I . S I T . . .
Y E N . C I I . C A P
A I T . H I P B O N E
T O E I N . T E N E T
T U R N O N . S Q M I
. C H O U . S U I T .
B R E A K T H E I C E
R E P L . T A M S . .
O S T E . Y V E T T E
T H I R D . A R A B S
H O O S I E R . D I N
S T N . E M T . O L E
. . L U I . R L S . .
```

379

```
B A S K . O N C D S
R H E O . O N F O O T
S I N O . P O L L O I
. E P E E . E T R E .
M L C A R R . R S S S
D O A . I A M S . .
T N N . C T U . S S I
. R A I D . H I N .
E L B E . O R I A N A
L E O V . N A C L . .
M A R I S A . A L E R
S H O V E L . H O H O
T Y N E R . N T S B
```

380

```
A B S . O W S . A V G
G A I . V E R . S A E
E N G R O S S . S N L
. K N E L T . G A E D
P R O B O S C I S . .
G U T . I L L S E E
A P H R O D I S I A C
S T E E L E . N R C .
. T E S S E L A T E
B O I S . T R U T H .
T A M . P O R C I N E
E T E . U R O . O U T
N Y S . S Y R . N T H
```

SOLUTIONS

381

S	P	U	R	N		D	E	B	T	
E	E	N	I	E		E	L	O	I	
E	Y	D	I	E		C	L	U	N	K
I	T	E	S			R	A	I	S	A
N	O	R		A	L	Y		L	E	T
	N	G	A	I	O		A	L	L	A
		R	O	T	U	N	D	A		
A	G	A	L		R	U	M	B	A	
T	I	D		P	S	T		A	V	A
O	V	U	L	E			R	I	A	L
R	E	A	I	R		C	E	S	T	A
	R	T	E	S		M	E	S	A	S
	S	E	S	E		A	L	E	R	T

382

	P	R	I	G		R	E	B	U	T
C	H	U	R	R		A	L	O	N	E
H	Y	D	R	O	P	H	O	B	I	A
E	S	O		A	A	A		B	C	S
S	I	L	E	N	T	L		L	E	E
S	O	F	T	E	R		H	E	F	T
			U	D	I	N	E			
A	L	L	I		A	O	R	T	I	C
S	A	E		A	R	T	D	E	C	O
Y	M	A		C	C	R		D	I	E
L	E	V	E	L	H	E	A	D	E	D
U	S	E	M	E		A	B	Y	S	S
M	A	N	O	F		L	A	S	T	

383

G	A	M		D	C	I		S	T	D
O	V	I		A	R	S		T	E	A
T	O	N	Y	S	O	P	R	A	N	O
T	I	N	E		S	Y	S	T	S	
O	R	E	A	D	S		S	E	I	S
		S	H	A	Q		S	O	L	A
L	B	O		B	U	G		F	E	W
A	I	T	S		E	R	A	T		
B	R	A	U		S	A	C	H	E	M
	D	F	L	A	T		T	E	R	I
B	E	A	U	T	I	C	I	A	N	S
I	R	T		R	O	B		R	I	T
B	S	S		I	N	C		T	E	Y

384

F	O	U	N	D		G	Y	P	S	Y
O	L	S	O	N		A	E	R	I	E
P	A	M	P	A	S	G	R	A	S	S
S	S	A		T	I	E		C	I	I
			J	E	T	S	E	T		
E	M	D	A	S	H		N	I	L	E
A	D	E	B	T		L	E	C	I	D
S	T	L	O		D	I	R	E	C	T
	I	T	S	A	G	O				
D	I	V		A	T	H		A	A	R
I	N	E	X	I	S	T	E	N	C	E
A	G	R	I	N		U	P	O	N	E
L	A	Y	I	T		P	I	X	E	L

SOLUTIONS

385

I	S	L	S			I	P	H	O	N	E
N	E	E	T		R	A	I	S	I	N	
N	E	C	E	S	S	I	T	A	T	E	
A	S	A	M	I		L	A	K	E	R	
T	O	R		N	S	F		A	R	O	
E	U	R	O		H	U	G				
	T	E	N	G	A	L	L	O	N		
		T	O	P		O	N	E	S		
R	A	L		R	E	F		A	S	L	
A	D	L	A	I		B	A	N	T	U	
S	M	A	L	L	M	I	N	D	E	D	
P	A	N	E	L	S		D	O	G	G	
S	N	O	C	A	T		I	N	G	E	

386

Y	O	S	H	I		C	H	E	R	I
A	L	O	A	N		H	E	M	A	N
L	E	F	T	S		A	S	P	C	A
T	I	T		T	W	I	S	T	E	R
A	N	I	T	R	A		Y	M	A	
	N	O	U	N	S		P	E	G	
O	P	T	I	C		H	O	R	S	E
N	A	H		T	A	U	R	O		
E	R	E		S	T	Y	M	I	E	
S	S	H	A	P	E	D		I	N	E
I	L	E	T	A		O	L	S	E	N
D	E	A	R	Y		W	E	E	P	S
E	Y	D	I	E		N	A	S	T	Y

387

S	E	S	E		A	L	E	R	T	S
K	E	W	L		L	I	Z	A	R	D
I	L	I	A		L	I	E	G	E	S
M	Y	S	T		P	I	K			
	S	E	E	R		I	M	S	O	
S	N	A		L	O	S	E	O	U	T
W	E	L	S	H		A	L	O	F	T
A	U	P	A	I	R	S		D	I	O
B	E	S	T		Y	E	S	M		
	I	T	D		P	U	S	S		
O	N	E	S	I	E		A	S	H	Y
R	E	E	F	E	R		S	I	A	L
L	L	O	Y	D	S		M	C	D	L

388

A	U	K		E	L	S		B	M	I
O	N	I		G	O	A		U	A	R
R	E	C		G	T	I		T	R	E
T	A	K	E	N	I	N		T	I	N
A	S	T	R	O		T	B	O	N	E
L	E	H	I	G	H		U	N	O	S
	E	C	S	T	A	S	Y			
A	B	B	A		C	U	T	O	U	T
S	E	U	S	S		C	L	U	N	Y
S	F	C		E	X	T	E	R	N	S
E	I	K		L	E	I		L	A	O
S	T	E		A	N	O		I	I	N
S	S	T		H	O	N		P	L	S

SOLUTIONS

389

C	H	I	M	P		S	A	W	E	D
R	E	N	E	E		A	R	A	D	O
E	A	S	E	R		N	O	L	I	E
D	R	E			T	S	A		K	T	S
O	T	C		U	T	A		I	O	S
	S	T	A	R	R		E	E	R	O
		I	N	B	U	I	L	T		
T	A	V	I		D	A	D	A	S	
I	L	O		A	E	C		L	E	S
C	T	R		F	L	O		K	E	A
T	I	O	G	A		C	A	I	N	E
A	M	U	S	T		C	U	E	I	N
C	A	S	T	E		A	S	S	N	S

390

H	A	P		F	T	S		O	S	A
A	P	A		L	E	K		N	E	G
S	P	U	M	O	N	I		A	C	S
E	L	L	E		K	N	U	R	L	
K	E	A	N	U		T	R	O	U	T
			U	N	W	I	E	L	D	Y
O	S	F		D	E	G		L	E	S
W	A	U	K	E	S	H	A			
L	Y	R	I	C		T	R	A	W	L
	S	C	R	I	P		U	D	A	Y
I	W	O		D	I	M	N	E	S	S
N	H	A		E	E	L		L	I	E
N	O	T		D	R	I		A	N	S

391

S	T	A	E	L		C	H	U	M	P
T	R	I	P	E		R	O	N	E	E
P	O	R	T	R	A	I	T	I	S	T
A	G	S		O	L	N		C	S	A
T	O	A		I	C	K	I	E	R	
S	N	C	C		O	L	A	F	S	
			A	S	H	E	N			
	A	M	T	O	O		S	E	S	E
	L	E	T	F	L	Y		B	E	L
D	O	L		A	I	M		E	A	L
U	N	D	E	R	C	H	A	R	G	E
A	Z	E	R	A		A	L	L	A	N
L	O	D	E	S		S	E	E	L	S

392

F	E	L	L	A		D	H	O	W	S
A	T	I	O	N		R	A	D	I	I
H	U	G	O	S		A	T	E	S	T
D	I	N	N	E	R	W	A	R	E	
		E	E	L	I	E	R			
B	B	O	Y		G	R	I	M	E	S
T	S	U		A	G	S		E	R	A
W	A	S	A	B	I		T	T	O	P
			N	A	N	N	I	E		
	O	R	A	N	G	E	B	O	W	L
S	H	A	R	D		W	I	R	E	S
W	I	L	C	O		T	A	I	N	T
F	O	E	H	N		S	E	C	T	S

SOLUTIONS

393

T	R	O	U	T			S	U	L	K
D	A	R	N	E	L		T	R	E	E
S	I	G	H	T	U	N	S	E	E	N
			A	R	I	S				
G	U	P	T	A		Y	E	N	S	
O	M	E			I	N	D	O	O	R
A	B	S	T	R	A	C	T	I	O	N
S	E	C	R	E	T			S	T	A
	R	I	L	E		A	B	Y	S	S
			C	I	R	O				
G	A	R	T	E	R	S	N	A	K	E
I	T	E	S		S	O	G	O	O	D
A	T	O	R			N	O	L	I	E

394

		P	R	I	M	P				
S	T	O	I	C	A	L		T	S	E
M	A	R	T	I	N	A		A	N	E
E	M	T			I	N	S	P	A	N
E	P	S	O	N		B	A	E	R	S
	S	O	L	A	R		Y	R	L	Y
		F	I	N	E	S	S	E		
E	D	E	N		N	A	A	C	P	
T	E	N	D	S		X	H	O	S	A
U	P	T	A	K	E			R	A	S
I	O	R		U	N	G	O	D	L	Y
S	T	Y		A	C	A	D	E	M	E
					S	E	G	E	R	

395

P	A	A	R			T	O	S	S	
A	G	N	U	S		I	D	T	A	G
P	A	I	G	E		E	D	A	T	E
A	T	M		A	F	I		F	O	R
C	H	A	G	R	I	N		F	U	M
Y	A	L	U		N	T	E	S	T	S
		K	A	R	A	O	K	E		
S	P	I	R	A	L		E	R	N	S
O	E	N		G	L	A	S	G	O	W
M	T	G		T	Y	P		E	V	E
A	U	D	I	O		P	L	A	I	D
S	L	O	O	P		L	A	N	C	E
	A	M	C	S			B	T	E	N

396

I	N	S	U	M		F	I	N	A	L
R	E	E	S	E		A	B	O	D	E
R	O	L	E	N		I	N	G	O	T
		L	A	U	E	R		R	G	S
A	B	E	S		S	P	E	E		
R	R	R		S	E	L	V	A	G	E
A	I	S	L	E		A	E	T	N	A
W	O	M	A	N	L	Y		S	A	T
		A	S	T	I		N	H	R	A
S	L	R		I	S	E	E	A		
L	I	K	E	N		A	R	K	I	N
O	P	E	R	E		S	T	E	I	N
T	O	T	A	L		E	S	S	I	E

SOLUTIONS

397

```
M R B I G ■ S C E N E
I N T R O ■ T O D O S
M A U R A ■ E L G I N
E S S ■ T H E L Y R E
■ ■ S I D L E ■ ■ ■
S P L I T S E C O N D
E D E L ■ ■ ■ T A R O
E Q U I L A T E R A L
■ ■ C U P I D ■ ■ ■
U T M O S T S ■ C A B
T R A S H ■ S U R G E
E E R I E ■ U N A R M
S E U S S ■ E U B I E
```

398

```
S E T ■ D I L A T E
K Y R A ■ O M E G A S
I C A L ■ E A T S U P
S K I M P S ■ ■ ■ ■
■ N A A N B R E A D
S O L ■ S T E E L I E
O T O E S ■ E L O R A
R E A L G A R ■ Q E D
B A D F O R Y O U ■
■ ■ ■ O S T E A L
S U D O K U ■ W N B A
O N U S E S ■ O C A S
H U R T L E ■ E S E
```

399

```
C U D G E L S ■ D D E
A N A H E I M ■ E E L
F E W I N N U M B E R
■ ■ R Y E ■ O T R O
B U T A ■ U N U S E D
B E A R U P O N ■ ■
B Y R D S ■ M T I D A
■ ■ E M I S S I O N
B E D L A M ■ H I T E
M A U L ■ A T A ■
O M N I P R E S E N T
C E N ■ J E T T I E S
S S E ■ S T R A N G E
```

400

```
L I S I ■ A S O R T
A S A N ■ C I T R U S
R E V S ■ O N R A M P
D R E I ■ N G O ■
■ ■ S T E V E D O R E
M A T U R E ■ E N C L
A R I ■ A R P ■ B M I
S E M S ■ T V T A P E
I D E N T I C A L ■
■ ■ U R B ■ R A P S
S I E G E L ■ T N T S
P O L L E E ■ A C A T
A S S Y R ■ N E S S
```

SOLUTIONS

401

R	S	S	S			A	B	A	B	A
A	T	T	A	R		L	O	R	E	N
D	U	A	N	E		E	R	R	E	D
O	C	T		M	I	X	T	A	P	E
N	C	O		I	S	A		Y	A	R
	O	R	O	N	O		I	S	T	S
		A	D	L	I	B				
S	S	G	T		A	N	N	A	N	
E	A	R		P	T	A		H	O	D
A	V	E	N	U	E	B		O	W	E
T	O	E	I	N		I	T	R	I	P
A	I	N	T	I		T	A	S	S	O
C	R	E	S	C			D	E	E	T

402

T	H	E	E		S	A	T	E	S	
Y	O	N	D		A	N	E	A	R	
P	R	I	M	A	D	O	N	N	A	
E	S	G		S	D	A	K			
B	E	M	U	S	E		S	T	A	S
		A	G	E	N	A		R	B	H
M	O	T	O	R		N	O	I	S	E
E	R	I		T	I	G	R	E		
L	O	C	A		C	L	I	N	I	C
		N	O	H	O			N	E	H
	D	I	S	M	I	S	S	I	V	E
	O	N	E	O	R		R	A	E	S
	B	A	L	O	O		S	L	R	S

403

W	O	N		I	C	H				
A	R	A		S	E	A		S	B	A
H	G	T		M	E	S	S	I	A	H
W	A	I	T	E		W	A	L	D	O
A	N	O	A			O	Y	V	E	Y
H	A	N	D	L	E	R		E	N	S
		A	S	U	N	D	E	R		
U	R	L		N	A	S	A	L	L	Y
T	E	P	E	E		R	I	A	A	
U	N	A	P	T		A	N	N	U	M
B	E	R	A	T	E	D		I	R	A
E	E	K		E	T	A		N	A	H
			S	E	R		G	S	A	

404

M	L	I		N	S	F				
A	I	N		A	T	O		S	T	E
R	E	D		T	O	U	C	H	E	D
G	R	I	M	E		R	U	E	R	S
I	N	S	C		A	L	L	P	R	O
N	E	S	C	A	F	E		H	E	N
		O	V	E	R	A	W	E		
I	A	L		R	E	F	E	R	T	O
C	R	U	S	O	E		R	D	A	S
K	A	B	O	B		T	E	S	L	A
E	C	L	A	I	R	S		P	K	G
S	E	E		C	T	A		I	T	E
			S	S	R		E	O	S	

SOLUTIONS

405

```
T A P I R . N I N N Y
U H U R U . O N E I S
C O N V E R T I B L E
K T S . H E F . O E R
. . . P L E A D . . .
A G U A . D I R E C T
T O N I C . R O K E R
C O U G A R . O G L E
. . . E L C I D . . .
G S A . O M S . K S U
I N C O R P O R E A L
G O T T I . L U A N N
O B E S E . A M N I A
```

406

```
H A S A T . D E L E S
A D O U R . E X E R T
M E R G E . N A D A L
. . E I E I O . A T O
I P S E . B U N . . .
D A P . A N N I E S .
I G O O N . C H A O S
. E T O I L E . G L O
. . M M E . D L I X .
A C R . A K N E E . .
C L E F T . S C E N A
T I T H E . F O Y E R
H O D A D . W R E A K
```

407

```
A M F . B C E . . . .
L E O P A R D . B O O
F I R E H Y D R A N T
. . G A S S . I L E R
A M E R . O T E L L O
B A T . T U R N A . .
A A M . H R E . N S A
. E L E G Y . D B L
S E N I O R . M C A T
A R O N . A C E H . .
I N T E R P O L A T E
D O S . V E R S I O N
. . . S S E . N A G
```

408

```
. N O O R . S F P D .
O O M P A . H E L O T
S W E E T P O T A T O
S I N N . O R A C H E
. . . . T S K T S K .
U N E A S E . . E N C
L I M P W R I S T E D
M A B . . F A L S E R
. . . I N H A L E . .
A L T A I C . P T U I
S E T T H E S T A G E
I S E E A . F I E L D
. E R S T . O N L Y .
```

SOLUTIONS

409

S	I	G	N	O		E	S	T	E	E
C	O	R	O	T		L	L	A	M	A
U	N	I	T	E		F	I	L	M	S
D	E	P	O	R	T		P	L	A	Y
			N	I	P	U	P			
A	G	C	Y		S	H	E	E	S	H
T	H	E	O	C		F	R	E	D	A
T	I	E	U	P	S		Y	E	S	M
		R	O	O	K	S				
A	P	A	L		S	A	L	T	E	D
P	I	X	I	E		R	O	M	E	O
S	C	O	F	F		S	P	E	L	L
E	S	N	E	S		T	E	N	S	E

410

	P	R	O	M		B	L	A	M	E
I	L	E	T	A		E	I	D	E	R
P	U	N	C	H	E	D	C	A	R	D
H	M	O		I	S	E		M	G	O
O	M	I	T		O	V	I	N	E	S
N	E	R	O		L	I	L			
E	T	S	E	Q		L	I	T	H	E
		I	U	M		A	R	A	G	
A	D	O	N	A	I		D	A	B	O
T	O	N		L	E	I		V	I	I
P	U	S	S	I	N	B	O	O	T	S
A	S	E	A	T		O	P	I	U	M
R	E	T	R	Y		S	E	S	E	

411

M	A	U	N	A		E	G	A	L	E
A	S	S	O	C		B	A	S	A	L
S	W	I	P	E		O	R	I	B	I
H	E	A	R	T	I	N	E	S	S	
		O	O	C	Y	T	E			
D	O	U	B	L	Y		H	E	L	M
I	N	N					I	B	E	
A	T	T	A		C	A	N	T	O	N
	I	N	A	L	I	E				
	S	M	O	K	E	S	T	A	C	K
I	L	E	D	E		L	T	G	E	N
P	O	L	E	R		E	L	O	P	E
A	B	Y	S	S		S	E	N	S	E

412

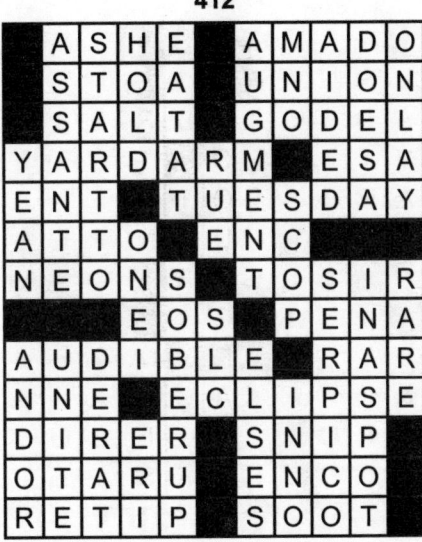

	A	S	H	E		A	M	A	D	O
	S	T	O	A		U	N	I	O	N
	S	A	L	T		G	O	D	E	L
Y	A	R	D	A	R	M		E	S	A
E	N	T		T	U	E	S	D	A	Y
A	T	T	O		E	N	C			
N	E	O	N	S		T	O	S	I	R
		E	O	S		P	E	N	A	
A	U	D	I	B	L	E		R	A	R
N	N	E		E	C	L	I	P	S	E
D	I	R	E	R		S	N	I	P	
O	T	A	R	U		E	N	C	O	
R	E	T	I	P		S	O	O	T	

613

413

R	I	V	E	T		E	L	L	A	S
O	N	I	C	E		L	A	I	L	A
A	C	C	T	S		E	X	F	B	I
D	L	I		S	O	G		E	E	N
B	I	O		A	M	I		P	E	T
E	N	U	F		M	A	W	R		
D	E	S	A	C		C	H	E	R	I
	C	A	H	N		A	S	E	T	
A	F	I		A	E	F		E	W	S
L	A	R		R	C	A		R	E	A
D	U	C	A	T		N	A	V	A	L
A	L	L	W	E		T	R	E	V	I
S	T	E	E	R		A	F	R	E	E

414

G	O	T	M	A	D		A	B	A	S
O	R	M	O	R	E		L	I	L	I
V	A	C	U	U	M	P	A	C	K	S
	T	B	A	R		A	A	S		
M	E	C	H	A	N	I	S	M		
U	D	O		D	O	W	E	R	S	
N	U	C	L	E	A	R	F	R	E	E
I	C	K	I	E	R		A	N	S	
	A	I	R	E	D	A	L	E	S	
R	I	T		I	W	I	N			
S	L	I	D	E	A	C	T	I	O	N
T	R	E	O		R	E	S	I	L	E
U	E	L	E		D	R	Y	I	N	G

415

	A	R	C	E	D		I	I	S
L	S	H	A	P	E	D		N	S	A
A	P	O	S	T	L	E		S	I	X
V	I	D	A		I	M	P	U	T	E
A	R	O	S	E		R	P	M	S	
S	E	D		N	O	H	O	P	E	
	E	L	G	R	E	C	O			
	U	N	I	S	O	N		R	Z	A
U	S	D	A		S	A	T	E	S	
N	O	R	M	A	L		C	A	R	S
U	F	O		P	A	G	E	B	O	Y
M	A	N		B	R	O	I	L	E	R
			A	N	N	E	S			

416

I	B	M		E	B	W			
P	U	E	R	I	L	E		P	T	L
O	R	D	I	N	A	L		R	A	I
	I	T	E	N		V	E	R	N	
D	U	C	T		K	E	E	P	O	N
U	N	I		C	E	L	L	O		
I	O	N		A	T	L		S	N	O
	E	M	M	Y	S		T	L	C	
H	O	B	N	O	B		W	E	E	D
I	S	A	O		L	A	H	R		
N	I	L		V	A	R	I	O	U	S
D	S	L		E	N	C	R	U	S	T
			R	K	O		S	E	E	

SOLUTIONS

417

```
K I P S ■ B O W L S
I S L E ■ U M A M I
D E A D L Y S I N S
D R U ■ E E K S ■
Y E S T E R ■ T O I T
■ I A M S O ■ U B U
S A B R A ■ S T T N G
O Y L ■ Y M C A S ■
B E E B ■ C A C H O U
■ E N G R ■ I S S
■ H O R S E S E N S E
■ R O L F E ■ L E I A
■ S P E W S ■ A S A S
```

418

```
C O A T I ■ G I S T
E R N O S ■ U B E R
D E I O N ■ S O C I O
A I M L E S S ■ R U N
R D A ■ W A Y ■ E N E
S A L S ■ G U T T E D
■ K E S ■ P A S ■
U N I Q U E ■ D E J A
S O N ■ N E C ■ R O T
A N G ■ D E L I V E R
R A D I I ■ A B I D E
■ G O T A ■ P E C O S
■ E M I L ■ S T E N T
```

419

```
S W A R D ■ T U L I P
S O D O I ■ U P D O S
A R I A S ■ B P L U S
■ M A R Q U E E ■
■ A U R ■ R S S S
N U P T I A L ■ A H S
A R R ■ E N A ■ B O T
I D O ■ T I S S U E S
F U G U ■ U T E ■
■ D I M N E S S ■
E L G I N ■ A S E A T
N S Y N C ■ M A M I E
T U N E R ■ E W I N G
```

420

```
A D A M N ■ C O E N
M O H A I R ■ A D D Y
E N I G M A ■ T O U T
■ O O M P A ■
M U G G Y ■ E R I K
O V O ■ T O R P O R
A E O L I A N H A R P
B A S E L Y ■ D E M
■ S E A L ■ C A S A S
■ R Y A N S ■
D I O N ■ S O T H A T
E N C E ■ P T I S A N
F A H D ■ E R N S T
```

SOLUTIONS

421

```
A S F O R ■ E S P O O
S C E N E ■ A U T R Y
T I M E C A P S U L E
■ ■ I S T O ■ P I E R
B O N ■ O U S E ■ ■
A K I N ■ T E N P I N
Y E S O R ■ A S O L O
H Y M N E D ■ E S E S
■ ■ L E O I ■ T R E
A V E O ■ O D O M ■
C O N C O M I T A N T
U L N A R ■ O R R I N
P E A L E ■ T A K E N
```

422

```
P R E S ■ A P A I N
L E A D ■ M A N N A
A N T I S O C I A L ■
N E A ■ P R O M S ■
B E T C H A ■ A P E X
■ ■ O I L S L I C K
S P A W N ■ H I N G E
G A L A X I E S ■ ■
T R I B ■ N I M B U S
■ M U R A L ■ S S A
■ H O N O R A R I U M
■ A N G I E ■ A D A S
■ N Y A L A ■ S E L A
```

423

```
S S W ■ K A A ■ C A L
C U E ■ N U L ■ U D O
A B L A T E D ■ R H O
R U L E ■ L O R R E S
A R E C A ■ ■ E Y R E
B B Q ■ S T I F F E N
■ U N C I V I L ■
A N I L I D E ■ A M U
S U P E ■ S E V E N
N O P R O B ■ N O T I
A V E ■ D E S E R T S
P A D ■ E A P ■ E L O
■ D N A ■ D E N ■
```

424

```
■ S H I P S ■ U T E P
■ A I D E S ■ T R E E
■ S T A R G A Z I N G
A H S ■ E T S ■ P S T
G A O L S ■ F O L I O
R Y N E ■ B O P E E P
■ ■ O F A R C ■ ■
A L E X I S ■ I S N O
N O S I R ■ R T H O N
I C K ■ M E E ■ R L S
S U I T A N D T I E ■
E S M E ■ C O I F S
S T O A ■ L S A T S ■
```

425

A	N	D		W	A	V			
Z	O	E		O	R	I		C	D	X
A	M	B		K	I	N	D	R	E	D
L	A	T	K	E		H	I	E	R	O
E	A	S	E			R	E	N	U	
A	M	O	N	G	S	T		P	S	T
	F	L	O	W	E	R	Y	
R	B	H		T	A	X	I	C	A	B
L	O	O	K			O	R	D	O	
E	T	N	A	S		O	T	A	R	U
S	H	O	T	P	U	T		W	A	R
S	A	R		A	I	R		L	T	S
		R	E	A		Y	E	E

426

V	O	I	L	A		I	S	L	E	T
I	D	T	A	G		L	A	U	R	A
B	E	S	T	S	E	L	L	I	N	G
E	D	I	E		T	B	A	
	N	O	S	E	D	I	V	E
W	A	R	C	R	Y			T	A	N
R	E	D	Y	E		N	T	E	S	T
A	R	A		G	O	I	N	T	O
P	O	S	T	P	A	I	D	
	E	A	U		I	A	G	O
B	E	L	L	Y	D	A	N	C	E	R
P	S	A	L	M		A	G	E	N	T
S	E	T	A	E		A	S	H	E	S

427

P	I	S	T	E		C	R	E	S	S
E	L	L	A	S		H	O	L	L	Y
A	L	A	M	E		A	L	I	E	N
P	I	T	A		O	F	F	S	E	T
O	N	E	R	O	S	E		S	P	H
D	I	S	A	R	M		F	A	Y	S
		C	U	O	M	O	
H	U	C	K		N	A	U	S	E	A
A	G	O		A	D	O	R	I	N	G
B	A	T	H	O	S		S	L	U	R
E	N	T	E	R		M	O	I	R	E
A	D	E	P	T		E	M	C	E	E
S	A	N	A	A		R	E	A	D	D

428

D	A	B		C	C	L	
B	R	U	S	H	U	P		C	F	L
L	E	C	T	E	R	N		H	A	T
	K	A	A	T		V	O	I	R
G	O	T	I	T		B	I	R	R	S
N	T	H	D	E	G	R	E	E	
U	S	E		D	I	I		O	R	C
	T	W	O	L	E	G	G	E	D
E	N	R	O	N		F	E	R	D	E
B	E	E	N		O	C	T	A	
R	A	N		S	H	A	M	P	O	O
O	R	D		R	O	S	E	H	I	P
		S	H	E		Y	D	S

429

D	O	H	A			G	A	F	F	E
E	R	A	T	O		A	M	O	R	E
M	A	L	T	V	I	N	E	G	A	R
	C	I	E	L			G	S	O	
C	R	Y	C	R	Y	C	R	Y		
C	E	O		F	A	R	E			
V	E	N	A	L		I	M	S	A	D
		D	O	I	T		O	N	E	
	B	O	W	W	I	N	D	O	W	
D	O	A		A	Q	U	A			
E	N	C	A	P	S	U	L	A	T	E
L	O	O	N	Y		E	L	S	I	E
I	N	N	I	E		S	H	A	K	

430

	S	E	M	I			I	M	A	S
F	L	U	F	F		A	W	A	I	T
R	A	N	D	I		S	O	R	E	L
O	V	I		T	W	I	N	K	L	E
N	E	C		S	A	D		E	L	O
D	R	E	A		R	E	T	R	O	
		P	A	L	S	Y				
	I	D	O	T	O		S	H	E	L
A	S	E		A	R	F		O	L	A
M	A	K	E	S	D	O		R	O	I
A	D	A	P	T		R	A	N	I	N
N	O	L	I	E		M	E	E	S	E
A	R	B	S			E	R	T	E	

431

B	O	R	A			P	T	R	A	P
F	O	E	S		S	O	R	D	I	D
A	R	A	T		E	L	I	S	S	A
S	T	R	O		U	A	E			
		R	U	T	S		D	A	T	A
P	I	A	N	I	S	T		P	H	D
H	O	N	D	A		O	F	P	I	E
A	L	G		S	A	M	O	A	N	S
R	E	E	D		G	E	O	L		
		E	K	E		T	O	P	S	
T	A	R	T	A	R		M	O	S	S
A	S	S	E	T	S		A	S	A	N
B	L	A	R	E		N	A	T	S	

432

E	R	L	E			W	N	B	A
D	A	I	R	Y		M	E	T	A	L
E	I	E	I	O		A	S	S	A	D
	S	T	O	I	C		B	S	A	
A	B	O	U		G	A	I			
C	A	V		B	A	D	D	O	G	
S	H	E	E	R		A	S	N	O	T
	T	R	U	I	S	M		E	R	O
		R	S	A		S	N	E	E	
I	A	T		T	O	M	E	I		
J	A	M	A	L		A	R	G	O	T
K	A	N	Y	E		R	A	H	A	B
L	A	T	E			C	T	R	S	

SOLUTIONS

433

S	E	Q	■	M	A	N	■	■	■
P	L	U	M	A	G	E	■	E	S	D
O	N	E	A	C	R	E	■	D	N	A
R	I	S	E	S	■	R	E	M	E	T
T	N	T	S	■	■	L	U	R	E	
S	O	I	■	A	T	T	E	N	D	S
■	O	F	F	R	O	A	D	■		
H	O	N	O	R	E	R	■	M	A	S
E	V	A	C	■	■	L	U	N	E	
S	O	B	I	G	■	A	U	S	S	I
S	I	L	■	A	L	A	S	K	A	N
E	D	E	■	F	O	R	H	I	R	E
■	■	F	A	E	■	E	I	S		

434

L	I	T	D	■	O	F	H	E	L	P
S	O	I	R	■	P	R	O	T	E	M
T	U	N	A	■	R	A	M	S	E	S
■	■	D	W	A	Y	N	E	■		
■	H	E	E	D	■	C	E	C	U	M
B	O	R	E	D	■	S	C	O	N	E
D	O	B	■	■	■	■	C	P	I	
R	H	O	D	A	■	F	A	K	I	R
M	A	X	I	M	■	E	L	A	N	
■	■	D	I	M	W	I	T	■		
C	R	I	N	G	E	■	S	I	A	N
U	N	L	O	A	D	■	T	E	T	E
L	A	O	T	S	E	■	S	L	O	T

435

L	U	F	F	S	■	A	L	C	O	A
I	N	H	O	T	■	N	E	I	G	H
T	H	A	R	P	■	T	W	E	R	E
■	■	G	A	T	O	■	L	E	M	
S	W	E	E	T	E	N	S	■		
E	A	S	T	■	T	I	E	B	A	R
M	A	S	S	P	R	O	D	U	C	E
S	C	O	T	I	A	■	I	T	A	N
■	■	O	N	D	E	M	A	N	D	
P	C	P	■	E	S	C	E			
T	A	L	O	N	■	O	N	E	T	O
U	H	U	R	U	■	N	T	E	S	T
I	N	G	O	T	■	O	S	S	E	O

436

A	C	C	R	A	■	R	E	A	D	A
T	R	Y	A	S	■	E	N	V	O	I
P	I	N	T	O	■	S	C	E	N	T
S	P	O	I	L	S	P	O	R	T	
■	■	S	T	O	N	E	R	■		
B	L	U	E	■	I	C	E	A	G	E
S	E	R	■	S	P	T	■	I	M	A
S	U	E	B	E	E	■	H	R	A	P
■	■	I	N	A	C	A	B	■		
■	S	H	A	N	T	Y	T	O	W	N
C	H	A	F	E	■	C	A	R	R	Y
C	O	U	R	T	■	A	R	N	I	E
S	E	T	A	T	■	D	I	E	T	S

SOLUTIONS

437

```
C L A C K ▮ U D A L L
A A R O N ▮ N O N O S
S M I L E ▮ S N E R T
A P P L E B E T T Y ▮
▮ ▮ ▮ I D T A G ▮ ▮ ▮
D U K E ▮ U T O P I A
A G E ▮ ▮ ▮ ▮ O L D
T O S S U P ▮ O L A V
▮ O P E D S ▮ ▮ ▮ ▮
▮ R U B B E R B A N D
T O M E I ▮ A O R T A
R E P I N ▮ T R E W S
A S S T D ▮ S N A T H
```

438

```
R E F U S E ▮ S P F S
A R I S T A ▮ U E L E
G A S C A P ▮ E N O W
▮ S H E S ▮ U L N A E
R U I N I N G ▮ Y T D
U R N S ▮ E L A M ▮
R E G U R G I T A T E
▮ T S A R ▮ T R I G
M C A ▮ D I G E S T S
C A C A O ▮ O S H A
J U K E ▮ M U T A N T
O S L O ▮ A D E L I E
B E E N ▮ H A R L A N
```

439

```
O L S E N S ▮ P P S S
R E A R U P ▮ O R E O
K I N S K I ▮ C O L I
▮ I T E N ▮ K C A R
S A T ▮ S N E E ▮
I C I ▮ I N T U N E
F E Z ▮ K N T ▮ N O W
T H E D O G ▮ T I E
▮ M A W R ▮ E D S
L I I I ▮ H A L S
O O R T ▮ E M O T E R
O N E R ▮ E I L E E N
M A S I ▮ L E A D E R
```

440

```
G L O W ▮ L E A D S ▮
U E L E ▮ P A N I C S
S T E N O G R A P H Y
S F O ▮ L A A ▮ P I S
E L L E N ▮ C R E S C
T Y E S ▮ T H E R M O
▮ S E V E R ▮
P A T I N A ▮ U L A N
S K I E D ▮ T N O T E
Y E R ▮ U T A ▮ C O X
C L A I R V O Y A N T
H A N S O M ▮ A T A T
▮ S E E S A ▮ M E L O
```

SOLUTIONS

441

W	O	R	T	H	■	A	A	L	T	O
A	M	I	E	S	■	C	L	U	M	P
R	O	L	L	T	H	E	D	I	C	E
N	O	E	L	■	E	Y	E	■		
■		A	U	R	■	N	T	W	T	
S	H	E	L	V	E	■	O	E	R	
I	M	P	L	A	U	S	I	B	L	E
N	O	I	■	N	I	N	E	T	Y	
O	S	S	O	■	D	M	D	■		
■		N	E	E	■	U	S	N	A	
F	I	R	E	C	R	A	C	K	E	R
U	B	O	A	T	■	S	T	I	N	T
N	O	T	D	O	■	E	S	T	E	S

442

A	C	M	E	■	D	A	R	N	A	Y
S	L	A	G	■	E	S	S	E	N	E
H	A	T	S	■	F	A	S	T	E	N
E	M	T	■	M	R	I	■	S	S	S
■		E	D	U	A	R	D	■		
R	A	R	E	F	Y	■	E	G	A	L
P	I	T	O	F	■	S	P	L	A	Y
I	N	O	R	■	S	H	O	E	R	S
■		O	L	E	A	T	E	■		
F	L	A	■	A	E	R	■	C	V	S
L	Y	C	E	U	M	■	C	L	E	O
U	N	R	E	E	L	■	M	U	I	R
S	N	E	E	R	Y	■	I	B	L	E

443

C	A	M	E	L	■	R	A	J	A	H
A	R	O	M	A	■	E	D	U	C	E
P	I	T	O	N	■	M	A	J	O	R
R	O	I	■	G	E	E	■	U	N	O
A	T	F	A	U	L	T	■	I	I	N
■		T	O	A	■	L	S	T	S	
■	W	O	R	R	I	S	O	M	E	■
L	I	N	A	■	N	I	N	■		
I	L	A	■	C	E	D	I	L	L	A
E	D	W	■	A	S	E	■	E	E	C
S	C	I	O	N	■	C	R	A	N	E
T	A	R	A	S	■	A	S	S	Y	R
O	T	E	R	O	■	R	A	H	A	B

444

U	H	U	R	A	■	T	A	C	S	
S	I	T	I	N	■	O	L	A	Y	
E	P	I	T	H	E	L	I	U	M	
D	S	L	■	E	L	L	E	S	■	
■		D	U	I	■	N	E	O	N	
P	H	R	A	S	A	L	■	W	O	E
R	U	E	D	E	■	A	M	A	Z	E
O	M	M	■	R	E	D	E	Y	E	D
B	E	A	V	■	T	Y	R	■		
■	S	I	S	I	S	■	G	O	D	
■	S	T	R	Y	C	H	N	I	N	E
■	T	E	E	N	■	I	M	B	U	E
■	K	R	O	C	■	P	E	E	P	S

SOLUTIONS

445

A	L	I	A			P	A	P	A	W	S
N	E	D	S		A	L	E	X	I	S	
D	B	L	S		C	A	S	E	I	N	
R	E	E	N	L	I	S	T				
E	C	H		O	F	T	E	N	E	R	
	A	S	M	Y		R	A	T	A		
U	L	N	A	E		L	E	V	E	L	
M	A	D	D		L	A	D	Y			
P	A	S	T	E	I	N		B	C	E	
		O	F	F	I	C	E	R	S		
P	R	O	S	I	T		R	A	I	N	
T	A	M	A	L	E		I	N	M	E	
S	P	A	Y	E	D		T	S	P	S	

446

C	I	D	E	R		Z	I	T	S	
S	N	O	R	E		A	C	H	E	
P	A	P	A	W		P	A	E	A	N
A	R	P	S		E	P	O	P	E	E
N	M	E		R	Y	A		A	E	R
	S	L	A	K	E		A	R	L	O
		G	L	O	B	U	L	E		
M	F	A	S		A	G	I	N	G	
E	E	N		M	N	O		T	A	S
T	U	G	R	I	K		H	T	M	L
A	D	E	E	R		S	O	R	B	O
	A	R	C	O		A	N	A	I	S
	L	S	T	S		D	E	P	T	H

447

A	B	C	D			S	T	R	A	I	T
N	E	H	I		W	H	O	L	L	Y	
T	R	O	U		I	R	A	T	E	R	
I	M	P	R	O	P	E	R				
		S	E	R	E	S		O	A	S	
B	A	T	T	Y		H	A	U	T	E	
A	L	I	I			L	T	R	S		
R	O	C	C	O		E	L	S	I	E	
S	T	K		L	A	Y	U	P			
		E	D	G	E	S	O	U	T		
S	A	L	I	V	A		I	K	E	A	
O	P	E	N	I	T		V	E	L	D	
A	P	I	E	C	E		E	N	E	S	

448

A	C	N	E	D		I	R	E	N	A
S	C	E	N	E		N	E	R	O	S
E	L	E	N	I		T	W	I	T	S
S	I	D	E	S	T	R	O	K	E	
			L	A	M	O	U	R		
P	R	E	D		T	S	K	T	S	K
C	T	S		C	A	T		A	A	R
T	E	S	L	A	S		S	K	Y	S
		U	N	T	A	M	E			
	S	K	A	T	E	B	O	A	R	D
S	A	O	N	E		Y	O	W	I	E
A	B	O	D	E		S	T	A	V	E
M	U	L	A	N		S	H	Y	E	R

622

449

L	A	S		T	I	E		B	S	O
O	V	I		I	N	T		O	A	F
W	E	T		G	R	A		A	R	F
C	R	O	C	H	E	T		R	A	S
A	S	N	O	T		S	A	D	H	E
L	E	T	M	E			G	I	S	T
		H	E	N		O	L	N		
A	R	E	A			B	E	G	O	T
F	I	F	T	Y		T	A	H	O	E
F	O	E		A	L	A	M	O	D	E
I	T	N		K	O	I		U	L	M
R	E	C		O	E	N		S	E	E
M	R	E		V	W	S		E	S	D

450

L	A	M	A		O	I	L	R	I	G
A	C	C	T		G	N	A	W	E	D
P	A	C	E	S	E	T	T	E	R	S
	I	C	E	T	E	A				
			E	S	K	I	M	O	S	
P	T	R	A	P		E	T	A	P	E
U	R	I	C			A	L	I	E	
M	I	E	N	S		I	L	L	E	R
P	O	L	E	C	A	T				
			U	R	S	I	N	E		
D	O	U	B	L	E	A	G	E	N	T
P	O	P	U	P	S		O	R	C	A
S	O	A	S	T	O		R	O	O	T

451

B	U	M	P	Y		V	S	O	P	
I	T	A	L	O		E	L	W	E	S
O	T	R	O	S		R	U	N	T	O
F	E	Y		H	E	M	M	E	R	S
U	R	L		I	C	E		R	I	A
E	L	A	M		H	I	L	O		
L	Y	N	D	E		L	E	C	A	R
		D	A	L	E		A	C	M	E
I	O	C		E	D	U		U	P	A
M	R	R	I	G	H	T		P	U	L
A	S	A	M	I		H	A	I	T	I
C	O	B	R	A		E	P	E	E	S
	N	S	E	C		R	O	R	E	M

452

A	M	B	I		F	B	I	M	E	N
L	O	O	M		L	A	N	A	T	E
P	R	O	P		A	I	S	L	E	S
S	T	R	E	E	T	R	O	D		
			T	O	L	D		E	P	A
G	R	A	I	N	Y		S	M	U	T
L	I	N	G	S		U	T	E	R	O
O	P	T	O		O	S	P	R	E	Y
P	E	I		T	O	N	I			
		M	I	S	C	R	E	A	N	T
I	F	O	N	L	Y		R	A	C	Y
C	A	N	N	O	T		R	H	I	N
C	O	Y	O	T	E		E	S	S	E

SOLUTIONS

453

A	A	S		P	I	P		C	T	A
S	C	H		I	N	A		A	U	S
S	E	L	F	E	V	I	D	E	N	T
O	T	E	A		E	R	A	S	E	R
C	O	P	C	A	R		K	U	D	U
			T	O	T	O		R	I	D
	S	P	O	K	E	S	M	A	N	
S	A	O		I	D	L	E			
T	U	R	K		S	O	S	O	O	N
A	T	T	A	I	N		S	T	L	O
P	E	R	I	T	O	N	I	T	I	S
L	E	A		E	B	W		O	V	I
E	D	Y		N	S	A		S	A	R

454

A	L	M	O	S	T			M	L	K
L	E	A	N	T	O	S		T	U	N
P	U	R	S	U	I	T		I	C	E
		E	N	T	R		D	C	L	
S	O	F	T	G		E	M	A	I	L
A	S	I		O	A	S				
B	U	T	T	E	R	K	N	I	F	E
		C	M	D		S	L	A		
A	L	I	B	I		G	A	M	U	T
P	O	D		G	R	I	S			
A	T	A		R	E	J	O	I	C	E
S	S	R		E	C	O	N	O	M	Y
T	A	E		T	E	E	N	I	E	

455

R	A	C	Y		P	A	G	E	
E	N	I	A	C		P	L	O	D	S
L	E	N	T	O		S	A	L	M	I
I	R	E		R	E	S	I	D	U	E
C	A	M	E	O	N		E	N	G	
	A	R	N	O		E	N	D	E	
A	F	T	R	A		F	U	J	I	S
N	A	O	S		G	U	R	U		
I	N	G		I	S	O	B	A	R	
M	A	R	T	I	N	I		I	B	E
A	T	A	I	L		O	N	L	O	W
L	I	P	P	Y		N	U	E	V	E
	C	H	I	A		N	E	E	D	

456

I	T	T	Y		D	E	T	O	O
F	A	H	E	Y		U	R	A	L	S
A	T	E	A	M		N	E	N	E	H
	T	H	I	N	G		D	N	A	
S	C	H		R	U	E	D	E		
A	B	R	A		N	O	R	M	A	L
B	E	E	C	H		N	O	B	I	D
U	S	E	R	I	D		P	I	L	L
	B	O	C	C	I		C	S	S	
R	O	E		K	I	S	S	Y		
I	T	A	L	O		N	O	C	A	N
P	O	R	E	R		O	F	L	A	W
E	S	S	A	Y		T	E	R	A	

SOLUTIONS

457

A	T	T	N			A	S	S	N
M	A	R	U		V	A	L	L	E	Y
I	L	E	R		E	S	P	R	I	T
D	I	A	S		R	A	H		
	S	E	E	S		A	S	K	A
D	I	U	R	N	A	L		A	N	I
C	A	R	Y	S		O	R	G	A	N
U	N	E		E	A	R	H	A	R	T
P	S	S	T		O	D	I	C	
		W	I	T		Z	I	N	C
I	M	P	O	S	E		O	O	O	H
G	R	A	P	P	A		M	U	N	I
A	T	O	M			E	S	E	S

458

A	P	S	I	S		M	A	C	E	D
B	I	T	T	E		A	L	A	N	A
A	S	A	I	R		S	A	N	D	P
C	T	R		A	N	T	E	D	U	P
A	I	T		P	M	S		Y	S	L
B	L	I	T	H	E		S	W	E	E
	N	A	S		T	A	R	
B	U	G	S		C	O	B	A	L	T
E	R	B		F	I	E		P	I	R
C	A	L	O	R	I	C		P	G	A
A	N	O	L	E		A	N	E	E	D
L	I	C	I	T		P	O	R	T	E
M	A	K	O	S		S	I	S	I	S

459

E	L	A	L		G	L	O	B	A	L
L	I	N	A		A	U	T	I	S	M
I	E	A	T		U	S	O	P	E	N
M	U	S	T	A	C	H	E		
		I	S	H		S	S	G	T
H	A	L	C	Y	O	N		T	A	R
A	R	P	E	L		O	O	O	L	A
R	E	N		A	N	O	M	A	L	Y
T	O	S	S		U	S	N	
		C	O	M	E	I	N	T	O
A	B	S	O	R	B		B	O	O	R
C	O	E	R	C	E		U	N	C	S
U	P	R	E	A	R		S	E	K	O

460

	H	O	B	O		J	A	D	E	D
P	E	P	I	N		U	M	A	M	I
R	H	I	N	O	P	L	A	S	T	Y
U	S	E	D		A	E	S		
		W	H	Y	S		L	I	B
R	O	S	E	U	P		S	E	L	A
T	A	K	E	T	H	E	C	A	K	E
E	K	E	D		O	N	A	P	A	R
S	S	W		G	N	A	R	
		D	U	E		C	I	A	O
S	U	B	S	I	S	T	E	N	C	E
O	L	M	O	S		A	L	T	H	O
T	A	W	S	E		P	Y	R	E	

SOLUTIONS

461

```
L E F T ■ B O O D L E
O N E L ■ O R D E A L
I N D C ■ E T A L I A
S A E ■ A S H ■ T R L
■ R E C K O N ■
G R A N N Y ■ O H H I
T O T O E ■ S T E E N
S E E K ■ M A D A M A
■ I V A N O V ■
A L E ■ E I S ■ Y T D
C O W A R D ■ I S A R
E V E N S O ■ T E R I
H E R E O F ■ T T O P
```

462

```
■ P A R K ■ S A G A ■
T U M O R ■ C U R V E
I R A B U ■ A D E E P
M E R ■ P E R I G E E
E L I ■ P A C ■ O N E
S Y L L ■ R E P R O S
■ L A M P R E Y ■
G L O B A L ■ P A B A
R E T ■ H U T ■ B A S
O V E R A G E ■ B R I
P I X E L ■ A H O R A
E N A M I ■ S I T I N
■ E S S A ■ E T T E ■
```

463

```
T W I R L ■ F A T S O
H E N N A ■ U R I E L
E N T R Y ■ L I M E D
F D R ■ L A C ■ E Y E
B Y A H A I R ■ C O S
I S N O ■ R U B O U T
■ S T A R M A N ■
F R I E D A ■ R S S S
E E G ■ V I A D U C T
D A E ■ I D S ■ M I R
O M N I S ■ S T I P E
R E C T O ■ T A N I S
A R E A R ■ S E G O S
```

464

```
A K C ■ C P U ■
L O L ■ A Y S ■ T C B
L A E R T E S ■ E E L
P L A T A ■ R O L L O
R A R E R ■ C L I O
O S S ■ A R E A M A P
■ I N C E N S E ■
D O G S T A R ■ A M T
I F H E ■ O S S E O
D U T C H ■ O U T D O
U S E ■ S E T S O U T
P E D ■ I N E ■ R S S
■ A D D ■ Y A Y
```

SOLUTIONS

465

T	O	L	U	■		N	A	A	C	P
A	R	U	N	■	C	O	S	T	A	S
B	U	L	B	■	O	G	L	A	L	A
■		L	O	A	F	S	■	R	E	L
S	M	A	L	L	F	■	I	B	M	
W	E	B	T	O	E	D	■			
M	A	Y	■	N	E	E	■	S	T	K
■		G	H	E	R	K	I	N		
H	I	C	■	O	R	I	E	N	T	
A	C	R	■	G	U	E	S	T	■	
S	H	A	R	E	S	■	E	C	C	E
N	O	Z	Z	L	E	■	T	H	U	D
T	R	Y	A	S	■	■	O	Y	E	S

466

467

468

P	H	A	S	E	■	N	G	A	I	O
I	S	L	I	P	■	E	A	T	N	O
P	I	L	E	I	■	Z	Z	T	O	P
■	E	T	C	S	■	E	O	N	S	
I	M	R	E	■	H	U	T			
S	A	G	■	N	E	S	T	L	E	
E	R	I	S	A	■	D	E	O	R	O
■	R	C	C	O	L	A	■	O	D	D
		R	S	A	■	I	K	E	A	
P	N	E	U	■	W	C	T	U	■	
D	U	M	P	Y	■	A	S	P	I	N
A	D	E	L	E	■	I	S	O	N	E
S	E	R	E	S	■	D	O	N	A	T

627

SOLUTIONS

469

M	E	D	I	A		B	J	O	R	K
I	T	E	M	S		B	U	R	I	N
R	O	M	A	N	C	A	N	D	L	E
	E	M	I	L		C	O	L	E	
A	L	A		T	U	F	T			
N	I	N	A		B	R	U	T	A	L
N	E	O	N	S		A	R	E	T	E
S	U	R	T	A	X		E	L	M	O
	I	C	E	L		E	E	S		
A	C	I	D		R	A	T	T		
C	H	L	O	R	O	P	H	Y	L	L
T	A	R	T	Y		S	E	P	I	A
I	S	E	E	A		E	N	E	M	Y

470

R	H	O	D	E	S			S	A	N
B	A	R	R	I	E		R	I	C	O
I	M	E	A	N	T		A	G	R	O
		M	E	T	A	P	H	O	R	
A	L	F	A			D	I	T		
C	O	A	T	S		A	D	L	A	I
A	S	C	I	I		N	T	E	S	T
R	E	E	C	E		O	R	S	E	R
	L	A	V			A	S	A	Y	
P	H	I	L	E	M	O	N			
R	O	F	L		A	U	S	T	I	N
A	T	T	Y		A	R	I	O	S	O
Y	E	S		M	S	T	A	R	S	

471

		O	G	S		T	D	S		
M	D	S		M	A	E		H	I	E
O	N	I		A	Z	A	L	E	A	S
C	A	T	C	H	A	F	E	W	Z	S
	T	E	A		O	V	O			
O	N	I	O	N		X	Y	L	E	M
S	A	N					V	C	R	
A	N	G	S	T		O	L	E	O	S
	T	I	A		F	A	R			
P	O	I	N	T	O	F	V	I	E	W
A	F	G	H	A	N	S		N	A	Y
U	N	H		M	O	E		E	N	E
L	O	T		I	S	T				

472

I	S	D	U	E		E	R	T	E	S
C	O	O	R	S		D	E	A	R	E
I	N	U	I	T		A	P	N	E	A
	A	B	E	A	T		E	D	I	N
I	T	L	L		R	U	N	E		
S	I	E		E	A	S	T	M	A	N
U	N	C		V	S	O		B	C	E
P	A	R	I	A	H	S		I	C	E
	O	N	C	E		S	C	U	T	
W	I	S	P		S	W	A	Y	S	
A	S	S	A	I		I	N	C	A	S
S	T	E	W	S		T	E	L	L	S
P	O	R	N	O		T	R	E	S	S

SOLUTIONS

473

A	W	W			A	P	I		C	U	D
F	E	A	R	F	U	L			I	N	E
R	E	T	I	T	L	E			N	R	C
I	V	E	S			I	S	A	D	O	R
C	I	R	C	E			L	Y	L	E	
A	L	I		T	R	E	A	C	L	E	
		N	O	T	F	A	I	R			
R	E	G	R	E	S	S		A	B	S	
A	S	H	E			T	O	W	I	T	
S	T	O	O	G	E		A	F	A	R	
P	A	L		A	M	O	R	O	S	O	
S	S	E		S	E	E	S	R	E	D	
			S	R	O		D	D	E		

474

N	O	S	Y		M	A	C	R	O	N	
I	F	H	E		A	G	A	S	S	I	
N	A	O	S		H	U	M	V	E	E	
E	N	R	O	L	L	E	E				
			T	R	U	E		O	D	O	R
U	N	S	N	A	R	L		E	N	O	
S	I	T	O	N		U	P	B	O	W	
N	C	O		N	U	R	T	U	R	E	
R	O	P	E		R	I	O	T			
			D	E	A	D	L	A	S	T	
B	R	O	G	A	N		E	N	Y	O	
S	U	V	A	R	I		M	T	N	S	
S	T	E	R	N	A		Y	E	C	H	

475

A	C	T	A	S		N	A	R	C	O	
L	E	E	L	A		E	N	O	L	A	
O	D	E	L	L		X	D	O	U	T	
W	I	N	T	E	R	T	I	M	E		
	A	H	M	E	D						
D	O	G	E		D	A	W	S	O	N	
S	P	E	R	M		Y	E	N	T	A	
S	T	R	E	A	M		A	E	O	N	
			L	A	T	K	E				
	C	H	I	M	P	A	N	Z	E	E	
B	L	O	B	S		R	E	E	D	Y	
B	E	L	I	E		T	S	A	D	E	
C	A	D	D	Y		Y	S	T	A	D	

476

	C	E	D	I		A	C	A	D
H	U	N	A	N		R	O	C	A
O	R	C	H	I	D		C	R	U	D
E	L	I		M	E	L	A	N	I	A
S	E	N		I	T	E		E	T	S
	W	A	S	T	E	A	W	A	Y	
		H	A	R	D	G				
	S	O	U	B	R	E	T	T	E	
A	M	U		L	E	R		R	D	A
K	I	T	T	E	N	S		I	D	E
E	L	L	E		T	H	E	A	I	R
E	E	E	S			I	S	L	E	Y
M	Y	T	H		P	A	S	S		

SOLUTIONS

477

S	L	O	S	H			S	A	L	A
K	O	W	T	O	W		U	P	I	N
E	R	N	A	N	I		D	O	S	S
D	E	S	T	I	N	E	D			
				D	R	E	S	S		
P	F	C	S		B	O	N	T	O	N
E	L	E	C	T	R	O	L	Y	T	E
R	I	C	H	I	E		Y	E	O	W
	T	A	M	L	A					
		A	L	K	A	L	O	I	D	
A	P	P	L		E	N	S	U	R	E
R	I	S	T		R	A	T	T	E	D
M	E	T	Z			T	S	A	D	E

478

A	S	A	S			T	A	E	L	S
S	O	M	E			O	L	D	I	E
E	S	P	N		B	R	E	W	U	P
C	O	H	E	R	E	N	T			
		I	C	U	S		A	R	L	O
C	A	B	A	R	E	T		E	O	N
A	M	I		A	R	C		C	E	O
S	B	A		L	I	E	D	O	W	N
H	I	N	T		O	L	E	N		
		S	K	U	L	L	C	A	P	
D	E	W	A	R	S		E	I	N	E
A	S	I	D	O			A	L	I	G
O	L	M	E	C			D	E	N	S

479

A	T	I	P		S	A	D	H	U	S
S	O	S	O		O	N	E	A	R	M
A	L	O	U		P	S	E	U	D	O
P	U	L	L	T	H	E	P	L	U	G
		A	T	A	I	L				
L	E	T	S	B	E			B	R	I
G	R	E		U	S	B		O	A	R
A	I	D		C	R	E	O	L	E	
		T	H	A	N	T				
E	N	D	P	R	O	D	U	C	T	S
L	E	O	I	I	I		R	A	G	S
M	I	C	M	A	C		E	M	I	T
O	N	S	A	L	E		S	P	F	S

480

			B	O	S	H		I	C	E
	D	I	O	N	N	E		N	H	L
N	E	W	Y	E	A	R	S	D	A	Y
A	M	I	C	A			A	I	R	S
N	O	S	E		V	O	Y	A	G	E
U	N	H		R	E	F	I	N	E	
			H	O	G	A	N			
	U	T	A	H	A	N		P	P	P
B	S	I	D	E	S		B	R	E	L
O	E	D	S			O	R	O	N	O
F	R	I	T	T	E	R	A	W	A	Y
F	I	E		O	H	W	E	L	L	
O	D	D		A	S	E	S			

SOLUTIONS

481

M	A	C	H	U		S	T	T	N	G
E	B	O	A	T		M	Y	H	A	T
T	R	U	R	O		E	P	E	E	S
E	A	N		P	Y	L	O	N		
		T	R	I	A	L		C	T	R
H	E	E	H	A	W		D	E	E	E
M	A	R	I	N		S	O	F	T	C
O	R	A	N		A	C	C	O	R	D
S	P	T		W	I	R	E	R		
		T	S	A	D	E		W	S	W
T	R	A	C	I		E	L	A	T	E
U	N	C	U	T		C	A	R	O	N
A	S	K	M	E		H	A	D	A	T

482

W	E	T	M	O	P		E	A	T	S
I	D	I	O	M	S		R	I	O	T
S	E	N	N	A	S		M	S	G	R
		I	A	N		D	A	L	A	I
E	M	E	R	I	T	A		E	S	P
R	I	S	C		O	T	S			
B	O	T	H	E	R	A	T	I	O	N
		Y	D	S		O	N	D	E	
A	P	T		H	O	L	I	D	A	Y
B	E	A	N	S		I	C	U		
Z	A	C	H		U	N	I	C	E	F
U	B	E	R		P	E	S	E	T	A
G	O	T	A		C	A	M	D	E	N

483

E	V	A	N	S		C	U	B	I	T
X	E	B	E	C		A	G	O	G	O
P	R	O	P	E	R	N	O	U	N	S
I	S	L		N	E	Z		G	O	S
R	E	L		E	S	O		H	R	E
E	D	A	M		T	N	O	T	E	S
			O	S	R	I	C			
L	I	O	T	T	A		S	E	R	I
A	C	R		I	I	I		N	O	M
M	A	I		C	N	N		G	N	P
B	R	E	A	K	T	H	E	I	C	E
D	U	N	N	O		E	E	L	E	D
A	S	T	O	N		R	E	D	Y	E

484

B	A	S	I	E				F	C	C
R	H	O	N	D	A		A	R	O	O
E	M	A	J	O	R		N	E	R	O
D	A	M	E		B	I	D	I	N	
E	D	I	C	T		N	E	G	R	I
			T	A	L	K	S	H	O	W
E	L	G		X	E	S		T	W	O
B	O	A	T	L	O	A	D			
B	Y	S	E	A		C	R	O	S	S
	A	L	L	W	E		A	P	P	L
E	L	A	L		N	E	W	T	O	Y
A	T	M	S		C	L	E	E	S	E
T	Y	P			O	R	D	E	R	

SOLUTIONS

485

I	S	A	W		T	A	P	E	T	A
T	H	R	O		E	L	I	N	O	R
C	O	M	O		C	I	N	D	E	R
H	E	A	L	T	H	F	O	O	D	
			E	L	I	E	L			
B	O	U	N	C	E		E	T	S	Y
U	K	R						A	T	O
N	A	N	O		O	M	A	S	U	M
			P	E	R	O	N			
	I	M	P	A	S	S	A	B	L	E
A	R	I	O	S	I		L	A	R	D
B	U	N	S	E	N		O	N	O	N
E	N	T	E	R	O		G	E	N	A

486

I	R	M	A		P	A	M	P	A
N	E	O	N	S		A	V	I	A	N
D	H	O	T	I		L	E	D	T	O
E	E	N		A	D	M		L	I	I
B	A	L	O	N	E	Y		I	N	N
T	R	I	G		A	R	A	F	A	T
	G	R	A	D	A	T	E	
O	F	H	E	L	P		C	C	L	I
N	U	T		L	A	B	O	R	E	R
A	T	F		U	N	U		I	S	A
P	I	L	A	R		R	O	S	S	I
A	L	I	V	E		P	L	I	E	S
R	E	T	A	R		E	S	N	E

487

U	M	D		E	E	R		L	P	N
L	A	U		V	S	O		I	R	A
A	C	C	R	E	T	E		N	O	N
	A	K	E	L	A		N	E	M	O
	R	D	S		B	A	R	E	
C	O	U	P		L	E	A	N	T	O
U	N	C		A	I	R		G	A	R
L	I	K	E	N	S		E	R	G	S
	G	O	S	H		L	A	T	
S	H	O	E		M	A	U	V	E
K	O	O		A	E	O	L	I	A	N
E	M	S		G	N	U		N	M	E
D	E	E		O	T	T		G	S	O

488

J	A	B	B	A		D	H	A	L
S	W	E	A	T		T	E	A	M	O
B	L	A	N	C		A	V	I	A	N
			G	O	O	G	O	L	
E	G	G	O		H	O	U	S	E	
D	O	E	R		H	U	R	T	L	E
E	M	T		B	E	T		O	C	S
L	A	S	T	I	N		S	N	A	P
	D	R	E	A	R		A	E	R	Y
		I	N	S	Y	N	C		
U	N	D	U	E		A	K	I	T	A
S	W	O	R	D		L	E	A	H	Y
C	A	F	E		A	R	T	I	E

SOLUTIONS

489

L	O	U	D				A	F	T	A
A	O	N	E		S	O	R	R	E	L
S	O	D	A		P	L	I	A	N	T
T	H	E	F	A	T	E	S			
		R	E	M		I	T	A	G	O
E	T	H	N	O		N	A	S	T	Y
G	O	A					P	O	E	
G	I	N	S	U		G	U	E	S	S
O	L	D	A	S		R	N	R		
			S	H	A	R	E	S	I	N
O	N	E	S	E	C		A	I	R	E
S	H	O	E	R	S		S	O	O	N
I	L	E	R				E	N	N	E

490

U	R	A	L	S			O	S	E	S
R	E	T	O	W		P	R	O	V	O
B	E	T	T	E	M	I	D	L	E	R
A	L	I		E	U	R		E	N	E
N	E	L		T	S	A		I	A	L
E	D	A	N		C	T	R	L	S	
			O	I	L	E	D			
	C	H	I	M	E		A	R	M	A
R	A	I		A	C	A		E	A	S
I	V	S		G	A	P		C	N	N
D	E	S	S	E	R	T	W	I	N	E
G	R	A	N	D		T	O	T	E	R
E	N	T	O			O	P	E	D	S

491

G	U	P	T	A		C	U	R	L	Y
U	H	A	U	L		O	L	S	O	N
T	O	L	E	T		R	U	S	S	E
S	H	O		O	O	F		S	E	Z
		M	I	S	C	U	E			
A	K	I	T	A	S		N	C	A	R
A	N	N	E	X		M	I	A	T	A
A	T	O	R		M	E	A	S	L	Y
		S	E	A	R	C	H			
A	R	N		R	I	C		E	S	C
Q	U	A	S	I		A	D	D	L	E
U	N	G	O	T		D	E	I	O	N
I	T	Y	O	U		E	R	N	E	S

492

A	L	E	A	K			I	L	R	E
R	A	M	R	O	D		L	E	O	V
M	A	T	E	R	I	A	L	I	Z	E
			C	A	Y	C	E			
A	W	M	A	N		T	G	I	F	
M	U	Y		N	I	A	C	I	N	
P	H	R	A	S	E	O	L	O	G	Y
S	A	N	C	H	O			S	H	R
	N	A	R	A		N	E	A	T	O
		O	R	S	O	N				
L	A	U	N	D	R	Y	L	I	S	T
E	S	P	Y		S	E	A	B	E	E
E	L	I	M			S	I	N	G	A

493

```
. S L I C E R . . . .
. T O W H E E . H O P
B E V E L E D . A C A
A L E R O . S H R U B
E M M E R . . I L L S
R O E . I H A V E I T
. . T I N A F E Y . .
O N E S E L F . S S S
R E N E . L O T T E .
B I D E T . A R R O W
I L E . A C T A E O N
T S R . L A U R E L .
. . . I N S E T S . .
```

494

```
C U B I T . C A D E T
U T I C A . A V I L A
D E F E R . R O A L D
. . O B S T A C L E .
S P C A . W W E . . .
C R A G . I A T E I T
A I L . A N Y . A T A
M I S S U S . S S R S
. . E D E . U E Y S .
. S P L I T E N D . .
S L E E T . A D O B E
G U A N O . C A U L S
T R U E R . H E T U P
```

495

```
O R T H O . . E C G
W E B A P P . A U R
E N A M E L . O C T O
M E R . N A U G H T Y
E W S . S I R L O I N
. . E T I E N N E .
. V I S A . G R E G
N I C O S I A .
E R E L O N G . A P E
A T L A N T A . L E T
R U E R . O R E I D A
T A S . W I N K A T
O L S . N O E L S
```

496

```
M A R R . B A A E D
U V E A . O M B R E
M I C K E Y F I N N
M A D E T I M E .
. . S H S . S A D A
P A R I A H S . B O S
L U A N N . C R E S S
O E R . S L A Y T O N
D R E A . U R E .
. . P U R E B R E D
. B L A C K D E A T H
. L I S L E . E S T A
. Y S T A D . R A U L
```

SOLUTIONS

497

R	E	L	O		A	C	C	E	N	T
O	N	U	S		S	A	I	L	E	R
I	D	D	O		S	L	E	D	G	E
L	O	I		D	U	A	L			
	C	R	U	M	B		N	A	N	
P	H	R	A	S	E	O	L	O	G	Y
I	D	O	N	T		O	U	T	I	E
E	Q	U	I	D	I	S	T	A	N	T
D	S	S		E	M	E	E	R		
	M	V	P	S		I	N	I		
A	R	A	B	I	A		U	Z	I	S
V	O	W	E	L	L		M	E	T	E
I	N	E	S	S	E		A	D	E	E

498

D	O	E	S		E	L	I	S	H	A
E	L	A	T		M	O	T	I	O	N
I	L	S	A		B	R	I	D	G	E
S	I	T	N		A	N	S	E		
T	E	N		D	R	E	S	S	E	D
	O	I	N	K		A	P	S	E	
W	A	R	N	S		N	I	L	L	A
W	I	T	S		A	N	D	I		
I	N	H	O	U	S	E		T	S	A
	E	M	T	S		A	T	P	S	
A	V	A	N	T	I		D	I	A	L
C	O	S	I	E	S		E	N	N	A
H	A	T	A	R	I		E	G	O	N

499

A	P	B	S		O	N	E	S	I	E
L	E	E	K		R	A	M	A	D	A
I	N	D	I	A	R	U	B	B	E	R
M	A	R		C	S	T		R	A	P
E	N	O	C	H		I	T	A	L	S
N	C	O	S		E	C	O			
T	E	M	P	O	R	A	R	I	L	Y
	A	U	R		I	S	A	O		
S	H	U	N	T		V	I	R	T	U
A	I	N		F	B	I		A	E	R
M	R	B	E	L	V	E	D	E	R	E
S	E	A	G	O	D		A	L	A	I
A	R	R	O	W	S		S	I	L	T

500

L	I	M	O		B	E	H	A	R
P	L	E	B	E		A	M	A	D	O
S	O	D	O	M		S	O	N	I	A
	S	I	L	E	N	T		N	O	R
A	T	T		R	E	I	N	A		
R	Y	E	S		H	O	O	H	A	S
T	O	R	I	C		N	O	M	S	G
S	U	R	T	A	X		K	O	N	A
	A	S	R	E	D		N	E	S	
E	R	N		C	R	E	A	T	E	
T	E	E	N	A		P	R	A	D	A
T	S	A	R	S		P	I	N	E	Y
E	T	N	A	S		D	A	D	E	